Montréal

Ninth edition

*"Between the St. Lawrence River
and its tributary...a lovely plateau...
is situated...amid grasslands...
with birds of many different colours
whose songs tamed our French people
in this wilderness."*

Histoire du Montréal, 1640-1672
François Dollier de Casson (1636-1701),
Sulpicien and *Seigneur* of the Island of Montréal.

Montréal's first historian, François Dollier de Casson
compiled his *Histoire du Montréal* between 1672 and 1673,
from which this description of the site on which Montréal was built
(present-day Pointe-à-Callière) is taken.

Travel better, enjoy more

ULYSSES

Travel Guides

Guide Update
Élodie Luquet

Update Contributor
Éric Bourbonnais

Research and Writing
François Rémillard (Exploring)
Benoît Prieur (Portrait)
Julie Brodeur, Pierre Daveluy,
Daniel Desjardins, Ambrose Gabriel,
Bernadette Hocke, Alain Legault

Publisher
Olivier Gougeon

Production Director
André Duchesne

Editing Assistance
Pierre Ledoux

Translation and Copy Editing
Cindy Garayt

Computer Graphics
Marie-France Denis
Isabelle Lalonde

Cartographers
Pascal Biet
Bradley Fenton

Photography
Cover page
Stéphan Poulin
Inside pages
© Tourisme Montréal
© www.vieux.montreal.qc.ca,
le photographe masqué
Patrick Escudero
Philippe Renault

Acknowledgements
We acknowledge the financial support of the Government of Canada through the Book
Publishing Industry Development Program (BPIDP) for our publishing activities. We would also
like to thank the Government of Québec for its tax credit for book publishing administered by
SODEC.

Library and Archives Canada Cataloguing in Publication

Main entry under title :

    Montréal

    (Ulysses travel guide)

    Translation of: Montréal.

    Includes index.

    ISSN 1483-2666

    ISBN 2-89464-742-5

    1. Montréal (Québec) - Guidebooks. I. Series.

FC2947.18.M6613 2006   917.14'28045 C97-302253-1

© June 2006, Ulysses Travel Guides
All rights reserved
Printed in Canada
ISBN 2-89464-742-5

Table of Contents

List of Maps	5	Tour J: Mont Royal	119
Map Symbols	6	Tour K: Westmount	125
Symbols Used In This Guide	6	Tour L: Outremont and Mile-End	128
My Montréal!	**7**	Tour M: Little Italy	134
Montréal In Due Time	8	Tour N: Sault-au-Récollet	137
Montréal *à la carte*	9	Tour O: Île Sainte-Hélène and Île Notre-Dame	141
Where is Montréal?	**12**	Tour P: Hochelaga-Maisonneuve	145
Portrait	**13**	Tour Q: Around the Lachine Canal	150
History	14	Tour R: West Island and Surroundings	160
The Language Question	25	**Outdoors**	**173**
Economy and Politics	26	Parks	174
Montréal's Communities	28	Outdoor Activities	177
Four Seasons and As Many Faces	29		
Literature	30	**Accommodations**	**185**
Film	32	Vieux-Montréal	188
Music	33	Downtown and Golden Square Mile	193
Visual Arts	34	Shaughnessy Village	199
Circus Arts	34	The McGill Ghetto and "The Main"	201
Practical Information	**37**	Quartier Latin	201
Entrance Formalities	38	The Village	205
Getting There and Getting Around	39	Plateau Mont-Royal	206
Useful Information, from A to Z	44	Notre-Dame-de-Grâce	206
		Côte-des-Neiges	206
Exploring	**55**	Hochelaga-Maisonneuve	207
Tour A: Vieux-Montréal	56	West Island and Surroundings	207
Tour B: Downtown	70		
Tour C: Montreal Museum of Fine Arts	82	**Restaurants**	**209**
Tour D: The Golden Square Mile	86	Vieux-Montréal	211
Tour E: Shaughnessy Village	94	Downtown and Golden Square Mile	215
Tour F: The McGill Ghetto and "The Main"	99	Shaughnessy Village	220
Tour G: Quartier Latin	104	The McGill Ghetto and "The Main"	222
Tour H: The Village	110	Quartier Latin	227
Tour I: Plateau Mont-Royal	115	The Village	229
		Plateau Mont-Royal	231

4

Restaurants *(continued)*

Westmount, Notre-Dame-de-Grâce
and Côte-des-Neiges   238

Outremont and Mile-End   239

Little Italy   245

Sault-au-Récollet   249

Île Sainte-Hélène
and Île Notre-Dame   249

Hochelaga-Maisonneuve   250

Around the Lachine Canal   252

West Island and Surroundings   254

Entertainment   261

Bars and Nightclubs   262

Gaming and Activities   271

Cultural Activities   272

Shopping   279

Accessories   280

Antiques   280

Art   281

Children   282

Cigars   283

Computers   283

Curiosities   283

Electronics   283

Fashion   283

Food   286

Gifts   289

Home Decor   290

Music   292

Outdoor Equipment   292

Pet Stores   293

Reading   293

Sex Shops   294

Travel Accessories   294

Appendix   295

Index   296

English-French Glossary   304

Our Guides   312

Contact Information   314

Write to Us   314

General Orientation   318

Table of Distances   319

Weights and Measures   319

Map Symbols   320

Symbols Used In This Guide   320

Table of Contents

List of Maps

Côte-des-Neiges
Accommodations 206

Downtown
Attractions 71

**Downtown and
Golden Square Mile**
Accommodations 195
Restaurants 217

**Fortifications of Montréal
circa 1750** 18

General Orientation 318

Golden Square Mile
Attractions 87

Hochelaga-Maisonneuve
Attractions 147
Accommodations 207
Restaurants 251

**Île Sainte-Hélène
and Île Notre-Dame**
Attractions 143
Restaurants 250

**Island of Montréal
and Surroundings** 11

**Lachine Canal (around the);
Little Burgundy
and Saint-Henri**
Attractions 151
Restaurants 252

**Lachine Canal (around the);
Pointe-Saint-Charles
and Verdun**
Attractions 157
Restaurants 253

Little Italy
Attractions 135
Restaurants 246

**The McGill Ghetto
and "The Main"**
Attractions 101
Accommodations 201
Restaurants 223

Mont Royal
Attractions 121

Outremont and Mile-End
Attractions 129
Restaurants 241

Plateau Mont-Royal
Attractions 117
Accommodations 205
Restaurants 233

Quartier Latin
Attractions 107
Accommodations 202
Restaurants 228

Sault-au-Récollet
Attractions 139
Restaurants 248

Shaughnessy Village
Attractions 95
Accommodations 200
Restaurants 221

Vieux-Montréal
Attractions 59
Accommodations 191
Restaurants 213

The Village
Attractions 111
Accommodations 204
Restaurants 230

West Island and Surroundings
Attractions 167
Restaurants 255

**West Island and Surroundings;
Lachine**
Attractions 163
Restaurants 254

Westmount
Attractions 126

**Westmount, Notre-Dame-
de-Grâce and Côte-des-Neiges**
Restaurants 239

Map Symbols

★ Attractions
▲ Accommodations
● Restaurants
▢ Sea, lake, river
▢ Forest or park
▢ Place
✪ National capital
★ Provincial or state capital
– – – – International border
·········· Provincial or regional border
+·+·+·+ Train track
▨▨▨▨ Tunnel

◎ Beach
 Bike path
▢ Building
🚐 Bus station
🚗 Car ferry
H Hospital
✈ International airport
🌟 Lookout
Ⓜ Metro station

🏛 Museum
Optional tour
🚢 Passenger ferry
≡ Stairs
Suggested tour
❶ Tourist information
📱 Train station
ULYSSES bookstore

Symbols Used In This Guide

≡ Air conditioning
bkfst incl. Breakfast included
♠ Casino
⋌ Fan
▤ Fax number
⌂ Fireplace
🏊 Fitness centre
● Kitchenette
@ Internet access in the room
# Mosquito net
P Parking
🐾 Pets allowed
≋ Pool
pb/sb Private and shared bathrooms
✳ Refrigerator
🍴 Restaurant
))) Sauna
sb Shared bathroom
🌿 Spa
☎ Telephone number
🚲 Travel by bike
🚍 Travel by bus
🚗 Travel by car
🚶 Travel by foot
Ⓜ Travel by metro
◉ Ulysses favourite
♿ Wheelchair access
◎ Whirlpool

Attraction Classification

★ ★ ★   Not to be missed
★ ★   Worth a visit
★   Interesting

Accommodation Classification

Unless otherwise noted, all prices indicated in this guide apply to a standard room for two people in peak season.

$ less than $60
$$ from $60 to $100
$$$ from $101 to $150
$$$$ from $151 to $225
$$$$$ more than $225

Restaurant Classification

Prices in this guide are for a meal for one person, excluding taxes and tip.

$ less than $15
$$ $15 to $25
$$$ $26 to $50
$$$$ more than $50

All prices in this guide are in Canadian dollars.

This guide's practical section features a grey border and lists this destination's useful addresses. You can refer to the following pictograms to find the information you need:

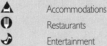

▲ Accommodations
● Restaurants
♪ Entertainment
🛍 Shopping

My
Montréal!

You only have a few days to discover Montréal and its secrets? You love nature, architecture or history? Whatever the length of your stay or your personal interests, this selection of attractions will help you plan the trip you want to make. Get ready to discover *your* Montréal!

Montréal In Due Time

■ One Day

To get a taste of Québec's metropolis, head to **Vieux-Montréal** for a stroll along Rue Saint-Paul, a charming cobblestone street that is lined with art galleries; visit the **Basilique Notre-Dame**, a masterpiece of Gothic Revival architecture, and the **Centre d'Histoire de Montréal**, to learn more about the origins of Ville-Marie. Toast the Happy Hour in one of the new **Quartier International's** happening bars, then head to lively **Rue Sainte-Catherine**, the city's famous commercial thoroughfare. Finally, if you'd like to discover the artists who've made their mark on Canadian art, you can visit the **Montreal Museum of Fine Arts** and the **Musée d'Art Contemporain**.

■ Two Days

A two-day stay means you'll get to dine at least once in one of the city's many renowned **restaurants**. Make sure you head up "The Main" to take in the colourful and eclectic crowd that provides the city with much of its cosmopolitan spirit. You can follow this up with a trek down the residential lanes and lively **Avenue du Mont-Royal** of the **Plateau Mont-Royal** neighbourhood, the perfect introduction to Francophone Montréal. Next, set your sights on the city's green lung, **Parc du Mont-Royal**, for a breathtaking view of the city. Devout Catholics and architecture buffs can visit the **Oratoire Saint-Joseph**, one of the most visited religious sites in all of Canada.

■ One Week

Once you've explored all of the above attractions, you can set some time aside to visit two of the city's well-to-do areas. First up is **Westmount**, a primarily English-speaking city within the city that features attractive Neo-Tudor residences that provide the area with an undeniably British flavour. Next is the Francophone counterpart to Westmount, **Outremont**, whose commercial arteries, lined with gourmet shops and fashion boutiques, border the the city's latest boho-hip district: **Mile-End**.

If architectural feats are what you're looking for, you can climb to the top of the world's highest leaning tower at the **Stade Olympique**: once up top, you'll marvel at the view of eastern Montréal and the famous **Pont Jacques-Cartier**. The **Jardin Botanique** and the **Biodôme,** both also located right by in the Hochelaga-Maisonneuve district, offer a fascinating look at our natural world thanks to their faithful replicas of various ecosystems, theme gardens and exhibition greenhouses.

Both the western part of the island and the **Old Port** are perfect for cyclists: you can rent a bike at the Old Port and visit the shores of the **Lachine Canal**, the birthplace of Canadian industry, or **Île Sainte-Hélène and Île Notre-Dame**, whose stunning **Biosphère**, a geodesic dome that features an environmental observation centre, can be seen from afar.

Montréal *à la carte*

■ Historic Montréal

On the origins of the city: **Pointe-à-Callière**, an archaeological and historical museum whose multimedia presentation provides an overview of the various stages of the founding of Montréal; the **Musée du Château Ramezay**, which served as a residence to the colony's first French administrators and, later, to insurgent Americans; the **Musée Stewart**, which is located at the **Fort de l'Île Sainte-Hélène**, takes visitors back in time to the conquest of the New World.

On the city's economic and political past: the **Fur Trade at Lachine National Historic Site** examines the fur trade, the lucrative commerce that spearheaded the city's economic development; **Pied-du-Courant prison**, where the *Patriotes* were executed in 1838 after having rebelled against the British Crown and fought for the emancipation of Québec,.

On the life of the city's residents: the **McCord Museum of Canadian History**, to learn everything about Montréal's day-to-day life during the 18th and 19th centuries; the **Centre d'Histoire de Montréal**, whose exhibits shine a spotlight on the different cultural communities that inhabit the city's neighbourhoods..

■ Cultural Montréal

The **Montreal Museum of Fine Arts**, where you'll find masterpieces from every period of art history, from Antiquity to contemporary design.

The **Musée d'Art Contemporain**, which features the most important collection of works by Québécois artist Paul-Émile Borduas, among many other artistic treasures.

TOHU, la Cité des Arts du Cirque, which is well on its way to placing Montréal at the head of the world's circus capitals.

Place des Arts, a cultural complex which is home to prestigious Québec dance and theatre companies. Its esplanade serves as a stage for some of the city's most important festivals, including the renowned **Festival International de Jazz de Montréal**.

■ Montréal, City of One Hundred Belltowers

Imposing churches: **Basilique Notre-Dame**, a masterpiece of Gothic Revival architecture; **Cathédrale Marie-Reine-du-Monde**, whose architectural style was inspired by St. Peter's Basilica in Rome; **Oratoire Saint-Joseph**, in important pilgrimage site which welcomes millions of visitors every year.

Beautiful churches hidden by downtown Montréal's skyscrapers: **St. James United Church** and its newly uncovered facade, in the heart of lively Rue Sainte-Catherine; **Basilique Saint-Patrick**, which was built for the city's Irish Catholic community; the Renaissance Revival-style **Église du Gesù**.

Testaments to Montrealers' religious faith: the Medieval-style **St. Andrew and St. Paul Presbyterian Church**, which was built for the city's well-to-do Scottish community; the **Église Saint-Jean-Baptiste**, whose construction was made possible by donations made by the Plateau Mont-Royal's working class residents; **St. George's Anglican Church**, a sandstone Gothic Revival architectural marvel.

■ Green Montréal

Craving green, wide-open spaces? **Parc du Mont-Royal** is the city's veritable "green lung;" **Parc Jean-Drapeau**, whose gardens and canals criss-cross Île Notre-Dame, is the perfect spot for a picnic; **Île-de-la-Visitation** and **Cap-Saint-Jacques Nature Parks** offer strollers and cross-country skiers charming trails within 30min of downtown Montréal.

To delve deeper into environmental issues: the **Biodôme** features replicas of various ecosystems that range from tropical forests to polar landscapes; the **Biosphère**, a stunning steel structure which houses an observation centre on Canada's different ecosystems; the **Jardin Botanique**, where visitors can explore some thirty theme gardens, including the splendid Jardin de Chine.

■ Multicultural Montréal

Montréal is home to a mosaic of cultural communities which you can discover while exploring the island's various neighbourhoods. Among these are **Little Italy**, where Italian immigrants settled after World War II, and which now boasts the lively *trattorias*, cafes and gourmet shops that surround the Marché Jean-Talon, and the city's small **Chinatown**, whose main pedestrian artery abounds with boutiques and restaurants.

■ Festive Montréal

Popular festivals: the **Festival International de Jazz de Montréal**, when the city swings to the rhythm of indoor and outdoor shows given by some of the biggest names in jazz; the **Just for Laughs Festival**, an annual mid-July event that features comedy's most renowned acts.

Spectacular events: Île Sainte-Hélène plays host to some of the world's foremost fireworks artists during the **International des Feux Loto-Québec**; the **Montréal High Lights Festival**, when some of the city's most impressive buildings are lit up to celebrate the magic of Montréal's winter nights.

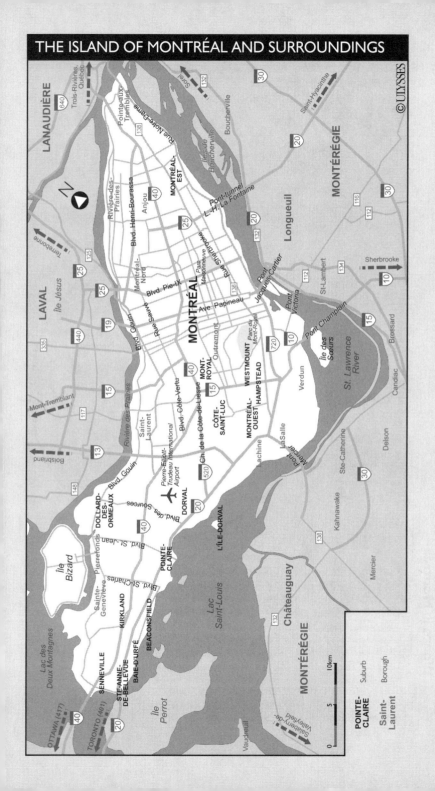

Where is Montréal?

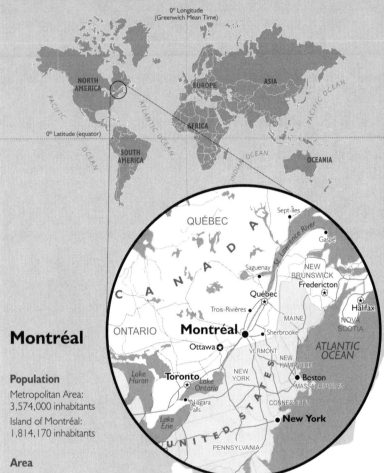

Montréal

Population

Metropolitan Area:
3,574,000 inhabitants

Island of Montréal:
1,814,170 inhabitants

Area

Island of Montréal: 499km²

Time Zone

GMT –5

Climate

Average temperature:
January: –10°C
(record low: –37,8°C in 1957)

July: 21°C
(record high: 37,6°C in 1975)

Average precipitation:
214cm of snow
736cm of rain

Highest Summit

Natural: Mont Royal,
at 233m

Urban: the 1000 De La
Gauchetière building, at 205m

Languages

Montréal is the second largest Francophone city in the world after Paris.

Percentage of population for whom French is the first language: 67,7%

Percentage of population for whom English is the first language: 12,6%

Allophone population: 19,7%

Cultural Diversity

More than a quarter of Montréal residents are immigrants.

The city's largest ethnic communities are Italian, Irish, English, Scottish, Haitian, Chinese and Greek.

Portrait

History	14	Literature	30
The Language Question	25	Film	32
Economy and Politics	26	Music	33
Montréal's Communities	28	Visual Arts	34
Four Seasons and As Many Faces	29	Circus Arts	34

Both Latin and Nordic, European and North American, cosmopolitan and metropolitan, the largest French-speaking city in the world after Paris and bilingual hub, Montréal is definitely an exceptional city. Visitors to the city appreciate it for many different reasons; it succeeds in delighting American tourists with its European charm and also manages to surprise overseas travellers thanks its haphazard character and nonchalance. Above all, Montréal holds nothing back and visitors often find what they are looking for without having to search too far.

Montréal is a city that exists in a balance between several different worlds: firmly planted in America yet looking towards Europe, claimed by two lands, Québec and Canada, and always, it seems, in the midst of social, economic and demographic changes.

It is difficult to define this city, especially since no postcard or cliché truly succeeds in evoking an image of it that is realistic or honest. If Paris has its great boulevards and squares, New York its skyscrapers and celebrated Statue of Liberty, what best symbolizes Montréal? Perhaps its numerous and beautiful churches, its Olympic Stadium, or its opulent Victorian residences?

Despite Montréal's rich architectural heritage, it is above all its unique, engaging atmosphere that appeals to people. Montréal is an enchanting city to visit and an exhilarating place to discover; it is generous, friendly and not at all mundane.

And when the time comes to celebrate jazz, film, comedy, francophone singers or Saint-Jean-Baptiste Day, hundreds of thousands of people flood into the streets, turning events into warm public gatherings. There is no doubt that Montréal is a big city that has managed to keep its human touch. For while its towering glass-and-concrete silhouette gives it the appearance of a North-American metropolis, Montréal has trouble hiding the fact that it is primarily a city of small streets and unique neighbourhoods, each with its own church, businesses, restaurants, and bars—in short, its own personality, shaped over the years by the arrival of people from all corners of the globe.

Elusive and mysterious, Montréal is nevertheless genuine, and is as mystical for those who experience it on a daily basis as it is for visitors immersed in it for only a few days.

History

To understand Montréal's place in the history of this continent, it is first of all necessary to consider the tremendous advantages afforded by its location. Occupying an island in the St. Lawrence River, the main route into northeastern North America, Montréal lies at the spot where maritime traffic encounters its first major obstacle, a series of rapids known as the Lachine Rapids.

From a commercial point of view, this geographical quirk worked to Montréal's advantage for many years, forcing vessels to stop here for transshipment. The city's commercial calling was further reinforced by the proximity of a number of other important waterways, guaranteeing it privileged access to the riches of an immense hinterland. These assets, moreover, have greatly favoured Montréal's growth and evolution throughout its history.

■ Origins

Before the regional balance was disrupted by the arrival of European explorers, what is known today as the island of Montréal was inhabited by the Iroquois nation. This people had probably recognized the location's exceptional qualities, which enabled it to flourish by dominating the St. Lawrence valley and by playing the role of commercial intermediary for the entire region.

In 1535 and 1541, Jacques Cartier, a navigator from Saint-Malo in the service of the king of France, became the first European to briefly explore the island. He took the opportunity to climb the mountain rising out of its centre, which he christened Mont Royal. (Following Jacques Cartier's 1535 voyage, an Italian named Giovanni Battista Ramusio, born in 1485, analyzed Cartier's discoveries and published *Delle Navigatiouo et Viaggi* in 1556, a work that included a map, called *La Terra de Hochelaga nella Nova Francia*, of the Mont Royal region, which he translated in Italian as *Monte Real*, the origins of "Montréal.")

In his ship's log, Cartier also mentioned a short visit to a large Aboriginal village apparently located on the side of the mountain. Inhabited by approximately 1,500 Iroquois, this village consisted of about 50 large dwellings protected by a high wooden palisade. All around, the villagers cultivated corn, squash and beans, thus meeting most of the dietary needs of their sedentary population. Unfortunately, Cartier left only a partial and sometimes contradictory account of this community, so that even today, the exact location of the village, as well as the name by which the Iroquois referred to it (Hochelaga or Tutonaguy?), remain unknown.

Another enduring mystery that still gives rise to much speculation is the astonishing and quick disappearance of this village after Cartier's visits. Some 70 years later, in 1603, when Samuel de Champlain travelled through the region, he found no trace of the Iroquoian community described by Cartier. The most popular hypothesis is that the Aboriginal people of the island of Montréal had fallen victim to trade rivals and finally been driven away from the island.

Champlain, the founder of New France, took an interest in the location's potential. In 1611, just three years after founding Québec City, he ordered that an area be cleared on the island. He viewed this spot, named Place Royale, as the starting point of a new colony or an outpost for the fur trade.

The project had to be postponed, however, since at the time the French, allied with the Algonquin and Huron, had to cope with attacks by the Five Nations of the Iroquois Confederacy. Supported by the merchants of New Amsterdam (which would later become New York), the Confederation was trying to seize complete control of the fur trade.

The founding of Montréal was thus delayed for a number of years and is not attributable to the efforts of Samuel de Champlain, who died in 1635.

Portrait - History

De Maisonneuve, Founder of Montréal

In the 17th century, the fur trade was the driving force behind France's bid to colonize Canada. Yet this lucrative trade was not the initial cause of the founding of Montréal; rather, it was the religious conversion of First Nations peoples.

Paul de Chomedey, Sieur de Maisonneuve, born in 1612 southeast of Paris, was not only chosen to carry out this mission but also designated as the new colony's first governor. De Maisonneuve left France in May 1641, leading an expedition of some 50 people, the Montréalistes de la Société Notre-Dame, a group that included Jeanne Mance. Jeanne Mance's ship reached Québec three months later without incident.

De Maisonneuve was not so fortunate, however, encountering violent storms along the way. In fact, he arrived so late that the founding of Montréal was postponed to the following year. The group spent the winter in Québec City. On May 17, 1642, de Maisonneuve founded Ville-Marie on the island of Montréal. A few years later, the name "Montréal" supplanted that of Ville-Marie.

In 1665, the governor of Montréal was summoned back to France indefinitely. He returned to Paris with a heavy heart, abandoning his duties and his beloved city and retiring among the Doctrine Chrétienne order of priests, where he died in 1676. He was likely buried in the order's former chapel, which was located in the vicinity of 17 Rue de Cardinal-Lemoine, in the 5e Arrondissement of Paris.

The founder of Montréal was a warm-hearted man of great intelligence and virtue. A monument to Paul de Chomedey, Sieur de Maisonneuve, erected in 1895, stands in Place d'Armes, in the heart of Old Montréal.

■ Ville-Marie (1642-1665)

The fur trade was the primary reason for the French colonization of Canada in those years; however, it does not appear to have been at the origin of the founding of Montréal.

The city, initially christened Ville-Marie, was established by a group of pious French men and women strongly influenced by the Jesuits' accounts of their time in America, as well as by the currents of religious revival that were then affecting Europe. Driven by idealism, they wanted to establish a small colony on the island in the hopes of converting natives and creating a new Christian society.

Paul de Chomedey, Sieur de Maisonneuve, was chosen to oversee this venture, and was later designated governor of the new colony. Heading an expedition of about 50 people, including Jeanne Mance, de Maisonneuve arrived in America in 1641 and founded Ville-Marie in May of the following year. From the beginning, great efforts were made to hasten the construction of the social and religious institutions that would form the heart of the town. In 1645, work was begun on the Hôtel-Dieu, the hospital Jeanne Mance had dreamed about. A few years later, the first school was opened, under the direction of Marguerite Bourgeoys. The year 1657 was marked by the arrival of the first priests from the Séminaire de Saint-Sulpice in Paris, who subsequently, and for many years to come, had a decisive influence on the city's development. Ironically, the primary goal behind the founding of Ville-Marie, the

Portrait - History

conversion of the Iroquois, had to be abandoned, or at least set aside for a certain period of time. In fact, just one year after their arrival, the French had to confront the Iroquois, who feared that the presence of colonists would disrupt the fur trade and put them at a disadvantage.

Before long, a permanent state of war set in, threatening the very survival of the colony several times. Finally, however, after nearly a quarter-century of hanging by only a thread, the colony was provided with military protection by King Louis XIV, who had been governing New France himself for two years. From that point on, Ville-Marie, which had already come to be known as Montréal, began to flourish.

■ The Fur Trade (1665-1760)

Although the church hierarchy still maintained its authority and the spiritual vocation of the town endured in people's minds, the protection afforded by the royal administration enabled Montréal to prosper as a military and commercial centre from 1665 on.

The arrival of French troops and the relative "pacification" of the Iroquois that ensued, especially after 1701 thanks to the signing of the Montréal peace treaty, finally made it possible to capitalize on the town's advantages as far as the fur trade was concerned. Since Montréal was the town located farthest up the St. Lawrence River, it soon surpassed Québec City as the hub of this lucrative commerce.

In addition, more and more young Montrealers called *coureurs des bois* were leaving the city and venturing deep into the hinterland to negotiate directly with native fur suppliers. Legalized in 1681, this practice gradually became more organized and hierarchical, and the *coureurs des bois* became for the most part paid employees of important Montréal merchants. Montréal, located at the gateway to the continent, also served as the starting point for France's intensive exploration of North America.

French expeditions, notably those led by Jolliet, Marquette, La Salle and La Vérendrye, kept pushing the borders of New France further and further. Pierre Le Moyne d'Iberville founded Louisiana in 1699, during one of these expeditions. In those years, France claimed the major part of present-day North America, an immense territory that enabled France to contain the expansion of the much more densely populated English colonies in the south, between the Atlantic and the Appalachians.

Supported by the royal administration, Montréal continued to grow slowly throughout this period. In 1672, a map was created, delimiting for the first time a number of the city's streets, the most important being Rue Notre-Dame and Rue Saint-Paul. Then, between 1717 and 1741, the wooden palisade surrounding the city was replaced by a stone wall over 5m high to reinforce the city's defences.

While the population grew somewhat slowly, it nevertheless spread beyond the areas outside the enclosure from the 1730s on. A clear social distinction gradually developed between the residents of these areas and those of the city centre, where, after a number of devastating fires, only stone buildings were permitted. The core of the city, protected by walls, was occupied mainly by members of the local aristocracy, wealthy merchants and social and religious institutions, while the outlying areas were inhabited primarily by artisans and peasants. With its numerous multi-level stone houses, the centre of Montréal already had the appearance and atmosphere of a small, peaceful French city by the middle of the 18th century.

Portrait - History

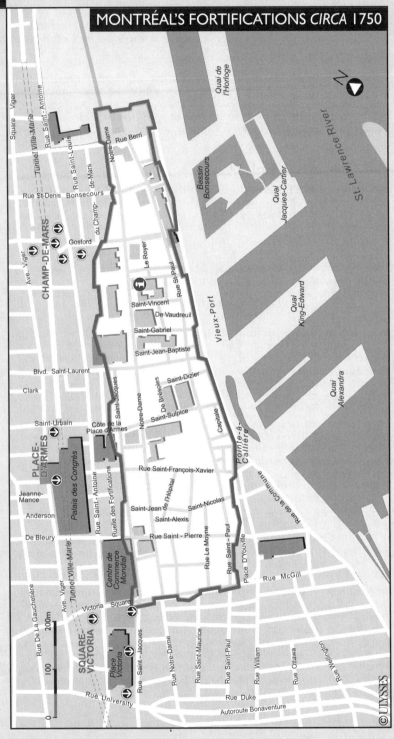

MONTRÉAL'S FORTIFICATIONS *CIRCA* 1750

© ULYSSES

The Seven Years War, which raged through Europe between 1756 and 1763, was to have enormous repercussions in America, which quickly became a battlefield. Québec City in 1759 and Montréal the following year fell into the hands of British troops. When the war ended in Europe, France officially ceded control of almost all its North-American possessions to England under the Treaty of Paris, thereby signing New France's death sentence. The fate of Montréal and its francophone population, numbering 5,733 inhabitants, was significantly altered as a result.

■ Transitional Years (1763-1850)

The first decades after the conquest (1760) were characterized by an atmosphere of uncertainty for the city's community. First of all, despite the return of a civilian government in 1764, French-speaking citizens continued to be edged out and excluded from the public administration and higher realms of decision-making, until 1774, when control of the lucrative fur trade passed into the hands of the conquerors, particularly a small group of merchants of Scottish extraction who would go on to form the Northwest Company in 1787.

In 1775-1776, the city was invaded once again, this time by American troops, who only stayed a few months. It was therefore at the end of the American Revolution that Montréal and other parts of Canada were faced with the first large waves of English-speaking immigrants, made up of Loyalists (American colonists wishing to maintain their allegiance to the British Crown). Later, from 1815 on, these individuals were followed by large numbers of newcomers from the British Isles, especially Ireland, which at the time was severely stricken by famine. The French-Canadian population, meanwhile, was growing at a remarkable pace due to a very high birth rate.

This rapid increase in the Canadian population had a positive effect on Montréal's economy as the urban and rural areas grew more and more dependent upon one another. The rapidly expanding rural areas, particularly in the part of the territory that would later become Ontario, formed a lucrative market for all sorts of products manufactured in Montréal. The country's agricultural production, particularly wheat, which inevitably passed through the port of Montréal before being shipped to Great Britain, ensured the growth of the city's port activities. Then, in the 1820s, an old dream was realized with the inauguration of a canal that made it possible to bypass the Lachine rapids.

In fact, Montréal's economy was already so diversified by that time that it was barely affected when, in 1821, the Hudson's Bay Company took over the Northwest Company, which had represented the city's interests in the fur trade until then. For many years the mainspring of Montréal's economy, the fur trade had become but one industry among many.

In the 1830s, Montréal earned the title of most populated city in the country, surpassing Québec City. A massive influx of English-speaking colonists disrupted the balance between French and English, and for 35 years, starting in 1831, there was an anglophone majority in Montréal.

Furthermore, the different ethnic communities had already started to band together in a pattern that would endure for many years to come: francophones lived mainly in the east end of the city, the Irish stayed in the southwest and the Anglo-Scottish remained in the west. These various ethnic groups did not, however, share the territory without problems. When the *Patriote* rebellions broke out in 1837-1838, Montréal became the scene of violent confrontations between the members of the Doric Club, composed of loyal British subjects, and the *Fils de la Liberté* (Sons of Liberty), made up

Portrait - History

of young francophones. It was actually after an inter-ethnic riot, leading to a fire that destroyed the parliament building, that Montréal lost its six-year-old title of capital of United Canada in 1849.

Although Montréal's urban landscape did not undergo any major changes during the first years of the English Regime, British-style buildings gradually began to appear in the 1840s. It was also at this time that the city's wealthiest merchants, mainly of Anglo-Scottish descent, gradually abandoned the Saint-Antoine neighbourhood and settled at the foot of Mont Royal. From that point on, less than a century after the conquest (1760), the British presence became an undeniable part of the city's makeup. It was also at this time that a crucial phase of Montréal's development began.

■ Industrialization and Economic Power (1850-1914)

Montréal experienced the most important period of growth in its history from the second half of the 19th century until World War I, thanks to rapid industrialization that began in the 1840s and continued in waves. From then on, the city ranked as Canada's undisputed metropolis and became the country's true centre of development.

The broadening of Canada's internal market—first with the creation of United Canada in 1840 and then, most importantly, the advent of Canadian Confederation in 1867—reinforced Montréal's industrial sector, whose products were increasingly replacing imports. The main forces that would long lie at the heart of the city's economy were the shoe, clothing, textile and food industries, as well as certain heavy industries, particularly rolling stock and iron and steel products. The geographical concentration of these activities near the port facilities and railroad tracks significantly altered the city's appearance.

The area around the Lachine Canal, the cradle of Canada's industrial revolution, followed by the Sainte-Marie and Hochelaga neighbourhoods, filled up with factories and inexpensive housing intended for workers. The industrialization of Montréal was intensified by the city's advantageous position as a transportation and communications hub for the entire Canadian territory, a position it worked to strengthen throughout this period. For example, starting in the 1850s, a channel was dug in the river between Montréal and Québec City, enabling larger ships to go upriver to the metropolis, thereby eliminating most of the advantages enjoyed by Québec City's port.

The railroad network that was beginning to extend over the Canadian territory also benefited Montréal by making the city the centre of its activities. Montréal's industries enjoyed privileged access to the markets of southern Québec and Ontario via the Grand Trunk network, and the west of the country via that of Canadian Pacific, which reached Vancouver in 1866. As far as both domestic and international trade were concerned, Montréal occupied a dominant position in the country during this period.

The city's rapid growth was equally exceptional from a demographic point of view; between 1852 and 1911, the population went from 58,000 to 468,000 (528,000 including the suburbs). This remarkable increase was due to the huge pull of the booming city. The massive waves of immigration from the British Isles, which had begun in the early 19th century, continued for several more years before slowing down significantly during the 1860s. This deceleration was then amply compensated for by an exodus of peasants from the Québec countryside, attracted to Montréal by the work offered in its factories.

The arrival of this mainly francophone population also led to a new reversal of the balance between French and English in Montréal. By 1866, the population became, and remains to this day, mainly francophone. An entirely new phenomenon began to take shape toward the end of the 19th century, when Montréal started attracting immigrants from places other than France and the British Isles. Initially, those who came in the greatest numbers were Eastern European Jews fleeing persecution in their own countries. At first, they grouped together mainly along Boulevard Saint-Laurent.

A considerable number of Italians also settled in Montréal, mostly, for their part, in the northern section of the city. Thanks to these waves of immigration, Montréal already had a decidedly multiethnic character by 1911, with more than 10% of its population of neither British nor French extraction.

The urbanization resulting from this population growth caused the city to spread out further, a phenomenon promoted by the creation of a streetcar network in 1892. The city thus expanded beyond its old limits on a number of occasions, annexing up to 31 new territories between 1883 and 1918.

At the same time, efforts were being made to lay out areas where Montrealers could spend leisure time, such as Parc du Mont-Royal (1874). As far as residential construction was concerned, British-inspired styles were most prevalent, notably in working-class neighbourhoods, where row houses with flat roofs and brick fronts predominated.

Furthermore, in order to offer low-cost housing to working-class families, these buildings frequently had two or three stories and were designed to accommodate at least as many families. Affluent Montrealers were increasingly settling on the flanks of Mont Royal, in a neighbourhood that would soon be known as the Golden Square Mile due to the great wealth of its residents. The industrial revolution had increased the socio-economic divisions within Montréal society. This phenomenon separated the main ethnic groups involved in an almost dichotomous fashion, since the upper middle class was almost entirely made up of Anglo-Protestants, while the majority of unspecialized workers consisted of French and Irish Catholics.

■ Between the Two Wars

From 1914 to 1945, a number of international-scale events hindered the city's growth and evolution. First of all, with the beginnings of World War I in 1914, Montréal's economy stagnated due to a drop in investments. It regained strength very quickly, however, thanks to the exportation of agricultural products and military equipment to Great Britain.

But those years were mostly marked in Montréal by a political battle waged between anglophones and francophones on the subject of the war. Francophones had mixed feelings about the British Empire and therefore protested at length against any Canadian participation in the British war effort. They were fiercely opposed to the conscription of Canadian citizens.

Anglophones, many of whom still had very strong ties with Great Britain, were in favour of Canada's full involvement. When, in 1917, the Canadian government finally made a decision and imposed conscription, francophones exploded with anger and Montréal was shaken by intense inter-ethnic tensions.

The war was followed by a few years of economic readjustment, and then by "the Roaring Twenties," a period of sustained growth stretching from 1921 to 1929. Dur-

Important Dates in Montréal's History

Fifth Century: Nomadic tribes settle in the St. Lawrence Valley and on the island known today as Montréal.

1535: On his second voyage to North America, Jacques Cartier sails up the river to the island of Montréal, where he visits an Iroquois village and climbs the mountain, naming it Mont Royal.

1642: Under the command of Paul de Chomedey, Sieur de Maisonneuve, a French colony, originally named Ville-Marie, is founded on the island. This small community survives with great difficulty for nearly a quarter of a century and very quickly abandons its initial plans to convert the Iroquois to Christianity.

1672: The main roads of Montréal, a city whose survival is now assured, are delineated for the first time.

1701: The French and First Nations sign a treaty, ushering in a period of peace and thus fostering the development of a fur trade centered around Montréal.

1760: Like Québec City the previous year, Montréal falls into the hands of British troops. The fate of the city and its inhabitants is drastically altered as a result.

1775-1776: While the American Revolution rages in the United States, the American army occupies Montréal for several months.

1831: Montréal surpasses Québec City in terms of population, thereby becoming

ing this time, development in Montréal picked up where it had left off before the war, and the city maintained its role as Canada's metropolis. Toronto, however, thanks to American investment and the development of Western Canada, was already starting to claim a more important place for itself.

Taller and taller buildings with designs reflecting American architectural trends gradually began to appear in Montréal's business centre. The city's population also started growing again, so much so that by the end of the 1920s, there were over 800,000 people living in Montréal, while the population on the island as a whole had already exceeded 1,000,000. Due to both the size of its population and the appearance of its business centre, Montréal already had all the attributes of a major North-American city.

The crisis that struck the world economy in 1929 had a devastating effect on Montréal, whose wealth was mainly based on exports. For an entire decade, poverty was widespread in the city, as up to a third of the population of working age was unemployed.

This dark period did not end until the beginning of World War II in 1939. From the start of this conflict, however, the controversy surrounding the war effort was rekindled, once again dividing the city's francophone and anglophone populations. The mayor of Montréal, Camillien Houde, who was opposed to conscription, was imprisoned between 1940 and 1944. Ultimately, Canada became fully involved in the war, putting its industrial production and army of conscripts at Great Britain's disposition.

■ Renewed Growth (1945-1960)

After many years of rationing and unfavourable upheavals, Montréal's economy emerged from the war stronger and more diversified than ever. What followed was a prosperous period during which the population's consumer demands could be met. For more than a decade, unemployment was almost nonexistent in Montréal, and the overall standard of living improved radically.

The growth of the Montréal urban area was equally remarkable from a demographic point of view, so much so that between 1941 and 1961, the population practically doubled, going from 1,140,000 to 2,110,000, while the population of the city itself passed the 1,000,000 mark in 1951. This population the main urban centre in Canada.

1837: Riots break out in Montréal, with the Fils de la Liberté (Sons of Liberty), a movement comprised of young French Canadians, opposing the Doric Club and its loyal British subjects.

1867: Canadian Confederation expands the domestic market, which, in the following years, is very beneficial to Montréal's development and industrialization.

1874: Creation of Parc du Mont-Royal by Frederick Law Olmsted, who designed New York City's Central Park.

1911: Due to immigration, 10% of Montréal's population is of neither British nor French extraction.

1951: Montréal's population surpasses one million, not including the rapidly expanding suburbs.

1966: Inauguration of the metro.

1967: The City of Montréal holds the successful Expo 67 World Fair.

1970: In October, a crisis breaks out when the Front de Libération du Québec (FLQ) kidnaps British diplomat James Cross and minister Pierre Laporte. The Canadian government reacts by enforcing martial law, and the Canadian army takes up position in Montréal.

1976: The Summer Olympic Games are held in Montréal.

1992: Montréal vibrantly celebrates the 350th anniversary of its founding.

2002: The towns that make up the Montréal Urban Community merge to form one city, Montréal.

explosion had several causes, first of which was the century-old exodus of rural inhabitants to the city, more widespread than ever, which resumed after coming to an almost complete halt during the Great Depression and World War II. Immigration also recommenced, the largest groups now arriving from southern Europe, especially Italy and Greece.

The increase in Montréal's population was also due to a sharp rise in the number of births, a veritable baby boom that affected Québec as much as it did the rest of North America. To meet the housing needs of this population, neighbourhoods located slightly on the outskirts of the city were quickly covered with thousands of new homes. In addition, suburbs even further removed from the downtown area emerged, fostered by the popularity of the automobile as an object of mass consumption. Suburbs also began developing off the island on the south shore of the river, around the access bridges, and to the north, on Île Jésus, now known as Laval. At the same time, downtown Montréal underwent some important changes, as the business section gradually shifted from Vieux-Montréal to the area around Boulevard René-Lévesque (formerly Boulevard Dorchester), where ever more imposing skyscrapers were springing up.

During this same period, the city was affected by a wave of social reforms aiming, in particular, at putting an end to the "reign of the underground." For years, Montréal had had a well-deserved reputation as a place where prostitution and gambling clubs flourished, thanks to the blind eye of some corrupt police officers and politicians. A public inquiry conducted between 1950 and 1954, during which lawyers Pacifique Plante and Jean Drapeau stood out in particular, led to a series of convictions and a significant improvement in the social climate.

At the same time, a desire for change manifested itself in the strong protest by Montréal's francophone intellectuals, journalists and artists against the all-powerful Catholic Church and the pervading conservatism of the times. However, the most striking phenomenon of this period remained French-speaking Montrealers' nascent awareness of their socio-economic alienation. Indeed, over the years, save certain exceptions, a very clear socio-economic split had developed between the city's two main groups.

Francophones earned lower average incomes than their anglophone colleagues, were more likely to hold subordinate positions, and their attempts at

Portrait - History

climbing the social ladder were mocked. And though the francophone population formed a large majority, Montréal projected the image of an Anglo-Saxon city due to its commercial signs and the supremacy of the English language in the main spheres of economic activity. Nevertheless, it wasn't until the early 1960s that the desire for change evolved into a series of accelerated transformations.

■ From 1960 to Today

The 1960s were marked by an unprecedented reform movement in Québec, a veritable race for modernization and change that soon became known as the Quiet Revolution. Québec francophones, particularly those living in Montréal, where the opposition between the two main ethnic groups was strongest, clearly expressed their desire to put an end to the anglophone minority's control over the province's societal development. A multitude of changes were initiated with this specific aim.

At the same time, the nationalist movement and its push for independence or increased political sovereignty for Québec found very fertile ground in Montréal. Indeed, the most important demonstrations in support of this cause were held here. It was also in Montréal that the **Front de Libération du Québec** (FLQ), a small cell of extremists wishing to "accelerate the decolonization of Québec," was most active.

Starting in 1963, the FLQ carried out a series of terrorist attacks in the city. Then, in October of 1970, a major political crisis broke out when certain members of the FLQ kidnapped British diplomat James Cross and Québec cabinet minister Pierre Laporte. On the pretext of curbing a dreaded climate of revolt, the federal government, headed by Pierre Elliott Trudeau, reacted quickly, enforcing martial law. The Canadian army took up position in Montréal, thousands of searches were conducted and hundreds of innocent people were imprisoned.

The crisis finally ended when James Cross' kidnappers obtained safeconduct to Cuba—not, however, before Pierre Laporte was found dead. The reaction of the Canadian government was harshly judged by many who accused it of having used the political context not only to bring the FLQ under control, but above all to try to halt the rise of the nationalist movement in Québec.

Over the years, the francophone majority made its presence felt more audibly in Montréal. Furthermore, the image projected by the city changed noticeably when successive provincial governments adopted language laws requiring commercial signs, which had up until then been in English, or at best in both languages, be written entirely in French. For many anglophones, however, these laws, combined with the rise of nationalism and entrepreneurship in Québec, were too difficult to accept, and a number of them left Montréal for good.

At the same time, Montréal, whose mayor at the time was Jean Drapeau, shone brightly on the international scene as it played host to a number of large-scale events, the most noteworthy being the 1967 World's Fair (Expo 67), the 1976 Summer Olympic Games and the 1980 Floralies Internationales (International Flower Show). From an economic standpoint, Montréal underwent profound changes with the decline of many branches of activity that had shaped its industrial structure for over a century. These were then partially replaced by massive investments in such leading industries as aeronautics, computers and pharmaceutical products.

In the mid-1970s, Montréal was also stripped of its title of Canadian metropolis by Toronto, which had been growing at a faster pace for several decades. The growing prominence of skyscrapers downtown, however, proved that Montréal's economy was nevertheless continuing to grow. The city's population also increased, so much so that the number of inhabitants in the Montréal urban area reached about 3,000,000.

This growth was mostly in the suburbs, however, which were becoming far removed from the city centre. Furthermore, with the influx of immigrants from around the world over the previous decades, Montréal became an increasingly complex cultural mosaic. More than ever, it had become a true international crossroads, while remaining the North-American metropolis of French culture.

The Language Question

The coexistence of two distinct cultural ideologies is one of the most fundamental elements of Montréal's makeup. More than anywhere else in Québec or Canada, two language communities, francophone and anglophone, share the same territory, the same city.

Montréal's language paradox is in fact much more complex than it seems, and has apparently been that way since the British Conquest of 1760. Visiting Montréal at the beginning of the 19th century, Alexis de Toqueville was surprised to observe the almost complete absence of the French language in public affairs and commerce. In fact, although francophones have always been in the majority in Montréal, except for a short period in the middle of the last century, the city projected an image almost as typically Anglo-Saxon as London, Toronto or New York for nearly 200 years. On business signs, in downtown department stores or during encounters, unexpected or not, between anglophones and francophones, the English language triumphed. Eventually, however, a new awareness on the part of francophones led to bitter disputes during the 1960s and initiated the process of restoring French to favour in Montréal.

Later, when Québec governments instituted several language laws, including the famous (or infamous) Bill 101 in 1977, the presence of the French language grew stronger in Montréal. The francization of the city did not, however, take place without greatly offending the sensibilities of the anglophone minority, who felt their rights were completely disregarded.

Many anglophones left Montréal in the mid-1970s, while activists denounced certain provisions of Québec's language laws, particularly those requiring business signs to be written in French only (today amended) and the mandatory integration of children of immigrants into French schools. However, despite appearances, things are far from being as simple as some people would like to believe; the anglophone community feels threatened that francophones still find themselves in a fairly precarious situation. The English language is still alive and well in Montréal.

Downtown, for example, in the heart of what people refer to as the second-largest francophone city in the world after Paris, English is used just as often as French. You have to venture farther east or north in the city to truly feel the francophone majority in Montréal.

Though the anglophone community still succeeds in integrating many new immigrants into its world, the provincial government's efforts to reverse this trend are starting to have an impact. Since English is the international language and is spoken by 98% of North Americans, its attraction as a means of cultural integration into North-American society is tremendous.

In their own way, therefore, Montréal's francophones and anglophones share the same fear—that of disappearing. Under circumstances such as these, how can Montréal, and Québec for that matter, maintain a balance between French and English that is acceptable to everyone? This question, which has been posed countless times, has yet to be answered and presumably won't be by means of simple principles. Montréal's bilingual population has always played a crucial role in this debate, so, until the issue is resolved, the precarious balance that exists between English- and French-speakers will continue.

Economy and Politics

Harshly affected by a loss of momentum in several primary industries that had long been the driving force behind its growth and wealth, Montréal's economy has neither the panache nor the power it once did. Many factories, some true symbols of Montréal's strength, have been swept away by technological changes or are quite simply only shadows of their former selves. And despite the growth of a number of other industries, particularly those related to high technology, the effects of this massive "deindustrialization" have not yet been entirely absorbed. These difficulties, reinforced by the middle-class exodus to the suburbs, a trend that has continued steadily since the 1950s, now project an image of a city leaning toward impoverishment.

Of course, Montréal is not the only city affected by these problems; they are the lot of many major North-American centres. The situation, moreover, is not hopeless, since this Québec metropolis has many assets capable of revitalizing its economy: the quality of its workforce, its bilingualism, its existing infrastructures and the possibilities of research and development offered by the four universities located within its limits. For the past few years, several large-scale projects have been attempting to boost Montréal's economy. A good example of these multiplying ventures is Technoparc, a space that was created in order to favour the establishment of new industries in the city; as a result, a number of them have already appeared. The fields of research and production are varied: biotechnology, pharmaceuticals, aerospace science, and information and telecommunications technologies.

On the political scene, municipal life was turned upside down in 2001, when the provincial government, headed first by Lucien Bouchard and then by Bernard Landry, decided to accelerate the municipal merger movement that had been undertaken during the 1990s. In spite of opposition from certain groups of suburban citizens, the merger of all Montréal Island communities was finalized on January 1, 2002. However, the coordination effort of the city's new 27 boroughs had barely started when the official provincial opposition of the day, headed by Jean Charest of the Liberal Party, promised to table a law that would re-create the former municipalities via democratic public consultation. Of course, the law was adopted as soon as the Québec Liberals took power in April of 2003. Following a year that was marked by several debates and the dismemberment of Montréal's new municipal entity, 89 referendums were held on June 20, 2004 in various municipalities across Québec, including 22 in the Montréal region. To win, the anti-merger camp needed to obtain not only a majority of votes, but also represent 35% of all registered voters. Most municipalities won back their independence, and 15 Montréal boroughs reclaimed their city status on January 1, 2006. The mergers and de-mergers have remained a touchy subject ever since and, though Montréal's economy does not seem to have suffered, the situation has tended to accentuate the linguistic and economic gaps between the various municipalities that were involved in the political muddle. In addition to these mergers and de-mergers, the city's mayor, Gérald Tremblay, has had to face a few political scandals since he took office in November of 2001.

On the federal scene, current Prime Minister Stephen Harper, the leader of the Conservative Party of Canada, leads the minority government that beat Paul Martin's Liberal Party in the January 2006 elections. In Québec, Jean Charest's Liberal Party replaced Bernard Landry's Parti Québécois at the head of the provincial government in April of 2003.

Québec's political life is deeply influenced, even monopolized, by the duality between the two levels of government: federal government and provincial government. Relations between these various levels of government are not always harmonious, and the City of Montréal frequently finds itself caught between the federal (Ottawa) and provincial (Québec City) capitals.

To fully understand the political situation in the province of Québec, one must first consider its historical context. When America was conquered by the British Empire in 1759, Québec City was the cradle of French culture, and the 1867 Confederation, which created Canada, was an event that had major repercussions on all French speakers in Québec. The most significant consequence was the fact that the French-Canadian population became a minority whose culture was very different from the English-speaking majority.

The type of government established in 1867 was a copy of the British model, giving legislative power to a Parliament elected by universal suffrage. The new constitution established a bi-level federal regime composed of the federal government and provincial governments. In Québec, this Parliament is known as the National Assembly, while in Ottawa, power belongs to the House of Commons. As a result of this new sharing of powers, the minority position of French speakers in Canada was confirmed. However, the province of Québec runs its own affairs in three domains that French speakers have always sought to preserve: education, culture and French civil law.

Québec has always favoured provincial autonomy in the face of a centralized federal government. From the first years of the constitution, some people, such as Honoré Mercier, opted for greater autonomy for the provinces. He maintained, most notably, that the rights of French Canadians were only efficiently protected in Québec. When he became the province's premier, he praised the French-Catholic character of Québec, but without challenging federalism. As a result of the influence of Québec's political leaders and the ethnic and linguistic tensions between francophones and anglophones, Québec would play an increasingly active role in the fight for provincial autonomy during the 20th century.

In the past 40 years, relations between the federal and provincial governments have taken a different turn. Indeed, the political life that took shape after the Quiet Revolution was marked by intense and troubled federal-provincial relations. The 1960s even saw the appearance of an extremist group, the Front de Libération du Québec (FLQ), which demanded Québec's independence.

For several years, the various governments that succeeded one another in Québec City all considered themselves to be the representative of a distinct language and culture, demanding distinct status as well as increased power for the province of Québec. The Québec government believed it knew the needs of the Québécois people better than the federal government and demanded the right to greater autonomy and power, and to the corresponding resources.

The event that radically changed the political stakes was the election of the Parti québécois in 1976. Soon, this party united the independent movements thanks mostly to the charismatic personality of its founder, René Lévesque. This political party, whose goal was Québec sovereignty, proposed a referendum on the national issue to the population of Québec in 1980, asking its permission to negotiate sovereignty-association with the rest of Canada. The Québécois people voted 60% against the project.

The same party, this time led by Jacques Parizeau, sent the population to the polls on the same question on October 31, 1995. The results were much closer, surprising even: 50.6% of the population voted against independence, while 49.4% voted for Québec's autonomy. The question has since been relegated to the back burners, yet is still present in most political speeches.

Montréal's Communities

Saturday night, on Rue Durocher in Outremont, dozens of Hasidic (orthodox) Jews dressed in traditional garb hurry to the nearby synagogue. A few hours earlier, as usual, a portion of Montréal's large Italian community met at Marché Jean-Talon to negotiate the purchase of products imported directly from Italy or simply to socialize with compatriots and discuss the latest soccer game between Milan and Turin.

These scenes, well known to all Montrealers, are only two examples of the vital community life of a number of the city's ethnic groups. In fact, Montréal's ethnic communities have countless meeting places and associations. And one need only take a brief stroll down Boulevard Saint-Laurent, also known as the Main, which divides the city between east and west and is lined with restaurants, grocery stores and other businesses with an international flavour, to be convinced of the richness and diversity of Montréal's population.

Indeed, Montréal often seems like a heterogeneous group of villages, which, without being ghettos, are mainly inhabited by members of one or another ethnic community. This sectioning of the city was initiated back in the 19th century by Montrealers of French and English descent—a division that still marks the city to a certain degree.

The east thus remains to a large extent francophone, while the west is anglophone. The most affluent members of the two communities live for the most part on opposite sides of Mont Royal, in Outremont and Westmount. With the arrival of immigrants from different ethnic backgrounds, several new neighbourhoods gradually fit into this puzzle. Very early, a small Chinese community, whose members had come to work in Canada when the railroads were being built, took up residence around Rue de la Gauchetière, west of Boulevard Saint-Laurent, which remains Montréal's Chinatown to this day.

The city's large Jewish community, for its part, first gathered a little higher on Boulevard Saint-Laurent and then settled further west, particularly in certain parts of Outremont, Côte-des-Neiges and Snowdon and in the municipalities of Côte-Saint-Luc and Hampstead, where its institutions flourished. Little Italy, often a very lively and colourful place with many cafés, restaurants and shops, occupies a large section in the northern part of the city, near Rue Jean-Talon and the Saint-Léonard area, where many Italians live.

Italians, for that matter, make up Montréal's largest ethnic community and add an undeniable energy to the city. Finally, a number of other more recently established communities also tend to gather in certain areas; for example, Greeks along Avenue du Parc, Haitians in Montréal-Nord, Portuguese around Rue Saint-Urbain and Jamaicans in Griffintown. In Montréal, it seems as if you almost travel from one country to another within the space of a few blocks.

Furthermore, today's Italian Montrealers no longer live in Little Italy, just as the Chinese no longer live in Chinatown. Most of Montréal's districts are characterized by the presence of several ethnic communities living in harmony. However, tension and friction, caused by misunderstandings and prejudice, has not completely disappeared. Adjustments are still necessary, especially in schools, but in general, Montréal has a true atmosphere of understanding. This cultural mosaic represents one of the city's greatest riches.

Four Seasons and As Many Faces

It is common knowledge that Montréal has at least as many different moods and personalities as there are seasons in a year. Indeed, this city truly lives in step with its often capricious climate, to which it has managed to adapt so as to reap all the possible benefits the weather has to offer.

In winter, for example, the season with which people most commonly identify this "northern" city, the temperature often wavers well below freezing and snow falls upon the city, yet it hardly misses a beat. This is because Montréal has become a world leader in "winter management," a veritable point of reference for a multitude of other major "cold" cities around the globe. During the winter months, day and night, an army of workers is available on call to remove the approximately 6.5-million cubic metres of snow that, on average, obstruct the city's streets every year.

To a large degree, Montrealers have also managed to circumvent the problems that can accompany a severe winter climate, notably by building an incredible underground city, one of the world's largest. Linked to one another by the metro system, these underground passageways, which cover almost 30km, make it possible to reach all sorts of office buildings, stores, restaurants, bars, hotels, cinemas, theatres and residential high-rises without ever having to step outside!

In short, be it the snow or the cold, nothing slows this city down. Of course, winter doesn't only bring problems; it also offers its share of pleasures and helps shape Montréal's character. Transformed by winter, the urban landscape lacks neither charm nor romanticism. The season's finest days offer an opportunity to enjoy a pleasant outing under the snow-laden trees, or a delightful visit to one of the city's outdoor skating rinks.

In addition, winter marks the awakening of a veritable passion, as typical of Montréal as any ever was: hockey. During the professional hockey season, the performance of Montréal's famous team, the Canadiens, is the topic of many conversations. Year after year, Montrealers manage to get through long winters, sometimes grumbling a little, but also enjoying the many joys the season has to offer.

Then, often abruptly, winter makes way for spring, an exhilarating season when Montréal takes on the appearance of a Mediterranean city. The first days of the season are always unforgettable, when the effect of the climate upon the city's inhabitants is most evident and Montrealers, transformed by the first rays of spring sun, seem to get back in touch with their Latin roots. It is finally possible to dress in lighter clothing, sit on a terrace or roam idly through the city streets. As if emerging from long months of hibernation, the crowds rush to Rue Saint-Denis, Boulevard Saint-Laurent and Parc du Mont-Royal.

This short, bucolic period of the year, when Montrealers are finally able to take advantage of the beautiful parks and main streets of their city, is only a prelude to the summer season—vacation time. Come summer, there is so much to do that Montrealers often choose to vacation in their own city. With the warm weather, Montréal comes to life, hosting numerous festivals to celebrate jazz, comedy, francophone singers and film, not to mention the traditional Saint-Jean-Baptiste Day, inevitably leading to gatherings of hundreds of thousands of people. In summer, Montréal is not exclusive, it is wide open.

The festivities continue until September; then, slowly, autumn settles in, and before fluttering to the ground, the leaves change colour, turning brilliant yellow, orange and red. But just as Montrealers prepare to bundle themselves up for another long, cold winter, they are given a brief respite known as Indian Summer, just to remind them how acutely their lives are lead by Mother Nature. Thus, the cycle starts anew.

Literature

As with much of modern literature in the Americas, Québec writing began with accounts of voyages by early explorers. These texts (including those by Jacques Cartier and various religious communities) were meant to inform Europeans about the "new" lands.

Toward the end of the 18th century and the beginning of the 19th, the oral tradition still dominated literary life in the New World. The Aboriginal way of life, the landscape of the country and the beginnings of French colonization all figure among the principal themes that were taken up by authors such as Père Sagard (*Le grand voyage au pays des Hurons*, 1632) and Baron de Lahontan (*Nouveaux voyages en Amérique septentrionale*, 1703). Later, the legends from this era were committed to paper, but there was no true literary movement until the end of the 19th century in Québec. At this point, some of the major themes were survival and praise for a simple, religious, country lifestyle. With few exceptions, the novels of this period are mostly of socio-historical interest. The novels of Antoine Gérin-Lajoie (*Jean Rivard le Défricheur*, 1862, and *Jean Rivard, Économiste*, 1864) are a good example of this quasi-propagandist tendency to heap praise on rural life. The glorification of the past, particularly the French-Regime era, also inspired several novelists. Few of the period's literary works, other than certain novels such as Laure Conan's *Angéline de Montbrun* (1884), are of much more than socio-historical interest. Traditional ideology also dominates much of the poetic output of the period. Louis-Honoré Fréchette was one of the rare poets who managed to avoid this political and philosophical straitjacket.

■ In French

Tradition continued to be the main characteristic of Québec literature well into the 1930s, though there were several innovative writers worth noting. Émile Nelligan, an early-20th-century poet, was influenced by Baudelaire, Rimbaud and Verlaine. Producing much of his work early on in life, he slowly sank into madness and today remains a mythic figure. Though country life remained a main feature in novels of the time, it began to be represented more realistically, as in *Maria Chapdelaine* (1916) by Louis Hémon, while Albert Laberge's writing (*La scouine*, 1918) tended to describe its mediocrity.

Literary works began to evolve toward modernism during the economic crisis and the Second World War. The era's literature still featured a predominantly rural setting, though the theme of individual alienation gradually started to appear. Novels set in the city, where the majority of the population now lived, began to appear. This is the case for *Bonheur d'occasion (The Tin Flute)* (1945) by Gabrielle Roy, a franco-Manitoban, and *Au pied de la pente douce* (1945) by Roger Lemelin.

Modernism took hold at the end of the Second World War, in spite of the strict political regime of Maurice Duplessis. Novels of the time were split into two categories, urban novels such as *Au pied de la pente douce* (1944) by Roger Lemelin and *Les Vivants, les morts et les autres* (1959) by Pierre Gélinas, and psychological novels like Robert Élie's *La Fin des songes* (1950) and André Giroux's *Le Gouffre a toujours soif* (1953). Prolific author Yves Thériault positioned himself somewhat outside these literary streams with the publication of his novels and stories (including *Agaguk* in 1958 and *Ashini* in 1960), which marked a whole generation of Quebecers between 1944 and 1962. Poetry flourished with the emergence of a number of great writers such as Gaston Miron, Alain Grandbois, Anne Hébert, Rina Lasnier and Claude Gauvreau. Gratien Gélinas' *Tit-Coq* marked the birth of Québec theatre, followed by various works by Marcel Dubé and Jacques Ferron. Among the numerous political essays that took position against the Duplessis regime, the most incisive and influential was undoubtedly the *Refus global* (1948), co-authored by a group of "automatic" painters.

During the Quiet Revolution, in the 1960s, political and social changes affected literary creation, leading to the "demarginalization" of authors. Several essays, such as Pierre de Vallières' *Nègres blancs d'Amérique* (1968), bear witness to this turbulent era of cultural upheaval and political opposition. The novel experienced a golden age, and new authors began to be established, such as Marie-Claire Blais (*Une saison dans la vie d'Emmanuel*, 1965), Hubert Aquin (*Prochain épisode*, 1965) and Réjean Ducharme (*L'avalée des avalés*, 1966). Poetry triumphed while theatre also went through an exciting period, with the emergence of Marcel Dubé and the ascension of such new playwrights as the illustrious Michel Tremblay. In addition, many poets, novelists and playwrights began to use *joual*, which is the spoken, popular form of Québec French.

Contemporary literature became richer and more diverse with the emergence of talents such as Victor-Lévy Beaulieu, Jacques Godbout (now deceased), Alice Parizeau, Roch Carrier, Jacques Poulain, Louis Caron, Suzanne Jacob and Yves Beauchemin, and more recently, Christian Mistral, Louis Hamelin, Robert Lalonde, Gaetan Soucy, Dany Laferrière, Ying Chen, Sergio Kokis, Denise Bombardier, Arlette Cousture, Marie Laberge, Lise Bissonnette, Chrystine Brouillet, Monique Proulx, Gil Courtemanche and Yann Martel.

In the 1980s, theatre became a far more important genre, with the staging of an abundance of quality productions, several of which integrated outside artistic expressions such as dance, song and video. The rising popularity of theatre in Montréal led to the opening of many new venues. Some of the brightest players on Montréal's contemporary theatre scene include companies such as Carbone 14, directors André Brassard, Dominic Champagne, Robert Lepage, Lorraine Pintal, René-Richard Cyr, Alexis Martin and playwrights Normand Chaurette, Marie Laberge, René-Daniel Dubois, Michel-Marc Bouchard, Jean-Pierre Ronfard (now deceased) and Wajdi Mouawad.

Humour has also always been an important part of Québec culture, and has been integral to societal changes. In the 1960s, the comedy troupe Les Cyniques ("the Cynics") produced biting criticisms of the clergy and political institutions, and so played a part in the Quiet Revolution. In the 1970s, Yvon Deschamps created characters who typified the exploited but "nice" Québec everyman, and brought about pain-

Portrait · Literature

ful self-awareness in the province. The years following the referendum in the early 1980s produced humour with elements of self-deprecation and the absurd signs of a disillusioned generation. This type of humour is typified in groups such as Ding et Dong and Rock et Belles Oreilles, and by comedian Daniel Lemire.

■ In English

The sharply comic prose of Mordecai Richler (1931-2001), as salty as smoked meat on rye, depicts life in the cold-water flats and small kosher delis of mid-town Montréal in the 1950s. Novels such as *The Apprenticeship of Duddy Kravitz* (1959), *The Street* (1969) and *St. Urbain's Horseman* (1971) portray a neighbourhood whose face is now changed but still recognizable on certain corners, such as Clark and Fairmount. Richler was also a frequent contributor to the *New Yorker*, with his crusty and controversial accounts of Québec politics. Other well-known literary voices of English Montréal include recently deceased poet Irving Layton, gravel-throated crooner/poet Leonard Cohen, novelist and essayist Hugh MacLennan and poet and novelist Mavis Gallant. On the stage, playwright David Fennario's *Balconville* (1979), which examines the lives of middle-class anglophones and francophones in Montréal, is one of the city's best-known works in English.

Montreal's latest literary star is writer Yann Martel. Born in Spain in 1963 to diplomat parents, Martel won the prestigious Booker Prize in 2002 for his novel *Life of Pi*, a fish tale of a story about a teenaged Indian boy shipwrecked on a lifeboat with a Bengal tiger.

Film

While some full-length films were made earlier, the birth of Québec cinema really did not occur until after World War II. Between 1947 and 1953, independent producers brought a number of literary adaptations to the screen, including *Un Homme et son Péché* (1948), *Séraphin* (1949), *La Petite Aurore l'Enfant Martyr* (1951) and *Tit-Coq* (1952). However, the arrival of television in the early 1950s resulted in a ten-year period of stagnation for the Québec film industry.

A cinematic renaissance during the 1960s occurred largely thanks to the support of the National Film Board (NFB-ONF). With documentaries and realistic films, directors focused primarily on a critique of Québec society. Among the many works of the era, *Pour la suite du monde* (1963), by Pierre Perreault and Michel Brault, was undoubtedly the most influential and innovative. Later, the full-length feature film dominated with the success of certain directors like Claude Jutras (*Mon Oncle Antoine*, 1971), Jean-Claude Lord (*Les Colombes*, 1972), Gilles Carle (*La Vraie Nature de Bernadette*, 1972), Michel Brault (*Les Ordres*, 1974), Jean Beaudin (*J.A. Martin Photographe*, 1977) and Frank Mankiewicz (*Les Bons Débarras*, 1979). The NFB-ONF and other government agencies provided most of the funding for these largely uncommercial works.

Significant feature films of recent years include those of Denys Arcand (*Le Déclin de l'empire américain*, 1986; *Jésus de Montréal*, 1989, both available in English), Jean-Claude Lauzon (*Un zoo la nuit*, 1987; *Léolo*, 1992), Léa Pool (*La Femme de l'hôtel*, 1984; *À corps perdu*, 1988; *Lost and Delirious*, 2001; *Le Papillon bleu*, 2004), Jean Beaudin (*Being at Home With Claude*, 1992), Charles Binamé (*Eldorado*, 1995; *Le Coeur au Poing*, 1998; *Séraphin, un homme et son péché*, 2002), François Girard (*The Red Violin*, 1998) and Robert Lepage (*Le confessionnal*, 1995; *Possible Worlds*, 2000, *La Face cachée de la lune*, 2003). Director Frédérick Back won Academy Awards for the superbly animated *Crac!* in 1981, and

The Man who Planted Trees in 1988. And let's not forget *La Grande Séduction* (2003) by Jean-François Pouliot, *20h17 rue Darling* (2003) by Bernard Émond, *Mambo Italiano* (2003) by Émile Gaudreault and *Gaz Bar Blues* (2003) by Louis Bélanger, which have benefited, along with Denys Arcand's *Les Invasions barbares* and Robert Lepage's *La Face cachée de la lune*, from a new trend that is hitting the movie industry in Québec. This new phenomenon, which finds movie-goers relating to more and more films, can be explained by two factors: better scripts that touch people, and American-style promotion and distribution of new movies throughout Québec and the world.

In addition, 2005 saw the Québec film industry beat 2003's previous box-office record thanks to such popular works as Bernard Émond's *La Neuvaine* (which won three prizes at Locarno, Switzerland's Festival International du Film), Jean-Marc Vallée's *C.R.A.Z.Y.* (named best Canadian film at Toronto's 2005 International Film Festival), Luc Dionne's *Aurore* and Ricardo Trogi's *Horloge biologique*.

Daniel Langlois has also made significant contributions to Québec cinema. A key player in the film industry, he has been very involved in the development of film centres and festivals. He founded Softimage, which designs special-effects software that has been used in several well-known feature-length films over the past several years. According to an industry magazine, 80% of animation and special-effects software produced in the world is designed by Montréal-based companies such as Softimage.

In addition to being the home of a booming movie-making industry, Montréal has been featured in several feature-length films, mostly from the United States. International producers and directors choose Montréal because it is a beautiful city with skilled professionals and excellent services. So next time you watch a movie, whether it is set in Boston or Munich, you might spot part of Montréal!

Music

Modernism was only introduced to the Québec music scene after the post-war years. This tendency intensified in the 1960s following the 1961 inauguration of the Semaine Internationale de la Musique Actuelle (International Week of New Music). Large orchestras such as the Orchestre symphonique de Montréal (OSM), started attracting larger crowds and the interest for modern music spread out from the city to Victoriaville, in the Lanaudière region, where a world-class avant-garde music festival is held every year (Festival International de Musique Actuelle de Victoriaville).

Popular song, which had always been an important part of Québec folklore, blossommed between the two World Wars thanks to the increasing popularity of radio and the improved quality of recording techniques. However, the work of pioneering songwriters such as Félix Leclerc and Raymond Lévesque was eclipsed by the growing popularity of Québécois adaptations of hit American and French songs.

Québec songwriters had to wait until the 1960s and the Quiet Revolution before being recognized on their own terms. Such artists as Claude Léveillé, Jean-Pierre Ferland, Gilles Vigneault and Claude Gauthier started attracting crowds in Québec's bars and cabarets with their nationalist songs that asserted French Québec's cultural identity. A defining moment came in 1968, when Robert Charlebois released the province's first French-language rock album. The scene was thus set for the development of francophone Québec music industry, a movement that even led to the success of certain francophone artists in Europe.

Portrait - Music

34

Certain non-francophone artists such as Leonard Cohen and folk singers Kate and Anne McGarrigle have enjoyed a long-standing international fan base, and up-and-comers like The Arcade Fire, The Dears, Wolf Parade and Rufus Wainwright have all been receiving much attention on the international scene in the last few years.

Visual Arts

Immersed as they were in the era's religious and nationalistic context, 19th-century Québec artworks mostly stand out for their attachment to an outdated aesthetic. Local painters were nonetheless encouraged by important Montréal art collectors and started following more innovative artistic movements around the turn of the 20th century. Landscape artists who celebrated Québec's natural beauty, such as Lucius R. O'Brien, appeared first. Others from the Barbizon School enjoyed some success through their depiction of the pastoral way of life, and subjectivism was progressively introduced by painters such as Edmund Morris.

The symbolist paintings of Ozias Leduc also demonstrated a tendency towards a subjective interpretation of reality, as did the early-20th-century sculptures of Alfred Laliberté. A few of the era's works also show a certain European influence, as is the case with the paintings of Suzor-Coté and, especially, the Matisse-inspired works of James Wilson Morrice. Morrice died in 1924 and is considered by many as the forerunner of Québec's modern art movement. However, several years passed before Québec's artists really caught up with contemporary world trends. Landscape and urban painter Marc-Aurèle Fortin was one of the rare local artists to make an impression during this period.

Modern Québec art really started affirming itself during the Second World War, with the innovative work of Alfred Pellan and Paul-Émile Borduas. Two major movements achieved prominence during the 1950s. First and foremost was the non-figurative movement, which can be divided into two strands: abstract expressionism, which includes such artists as Marcelle Ferron, Marcel Barbeau, Pierre Gauvreau and, especially, Jean-Paul Riopelle; and geometric abstraction, as typified by artists such as Jean-Paul Jérôme, Fernand Toupin, Louis Belzile and Redolphe de Repentigny. The second major post-war movement was the figurative style, which was adopted by artists like Jean Dallaire and Jean-Paul Lemieux.

These post-war movements continued into the 1960s, as geometric abstraction became even more popular with the arrival of new artists such as Guido Molinari, Claude Tousignant and Yves Gaucher. Etching and engraving techniques became popular, performance art was introduced and contemporary artists started being called upon to provide works of art for public spaces. The diversification of techniques and styles became widespread at the beginning of the 1970s, leading to the field's current state of extreme eclecticism.

Circus Arts

Cirque du Soleil, Cirque Éloize and Cirque Éos have given Québec an international presence and recognition the province has never before enjoyed. In the last few years, the talented Québécois artists who stage these circus companies' shows have gained a solid reputation as they tour the world and perform for millions of people of all ages.

■ Cirque du Soleil

The idea for Cirque du Soleil appeared in 1984 in Baie-Saint-Paul, in the Charlevoix region, where a group of acrobats on stilts were providing entertainment at a country fair. This is where founder Guy Laliberté and member-founder Gilles Saint-Croix first met.

Before making its way around the world, Cirque du Soleil first toured throughout Québec to survive. Then came an offer from Los Angeles, a chance to break into new markets and invest in the company's future; it embarked on a series of tours, with one show, one big tent and 200 employees, artists and craftspeople. One of our age's most important circus companies was the result of a mix of Guy Laliberté's vision, the creative drive of Franco Dragone, the director of Cirque du Soleil's first show, the talent of its technicians, and the sensibilities of its artists and performers.

Today, with some 3,000 employees, including more than 600 artists from 40 different countries, Cirque du Soleil is managed like a multinational corporation. Several permanent performance halls have been set up around the world, including in Las Vegas, Disney World (Florida) and Japan, and the company has travelled to Australia, New-Zealand, Europe and Brazil.

What sets Cirque du Soleil apart is the fact its shows combine elements taken from theatre, dance and traditional circuses (an important exception being that they do not feature animals). Furthermore, the shows follow a non-stop narrative, with no intermission and no downtime between the various parts of the story to break up the rhythm. A large team of talented artists is put to the task: choreographers, lighting engineers, composers and a whole slew of others combine to create a marvellously enchanting *tableau vivant*. Cirque du Soleil is currently examining the possibility of setting up a permanent performance facility in Montréal, which is already the company's administrative headquarters. Montrealers will undoubtedly be following this story closely.

■ Cirque Éloize

Cirque Éloize was founded in 1993 by seven young Îles de la Madeleine residents who had moved to Montréal to study at the École Nationale du Cirque (circus school). This company has since been garnering rave reviews all around the world, and the troupe is renowned for the poetry and originality of its shows, in which acrobatics, dance, music and song come together in a beautiful dream-like whole.

Barely ten years after its creation, Cirque Éloize has already visited some 200 cities in 20 countries and staged more than 2,000 shows, with two different troupes presently touring the world. The circus company has recently come full circle by setting up its permanent residence in the former Dalhousie train station, in Old Montréal, the same site that housed the École Nationale du Cirque from 1986 to 2003 (the circus school has since relocated to a building on the site of TOHU, la Cité des Arts du Cirque).

■ Cirque Éos

Cirque Éos was founded in the Québec City region in 1998, a few years after the École de Cirque de Québec was created. The circus company's founders aimed to provide Québec's up-and-coming artists and performers with a professional environment where they could develop their talents while taking advantage of the growing popularity of circus arts.

Portrait – Circus Arts

Cirque Éos' fascinating productions and colourful characters set it apart from other circus companies. International demand for the company's shows has been growing non-stop, and spectators of all ages delight in an imaginary world that features tight-rope walkers, jugglers, acrobats, actors, trapezists and dancers.

■ TOHU, la Cité des Arts du Cirque

TOHU, la Cité des Arts du Cirque is a non-profit organization that was jointly founded in Montréal in 1999 by En Piste (an association of Québec circus professionals), the École Nationale de Cirque and Cirque du Soleil. Its objectives are to make Montréal a world capital in the field of circus arts, to participate in the restoration of the site of the former Miron quarry where TOHU is located (now the Complexe Environne-mental Saint-Michel) and to revitalize the surrounding Saint-Michel neighbourhood.

The idea behind this "circus arts district" was to create a single site that would bring together all of the facilities that go into the creation, training, production and pro-motion of circus arts. Five years after TOHU's founding, this dream has become a reality: the circus complex now includes the world headquarters of Cirque du Soleil (with 1,600 employees on site) and its artists' accommodations; the École Nationale de Cirque, which also includes the offices of the En Piste association; and the TOHU pavilion. The pavilion is the complex's only public space and a unique example of "green" architecture. It doubles as the entrance to the Complexe Environnemental Saint-Michel and features Canada's first circular performance hall and a large outdoor performance space with a collapsible big tent that can seat 1,700 spectators.

Practical Information

Entrance Formalities 38

Getting There and Getting Around 39

Useful Information, from A to Z 44

Practical Information

The information in this chapter will help you better plan your trip, not only in advance, but also once you've arrived in Montréal. It provides important details on entrance formalities for visitors from other countries as well as tips on getting into and around the city.

Entrance Formalities

■ Customs

Smokers (the legal age for purchasing tobacco products in Québec is 18) can bring in a maximum of 200 cigarettes, 50 cigars, 200g of tobacco or 200 tobacco sticks.

For **alcohol** (the legal age for purchasing and consuming alcohol in Québec is 18), the limit is 1.5 litres of wine (or approximately two bottles per person), 1.14 litres of liquor, and 24 355ml cans or 341ml bottles of beer.

For further information on Canadian customs' rules and regulations, contact the **Canada Border Services Agency** (☎800-461-9999 from inside Canada, ☎204-983-3500 or 506-636-5067 from outside Canada; www.cbsa-asfc.gc.ca).

There are very strict rules regarding the importation of **plants** or **flowers**; it is therefore not recommended that visitors bring any of these types of gifts or products into the country. If however you deem that this is indispensable, we strongly advise that you contact the **Canadian Food Inspection Agency** (www.inspection.gc.ca) or your home country's Canadian consulate **before** you leave for Canada.

If you are travelling with your **pet**, you will need to present a rabies-vaccination certificate (provided by a veterinarian). The animal's vaccination must have been administered **at least 30 days before** your departure and not be more than one year old.

■ Passport and Visa

A valid passport is usually sufficient for most visitors from Western Europe and the United States planning to stay less than three months in Canada. You may be required to present your return ticket and proof of sufficient funds to cover your stay.

Travel To or Through the United States

European visitors who wish to continue their journey to the United States, either for leisure or business, no longer need to have a visa. They must, however:

• have a return plane ticket;

• present a biometric passport, except if they have a valid machine-readable passport issued before October 26, 2005; failing this, a visa will be required;

• plan a stay of a maximum of 90 days (the trip cannot be extended on site, and visitors cannot change their status, accept a job or study in the U.S.);

• fill out the Visa Waiver Programme form (I-94W) given by the airline during your flight.

Extended Visits

Visitors must submit a request to extend their visit **written 3 weeks before** the expiration of the first three months of their visit or of their visa (the date is usually written in your passport) to a **Citizenship and Immigration Canada** (www.cic.gc.ca) office. To make a request you must have a valid passport, a return ticket, proof of sufficient funds to cover the stay, as well as the $75 non-refundable filing fee. In some cases (work, study), however, the request must be made **before** arriving in Canada.

Getting There and Getting Around

■ By Plane

Montréal-Pierre Elliott Trudeau International Airport

The Montréal-Dorval International Airport was recently renamed Montréal-Pierre Elliott Trudeau International Airport after the former Canadian Prime Minister. This airport, which is also simply refered to as "**Montréal-Trudeau**," is about a 20min drive from downtown Montréal. To reach the downtown area, take Highway 20 East to the junction with the Ville-Marie Highway (720) and follow directions to "Centre-ville, Vieux-Montréal."

For information regarding airport services (arrivals and departures), contact the **Aéroports de Montréal (ADM)** Information Centre (☎514-394-7377 or 800-465-1213, www.admtl.com).

By Shuttle

The **Aérobus**, affiliated to the **La Québécoise** bus company (☎514-842-2281, www.autobus.qc.ca), offers a shuttle service between the downtown area (Station Centrale), a few major hotels and the Montréal-Trudeau airport. You can get more information on the Aérobus shuttle by calling **Aéroports de Montréal (ADM)**.

You can purchase your ticket from the airport ticket office or at **Station Centrale** (505 Boulevard de Maisonneuve Est, Métro Berri-UQAM, ☎514-842-2281).

Main Airlines

Regular Flights

Air Canada	☎888-247-2262	www.aircanada.com
Air France	☎800-667-2747	www.airfrance.com
Air New Zealand	☎800-663-5494	www.airnewzealand.com
American Airlines	☎800-433-7300	www.aa.com
British Airways	☎888-334-3448	www.britishairways.com
Delta Airlines	☎800-221-1212	www.delta.com
KLM	☎800-225-2525	www.nwa.com
Lufthansa	☎800-563-5954	www.lufthansa.com
Swiss Airlines	☎877-359-7947	www.swiss.com
US Airways	☎800-428-4322	www.usairways.com

Charter Flights

Air Transat	☎877-872-6728	www.airtransat.com
Corsair	☎800-567-0025	www.corsair.fr
Zoom Airlines	☎866-359-9666	www.flyzoom.com

Domestic Flights

Air Canada Jazz	☎888-247-2262	www.flyjazz.ca
Canjet	☎800-809-7777	www.canjet.com
WestJet	☎888-937-8538	www.westjet.com

Practical Information – Getting There and Getting Around

From the Montréal-Trudeau airport to downtown: every 20 min from 7am to 2am. Stops at five major hotels (Marriott Château Champlain, Delta Centre-ville, Fairmont Reine-Élizabeth, Sheraton, Delta Montréal), arrival at Station Centrale. Rate: $13 one-way; $22.75 return.

From downtown to Montréal-Trudeau airport: every 20min from 4am to 11pm. Departure from Station Centrale, stops at five major hotels (Marriott Château Champlain, Delta Centre-ville, Fairmont Reine-Élizabeth, Sheraton, Delta Montréal). Rate: $13 one-way; $22.75 return.

There is also a free **shuttle service** *(reservations:* ☎*514-843-4938)* that links the Station Centrale bus station and a few other downtown hotels.

By Public Transport

From the Montréal-Trudeau airport, you can also use public transport thanks to the **Société de Transport de Montréal (STM)** *(*☎*514-288-6287, www.stm.info)* to reach downtown. Take the 204 bus east to the Dorval train station. From there, take the 211 bus east to the Lionel-Groulx métro station.

By Taxi

The Montréal-Trudeau airport is served by a fleet of 260 taxi cabs. Taxi service is offered from 6am until the last flight. The rate is $31 for trips between the airport and downtown Montréal. All taxis serving Montréal-Trudeau airport are supposed to accept major credit cards.

Car Rentals

The major car-rental companies have offices at the Montréal-Trudeau airport.

Mont-Tremblant International Airport

Mont-Tremblant International Airport *(150 Chemin Roger-Hébert, Rivière-Rouge,* ☎*819-425-7919 or 877-425-7919, www. mtia.ca)*, the newest Canadian international airport, is located 30min north of the Mont-Tremblant resort. It welcomes large carriers from Toronto and New York, small private planes and corporate jets, and offers all the airport and passenger services that one expects from an international airport. Its terminal is unique thanks to its log architecture and features, among other things, hotel-reservation services and a car-rental agency, as well as catering services, limousines and taxis.

■ By Car

Getting into the City

When coming from Québec City, there are two possible routes: take either Highway 20 West to the Champlain Bridge *(pont)*, then Highway 10 (Autoroute Bonaventure), which leads directly downtown, or take Highway 40 West to Highway 15 South (Autoroute Décarie), and then follow the signs for downtown *(centre-ville)*.

From Ottawa, take Highway 40 East to Highway 15 South (Autoroute Décarie), and then follow the signs for downtown *(centre-ville)*.

Visitors arriving from Toronto will arrive via Highway 20 East. Continue along it and then take Autoroute 720 (the Ville-Marie) and follow the signs for downtown *(centre-ville)*.

From the United States, via either Highway 10 or Highway 15, you will take the Champlain Bridge and Highway 10 (Autoroute Bonaventure).

Getting Around the City

Since Montréal is well served by public transportation and taxis, having a car is not essential to visit the city, especially since most of the sights are located relatively close to one another, and all of the suggested tours can be done on foot, except the West Island. Nevertheless, it is quite easy to get around by car. Parking lots, though quite expensive, are numerous in the downtown area. Parking on the street is possible, but be sure to read the signs carefully. Ticketing of illegally parked cars is strict and expensive.

Things to Consider

Winter Driving: During snow removal after a storm, special parking signs are placed on the side of the road that tell drivers when to move their cars. As well, tow trucks with distinctive, blaring warning sirens go by while clearing the snow to remind drivers to move their cars or be towed.

Driving and the Highway Code: When a **school bus** (usually yellow) has stopped and has its signals flashing, you must come to a complete stop, no matter what direction you are travelling in. Failing to stop at the flashing signals is considered a serious offense and carries a heavy penalty.

Seat belts must be worn in both front and back seats at all times.

On certain major thoroughfares, the right lane is **reserved for buses**. They are indicated by a white diamond and signs indicating the hours to avoid driving in the lane, except of course when turning right.

Turning right on a red light is forbidden in Montréal but permitted anywhere else in Québec, except at intersections where it is otherwise indicated.

Signs marked "**Arrêt**" (Stop) in white against a red background must always be respected. Come to a complete stop even if there is no apparent danger.

The only drawback to driving in Montréal is the dreaded **one-way street**. Montréal is full of one-way streets, and you may find yourself literally going around in circles. For example, a street may be one-way north for a section and then suddenly switch to one-way south. Luckily, however, streets usually alternate in direction; if one is one-way north, generally the next will be one-way south. Always check traffic signs carefully!

Car Rental

Vacation packages that include flight, hotel and car, or simply hotel and car, are generally less expensive than renting a car on the spot. Many travel agencies have agreements with the major car-rental companies (Avis, Budget, Hertz, etc.) and offer good deals; contracts often include added bonuses (reduced show ticket prices, for example).

When renting a car, find out if the contract includes unlimited kilometres or not and if the insurance offered provides full coverage (accident, property damage, hospital costs for you and passengers, theft).

Certain credit cards, such as Gold cards, automatically provide holders with collision and theft insurance for their rental vehicles; we suggest you check if your credit card provides this insurance before you rent a vehicle.

Practical Information · Getting There and Getting Around

Main Car Rental Agencies		
Avis	☎ 800-331-1212	www.avis.com
Budget	☎ 800-268-8970	www.budget.ca
Discount	☎ 888-310-2277	www.discountcar.ca
Dollar	☎ 800-848-8268	www.dollarcanada.ca
Enterprise	☎ 800-261-7331	www.enterprise.com
Hertz	☎ 800-263-0678	www.hertz.ca
National	☎ 800-227-7368	www.nationalcar.ca
Thrifty	☎ 800-847-4389	www.thrifty.com

Remember:

- To rent a car in Québec, you must be at least 21 years of age and have had a driver's license for **at least** one year. If you are between 21 and 25, certain companies will ask for a $500 deposit, and in some cases they will also charge an extra sum for each day you rent the car. These conditions do not apply for those over 25 years of age.

- A credit card is needed for the deposit. The credit card must be in the same name as the driver's permit.

- Most rental cars have an automatic transmission.

- Child safety seats cost extra.

Accidents and Emergencies

In case of serious accident, fire or other emergency, dial ☎911 or 0. If you run into trouble on the highway, pull onto the shoulder of the road and turn on your vehicle's hazard lights. If you're driving a rental car, you should contact the rental agency as soon as possible.

If an accident occurs, always fill out an accident report. In case of a disagreement as to who is at fault, ask a police officer for assistance.

■ By Bus

Station Centrale *(505 Boulevard de Maisonneuve Est, at the corner of Rue Berri,* ☎514-842-2281; *Berri-UQAM metro)* is Montréal's main bus station. It is served by such companies as **Greyhound** *(*☎800-661-8747, *www.greyhound.ca)* and **Orléans Express** *(*☎888-999-3977, *www.orleansexpress.com)*, which link most major Canadian and American cities. The terminal is located in a building above the Berri-UQAM metro station and features a tourist-information desk and car-rental kiosks.

■ By Train

The Montréal train station, **Gare Centrale** *(895 rue De La Gauchetière O., metro Bonaventure,* ☎514-989-2626 or 888-842-7245, *www.viarail.ca)* is located right downtown.

■ By Boat

All maritime shuttles that link the municipalities located on the north and south shores of the St. Lawrence accept pedestrians and cyclists. Before heading out to the docks, however, call ahead to find out about schedules.

Croisières AML *(*☎514-281-8000, *www.croisieresaml.com)*, which runs the **Maritime Shuttles of the St. Lawrence**, links the Old Port of Montréal (Jacques-Cartier dock) and Île Sainte-Hélène *(mid-Jun to early Sep every day, mid-May to mid-Jun and early Sep to mid-Oct Sat-Sun; $5)* and the Port de Plaisance de Longueuil *(same rates and schedule)*.

Croisières Navark's *(*☎514-871-8356, *www.navark.net)* ferry *($3.50, includes admission to the Parc National des Îles-de-Boucherville; Sat-Sun and holidays in summer)* links the Parc de la Promenade Bellerive (in eastern Montréal) to Île Charron and its national park. Croisières Navark also offers a **shuttle** service *($5; Sat-Sun and holidays in summer; the crossing takes 50min)* on Lac Saint-Louis, between the Lachine marina and Châteauguay's Parc de la Commune, near Île Saint-Bernard.

■ Public Transportation

Bus and Metro

Visitors are strongly advised to take advantage of Montréal's public-transportation system, which consists of an extensive network of buses and subway trains (the metro) that serve the region well. Metro stations are identified by a blue sign with a white arrow pointing downwards and the word "Métro." Bus stops, indicated by a blue-and-white sign, are usually located at street corners.

A pass entitling the holder to unlimited use of the public-transportation services of the **Société de Transport de Montréal (STM)** *(www.stm.info)* for one month costs $63 and $18.50 for one week. The monthly pass goes on sale a few days before the start of each month. Tourist cards, valid for one day *($9)* or three consecutive days *($17)* also entitle the holder to unlimited use of public-transportation services. For shorter stays or less moving about, visitors can purchase six tickets for $11.50, or single tickets at $2.50 each. Children benefit from reduced fares. Tickets and passes can be purchased at all metro stations. **Take note that bus drivers do not sell tickets and do not give change.**

The metro's green and orange lines operate from Monday to Friday and Sunday from 5:30am to 12:30am, and Saturday from 5:30am to 1am. The yellow line operates from Monday to Friday and Sunday from 5:30am to 1am, and Saturday from 5:30am to 1:30am. The blue line, for its part, operates every day from 5:30am to midnight.

Most bus lines follow the same schedule. However, there are night buses, which are indicated at each stop by a crescent moon. Night buses circulate more or less regularly between 12am and 5am along the city's main thoroughfares. All major stops on the bus network feature a small sign displaying schedules and routes.

If a trip involves a transfer (from one bus to another, from the bus to the metro or vice versa), the passenger must ask the bus driver for a transfer ticket when getting on, or take one from a transfer machine in the metro station. Free subway maps are available inside all stations, as are timetables for the buses that stop at that station.

Note that there is a service offered to women who might need to get off the bus between stops. This service is available after 9pm, provided that passengers alert the driver in advance and that the drop-off location is safe. Furthermore, certain specially equipped STM buses are wheelchair-accessible.

The Berri-UQAM metro station is where you will find the Planibus, which is the detailed schedule and route of each bus. During office hours, this is also where you can pick up objects that may have been lost in the metro or bus.

For more information on the public-transportation system and bus schedules, call ☎ (514) 786-4636 or 288-6287 (which corresponds to the word AUTOBUS, French for "bus", on a telephone dial pad) or visit the Web site www.stm.info.

Commuter Trains

Commuter trains are run by the **Agence Métropolitaine de Transport (AMT)** *(☎514-287-8726, www.amt.qc.ca)*. There are five commuter railway lines with several train stations, and passengers can board with a bicycle: Montréal/Dorion-Rigaud, Montréal/Deux-Montagnes, Montréal/Blainville, Montréal/Mont-Saint-Hilaire and Montréal/Delson. You can purchase train tickets at several places, namely at the Gare centrale and the Lucien-L'Allier, Vendôme, Du Parc and Sainte-Thérèse metro stations, as well as at the ticket counters located at Le Carrefour and the Angrignon, Centre-Ville, Henri-Bourassa Nord, Longueuil and Radisson terminals. Note that schedules and rates vary.

■ By Taxi

Taxi Co-op
☎ (514) 725-9885

Taxi Diamond
☎ (514) 273-6331

Taxi Royal
☎ (514) 274-3333

■ By Bicycle

One of the most enjoyable ways to get around in the summer is by bicycle. Bike paths allow cyclists to explore various neighbourhoods in the city. To help you find your way around, a free map of paths is available at the tourist-information office. You can also purchase the booklet *Biking Montréal* (Ulysses Travel Guides).

The **Société de Transport de Montréal (STM)** (☎514-786-4643, *www.stm.info*) allows passengers to board the metro with their bicycle, on the following conditions:

Passengers must be at least 16 years old or, if they're younger, be accompanied by an adult. They can board with their bicycle between 10am and 3pm, or after 7pm, from Monday to Friday; on Saturdays, Sundays and holidays, they can travel the metro with their bicycle all day. They must travel in the first metro car, but pedestrians have priority, and they cannot board the car if there are already four bicycles in it. In addition, they cannot travel the metro with their bike during large-scale events such as the La Ronde fireworks or the car races on Île Notre-Dame.

At all times, cyclists can park their bicycle near a metro station; the STM provides several bike racks.

You can also travel with your bicycle on commuter trains, which are run by the **Agence Métropolitaine de Transport (AMT)** (☎514-287-8726, *www.amt.qc.ca*).

Since drivers are not always attentive, cyclists should be alert, respect road signs (as is required by law) and be careful at intersections. Bicycle helmets are not mandatory in Montréal, but wearing one is strongly recommended.

For more information on recognized organizations, rental shops and top cycling spots, refer to the Outdoor Activities chapter, Cycling section, of this guide.

■ On Foot

Montréal is an easy city to get around. Its north-south and east-west grid of streets makes an almost perfect checkerboard.

The east-west arteries are divided by Boulevard Saint-Laurent, where street numbers begin at zero and increase eastward and westward, with the direction usually designated in the address.

On north-south arteries, addresses begin at zero at the river (south of the island). Therefore, no. 4176 on Rue Saint-Denis roughly corresponds to no. 4176 on Rue Papineau or Rue Saint-Urbain. The map on p 318 provides a quick orientation to the city.

Useful Information, from A to Z

■ Advice for Smokers

Cigarette smoking is increasingly considered taboo and is being prohibited in more and more public places, such as:

- shopping centres
- buses and the metro
- government offices

Since May 31, 2006, smoking is forbidden in most public places, including bars and restaurants. Cigarettes are generally sold in grocery stores and newsstands, and you must be at least 18 years old to purchase tobacco products.

■ Business Hours

Banks

Banks are generally open Monday to Friday from 10am to 3pm. Many are also open Thursdays and Fridays until 6pm, and sometimes until 8pm. The city's banks have a well-developed network of 24-hour automatic teller machines.

Post Offices

The two largest post offices (see below) are open from 9am to 5:30pm Monday to Friday (*Canada Post, ☎800-267-1177, www.canadapost.ca)*. There are many smaller post offices throughout Québec, located in shopping malls, *dépanneurs* (convenience stores) and even pharmacies; these post offices are open much later and sometimes even on Saturdays.

1250 Rue University
☎ (514) 846-5401

1695 Rue Ste-Catherine Est
☎ (514) 522-3220

Stores

By law, stores can be open the following hours:

- Monday to Wednesday from 10am to 6pm
- Thursday and Friday from 10am to 9pm
- Saturday from 9am or 10am to 5pm
- Sunday from noon to 5pm

Dépanneurs (convenience stores that sell food, beer and cigarettes) are found throughout Québec and are open later, sometimes even 24hrs a day.

■ Canadian Embassies and Consulates Abroad

For a complete list of consular services abroad, visit the Canadian government Web site: www.dfait-maeci.gc.ca

United Kingdom

Canada High Commission
38 Grosvenor Street, GB-London W1X 4AA
▤ (207) 258-6506
www.dfait-maeci.gc.ca/canada-europa/united_kingdom

United States

501 Pennsylvania Ave., NW
Washington DC, 20001
☎ (202) 682-1740
▤ (202) 682-7701
www.dfait-maeci.gc.ca/can-am/washington

Canadian Consulate General
1175 Peachtree St., 100 Colony Sq., Suite 1700
Atlanta, GA 30361-6205
☎ (404) 532-2000
▤ (404) 532-2050

Canadian Consulate General
3 Copley Pl., Suite 400, Boston, MA 02116
☎ (617) 262-3760
▤ (617) 262-3415

Canadian Consulate General
Two Prudential Plaza
180 N. Stetson Ave., Suite 2400, Chicago, IL 60601
☎ (312) 616-1860
▤ (312) 616-1878

Canadian Consulate General
750 N. St. Paul St., Suite 1700, Dallas, TX 75201
☎ (214) 922-9806
▤ (214) 922-9815

Canadian Consulate General
600 Renaissance Center, Suite 1100
Detroit, MI 48243-1798
☎ (313) 567-2340
▤ (313) 567-2164

Canadian Consulate General
550 South Hope St., 9th Floor
Los Angeles, CA 90071-2627
☎ (213) 346-2700
▤ (213)346-2767

Canadian Consulate General
200 South Biscayne Blvd., Suite 1600, First Union Financial Center, Miami, Fl 33131
☎ (305) 579-1600
▤ (305) 374-6774

Canadian Consulate General
701 Fourth Ave. S., Suite 901
Minneapolis, MN 55415-1899
☎ (612) 332-7486
▤ (612) 332-4061

Canadian Consulate General
1251 Ave. of the Americas
New York, NY 10020-1175
☎ (212) 596-1628
▤ (212) 596-1790

Canadian Consulate General
412 Plaza 600 Building, Sixth Avenue and Stewart Street, Seattle, WA, 98101-1286
☎ (206) 443-1777
▤ (206) 443-9735

■ Children

Generally, children under five travel for free, and those under 12 are eligible for fare reductions. The same rules apply for various leisure activities and shows, so find out before you purchase tickets. High chairs and children's menus are available in most restaurants, while a few of the larger stores provide a baby-sitting service while parents shop.

■ Climate

Montréal enjoys generally pleasant weather. Well, at least compared to the rest of Québec! Temperatures can rise above 30oC in summer and drop to –25oC in winter. The heat wave that generally hits in July plunges the city into its usual summertime torpor: Mont-realers slow down and head to the city's public pools to cool off. Every season influences not only the scenery, but also the lifestyle and behaviour of the local population.

Weather Forecasts

For weather forecasts, call ☎(514) 283-3010. You can also tune in to **Météomédia**, channel 17 on cable television, or visit the Web site www.meteomedia.com. For road conditions, call ☎(514) 284-2363 in Montréal and ☎888-355-0511 anywhere else in Québec.

■ Drugs

Drugs are strictly forbidden (even "soft" drugs). Drug users and dealers caught with drugs in their possession risk severe consequences.

■ Electricity

Voltage is 110 volts throughout Canada, the same as in the United States.

Electrical plugs are two-pinned and flat, and adaptors are available here.

■ Emergencies

You can call for help anywhere in Québec by dialling ☎911. Certain regions outside large urban centres have their own emergency telephone number; in these cases, dial 0.

■ Financial Services

Banks

Banks are generally open Monday to Friday, from 9am to 3pm. The best way to withdraw cash is to use your bank card (ATM card). Be aware however that your bank will charge you fixed fees for this service (for example, $5CAN per transaction), and that it is best to avoid making several small withdrawals.

Exchange Rates*		
$1 CAD	=	$0.88 USD
$1 CAD	=	£0.50
$1 CAD	=	0.73 euro
$1 USD	=	$1.13 CAD
£1	=	$1.99 CAD
1 euro	=	$1.36 CAD
*Samples only—rates fluctuate		

Credit Cards

Most credit cards are useful for cash withdrawal and are accepted almost everywhere. A credit card can be essential when renting a car to avoid tying up large sums of money when paying the rental deposit. Some car-rental agencies may even refuse to rent cars to travellers who do not hold a credit card. The most commonly accepted credit cards are Visa, MasterCard, and, to a lesser extent, American Express.

Traveller's Cheques

Traveller's cheques can be cashed in banks upon presentation of personal identification (for a fee) and are generally accepted in most businesses.

Currency

The monetary unit is the dollar ($), which is divided into cents (¢). One dollar=100 cents.

Bills come in 5, 10, 20, 50 and 100 dollar denominations; coins come in one, 5, 10 and 25 cent pieces and in 1 and 2 dollar coins.

Francophones sometimes speak of *"piastres"* and *"sous,"* which are dollars and cents respectively. On occasion, especially in everyday language, you might be asked for a *"trente sous"* (30-cent piece); what the person really wants is a 25-cent piece. A *"cenne noire"* (black cent), furthermore, is a one-cent piece. In English, Europeans may be surprised to hear "pennies" (1¢), "nickels" (5¢), "dimes" (10¢), "quarters" (25¢), "loonies" ($1) and even "toonies" ($2).

■ Foreign Consulates in Montréal

Consulate General of the United States of America
1155 Rue St-Alexandre
☎ (514) 398-9695
▤ (514) 398-0973
http://montreal.usconsulate.gov

Consulate General of Great Britain
1000 De La Gauchetière Ouest, Suite 4200
☎ (514) 866-4315
▤ (514) 866-0202
www.fco.gov.uk

■ Gay and Lesbian Life

Montréal offers many services to the gay and lesbian community. These are mostly concentrated in the part of town known as **The Village**, located on Rue Sainte-Catherine between Amherst and Papineau streets, as well as on the adjoining streets.

Centre d'Information Touristique du Village (see p 53).

In Montréal, a phone line is provided to find out about activities in the city: **Gai-Écoute** *(support and information line, Mon-Fri 8am to 3am, Sat-Sun 11am to 3am; ☎514-866-0103 or 888-505-1010)*. Another option is the **Centre Communautaire des Gais et Lesbiennes** *(2075 Rue Plessis, ☎514-528-8424)*, which offers all kinds of activities, such as dancing, language classes, music, etc.

The **Défilé de la Fierté Gaie et Lesbienne** (the Pride Parade) takes place on the first weekend in August on Boulevard René-Lévesque and ends at Parc Émilie-Gamelin with various performances *(information: Divers-cité, 4067 Boulevard St-Laurent; ☎514-285-4011)*.

Several free magazines containing information concerning the gay and lesbian communities are available in bars and other establishments serving the gay and lesbian communities: *RG*, *Fugues* and *La Voix du Village*.

■ Guided Tours

Various companies organize tours of Montréal, offering visitors interesting ways to explore the city. Walking tours lead to an intimate discovery of the city's neighbourhoods, while bus tours provide a perspective of the city as a whole. Boat cruises highlight another facet of the city, this time in relation to the river. Though there are numerous options, consider the walking, bus and boat tours offered by the following companies.

On Foot

Architectours (Héritage Montréal)
☎ (514) 286-2662
www.heritagemontreal.qc.ca
These walking tours criss-cross neighbourhoods focusing on architecture, history and town planning. Tours are organized from mid-August to mid-October on weekends; they last about two hours and cost $12 per person.

Practical Information – Useful Information, from A to Z

L'Autre Montréal

in summer for all, in winter for groups only
2000 Boulevard St-Joseph Est
☎ (514) 521-7802
www.autremontreal.com

This organization reveals the hidden face of Montréal, through its hippest neighbourhoods and little-known nooks and crannies. Some tours are thematic (for example, "Women in the City"). They last on average three hours and cost $15 per person.

Guidatour

in summer for all, in winter for groups only
477 Rue St-François-Xavier, Suite 300
☎ (514) 844-4021
www.guidatours.qc.ca

Every day from June to October, this company organizes tours along the city's major arteries, allowing visitors to discover Montréal's history, its growth, its architecture and its culture. You can even tour the city in costume dress. Tours last about 1.5hrs and cost from $15 to $25 per person.

Theme Tours

There are several animated tours highlighting the characteristics of each neighbourhood through various themes. For example, the **Old Montréal Ghost Trail** *(☎514-868-0303, www.phvm.qc.ca)* invites you to discover Montréal's legends, famous characters and historic crimes.

The **Monde de Michel Tremblay sur un "plateau"** tour *(☎514-844-4021, www. guidatour.qc.ca)*, for its part, offers an excursion to the heart of the Plateau Mont-Royal district, in the spirit of characters and places in the novels of this famous Montréal author.

A guide playing the role of the patriot chief's wife in the **Le Vieux-Montréal de Julie Papineau 1 et 2** tour *(☎514-844-4021, www. guidatour.qc.ca)* leads a 19th-century–style tour of Old Montréal.

By Bus

Autocar Impérial

1255 Rue Peel, corner Rue Ste-Catherine
(Centre Infotouriste)
☎ (514) 871-4733
www.autocarimperial.com

This company offers a 3h general tour *($35)* or a tour on an air-conditioned, luxurious bus with panoramic windows, as well as visits aboard a double-decker bus. Two-day visits, with nine possible stopovers, provide an interesting option for those who wish to take their time exploring Montréal. These tours let you spend more time at an attraction before joining another group later.

By Boat

Croisières AML Montréal

Quai King-Edward, Old Port
☎ (514) 842-9300
www.croisieresaml.com

Visitors can enjoy various cruises on the river starting at $24. The duration and cost of these excursions vary depending on the package. Evening dinner cruises are also offered.

Amphi-Bus

Departure from the corner of Rue de La Commune and Boulevard St-Laurent
☎ (514) 849-5181

The Amphi-Bus is an "amphibious" bus. From May to late October, it offers guided tours of Old Montréal and the Old Port on land and water for $23.75, an experience that is sure to please children!

Le Bateau-Mouche

Quai Jacques-Cartier, Old Port
☎ (514) 849-9952
www.bateau-mouche.com

Cruises along the river offer an interesting perspective of Montréal. During the day, a cruise costs $25 and lasts 1hr. Departures every day at 10am, 11:30am (with lunch included, last 1.5hrs), 1:30pm, 3pm and 4:30pm, from May to October. Evening tours, during which dinner is served, last 3.5hrs and cost between $80 and $140; departure at 7pm.

■ Health

Vaccinations are not necessary for people coming from Europe or the United States. However, it is strongly suggested, particularly for medium or long-term stays, that visitors take out health and accident insurance. There are different types, so it is best to shop around. Bring along all medication, especially prescription medicine. Unless otherwise stated, water is drinkable throughout Québec.

■ Insurance

Cancellation

Your travel agent will usually offer you cancellation insurance when you buy your airline ticket or vacation package. This insurance allows you to be reimbursed for the ticket or package deal if your trip must be cancelled due to serious illness or death.

Theft

Most residential insurance policies protect some of your goods from theft, even if the theft occurs in a foreign country. To make a claim, you must fill out a police report.

Illness

This is the most useful kind of insurance for travellers, and should be purchased prior to departure. Your insurance plan should be as complete as possible because health-care costs can add up quickly. When buying insurance, make sure it covers all types of medical costs, such as hospitalization, nursing services and doctors' fees. Make sure your limit is high enough, as these expenses can be costly. A repatriation clause is also vital in case the required care is not available on site. Furthermore, since you may have to pay immediately, check your policy to see what provisions it includes for such situations. To avoid any problems during your vacation, always keep proof of your insurance policy with you.

■ Language

Quebecers are very proud of their language and have struggled long and hard to preserve it while surrounded on all sides by English speakers. The accent and vocabulary are different from European French and have a charm all their own.

When writing a guide to a region where the use and preservation of language are a part of daily life, certain decisions have to be made. We have tried to keep our combined use of English and French consistent throughout this guide. The official language in Québec is French, so when providing the names of attractions and other establishments, we have retained the official French name, except where an official English name exists. In such cases, we provide both in the text and index. This will allow readers to make the connection between the guide and the street signs they will be seeing. English style has been used in the text itself, to preserve readability. In Montréal, visitors will hear English almost as much as French, so English-speaking visitors to Montréal will often be able to take a break from practicing their French, if they want. Just remember, a valiant effort and a sincere smile go a long way!

A complete list of all local expressions would be too long to include. Travellers interested in knowing a bit more on the subject can refer to *Canadian French for Better Travel*, published by Ulysses Travel Guides, the *Dictionnaire de la Langue Québécoise* by Léandre Bergeron, published by Éditions VLB, or the excellent *Dictionnaire Pratique des Expressions Québécoises*, published by Éditions Logiques.

Language Courses

Visitors who plan an extended stay in Montréal may want to consider French lessons. A knowledge of French will reveal a whole other side of the city's vibrant culture. Canadian citizens can learn French for free at local CEGEPs (community colleges), while landed immigrants and refugees are offered French classes by Immigration Québec.

Practical Information – **Useful Information, from A to Z**

Everybody else must take courses either from the universities, the YMCA or private language schools. Here are a few private schools to try:

Berlitz Language Centre
☎ (514) 288-3111 or 387-2566

Centre Linguista
☎ (514) 397-1736

Language Studies Canada
☎ (514) 939-9911

■ Laundromats

These are found almost everywhere. In most cases, detergent is sold on the premises. Although change machines are sometimes provided, it is best to bring plenty of quarters with you.

■ Museums

Most museums charge admission; however, permanent exhibits at some museums are free on Wednesday evenings from 6pm to 9pm, while reductions are offered for temporary exhibits. Reduced prices are available for seniors, children and students. Call ahead for further details.

The Montreal Museums Pass is offered by the **Board of Montreal Museum Directors** (☎514-845-6873, *www.museesmontreal.org*) and provides free admission to 30 museums and major Montréal attractions, as well as the public-transit system for three consecutive days, for a very reasonable price of $39.

The Montreal Museums Pass can be purchased in the following establishments:

• most participating museums and attractions;

• the **Old Montréal Tourist Welcome Centre** *(174 Rue Notre-Dame Est,* ☎*514-874-1696)*;

• certain Montréal hotels.

■ Newspapers

International newspapers can easily be found in Montréal. The major Montréal newspapers are, in French, *Le Devoir*, *La Presse* and *Le Journal de Montréal*, and in English, *The Gazette*. Four free weekly newspapers are also available: *Hour* and *The Mirror* in English and *Voir* and *Ici* in French. They can be found in many public places such as bars, restaurants et certain boutiques. All four are free and provide information on Montréal's entertainment scene.

■ Pets

If you have chosen to travel with your pet, note that animals are not admitted in most businesses, including food stores, restaurants and cafés. Small pets are allowed on the public-transportation system, as long as they are in a cage or in the arms of their owner. Finally, you can walk your dog in all Montréal parks, as long as it is kept on a leash and you pick up its droppings.

In the Plateau Mont-Royal sector, **Parc La Fontaine** (see p 174), among other urban green spaces, provides a fenced-in area where dogs can run free; several other parks in the city also provide dog runs.

■ Public Holidays

The following is a list of public holidays in Québec. Most administrative offices and banks are closed on these days.

New Year
January 1st and 2nd

Easter Monday and/or Good Friday
Variable

Journée nationale des Patriotes
Monday before May 25th

Saint-Jean-Baptiste Day
(Québec's national holiday)
June 24th

Canada Day
July 1st

Labour Day
First Monday in September

Thanksgiving
Second Monday in October

Remembrance Day
November 11th

Christmas Day and Boxing Day
December 25th and 26th

funds are done at the border or by filling out a GST refund form (GST 176).

For information:

from Canada
☎ 800-668-4748

outside Canada
☎ (902) 432-5608
www.cra-arc.gc.ca/tax/nonresidents/visitors

■ Senior Citizens

Seniors who would like to meet people their age can do so through the umbrella association below, which brings together most organizations for senior citizens and provides information about activities and local clubs throughout Québec.

Reduced transportation fares and entertainment tickets are often available to seniors. Do not hesitate to ask or contact the **Mouvement des aînés du Québec** *(4545 Avenue Pierre-De Coubertin, C.P. 1000, Succursale M, Montréal, H1V 3R2,* ☎ *514-252-3017 or 800-828-3344, www.fadoq.ca).*

■ Taxes

The ticket price on items usually **does not include tax**. There are two taxes, the GST (federal Goods and Services Tax, TPS in French) of 7% and the PST (provincial sales tax, TVQ in French) at 7.5% on goods and services. They are cumulative, therefore you must add about 15% in taxes to the price of most items and at restaurants. A **special tax is charged on accommodations** (see p 186).

There are some exceptions to this taxation system, such as books, which are only taxed 7%, and food (except for ready-made meals), which is not taxed at all.

Tax Refunds for Non-Residents

Non-residents can reclaim the GST they paid on their purchases. It is therefore important to save all receipts. Tax re-

■ Telecommunications

The area code for the island of Montréal is 514. The area code for the region around the island is 450. Calls between these two regions are still local but you must dial the area code before the number.

Note that all 10 digits (area code + telephone number) will need to be dialled after June 17th, 2006 for all telephone numbers located in the 514 and 450 area-code regions. Furthermore, a second area code (438) will be progressively introduced for telephone numbers of the island of Montréal.

Long-distance calls require that you dial 1 followed by the area code, then the seven-digit number. To call the U.K., dial 011-44 followed by the local area code and number.

Telephone numbers preceded by **800**, **866**, **877** or **888** are toll-free. Some toll-free numbers in the United States can be reached from Canada. To reach an operator, dial **0**.

Less expensive than in Europe, public telephones can be found pretty much everywhere. Unlimited-time local calls cost 25¢. For long-distance calls, stock up on quarters or purchase a telephone card. These are available at newsstands, some convenience stores, drug stores, gas stations and the various phone companies' automatic distributors that can be found in many public spaces.

■ Time Zone

Québec is in the Eastern Standard Time zone, as is most of the eastern United States. It is 3hrs ahead of the west coast of the continent. There is a six-hour time difference between Québec and most continental European countries and a difference of five hours between Québec and the United Kingdom. The entire province of Québec operates on Eastern Standard Time (except Îles de la Madeleine, which are an hour ahead). However, the government of Québec plans to follow the United States' example by extending eastern daylight-saving time starting in 2007 (daylight-saving time would start three weeks earlier in March and end one week later in November).

■ Tipping

In general, tipping applies to all table service: restaurants, bars and nightclubs (no tipping in fast-food restaurants). Tipping is also standard in taxis.

The tip is usually about 15% of the bill before taxes, but varies, of course, depending on the quality of service.

Unlike in Europe, tips are not included in the bill, so it is up to the client to calculate it and give it to the server. Service and tip mean the same thing in North America.

■ Tourist Information

In Europe

Visitors from the UK, the Netherlands and Scandinavia can obtain province-wide information from the following source:

Tourisme Québec International Representation
35-37 Grosvenor Gardens House
London, SW1W 0BS
☎ (44 20) 7233-8011
🖷 (44 20) 7233-7203
info@destinationquebec.de

United Kingdom
General Delegation of Québec
59 Pall Mall, London, Great Britain SW1Y 5JH
☎ (44 20) 7766-5900
🖷 (44 20) 7930-7938
www.mri.gouv.qc.ca

In the United States
General Delegation of Québec
One Rockefeller Plaza, 26th Floor,
New York, NY 10020-2102
☎ (212) 397-0200 or 843-0950
🖷 (212) 757-4753 or 376-8984
www.mri.gouv.qc.ca/usa

On the Internet

You can also find tourist information on the Internet. The following sites may be of interest:

Quebecers and visitors alike will want to visit the site posted by the **Ministère du Tourisme** *(www.bonjourquebec.com)*, which provides access to the various regional tourist associations and even gives a virtual tour of Québec.

Check the **Ulysses Travel Guides** site *(www. ulyssesguides.com)* for new information on Québec, updated regularly.

You can also visit the following Web sites:

http://voyagez.branchez-vous.com
www.canoe.qc.ca
www.toile.ca
www.petitmonde.ca

The site of the **Office des Congrès et du Tourisme du Grand Montréal (OCTGM)** *(www. tourisme-montreal.org)* is overflowing with practical and cultural information about the city of Montréal. It also has a calendar of the countless festivals and events that liven up the city in both summer and winter.

Various Montréal magazines and newspapers also have their own Web sites, such as the English weeklies **Hour** *(www.hour.ca)* and **Mirror** *(www.montreal mirror.com)*, and Montréal's English daily newspaper, **The Gazette** *(www.canada. com/montrealgazette)*.

The **montrealplus.ca** site provides information on restaurants, bars, cinemas, music, culture, sports and hobbies, boutiques, hotels and tourist attractions.

In Montréal

Tourisme Québec
Case Postale 979, Montréal, H3C 2W3
☎ (514) 873-2015 or 877-266-5687
www.bonjourquebec.com

Centre Infotouriste de Montréal
early Jun to early Sep 8:30am to 7:30pm, rest of the year every day 9am to 6pm
1255 Rue Peel, corner Rue Ste-Catherine
Peel metro
☎ (514) 873-2015
The centre provides detailed information, maps, flyers and accommodation information for Montréal and all the tourist regions of Québec.

Bureau d'Accueil Touristique du Vieux-Montréal (Old Montréal)
Jun to Sep every day 9am to 7pm, Sep to May every day 9am to 1pm and 2pm to 5pm
174 Rue Notre-Dame Est
Champ-de-Mars metro
☎ (514) 874-1696

Centre d'Information Touristique du Village (CITV)
Mon-Fri 10am to 6pm, closed on holidays
576 Rue Ste-Catherine Est (corner Rue St-Hubert, facing Parc Émilie-Gamelin)
Berri-UQAM metro
☎ (514) 842-4500, ext. 4788 or
877-616-0060, ext. 4788
www.ccgq.ca/citv.htm
Information on Montréal's Gay Village and its surroundings.

■ Travellers with Disabilities

Kéroul is a non-profit organisation that collaborates with Tourisme Québec to develop, promote and provide information on tourism infrastructures and cultural events that are accessible to people with disabilities throughout the province. Kéroul, in collaboration with Ulysses, also publishes the *Québec Accessible* guide, which lists the tourist and entertainment facilities that are accessible to disabled people. *Québec Accessible* is available at Ulysses and most local bookstores.

Association Québécoise de Loisir pour Personnes Handicapées
4545 Avenue Pierre-De Coubertin
C.P. 1000, Succursale M, Montréal, H1V 3R2
☎ (514) 252-3144
▤ (514) 252-8360
www.aqlph.qc.ca
For further information:

Keroul
4545 Avenue Pierre-De Coubertin
C.P. 1000 Succursale M, Montréal, H1V 3R2
☎ (514) 252-3104
▤ (514) 254-0766
www.keroul.qc.ca
For Canada-wide information, the following government Web site provides useful links: www.accesstotravel.gc.ca.

■ Weights and Measures

Although the metric system has been in use in Canada for more than 20 years, some people continue to use the Imperial system in casual conversation. Here are some equivalents:

Weights
1 pound = 454 grams (g)
1 kilogram (kg) = 2.2 pounds

Linear Measure
1 inch = 2.54 centimetres (cm)
1 foot = 30 centimetres (cm)
1 mile = 1.6 kilometre (km)

Land Measure
1 acre = 0.4047 hectare (ha)
1 hectare (ha) = 2.471 acres

Volume Measure
1 U.S. gallon = 3.79 litres (l)
1 U.S. gallon = 0.83 imperial gallon

Temperature
To convert °F into °C: subtract 32, divide by 9, multiply by 5
To convert °C into °F: multiply by 9, divide by 5, add 32.

■ Wine, Beer and Alcohol

In Québec, the sale of alcohol is regulated by a provincial authority, the Société des Alcools du Québec (SAQ). The best wines, beers and spirits are sold in SAQ stores. The shops are conveniently located throughout the Montréal area.

To find the nearest outlet, call ☎(514) 873-2020 or visit the SAQ's Web site: www.saq.com.

Beer

Two large brewing companies, Labatt and Molson, share the greater portion of the provincial market. Each produces various types of beer, mainly lagers, with varying levels of alcohol. In bars, restaurants and nightclubs, beer on tap, sometimes referred to as "draft" (even in French), is less expensive than bottled beer.

Beside these "macro-breweries," micro-breweries have been sprouting up over the last several years and their beers are very popular in Québec for their variety and flavour. Some of the better-known micro-breweries are Unibroue, McAuslan, Brasseurs RJ and Brasseurs du Nord.

N.B. The legal drinking age in Québec is **18**.

Exploring

Tour A: Vieux-Montréal	56	Tour J: Mont Royal	119
Tour B: Downtown	70	Tour K: Westmount	125
Tour C: Montreal Museum of Fine Arts	82	Tour L: Outremont and Mile-End	128
		Tour M: Little Italy	134
Tour D: The Golden Square Mile	86	Tour N: Sault-au-Récollet	137
Tour E: Shaughnessy Village	94	Tour O: Île Sainte-Hélène and Île Notre-Dame	141
Tour F: The McGill Ghetto and "The Main"	99	Tour P: Hochelaga-Maisonneuve	145
Tour G: Quartier Latin	104	Tour Q: Around the Lachine Canal	150
Tour H: The Village	110	Tour R: West Island and Surroundings	160
Tour I: Plateau Mont-Royal	115		

Exploring

T he tours and main attractions described in this chapter are rated according to a star system to ensure you don't miss the city's must-sees, even if you're only in Montréal for a short stay.

★   Interesting
★★   Worth a visit
★★★   Not to be missed

The name of each attraction is followed by information in brackets, such as opening hours, address and telephone number. The admission rate (for one adult) is also indicated. Note that most establishments offer discounts for children, students, senior citizens and families.

Suggested Tours

A	Vieux-Montréal	★★★	p 56
B	Downtown	★★★	p 70
C	Montreal Museum of Fine Arts	★★	p 82
D	The Golden Square Mile	★	p 86
E	Shaughnessy Village	★	p 94
F	The McGill ghetto and "The Main"	★	p 99
G	Quartier Latin	★★	p 104
H	The Village	★	p 110
I	Plateau Mont-Royal	★★	p 115
J	Mont Royal	★★	p 119
K	Westmount	★	p 125
L	Outremont and Mile-End	★	p 128
M	Little Italy	★	p 134
N	Sault-au-Récollet	★	p 137
O	Île Sainte-Hélène and Île Notre-Dame	★★	p 141
P	Hochelaga-Maisonneuve	★★	p 145
Q	Around the Lachine Canal	★	p 150
R	West Island and Surroundings	★★	p 160

Tour A: Vieux-Montréal
★★★

⏱ *one day*

In the 18th century, Montréal, like Québec City, was surrounded by stone fortifications (see the map of Montréal's fortifications circa 1750, p 18). Between 1801 and 1817, these ramparts were demolished by local merchants who saw them as an obstacle to the city's development. The network of old streets, compressed after nearly a century of confinement, nevertheless remained in place. Today's Vieux-Montréal, or Old Montréal, thus corresponds quite closely to the area covered by the fortified city.

During the 19th century, this area became the hub of commercial and financial activity in Canada. Banks and insurance companies built sumptuous head offices here, leading to the demolition of almost all buildings erected under the French Regime.

The area was later abandoned for nearly 40 years in favour of today's modern downtown area. Finally, the long process of breathing new life into Old Montréal got underway during the preparations

Exploring

June's traditional Chinese Dragon Parade, with the Marché Bonsecours in the background.
© *Tourisme Montréal*

The Second Empire-style Hôtel de Ville towers over Old Montréal.
© *Tourisme Montréal*

The majestic Basilique Notre-Dame, a masterpiece of Gothic Revival architecture.
© *www.vieux.montreal.qc.ca, le photographe masqué*

The metro serves Montréal's sprawling underground city.
© *Tourisme Montréal*

Square Dorchester and its surroundings provide a good example of downtown Montréal's eclectic architectural styles.
© *Tourisme Montréal*

La Foule Illuminée, a sculpture by artist Raymond Mason, stands in front of the twin BNP / Banque Laurentienne towers.
© *Philippe Renault*

The Place Ville-Marie esplanade and its huge Christmas tree face Avenue McGill College.
© *Tourisme Montréal*

for Expo 67 and continues today with numerous conversion and restoration projects. This revitalization has even gotten a second wind since the late 1990s. In fact, several high-end hotels have been established in historic buildings, while many Montrealers have rejuvenated the neighbourhood by making it their home.

›› Ⓜ *This tour starts at the western tip of Vieux-Montréal, on Rue Saint-Jacques (Square-Victoria metro).* **Square Victoria** *(see p 81), located behind you, is described in the Quartier International section of the downtown Montréal tour.*

Rue Saint-Jacques was the main artery of Canadian high finance for over a century. This role is reflected in its rich and varied architecture, which serves as a veritable encyclopedia of styles from 1830 to 1930. In those years, the banks, insurance companies and department stores, as well as the nation's railway and shipping companies, were largely controlled by Montrealers of Scottish extraction, who had come to the colonies to make their fortune.

The modern downtown area stands in the background, where glass and steel skyscrapers tower over wide boulevards, marking a sharp contrast with the old part of the city where stone buildings predominate on narrow, compact streets.

Begun in 1928 according to plans by New York skyscraper specialists York and Sawyer, the former head office of the **Banque Royale / Royal Bank** ★★ *(360 Rue St-Jacques; Square-Victoria metro)* was one of the last buildings erected during this era of prosperity. The 22-storey tower has a base inspired by Florentine palazzos, which corresponds to the scale of neighbouring buildings. Inside the tower, visitors can admire the high ceilings of this "temple of finance," built at a time when banks needed impressive buildings to win customers' confidence. The walls of the great hall are emblazoned with the heraldic insignia of eight of the 10 Canadian provinces, as well as those of Montréal (St. George's Cross)

and Halifax (a yellow bird), where the bank was founded in 1861.

The **Banque Molson / Molson Bank** ★ *(288 Rue Saint-Jacques; Square-Victoria metro)* was founded in 1854 by the Molson family, famous for the brewery established by their ancestor, John Molson (1763-1836), in 1786. The Molson Bank, like other banks at the time, even printed its own paper money—an indication of the power wielded by its owners, who contributed greatly to the city's development. The head office of the family business looks more like a patrician residence than an anonymous bank. Completed in 1866, it is one of the earliest examples of the Second Empire, or Napoleon III, style to have been erected in Canada. This French style, modelled on the Louvre and the Paris Opera, was extremely popular in North America between 1865 and 1890. Above the entrance, visitors will see the sandstone carvings of the heads of William Molson and two of his children. The Molson Bank merged with the Bank of Montréal in 1925.

››› ⋏ *Walk along Rue Saint-Jacques; you'll soon reach Place d'Armes.*

Under the French Regime, **Place d'Armes** ★★ *(Place-d'Armes metro)* was the heart of the city. Used for military manoeuvres and religious processions, the square was also the location of the Gadoys well, the city's main source of potable water. In 1847, the square was transformed into a lovely, fenced-in Victorian garden, which was destroyed at the beginning of the 20th century to make room for a tramway terminal. In the meantime, a **monument to Maisonneuve** ★★ was erected in 1895. Executed by sculptor Philippe Hébert, it shows the founder of Montréal, Paul de Chomedey, Sieur de Maisonneuve, surrounded by prominent figures from the city's early history, namely Jeanne Mance, founder of the Hôtel-Dieu hospital, Lambert Closse and his dog Pilote, and Charles LeMoyne, the head of a family of famous explorers. An Iroquois warrior completes the tableau.

The square, which is in fact shaped like a trapezoid, is surrounded by several noteworthy buildings. The **Banque de Montréal** ★★ *(119 Rue St-Jacques; Place-d'Armes metro)*, or Bank of Montreal, founded in 1817 by a group of merchants, is the country's oldest banking institution. Its present head office takes up an entire block on the north side of Place d'Armes. A magnificent building created by John Wells in 1847 and modelled after the Roman Pantheon, it occupies the place of honour in the centre of the block. Its Corinthian portico is a monument to the commercial power of the Scottish merchants who founded the institution. The columns' capitals, for their part, were severely damaged by pollution and replaced in 1970 with aluminum replicas. The pediment includes a bas-relief depicting the bank's coat of arms carved out of Binney stone in Scotland by Her Majesty's sculptor, Sir John Steele.

The interior was almost entirely redone in 1904-05 by celebrated New York architects McKim, Mead and White (Boston Library, Columbia University in New York City). On this occasion, the bank was endowed with a splendid banking hall, designed in the style of a Roman basilica, with green syenite columns, gilded bronze ornamentation and beige marble counters. A small **Numismatic Museum** *(free admission; Mon-Fri 10am to 4pm)*, located in the lobby of the more recent building, displays bills from different eras, as well as an amusing collection of mechanical piggy banks. Across from the museum, visitors will find four bas-reliefs carved out of an artificial stone called *coade*, which once graced the facade of the bank's original head office. These were created in 1819, after drawings by English sculptor John Bacon.

The surprising red-sandstone tower at number 511 Place d'Armes was erected in 1888 for the New York Life insurance company by architects Babb, Cook and Willard. Although it only has eight floors, it is regarded as Montréal's first skyscraper. The stone used for the facing was imported from Scotland. At the time, this type of stone was transported in the holds of ships, where it served as ballast until it was sold to building contractors at the pier. The edifice next door *(507 Place-d'Armes)* is adorned with beautiful Art-Deco details. It was one of the first buildings over 10 stories to be erected in Montréal after a regulation restricting the height of structures was repealed in 1927.

⋯ ⚊ *On the south side of Place d'Armes, visitors will find the Basilique Notre-Dame and the Vieux Séminaire, which are described below.*

In 1663, the seigneury of the island of Montréal was acquired by the Sulpicians from Paris, who remained its undisputed masters up until the British conquest of 1760. In addition to distributing land to colonists and laying out the city's first streets, the Sulpicians were responsible for the construction of a large number of buildings, including Montréal's first

★ **ATTRACTIONS**

1.	BX	Banque Royale / Royal Bank
2.	BX	Banque Molson / Molson Bank
3.	CX	Place d'Armes / Monument to Maisonneuve
4.	CX	Banque de Montréal / Numismatic Museum
5.	CX	Basilique Notre-Dame
6.	CX	Vieux Séminaire Saint-Sulpice
7.	CY	Cours Le Royer
8.	CY	Place Royale
9.	CY	Pointe-à-Callière, Musée d'Archéologie et d'Histoire de Montréal / Maison de la Douane
10.	BY	Place D'Youville
11.	BY	Centre d'Histoire de Montréal
12.	BY	Hôpital Général des Sœurs Grises
13.	BZ	Musée Marc-Aurèle-Fortin
14.	AY	Fonderie Darling
15.	AZ	Cognicase building
16.	DY	Vieux-Port de Montréal / Old Port
17.	CY	Centre des Sciences de Montréal
18.	DX	Auberge Saint-Gabriel
19.	DX	Centre de Céramique Bonsecours
20.	DX	Palais de Justice
21.	DX	Édifice Ernest-Cormier
22.	DX	Former Palais de Justice
23.	DX	Place Jacques-Cartier / Colonne Nelson
24.	DX	Hôtel de Ville
25.	DX	Place Vauquelin
26.	DX	Champ-de-Mars
27.	DX	Place De La Dauversière
28.	DX	Musée du Château Ramezay
29.	EX	Sir George-Étienne-Cartier National Historic Site
30.	EX	Cathédrale Schismatique Grecque Saint-Nicolas (former)
31.	EX	Gare Viger
32.	EX	Gare Dalhousie
33.	EX	Chapelle Notre-Dame-de-Bon-Secours / Musée Marguerite-Bourgeoys
34.	EX	Maison Pierre du Calvet
35.	EX	Maison Papineau
36.	EY	Marché Bonsecours
37.	DY	Pavillon Jacques-Cartier
38.	EY	Tour de l'Horloge

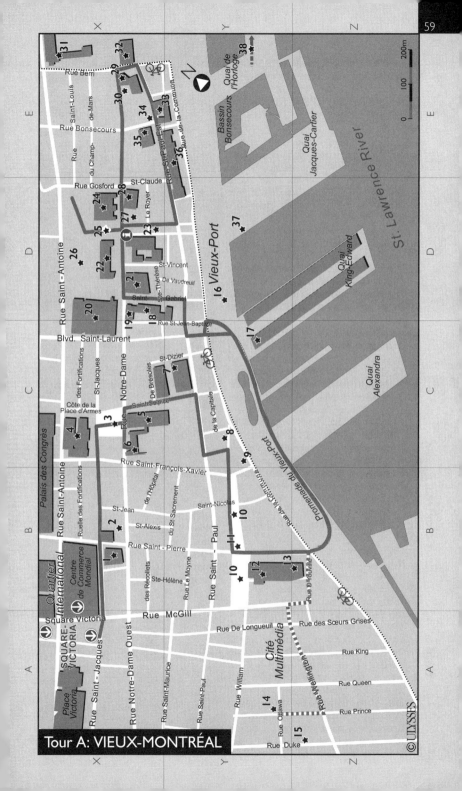

Tour A: VIEUX-MONTRÉAL

parish church (1673). Dedicated to *Notre Dame* (Our Lady), this church had a beautiful Baroque facade, which faced straight down the centre of the street of the same name, creating a pleasant perspective characteristic of classical French town-planning.

At the beginning of the 19th century, however, this rustic little church cut a sorry figure when compared to the Anglican cathedral on Rue Notre-Dame and the new Catholic cathedral on Rue Saint-Denis, neither of which still stands today. The Sulpicians therefore decided to make a move to surpass their rivals once and for all. In 1823, to the great displeasure of local architects, they commissioned New York architect James O'Donnell, who came from an Irish Protestant background, to design the largest and most original church north of Mexico.

Basilique Notre-Dame ★★★ *($4; Mon-Fri 8am to 4:30pm, Sat 8am to 4pm, Sun 12:30pm to 4pm; 110 Rue Notre-Dame Ouest, ☎514-842-2925 or 866-842-2925; Place-d'Armes metro)*, built between 1824 and 1829, is a true North-American masterpiece of Gothic Revival architecture. It should be seen not as a replica of a European cathedral, but rather as a fundamentally neoclassical structure characteristic of the Industrial Revolution, complemented by a medieval-style decor that foreshadowed the historicism of the Victorian era. These elements make the building simply remarkable.

O'Donnell was so pleased with his work that he converted to Catholicism before his death, so that he could be buried under the church. Between 1874 and 1880, the original interior, considered too austere, was replaced by the fabulous polychromatic decorations found today. Executed by Victor Bourgeau, then the leading architect of religious buildings in the Montréal region, along with about 50 artists, it is made entirely of wood, painted and gilded with gold leaf. Particularly noteworthy features include the baptistery, decorated with frescoes by Ozias Leduc, and the powerful electro-pneumatic Casavant organ

Spotlight on the City

For almost five years now, Montréal has had its own *Plan Lumière*, a lighting program whose mission is to illuminate the city after dark and make it as attractive by nightfall as it is by daylight. The concept of highlighting the city's architectural heritage in this way, which has been all the rage in Europe for the last 20 years or so, is the work of Gilles Arpin, the leading Québec expert in urban lighting.

Lampposts and carefully positioned floodlights make Montréal's monuments and public squares emerge out of the shadows and reveal aspects of their architecture that might otherwise go unnoticed in the light of day. The entire program is controlled by computer. You need only walk around downtown or Old Montréal to appreciate most of these permanent night-time landscapes.

with 7,000 pipes, often used during the numerous concerts given at the basilica. Lastly, there are the stained-glass windows by Francis Chigot, a master glass artist from France, which depict various episodes in the history of Montréal. They were installed in honour of the church's centennial.

To the right of the chancel, a passage leads to the Chapelle du Sacré-Cœur (Sacred Heart Chapel), added to the back of the church in 1888. Nicknamed *"Chapelle des Mariages"* (Wedding Chapel) because of the countless nuptials held there every year, it was seriously damaged by fire in 1978. The spiral staircases and the side galleries are all that remain of the exuberant, Spanish-style Gothic Revival decor of the original. Architects Jodoin, Lamarre and Pratte decided to tie in these vestiges with a modern design, completed in 1981, and included a lovely sectioned vault with skylights, a large bronze reredos by Charles Daudelin and a Guilbault-Thérien mechanical organ.

The **Vieux Séminaire Saint-Sulpice** ★ *(130 Rue Notre-Dame Ouest; Place-d'Armes metro)*, or old seminary, was built in 1683 in the style of a Parisian *hôtel particulier*, with a courtyard in front and a garden in back. It is the oldest building in the city. For more than three centuries, it has been occupied by Sulpician priests who, under the French Regime, used it as a manor from which they managed their vast seigneury. At the time of the building's construction, Montréal was home to barely 500 inhabitants and was constantly being terrorized by Iroquois attacks. Under those circumstances, the seminary, although modest in appearance, represented a precious haven of European civilization in the middle of the wilderness. The public clock at the top of the facade was installed in 1701, and may be the oldest one of its kind in the Americas.

⋯ ⅄ *Take Rue Saint-Sulpice, which runs alongside the basilica.*

The immense warehouses of the **Cours Le Royer** ★ *(corner of Rue St-Sulpice and Rue St-Paul; Place-d'Armes metro)* belonged to the *religieuses hospitalières* (nursing sisters) of Saint-Joseph, who rented them out to importers. Designed between 1860 and 1871 by Michel Laurent and Victor Bourgeau, who seldom worked on commercial structures, they are located on the site of Montréal's first Hôtel-Dieu hospital, founded by Jeanne Mance in 1643. The warehouses, covering a total of 43,000m², were converted into apartments and offices between 1977 and 1986. The small Rue Le Royer was excavated to make room for an underground parking lot, now covered by a lovely pedestrian mall.

Old Montréal features a large number of 19th-century warehouses with stone frames used to store the goods unloaded from ships at the nearby port. Certain elements of their design—their large glass surfaces, intended to reduce the need for artificial gas lighting and consequently the risk of fire, their wide open interior spaces, the austere style of their Victorian facades—make these buildings the natural precursors of modern architecture. Many of the warehouses have been converted into hotels.

⋯ ⅄ *Turn right on Rue Saint-Paul, towards Place Royale, which lies on the left side of the street.*

Rue Saint-Paul is Montréal's oldest street. It was drawn by land surveyor Bénigne de Basset in 1672 according to urban planner and historian Dollier de Casson's plans, and was Montréal's main commercial artery for a long time. It is probably Old Montréal's most emblematic street, lined with 19th-century stone buildings that are home to art galleries, arts-and-crafts shops and jazz clubs, making it a very pleasant place for a stroll.

Heads Up!

→ Time for lunch? Head to **Olive + Gourmando** (see p 212), a charming bistro-bakery on Rue Saint-Paul.

Montréal's oldest public square, **Place Royale** *(Place-d'Armes metro)*, dates back to 1657. Originally a market square, it later became a pretty Victorian garden surrounded by a cast-iron fence. In 1991, it was raised in order to make room for an archaeological observation site. It now links the Musée d'Archéologie de Montréal to the **Maison de la Douane**, the former customs house, on the north side. The latter is a lovely example of British neoclassical architecture transplanted into a Canadian setting. The building's austere lines, accentuated by the facing of local grey stone, are offset by the appropriate proportions and simplified references to antiquity. The old customs house was built in 1836 by John Ostell, who had just arrived in Montréal. It is now an integral part of the Pointe-à-Callière museum.

Exploring – Vieux-Montréal

Pointe-à-Callière, Musée d'Archéologie et d'Histoire de Montréal ★★ *($11; Sep to Jun Tue-Fri 10am to 5pm, Sat and Sun 11am to 5pm; Jul and Aug Mon-Fri 10am to 6pm, Sat and Sun 11am to 6pm; 350 Place Royale, Place-d'Armes metro,* ☎*514-872-9150, www. pacmusee.qc.ca)* is an archaeology and history museum that lies on the exact site where Montréal was founded on May 18, 1642: **Pointe à Callière**. The Saint-Pierre river used to flow alongside the area now occupied by Place d'Youville, while the muddy banks of the St. Lawrence reached almost as far as the present-day Rue de la Commune. The first colonists built Fort Ville-Marie out of earth and wooden posts on the isolated point of land created by these two bodies of water. Threatened by Iroquois flotillas and flooding, the leaders of the colony soon decided to establish the town on Côteau Saint-Louis, the hill now bisected by Rue Notre-Dame. The site of the fort was then occupied by a cemetery and the château of Governor de Callière, hence the name.

The museum uses the most advanced techniques available to provide visitors with a survey of the city's history. Attractions include a multimedia presentation, a visit to the vestiges discovered on the site, excellent models illustrating the stages of Place Royale's development, holograms and thematic exhibitions. Designed by architect Dan Hanganu, the museum was established in 1992, the city's 350th anniversary.

⋯ ⃗ *Head towards Place d'Youville, west of the museum.*

Stretching from Place Royale to Rue McGill, **Place d'Youville** owes its elongated shape to its location on top of the bed of the Rivière Saint-Pierre, which was canalized in 1832.

In the heart of Place d'Youville stands the former no. 3 fire station, one of Québec's rare examples of Flemish-inspired architecture. The station is now home to the **Centre d'Histoire de Montréal** ★ *($4.50; May to Aug Tue-Sun 10am to 5pm, Sep to Apr Wed-Sun 10am to 5pm; 335 Place d'Youville,* ☎*514-872-3207, www.ville.montreal.qc.ca/*

chm). A lovely exhibit showcasing various objects relating Montréal's history is presented on the first floor. Thanks to lively presentations, visitors can follow the city's evolution and learn about significant events, such as Expo 67, discover daily life in various eras, hear about major strikes in the city and see how several heritage buildings were demolished. Sound effects, among other things, play a particularly important role here, as you can hear taped testimonies of Montrealers of various origins talking about their city. On the top floors are temporary exhibits, as well as a glassed-in overpass from which you can admire Old Montréal.

Marché Sainte-Anne used to be located west of Rue Saint-Pierre and was the seat of the Province of Canada's Parliament from 1840 to 1849, when Orangemen burned the building down following the adoption of a compensatory law aimed at both English- and French-speaking victims of the 1837-1838 Rebellions. This marked the end of Montréal's political vocation: Canada's Parliament was subsequently moved to Toronto, then Québec City and, finally, Ottawa in 1847.

⋯ ⃗ *Turn left on Rue Saint-Pierre.*

The Sœurs de la Charité (Sisters of Charity) are better known as the Sœurs Grises (Grey Nuns), a nickname given to these nuns who were falsely accused of selling alcohol to natives and getting them drunk (in French, *gris* means both grey and tipsy). In 1747, the founder of the community, Sainte Marguerite d'Youville, took charge of the former Hôpital des Frères Charon, established in 1693, and transformed it into the **Hôpital Général des Sœurs Grises** ★ *(138 Rue St-Pierre; Square-Victoria metro)*, a shelter for the city's homeless children. The west wing and the ruins of the chapel are all that remain of this complex, built during the 17th and 18th centuries in the shape of an *H*. The other part, which made up another of the old city's classical perspectives, was torn open when Rue Saint-Pierre was extended through the middle of the chapel. The right transept and part of the apse, visible on the right, have been reinforced in order to accommodate a work of art representing the text of the congregation's letters patent.

The small **Musée Marc-Aurèle-Fortin** *($5; Tue-Sun 11am to 5pm; 118 Rue St-Pierre,* ☎*514-845-6108, www.museemafortin.org; Square-Victoria metro)*, which has only a few rooms, is entirely dedicated to the work of Marc-Aurèle Fortin. Using his own unique style, Fortin painted picturesque Québec scenes. Paintings executed on a black background and majestic trees are just a few of his trademarks.

Fonderie Darling *($2, free admission Thu; 745 Rue Ottawa,* ☎*514-392-1554, www.quartierephemere.org; Square-Victoria metro)* is well worth the detour. The former Darling Foundry, located in what is now the Cité Multimédia, was converted into an arts centre thanks to an initiative of Quartier Éphémère, an organization devoted to preserving the city's industrial heritage. Established in the industrial district in 1880, the foundry contributed to the development of Montréal's port. After being abandoned for many years, the building was renovated and is now a centre for the creation, production and promotion of works by young artists, and contains offices, art studios, a sound studio, an art gallery with an exhibit space and a café-restaurant named ArtBar Cluny.

Fonderie Darling is located in what is now called the **Cité Multimédia de Montréal** ★, which takes up a large chunk of the southwestern part of Old Montréal, i.e. the old Faubourg des Récollets. These buildings house several companies in the movie and multimedia industries, which brings a lot of life to a district that is now teeming with young workers all day long. The **Cognicase building** ★ *(111 Rue Duke)* is definitely worth a look for its unique architecture.

▸▸▸ 🕅 *Retrace your steps and cross Rue de la Commune to the Promenade du Vieux-Port, which runs alongside the St. Lawrence.*

The port of Montréal is the largest inland port on the continent. It stretches 25km along the St. Lawrence River,

from Cité du Havre to the refineries in the east end. The **Vieux-Port de Montréal / Old Port** ★ *(www.vieuxportdemontreal.com; Place-d'Armes or Champ-de-Mars metro)* corresponds to the historic portion of the port, located in front of the old city. Abandoned because of its obsolescence, it was revamped between 1983 and 1992, following the example of various other centrally located North-American ports. The old port encompasses a lovely park, laid out on the embankments and coupled with a promenade, which runs alongside the piers, or *quai*, offering a "window" on the river and the few shipping activities that have fortunately been maintained. The layout emphasizes the view of the water, the downtown area and Rue de la Commune, whose wall of neoclassical grey-stone warehouses stands before the city, one of the only examples of so-called "waterfront planning" in North America.

From the port, visitors can set off on an excursion on the river and the Lachine Canal aboard the **Bateau-Mouche** *($20.65; mid-May to mid-Oct, departures every day at 10am, 11:30am, 1:30pm, 3pm and 4:30pm; quai Jacques-Cartier,* ☎*514-849-9952 or 800-361-9952, www.bateaumouche.ca)*, whose glass roof enables passengers to fully appreciate the beauty of the surroundings. These guided tours last 1.5hrs. At night, you can also enjoy dinner and dancing on the boat. The ***navettes fluviales***, or river shuttles, *($5;* ☎*514-281-8000)* ferry passengers to Île Sainte-Hélène and Longueuil, offering a spectacular view of the old port and Old Montréal along the way.

On the right, directly in line with Rue McGill, visitors will find the mouth of the **Canal de Lachine / Lachine Canal** ★, inaugurated in 1825. This waterway made it possible to bypass the formidable rapids known as the Rapides de Lachine, upriver from Montréal, thus providing access to the Great Lakes and the American Midwest. The canal also became the cradle of the industrial revolution in Canada since spinning and flour mills were able to harness its power, as well as a direct means of taking in supplies and

Exploring – Vieux-Montréal

sending out shipments (from the boat to the factory and vice versa).

Closed in 1970, 11 years after the St. Lawrence seaway was opened in 1959, the canal was turned over to the Canadian Parks Service. A bicycle path now runs alongside it, continuing on to the Old Port. The locks, restored in 1991, lie adjacent to a park and a boldly designed lock-keeper's house. Behind the locks stands the last of the old port's towering **grain silos**. Erected in 1905, this reinforced concrete structure gained the admiration of Walter Gropius and Le Corbusier when they came here on a study trip. It is now illuminated as if it were a monument. In front, visitors will see the strange pile of cubes that form **Habitat 67** ★★ (see p 141) on the right, and the **Gare Maritime Iberville du Port de Montréal** (☎514-286-7011), the harbour station for liners cruising the St. Lawrence, on the left.

The **Centre des Sciences de Montréal** (*$10; May to Aug every day 10am to 6pm, Sep to Apr Mon-Fri 9am to 3:30pm, Sat-Sun 10am to 5pm; Quai King-Edward,* ☎*514-496-4724 or 877-496-4724, www.centredessciencesdemontreal. com; Place-d'Armes metro),* an interactive science-and-entertainment complex set up in a modern building, invites you to discover the secrets of the world of science and technology while having a great time. The centre features three interactive exhibition halls where participants can enjoy science experiments, games of skill and several cultural and educational activities. The centre also boasts an **IMAX** theatre, the Immersion Interactive Cinema, restaurants and boutiques.

▸▸▸ 🧍 *Walk along the promenade to **Boulevard Saint-Laurent** (see p 99).*

Boulevard Saint-Laurent, one of the city's main arteries, serves as the dividing line between east and west not only as far as place names and addresses are concerned, but also from a linguistic point of view. Traditionally, there has always been a higher concentration of English-speakers in the western part of the city and French-speakers in the eastern part,

while ethnic minorities of all different origins are concentrated along Boulevard Saint-Laurent.

▸▸▸ 🧍 *Head up Boulevard Saint-Laurent to Rue Saint-Paul. Turn right, then left onto narrow Rue Saint-Gabriel.*

It was on this street that Richard Dulong opened an inn in 1754. Today, the **Auberge Saint-Gabriel** *(426 Rue St-Gabriel,* ☎*514-878-3561; Place-d'Armes metro),* the oldest Canadian inn still in operation, is a restaurant (see p 214). It occupies a group of 18th-century buildings with sturdy fieldstone walls.

The **Centre de Céramique Bonsecours** *(schedule varies; 444 Rue St-Gabriel,* ☎*514-866-6581, www.centreceramiquebonsecours.net; Place-d'Armes metro),* a training, research, creation and promotion centre for ceramics in Québec, also houses an art gallery. It was founded about 20 years ago in the former Caserne Saint-Gabriel, the oldest firehouse in Montréal that is still standing. This Victorian-style structure was built in 1871-1872 by architect J.J. Browne.

▸▸▸ 🧍 *Turn right on Rue Notre-Dame.*

Having passed through the financial and warehouse districts, visitors now enter an area dominated by civic and legal institutions; no fewer than three courthouses lie along Rue Notre-Dame. Inaugurated in 1971, the massive new **Palais de Justice** *(1 Rue Notre-Dame Est; Champ-de-Mars metro),* or courthouse, dwarfs the surroundings. A sculpture by Charles Daudelin entitled *Allegropole* stands on its steps. A mechanism makes it possible to open and close this stylized "hand of justice."

From the time it was inaugurated in 1926 until it closed in 1970, the **Édifice Ernest-Cormier** ★★ *(100 Rue Notre-Dame Est; Champ-de-Mars metro)* was used for criminal proceedings. The former courthouse was converted into a conservatory and was named after its architect, the illustrious Ernest Cormier, who also designed the main pavilion of the Université de Montréal and the doors of the United Nations Headquarters in New York City.

The Édifice Ernest-Cormier returned to its original use in 2004, as the Court of Appeal of Québec. The courthouse is graced with outstanding bronze sconces, cast in Paris at the workshops of Edgar Brandt. Their installation in 1925 ushered in the Art Deco style in Canada. The main hall, faced with travertine and topped by three dome-shaped skylights, is worth a quick visit.

The former **Palais de Justice** ★ *(155 Rue Notre-Dame Est; Champ-de-Mars metro)*, the oldest courthouse in Montréal, was built between 1849 and 1856 by John Ostell and Henri-Maurice Perrault, on the site of the first courthouse, which was erected in 1800. It is another fine example of Canadian neoclassical architecture. After the courts were divided in 1926, the old Palais was used for civil cases, judged according to the Napoleonic Code. Since the opening of the new Palais to its left, the old Palais has been converted into an annex of city hall, located to the right.

﹒﹒﹒ ⚲ *Continue along Rue Notre-Dame. Place Jacques-Cartier will appear on your right.*

Place Jacques-Cartier ★ *(Champ-de-Mars metro)* was laid out on the site once occupied by the Château de Vaudreuil, which burned down in 1803. The former Montréal residence of the governor of New France was without question the most elegant private home in the city. Designed by engineer Gaspard Chaussegros de Léry in 1723, it had a horseshoe-shaped staircase leading up to a handsome cut-stone portal, two projecting pavilions (one on each side of the main part of the building), and a formal garden that extended as far as Rue Notre-Dame. After the fire, the property was purchased by local merchants, who decided to give the government a small strip of land, on the condition that a public market be established there, thus increasing the value of the adjacent property that remained in private hands. This explains Place Jacques-Cartier's oblong shape.

Merchants of British descent sought various means of ensuring their visibility and publicly expressing their patriot-

ism in Montréal. They quickly formed a much larger community in Montréal than in Québec City, where government and military headquarters were located. In 1809, they were the first in the world to erect a monument to Admiral Horatio Nelson, who defeated the combined French and Spanish fleets in the Battle of Trafalgar. Supposedly, they even got French-Canadian merchants drunk in order to extort a financial contribution from them for the project. The base of the **Colonne Nelson**, or Nelson Column, was designed and executed in London according to plans by architect Robert Mitchell. It is decorated with bas-relief depicting the exploits of the famous admiral at Abukir, Copenhagen, and of course Trafalgar. The statue of Nelson at the top was originally made of an artificial type of stone, but after being damaged time and time again by protestors, it was finally replaced by a fibre-glass replica in 1981. The column is the oldest extant monument in Montréal.

At the other end of Place Jacques-Cartier, visitors will see the **Quai Jacques-Cartier** and the river, while **Rue Saint-Amable** lies tucked away on the right, at the halfway mark. During summer, artists and artisans gather on this little street, selling jewellery, drawings, etchings and caricatures.

Under the French Regime, Montréal, following the example of Québec City and Trois-Rivières, had its own governor, not to be confused with the governor of New France. The situation was the same under the English Regime. It wasn't until 1833 that the first elected mayor, Jacques Viger, took control of the city. This man, who was passionate about history, gave Montréal its motto (*Concordia Salus*) and coat of arms, composed of the four symbols of the "founding" peoples, namely the French *fleur de lys*, the Irish clover, the Scottish thistle and the English rose, all linked together by the Canadian beaver.

After occupying a number of inadequate buildings for decades (a notable example was the Hayes aqueduct, an edifice containing an immense reservoir of water, which one day cracked while a

Exploring - Vieux-Montréal

meeting was being held in the council chamber just below), the municipal administration finally moved into its present home in 1878. The **Hôtel de Ville ★** *(275 Rue Notre-Dame Est; Champ-de-Mars metro)*, or city hall, a fine example of the Second Empire, or Napoleon III, style, is the work of Henri-Maurice Perrault, who also designed the neighbouring courthouse. In 1922, a fire destroyed the interior and roof of the building which was later restored in 1926 on the model of the city hall in Tours, France. Exhibitions are occasionally presented in the main hall, which is accessible via the main entrance. Visitors will also be interested to learn that it was from the balcony of this building that France's General de Gaulle cried out his famous *"Vive le Québec libre!"* ("Freedom for Québec!") in 1967, to the great delight of the crowd gathered in front of the building.

⋯ ⋏ *Head to the rear of the Hôtel de Ville by way of the lovely* **Place Vauquelin**, *the continuation of Place Jacques-Cartier.*

The statue of Admiral Jean Vauquelin, defender of Louisbourg at the end of the French Regime, was probably put here to counterbalance the monument to Nelson, a symbol of British control over Canada. Go down the staircase leading to the **Champ-de-Mars**, modified in 1991 in order to reveal some vestiges of the fortifications that once surrounded Montréal. Gaspard Chaussegros de Léry designed Montréal's ramparts, erected between 1717 and 1745, as well as those of Québec City. The walls of Montréal, however, never lived through war, as the city's commercial calling and location ruled out such rash acts. The large, tree-lined lawns are reminders of the Champ-de-Mars' former vocation as a parade ground for military manoeuvres until 1924. A view of the downtown area's skyscrapers opens up through the clearing.

⋯ ⋏ *Head back to Rue Notre-Dame.*

Facing City Hall, on the south side of Rue Notre-Dame, is the beautiful **Place De La Dauversière ★**, which is home to several works of public art, notably the statue of one of Montréal's former mayors, Jean Drapeau. A very popular mayor, Mr. Drapeau reigned over "his" city for nearly 30 years.

The **Musée du Château Ramezay ★★** *($7.50; summer every day 10am to 6pm, rest of the year Tue-Sun 10am to 4:30pm; 280 Rue Notre-Dame Est, ☎514-861-3708, www. chateauramezay.qc.ca; Champ-de-Mars metro)* is located in the humblest of all the "châteaux" built in Montréal, and the only one still standing. The Château Ramezay was built in 1705 for the governor of Montréal, Claude de Ramezay, and his family. In 1745, it fell into the hands of the Compagnie des Indes Occidentales (The French West Indies Company), which made it its North-American headquarters. Precious Canadian furs were stored in its vaults awaiting shipment to France. After the conquest (1760), the British occupied the house, before being temporarily removed by American insurgents who wanted Québec to join the nascent United States. Benjamin Franklin even came to stay at the château for a few months in 1775, in an attempt to convince Montrealers to become American citizens.

In 1895, after serving as the first building of the Montréal branch of the Université Laval in Québec City, the château was converted into a museum, under the patronage of the Société d'Archéologie et de Numismatique de Montréal, founded by Jacques Viger. Visitors will still find a rich collection of furniture, clothing and everyday objects from the 18th and 19th centuries here, as well as many Aboriginal artifacts. The Salle de Nantes is decorated with beautiful Louis XV-style mahogany panelling, designed by Germain Boffrand and imported from the Nantes office of the Compagnie des Indes (circa 1725).

The museum also features cultural activities on Sundays. For example, on the first Sunday of the month, you can attend play readings. In addition, Château Ramezay now features a new indoor green space, the "neo-formal" Jardin du Gouverneur garden, as well as the Café du Château and the Marie-Charlotte shop.

⋯ 🅰 *Walk along Rue Notre-Dame to Rue Berri.*

At the corner of Rue Berri lies the **Sir George-Étienne-Cartier National Historic Site ★** *($4; early Sep to late Dec and early Apr to late May Wed-Sun 10am to noon and 1pm to 5pm, late May to early Sep every day 10am to 6pm, closed Jan to Mar; 458 Rue Notre-Dame Est, ☎514-283-2282, www.pc.gc.ca/cartier; Champ-de-Mars metro)*, consisting of twin houses inhabited successively by George-Étienne Cartier, one of the Fathers of Canadian Confederation. Inside, visitors will find a reconstructed mid-19th-century French-Canadian bourgeois home. Interesting educational soundtracks accompany the tour and add a touch of authenticity to the site.

The neighbouring building, at number 452, is the former **Cathédrale Schismatique Grecque Saint-Nicolas**, built around 1910 in the Romanesque-Byzantine Revival style.

Rue Berri marks the eastern border of Old Montréal, and thus the fortified city of the French Regime, beyond which extended the Faubourg Québec, excavated in the 19th century to make way for railroad lines. This explains the sharp difference in height between the hill known as Côteau Saint-Louis and the Viger and Dalhousie stations.

Gare Viger, visible on the left, was inaugurated by Canadian Pacific in 1897 in order to serve the eastern part of the country. Its resemblance to the Château Frontenac in Québec City is not a coincidence; both buildings were designed for the same railroad company and by the same architect, an American named Bruce Price. The Château-style station, closed in 1935, also included a prestigious hotel and large stained-glass train shed that has since been destroyed.

The smaller **Gare Dalhousie** *(514 Rue Notre-Dame Est; Champ-de-Mars metro)*, located near the Maison Cartier, was the first railway station built by Canadian Pacific,

a company established for the purpose of building a Canadian transcontinental railroad. The station was the starting point of the first transcontinental train headed for Vancouver on June 28, 1886. Canadian Pacific seems to have had a weakness for foreign architects, since it was Thomas C. Sorby, Director of Public Works in England, who drew up the plans for this humble structure.

For a long time, Gare Dalhousie was home to the École Nationale de Cirque de Montréal, which recently moved to a building located in what is now known as **TOHU, la Cité des Arts du Cirque ★** (see p 140), in the northern section of the island of Montréal. The Eloize circus company has since taken its place at Gare Dalhousie.

From the top of Rue Notre-Dame, the port's former refrigerated warehouse, made of brown brick, is visible, as well as Île Sainte-Hélène, in the middle of the river. This island, along with Île Notre-Dame, was the site of Expo 67.

⋯ 🅰 *Turn right on Rue Berri, and right again on Rue Saint-Paul, which offers a lovely view of the Marché Bonsecours dome. Continue straight ahead to Chapelle Notre-Dame-de-Bonsecours.*

This site was originally occupied by another chapel, built in 1658 upon the recommendation of Saint Marguerite Bourgeoys, founder of the congregation of Notre-Dame. The present **Chapelle Notre-Dame-de-Bonsecours ★** *(400 Rue St-Paul Est; Champ-de-Mars metro)* dates back to 1771, when the Sulpicians wanted to establish a branch of the main parish in the eastern part of the fortified city. In 1890, the chapel was modified to suit contemporary tastes, and the present stone facade was added, along with the "aerial" chapel looking out on the port. Parishioners asked for God's blessing on ships and crews bound for Europe from this chapel. The interior, redone at the same time, contains a large number of votive offerings from sailors saved from shipwrecks. Some are in the form of model ships, hung from the ceiling of the nave.

Exploring – Vieux-Montréal

Children's Favourite
Attractions in Montréal

Vieux-Montréal

A whole range of activities for children are offered at the **Old Port**, including shows where performers make sure everyone is entertained.

The **Centre des Sciences de Montréal** provides young and old with hours of educational fun. Also on site is an **IMAX** cinema and the **Immersion Interactive Cinema**, which children particularly enjoy.

Downtown

In order to introduce the very young to the wonderful world of astronomy, the **Planétarium de Montréal** has visual presentations for different ages that deal with subjects such as the solar system and the seasons.

In summer, the **Musée des Beaux-Arts**, or Museum of Fine Arts, organizes day camps aimed at awakening children's creativity.

During Sunday workshops at the **Musée d'Art Contemporain**, children get to learn various techniques used in painting and crafts.

Île Sainte-Hélène and Île Notre-Dame

The young and the young at heart will want to head to **La Ronde**, an amusement park with thrilling rides.

Maisonneuve

The **Biodôme**, with its reconstructed biospheres inhabited by indigenous plants and animals, never fails to fascinate children.

The mission of the **Insectarium** is to educate the public, particularly children, about insects by displays and interpretation.

The West Island and Surroundings

The **Fur Trade at Lachine National Historic Site** features an exhibit on this important activity, which was significant in the development of Montréal. Educational interactive games, as well as real furs you can touch, bring the past to life.

Exploring - Vieux-Montréal

Between 1996 and 1998, excavations below the chapel's nave uncovered several artifacts, including some dating from the colony's early days. Today, the **Musée Marguerite-Bourgeoys** ★ *($6; May to Oct every day 10am to 5:30pm, Nov to mid-Jan every day 11am to 3:30pm, Mar to late Apr every day 11am to 3:30pm, closed mid-Jan to early Mar; 400 Rue St-Paul Est, ☎514-282-8670, www.marguerite-bourgeoys.com)* displays these interesting archaeological finds. But there is even more to explore: adjoining the Notre-Dame-de-Bon-Secours chapel, it leads from the top of the tower, where the view is breathtaking, to the depths of the crypt, where the old stones tell their own story. Learn about the life of Marguerite Bourgeoys, a pioneer of education in Québec, admire her portrait and discover the mystery surrounding her. Guided tours of the archaeological site surrounding the foundations of the stone chapel, the oldest in Montréal, are offered.

⋯ ⃗ *Turn right on Rue Bonsecours.*

The **Maison Pierre du Calvet**, at the corner of Rue Bonsecours (no. 401), was built in 1725 and is representative of 18th-century French urban architecture adapted to the local setting, with thick walls made of fieldstone embedded in mortar, storm windows doubling the casement windows with their little squares of glass imported from France, and high firebreak walls, then required by local regulations as a means of limiting the spread of fire from one building to the next. One of Montréal's best hostelries has been located in the house for many years: **Auberge-Restaurant Pierre du Calvet** (see p 190 and 215).

A little higher on Rue Bonsecours, visitors will find the **Maison Papineau** *(440 Rue Bonsecours; Champ-de-Mars metro)* inhabited long ago by Louis-Joseph Papineau (1786-1871), lawyer, politician and head of the French-Canadian nationalist movement until the insurrection of 1837. Built in 1785 and covered with a wooden facing made to look like cut stone, it was one of the first buildings in Old Montréal to be restored (1962).

Heads Up!

→ Looking for some artwork? Stroll down the picturesque stone sidewalks of narrow **Rue Saint-Paul**, where you'll find several art galleries.

The **Marché Bonsecours** ★ ★ *(300 Rue St-Paul Est, www.marchebonsecours.qc.ca)* was erected between 1845 and 1850. The lovely grey-stone neoclassical edifice with sash windows is located between Rue Saint-Paul and Rue de la Commune.

The building is adorned with a portico supported by cast-iron columns moulded in England, and topped by a silvery dome, which for many years served as the symbol of the city at the entrance to the port. The public market, closed in the early 1960s following the advent of the supermarket, was transformed into municipal offices, then an exhibition hall before finally partially reopening in 1996. The market now presents an exhibition and features arts-and-crafts shops. The building originally housed both the city hall and a concert hall upstairs. The market's old storehouses, recently renovated, can be seen on Rue Saint-Paul. From the large balcony on Rue de la Commune, you can see the partially reconstructed Bonsecours dock, where paddle-wheelers, full of farmers who came to the city to sell their produce, used to moor.

⋯ ⃗ *Walk to Place Jacques-Cartier.*

At the southern end of Place Jacques-Cartier rise the multiple metallic points of the **Pavillon Jacques-Cartier**. Inside you'll find a cafeteria and bar-terrace, as well as a promenade extending all the way to the southeastern edge of the pier upon which the pavilion stands.

The **Tour de l'Horloge** ★ *(early May to late Sep; at the end of Quai de l'Horloge, ☎514-496-7678; Champ-de-Mars metro)* is visible to the east from the end of Quai Jacques-Cartier. Painted a pale yellow, the structure is actually a monument erected in 1922 in memory of merchant marine sailors who died during WWI. It was inaugurated by the Prince of Wales (who became Edward VIII) during one of his many visits to Montréal. An observatory at the top of the tower provides a clear view of Île Sainte-Hélène, the Jacques-Cartier bridge and the eastern part of Old Montréal. Standing on Place Belvédère at the base of the tower, one has the impression of standing on the deck of ship as it glides slowly down the St. Lawrence and out to the Atlantic Ocean.

⋯ ⃗ ⓜ *To return to the metro, walk back up Place Jacques-Cartier, cross Rue Notre-Dame, Place Vauquelin and finally*

Exploring – Vieux-Montréal

Champ-de-Mars, to the metro station of the same name.

Tour B: Downtown
★ ★ ★

 one day

Downtown skyscrapers give Montréal a typically North-American look. Nevertheless, unlike most other cities on the continent, there is a certain Latin spirit here, which seeps in between the towering buildings, livening up this part of Montréal both day and night. Bars, cafés, department stores, shops and head offices, along with two universities and numerous colleges, all lie clustered within a limited area at the foot of Mount Royal.

At the beginning of the 20th century, Montréal's central business district gradually shifted from the old city to what was up until then a posh residential neighbourhood known as the **Golden Square Mile** (see p 86), inhabited by upper-class Canadians. Wide arterial streets such as Boulevard René-Lévesque (then known as Dorchester Street) were lined with palatial residences surrounded by shady gardens. The city centre underwent a radical transformation in a very short time (1960-1967), marked by the construction of Place Ville-Marie, the metro, the underground city, Place des Arts and various other infrastructures that still exert an influence on the area's development.

⋯ **⚲ Ⓜ** *This tour kicks off underground at the Peel metro station. From here, head to* **Cours Mont-Royal** *and Rue Peel.*

Montréal has the most extensive **underground city** (see p 73) in the world. Greatly appreciated in bad weather, it provides access to more than 2,000 shops and restaurants, as well as movie theatres, apartment and office buildings, hotels, parking lots, the train station, the bus station, Place des Arts and even the Université du Québec à Montréal (UQAM) via tunnels, atriums and indoor plazas.

The **Cours Mont-Royal** ★ ★ *(1455 Rue Peel; Peel metro)* are linked to this sprawling network, which centres around the various metro stations. A multi-purpose complex, Les Cours consists of four levels of stores, offices and apartments laid out inside the former Mount Royal Hotel. With its 1,100 rooms, this Jazz Age palace, inaugurated in 1922, was the largest hotel in the British Empire. Aside from the exterior, all that was preserved during the 1987 remodelling was a portion of the lobby's ceiling, from which the former chandelier of the Monte Carlo casino is suspended. The four 10-storey *cours* (inner courts) are definitely worth a visit, as is a stroll through what may be the best-designed shopping centre in the downtown area. The building that looks like a small Scottish manor across the street is the head office of the Seagram distillery.

⋯ **⚲** *Head south on Rue Peel to Square Dorchester.*

At Montreal's tourist office, the **Centre Infotouriste** *(1255 Rue Peel, corner Rue Ste-Catherine Ouest,* ☎*877-266-5687, www. tourisme-montreal.org; Peel metro)*, visitors will find representatives from a number of tourism-related enterprises, such as tourist-information offices and the Greyhound bus company.

From 1799 to 1854, **Square Dorchester** ★ *(Peel metro)* was occupied by Montréal's Catholic cemetery, which was later moved to Mount Royal, where it is still located. In 1872, the city turned the free space into two squares, one on either side of Dorchester Street (now Boulevard René-Lévesque). The northern portion is called Square Dorchester, while the southern part was renamed Place du Canada to commemorate the 100th anniversary of Confederation (1967). A number of monuments adorn Square Dorchester. In the centre is an equestrian statue dedicated to Canadian soldiers who died during the Boer War in South Africa, while around the perimeter stand a handsome statue of Scottish poet Rob-

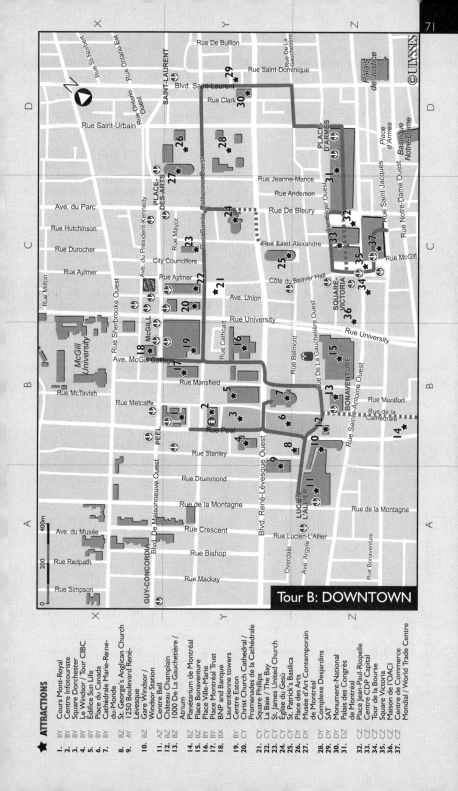

71

Tour B: DOWNTOWN

★ ATTRACTIONS

1.   BY   Cours Mont-Royal
2.   BY   Centre Infotouriste
3.   BY   Square Dorchester
4.   BY   Le Windsor / Tour CIBC
5.   BY   Édifice Sun Life
6.   BY   Place du Canada
7.   BY   Cathédrale Marie-Reine-
          du-Monde
8.   BZ   St. George's Anglican Church
9.   AY   1250 Boulevard René-
          Lévesque
10. BZ   Gare Windsor /
          Windsor Station
11. AZ   Centre Bell
12. BZ   Château Champlain
13. BZ   1000 De La Gauchetière /
          Atrium
14. BZ   Planétarium de Montréal
15. BY   Place Bonaventure
16. BY   Place Ville-Marie
17. BY   Place Montréal Trust
18. BX   BNP and Banque
          Laurentienne towers
19. BY   Centre Eaton
20. CY   Christ Church Cathedral /
          Promenades de la Cathédrale
21. CY   Square Phillips
22. CY   La Baie / The Bay
23. CY   St. James United Church
24. CY   Église du Gesù
25. CY   St. Patrick's Basilica
26. DY   Place des Arts
27. DY   Musée d'Art Contemporain
          de Montréal
28. DY   Complexe Desjardins
29. DY   SAT
30. DY   Monument-National
31. DZ   Palais des Congrès
          de Montréal
32. CZ   Place Jean-Paul-Riopelle
33. CZ   Centre CDP Capital
34. CZ   Tour de la Bourse
35. CZ   Square Victoria
36. CZ   Maison de l'OACI
37. CZ   Centre de Commerce
          Mondial / World Trade Centre

©ULYSSES

ert Burns, styled after Bartholdi's Roaring Lion and donated by the Sun Life insurance company, and Émile Brunet's monument to Sir Wilfrid Laurier, Prime Minister of Canada from 1896 to 1911. The square also serves as the starting point for guided bus tours.

Le Windsor ★ *(1170 Rue Peel, www.lewindsor. com; Peel metro)*, the hotel where members of the royal family used to stay during their visits to Canada, no longer exists. The prestigious Second Empire–style edifice, built in 1878 by architect W. W. Boyington of Chicago, was ravaged by fire in 1957. All that remains is an annex erected in 1906, which was converted into an office building in 1986. The ballrooms and lovely Peacock Alley have, however, been preserved. An impressive atrium, visible from the upper floors, has been constructed for the building's tenants. The handsome **Tour CIBC**, designed by Peter Dickinson (1962), stands on the site of the old hotel. Its walls are faced with green slate, which blends harmoniously with the dominant colours of the buildings around the square, the greyish beige of stone and the green of oxidized copper.

The **Édifice Sun Life** ★ ★ *(1155 Rue Metcalfe; Peel metro)*, erected between 1913 and 1933 for the powerful Sun Life insurance company, was for many years the largest building in the British Empire. It was in this "fortress" of the Anglo-Saxon establishment, with its colonnades reminiscent of ancient mythology, that the British Crown Jewels were hidden during World War II. In 1977, the company's head office was moved to Toronto, in protest against provincial language laws excluding English. Fortunately, the chimes that ring at 5pm every day are still in place and remain an integral part of the neighbourhood's spirit.

Place du Canada ★ *(Bonaventure metro)*, the southern portion of Square Dorchester, is the setting for the annual Remembrance Day ceremony (November 11th), which honours Canadian soldiers killed in the two World Wars and the Korean War. Veterans reunite around the War Memorial, which occupies the place of

honour in the centre of the square. A more imposing monument to Sir John A. Macdonald, Canada's first Prime Minister, elected in 1867, stands alongside Boulevard René-Lévesque.

A number of churches were clustered around Square Dorchester before it was even laid out in 1872. Unfortunately, only two of the eight churches built in the area between 1865 and 1875 have survived. One of these is **Cathédrale Marie-Reine-du-Monde** ★ ★ *(Boulevard René-Lévesque Ouest at the corner of Mansfield; Bonaventure metro)*, the seat of the archdiocese of Montréal and a reminder of the tremendous power wielded by the clergy up until the Quiet Revolution. It is exactly one third the size of St. Peter's in Rome. In 1852, a terrible fire destroyed the Catholic cathedral on Rue Saint-Denis, so the ambitious Monseigneur Ignace Bourget (1799-1885), who was bishop of Montréal at the time, seized the opportunity to work out a grandiose scheme to outshine the Sulpicians' Basilique Notre-Dame and ensure the supremacy of the Catholic Church in Montréal. What could accomplish this better than a replica of Rome's St. Peter's, right in the middle of the Protestant neighbourhood? Despite reservations on the part of architect Victor Bourgeau, the plan was carried out. The bishop even sent Bourgeau to Rome to measure the venerable building. Construction began in 1870 and was finally completed in 1894. The copper statues of the 13 patron saints of Montréal's parishes were installed in 1900.

Modernized during the 1950s, the interior of the cathedral is no longer as harmonious as it once was. Nevertheless, there is a lovely replica of Bernini's baldaquin, executed by sculptor Victor Vincent. The bishops and archbishops of Montréal are interred in the mortuary chapel on the left, where the place of honour is occupied by the recumbent statue of Monseigneur Bourget. An outdoor monument reminds visitors of this individual, who did so much to strengthen the bonds between France and Canada.

Underground City

The construction of Place Ville-Marie in 1962, with its basement shopping mall, marks the start of what is now known as the "underground city." The development of this "city under the city" was hastened by the construction of the metro, which started in 1966. Within a short time, many of the downtown area's main businesses, office buildings and hotels were strategically linked to the underground pedestrian network and, by extension, the metro.

Today, five main areas make up what has now become the world's largest underground city. The first is located in the heart of the metro system, around the Berri-UQAM station. It provides access to the Université du Québec à Montréal (UQAM) buildings, Place Dupuis, the Bibliothèque Nationale and the bus station (Station Centrale).

The second is located between the Place-des-Arts and Place-d'Armes stations and features an exceptional cultural ensemble, providing access to Place des Arts, the Musée d'Art Contemporain, Complexe Desjardins, Complexe Guy-Favreau and the Palais des Congrès. The third area is located beneath the business district that surrounds the Square-Victoria metro station.

The underground city's bustling fourth zone spreads out around the McGill, Peel and Bonaventure metro stations. It includes the La Baie (The Bay) department store, the Centre Eaton, Les Ailes de la Mode, Promenades de la Cathédrale, Place Montréal Trust and Cours Mont-Royal shopping malls, as well as Place Bonaventure, the 1000 De La Gauchetière complex, the Gare Centrale train station and Place Ville-Marie.

Finally, a fifth zone can be found in the commercial sector that surrounds the Atwater metro station and neighbouring Westmount Square and Place Alexis-Nihon.

··· ⚲ *Upon exiting the cathedral, turn left on Boulevard René-Lévesque and walk to Rue Peel and the splendid St. George's Anglican Church.*

The beautiful Gothic Revival–style **St. George's Anglican Church**'s ★ ★ *(at the corner of Rue De La Gauchetière and Rue Peel; Bonaventure metro)* delicately sculpted sandstone exterior conceals an interior covered with lovely, dark woodwork. Particularly noteworthy are the remarkable ceiling, with its exposed framework, the woodwork in the chancel and the tapestry from Westminster Abbey, used during the coronation of Queen Elizabeth II.

The elegant 47-storey **1250 Boulevard René-Lévesque** ★ building *(1250 Boulevard René-Lévesque Ouest; Bonaventure metro)*, formerly the IBM-Marathon tower and forming part of the backdrop of St. George's, was completed in 1991 by famous New York architects Kohn, Pedersen and Fox. Its winter bamboo garden is open to the public.

In 1887, the head of Canadian Pacific, William Cornelius Van Horne, asked his New York friend Bruce Price (1845-1903) to draw up plans for **Gare Windsor / Windsor Station** ★ ★ *(at the corner of Rue De La Gauchetière and Rue Peel; Bonaventure metro)*, a modern train station that would serve as the terminal for the transcontinental railroad, completed the previous

Exploring – Downtown

year. At the time, Price was one of the most prominent architects in the eastern United States, where he worked on residential projects for high-society clients, as well as skyscrapers like the American Surety Building in Manhattan. Later, he was put in charge of building the Château Frontenac in Québec City, thus establishing the Château style in Canada.

The massive-looking Gare Windsor, with its corner buttresses, Roman arches outlined in stone and series of arcades, is Montréal's best example of the Romanesque Revival style as interpreted by American architect Henry Hobson Richardson. Its construction established the city as the country's railway centre and initiated the shift of commercial and financial activity from the old town to the Golden Square Mile. Abandoned in favour of the Gare Centrale after World War II, Windsor Station was used only for commuter trains up until 1993. Today, the Gare Windsor houses many stores and offices, and its waiting hall is used for various events.

••• ⋀ *Walk down Rue De La Gauchetière to get to the Centre Bell.*

The **Centre Bell** *($8; 1hr 15min guided tours every day at 9:45am and 1:15pm; 1260 Rue De La Gauchetière Ouest, ☎514-932-2582; Bonaventure metro)*, built on the platforms of Windsor Station, now blocks all train access to the venerable old station. Opened in 1996 (when it was called the Molson Centre; Bell Canada purchased the rights in 2002), this immense, oddly shaped building succeeds the Forum on Sainte-Catherine as the home of the National Hockey League's Montréal Canadiens.

The amphitheatre can seat 21,247 people and boasts 138 glassed-in private boxes sold to Montréal companies for hefty sums. The National Hockey League's regular season runs from October to April, and play-offs can carry on into June. Two thousand tickets are sold at the Bell Centre on each game day, making it possible to get good last-minute seats. The Bell Centre also pres-

ents a wide array of concerts and family shows.

The **Cité du Commerce Électronique** is a developing sector bordered by Saint-Antoine, Lucien-L'Allier and De la Montagne streets and René-Lévesque boulevard. In the last few years, buildings have sprung up here to welcome the headquarters of Web-solution and e-commerce companies, such as CGI.

••• ⋀ *Retrace your steps to get to Château Champlain, which is located south of Place du Canada.*

Built in 1966, the Marriott **Château Champlain** ★ *(1 Place du Canada; Bonaventure metro)*, nicknamed the "cheese grater" by Montrealers due to its many arched, convex openings, was designed by Québec architects Jean-Paul Pothier and Roger D'Astous. The latter is a disciple of American architect Frank Lloyd Wright, with whom he studied for several years. The hotel is not unlike some of the master's late works, characterized by rounded, fluid lines.

1000 De La Gauchetière *(1000 Rue De La Gauchetière; Bonaventure metro)*, a 51-storey skyscraper, was completed in 1992. It houses the terminus for buses linking Montréal to the South Shore, as well as the **Atrium**, an indoor skating rink open year-round *($5.50, skate rentals $5; schedule changes frequently; ☎514-395-0555, www.le1000.com)*. Its architects wanted to set the building apart from its neighbours by crowning it with a copper-covered point. Its total height is the maximum allowed by the city, namely the height of Mount Royal. The ultimate symbol of Montréal, the mountain may be not surpassed under any circumstances.

••• ⋀ *A short side trip from this tour leads to the Planétarium de Montréal. To get there, head south on Rue de la Cathédrale.*

The **Planétarium de Montréal** ★ *($6.50; every day, presentations last 45min; schedule changes frequently; 1000 Rue Saint-Jacques Ouest, ☎514-872-4530; Bonaventure metro)* projects astronomy films onto a 20m hemispheric dome. The universe and its mysteries are explained in a way that makes this marvellous, often poorly understood world accessible to all. Guest lecturers provide commentaries on the presentations.

⋯ 🕺 *Head onto Rue De La Gauchetière. Place Bonaventure will appear on your right.*

An immense, grooved concrete block with no facade, **Place Bonaventure ★** *(1 Place Bonaventure; Bonaventure metro)*, which was completed in 1966, is one of the most revolutionary works of modern architecture of its time. Designed by Montrealer Raymond Affleck, it is a multi-purpose complex built on top of the railway lines leading into the Gare Centrale. It contains a parking area, a bi-level shopping centre linked to the metro and the underground city, two large exhibition halls, wholesalers, offices and an intimate 400-room hotel laid out around a charming hanging garden, worth a short visit. Place Bonaventure is linked to the metro station of the same name, designed by architect Victor Prus (1967). With its brown-brick facing and bare concrete vaults, the station looks like an early Christian basilica.

A railway tunnel below Mount Royal to the downtown area was built in 1913. The tracks ran under Avenue McGill College, then multiplied at the bottom of a deep trench, which stretched between Rue Mansfield and Rue University. In 1938, the subterranean **Gare Centrale** was built, marking the true starting point of the underground city. Camouflaged since 1957 by the Hôtel Reine-Elizabeth, it has an interesting, streamlined Art-Deco waiting hall.

⋯ 🕺 *Head back onto Rue Mansfield, which runs alongside Cathédrale Marie-Reine-du-Monde. The imposing Sun Life building can be seen in the background. Turn right on Boulevard René-Lévesque.*

Place Ville-Marie ★★★ *(1 Place Ville-Marie; Bonaventure metro)* was erected above the northern part of the former open-air trench in 1959. Famous Chinese-American architect I.M. Pei (Louvre Pyramid, Paris; East Building of the National Gal-

lery of Art, Washington, DC) designed the multipurpose complex built over the railway tracks and containing vast shopping arcades now linked to most of the surrounding edifices. It also encompasses a number of office buildings, including the famous cruciform aluminum tower, whose unusual shape enables natural light to penetrate all the way into the centre of the structure, while at the same time symbolizing Montréal, a Catholic city dedicated to the Virgin Mary.

In the middle of the public area, a granite compass card indicates true north, while **Avenue McGill College**, which leads straight toward the mountain, indicates "north" as it is perceived by Montrealers in their everyday life. This artery, lined with multicoloured skyscrapers, was still a narrow residential street in 1950. It now offers a wide view of Mount Royal, crowned by a **metal cross** (see p 119).

⋯ 🕺 *Cross Place Ville-Marie and take Avenue McGill College to Rue Sainte-Catherine Ouest.*

Avenue McGill College was widened and entirely redesigned in the 1980s. Walking along it, visitors will see several examples of eclectic, polychromatic postmodern architecture composed largely of granite and reflective glass. **Place Montréal Trust** *(at the corner of Rue Sainte-Catherine; McGill metro)* is one of a number of Montréal shopping centres topped by an office building and linked to the underground city and the metro by corridors and private plazas.

The **twin BNP** and **Banque Laurentienne towers ★** *(1981 Avenue McGill College; McGill metro)*, certainly the best designed buildings on Avenue McGill College, were built in 1981 by the architectural firm Webb, Zerafa, Menkès, Housden Partnership (Tour Elf-Aquitaine, Paris; Royal Bank, Toronto). Their bluish glass walls set off a sculpture entitled *La Foule Illuminée* (The Illuminated Crowd) by Franco-British artist Raymond Mason.

⋯ 🕺 *Return to Rue Sainte-Catherine.*

Exploring - Downtown

Rue Sainte-Catherine is Montréal's main commercial artery. It stretches along 15km, changing in appearance several times along the way. Around 1870, it was still lined with row houses; by 1920, however, it had already become an integral part of life in Montréal. Since the 1960s, a number of shopping centres linking the street to the adjacent metro lines have sprouted up among the local businesses. The **Centre Eaton** *(705 Rue Ste-Catherine Ouest; McGill metro)* is the most recent of these. It is composed of a long, old-fashioned gallery lined with five levels of shops and restaurants, and is linked to Place Ville-Marie by a pedestrian tunnel.

The **Eaton** department store *(677 Rue Ste-Catherine Ouest; McGill metro)*, one of the largest department stores on Ste-Catherine and an institution across Canada, went bankrupt in 1999 and had to close its doors. The imposing nine-storey building now houses another department store, **Les Ailes de la Mode**. Its magnificent Art-Deco dining room on the ninth floor, designed by Jacques Carlu and completed in 1931, is a historic monument, but is not currently open to the public.

The first Anglican cathedral in Montréal stood on Rue Notre-Dame, not far from Place d'Armes. After a fire in 1856, **Christ Church Cathedral** ★★ *(at the corner of Rue University; McGill metro)* was relocated to be closer to the community it served, in the heart of the nascent Golden Square Mile. Using the cathedral of his hometown, Salisbury, as his model, architect Frank Wills designed a flamboyant structure, with a single steeple rising above the transepts. The plain interior contrasts with the rich ornamentation of the Catholic churches included in this walking tour. A few beautiful stained-glass windows from the workshops of William Morris provide the only bit of colour. The steeple's stone spire was destroyed in 1927 and replaced by an aluminum replica; otherwise, it would have eventually caused the building to sink. The problem, linked to the instability of the foundation, was not resolved, however, until a shopping centre, the **Promenades**

de la Cathédrale, was constructed under the building in 1987. Christ Church Anglican Cathedral thus rests on the roof of the mall. At the same time, a postmodern glass skyscraper topped by a "crown of thorns" was erected behind the cathedral. At its base is a little garden that honours architect Raoul Wallenberg, a Swedish diplomat who saved several Hungarian Jews from Nazi deportation during the Second World War.

It was around **Square Phillips** ★ *(at the corner of Rue Union and Rue Ste-Catherine; McGill metro)* that the first stores appeared along Rue Sainte-Catherine, which was once strictly residential. Henry Morgan moved Morgan's Colonial House, now **La Baie / The Bay** *(McGill metro)*, here after the floods of 1886 in the old city. Henry Birks, descendant of a long line of English jewellers, arrived soon after, establishing his famous shop in a handsome beige sandstone building on the west side of the square. In 1914, a monument to King Edward VII, sculpted by Philippe Hébert, was erected in the centre of Square Phillips. Downtown shoppers and employees alike come here to relax.

Heads Up!

Time for a quick snack? Stop by **Le Grand Comptoir** (see p 216), facing Phillips Square, for an inexpensive light meal.

A former Methodist church designed in the shape of an auditorium, **St. James United Church** ★ *(463 Rue Ste-Catherine Ouest; McGill metro)* originally had a complete facade looking out onto a garden. In 1926, in an effort to counter the decrease in its revenue, the community built a group of stores and offices along the front of the building on Rue Sainte-Catherine, leaving only a narrow passageway into the church. Visitors can still see the two Gothic Revival–style steeples set back from Rue Sainte-Catherine. St. James United Church recently underwent outdoor renovations to the tune of two million dollars. The removal of the shops and offices that hid its facade re-

St. James United Church Finally Unveiled!

St. James United Church was built in 1889 and designed by Montréal architect Alexander F. Dunlop. Commercial buildings, the religious community's then major source of revenue, had hidden this national historic monument's facade since 1926. Rue Sainte-Catherine strollers had to wait nearly 80 years before demolition work was undertaken to reveal its French-Gothic-cathedral-style towers, red sandstone facade and new rosace.

vealed an impressive structure. A large green space will be added in the coming years, greatly improving the quality of life of downtown residents.

··· 人   *Turn right on Rue De Bleury.*

After a 40-year absence, the Jesuits returned to Montréal in 1842 at Monseigneur Ignace Bourget's invitation. Six years later, they founded Collège Sainte-Marie, where several generations of boys would receive an outstanding education. **Église du Gesù** ★ ★ *(1202 Rue De Bleury; Place-des-Arts metro)* was originally designed as the college chapel. The grandiose project begun in 1864 by architect Patrick C. Keely of Brooklyn, New York, was never completed, however, due to lack of funds. Consequently, the church's Renaissance Revival–style towers remain unfinished. The *trompe-l'œil* decor inside was executed by artist Damien Müller. Of particular interest are the seven main altars and surrounding parquetry, all fine examples of cabinet work. The large paintings hanging from the walls were commissioned from the Gagliardi brothers of Rome. The Jesuit college, erected to the south of the church, was demolished in 1975, but the church was fortunately saved and then restored in 1983.

··· 人   *Visitors can take a short side trip to St. Patrick's Basilica. To do so, head south on Rue de Bleury. Turn right on Boulevard René-Lévesque, then left on little Rue Saint-Alexandre. Enter the church through one of the side entrances.*

Fleeing misery and potato blight, a large number of Irish immigrants came to Montréal between 1820 and 1860 and helped construct the Lachine Canal and the Victoria bridge. **St. Patrick's Basilica** ★ ★ *(460 Boulevard René-Lévesque Ouest; Place-des-Arts metro)*, was built to meet a pressing new demand for a church to serve the Irish-Catholic community. When it was inaugurated in 1847, St. Patrick's dominated the city below. Today, it is well hidden by the skyscrapers of the business centre. Architect Pierre-Louis Morin and Père Félix Martin, the Jesuit superior, designed the plans for the edifice, built in the Gothic Revival style favoured by the Sulpicians, who financed the project. One of the many paradoxes surrounding St. Patrick's is that it is more representative of French than Anglo-Saxon Gothic architecture. The high, newly restored interior is spectacular in pale green, pink and gold. Each of the pine columns that divide the nave into three sections is a whole tree trunk, carved in one piece.

··· 人   *Head back to Rue Sainte-Catherine.*

Within the next few years, the sector around the intersection of Sainte-Catherine and Jeanne-Mance streets will become the **Quartier des Spectacles**: among other sites, it will feature the Complexe Spectrum and the Place des Festivals (agora), at the southwestern corner.

During the rush of the Quiet Revolution, the government of Québec, inspired by cultural complexes like New York's Lincoln Center, built **Place des Arts** ★ *(175 Rue Sainte-Catherine Ouest, ☎514-842-2112, www.pda.qc.ca; Place-des-Arts metro)*, a collection of five halls for the performing arts. Salle Wilfrid Pelletier, in the centre, was inaugurated in 1963 (2,982 seats). It accommodates both the Montreal Symphony Orchestra and the Opéra de Montréal.

Exploring - Downtown

The cube-shaped Théâtre Maisonneuve, on the right, contains three theatres: Théâtre Maisonneuve (1,453 seats), Théâtre Jean-Duceppe (755 seats) and the intimate Studio-Théâtre (138 seats). The Cinquième Salle (350 seats) was built in 1992 during construction of the Musée d'Art Contemporain. Place des Arts is linked to the governmental section of the underground city, which stretches from the Palais des Congrès convention centre to Avenue du Président-Kennedy. Developed by the various levels of government, this portion of the underground network distinguishes itself from the private section, centered around Place Ville-Marie, farther west.

Place des Arts' esplanade also serves as a kind of cultural central square in the heart of the downtown sector. Many of Montréal's major cultural events are held here, and it's also where many of the Montréal International Jazz Festival's biggest outdoor shows are presented, attracting thousands of music fans.

The **Musée d'Art Contemporain de Montréal** ★★ *($8, free admission Wed 6pm to 9pm; Tue-Sun 11am to 6pm, Wed 11am to 9pm; 185 Rue Ste-Catherine Ouest, at the corner of Rue Jeanne-Mance, ☎514-847-6226, www.macm.org; Place-des-Arts metro)*, Montréal's museum of modern art, was moved to this site in 1992. Both its size and the sheer volume of its collection, which includes more than 7,000 works, make it the largest contemporary-art museum in Canada. The long, low building, erected on top of the Place des Arts parking lot, contains eight rooms where post-1940 works of art from both Québec and abroad are exhibited. The interior, which has a decidedly better design than the exterior, is laid out around a circular hall. The museum's permanent exhibit features the largest collection of works by Paul-Émile Borduas, while its temporary exhibits usually favour multimedia creations. Among the museum's other facilities are the Olivieri bookshop, which specializes in monographs on Canadian artists and essays on art, and the La Rotonde restaurant, located

above the Place des Arts esplanade. On the lower level, an amusing metal sculpture by Pierre Granche entitled *Comme si le temps... de la Rue* ("As if time... from the street") shows Montréal's network of streets crowded with helmeted birds in a sort of semicircular theatre.

Since 1976, the head office of the Fédération des Caisses Populaires Desjardins, the credit union, has been located in the vast **Complexe Desjardins** ★ *(Rue Sainte-Catherine Ouest, www.complexedesjardins.com; Place-des-Arts metro)*, which also houses a large number of government offices. The building's large atrium surrounded by shops is very popular during the winter months. A variety of shows are presented in this space, which is surrounded by boutiques, a food court and the **Hyatt Regency Montréal**'s (see p 198) adjacent tower.

It Don't Mean a Thing If It Ain't Got That Swing: The Montreal Jazz Fest

From the small festival that was created in 1980 by Alain Simard, André Ménard and Denyse McCann on Île Sainte-Hélène to today's major entertainment juggernaut headed by Spectra, the recipe that has made this the world's largest jazz festival has remained the same: an eclectic program that features artists from around the world, from local up-and-comers to the biggest names in jazz, and a wide selection of free outdoor concerts that attracts more than one million music lovers to the city's downtown core every summer *(☎514-871-1881, www.montrealjazzfest.com)*.

You'll be walking down a quite different Rue Sainte-Catherine between Rue Saint-Urbain and Boulevard Saint-Laurent, a nocturnal version of the street where strip joints, sex shops and concert halls predominate. This is one of the many faces of Montréal, and it makes a lively contrast with the polite commercial endeavours of the street's daytime incarnation.

··· ⚲ *Turn right on Boulevard Saint-Laurent.*

The **SAT** (Société des Arts Technologiques) *(1195 Boulevard St-Laurent, ☎514-844-2033, www.sat.qc.ca; St-Laurent metro)* is a multidisciplinary centre for creation and promotion in the field of development and preservation of digital culture. It presents arts-related events, including concerts and DJ sets, on a regular basis.

Erected in 1893 for the Société Saint-Jean-Baptiste, which is devoted to protecting the rights of French-speakers, the **Monument-National** ★ *(1182 Boulevard St-Laurent; Saint-Laurent metro)* was intended to be a cultural centre dedicated to the French-Canadian cause. It offered business courses, became the favourite platform of political orators and presented shows of a religious nature. However, during the 1940s, it also hosted cabaret shows and plays, launching the career of many a Québec performer, including Olivier Guimond Sr. and Jr. The building was sold to the National Theatre School of Canada in 1971. As Canada's oldest theatre, it was artfully restored for its 100th anniversary.

··· ⚲ *Cross Boulevard René-Lévesque, then turn right on Rue De La Gauchetière.*

Montréal's **Chinatown** ★ *(Rue De La Gauchetière; Place-d'Armes metro)* may be rather small, but it is nonetheless a lovely place to explore. A large number of the Chinese who came to Canada to help build the transcontinental railroad, completed in 1886, settled here at the end of the 19th century. Though they no longer live in the neighbourhood, they still come here on weekends to stroll about and stock up on traditional products. Rue De La Gauchetière has been converted into a pedestrian street lined with restaurants and framed by beautiful Chinese-style gates.

··· ⚲ *Turn left on Rue Saint-Urbain and enter the Palais des Congrès de Montréal, on the corner of Avenue Viger. This building is part of the new "Quartier International de Montréal" district.*

The new **Quartier International de Montréal (QIM)** ★★ *(www.qimtl.qc.ca)* business sector is the result of a major overhaul of the area located between Saint-Urbain, Saint-Jacques, University and Viger streets. The project, which was overseen by architects and urban planners Clément Demers and Réal Lestage, won several prizes, including the prestigious *PMI Project of the Year*, awarded by the Project Management Institute in 2005. The area was long marred by the Ville-Marie expressway and neglected by Montrealers, but the QIM has made it a window onto Montréal's international economic activities.

The project entailed a profound urban restructuring effort that included the renovation of existing structures such as the Palais des Congrès, the addition of pedestrian walkways and green spaces and the construction of ultra-modern

Exploring – Downtown

buildings to house new businesses and hotels, all with the mandate of attracting foreign investors and improving local residential spaces. A 40% increase in pedestrian surfaces in this transitional area between downtown and Old Montréal was created by covering the Ville-Marie expressway between Rue De Bleury and Rue Saint-Alexandre, and a series of poles bearing the flags of several of the world's countries now lines Rue University.

If you wish to learn more about this neighbourhood, we suggest you take part in one of the guided tours offered by **Héritage Montréal** (see p 47).

To the west of Rue Saint-Urbain lies Montreal's convention centre, the **Palais des Congrès de Montréal** ★ *(201 Avenue Viger Ouest,* ☎*514-871-3170, www.congresmtl. com; Place-d'Armes metro),* a forbidding mass of concrete erected over the Ville-Marie highway, which contributes to the isolation of the old city from downtown. After an expansion in 2002, the Palais des Congrès doubled in size and now features two entrances.

The new section opens onto street level. Its huge coloured-glass facade, on Rue De Bleury, creates light effects both inside and outside the Palais des Congrès. It overlooks a new public square, **Place Jean-Paul-Riopelle** ★★, at the corner of Saint-Antoine and De Bleury streets, where you will find an immense bronze sculpture-fountain created by Riopelle himself and entitled *La Joute,* complete with water jets and flames. Facing it is a new building with a unique architectural style, the **Centre CDP Capital** ★, headquarters of the Caisse de Dépôt et Placement du Québec (CDP). Two works of art also enhance the Palais des Congrès: *Translucide,* a diptych by multimedia artists Michel Lemieux and Victor Pilon, among others, and *La Poussée Vers le Haut,* a mineral garden by Francine Larivée, on the roof. Two landscapes complete the decor: *Nature Légère / Lipstick Forest,* a surreal garden composed of 52 pink-concrete tree trunks, and *L'Esplanade,* where 31 heaps of dirt are linked by trails of Montréal-style limestone and planted

Jean-Paul Riopelle

Jean-Paul Riopelle was one of Québec's most renowned painters, and its best-known internationally. Many of the impressive number of paintings he created are exhibited throughout the world. This legendary character, an abstract painter famous for his huge mosaics, left his mark on the world of contemporary art. He was born in Montréal in 1923, and his career took off with the Automatism movement in the 1940s. He was also one of the 16 co-signatories of the *Refus Global,* a cultural and political manifesto. He lived in Paris for several years but returned to the province of Québec during the last years of his life. He died on March 12, 2002, in his manor on Île aux Grues, on the St. Lawrence River, in the migration path of the snow geese he held so dear to his heart.

with decorative crab-trees, the floral emblem of the City of Montréal since May 1995. Among the works of public art that are found at the Palais des Congrès is also a sculpture by Charles Daudelin, *Éolienne V,* a stainless-steel mobile.

The **Tour de la Bourse** ★ *(Place Victoria,* ☎*514-871-2424),* or the stock exchange tower, dominates the surroundings. It was erected in 1964 according to a design by famous Italian engineers Luigi Moretti and Pier Luigi Nervi, to whom we owe the Palazzo dello Sport (sports stadium) in Rome and the Exhibition Centre in Turin. The elegant 47-storey black tower that houses the stock exchange's offices and trading floor is one of several Montréal buildings that were designed by foreign architects. Initial plans had called for three identical towers, and its construction was meant to revitalize the city's financial district, which had been abandoned after economic activity was transferred to the area around Dorchester square after the 1929 crash.

In the 19th century, **Square Victoria** *(Square-Victoria metro)* was a Victorian garden surrounded by Second Empire and Renaissance Revival stores and office buildings. Only the narrow building at 751 Rue McGill remains from that era. Recently, Square Victoria was completely redesigned according to its original layout and has become one of the focal points in the Quartier International de Montréal. Square Victoria will eventually be given back its former shape and size, as well as its restored statue of Queen Victoria.

Recently, what is known as "Entourage Grimard" was officially reopened; named after architect Hector Grimard, who designed the gate to the Parisian "Metropolitain"—an Art-Nouveau piece that was created in the early 1900s—, it was loaned in 1966 by the Régie autonome des transports parisiens (RATP) to the Montréal metro so that it could be installed in one of its stations. During the inauguration of the "Entourage," which is set up at the outside entrance to the Square-Victoria metro, the RATP offered the gate as a gift to the Société de Transport de Montréal.

The headquarters of the two organizations that control international civil aviation, IATA (the International Air Transport Association) and ICAO (the International Civil Aviation Organization) are located in Montréal. The latter is a United Nations organization that was founded in 1947 and is located in the **Maison de l'OACI** *(at the corner of Rue University and Rue St-Antoine Ouest)*, which houses the delegations of its 189 member countries. The back of the building, which has been connected to the Cité Internationale de Montréal, is visible from Square Victoria. Completed in 1996, it was designed by architect Ken London, who was somewhat inspired by Scandinavian architecture of the 1930s. *Miroir aux Alouettes*, a "stained-glass totem" by artist Marcelle Ferron, stands in front of the western facade of the building.

⋆⋆⋆ ⋏ *Enter the covered passageway of the Centre de Commerce Mondial.*

World trade centres are exchange organizations intended to promote international trade. Montréal's **Centre de Commerce Mondial / World Trade Centre ★** *(Rue McGill; Square-Victoria metro)*, completed in 1991, is a new structure hidden behind an entire block of old facades. An impressive glassed-in passageway stretches 180m through the centre of the building, along a portion of the Ruelle des Fortifications, a lane marking the former location of the northern wall of the fortified city. Alongside the passageway, visitors will find a fountain and an elegant stone stairway, which provide the setting for a statue of Amphitirite, Poseidon's wife, taken from the municipal fountain in Saint-Mihiel-de-la-Meuse, France. This work of art dates back to the mid-18th century; it was created by Barthélémy Guibal, a sculptor from Nîmes, France, who also designed the fountains gracing Place Stanislas in Nancy, France. Visitors will also find a portion of the Berlin Wall, a gift from the City of Berlin on the occasion of the 350th anniversary of Montréal's foundation.

⋆⋆⋆ ⋏ *Climb the stairway, then walk along the passageway to the modest lobby entrance of the Hôtel Inter-Continental. Turn right onto the footbridge leading to the Nordheimer building.*

The Nordheimer building was restored in order to accommodate the hotel's reception halls, which are linked to the trade centre. Erected in 1888, it originally housed a piano store and a small concert hall where many great artists performed, including Maurice Ravel and Sarah Bernhardt. The interior, with its combination of dark woodwork, moulded plaster and mosaics, is typical of the late 19th century, characterized by exuberant eclecticism and lively polychromy. The facade, facing Rue Saint-Jacques, combines Romanesque Revival elements, as adapted by American architect Henry Hobson Richardson, with elements from the Chicago School, notably the multi-windowed metallic roof.

Exploring – Downtown

›› 人 Ⓜ *Exit via 363 Rue Saint-Jacques. This is where the **Vieux-Montréal** tour begins (see p 56). You can also get back on the metro at the Place-d'Armes station, which is connected to the World Trade Centre.*

Tour C:
Montreal Museum
of Fine Arts
★★

 at least two hours

The **Musée des Beaux-Arts de Montréal/ Montreal Museum of Fine Arts** *(free admission for the permanent collection; $12-$15 for temporary exhibitions, half-price Wed 5pm to 9pm; open Tue-Sun 11am to 5pm, Wed until 9pm; 1379-1380 Rue Sherbrooke Ouest, ☎514-285-2000, www.mbam.qc.ca; Guy-Concordia metro and bus no. 24)*, located in the heart of the downtown area, is the oldest and largest museum in Québec. It houses a variety of collections that illustrate the evolution of the fine arts from antiquity to the present day. The museum occupies two separate buildings on either side of Rue Sherbrooke Ouest: the Michal and Renata Hornstein Pavilion and Liliane and David M. Stewart Pavilion at no. 1379 and the Jean-Noël Desmarais Pavilion at no. 1380. Only 10% of the permanent collection, which contains over 25,000 pieces in all, is on display. Furthermore, as many as three world-class temporary exhibitions can be presented at the museum simultaneously, which accounts for a significant portion of the institution's activity.

Known until 1949 as the Art Association of Montreal, the museum was founded in 1860, when the city was at the height of its glory, by a group of affluent art-loving Montrealers of British origin. The core of the permanent collection still reflects the taste of these wealthy families of English and Scottish descent, who donated many works to the museum. It wasn't until nearly 20 years later, however, that the museum was set up in a permanent exhibition space. With funds donated by

local patron of the arts Benaiah Gibb, a modest gallery, which no longer exists, was built on the southeast corner of Square Phillips and Rue Sainte-Catherine Ouest in 1879.

A subscription campaign was launched in 1909 to finance the construction of a more prestigious home for the museum, which would be erected on Rue Sherbrooke Ouest, in the heart of the Golden Square Mile, the upper-class residential neighbourhood that has since become the downtown core of modern-day Montréal. This building, the present Michal and Renata Hornstein Pavilion, was inaugurated in 1912. Architects and brothers Edward and William Sutherland Maxwell graced it with an elegant, white Vermont-marble facade in the Classical Revival style, with lines reminiscent of ancient Rome. Expanded twice towards the back, in 1939 and in 1975, the building nonetheless ultimately proved to be too small.

Since demolishing the neighbouring buildings to the north and west was out of the question, the museum's directors turned their attention to the property across the street, proposing an original solution and offering quite a challenge to their architect, Moshe Safdie, already well known for designing Habitat 67 and the National Gallery in Ottawa. The new wing, named after Jean-Noël Desmarais, the father of arts patron Paul Desmarais, was inaugurated in 1991. On the left, it has a white marble facade that echoes the Maxwell brothers' museum, while incorporated into its right side is the red-brick facade of a former apartment building (1905). A series of underground passageways running beneath Rue Sherbrooke Ouest makes it possible to walk from the Jean-Noël Desmarais Pavilion to the Michal and Renata Hornstein Pavilion without ever stepping outside. A major 100-million-dollar expansion project was announced by the Musée des Beaux-Arts de Montréal's board of directors in 2003. Among the real-estate properties that are coveted by the museum for their collections of Canadian art is the splendid **Erskine & American United Church** ★ (see p 92).

In addition to the usual exhibitions, the Museum of Fine Arts offers visitors the following services and facilities: a bookstore specializing in art and architecture (Jean-Noël Desmarais Pavilion, level 1); a gift shop (Jean-Noël Desmarais Pavilion, level 1); a cafeteria (Jean-Noël Desmarais Pavilion, level 2); a library containing over 75,000 volumes on art (Michal and Renata Hornstein Pavilion); an art gallery (Jean-Noël Desmarais Pavilion, level 1); guided tours for groups of 10 or more *(for reservations, call* ☎*514-285-1600, ext. 440)*; an educational and cultural service that organizes conferences, concerts and film screenings at the Maxwell-Cummings Auditorium (Michal and Renata Hornstein Pavilion), as well as art workshops for children and adults in the StudiO (Jean-Noël Desmarais Pavilion, level 1).

There are a number of ways to visit the Musée des Beaux-Arts de Montréal. We have outlined a whirlwind tour of the permanent collection, starting at the main entrance of the museum *(Jean-Noël Desmarais Pavilion)*. Those who prefer to start out with the Canadian Art, Inuit or pre-Columbian collections can enter the museum through the big oak doors of the Michal and Renata Hornstein Pavilion *(1379 Rue Sherbrooke Ouest)*. Note that this tour may change in the near future, as plans are under way for a restructuring of the museum's permanent collection.

To find your way around the museum, please refer to the layout map available at the museum's ticket counter.

⋯ ⚲ *Cross the museum's spacious hall and take the elevator to the fourth level.*

Head left to the galleries containing the **Old Masters collection ★ ★** *(Jean-Noël Desmarais Pavilion, level 4)*, which includes paintings, furniture and sculptures from the Middle Ages, the Renaissance and the baroque and classical periods, offering a vast panorama of the history of European art from 1000 CE to the end of the 18th century. The medieval art on display includes fragments of stained-glass windows from the Abbaye de Saint-Germain-des-Prés (circa 1245) and a lovely *Crowning of the Virgin* by Nicolò di Pietro Gerini (circa 1390).

Among the most significant works from the Renaissance are *Portrait of a Man* by Hans Memling (1490), *The Return from the Inn* by Bruegel the Younger (1620), *Portrait of a Man from the House of Leiva* by El Greco (1580) and a superb triptych attributed to Jan de Beer and depicting the *Annunciation*, the *Adoration of the Shepherds* and the *Flight to Egypt* (circa 1510).

The 17th and 18th centuries are represented by a large number of Flemish works, reflecting the fondness of the affluent residents of the Golden Square Mile for these paintings, with their complex light effects. Of note is the *Portrait of a Young Woman* by Rembrandt (circa 1665) and the *Adoration of the Shepherds* by Nicolaes Maes (1658). English painters figure prominently in the last room of this section, in works like *Rustic Courtship* (circa 1755) and the *Portrait of Mrs. George Drummond* (1779), both by Thomas Gainsborough. Paintings by Canaletto and Tiepolo also adorn the walls of this gallery.

⋯ ⚲ *Head to the* **Belvedere***, a sort of aerial promenade over the lobby, where you can admire Mount Royal and the buildings along Sherbrooke street.*

Go down to level 3, where you'll find the Glass Court, the space used for temporary exhibitions, which offers an impressive view of the urban chaos of downtown Montréal's rooftops, along with the museum's collection of **19th- and 20th-century European Art ★** *(Jean-Noël Desmarais Pavilion, level 3)*. Since the wealthy residents of the Golden Square Mile were quite fond of the Barbizon School, the collection includes a number of works by Corot *(l'Île heureuse, 1868)* and Daumier *(Nymphes Pursued by Satyrs, 1848)*, as well as a few impressionist pieces by Sisley, Pissaro and Monet. More recent works include the arresting *Portrait of the Lawyer Hugo Simons* (1925) by Otto Dix and *Seated Woman, Back Turned to the Open Window* by Matisse (circa 1922).

Exploring ▪ Montreal Museum of Fine Arts

Get back on the elevator and go down to level S2 (the second lower level), where you'll find 6m-high galleries that look as if they were made for giants. These are perfectly suited for the large pieces in the **Contemporary Art collection ★** *(Jean-Noël Desmarais Pavilion, level S2)*, which consists chiefly of works by Canadian artists. The museum occasionally uses some of the space on level S2 for temporary international exhibitions of contemporary art.

Another section is devoted to **Pre-Columbian Art ★** *(Benaiah Gibb Pavilion, level 1)* from Mexico and Central and South America. Here, you can admire a piece of Peruvian tapestry dating back 2,000 years. Among the ceramic objects, you'll find depictions of a standing warrior (Jalisco, 300-500 CE) and a handsome stirrup-spout vessel with portrait head (Mochica, 200-600 CE).

Follow the passageway that runs alongside the ramp/staircase to the **Galleries of Ancient Cultures ★** *(Jean-Noël-Desmarais Pavilion, level S2)*, which stretch below Rue Sherbrooke and contain collections of decorative arts from Africa, Oceania, Asia, the Arab world and the ancient civilizations of the Near East, Greece and Rome. Among the many items on display are an interesting Assyrian bas-relief from the palace of Assurnasirpal II, a lead sarcophagus found in Tyre and a large basin, originally inlaid with silver, which belonged to the Sultan of Aleppo and Damascus (13th century).

Take the elevator at the north end of the galleries to the entrance hall of the Michal and Renata Hornstein Pavilion. Designed in the spirit of the École des Beaux-Arts, it leads to a monumental staircase, which you must climb in order to reach the temporary exhibition galleries and the **collection of Canadian Art ★★★** *(Michal and Renata Hornstein Pavilion, level 2)*, the true highlight of the museum. Presented in chronological order, this collection enables viewers to relive Canadian history through paintings, sculptures, furniture and ecclesiastical silver.

In the first gallery, visitors learn about everyday life in the Canada of yesteryear through lovely paintings by Paul Kane (*Mah Min* and *Caw Wacham*, circa 1848), Cornelius Krieghoff (*Montmorency Falls*, 1853) and many others (such as *View of Quebec City* by Fred Holloway, 1853). Portrait painters Théophile Hamel (1817-1870) and Antoine Plamondon (1804-1895), for their part, depicted the aristocracy of their era. On the right is the small Arthur Lismer room, dedicated to artist Alfred Laliberté (1878-1953). It features several plaster reproductions of bronzes depicting various French-Canadian trades and customs.

In the gallery devoted to the Victorian era, visitors can admire the academic style of Paul Peel's *The Spinner* (around 1890) and the shimmering January light in William Brymner's *Champ-de-Mars, Winter* (1892). In Canada, the first 30 years of the 20th century were marked by a veritable explosion of colour, as shown in Emily Carr's *Indian War Canoe* (1912) and Tom Thomson's *In the Northland* (1915). This section also contains paintings by other members of the Group of Seven, including *Cathedral Mountain* by Arthur Lismer (1928).

Slightly set back on the left is a small gallery dedicated to **Inuit Art ★** *(Michal and Renata Hornstein Pavilion, level 2)*. Visitors will mostly find recent pieces, including *Homme au Tambour*, a stone sculpture by artist Aibilic Echalook (1965-1970) and *Histoire de Chasse* by Alain Iyerack (1920), which both provide a glimpse into the customs of these Arctic people. An adjoining gallery dedicated to **Canadian Decorative Arts** contains a treasure trove of religious artefacts, including some pieces by François Ranvoyzé (late 18th century) and Laurent Amiot. Some of the furniture on display dates back to the French Regime, while other items were created during the 1930s, including some pieces by Jean-Marie Gauvreau, who founded the École du Meuble de Montréal (Montréal Furniture School) in 1935.

The next sections display works influenced by the Art Deco style, such as

The Refus Global

"Supporters of the status quo suspect us of endorsing the 'Revolution,' supporters of the 'Revolution' of being mere rebels: '... we oppose the established order, but only to transform it, not change it.'"

Extract from the *Refus Global* manifesto, 1948

Paul-Émile Borduas and 15 other signatories

The *Refus Global*, which spawned the 1960s' Quiet Revolution, is a manifesto that denounced the political and religious conformity that made 1940s Québec a stifling and hostile environment that hindered individual and collective creativity. Signed in 1948 by painter Paul-Émile Borduas (1905-1960) and 15 other artists, including Jean-Paul Riopelle, the manifesto marked the beginning of a radical shift in Québec society. Following its publication, which caused a huge uproar, Borduas was fired from his teaching post at Montréal's École du Meuble and, a few years later, sought exile in Paris.

Adrien Hébert's *Montreal Harbour* (circa 1925) and a few colourful works by Alfred Pellan (*Sujet d'Ambassade*, 1950; *Nappe Carrelée*, 1942). Two of the most noteworthy sculptures on this level are Robert Tait Mackenzie's *The Plunger* (1923) and Sylvia Daoust's *My Brother* (1931). Finally, the last section on the right focuses on **Native American Art**, with such notable items as late-19th-century and early-20th-century masks and daggers made of wood and mother-of-pearl.

You'll reach the next level by going down the nearby large staircase with a glass banister. The museum's **Contemporary Decorative Arts ★★** collection is located here *(Liliane and David M. Stewart Pavilion, level 1)*. This gallery mostly features items from temporary exhibits focusing on various designers from around the world. These include the "Liliane and David M. Stewart collection," with furnishings and decorative objects dating from 1935 and later. Notable pieces include works by artists Niki de Saint-Phalle (*Table and Stool*, 1980), Ettore Sottsass (*Mobile Giallo Cabinet*, 1988), Salvador Dalí (*Chessboard*, 1964-1971) and Pablo Picasso (*Tripod Vase*, 1951-1953), as well as designers Philippe Starck and Isamu Noguchi. Among the gallery's other pieces are an interesting English Porcelain collection, some silver, glass and crystal items, and part of Georges Clemenceau's stunning collection of 3,000 Japanese incense boxes, which was acquired by the museum.

The exit leads to the Michal and Renata Hornstein Pavilion's secondary hall, where you'll find the **Mediterranean Archaeology** exhibit *(Michal and Renata Hornstein Pavilion, level 1)*. Works presented here include sculptures, Corinthian vases and a superb mosaic carpet that used to adorn the floors of the Eastern Mediterranean's first Catholic churches.

⋯ ⋏ *You can exit the museum through the front doors of the Michal and Renata Hornstein Pavilion.*

You can go for a stroll in the **Max and Iris Stern Sculpture Garden**, which runs along the Michal and Renata Hornstein Pavilion. This recently inaugurated garden honours art collector and patron Max Stern. A great discoverer of new talent, this gallery owner played an important part in the promotion of modern Canadian art. His Dominion Gallery in Montréal has presented notable exhibits on Paul-Émile Borduas and Emily Carr.

Exploring – Montreal Museum of Fine Arts

··· 🚶 *If you need to return to the main lobby of the Jean-Noël Desmarais Pavilion, take the elevator down to level S2 and follow the passageway to the other elevators. Go up to level 1, where the cloakroom, bookstore and boutique are located (the cafeteria and bistro are on level 2).*

Tour D:
The Golden Square Mile
★

 three to four hours, not counting your visit to the Museum of Fine Arts

The Golden Square Mile was the residential neighbourhood of the Canadian upper class between 1850 and 1930. Since the early 20th century, the shady streets lined with sumptuous Victorian houses have gradually given way to the city's modern business centre. At its apogee, around 1900, the Golden Square Mile was bounded by Avenue Atwater to the west, Rue de Bleury to the east, Rue De La Gauchetière to the south and the mountain, Mount Royal, to the north. In those years, an estimated 70% of the country's wealth lay in the hands of local residents, the majority of whom were of Scottish descent. Only a few houses from this era remain, most of which are clustered north of Rue Sherbrooke, the Golden Square Mile's luxurious main street.

··· 🚶 Ⓜ *From the McGill metro station, head north on Avenue McGill College toward the campus of McGill University. The tour starts on Rue Sherbrooke.*

The **Maison William Alexander Molson** *(888 Rue Sherbrooke Ouest; McGill metro)* provides a good idea of Rue Sherbrooke's modest scale and residential character back in the early 20th century. It was built in 1906 according to a design by Robert Findlay, favourite architect of the famous Molsons, a name associated with beer brewing for two centuries. William Alex-

ander Molson chose a different path, however, becoming an eminent doctor. After his death in 1920, this Elizabethan Revival–style house served first as the head office of the Anglin-Norcross construction company and was then used by McGill University's Institute of Space Research. The Banque Commerciale Italienne du Canada took over the building in 1993.

The **Musée McCord d'Histoire Canadienne / McCord Museum of Canadian History** ★★ *($10, free admission first Sat of every month 10am to noon; Tue-Fri 10am to 6pm, Sat and Sun 10am to 5pm, Mon on holiday weekends and summer every day 10am to 5pm; 690 Rue Sherbrooke Ouest, ☎514-398-7100, www.musee-mccord.qc.ca; McGill metro and bus no. 24)* occupies a building formerly used by the McGill University Students' Association. Designed by architect Percy Nobbs (1906), this handsome building of English baroque inspiration was enlarged toward the back in 1991. Along Rue Victoria, visitors can see an interesting sculpture by Pierre Granche entitled *Totem Urbain/Histoire en Dentelle* ("Urban totem/History in lace"). For anyone interested in the First Nations and daily life in Canada in the 18th and 19th centuries, this is *the* museum to see in Montréal. It houses a large ethnographic collection, as well as collections of costumes, decorative arts, paintings, prints and photographs, including the famous Notman photography collection, composed of 450,000 photos, including 200,000 glass negatives and constituting a veritable portrait of Canada at the end of the 19th century.

McGill University ★★ *(805 Rue Sherbrooke Ouest; McGill metro)* was founded in 1821, thanks to a donation by fur-trader James McGill. It is the oldest of Montréal's four universities. Throughout the 19th century, the institution was one of the finest jewels of the Golden Square Mile's Scottish bourgeoisie. The university's main campus lies nestled in greenery at the foot of Mount Royal. The entrance is located at the northernmost end of Avenue McGill College, at the Roddick Gates, which contain the university's clock and chimes. On the right are

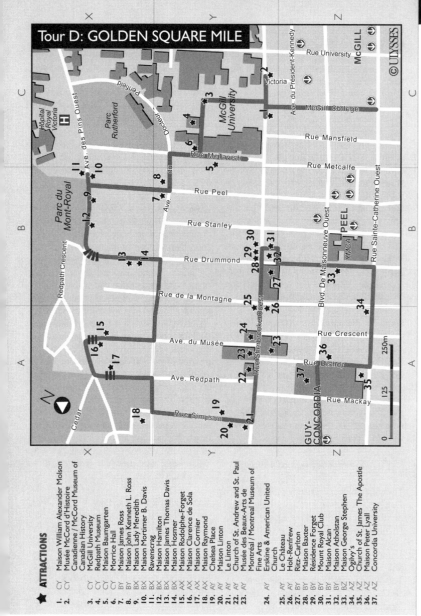

Tour D: GOLDEN SQUARE MILE

© ULYSSES

★ **ATTRACTIONS**

1. CY Maison William Alexander Molson
2. CY Musée McCord d'Histoire Canadienne / McCord Museum of Canadian History
3. CY McGill University
4. CY Redpath Museum
5. CY Maison Baumgarten
6. CY Morrice Hall
7. BY Maison James Ross
8. BY Maison John Kenneth L. Ross
9. BY Maison Lady Meredith
10. BX Maison Mortimer B. Davis
11. BX Ravenscrag
12. BX Maison Hamilton
13. BX Maison James Thomas Davis
14. BX Maison Hosmer
15. AX Maison Rodolphe-Forget
16. AX Maison Clarence de Sola
17. AX Maison Cormier
18. AX Maison Raymond
19. AY Chelsea Place
20. AY Maison Linton
21. AY Le Linton
22. AY Church of St. Andrew and St. Paul
23. AY Musée des Beaux-Arts de Montréal / Montréal Museum of Fine Arts
24. AY Erskine & American United Church
25. AY Le Château
26. AY Holt-Renfrew
27. BY Ritz-Carlton
28. BY Maison Baxter
29. BY Residence Forget
30. BY Mount Royal Club
31. BY Maison Alcan
32. BY Maison Atholstan
33. BZ Maison George Stephen
34. AZ Ogilvy's
35. AZ Church of St. James The Apostle
36. AZ Maison Peter Lyall
37. AZ Concordia University

Exploring – The Golden Square Mile

---

two Romanesque Revival buildings designed by Sir Andrew Taylor to house the physics (1893) and chemistry (1896) departments. The Faculty of Architecture now occupies the second building. A little farther along, visitors will see the Macdonald Engineering Building, a fine example of the English baroque-revival style, with a broken pediment adorn-

ing its rusticated portal (Percy Nobbs, 1908). At the end of the drive stands the oldest building on campus, the Arts Building (1839). For three decades, this austere neoclassical structure by architect John Ostell was McGill University's only building. It houses Moyse Hall, a lovely theatre dating back to 1926, with a design inspired by antiquity (Harold Lea Fetherstonaugh, architect).

The profile of the unusual **Redpath Museum** *(voluntary contribution; in summer Mon-Thu 9am to 5pm, Sun 1pm to 5pm; in winter Mon-Fri 9am to 5pm, Sun 1pm to 5pm; 859 Rue Sherbrooke Ouest, ☎514-389-4086, www.mcgill.ca/redpath; McGill metro)* stands out to the left. It is a protorationalist openwork building concealed behind a composite facade, the work of architects Hutchison and Steele. Precious objects relating to archaeology, botany, geology and palaeontology, accumulated by the university's researchers and professors, have been collected here. This was the first building in Québec designed specifically as a museum, and it also serves as a rare example of a building with an iron and stone framework not intended for industrial or commercial purposes.

South of the museum, visitors will see the library and Redpath Hall, equipped with a French-style mechanical organ. Baroque music concerts are often held in this lovely hall dominated by its visible wooden frame. Take note of the gargoyles and lavishly sculpted columns of the library, among the most sophisticated examples of the Romanesque Revival style in Canada.

··· ⚶ *Take the lane that leads to Rue McTavish.*

The **Maison Baumgarten** *(3450 Rue McTavish; McGill metro)*, located a little lower on Rue McTavish, serves as the McGill Faculty Club. It houses a restaurant, reading rooms and pool tables from the former residences of the Golden Square Mile, now owned by McGill University. The house was built in stages between 1887 and 1902 for Alfred Friedrich Moritz Baumgarten, son of the personal physician of King Frédéric-Auguste of Saxony, chemist, inspector of German sugar refineries and founder of the Saint-Laurent sugar refinery in Montréal. His house stands out from the other bourgeois residences in the Golden Square Mile because of its sobre exterior and three levels of reception rooms. On the first floor of the stairwell, the privileged individuals offered access into the club

can enjoy a bird's-eye view of the Battle of Arras (17th century), brought back from France by Sir Arthur Currie, rector of the university. On the north side stands **Morrice Hall** *(3485 Rue McTavish)*, a Gothic Revival–style building erected in 1881, which once housed the Presbyterian Theological College of Montréal.

··· ⚶ *Walk uphill on Rue McTavish. Visitors can enjoy a view of* **Ravenscrag** *(see p 89) on the hillside before turning left on Avenue Docteur-Penfield, then right onto Rue Peel.*

Maison James Ross ★ *(3644 Rue Peel; Peel metro)* was built in 1890 according to a design by American architect Bruce Price (Windsor Station, Château Frontenac in Québec City) for the head engineer of Canadian Pacific. Expanded on several occasions, it was once the scene of glittering receptions. With its resemblance to a medieval castle, it contributes to the charm of the Golden Square Mile. Particularly noteworthy is the combination of colours of its exterior, made up of a mixture of buff-coloured sandstone, pink granite and red slate. James Ross owned an exceptional collection of paintings, including works by Rembrandt, Rubens, Reynolds, Courbet, Corot, Millet, Rossetti and Edward Burne-Jones. In 1948, the house became the McGill University Faculty of Law. It lost a considerable portion of its large garden when Avenue Docteur-Penfield was laid out in 1957.

Maison John Kenneth L. Ross ★ *(3647 Rue Peel; Peel metro)* was originally the residence of James Ross' son, who lived in grand style for several years, accumulating yachts and race horses and travelling extensively. Once his father's fortune was exhausted, however, he had to sell the precious family collection of paintings at Christie's in London, a useless sacrifice in the end since the crash of 1929 ruined him anyway. His house (1909), a fine example of the Beaux-Arts style, is the work of brothers Edward and William Sutherland Maxwell, the favourite architects of Montréal's Scottish bourgeoisie. It is now an annex of the McGill University Faculty of Law.

··· ⚶ *Go up Rue Peel to Avenue des Pins.*

In another era, children used to sleigh down Rue Peel, which, like all city streets during the long winter months, was covered with a thick layer of snow.

Maison Lady Meredith ★ *(1110 Avenue des Pins Ouest)* is perhaps Montréal's best example of the trend toward eclecticism, polychromy and the picturesque that swept through North America in the last two decades of the 19th century. Visitors will discover on its facades a mixture of styles ranging from Romanesque to late 18th century, as well as strong hues and a marvellous jumble of towers, inlays, bay windows and chimneys. The house was built in 1894 for Andrew Allan, who gave it to his daughter when she married Henry Vincent Meredith, the president of the Bank of Montreal at the time.

Maison Mortimer B. Davis ★ *(1020 Avenue des Pins Ouest)* was once the residence of the founder of the Imperial Tobacco Company, Mortimer Barnett Davis. It was later occupied by Sir Arthus Purvis and then sold to McGill University. Purvis was responsible for the secret shipment of North-American-made arms to Europe during World War II, enabling Great Britain to avoid a Nazi invasion. The Davis house was designed in the Beaux-Arts style, recognizable by the balustrade along the top, the wrought-iron balconies supported by brackets and the grandiose, symmetrical design.

At the time, Montréal was not a political capital: it was above all a commercial city endowed with an important port. Its castle was not that of a king, but rather that of a financial and commercial magnate. **Ravenscrag** ★★ *(1025 Avenue des Pins Ouest)* could indeed be labelled the castle of Montréal thanks to its prominent location overlooking the city, its exceptional size (originally over 60 rooms) and its history, which is rich in memorable receptions and prestigious hosts. This immense residence was built from 1861 to 1864 for the fabulously wealthy Sir Hugh Allan, who at the time had a near monopoly on sea transport between Europe and Canada. From the central tower of his house, this "monarch" could keep a close eye on the comings and goings of his ships at the port.

Sir Hugh Allan's house is one of the best North-American examples of the Renaissance Revival style, inspired by Tuscan villas and characterized, notably, by an irregular plan and an observation tower. The interior, almost entirely destroyed when the building was converted into a psychiatric institute (1943), used to include a Second Empire–style ballroom that was able to accommodate 200 polka dancers. Interesting aspects around the building include a cast-iron entry gate, a gate house and luxurious stables that are now used as offices.

⋯ ⋏   *Head west on Avenue de Pins.*

Maison Hamilton *(1132 Avenue des Pins Ouest)* has a unique and personal design endowed by the Maxwell brothers, who had developed their own style, characterized by a gradual widening of their structures toward the base and whimsical little openings distributed in a carefully studied disorder. The Hamilton house (1903) has Arts & Crafts elements, as well as features foreshadowing the Art Deco style, such as the zigzag pattern of the bricks on the first floor.

⋯ ⋏   *Go down the stairway leading to Promenade Sir-William-Osler.*

Maison James Thomas Davis ★ *(3654 Promenade Sir-William-Osler)* originally belonged to a building contractor who equipped his house with a reinforced concrete structure. The design for this Elizabethan–style "manor" was also drawn up by the Maxwells (1908). Those who enter the house will find the lovely original tapestries still in place, in addition to remounted paintings by Canadian artist Maurice Cullen. Like so many old residences in the neighbourhood, the Davis house now belongs to McGill University.

Maison Hosmer ★ *(3630 Promenade Sir-William-Osler)* is without question the most exuberant Beaux-Arts–style house in Montréal. Thick mouldings, twin columns and cartouches, all carved in red

Growing up English in Montreal

Montreal is my home, not *Montréal*, and when I think of this city and its sights I think of the Olympic Stadium, the Botanical Gardens, the Montreal Museum of Fine Arts, Old Montreal, Mount Royal, Beaver Lake and St. Joseph's Oratory. I know the names of these places should technically be in French, but as an Anglophone they have different names because they are part of my city.

As a Montrealer of Anglo-Saxon descent, I grew up in the Anglo stronghold of Montréal and by extension of Québec, that former cottage-country we affectionately call the West Island. I was at an English elementary school when Bill 101 was announced, and thought he was a newscaster! My parents had the good sense to enroll me in French immersion, yet my existence was decidedly anglophile. After English high school, I moved downtown; this time we made our home in Westmount, another of the few Anglophone enclaves. I attended an English CÉGEP, and then went on to McGill University for a degree in English Literature.

Ironically, it was during these years that I began to make Francophone friends. Initially, I realized how different we were when they insisted on greeting me with kisses, one on each cheek (called "*la bise*," by the way). Then I tried to get them to explain Bill 101. Why was it necessary to deny me what I thought was a basic right and why did I detect fear amongst them? They explained that they were here before us, so naturally they felt justified in wanting to preserve their distinct culture, and surrounded by a sea of English, measures had to be taken. Yet my Anglophone heritage has been greatly enhanced by its location within a Francophone environment, and I also intend to preserve the distinct culture that has resulted. To me, Montreal is a unique city precisely because we are both here.

Visitors to Montréal always wonder what I am doing here. Why do I choose to live in a city where signs in my language used to be illegal (now they must simply be less prominent), where the locals refer to me as a *tête carrée* (square head), where the spots I cherish no longer have names I recognize? Well, I live here because I was born and raised here. I choose to live here because, although I am not Francophone, I understand those signs and at least some of the politics behind them, and because I understand why they call me a "*tête carrée;*" it is the same reason I call them "frog" and "Pepsi." Of course we have our differences, so naturally we have our silly names for each other. Fundamentally we are all Quebecers and we are defined by these differences. I am a Canadian, yet I cannot imagine having to live in any other province or to identify with any other provincial mind-set. I relish the warm welcome of shopkeepers when my accent betrays me and they think I am a tourist. I am proud when people cannot detect my English accent, relieved when I return to the West Island and see that I could still exist exclusively in English. It is then that I know I fit in, that I am at home in both English and French. You see, I love Schwartz's Deli just as much as I love La Binerie Mont-Royal. I eat both *tourtière* and plum pudding at Christmas. I paint *fleurs de lys* on my cheeks on June 24th and maple leaves on July 1st.

Jennifer McMorran

Exploring - The Golden Square Mile

sandstone imported from Scotland, were sure to impress both visitors and business rivals. Edward Maxwell drew up the plans while his brother William was studying at the École des Beaux-Arts in Paris. The sketches sent from across the Atlantic clearly had a great influence on the design of this house, erected in 1900 for Charles Hosmer, who had ties with Canadian Pacific and 26 other Canadian companies. Each room was designed in a different style in order to serve as a showcase for the Hosmer family's diverse collection of antiques. The family lived here until 1969, at which time the house became part of McGill University's Faculty of Medicine.

››› ⚶ *Turn right on Avenue Docteur-Penfield, then right again on Avenue du Musée.*

Few residences in the Golden Square Mile were built for members of the French-Canadian elite. These individuals, generally less affluent than their British colleagues, preferred the area around Square Saint-Louis. Rodolphe Forget (1861-1919) was thus regarded as an exception. This distinguished Francophile founded the Banque Internationale du Canada, was a member of the council of the Société Générale and took part in the founding of the Franco-Canadian Crédit Foncier. The **Maison Rodolphe-Forget** ★ *(3685 Avenue du Musée)*, inspired by Parisian *hôtels particuliers* of the Louis-XV era, was designed in 1912 by Jean Omer Marchand, the first French-Canadian graduate of the École des Beaux-Arts in Paris. Famous Québec suffragette Thérèse Casgrain, daughter of Rodolphe Forget, spent her early childhood here. The building is now part of the Russian consulate.

››› ⚶ *Climb the stairs on Avenue du Musée. At the top, you will get a lovely view of the downtown area and the river.*

The **Maison Clarence de Sola** ★ *(1374 Avenue des Pins Ouest)* is an extremely exotic Hispano-Moorish style residence that clearly stands out against the urban landscape of Montréal. The contrast is even more amusing the day after a snowstorm. The house was erected in 1913 for Clarence de Sola, the son of a rabbi of Portuguese-Jewish descent.

››› ⚶ *Head west on Avenue des Pins.*

The **Maison Cormier** ★★ *(1418 Avenue des Pins Ouest)* was designed in 1930 for personal use by Ernest Cormier, architect of the **Université de Montréal** ★ (see p 124) and the Supreme Court in Ottawa. He experimented with the house, giving each side a different look—Art Deco for the facade, monumental for the east side and distinctly modern for the back. The interior was planned in minute detail. Cormier created most of the furniture, while the remaining pieces were acquired at the 1925 Exposition des Arts Décoratifs in Paris. Though the facade on Avenue des Pins appears quite small, the house actually has four aboveground floors on the other side thanks to the steep incline of the terrain south of the avenue. The entire building, now listed as a historic monument, has been carefully restored.

››› ⚶ *Go down the stairs on the left, which lead to Avenue Redpath. Turn right on Avenue Docteur-Penfield.*

The **Maison Raymond** *(1507 Avenue Docteur-Penfield; Guy-Concordia metro)* was one of the last single-family residences to be erected in the Golden Square Mile (1930) and is still inhabited today. It belongs to the family of businessman Aldéric Raymond, who owned the Montréal Forum in the 1950s, as well as several big hotels in the city. It is another excellent example of the French Beaux-Arts style.

››› ⚶ *Go down Rue Simpson toward Rue Sherbrooke.*

Chelsea Place ★ *(on the east side of Rue Simpson; Guy-Concordia metro)* is a subtle grouping of Neo-Georgian–style residences built on a more modest scale than the homes seen thus far. It was erected in 1926 according to plans by architect Ernest Isbell Barott, in the years when Montréal's Scottish bourgeoisie was starting to decline. Decimated by the Great War, burdened by taxes (which were practically nonexistent before 1914) and

Exploring – The Golden Square Mile

suffering from a shortage of servants, many businessmen were forced to sell their "palaces" and move into more practical dwellings. Of particular interest is the lovely central garden, giving Chelsea Place a unique style, both communal and refined. Summerhill Terrace, located on the west side of Rue Simpson, is a similar grouping built by the same architect.

Maison Linton *(3424 Rue Simpson; Guy-Concordia metro)* is one of the most successful examples of the Second Empire style in Montréal. Don't be fooled by the exterior: the facade on Rue Simpson is in fact the east side of the house, whose main facade originally looked south out onto a vast lawn stretching all the way to Rue Sherbrooke. The portico and staircase were dismantled, then reconstructed facing Rue Simpson when the **Le Linton** *(1509 Rue Sherbrooke Ouest; Guy-Concordia metro)* apartment building was erected in 1907. The little cartouches, the openings with segmented arches and above all the mansard roof are all characteristic of the Second Empire, or Napoleon III, style. The house was erected in 1867 according to a design by Cyrus P. Thomas. An underground garage was built all around it in 1990, but its interior remains just as it was at the end of the 19th century, from the fireplaces to the embossed wallpaper and lavish mouldings on the ceilings.

⠀⠀⠀ 🚶 *Turn left on Rue Sherbrooke.*

Heads Up!

Feel like browsing through art galleries? The "museum district" features several interesting ones. The **Canadian Guild of Crafts** (see p 282) gallery is particularly recommended.

The lovely presbyterian **Church of St. Andrew and St. Paul** ★★ *(at the corner of Rue Redpath; Guy-Concordia metro)* was one of the most important institutions of the Scottish elite in Montréal. Built in 1932 by architect Harold Lea Fetherstonaugh as the community's third place of worship, it illustrates the endurance of the medieval style in religious architecture. The stone interior is graced with magnificent commemorative stained-glass windows. Those along the aisles came from the second church and are for the most part significant British pieces, such as the windows of Andrew Allan and his wife, produced by the workshop of William Morris after sketches by the famous English Pre-Raphaelite painter Edward Burne-Jones. The Scottish-Canadian Black Watch Regiment has been affiliated with the church ever since it was created in 1862.

The **Musée des Beaux-Arts de Montréal / Montreal Museum of Fine Arts** ★★, located in two buildings on either side of Rue Sherbrooke Ouest, is described in Tour C (see p 82).

Erected in 1892, the **Erskine & American United Church** ★ *(at the corner of Avenue du Musée)* is an excellent example of the Romanesque Revival style as interpreted by American architect Henry Hobson Richardson. The textured sandstone, large arches flanked by either squat or disproportionately elongated columns, and sequences of small, arched openings are typical of the style. The auditorium-shaped interior was remodelled in the style of the Chicago School in 1937. The lower chapel (along Avenue du Musée), contains lovely, brilliantly coloured Tiffany stained-glass windows.

A symbol of its era, **Le Château** ★ *(1321 Rue Sherbrooke Ouest; Guy-Concordia or Peel metro)*, a handsome Château-style building, was erected in 1925 for a French-Canadian businessman by the name of Pamphile du Tremblay, owner of the French-language newspaper *La Presse*. Architects Ross and Macdonald designed what was at the time the largest apartment building in Canada. The Royal Institute awarded these architects a prize for the design of the fashionable **Holt Renfrew** *(1300 Rue Sherbrooke Ouest)* store that stands across the street in 1937. With its rounded, horizontal lines, the store is a fine example of the streamlined Art Deco style.

The last of Montréal's old hotels, the **Ritz-Carlton** ★ *(1228 Rue Sherbrooke Ouest; Guy-Concordia or Peel metro)* was inaugurated in 1911 by César Ritz himself. For many years, it was the favourite gathering place of the Montréal bourgeoisie. Some people even stayed here year-round, living a life of luxury among the drawing rooms, garden and ballroom. The building was designed by Warren and Wetmore of New York City, the well-known architects of Grand Central Station on New York's Park Avenue. Many celebrities have stayed at this sophisticated luxury hotel over the years, including Richard Burton and Elizabeth Taylor, who were married here in 1964.

››› ⚲ *Continue along Rue Sherbrooke to the entrance of Maison Alcan.*

Three noteworthy buildings lie across the street. **Maison Baxter** *(1201 Rue Sherbrooke Ouest; Peel metro)*, on the left, boasts a beautiful stairway. **Résidence Forget** *(1195 Rue Sherbrooke Ouest; Peel metro)*, in the centre, was built in 1883 for Louis-Joseph Forget, one of the only French-Canadian magnates to live in this neighbourhood during the 19th century. The building on the right is the **Mount Royal Club** *(1175 Rue Sherbrooke Ouest; Peel metro)*, a private club frequented essentially by business people. Built in 1905, it is the work of Stanford White, of the famous New York firm McKim, Mead and White, architects of the head office of the **Bank of Montréal** (see p 58) on Place d'Armes.

Maison Alcan ★ *(1188 Rue Sherbrooke Ouest; Peel metro)*, head office of the Alcan aluminum company, is a fine example of historical preservation and inventive urban restructuring. Five buildings along Rue Sherbrooke, including the lovely **Maison Atholstan** *(1172 Rue Sherbrooke Ouest)*, the first Beaux-Arts–style structure erected in Montréal (1894), have been carefully restored and joined in the back to an atrium, which is linked to a modern aluminum building. The garden running along the south wall of the modern part provides a little-known passageway between Rue Drummond and Rue Stanley.

››› ⚲ *Enter the atrium through the Sherbrooke entrance. Exit through the garden on Rue Drummond.*

Heads Up!

Hungry for a quick bite? **La Brûlerie Saint-Denis** (see p 216) is tucked away in Maison Alcan's little garden and provides a nice bit of greenery in the heart of the Golden Square Mile district. Get your java fix and a tasty light meal at this branch of the famous Saint-Denis street coffee shop.

››› ⚲ *Turn left on Rue Drummond.*

Lord Mount Stephen, born in Stephen Croft, Scotland, was a determined man. Co-founder and first president of Canadian Pacific, he built a transcontinental railroad stretching over 5,000km from New Brunswick to British Columbia. His house, **Maison George Stephen** ★★ *(1440 Rue Drummond; Peel metro)* is a veritable monument to Montréal's Scottish bourgeoisie.

The house was built between 1880 and 1883 by William Tutin Thomas at a cost of $600,000, an astronomical sum at the time. Stephen called upon the best artisans in the world who covered the interior walls with marble, onyx and woodwork made of rare materials, such as English walnut, Cuban mahogany and Sri Lankan satinwood. The ceilings are so high that the house seems to have been built for giants. Since 1925, it has been owned by the Mount Stephen Club, a private club for business people.

››› ⚲ *Turn right on **Rue Sainte-Catherine** (see p 76); 15km long, it is Montréal's main commercial artery.*

Ogilvy's department store *(1307 Rue Ste-Catherine Ouest; Peel metro)*, the most elegant of Montréal's department stores, was purchased several years ago by a group of French-Canadian businessmen. The new owners have striven to preserve the original character of this Scottish Montréal institution, whose atmosphere

Exploring – The Golden Square Mile

is enlivened each day at noon by a bag-pipe player. The Tudor room on the top floor is often used for concerts and receptions. Across the street is a group of neoclassical houses dating back to 1864 (groupings such as these are known as "terraces"), which are among the last houses on the street to have survived to the present day.

Rue Crescent ★ *(Guy-Concordia metro)*, located immediately east of the museum, has a split personality. To the north of Boulevard de Maisonneuve, the street is lined with old row houses, which now accommodate antique shops and luxury boutiques, while to the south, it is crowded with night clubs, restaurants and bars, most with sunny terraces lining the sidewalks. For many years, Rue Crescent was known as the English counterpart of Rue Saint-Denis. Though it is still a favourite among American visitors, its clientele is more diversified now.

The **Church of St. James The Apostle** *(1439 Rue Sainte-Catherine Ouest; Guy-Concordia metro)* was built in 1864. At the time, it was located in the middle of a field, not far from where local cricket games were played, thus earning it the nickname "St. Cricket in the Fields." Before long, Rue Sainte-Catherine was lined with row houses. These have since made way to commercial buildings.

⋯ ☴ *Turn right on Rue Bishop.*

Throughout the 19th century, a large number of Scots emigrated to the British colonies. The market in their own land was controlled by the London upper class, who prevented the Scots from expanding their modest businesses. In those years, Montréal was the primary destination of these merchants, industrialists and inventors from Glasgow and Inverness. They were anxious to open stores or factories in this new country, which, with its rapidly growing population, needed everything. Peter Lyall was one of these immigrants. Immediately after his arrival from Castletown in 1870, he founded a construction company that prospered and was even commissioned to rebuild the Canadian Parliament after

the fire of 1916. Located south of Boulevard de Maisonneuve, **Maison Peter Lyall** *(1445 Rue Bishop; Guy-Concordia metro)*, his eclectic, polychrome, delightfully picturesque residence, looks like a big gingerbread house. It has been converted into business and office spaces.

Across the street lies **Concordia University**'s main campus, Montréal's second English university and the most recent (1974) of the city's four universities.

⋯ ☴ *To return to the starting point of the tour, head east on Boulevard de Maisonneuve or Rue Sainte-Catherine, the more pleasant of the two. The entrance to the McGill metro station is located near the corner of Avenue McGill College. However, the Guy-Concordia metro station is closer; turn left onto Boulevard De Maisonneuve. The entrance to the station is on the corner of Rue Guy.*

Tour E: Shaughnessy Village
★

🕐 *three hours*

When the Sulpicians took possession of the island of Montréal in 1663, they kept a portion of the best land for themselves, then set up a farm and a native village there in 1676. Following a fire, the native village was relocated several times before being permanently established in Oka. A part of the farm, corresponding to the area now known as Westmount, was then granted to French settlers. The Sulpicians planted an orchard and a vineyard on the remaining portion. Starting around 1870, the land was separated into lots. Part of it was used for the construction of mansions, while large plots were awarded to Catholic communities allied with the Sulpicians. It was at this time that Shaughnessy House was built—hence the name of the neighbourhood. During the 1970s, the number of local inhabitants increased considerably,

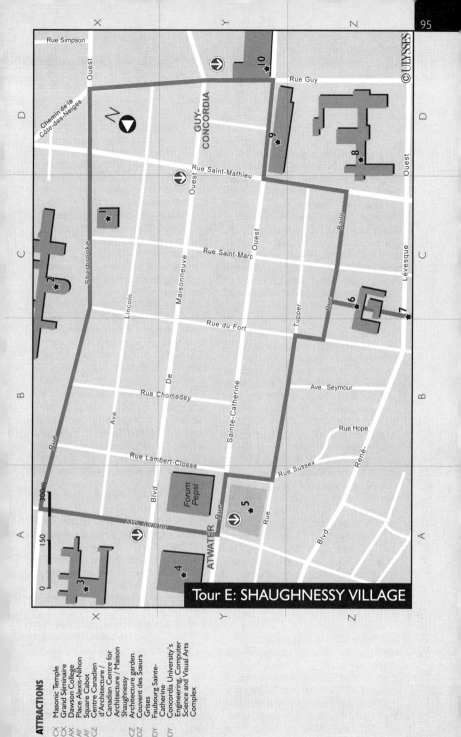

© ULYSSES

GUY-
CONCORDIA

ATWATER

Rue Simpson
Chemin de la Côte-des-Neiges
Ouest
Rue Guy
Rue Saint-Mathieu
Ouest
Rue Saint-Marc
Ouest
Sherbrooke
Rue du Fort
Lincoln
Maisonneuve
De
Sainte-Catherine
Baile
Tupper
Rue
Lévesque
Ave. Seymour
Rue Hope
Rue Chomedey
Ave.
Rue Lambert-Closse
Rue Sussex
René-
Blvd.
Forum
Pepsi
Rue
Ave. Atwater
Blvd.

300m
0   150

Tour E: SHAUGHNESSY VILLAGE

★ **ATTRACTIONS**

1. CX Masonic Temple
2. CX Grand Séminaire
3. AX Dawson College
4. AY Place Alexis-Nihon
5. AY Square Cabot
6. CZ Centre Canadien
       d'Architecture /
       Canadian Centre for
       Architecture / Maison
       Shaughnessy
7. CZ Architecture garden
8. DZ Couvent des Sœurs
       Grises
9. DY Faubourg Sainte-
       Catherine
10. DY Concordia University's
        Engineering, Computer
        Science and Visual Arts
        Complex

making Shaughnessy Village the most densely populated area in Québec.

••• 🚶 Ⓜ *From Rue Guy (Guy-Concordia metro), turn left on Rue Sherbrooke.*

Masonic lodges, which had already existed in New France, increased in scale with British immigration. These associations of freethinkers were not favoured by the Canadian clergy, who denounced their liberal views. Ironically, the **Masonic Temple** ★ *(1850 Rue Sherbrooke Ouest; Guy-Concordia metro and bus no. 24)*, one of Montréal's Scottish lodges, stands opposite the Grand Séminaire, where Catholic priests are trained. The edifice, built in 1928, enhances the secret, mystical character of Freemasonry with its impenetrable, windowless facade, equipped with antique vessels and double-headed lamps.

The Sulpicians' farmhouse was surrounded by a wall linked to four stone corner towers, earning it the name Fort des Messieurs. The house was destroyed when the **Grand Séminaire** ★★ *(guided tours Jun to Aug Tue-Sat at 1pm and 3pm; 2065 Rue Sherbrooke Ouest; Guy-Concordia metro and bus no. 24)* was built (1854-1860), but two towers, erected in the 17th century according to plans by François Vachon de Belmont, superior of the Montréal Sulpicians, can still be found in the institution's shady gardens. It was in one of these that Saint Marguerite Bourgeoys taught young Aboriginal girls. Around 1880, the long neoclassical buildings of the Grand Séminaire, designed by architect John Ostell, were topped by a mansard roof by Henri-Maurice Perrault. Information panels on Rue Sherbrooke, directly in line with Rue du Fort, provide precise details about the farm buildings.

It is well worth entering the Seminary to see the lovely Romanesque Revival–style chapel designed by Jean Omer Marchand in 1905. The ceiling beams are made of cedar from British Columbia, while the walls are covered with stones from Caen. The 80m-wide nave is lined with 300 hand-carved oak pews. Sulpicians who have died in Montréal since

the 18th century are interred beneath it. The Sulpician order was founded in Paris by Jean-Jacques Olier in 1641, and its main church is the Saint-Sulpice in Paris, which stands on the square of the same name.

The Congrégation de Notre-Dame, founded by Saint Marguerite Bourgeoys in 1671, owned a convent and a school in Old Montréal. Reconstructed in the 18th century, these buildings were expropriated by the city at the beginning of the 20th century as part of a plan to extend Boulevard Saint-Laurent all the way to the port. The nuns had to leave the premises and settle into a new convent. The congregation thus arranged for a convent to be built on Rue Sherbrooke, according to a design by Jean Omer Marchand (1873-1936), the first French-Canadian architect to graduate from the École des Beaux-Arts in Paris. The immense complex now bears witness to the vitality of religious communities in Québec before the Quiet Revolution of 1960.

The decline of religious practices and lack of new vocations forced the community to move into more modest buildings. **Dawson College** ★ *(3040 Rue Sherbrooke Ouest; Atwater metro)*, an English-language college or CÉGEP (*collège d'enseignement général et professionnel*), has been located in the original convent since 1987. The yellow-brick building, set on luxurious grounds, is probably the most beautiful CÉGEP in Québec. It is now directly linked to the subway and underground city. The Romanesque Revival–style chapel in the centre has an elongated copper dome reminiscent of Byzantine architecture. It now serves as a library and has barely been altered.

••• 🚶 *Head south on Avenue Atwater, then turn left on Rue Sainte-Catherine Ouest. Pass by the old Montreal Forum, now converted into a huge entertainment complex.*

On Avenue Atwater stands **Place Alexis-Nihon**, a multi-purpose complex containing a shopping mall, offices and apartments that is linked to the underground city. **Square Cabot** used to be the terminal for all buses serving the western part of the city.

Turn right on Rue Lambert-Closse, then left on Rue Tupper.

Between 1965 and 1975, Shaughnessy Village witnessed a massive wave of demolition. A great many Victorian row houses were replaced by high-rises, whose rudimentary designs, characterized by an endless repetition of identical glass or concrete balconies, are often referred to as "chicken coops." **Avenue Seymour ★** *(Atwater metro)* is one of the only streets in the area to have escaped this wave, which has now been curbed. Here, visitors will find charming houses made of brick and grey stone, with Queen Anne, Second Empire or Romanesque Revival details.

⋯ ⋏ *Turn right on Rue du Fort and then left on small Rue Baile (watch out for the fast-moving traffic heading to the highway on-ramp).*

Founded in 1979 by Phyllis Lambert, the **Centre Canadien d'Architecture / Canadian Centre for Architecture ★ ★ ★** *($10, free admission Thu 5:30pm to 9pm; Wed-Sun 10am to 5pm, Thu to 9pm; 1920 Rue Baile, ☎514-939-7026, www.cca.qc.ca; Guy-Concordia metro and bus no. 15 or 150)* is both a museum and a centre for the study of world architecture. Its collections of plans, drawings, models, books and photographs are the most important of their kind in the world.

Heads Up!

Want to read up on Montréal? Amateur urban planners can spend hours in the **Canadian Centre for Architecture**'s library (see above) uncovering the secrets behind the city's architecture and town planning.

The Centre, erected between 1985 and 1989, has six exhibition rooms, a bookstore, a library, a 217-seat auditorium and a wing specially designed for researchers, as well as vaults and restoration laboratories. The main building, shaped like a *U*, was designed by Peter Rose, with the help of Phyllis Lambert. It is covered with grey limestone from the Saint-Marc quarries near Québec City. This material, which used to be extracted from the Plateau Mont-Royal and Rosemont quarries in Montréal, also adorns the facades of many of the city's houses.

The centre surrounds the **Maison Shaughnessy**, whose facade looks out onto Boulevard René-Lévesque Ouest. This house is in fact a pair of residences, built in 1874 by architect William Tutin Thomas. It is representative of the mansions that once lined Boulevard René-Lévesque (formerly Dorchester Street).

In 1974, it was at the centre of an effort to salvage the neighbourhood, which had been torn down in a number of places. The house, itself threatened by demolition, was purchased at the last moment by Phyllis Lambert; she set up the offices and reception rooms of the Canadian Centre for Architecture inside. The building was named after Sir Thomas Shaughnessy, a former president of the Canadian Pacific Railway Company, who lived in the house for several decades. Neighbourhood residents who formed an association subsequently chose to name the entire area after him.

The amusing **architecture garden ★** *(facing the Canadian Centre for Architecture, on the south side of Boulevard René-Lévesque)*, by artist Melvin Charney, lies across from Shaughnessy House between two highway on-ramps. It illustrates the different stages of the neighbourhood's development using a portion of the Sulpicians' orchard on the left, stone lines to indicate borders of 19th-century properties and rose bushes reminiscent of the gardens of those houses. A promenade along the cliff that once separated the wealthy neighbourhood from the working-class sector below offers a view of the lower part of the city (Little Burgundy, Saint-Henri, Verdun) and the St. Lawrence River. Some of the highlights of this panorama are represented in a stylized manner, atop concrete posts.

Exploring – Shaughnessy Village

The Pull of Montréal

I arrived here from Calgary, didn't know a soul, and ran into my best friend from kindergarten on Saint-Laurent boulevard four days later. What can I say? Montréal is a magnetic city.

I have no statistics, but Montréal's vibrant reputation moves a huge crowd of young people from across the country to come and soak up their own part of the ethnic mix. Though the prospect of learning and re-learning French puts some people off, a surprising number of English-speaking Canadians seek out Montréal, eager to experience another culture and language. The good thing about the city is that you can do both—spend the day putting accents on your *e*'s and the evening watching movies made in Toronto. This cohabitation survives, running along the usual love-hate roller coaster, sending out sparks from Vancouver to Halifax.

We all unpack our bags here, but after that, similarities are difficult to define. I would say Anglos who choose Montréal have a penchant for diversity and a love of things exotic. We are travellers at heart, but need to feel at home— many of us are clustered in the Plateau area. We are willing to accept a small English-speaking community in exchange for a city with soul. We are glad political, linguistic and cultural debates are part of everyday conversation—life would be so boring without them!

Something about Montréal fascinates those of us from the more homogeneous parts of Canada, and makes us want to try living in a city where everyone from symphony conductors to grocery-store clerks must speak a few words in at least two languages. Something about the kaleidoscope of equally adamant points of view being expressed simultaneously on any given day brings curious minds pouring on to the island. And then sometimes, not always, something about the contradictions and quirks of our adopted home makes us stay.

Carol Wood

··· ⅄ *Head east on Boulevard René-Lévesque. Turn left on Rue Saint-Marc, then right on Rue Baile and head to the corner of Rue Saint-Mathieu, where you'll turn left.*

Like the Congrégation de Notre-Dame, the Sœurs Grises had to relocate their convent and hospital, which used to be situated on Rue Saint-Pierre in Old Montréal (see p 62). They obtained part of the Sulpicians' farm, where a vast convent, designed by Victor Bourgeau, was erected between 1869 and 1874.

The former **Couvent des Sœurs Grises ★** *(1185 Rue St-Mathieu, ☎ 514-937-9501; Guy-Concordia metro)*, which now houses the Mother House college, is the product of an architectural tradition developed over the centuries in Québec. The chapel alone reveals a foreign influence, namely the Romanesque Revival style favoured by the Sulpicians, as opposed to the Renaissance and Baroque Revival styles preferred by the church.

Upon request, it is possible to enter the Chapelle de l'Invention-de-la-Sainte-Croix, in the centre of the convent. Its stained-glass windows come from the Maison Champigneule in Bar-le-Duc, France. In 1974, the convent was supposed to be demolished and replaced by high-rises. Fortunately, Montrealers protested and the buildings were saved. Today, the convent is a listed historic monument.

⋯ ⋏ *Turn right on Rue Sainte-Catherine Ouest.*

At the **Faubourg Sainte-Catherine** ★ *(1616 Rue Ste-Catherine Ouest; Guy-Concordia metro)*, a large converted, glass-roofed garage, visitors will find a market made up of small specialty shops selling local and imported products, and a fast-food area.

You'll find Concordia University's new **Engineering, Computer Science and Visual Arts Complex** *(1515 Rue Ste-Catherine Ouest)* at the corner of Guy and Sainte-Catherine streets. Further north, at the corner of Rue Guy and Boulevard De Maisonneuve, is where another similar building is expected to be built in 2007 to house one of Montréal's most prestigious business schools: the John Molson School of Business. These two pavilions are part of the "Quartier Concordia" (Concordia neighbourhood) project, which aims to modernise the university's rather timeworn infrastructures and meet the demands of its ever-growing student population. Note the ultramodern style of the new pavilion, whose glass exterior and wood-panelled interior recall two of Montréal's other recent architectural undertakings: the **Bibliothèque Nationale du Québec** (see p 108) and the **Insititut de Tourisme et d'Hôtellerie du Québec** (see p 104).

⋯ ⋏ Ⓜ *To return to the Guy-Concordia metro station, turn left on Rue Guy.*

Tour F: The McGill Ghetto and "The Main" ★

 three hours

This tour starts in the **McGill Ghetto**, the area where many McGill University students reside (see p 86). The university's main campus is located west of Rue University. The many American students who are enrolled at McGill have converted some of the ghetto's residences into fraternity houses. You'll have no trouble spotting these private clubs: exterior signs in ancient Greek identify each fraternity.

This tour also provides an overview of the history of one of Montréal's important religious communities. In 1860, the *religieuses hospitalières* of Saint-Joseph (nursing nuns) left the Hôtel-Dieu hospital founded by Jeanne Mance in 1643 in Old Montréal and moved to Avenue des Pins. Victor Bourgeau designed the new hospital, located in what was then open country. In the following years, the nuns gradually sold off the remaining property in lots, laying out streets soon to be lined with Victorian row houses. A number of these row houses were threatened by demolition after the unveiling of a gigantic real-estate development project in 1973. However, neighbourhood residents fought the developers, who in the end only succeeded in tearing down a few of the coveted buildings. The houses that were saved are now part of the Milton Park project, the largest housing cooperative in Canada.

Finally, visitors will explore **Boulevard Saint-Laurent**, commonly known to Montrealers as "The Main." At the end of the 18th century, the Faubourg Saint-Laurent sprung up along the street of the same name, which led inland from the river. In 1792, the city was officially divided into east and west sections, with this artery marking the boundary. Then, in the early 20th century, the addresses of east-west streets were reassigned so that they all began at Boulevard Saint-Laurent.

Meanwhile, around 1880, French-Canadian high society came up with the idea of turning the boulevard into the "Champ-Élysées" of Montréal. The west side was destroyed in order to make the street wider and to reconstruct new buildings in Richardson's Romanesque Revival style, which was all the rage at the end of the 19th century. Populated by the successive waves of immigrants who arrived at the port, Boulevard Saint-Laurent never, however, attained the heights of

Exploring – The McGill Ghetto and "The Main"

glory anticipated by its developers. But the section between Boulevard René-Lévesque and Boulevard de Maisonneuve did become the hub of Montréal nightlife in the early 20th century. Indeed, the city's big theatres, like the Français, where Sarah Bernhardt performed, were located around here. During the Prohibition era (1919-1930), the area became run-down. Every week, thousands of Americans came here to frequent the cabarets and brothels, which abounded in this neighbourhood until the late 1950s.

⋯ ⋏ Ⓜ *The tour starts at the exit of the McGill metro station. Head north on Rue University until Rue Sherbrooke.*

Royal Victoria College *(555 Rue Sherbrooke Ouest; McGill metro)* was once a professional school for young women from well-to-do families. Today, it houses McGill University's Faculty of Music, as well as the 300-seat Pollack Hall, a perfect place for chamber music. On the front steps of the building, designed by American architect Bruce Price (1899), is a lovely bronze statue of Queen Victoria executed by her daughter, the talented Princess Louise. Walking up Rue University, visitors will see the Montreal High School, a pale-yellow brick building.

The **Montreal Diocesan Theological College** ★ *(3473 Rue University; McGill metro)* is dedicated to the training of Anglican priests. With its densely ornamented walls of beige sandstone and red brick, the 1896 Gothic Revival–style building is representative of the picturesque, polychrome period of the end of the Victorian era.

⋯ ⋏ *Turn right on Rue Milton.*

The **Maison Hans Selye** *(659 Rue Milton; McGill metro)* is located at the corner of University and Milton streets. The famous Dr. Hans Selye, a stress specialist, lived and worked here during the 1940s and 1950s.

⋯ ⋏ *Turn left on Avenue Lorne. Continue up beyond Rue Prince-Arthur to Lorne Crescent, a residential street that is little known, even to Montrealers.*

On this street, visitors will find some interesting semi-detached Victorian houses (circa 1875). During the Vietnam War, American protesters dodging the U.S. draft took refuge in this neighbourhood.

⋯ ⋏ *Turn right on Rue Aylmer, then left on Rue Prince-Arthur.*

Complexe La Cité *(at the corner of Avenue du Parc and Rue Prince-Arthur)* has been renamed "Place du Parc." Spread over four blocks on both sides of Rue Prince-Arthur, it is the only completed portion of an extensive urban-renewal project involving the destruction of most of the Victorian buildings on Rue Hutchison, Rue Jeanne-Mance and Rue Sainte-Famille. La Cité, erected between 1973 and 1977, is one of the only complexes of this size in the world to have been designed by a woman, architect Eva Vecsei. It includes high-rise apartment buildings, a hotel, a shopping centre, a movie theatre and a large health club.

⋯ ⋏ *Cross Avenue du Parc.*

The former **First Presbyterian Church** *(3666 Rue Jeanne-Mance)*, at the corner of Rue Prince-Arthur, was erected in 1910 for American Presbyterians. It underwent a radical transformation in 1986 when apartments were laid out under the nave and all the way to the top of its steeple. Behind the church lies the former Strathearn School, now occupied by local community organizations, while the small German Lutheran **St. John Church** stands across the street. East of Rue Jeanne-Mance is an opening offering a view of an alley that was given a complete face-lift in 1982. After the creation of a residential cooperative, the numerous sheet-metal sheds and wooden walkways were replaced by small grassy yards enclosed by fences.

Turn left on Rue Sainte-Famille, which offers two interesting perspectives, one on the chapel of the Hôtel-Dieu on Avenue des Pins to the north, and the other on the UQAM School of Design on Rue Sherbrooke to the south. The street is reminiscent of classical French town-planning, several examples of which

Tour F: THE McGILL GHETTO AND "THE MAIN"

Ave. du Mont-Royal Est

N

W — W

Parc du Mont-Royal

Parc Jeanne-Mance

Marie-Anne Ouest

Parc du Portugal

Marie-Anne Est

0   150   300m

Monument to Sir-George-Étienne-Cartier

Ave. de l'Esplanade
Rue Saint-Urbain
Rue Clark
Rue Rachel

Ave. du Parc

Duluth Ouest   Duluth Est

X — X

Bagg
Napoléon

Rue St-Dominique
Ave. de l'Hôtel-de-Ville

Hôtel-Dieu de Montréal H

St-Cuthbert

Roy

Molson Stadium

7   6
Ave. des Pins Ouest   Ave. des Pins Est

Guilbault

8

Ave. Coloniale
Rue De Bullion
Ave. Laval
Ave. Henri-Julien
Rue Drolet

Y — Y

Rue University
Croissant
Rue Aylmer
Rue Durocher
Rue Hutchinson

Prince-Arthur Ouest

5

4

Ave. du Parc
Rue Jeanne-Mance
Rue Ste-Famille

Blvd. Saint-Laurent

Prince-Arthur Est

Square Saint-Louis

3

2

Rue Milton

9   10
11   12

Rue Sherbrooke Est

Z — Z

Rue Sherbrooke Ouest

1

Rue De Bleury

13
14

Rue Ontario

McGILL

Ave. du Président-Kennedy

Blvd. De Maisonneuve Ouest

PLACE-DES-ARTS

SAINT-LAURENT

©ULYSSES

★ ATTRACTIONS

1.	AZ	Royal Victoria College
2.	AZ	Montreal Diocesan Theological College
3.	AY	Maison Hans Selye
4.	AY	Complexe La Cité
5.	BY	First Presbyterian Church (former)
6.	BY	Musée des Hospitalières
7.	BY	Hôtel-Dieu
8.	BY	Ex-Centris

9.	BZ	Conseil des Arts de Montréal
10.	BZ	Maison Notman
11.	BZ	Édifice Godin
12.	CZ	Musée Juste Pour Rire / Just for Laughs Museum
13.	BZ	Édifice Grothé
14.	BZ	Jules Saint-Michel, Luthier – Économusée de la Lutherie

Main Madness!

Summer is a festive time on the Main. Boulevard Saint-Laurent businesses have been banding together twice every year since 1979 to hold a huge sidewalk sale. One of the city's busiest streets is then closed off to traffic and pedestrians get to enjoy the eclectic ambiance of these events, as they check out the bohemian crowd, shop for bargains and savour mangoes and pina coladas on outdoor terraces. *(Main Madness; Jun 16-19 and Aug 25-28 2006; ☎514-286-0334, www.boulevardsaintlaurent.com).*

could once be found in Old Montréal. Celebrated physicist Ernest Rutherford lived at 3702 Rue Sainte-Famille while he was teaching at McGill. A little farther up the street, visitors will find six residential buildings with vaguely Art Nouveau–style details. These were erected by the nuns in 1910 to house the doctors working at the Hôtel-Dieu *(3705 to 3739 Rue Ste-Famille)*.

The **Musée des Hospitalières** ★ *($6; mid-Jun to mid-Oct, Tue-Fri 10am to 5pm, Sat and Sun 1pm to 5pm; mid-Oct to mid-Jun, Wed-Sun 1pm to 5pm; 201 Avenue des Pins Ouest, ☎514-849-2919; Place-des-Arts or Sherbrooke metro and bus no. 55 or 144)* is located in the former chaplain's lodgings, next door to the hospital chapel. It provides a detailed account of both the history of the Filles Hospitalières de Saint-Joseph, a community founded at the Hôtel-Dieu de La Flèche (Anjou, France) in 1634, and the evolution of medicine over the last three centuries. Visitors can see the former wooden stairway of the Hôtel-Dieu de La Flèche (1634), given to the City of Montréal by the French region of Sarthe in 1963. The piece was skilfully restored by the Compagnons du Devoir and incorporated into the museum's beautiful entrance hall, the work of architects D'Anjou, Bernard and Mercier (1992).

The **Hôtel-Dieu** ★ *(3840 Rue St-Urbain; Place-des-Arts or Sherbrooke metro and bus no. 55 or 144)* is still one of Montréal's major hospitals. The institution and the city were founded almost simultaneously as part of a project initiated by a group of devout Parisians led by Jérôme Le Royer de La Dauversière.

Thanks to the wealth of Angélique Faure de Bullion, wife of the superintendent of finances under Louis XIV, and the devotion of Jeanne Mance, from Langres, the institution grew rapidly on Rue Saint-Paul in Old Montréal. However, lack of space, polluted air and noise in the old city forced the nuns to move the hospital to their farm in Mont-Sainte-Famille in the mid-19th century. The complex has been enlarged many times and is centered around a lovely neoclassical chapel with a dome and a facade reminiscent of urban churches in Québec under the French Regime. The interior, simplified in 1967, has, however, been divested of several interesting remounted paintings.

⋯ ⋏ *Head east on Avenue des Pins to Boulevard Saint-Laurent.*

The portion of Boulevard Saint-Laurent located within the limits of the Hôtel-Dieu area is lined with an assortment of specialty food shops selling products from Eastern Europe, bookstores, second-hand shops and fashionable restaurants and cafés.

The bustling section of Boulevard Saint-Laurent between Boulevard René-Lévesque and Avenue du Mont-Royal is expected to receive a major overhaul by 2007. The new face of the Main is expected to include wider sidewalks, new street furniture and parking areas that will facilitate car traffic on one of the city's busiest arteries.

Exploring – The McGill Ghetto and "The Main"

Heads Up!

→ Up for some window-shopping? **Boulevard Saint-Laurent** south of Avenue des Pins is home to several fashion boutiques. Stop by on your way to one of the area's many hip eateries.

••• ☥ *Turn right on Boulevard Saint-Laurent.*

The first street you'll come upon is **Rue Prince-Arthur**, a pedestrian street that was Montréal's bastion of hippie culture during the 1960s. Here, visitors will find a cluster of family restaurants, with terraces stretching all the way to the middle of the street. On summer evenings, a dense crowd gathers between the buildings to applaud street performers. Rue Prince-Arthur also provides access to **Square Saint-Louis** ★★ (see p 105) and Rue Saint-Denis *(Sherbrooke metro)*.

Ex-Centris ★ *(3536 Boulevard St-Laurent, ☎514-847-2206, www.ex-centris.com; Saint-Laurent metro and bus no. 55)* is located in a stone building that blends in well with the older buildings next to it. A movie and new-media complex, Ex-Centris was opened in 1999 by Daniel Langlois, who financed the entire construction from beginning to end. The complex shows the best independent films, produced either locally or internationally, in three magnificent rooms of different sizes.

Heads Up!

→ Ready for lunch? For a laid-back, colourful ambiance, head to **Euro Deli** (see p 222). Film aficionados in the mood for something a little classier can opt for **Café Méliès** (see p 226), across the street.

••• ☥ *Turn right on Rue Milton and then left on Rue Saint-Urbain.*

The **Conseil des Arts de Montréal** *(3450 Rue St-Urbain)*, the city's arts council, occupies the former École d'Architecture de Montréal, erected in 1922. Ernest

Cormier's former studio (1923), a small red-brick building with stained glass, stands on the grounds of the school. The Conseil rents it to Québec artists wishing to withdraw from the world for a certain period of time in order to create a specific work. At the corner of Rue Sherbrooke stands the former École des Beaux-Arts.

••• ☥ *Turn left on Rue Sherbrooke.*

Montréal photographer William Notman, known for his Canadian scenes and portraits of 19th-century bourgeoisie, lived in the **Maison Notman** ★ *(51 Rue Sherbrooke Ouest; Place-des-Arts metro)* from 1876 to 1891. The inexhaustible Notman photographic archives may be viewed at the **McCord Museum of Canadian History** ★★ (see p 86). The house, erected in 1844 according to a design by John Wells, is a fine example of the Greek Revival style as it was interpreted in Scotland in those years. Its extreme austerity is broken only by some small, decorative touches, such as the palmettes and rosettes of the portico. From 1894 to 1990, the residence served as a hospital, St. Margaret's Home for the Incurables, which provided extended care for the elderly.

The neighbouring gas station enjoys a prime location at the corner of two of the city's main streets, Boulevard Saint-Laurent and Rue Sherbrooke. The residence of the Molson family, famous brewers and bankers, once stood here.

••• ☥ *Head south on Boulevard Saint-Laurent.*

The **Édifice Godin** ★ *(2112 Boulevard St-Laurent; Saint-Laurent metro)*, located at the corner of Rue Sherbrooke, is quite certainly the most daring example of early 20th-century modern architecture in Canada (1914). With its visible reinforced concrete structure, the building is evidence of the experiments of Auguste Perret and Paul Guadet, while the addition of a few subtle Art Nouveau curves gives it a very Parisian appearance. The building, designed by architect Joseph-Arthur Godin, to whom we also owe the **Saint-Jacques** ★ (see p 106), was originally intended to be residential, but its novelty frightened off potential renters—so much so that it remained empty for a number of years after being completed and was finally converted into a clothing factory.

In 2004, this historic building was renovated at a cost of close to 35 million dollars to welcome the luxurious **Hôtel Godin** (see p 196), with its 140 or so rooms.

Set up inside the former Ekers brewery, the **Musée Juste Pour Rire / Just for Laughs Museum** ★ *($9 and up, depending on activities or shows; Tue-Sun upon reservation only, groups of 15 people or more; 2111 Boulevard Saint-Laurent, ☎514-845-4000, www.hahaha.com; Saint-Laurent metro)* opened in 1993. This museum, the only one of its kind in the world, explores the different facets of humour using a variety of film clips and sets. Visitors are equipped with infrared headphones, which enable them to follow the presentation. The building itself was renovated and redesigned by architect Luc Laporte and features some 3,000m² of exhibition space. The museum also houses a concert hall, **Le Cabaret Music-Hall** (see p 274).

Boulevard Saint-Laurent changes appearance several times from one end to the other. For a brief stretch, it takes on an industrial air and then regains its busy commercial look. Located at the corner of Rue Ontario, the **Édifice Grothé** *(2000 Boulevard St-Laurent; Saint-Laurent metro)*, the former Grothé cigar factory, is an austere red-brick edifice dating back to 1906 that has been converted into residences. In the early 20th century, when transportation, energy and the big banks were controlled by British magnates, French-Canadian strength, as the Grothé company proves, lay in the food and tobacco industries.

Near the intersection of Boulevard Saint-Laurent and Rue Ontario, south of Rue Sherbrooke, is **Jules Saint-Michel, Luthier – Économusée de la Lutherie** *($6 private tour; Mon-Fri 2pm to 5pm; 57 Rue Ontario Ouest, ☎514-288-4343)*. The Économusée de la Lutherie is the best place to see how a violin is made; this instrument's shape has not changed in 450 years. For ex-

ample, you will learn the different parts that make up a violin, who were the greatest instrument-makers in history, and what role Québec has played in this field. Violin-maker Jules Saint-Michel will let you tour his shop, workshop and museum.

⋯ 🚶 Ⓜ️ *The current tour ends at the Saint-Laurent metro station, at the corner of Boulevard de Maisonneuve.*

Tour G: Quartier Latin ★★

 three hours

People come to the Quartier Latin, a university neighbourhood centered around Rue Saint-Denis, for its theatres, cinemas and countless outdoor cafés, which offer a glimpse of its heterogeneous crowd of students and revellers. The area's origins date back to 1823, when Montréal's first Catholic cathedral, Église Saint-Jacques, was established on Rue Saint-Denis. This prestigious edifice quickly attracted the cream of French-Canadian society—mainly old noble families who had remained in Canada after the conquest—to the area. In 1852, a fire ravaged the neighbourhood, destroying the cathedral and Monseigneur Bourget's palace in the process. Painfully reconstructed in the second half of the 19th century, the area remained residential until the Université de Montréal was established here in 1893, marking the beginning of a period of cultural turmoil that would eventually lead to the Quiet Revolution of the 1960s. The Université du Québec à Montréal (UQAM), founded in 1969, has since taken over the Université de Montréal, which is now located on the north side of Mount Royal. The presence of the university has ensured the quarter's prosperity.

⋯ 🚶 Ⓜ️ *This tour starts at the exit of the Sherbrooke metro station.*

The **Institut de Tourisme et d'Hôtellerie du Québec (ITHQ)** *(3535 Rue St-Denis, ☎514-*

Finally!

For 30 years, the rather unseemly building that housed the Insititut de Tourisme et d'Hôtellerie du Québec was an eyesore that marred the landscape of the very pretty Saint-Louis Square located across Rue Saint-Denis. Fortunately, extensive renovations were completed in 2005 to restore the establishment's image and provide it with a building that is better suited to the institution's vocation.

282-5108, www.ithq.qc.ca; Sherbrooke metro), a school devoted to the tourism and hotel industries, was recently renovated and now presents an ultramodern glass facade. Top-notch cooking, tourism and hostelry courses are given here, and the establishment also features a hotel (**Hôtel de l'Institut**, see p 204) and a restaurant (**Le Restaurant de l'Institut**, see p 229), where you can get a foretaste of a potential future great chef's creations. You can also sign up for a cooking class to perfect your technique or take part in a "meal-course" to discover a few of this school's mouth-watering gourmet recipes.

▸▸▸ ⚲ *Cross Rue Saint-Denis to get to Square Saint-Louis.*

In 1848, the City of Montréal had a water reservoir built at the top of the hill known as Côte-à-Barron. In 1879, it was dismantled and the site was converted into a park by the name of **Square Saint-Louis ★★** *(Sherbrooke metro)*. Developers built beautiful Second Empire–style homes around the square, making it the nucleus of the French-Canadian bourgeois neighbourhood. These groups of houses give the area a certain harmonious quality that is rarely found in Montréal's urban landscape. **Rue Prince-Arthur** (see p 103) extends west from the square.

Turn left onto **Avenue Laval**, one of the only streets in the city where the Belle Époque atmosphere is still very tangible. Abandoned by the French-Canadian bourgeoisie in 1920, the houses were converted into rooming houses before attracting the attention of local artists, who began restoring them one by one. Poet Émile Nelligan (1879-1941) lived at number 3688 with his family at the turn of the 20th century. A bronze bust by artist Roseline Granet in memory of the poet was recently inaugurated and stands at the corner of Avenue Laval and Square Saint-Louis.

The Union des Écrivains Québécois (Québec Writers' Association) house occupies number 3492, the former home of filmmaker Claude Jutra, who directed such films as *Mon Oncle Antoine*. A number of other artists, including singer Pauline Julien and her late husband, poet and politician Gérald Godin, writers Michel Tremblay and Yves Navarre, and pianist André Gagnon, live or have lived in the area around Square Saint-Louis and Avenue Laval.

Mont-Saint-Louis ★ *(244 Rue Sherbrooke Est; Sherbrooke metro)*, a former boys' school run by the brothers of the Écoles Chrétiennes, was built facing straight up Avenue Laval in 1887. The long facade punctuated with pavilions, grey stone walls, openings with segmental arches and mansard roof, make this building one of the most characteristic examples of the Second Empire style as adapted to suit Montréal's big institutions. The school closed its doors in 1970 and the edifice was converted into an apartment building in 1987, at which time an unobtrusive parking lot was built under the garden.

Journalist, poet and Member of Parliament Louis Fréchette (1839-1908) lived in the **Maison Fréchette** *(306 Rue Sherbrooke Est; Sherbrooke metro)* a Second Empire-style house. Sarah Bernhardt stayed here on several occasions during her North-American tours.

Exploring – Quartier Latin

›› 𝔸 *Turn right on Rue Saint-Denis and walk down "Côte-à-Barron" toward the Université du Québec à Montréal.*

Montée du Zouave, the hill on the right known today as **Terrasse Saint-Denis**, was the favourite meeting place of Québec's poets and writers a century ago. The group of houses was built on the site of the home of Sieur de Montigny, a proud papal Zouave.

Montréal architect Joseph-Arthur Godin was one of the precursors of modern architecture in North America. In 1914, he began construction on three apartment buildings with visible reinforced concrete frames in the Quartier Latin area. One of these is the **Saint-Jacques ★** *(1704 Rue St-Denis; Berri-UQAM metro)*. Godin blended this avant-garde concept with subtle Art-Nouveau curves, giving the buildings a light, graceful appearance. The venture was a commercial failure, however, leading Godin to bankruptcy and ending his career as an architect.

The former **Bibliothèque Nationale ★** *(1704 Rue St-Denis; Berri-UQAM metro)*, or national library, was originally built for the Sulpicians, who looked unfavourably upon the construction of a public library on Rue Sherbrooke. Even though many works were still on the *Index*, therefore forbidden reading for the clergy, the new library was seen as unfair competition. Known until 1967 as Bibliothèque Saint-Sulpice, this branch of the Bibliothèque Nationale du Québec was designed in the Beaux-Arts style by architect Eugène Payette in 1914. This style, a synthesis of classicism and French Renaissance architecture, was taught at the École des Beaux-Arts in Paris, hence its name in North America. The interior is graced with lovely stained-glass windows created by Henri Perdriau in 1915. The Bibliothèque Nationale's collections were transferred to its new location, at the corner of Rue Berri and Boulevard De Maisonneuve (see p 108).

Heads Up!

↪ Tea time? The charming little **Camellia Sinensis** (see p 227) tea shop on Rue Émeri offers one of the best selections of fine teas in Montréal. A good spot for a quick break in the heart of the bustling Quartier Latin area.

The **Théâtre Saint-Denis** *(1594 Rue St-Denis,* ☎ *514-790-1111; Berri-UQAM metro)* is made up of two theatres, which are among the most popular in the city. During summer, the Festival Juste pour Rire, also known as the Just for Laughs Festival, is presented here. The theatre opened in 1916, and has since welcomed big names in show business from the world over. Modernized several times over the years, it was completely renovated yet again in 1989. As visitors can see, the top of the original theatre is higher than the recently added pink-granite facade.

At the corner of Boulevard De Maisonneuve are the offices of **NFB Montréal** *(Tue-Sun noon to 9pm; 1564 Rue St-Denis,* ☎ *514-496-6887, www.onf.ca)*, Montréal's distribution and consultation branch of the **National Film Board of Canada (NFB)**. NFB Montréal includes the **Cinérobothèque** *($5.50 for 2hrs, $3 for 1hr)*, which provides users with 21 viewing units (individual and double) so that they can view various films. In addition, the complex features two theatres that present documentaries and movies. You can also rent NFB archival films and get videocassettes and

★ **ATTRACTIONS**

1.	BV	Institut de Tourisme et d'Hôtellerie du Québec (ITHQ)	10.	BX	Salle Pierre-Mercure
2.	BV	Square Saint-Louis	11.	BX	Bibliothèque Nationale du Québec
3.	AW	Mont-Saint-Louis	12.	BX,BY	Université du Québec à Montréal (UQAM)
4.	BW	Maison Fréchette	13.	BY	Chapelle Notre-Dame-de-Lourdes
5.	BW	Saint-Jacques	14.	CX	Parc Émilie-Gamelin
6.	BW	Bibliothèque Nationale (former)	15.	CZ	École des Hautes Études Commerciales (former)
7.	BX	Théâtre Saint-Denis	16.	BZ	Square Viger
8.	BX	NFB Montréal / Cinérobothèque	17.	BZ	Union Française
9.	BX	Cinémathèque Québécoise	18.	BZ	Église Saint-Sauveur

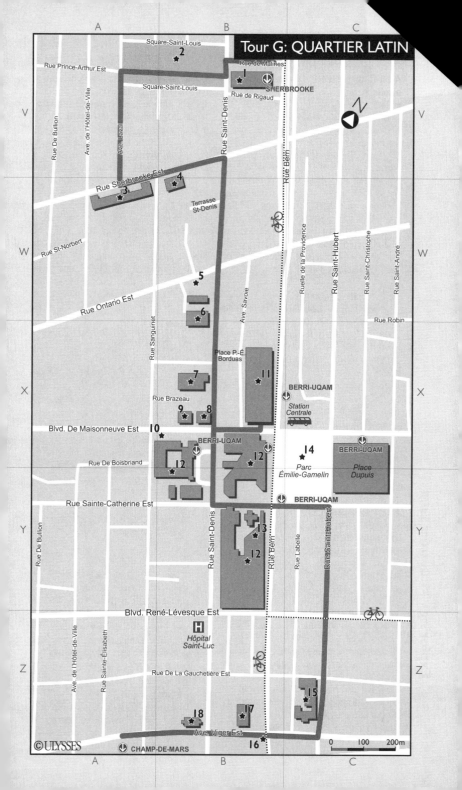

Tour G: QUARTIER LATIN

as well as promotional products ...CinéBoutique.

...urther west, the **Cinémathèque Qué-** ... ★ *(free admission to exhibits, $7 for screenings; closed Mon; 335 Boulevard De Maisonneuve Est,* ☎*514-842-9763, www. cinematheque.qc.ca)* is another great place for movie lovers. It features a collection of 25,000 Canadian, Québécois and foreign films, as well as several pieces of equipment that date back to the early days of cinema. The Cinémathèque contains, in addition, theatres, exhibit spaces, a "mediatheque" and a shop, as well as a café-bar. Facing it is a concert hall affiliated to the Université du Québec à Montréal, the **Salle Pierre-Mercure** of the Centre Pierre-Péladeau.

Further east on Boulevard De Maisonneuve is the new **Bibliothèque Nationale du Québec** ★ ★ *(Tue-Fri 10am to 10pm, Sat-Sun 10am to 5pm; 475 Boulevard De Maisonneuve Est,* ☎*514-873-1100. www.bnquebec. ca)*, which opened on April 30, 2005 and is commonly known as "La Grande Bibliothèque." This major new addition to Montréal's cultural landscape cost nearly 100 million dollars and is housed in a bright and airy, luxurious six-storey building located on the site of the former Palais du Commerce. The edifice's design features contrasting wood and glass elements and the library contains over four million titles, making it the most important collection of books and multimedia documents in the province. Though some say the establishment's inauguration marks the death of neighbourhood libraries, others argue that it meets the modern needs of the major cultural metropolis that is Montréal, especially after UNESCO named it a "World Book Capital City" in 2005. Start your visit at the library's entrance, where you'll be greeted by the *Espace Fractal* "knowledge tree", a veritable bouquet of aluminium sparks created by Québec artist Jean-Pierre Morin. Take one of the panoramic elevators to the library's top floor for an unbeatable view of the city. Among the library's other contemporary works of art are the *Vous Êtes Ici* glass curtain wall on the Avenue Savoie facade by Dominique Blain and the glass *Voix*

Sans Bruit piece by Louise Viger on the metro level.

Unlike most North-American universities, whose buildings are contained within a specific campus, the campus of the **Université du Québec à Montréal (UQAM)** ★ *(Berri-UQAM metro)* is integrated into the city fabric like French and German universities built during the Renaissance. It is also linked to the underground city and the metro. The university is located on the site once occupied by the buildings of the Université de Montréal and the Église Saint-Jacques, which was reconstructed after the fire of 1852. Only the wall of the right transept and the Gothic Revival steeple were integrated into the Pavillon Judith-Jasmin (1979), and these elements have since become the symbol of the university. UQAM is part of the

Tête à Papineau

The son-in-law of Louis-Joseph Papineau, artist Napoléon Bourassa—whose masterpiece Notre-Dame-de-Lourdes chapel was erected on Sainte-Catherine street in Montréal in 1876—lived in a large house located on Rue St-Denis (no. 1242), near the aforementioned chapel. On the house's facade is Papineau's head ("*tête à Papineau*").

The heroic instigator of the Patriote movement, Louis-Joseph Papineau remains without question a major player in the dismantling of a political regime that was unacceptable to the people of Lower Canada. His reputation as a man of high intelligence survives to this day in the popular French-language expression "*Ça ne prends pas la tête à Papineau!*" (meaning "It doesn't take Papineau's brains!" or "It's not rocket science!").

Université du Québec, founded in 1969 and established in cities across the province. Every year, over 40,000 students attend this flourishing institution of higher learning.

Artist Napoléon Bourassa lived in a large house on Saint-Denis Street (no. 1242): note the facade and its "tête à Papineau." **Chapelle Notre-Dame-de-Lourdes** ★ *(430 Rue Ste-Catherine Est; Berri-UQAM metro)*, erected in 1876, was his greatest achievement. It was commissioned by the Sulpicians, who wanted to secure their presence in this part of the city. Its Roman-Byzantine style is in some way a summary of its author's travels. The little chapel's recently restored interior, adorned with Bourassa's vibrantly coloured frescoes, is a must-see.

⋯ ⋏ *Retrace your steps and turn right on Rue Sainte-Catherine Est.*

Parc Émilie-Gamelin ★ *(at the corner of Rue Berri and Rue Ste-Catherine; Berri-UQAM metro)*, laid out in 1992 for Montréal's 350th anniversary, is a large public space that honours the memory of the founder of the Soeurs de la Providence religious order, whose asylum occupied this site until 1960. At the north end, visitors will find a few unusual metal sculptures by Melvin Charney, who also designed the garden of the **Canadian Centre for Architecture** ★★★ (see p 97).

North of the park lies the bus terminal (Station Centrale), built on top of the Berri-UQAM metro station where three of the city's four metro lines converge. To the east, Place Dupuis, with stores, offices and a hotel, is located on the site of the former Dupuis Frères department store. A few businesses that are dear to Montrealers, such as the Archambault record shop, still grace Rue Sainte-Catherine Est. The part of this street between Rue Amherst and Avenue Papineau is known as Montréal's **Gay Village** (see p 110).

⋯ ⋏ *Turn right on Rue Saint-Hubert, then right again on Avenue Viger.*

You may find that the many major roads that criss-cross this part of the Quartier Latin neighbourhood make it a less interesting area to visit than Rue Saint-Denis. The Ville-Marie expressway, in the southern part of this tour, is notable for having disfigured a historic part of the city whose rich architectural heritage includes the magnificent Beaux-Arts building on Avenue Viger that used to house the École des Hautes Études Commerciales de Montréal business school.

A symbol of the social ascent of a certain class of French-Canadian businessmen in the early 20th century, the former **École des Hautes Études Commerciales** ★★ *(535 Avenue Viger; Berri-UQAM or Champ-de-Mars metro)* business school profoundly altered Montréal's managerial and financial circles. Prior to the school's existence, these fields were dominated by Canadians of British extraction. This imposing building's Parisian Beaux-Arts architecture (1908), characterized by twin columns, balustrades, a monumental staircase and sculptures, bears witness to the Francophile leaning of those who built it. In 1970, this business school, known as HEC, joined the campus of the Université de Montréal on the north side of Mount Royal. This beautiful building now houses the Centre d'Archives de Montréal – Archives Nationales du Québec.

Before moving to the Square Saint-Louis area around 1880, members of the French-Canadian bourgeoisie settled around **Square Viger** *(Avenue Viger; Berri-UQAM or Champ-de-Mars metro)* during the 1850s. Marred by the underground construction of Autoroute Ville-Marie (1977-79), the square was redesigned in three sections by as many artists, who opted for an elaborate design, as opposed to the sober style of the original 19th-century square. In the background, visitors will see the former castle-like **Gare Viger** (see p 67).

The **Union Française** *(429 Avenue Viger Est; Berri-UQAM or Champ-de-Mars metro)*, Montréal's French cultural association, has occupied this old, aristocratic residence since 1909. Lectures and exhibitions on France and its various regions are held here. Every year, Bastille Day (July 14) is celebrated at Square Viger, across the street. The house, attributed to architect Henri-Maurice Perrault, was built in 1867 for shipowner Jacques-Félix Sincennes, founder of the Richelieu and Ontario Navigation Company. It is one of the oldest examples of Second Empire architecture in Montréal.

At the corner of Rue Saint-Denis is the **Église Saint-Sauveur** *(329 Avenue Viger; Berri-UQAM or Champ-de-Mars metro)*, a Gothic Revival church built in 1865 by architects Lawford and Nelson. From 1922 to 1995, it was the seat of Montréal's Syrian Catholic community. Like several other deserted religious sites in Montréal, the church is now for sale and could fall prey to unscrupulous demolishers and developers, despite the works of art it contains.

⋯ 🚶 Ⓜ *Continue along Avenue Viger to get to the Champ-de-Mars metro station.*

Tour H: The Village ★

 three hours

This neighbourhood, located on the edge of the downtown area, developed in the late 18th century when Old Montréal extended eastward. Originally known as "Faubourg Québec" because it ran alongside the road leading to Québec City, it was renamed "Quartier Sainte-Marie" after becoming industrialized, then nicknamed "Faubourg à M'lasse" around 1880, when hundreds of barrels of sweet-smelling molasses began to be unloaded every day onto the wharves of the nearby port (*mélasse* is the French word for molasses).

In the mid-1960s, civil servants affixed the somewhat bland name "Centre-Sud" to the neighbourhood. This was before the homosexual community took it over in 1980 and made it the "Gay Village." Despite its many names, The Village is

a place with a lot of spirit, which has always been marked by poverty and life on the fringe. Occasionally ugly and in poor taste, it is full of activity and can be fascinating if given a chance.

The Village is divided into three zones of varying sizes from south to north: the port and industrial area, almost impassable on foot as it is blocked by Autoroute Ville-Marie, which was built between 1974 and 1977; the Cité des Ondes, home to Radio-Canada, whose 1970 construction led to the demolition of a third of the neighbourhood; and finally, Rue Sainte-Catherine, where visitors will find a large concentration of cafés, nightclubs, restaurants and bars.

⋯ 🚶 Ⓜ *From the Berri-UQAM metro station, head east on Rue Sainte-Catherine.*

In 1979, **Place Dupuis** *(facing Parc Émilie-Gamelin; Berri-UQAM metro)* replaced the Dupuis Frères department store, the French-Canadian counterpart of stores like Eaton and Ogilvy's in downtown Montréal. The section of Rue Sainte-Catherine around Rue Saint-Hubert was, moreover, considered the commercial hub of French-Canadian Montrealers up until the mid-20th century.

A little farther east, visitors will find the former **Pilon Clothing Store** *(915 Rue Ste-Catherine Est)*. Its protorationalist, stone-frame structure dates back to 1878, making it the oldest commercial building in the neighbourhood. The lovely Art-Deco facade at number 916 once belonged to the **Pharmacie Montréal** (1934), the first institution of its type in Québec to make home deliveries and stay open both day and night.

Those interested in the history of industry and labour and how the industrial revolution transformed this district won't want to miss the **Écomusée du Fier Monde** ★ *($6; Wed 11am to 8pm, Thu-Fri 9:30am to 4pm, Sat and Sun 10:30am to 5pm; 2050 Rue Amherst,* ☎*514-528-8444, www.ecomusee. qc.ca; Berri-UQAM or Sherbrooke metro)*. The museum is located north of Rue Ontario in an old bathhouse known as the Bain Généreux, built in 1927 and mod-

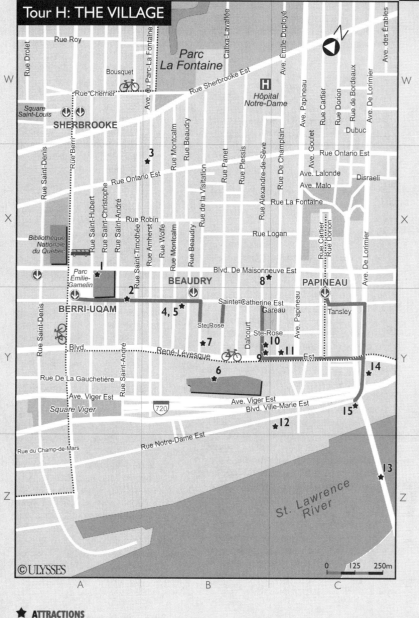

Tour H: THE VILLAGE

Rue Roy

Rue Drolet

Bousquet

Rue Cherrier

Square
Saint-Louis

SHERBROOKE

Parc
La Fontaine

Calixa-Lavallée

Ave. Émile-Duployé

Rue Sherbrooke Est

Hôpital
Notre-Dame

Ave. Papineau

Rue Cartier

Rue Dorion

Rue de Bordeaux

Ave. De Lorimier

Ave. des Érables

Dubuc

Rue du Parc-La Fontaine

Rue Saint-Denis

Rue Berri

Ave. du Parc-La Fontaine

Rue Ontario Est

★ 3

Rue Montcalm

Rue Beaudry

Rue Panet

Rue Plessis

Rue Alexandre-de-Sève

Rue De Champlain

Ave. Goulet

Rue Ontario Est

Ave. Lalonde

Ave. Malo

Disraeli

Bibliothèque
Nationale
du Québec

Rue Saint-Hubert

Rue Saint-Christophe

Rue Saint-André

Rue Robin

Rue Saint-Timothée

Rue Amherst

Rue Wolfe

Rue Montcalm

Rue Beaudry

Rue de la Visitation

Rue La Fontaine

Rue Logan

Rue Cartier
Rue Dorion

Ave. De Lorimier

Parc
Émilie-
Gamelin

★ 1

Blvd. De Maisonneuve Est

BEAUDRY

8 ★

PAPINEAU

BERRI-UQAM

★ 2

4, 5 ★

Sainte-Catherine Est

Gareau

Ave. Papineau

Tansley

Ste-Rose

Dalcourt

Ste-Rose

10 ★

★ 11

Rue Saint-Denis

★ 7

Blvd.
René-Lévesque

9 ★

Est

★ 14

Rue De La Gauchetière

Rue Saint-André

6 ★

Ave. Viger Est

15 ★

Square Viger

720

Ave. Viger Est

Blvd. Ville-Marie Est

★ 12

Rue du Champ-de-Mars

Rue Notre-Dame Est

★ 13

St. Lawrence
River

©ULYSSES

0   125   250m

★ ATTRACTIONS

1.	AX	Place Dupuis
2.	AY	Pilon Clothing Store / Pharmacie Montréal (former)
3.	BX	Écomusée du Fier Monde
4.	BY	Ouimetoscope
5.	BY	Théâtre National (former)
6.	BY	Maison de Radio-Canada
7.	BY	Église Saint-Pierre-Apôtre
8.	BX	TVA

9.	BY	École Sainte-Brigide (former)
10.	BY	Église Sainte-Brigide
11.	CY	Cathedral of St. Peter and St. Paul
12.	CY	Molson Brewery
13.	CZ	Pont Jacques-Cartier
14.	CY	Prison du Pied-du-Courant / Monument to the Patriotes / Centre d'Exposition de la Prison-des-Patriotes
15.	CY	Craig Pumping Station

elled after the Butte-aux-Cailles pool in Paris. The social and economic history of this south-central neighbourhood is presented in a wonderfully rehabilitated interior.

Heads Up!

Are you an antique buff? Stroll down **Rue Amherst**, where you'll find most of the Village's antique shops and second-hand stores.

••• *Montréal's Gay Village starts east of Rue Amherst.*

Originally clustered in the "West" along Rue Stanley and Rue Drummond, gay bars were considered too conspicuous by some local real-estate developers and town councillors. The continual badgering and periodic attempts to "clean house" led bar owners, then renters in the downtown area, to purchase inexpensive buildings in the Centre-Sud in hopes of running their businesses as they pleased. Thus was born the **Gay Village** *(Rue Ste-Catherine Est, between Rue Amherst and Rue Papineau; Berri-UQAM, Beaudry or Papineau metro)*, a concentration of establishments catering to a homosexual clientele (saunas, bars, restaurants, clothing stores and hotels). Far from being hidden or mysterious, many of these establishments open out onto the street with terraces and gardens during the warm summer months.

Heads Up!

Feel like stepping out? Don't miss the shows at **Le Cabaret Mado** (see p 268). The mythical stage of this gay Montréal nightlife institution provides a lively 1920s-Berlin cabaret atmosphere.

Filmmaker, distributor and theatre-owner Léo-Ernest Ouimet (1877-1973) pioneered Montréal's film industry. In 1906, he built the **Ouimetoscope** *(1206 Rue Ste-Catherine Est; Beaudry metro)*, the first theatre designed for and devoted exclu-

sively to film in all of Canada. Moved, modernized then recently closed, the Ouimetoscope is nothing but a memory now. Immediately east lies the former **Théâtre National** *(1220 Rue Ste-Catherine Est)*, whose pretty little Renaissance Revival–style theatre, inaugurated in 1900, is still intact. As indicated on a plaque outside the entrance, this theatre, which once specialized in burlesque and vaudeville, was run for many years by the hilarious Rose Ouellette, known as "La Poune." A few other old theatres dot Rue Saint-Catherine on the way to the Jacques-Cartier bridge.

••• 🚶 *Turn right on Rue de la Visitation. You'll notice the Radio-Canada building behind the church's silver bell tower.*

From the end of small Rue Beaudry, you will see an oversized structure set like an island in the middle of a vast parking lot. This is the **Maison de Radio-Canada** *(1400 Boulevard René-Lévesque Est; Beaudry metro)*, built between 1970 and 1973 by Scandinavian architect Tore Bjornstad. The building accommodates the province's French-language and local English-language programming of the CBC, or Canadian Broadcasting Corporation (Société Radio-Canada in French), the national radio and television network. When it was built, the traditional urban fabric of the neighbourhood was completely erased. Nearly 5,000 people (678 families) had to be relocated. Even 20 years before Radio-Canada was built, the width of Boulevard René-Lévesque (formerly Dorchester Street) had been tripled, separating the south part of the neighbourhood from the north. Radio-Canada offers guided tours of its studios, newsroom and museum every Wednesday *($8.50; French and English tours are available; reservations required:* ☎*514-597-7787)*.

The **Église Saint-Pierre-Apôtre** ★ ★ *(1201 Rue de la Visitation; Beaudry metro)* is part of the monastery of the Oblate priests, who settled in Montréal in 1848 thanks to the assistance of Monseigneur Ignace Bourget. The building, completed in 1853, is a major work of Québec Gothic Revival architecture, as well as prolific architect Victor Bourgeau's first project in this style.

Notable elements include the flying buttresses, exterior supports for the walls of the nave, rarely used in Montréal, and the spire, which measures 70m at its tallest point, an exceptional height for the time. The finely decorated interior reveals a number of other uncommon elements, such as the limestone pillars separating the nave from the side aisles, here in a land where church structures were usually made entirely of wood. Some of the stained-glass windows from the Maison Champigneule in Bar-le-Duc, France, deserve careful examination, including the 9m-tall St. Peter in the Choir (1854).

››› ✕ *Walk up Rue de la Visitation, then turn right on little Rue Sainte-Rose.*

On the way, you will pass alongside the neoclassical presbytery of Saint-Pierre-Apôtre and the former buildings of the Maîtrise Saint-Pierre, a choir school and priests' residence, which has been converted into a community centre. Rue Sainte-Rose is a picturesque street, lined to the north with a series of working-class homes with mansard roofs. It has preserved part of its old-fashioned appearance. Since 1975, a number of neighbourhood houses have been restored by executives and artists working at nearby Radio-Canada.

››› ✕ *Turn left on Rue Panet, then right on Rue Sainte-Catherine.*

Cross small **Rue Dalcourt**, a secondary street between two main arteries patterned after London's mews. It is lined with cramped housing, intended in the past for the poorest workers. In 1982, Rue Dalcourt was redesigned by the City of Montréal as part of its Place au Soleil (Place in the Sun) program.

The offices of the **TVA** *(1425 Rue Alexandre-de-Sève, corner Boulevard De Maisonneuve Est; Papineau metro)* television network occupy an entire block. Founded in 1961 by Alexandre de Sève under the name Télé-Métropole, this private television network out-rated Radio Canada

among working-class viewers for many years. Some of the network's studios are located inside the former Théâtre Arcade and the Pharmacie Gauvin (1911), a handsome four-storey building made of glazed, white terra cotta. TVA, along with Radio-Canada and Télé-Québec, forms a veritable Cité des Ondes ("on-air city") in eastern Montréal.

››› ✕ *Turn right on Rue Alexandre-de-Sève.*

The red-brick building on the left, preceded by a neighbourhood park, is the former **École Sainte-Brigide** *(1125 Rue Alexandre-de-Sève; Papineau metro)*, opened by the Frères des Écoles Chrétiennes in 1895. It was converted into a retirement home in 1989.

The high concentration of Catholic workers in the Faubourg à M'lasse at the end of the 19th century, combined with the competition still being waged between the bishopric and the Sulpicians at that time, justified the 1878 construction of a second church only a few hundred metres from the Église Saint-Pierre-Apôtre. **Église Sainte-Brigide** ★ *(1153 Rue Alexandre-de-Sève; Papineau metro)* was designed by architect Louis-Gustave Martin (Poitras et Martin) in the Romanesque Revival style that was then advocated by the Sulpicians. The interior of the church, which belongs to a deteriorating parish, has undergone few changes since its construction and contains lovely lamps dating back to the end of the 19th century, as well as a jumble of dingy plaster statues serving as eloquent witnesses of better days.

››› ✕ *Walk east on Boulevard René-Lévesque.*

The **Cathedral of St. Peter and St. Paul** ★ *(1151 Rue De Champlain; Papineau metro)* is Montréal's Russian Orthodox Cathedral. The building, a former Episcopal church, was erected in 1853. Those who attend Sunday Mass can see a lovely collection of icons and treasures from Russia, as well as listen to the spellbinding chants of the choir.

The **Molson Brewery** *(1650 Rue Notre-Dame Est)* is visible from Boulevard René-Lé-

Exploring – The Village

vesque. Those who want a closer look should be very careful crossing the busy streets of the area. The brewery's entrance hall contains enlargements of photographs from the company archives, as well as a souvenir shop. Across the street, a monument commemorates the *Accommodation*, the first steamship launched on the St. Lawrence by the Molson family (1815).

The Molson Brewery was opened back in 1786 in the Faubourg Québec by an Englishman named John Molson (1763-1836). It would later become one of the most successful businesses in Canada. This brewery, rebuilt and expanded many times, still stands alongside the port. The Molsons, for their part, remain one of the pillars of Montréal's upper class. Involved in banking (see p 57), construction, rail transport and shipping, the family has never deviated from its first rule of conduct, which is to innovate constantly.

At the beginning of the 19th century, a bourgeois neighbourhood with an Anglican church and market square (Avenue Papineau) surrounded the brewery. The last signs of those years disappeared when Autoroute Ville-Marie was built in 1974.

••• 🏃 *Continue eastward on Boulevard René-Lévesque. Go under the Jacques-Cartier bridge, then turn right onto Avenue De Lorimier. Cross Avenue De Lorimier at the corner of Avenue Viger to reach the head office of the Québec liquor commission, the Société des Alcools du Québec, located inside Montréal's former penitentiary, better known by its former name, Pied-du-Courant.*

The **Pont Jacques-Cartier** ★ ★ bridge was inaugurated in 1930. Up until then, the Pont Victoria, completed in 1860, was the only means of reaching the South Shore, aside from the ferry. The Jacques-Cartier bridge also made it possible to link Île Sainte-Hélène directly to the central neighbourhoods of Montréal. It was a true nuisance to build because city councillors couldn't agree on a plan that would avoid demolishing all sorts of buildings. It was finally decided that

the bridge should be curved on its way into Montréal, earning it the nickname "pont croche" (the crooked bridge). Today, it is possible to cross the Jacques-Cartier bridge on foot (there is a wide pedestrian walk and central belvedere), by bicycle (bike path shared with pedestrians) and of course by car, which is what thousands of motorists do every day to get to work.

Prison du Pied-du-Courant ★ ★ *(2125 Place des Patriotes; Papineau metro)* is thus named (literally "Foot-of-the-Current") because it is located in front of the river, at the foot of the Sainte-Marie current, which used to create resistance for ships entering the port. Built between 1830 and 1836 by George Blaiklock, it is a long, neoclassical cut-stone building with a gate made of the same material. It is the oldest public building still standing in Montréal.

In 1894, a house for the prison warden was added at the corner of Avenue de Lorimier. In 1912, the last prisoners left Pied-du-Courant, which became the head office of the Commission des Liqueurs, the liquor commission, in 1922. Over the years, annexes and warehouses were added to the old forgotten prison. Between 1986 and 1990, however, the Québec government proceeded to demolish the additions and restore the prison, rekindling old memories of tragic events that took place shortly after it was opened.

It was within these walls that 12 of the Patriotes who participated in the armed rebellion of 1837-38, an attempt to emancipate Québec, were executed. One of them was the Chevalier de Lorimier, after whom the neighbouring street was named. Five hundred others were imprisoned here before they were deported to the penal colonies of Australia and Tasmania in the South Pacific. A handsome **Monument to the Patriotes** ★ by Alfred Laliberté stands on the grounds of the former prison. The Gothic Revival warden's residence now houses the reception rooms of the Société des Alcools du Québec (SAQ).

Located in the basement of the Édifice du Pied-du-Courant is the new **Centre d'Exposition de la Prison-des-Patriotes** *(free admission; Wed-Fri noon to 5pm, Sat-Sun 9:30am to 5pm; 903 Avenue De Lorimier,* ☎*450-787-9980; Papineau metro)*, an SAQ project that is run by the Maison Nationale des Patriotes and the Musée de Saint-Eustache et de ses Patriotes. Here, you can enjoy a theme exhibit on the 1837 and 1838 rebellion, which features seven sections: Introduction, Economy, Identity, Politics, Before Arms, To Arms! and Conclusion.

On your way out of the exhibition centre you'll notice the **Craig Pumping Station** *(corner Rue Notre-Dame Est and Avenue De Lorimier,* ☎*514-393-3937, www.champlibre. com)*, under the Jacques-Cartier bridge. This former pumping station was used to regulate the St. Lawrence's waters and was closed at the end of the 1950s. Over the last few years, Champ Libre, a non-profit organization that fights for the preservation of Montréal's architectural heritage, has been striving to give new life to this 19th-century structure by presenting various shows and exhibits in the station.

⋯ 🚶 Ⓜ *To return to Rue Sainte-Catherine, head north on Avenue De Lorimier, then turn left toward the Papineau metro station.*

Tour I: Plateau Mont-Royal
★★

🕐 *three hours*

If there is one neighbourhood that best defines Montréal, it is definitely the Plateau Mont-Royal. Thrown into the spotlight by writer Michel Tremblay, one of its illustrious sons, the "Plateau" is a neighbourhood of penniless intellectuals, young professionals and old French-speaking working-class families. Its long streets are lined with duplexes and triplexes adorned with amusingly contorted exterior staircases leading up

to the long, narrow apartments that are so typical of Montréal. Flower-decked balconies made of wood or wrought iron provide box-seats for the spectacle on the street below.

The Plateau is bounded by the mountain to the west, the Canadian Pacific railway tracks to the north and east, and Rue Sherbrooke to the south. It is traversed by a few major streets lined with cafés and theatres, such as Rue Saint-Denis and Avenue Papineau, but is a tranquil area on the whole. A stroll through this area is a must for visitors who want to grasp the spirit of Montréal.

⋯ 🚶 Ⓜ *This tour starts at the exit of the Mont-Royal metro station. Turn right on Avenue du Mont-Royal.*

The **Sanctuaire du Saint-Sacrement** ★ *(500 Avenue du Mont-Royal Est; Mont-Royal metro)* and its church, Église Notre-Dame-du-Très-Saint-Sacrement, were built at the end of the 19th century for the community of priests of the same name. The somewhat austere facade of the church conceals an extremely colourful interior with an Italian-style decor designed by Jean-Baptiste Resther. This sanctuary, dedicated to the "Eternal Exhibition and Adoration of the Eucharist," is open for prayer and contemplation every day of the week. Baroque music concerts are also occasionally presented here.

Continue heading east on **Avenue du Mont-Royal**, blending in with the neighbourhood's widely varied inhabitants on their way in and out of an assortment of businesses, ranging from shops selling knick-knacks for a dollar to used records and books.

Heads Up!

Curious about the famous Montréal bagel? Make sure you stop by **St. Viateur Bagel & Café** (see p 242). You'll find authentic hot-from-the-wood-oven bagels in this veritable Montréal institution.

⋯ 🚶 *Turn right on Rue Fabre.*

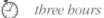

Exploring – Plateau Mont-Royal

Rue Fabre features some good examples of Montréal-style housing. Built between 1900 and 1925, the houses contain between two and five apartments, all with private outdoor entrances. Decorative details vary from one building to the next. Visitors will see Art-Nouveau stained glass, parapets, cornices made of brick or sheet metal, balconies with Tuscan columns and ornamental ironwork shaped in ringlets and cables.

··· 🅇 *Turn left on Rue Rachel.*

At the end of Rue Fabre, visitors will find **Parc La Fontaine** ★ *(Sherbrooke metro)*, the Plateau's main green space, laid out in 1908 on the site of an old military shooting range. Monuments to Sir Louis-Hippolyte La Fontaine, Félix Leclerc and Dollard des Ormeaux have been erected here. The park covers an area of 36ha and is embellished with two artificial lakes and shaded paths for pedestrians and cyclists. There are tennis courts and bowling greens for summer-sports enthusiasts, and in the winter, the frozen lakes form a large rink that is illuminated at night. The Théâtre de Verdure outdoor theatre is also located here. Every weekend, the park is crowded with people from the neighbourhood who come here to make the most of beautiful sunny days.

Heads Up!

For a cup of savoury Italian espresso or cappuccino, we suggest you head to **Café Bicicletta** (see p 231). This charming bistro-café faces Parc La Fontaine and is popular with local cyclists.

··· 🅇 *To cross the park, head down Avenue Calixa-Lavallée or stroll down one of the trails that border the park's ponds and lead*

to the corner of Rue Cherrier and Avenue du Parc-La-Fontaine.

The monument to Sir Louis-Hippolyte La Fontaine (1807-1864), after whom the park was named, is located across the street. Regarded as the father of responsible government in Canada, La Fontaine was also one of the main defenders of the French language in the country's institutions. You'll pass **École Le Plateau** (1930) at 3700 Avenue Calixa-Lavallée. This Art-Deco building was designed by architects Perrault and Gadbois. An obelisk dedicated to Général de Gaulle, by French artist Olivier Debré, towers over the long **Place Charles-de-Gaulle** *(at the corner of Avenue Émile-Duployé; Sherbrooke metro)*, located alongside Rue Sherbrooke. The monument is made of blue granite and stands 17m high. It was given to the City of Montréal by the City of Paris in 1992, on the occasion of Montréal's 350th anniversary. **Hôpital Notre-Dame**, one of the city's major hospitals, stands across the street. From here, you'll also notice the stately building that housed the former **Bibliothèque Centrale de Montréal** ★ *(1210 Rue Sherbrooke Est)*. The library's collection has since been moved to the new **Bibliothèque Nationale du Québec** ★ ★ (see p 108), which opened in April of 2005 in the Quartier Latin neighbourhood.

··· 🅇 *Take Rue Cherrier, which branches off from Rue Sherbrooke across from the monument.*

Rue Cherrier, along with Square Saint-Louis at its west end, once formed the nucleus of the French-Canadian bourgeois neighbourhood. At number 840, visitors will find the **Agora de la Danse**, where the studios of various dance companies are located. The red-brick building, completed in 1919, originally served as the Palestre Nationale, a sports centre for neighbourhood youth and the scene

Exploring – Plateau Mont-Royal

★ **ATTRACTIONS**

1.	AW	Sanctuaire du Saint-Sacrement
2.	CY	Parc La Fontaine
3.	CY	École Le Plateau
4.	CZ	Place Charles-de-Gaulle
5.	CZ	Hôpital Notre-Dame
6.	BZ	Bibliothèque Centrale de Montréal (former)
7.	BZ	Agora de la Danse
8.	AZ	Église Saint-Louis-de-France
9.	AZ	Institut des Sourdes-Muettes (former)
10.	AX	Église Saint-Jean-Baptiste
11.	AX	Collège Rachel
12.	AX	Hospice Auclair (former)

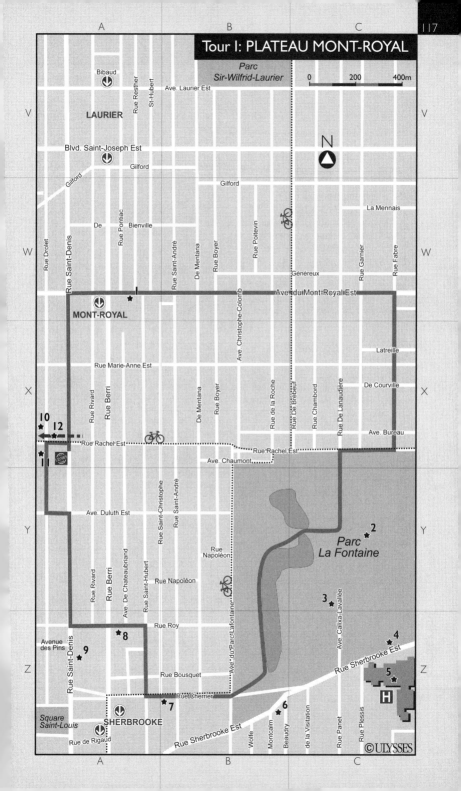

of many tumultuous public gatherings during the 1930s.

⋯ 🚶 *Turn right on Rue Saint-Hubert, lined with fine examples of vernacular architecture. Turn left on Rue Roy.*

Église Saint-Louis-de-France was built in 1936 as a replacement for the original church, destroyed by fire in 1933. From here you'll notice the **Parc du Mont-Royal ★ ★ ★** (see p 119), which stands over the city, in the background.

At the corner of Rue Saint-Denis stands the former **Institut des Sourdes-Muettes** *(3725 Rue St-Denis, at the corner of Avenue des Pins; Sherbrooke metro)*, a large, grey-stone building made up of numerous wings and erected in stages between 1881 and 1900. Built in the Second Empire style, it covers an entire block and is typical of institutional architecture of that period in Québec. It once took in the region's deaf and mute girls and women. The strange chapel with cast-iron columns, as well as the sacristy, with its tall wardrobes and surprising spiral staircase, are now where special masses for deaf people are celebrated.

⋯ 🚶 *Head north on Rue Saint-Denis.*

Between Boulevard De Maisonneuve, to the south, and Boulevard Saint-Joseph, to the north, **Rue Saint-Denis** is lined with numerous outdoor cafés and beautiful shops, established inside Second Empire–style residences built during the second half of the 19th century. Visitors will also find many bookstores, tea rooms and restaurants that have become veritable Montréal institutions over the years.

Heads Up!

→ Why not kick your day off with a tasty brunch? Sunny **Côté Soleil**'s (see p 234) generous brunch is perfect for a family breakfast.

⋯ 🚶 *Turn left on Avenue Duluth and then right on Rue Drolet.*

Rue Drolet offers a good example of the working-class dwellings that were built in the Plateau area during the 1870s and 1880s before the advent of the typical two- and three-storey houses with exterior staircases that we've already seen on Rue Fabre. The colourful houses may surprise you, with their light green, salmon pink, dark blue or violet ivy-covered brick exteriors. Continue north to the corner of Rachel and Drolet streets to get to Église Saint-Jean-Baptiste.

Église Saint-Jean-Baptiste ★ ★ *(309 Rue Rachel; Mont-Royal metro)*, dedicated to the patron saint of French Canadians, is a gigantic symbol of the solid faith of the Catholic working-class inhabitants of the Plateau Mont-Royal at the turn of the 20th century who, despite their poverty and large families, managed to amass considerable amounts of money for the construction of sumptuous churches. The exterior was built in 1874 by architect Émile Vanier. The interior was redone after a fire and is now a veritable Baroque Revival masterpiece designed by Casimir Saint-Jean that should not be missed. The pink-marble and gilded wood baldaquin in the chancel (1915) shelters the altar, which is made of white Italian marble and faces the large Casavant organs—among the most powerful in the city—in the jube. Concerts are frequently given at this church, which can seat up to 3,000 people.

The old **Collège Rachel**, built in 1876 in the Second Empire style, stands across the street from the church. Finally, west of Avenue Henri-Julien, visitors will find the former **Hospice Auclair** (1894), with its semi-circular entrance on Rue Rachel.

⋯ 🚶 Ⓜ *Before heading north on Rue Saint-Denis to get to Avenue du Mont-Royal and the metro station, why not stop by the* **Librairie Ulysse** *travel bookstore (4176 Rue St-Denis)?*

Tour J: Mont Royal
★★

 one day

Montréal's central neighbourhoods were built around Mount Royal, an important landmark in the cityscape. Known simply as "the mountain" by Montrealers, this squat mass, measuring 233m at its highest point, is composed of intrusive rock. It is in fact one of the seven hills of the St. Lawrence plain in the Montérégie region. A "green lung" rising up at the far end of downtown streets, it exerts a positive influence on Montrealers who, as a result, never really lose touch with nature.

The mountain actually has three summits; the first is occupied by Parc du Mont-Royal, the second by the Université de Montréal, and the third by Westmount, a wealthy neighbourhood with lovely English-style homes which, up until recently, was an independent city. In addition to these areas, there are Catholic, Protestant and Jewish cemeteries, which, considered as a whole, form the largest necropolis in North America.

⋯ 🚶 🚌 Ⓜ *To reach the starting point of the tour, take bus no. 11 from the Mont-Royal metro station, located on the Plateau Mont-Royal, and get off at the Belvédère Camillien-Houde.*

⋯ 🚗 *If you're driving, head west on Avenue du Mont-Royal and turn onto Voie Camillien-Houde to get to the belvedere (the parking lot is on your left).*

From the **Belvédère Camillien-Houde ★★** *(Voie Camillien-Houde)*, a lovely scenic lookout, visitors can look out over the entire eastern portion of Montréal. The Plateau Mont-Royal lies in the foreground, a uniform mass of duplexes and triplexes, dominated in a few places by the oxidized copper bell towers of parish churches, while the Rosemont and Maisonneuve districts lie in the background as the Olympic Stadium towers over them.

⋯ 🚶 *Climb the staircase at the south end of the parking lot and follow Chemin Olmsted on the left, which leads to the chalet and main lookout. You will pass the mountain's cross on the way.*

The **Mount Royal Cross** stands on the side of Chemin Oldsted and commemorates the moment when the city's founder, Paul Chomedey, Sieur de Maisonneuve, scaled the mountain in January of 1643 to place a wooden cross in thanks to the Virgin Mary for sparing the fort of Ville-Marie from a devastating flood.

Pressured by the residents of the Golden Square Mile, who saw their favourite playground being deforested by various firewood companies, the City of Montréal created **Parc du Mont-Royal ★★★** *(www.lemontroyal.qc.ca)* in 1870. Frederick Law Olmsted (1822-1903), the celebrated designer of New York's Central Park, was commissioned to design the park. He decided to preserve the site's nat-

The *Tam-Tams*

The slope of Mount Royal facing Avenue du Parc has been the site of a colourful impromptu party, known simply as the *Tam-Tams*, every Sunday afternoon in summer for several years now. Weather permitting, people of all stripes and ages gather here in a bohemian atmosphere.

Dozens of percussionists settle at the foot of the huge monument to Sir George-Étienne Cartier—one of the fathers of Confederation—and improvise lively world-beat rhythms throughout the afternoon. Hordes of dancers groove to the frenzied beat of African congas and other drums, while a merry crowd of onlookers enjoys a picnic or sunbathes on the grass.

Exploring - Mont Royal

ural character, limiting himself to a few lookout points linked by winding paths. Inaugurated in 1876, the park, which covers 101ha on the southern part of the mountain, is cherished by Montrealers as a place to enjoy fresh air. Since 2003, Mount Royal and its three summits are protected by the Government of Québec as a historic and natural district.

The **Chalet du Mont Royal** ★★★ *(Mon-Sat 10:30am to 8pm; Parc du Mont-Royal, ☎514-872-3911)*, located in the centre of the park, was designed by Aristide Beaugrand-Champagne in 1932 as a replacement for the original structure, which was about to collapse. During the 1930s and 1940s, big bands gave moonlit concerts on the steps of the building. The interior is decorated with 17 remounted paintings depicting scenes from Canadian history. They were commissioned from some of Québec's great painters, such as Marc-Aurèle Fortin and Paul-Émile Borduas. The chalet underwent major renovations in 2003, and its paintings were restored.

Nevertheless, people go to the chalet mainly to stroll along the lookout and take in the exceptional **view** ★★★ of downtown from the **Belvédère Kondiaronk** (named after the Huron-Wendat chief who negotiated the Great Peace treaty in 1701). The view is at its best in the late afternoon and evening, when the skyscrapers light up the darkening sky.

··· ⚹ *Take the gravel road that leads to the parking lot of the chalet and Voie Camillien-Houde. One of the entrances to the Mount Royal Protestant Cemetery lies on the right.*

The **Mount Royal Protestant Cemetery** ★★ *(Voie Camillien Houde)* ranks among the most beautiful spots in the city. Designed as an Eden for the living visiting the deceased, it is laid out like a landscape garden in an isolated valley, giving visitors the impression that they are a thousand miles from the city, though they are in fact right in the centre of it. The wide variety of hardwood and fruit trees attract species of birds found nowhere else in Québec. Founded by the Anglican, Presbyterian, Unitarian, Meth-

odist and Baptist churches, the cemetery opened in 1852. Some of its monuments are true works of art, executed by celebrated artists. The families and eminent personalities buried here include the Molson brewers, who have the most impressive and imposing mausoleum, shipowner Sir Hugh Allan, and numerous other figures from the footnotes and headlines of history, such as Anna Leonowens, governess of the King of Siam in the 19th century and the inspiration for the play *The King and I*.

On the left, on the way to Lac aux Castors (Beaver Lake), visitors will see the last of the mountain's former farmhouses. **Maison Smith** *(1620 Chemin Remembrance, ☎514-843-8240, www.lemontroyal.qc.ca)* is the headquarters of Les Amis de la Montagne, an organization that offers all kinds of exhibits and activities in collaboration with the Centre de la Montagne. Maison Smith also features a permanent exhibit on the flora, fauna, geology and history of Mount Royal.

The small **Lac aux Castors / Beaver Lake** *(alongside Chemin Remembrance)* was created in 1958 in what used to be a swamp. In winter, it becomes a lovely skating rink. This part of the park also has grassy areas and a sculpture garden. It is laid out in a more conventional manner than the rest, violating Olmsted's purist directives.

Heads Up!

Feel like going for a skate? **Lac aux Castors**, in the heart of Parc du Mont-Royal, is the perfect place to practice your figure-eights.

··· ⚹ *Follow the trail that leads to Chemin Remembrance, at the entrance to Notre-Dame-des-Neiges cemetery.*

The **Cimetière Notre-Dame-des-Neiges** ★★ *(Chemin Remembrance, www.cimetierenddn. org; bus no. 11)*, Montréal's largest cemetery, is a veritable city of the dead, as more than 800,000 people have been buried here since it opened in 1855. It replaced the cemetery in Square Do-

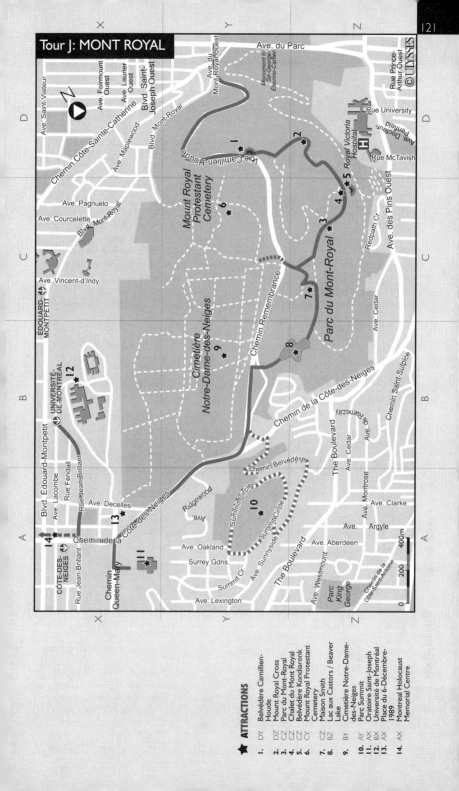

Tour J: MONT ROYAL

121

©ULYSSES

★ ATTRACTIONS

1. DY Belvédère Camillien-
          Houde
2. DZ Mount Royal Cross
3. CZ Parc du Mont-Royal
4. CZ Chalet du Mont Royal
5. CZ Belvédère Kondiaronk
6. CY Mount Royal Protestant
          Cemetery
7. CZ Maison Smith
8. BZ Lac aux Castors / Beaver
          Lake
9. BY Cimetière Notre-Dame-
          des-Neiges
10. AY Parc Summit
11. AX Oratoire Saint-Joseph
12. BX Université de Montréal
13. AX Place du 6-Décembre-
          1989
14. AX Montreal Holocaust
          Memorial Centre

Cimetière Notre-Dame-des-Neiges

The Notre-Dame-des-Neiges cemetery opened in 1855 and covers land that was once the north shore of a lost island in the former Champlain Sea (the site of present-day Mount Royal) following the thaw of the Laurentide ice sheet (a 3km-thick continental glacier) 10,000 years ago. Non-fossilized seashells were discovered in the sandy sediment of this ancient post-glacial beach when the site was temporarily used as a dump site.

On May 29, 1855, Mrs. Jane Gilroy, wife of Thomas McCready, then a Montréal municipal councilor, was the first person to be buried in the new cemetery. Standing on lot F56, the epitaph on her granite monument is, surprisingly, still legible, unlike other historic gravestones that often eroded because of the poor quality of the material they were made of—mostly limestone, which is soluble. Since the burial of Mrs. Gilroy, almost one million people have been laid to rest here, making Cimetière Notre-Dame-des-Neiges the second-largest cemetery in North America, after Arlington Cemetery in Washington. A walk through the 55km of trails that criss-cross the site proves that this cemetery is a unique treasure, as much for its architectural, cultural and historical facets as for its natural setting.

Not only do people come to Cimetière Notre-Dame-des-Neiges for its tranquility, greenery and birds, but also to admire the often magnificently carved gravestones. To better plan your walk, pick up a detailed map of the cemetery at the reception area, across from Chapelle de la Résurrection. Sumptuously detailed monuments attest to a dominant upper class, and many sections of the cemetery are recommended for the sheer beauty of these memorials.

One area you should not miss is section T, with its majestic monuments and dozens of crypts that seem right out of a classic horror film. The Veterans section, with hundreds of small, grey tombstones lined up in perfect rows, is also worth seeing. As well, the ethnic sections are often worth a detour for a glimpse into other funerary traditions; for example, the Chinese section (U598-604), where every monument bears an image of the deceased. The orthodox section is full of gravestones decorated with multicoloured beds of flowers, and most of them have epitaphs in gold letters.

In addition to rich families proudly displaying their wealth in sculpted granite, the working classes are also represented in section FT (*fosse temporaire*, or temporary grave), where, as the name suggests, families can rent lots for a period of 10 years. Some of these families could not afford expensive monuments, which explains the presence of several little wooden crosses scattered about this section.

A visit to the Cimetière Notre-Dame-des-Neiges would not be complete without a look at the many commemorative monuments scattered about the cemetery. Among the most eye-catching is the one belonging to the Société Saint-Jean-Baptiste (lot C24), which stands on the grave of its founder, Ludger Duvernay. There is also a magnificent black granite monument for the Union des Artistes (O203), honouring actors who left their mark on Québec theatre.

Finally, the most impressive of all is a tribute to the many Patriots of 1837-38 (lot B261) who fell in battle against the English and were hanged or exiled.

Of the hundreds of thousands of people buried here, a significant number are historic figures, including politicians Robert Bourassa (secteur E), former Prime Minister of Québec, and Georges-Étienne Cartier (lot 01), who was one of the Founding Fathers of Canada.

Many artists have also been laid to rest here, including Philippe Aubert-de-Gaspé (lot G26), the author of the first French-Canadian novel, famous Québec theatre actors Olivier Guimond and his father Ti-Zoune (lot GA1341), Émile Nelligan (lot N588), one of Québec's most admired poets, and Marie Travers, a popular 1930s singer better known as *La Bolduc* (TROIE1912).

Admiring the many interesting gravestones along the paths is like taking a walk back into the past. Who knows? Perhaps you will come across a familiar name, or read an epitaph that will remind you of something. Even if it has never occurred to you to visit a cemetery, Notre-Dame-des-Neiges is a moving experience that you will not regret.

minion (now Square Dorchester), which was deemed too small. Unlike the Protestant cemetery, it has a conspicuously religious character, clearly identifying it with the Catholic faith. Accordingly, two heavenly angels flanking a crucifix greet visitors at the main entrance on Chemin de la Côte-des-Neiges.

The "two solitudes" (Canadians of French Catholic and Anglo-Saxon Protestant extraction) thus remain separated even in death. The tombstones read like a who's who in the fields of business, arts, politics and science in Québec. An obelisk dedicated to the Patriotes of the rebellion of 1837-38 and numerous monuments executed by renowned sculptors lie scattered alongside the 55km of roads and paths that criss-cross the cemetery. Both the cemetery and the roads leading to it offer a number of views of the Oratoire Saint-Joseph.

▸▸▸ *Upon exiting the cemetery on Chemin Remembrance, take bus no. 11 to get to Oratoire Saint-Joseph.*

On your way to the oratory you'll pass **Parc Summit** *(Summit Circle; Côte-des-Neiges metro)*, a veritable urban forest and bird sanctuary that is Westmount's largest park. Some say its **belvedere** provides

even more spectacular views of Montréal than the famous Kondiaronk lookout, especially at sunset.

Oratoire Saint-Joseph ★★ *(free admission; every day 7am to 8:30pm, Mass every day, Christmas manger from Nov to Mar; 3800 Chemin Queen Mary, ☎514-733-8211, www. saint-joseph.org; Côte-des-Neiges metro).* The enormous oratory, topped with a copper dome, is the second-largest dome in the world after that of St. Peter's in Rome and stands on a hillside, accentuating its mystical aura. From the gate at the entrance, there are over 300 steps to climb to reach the oratory. The oratory was built between 1924 and 1967, thanks to the efforts of the blessed Frère André, porter of Collège Notre-Dame (across the street), to whom many miracles are attributed. A veritable religious complex, the oratory is dedicated to both Saint Joseph and its humble creator. It includes the lower and upper basilicas, the crypt of Frère André and a museum. Visitors will also find the porter's first chapel, built in 1904, a cafeteria, a hostelry and a store selling devotional articles.

The oratory is one of the most important centres of worship and pilgrimage in North America. Each year, it attracts some 2,000,000 visitors. The building's

Exploring – Mont Royal

neoclassical exterior was designed by Dalbé Viau and Alphonse Venne, while the essentially modern interior is the work of Lucien Parent and French Benedictine monk Dom Paul Bellot, the author from Saint-Benoît-du-Lac in the Eastern Townships. It is well worth visiting the upper basilica to see the stained-glass windows by Marius Plamondon, the altar and crucifix by Henri Charlier, and the astonishing gilded chapel at the back. The oratory has an imposing Beckerath-style organ, which can be heard on Wednesday evenings in summer. Outside, visitors can also see the chimes, made by Paccard et Frères and originally intended for the Eiffel Tower, as well as the beautiful Chemin de Croix (Way of the Cross) by Louis Parent and Ercolo Barbieri, in the gardens on the side of the mountain. Measuring 263m, the oratory's observatory, which commands a sweeping view of the entire city, is the highest point on the island.

St. Joseph's Oratory is currently undergoing major renovations that represent a 45-million-dollar investment. This is mainly to restructure its areas and traffic ways and to build a new reception pavilion. The project will also renovate and install elevators and escalators to facilitate the comings and goings of visitors, as well as improve safety. The reception area is now located at the Pavillon des Pèlerins, facing the shop, while the main office was moved to the entrance that leads to the votive chapel. Since May 2003, this is where pilgrims come to have religious objects blessed.

⋯ ⊼ Ⓜ *The next attraction is slightly removed from the present tour, and you should expect to spend an extra hour visiting it.*

Aiming to preserve its monopoly on French-language university education in Québec, after many attempts, Québec City's Université Laval finally opened a branch of its institution at Château Ramezay in 1876. A few years later, it moved to Rue Saint-Denis, giving birth to the **Quartier Latin** (see p 104). The **Université de Montréal** ★ *(2900 Boulevard Édouard-Montpetit, www.umontreal.ca; Université-de-Montréal metro)* finally became autono-

mous in 1920, enabling its directors to develop grandiose plans. Ernest Cormier (1885-1980) was approached about designing a campus on the north side of Mount Royal. The architect, a graduate of the École des Beaux-Arts in Paris, was one of the first to acquaint North Americans with the Art-Deco style.

The plans for the main building evolved into a refined, symmetrical Art-Deco structure faced with pale-yellow bricks and topped by a central tower, visible from Chemin Remembrance and Cimetière Notre-Dame-des-Neiges. Begun in 1929, construction on the building was interrupted by the stock-market crash, and it wasn't until 1943 that the first students entered the main building on the mountain. Since then, a host of pavilions has been added, making the Université de Montréal the second-largest French-language university in the world, with a student body of over 58,000.

The École Polytechnique of the Université de Montréal, which is also located on Mount Royal, was the scene of a tragedy that marked the city and all of Canada. On December 6, 1989, 13 female students and one female university employee were murdered in cold blood inside the École Polytechnique. To keep the memory of these women alive, and that of all female victims of violence, the **Place du 6-Décembre-1989** *(corner Rue Decelles and Chemin Queen-Mary)* was erected on December 6, 1999, to commemorate the 10th anniversary of the massacre. There, artist Rose-Marie Goulet erected her *Nef pour Quatorze Reines* (Nave for Fourteen Queens), inscribed with the names of the victims of the Polytechnique massacre.

⋯ ⊼ Ⓜ *You can get back on the metro at the Côte-des-Neiges station, near the corner of Avenue Lacombe and Chemin de la Côte-des-Neiges.*

Outside the tour but easily accessible by metro is the **Montreal Holocaust Memorial Centre** *(free admission; Mon, Tue and Thu 10am to 5pm, Wed 10am to 9pm, Fri 10am to 3pm, Sun 10am to 4pm; 5151 Chemin de la Côte-Ste-Catherine, ☎514-345-2605; Côte-*

Ste-Catherine metro and bus no. 129). A history museum, the Montreal Holocaust Memorial Centre displays, among other things, works of arts and photographs, as well as souvenirs and archives relating to the Holocaust. Here, the lives of those who were affected by this tragedy are openly exposed to all.

Tour K: Westmount ★

⏱ *three hours*

This wealthy residential city of over 20,000 inhabitants is enclosed in the territory of the City of Montréal. It has long been regarded as the bastion of the Anglo-Saxon elite in Québec; indeed, after the Golden Square Mile was invaded by the business centre, Westmount assumed its role. Its shady, winding roads on the southwestern side of the mountain are lined with Neo-Tudor and Neo-Georgian residences, most of which were built between 1910 and 1930. Upper Westmount offers some lovely views of the Notre-Dame-de-Grâce and Côte-des-Neiges neighbourhoods, as well as the city below.

⋯ 🚶 ⓜ *This tour kicks off at the Atwater metro station, on the corner of Avenue Wood and Boulevard De Maisonneuve Ouest.*

Architect Ludwig Mies van der Rohe (1886-1969), one of the leading masters of the modernist movement and the head of Bauhaus in Germany, designed **Westmount Square ★★** *(at the corner of Avenue Wood and Boulevard De Maisonneuve Ouest; Atwater metro)* in 1964. The complex is typical of the architect's North-American work, characterized by the use of black metal and tinted glass. It includes an underground shopping centre topped by three towers containing offices and apartments. The public areas were originally covered with veined white travertine, one of Mies' favourite materials, which was later replaced by a layer of granite, more resistant to the harsh climactic effects of freezing and thawing.

On **Avenue Greene** *(Atwater metro)*, a small street with a typically English-Canadian character, visitors will find several of Westmount's most fashionable shops. In addition to service-oriented businesses, there are art galleries, antique shops and bookstores filled with lovely coffee-table books.

Heads Up!

Up for a lovely stroll? Head down the red brick sidewalks of **Avenue Greene**, a charming Westmount commercial artery.

⋯ 🚶 *Turn left on Rue Sherbrooke and walk to the corner of Avenue Kitchener.*

Erected in 1928, Westmount's English Catholic church, the **Church of The Ascension of Our Lord ★** *(corner Avenue Kitchener; Atwater metro)* is evidence of the staying power of the Gothic-Revival style in North-American architecture and the historical accuracy, ever more apparent in the 20th century, of buildings patterned after ancient models. With its rough stone facing, elongated lines and detailed sculptures, it looks like an authentic church from a 14th-century English village.

Westmount is like a piece of Great Britain in North America. Its **City Hall ★** *(4333 Rue Sherbrooke Ouest, www.westmount. org)* was built in the Neo-Tudor style, inspired by the architecture of the age of Henry VIII and Elizabeth I, which was regarded during the 1920s as the national style of England because it originated from the British Isles. The style is characterized in part by horizontal openings with multiple stone transoms, bay windows and flattened arches. The impeccable green of a lawn-bowling club lies at the back, frequented by members wearing their regulation whites.

⋯ 🚶 *Take Chemin de la Côte-Saint-Antoine to King George Park.*

In Québec, the term *côte*, which translates literally as "hill," usually has nothing to

Exploring – Westmount

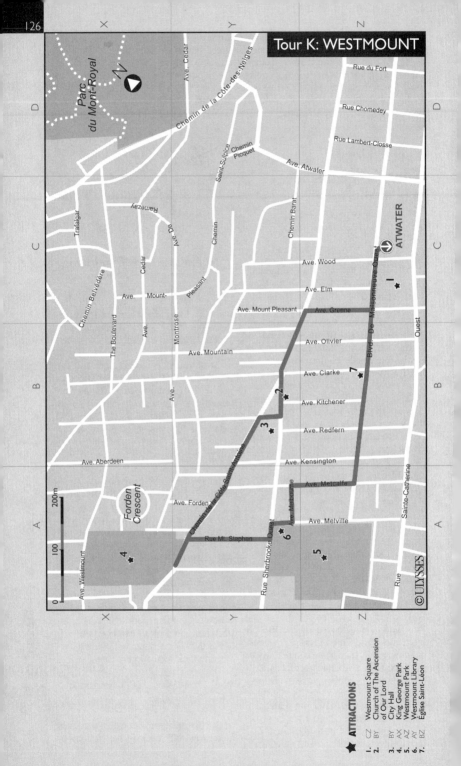

Tour K: WESTMOUNT

Parc
du Mont-Royal

Rue du Fort

Rue Chomedey

Rue Lambert-Closse

Chemin de la Côte-des-Neiges

Saint-Sulpice

Chemin
Picquet

Ave. Atwater

Trafalgar

Ramezay

Chemin

Chemin Barat

ATWATER

Ave. De

Chemin Belvédère

Cedar

Chemin

Ave. Mount-

Pleasant

Ave. Wood

Ave. Elm

Blvd. De Maisonneuve Ouest

The Boulevard

Ave.

Montrose

Ave. Mount Pleasant

Ave. Greene

Ave. Olivier

Ave. Mountain

Ave. Clarke

Ave.

Ave. Kitchener

Ave. Redfern

Ave. Aberdeen

Ave. Kensington

Ave. Metcalfe

Sainte-Catherine

Forden
Crescent

Ave. Forden

Chemin de la Côte-Saint-Antoine

Ave. Melville

Ave. Westmount

Rue Mt. Stephen

Rue Sherbrooke Ouest

Ave. Metcalfe

Ave. Melville

200m

100

0

©ULYSSES

★ ATTRACTIONS

1. CZ Westmount Square
2. BY Church of The Ascension
       of Our Lord
3. BY City Hall
4. AX King George Park
5. AZ Westmount Park
6. AY Westmount Library
7. BZ Église Saint-Léon

do with the slope of the land, but is rather a leftover division of the seigneurial system of New France. The roads linking one farm to the next ran along the tops of the long rectangles of land distributed to colonists. As a result, these plots of land gradually became known as *côtes*, from the French word for "side," *côté*. **Côte Saint-Antoine** is one of the oldest roads on the island of Montréal. Laid out in 1684 by the Sulpicians on a former Aboriginal trail, it is lined with some of Westmount's oldest houses. At the corner of Avenue Forden is a **milestone** dating back to the 17th century, discreetly identified by the pattern of the sidewalk, which radiates out from it. This is all that remains of the system of road signs developed by the Sulpicians for their seigneury on the island of Montréal.

For those who would like to immerse themselves in a Mid-Atlantic atmosphere, a blend of England and America, **King George Park** *(north of Avenue Mount Stephen)* offers the perfect combination: a football field and tennis courts in a country setting. Here, visitors will find the remains of a natural grouping of acacias, an extremely rare species at this latitude due to the harsh climate. The trees' presence is an indication that this area has the mildest climate in Québec, a result of both the southwestern slant of the land and the warm air coming from the nearby Lachine rapids.

⋯ 🜊 *Go down Avenue Mount Stephen to return to Rue Sherbrooke.*

Westmount Park ★ *(4575 Rue Sherbrooke Ouest)* was laid out on swampy land in 1895. Four years later, Québec's first public library, the **Westmount Library**, was erected on the same site. Up until then, religious communities had been the only ones to develop this type of cultural facility, and the province was therefore somewhat behind in this area. The red-brick building is the product of the trends toward eclecticism, picturesqueness and polychromy that characterized the last two decades of the 19th century. Head down the passageway that leads to the Westmount Conservatory, whose greenhouses regularly present floral ex-

hibits, and Victoria Hall, a former cultural centre that was built in 1924 in the same Tudor style as the city hall. Its recently inaugurated art gallery shows works by local Westmount artists.

⋯ 🜊 *From the park, head east on Avenue Melbourne, where there are some fine examples of Queen Anne-style houses. Turn right on Avenue Metcalfe, then left on Boulevard de Maisonneuve.*

At the corner of Avenue Clarke stands the **Église Saint-Léon** ★, the only French-language Catholic parish in Westmount. The sober, elegant Romanesque Revival facade conceals an exceptionally rich interior decor begun in 1928 by artist Guido Nincheri. Nincheri was provided with a large sum of money to decorate the church using no substitutes and no artifices. Accordingly, the floor and the base of the walls are covered with the most beautiful Italian and French marble available, while the upper portion of the nave is made of Savonnières stone and the chancel of the most precious Honduran walnut, hand-carved by Alviero Marchi. The complex stained-glass windows depict various scenes from the life of Jesus Christ, including a few individuals from the time of the church's construction that visitors will be amused to discover among Biblical figures. Finally, the entire Christian pantheon is represented in the chancel and on the vault in vibrantly coloured frescoes, executed in the traditional manner of egg-wash. This technique (used, notably, by Michelangelo) consists of making pigment stick to a wet surface with a coating made of egg, which becomes very hard and resistant when dry.

⋯ 🜊 Ⓜ *Continue on Boulevard De Maisonneuve Ouest to cross the former francophone part of Westmount. Turn right on Avenue Greene. An underground corridor leads from Westmount Square to the Atwater metro station.*

Exploring - Westmount

Tour L: Outremont and Mile-End

★

 three hours

Heads Up!

→ Looking to add to your wardrobe? Many of Montréal's top fashion designers can be found in this area. For a sampling of their creations, head to **L'Assomoir** (see p 271), a hip watering hole that often presents mini fashion shows during happy hour.

On the other side of Mount Royal is the borough of **Outremont**, which, like Westmount (its anglophone counterpart on the south side of the mountain), clings to the side of the mountain and has, over the course of its development, welcomed a fairly well-off population, including many influential Quebecers.

Outremont was once a municipality and has long been a sought-after residential area. In fact, recent research suggests that the mysterious Aboriginal village of Hochelaga, which disappeared between the voyages of Jacques Cartier and De Maisonneuve (16th and 17th centuries), was probably situated in this region. Furthermore, Chemin de la Côte-Sainte-Catherine, the main road around which Outremont developed, supposedly attests to Aboriginal activity in the area and follows a former communication route cleared by Aboriginals to enable them to skirt the mountain.

The Europeans first used the territory known today as Outremont for market gardening during the 17th and 18th centuries. It was later used for horticultural purposes and, being a rural area close to the city, as a vacation spot for middle-class Montrealers in the 19th century. Agricultural goods produced here at the time were popular and served at important tables throughout the American Northeast. Montréal's urban expansion brought an end to Outremont's agricultural vocation in the late 19th century and led to the development of the essentially residential municipality that is found here today.

⋯ ⋏ 🚌 Ⓜ *Our suggested tour of Outremont runs along Chemin de la Côte-Sainte-Catherine, beginning at the corner of Avenue du Mont-Royal (Mont-Royal metro and bus no. 11).*

A means of circling the mountain, **Chemin de la Côte-Sainte-Catherine** curves for a good part of its length, at an angle from the grid network of local streets. The *côte*, or slope, serves as the border between two types of terrain, while at the same time separating what has come to be known as "Outremont-en-haut" (Upper Outremont), perched atop the mountain, from the rest of the borough. Initially, many imposing residences were built along this large boulevard in order to take advantage of the sharp incline of the south side (the homes of the heirs of the famous cigar manufacturer Grothé are located at numbers 96 and 98). The land all along the road has been laid out in accordance with this slope. For example, some entrances and facades face Avenue Maplewood, located in the back; yards are terraced; wooded areas are left intact to prevent erosion and low retaining walls have been constructed.

For the past 30 years, however, the sporadic and controversial development of prestigious high-rises on the north side has somewhat altered the general appearance of the street, or at least the section between Boulevard Mont-Royal and Avenue Laurier. Relatively unoriginal in style, these high-rises, which the municipality hoped would make the street look something like New York's Fifth Avenue, have often replaced older, more interesting residences, such as those of the Berthiaume-Du Tremblay group, owner of the French-language newspaper *La Presse*, which stood at the corner of Avenue Bloomfield *(replaced by the Le Tournesol tower at number 205).*

⋯ ⋏ *Walk to the corner of Avenue Bloomfield and Avenue Laurier.*

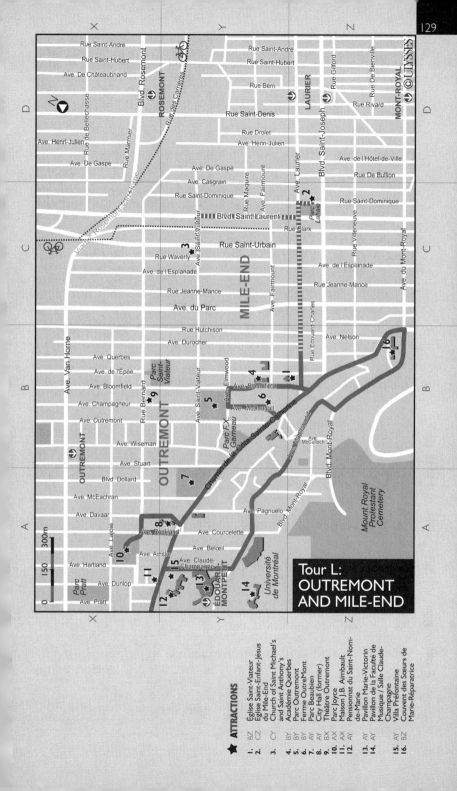

Tour L:
OUTREMONT
AND MILE-END

★ **ATTRACTIONS**

1.	BZ	Église Saint-Viateur
2.	CZ	Église Saint-Enfant-Jésus du Mile-End
3.	CY	Church of Saint Michael's and Saint Anthony's
4.	BY	Académie Querbes
5.	BY	Parc Outremont
6.	BY	Ferme Outremont
7.	AY	Parc Beaubien
8.	AY	City Hall (former)
9.	BX	Théâtre Outremont
10.	AX	Parc Joyce
11.	AX	Maison J.B. Aimbault
12.	AY	Pensionnat du Saint-Nom-de-Marie
13.	AY	Pavillon Marie-Victorin
14.	AY	Pavillon de la Faculté de Musique / Salle Claude-Champagne
15.	AY	Villa Préfontaine
16.	BZ	Couvent des Sœurs de Marie-Réparatrice

At the corner of Laurier and Bloomfield, visitors will find the **Église Saint-Viateur** ★, which dates back to the 1910s. Its remarkable interior, inspired by the Gothic Revival style, was decorated by artists renowned in the fields of painting (Guido Nincheri), glass-working (Henri Perdriau), cabinet-making (Philibert Lemay) and sculpting (Médard Bourgault and Olindo Gratton). The ceiling vaults, covered with paintings depicting the life of Saint Viateur, are quite exceptional.

Avenue Laurier ★ is one of three trendy shopping streets in the municipality that are popular among well-off Outremont and Montréal residents. The avenue has been given a facelift, contributing a certain stylishness to the local specialty shops.

Don't hesitate to venture east beyond Avenue du Parc to Boulevard Saint-Laurent, with Avenue Fairmount and Avenue Saint-Viateur to the north. You're now within the heart of the **Mile-End** ★ district, a bustling bourgeois-bohemian neighbourhood that has welcomed several waves of immigration in the past. Mile-End is very representative of Montréal's cultural diversity, as much for its residents as for its many businesses, including cafés, restaurants and boutiques that are frequented by a multilingual, eclectic clientele. The neighbourhood has a distinctly working-class flavour, as many factories set up here during the 19th century, most notably quarries and tanneries.

The best way to get a feel for the area is probably to simply stroll down its main streets and savour its eclectic atmosphere. At the corner of Avenue Laurier and Boulevard Saint-Laurent you'll come upon a strange castle set up amidst residential buildings. It was built in 1905 and has served several different functions: it has been Saint-Louis-du-Mile-End's city hall, a bank, a post office, a prison and now a fire station. Across Boulevard Saint-Laurent, to the south, is Parc Lahaie, which borders a Baroque-style church: **Église Saint-Enfant-Jésus du Mile-End** ★ *(5039 Rue St-Dominique)*. The church was designed by architect Victor

Bourgeau during the 19th century and its dome contains artworks by Ozias Leduc. If there's one church you should visit in the Mile-End, however, it's the **Church of Saint Michael's and Saint Anthony's** ★ *(5580 Rue St-Urbain)*. The church's construction was overseen by architect Aristide Beaugrand-Champagne, who, surprisingly enough, chose a Byzantine-inspired style for this Catholic church that contrasts sharply with the surrounding working-class residential area. Initially built for the area's Irish community, the church now welcomes the neighbourhood's large Portuguese population. Its imposing dome measures 23m in diameter, to which two semi-cupolas were added. Before the Saint-Joseph oratory's construction, this used to be the city's highest domed structure.

Heads Up!

Hungry for an authentic Montréal bagel? Head to the **Fairmount Bagel Bakery** (see p 240), where twenty different varieties are offered, 24 hours a day. The perfect late-night stop on your way out of one the area's many bars.

⋯ ⟨ *If you've been exploring the Mile-End district, head back to Avenue Laurier near Église Saint-Viateur and turn onto Avenue Bloomfield.*

Avenue Bloomfield is believed to have been named after a farm that was once located here, where the harvest would have been typical of the market gardening and fruit growing of the time. Today, the avenue serves as a reminder of the first urban-style lots that would eventually line the city streets from east to west.

The overall layout of this winding street is very pleasant, with large trees, spacious front yards and distinctive architecture. Several buildings are worth a look. The **Académie Querbes**, from numbers 215 to 235, was built in 1914. The architectural detail—monumental entrance and stone galleries reaching all the way to the third floor—is quite original for the period. Furthermore, the facilities were ahead of their time, including a swimming pool, bowling alley and gymnasium. The canopy-shaped balconies over the entrances of numbers 249 and 253 have been unusually styled as loggias. The building at number 261 was designed by the same architect as the latter two houses, and was once the home of Canon Lionel Groulx, a priest, writer, history professor and prominent Québec nationalist. The building now houses a foundation bearing his name. Number 262 stands out for its facade, made of alternating red brick and grey stone. A little further, facing Parc Outremont at number 345, is a house that was built in 1922 by and for architect Aristide Beaugrand-Champagne, which is distinguished by its cathedral roof and white stucco.

··· ⋏ *Turn left on Avenue Elmwood.*

Parc Outremont is one of the municipality's many popular parks, used for both sports and leisure activities. Laid out a century ago on swamplands supplied with water by a stream flowing from the neighbouring hills, it gives the area a serene beauty. Occupying the place of honour in the middle of the Bassin McDougall is a fountain resembling the *Groupes d'Enfants* that adorns the grounds of the Château de Versailles in Paris. A monument to the citizens of Outremont who died during World War I faces the street.

··· ⋏ *Turn left on Avenue McDougall.*

Avenue McDougall is particularly interesting, in part for the house at numbers 221 and 223, which occupies a very important place in the history of Outremont: the **Ferme OutreMont**, built for L.-T. Bouthillier between 1833 and 1838. From 1856 to 1887, the farm was the family residence of a financier named McDougall. It later became a horticultural school for the deaf run by the clergymen of Saint-Viateur.

This was the scene of the first Mass ever celebrated in Outremont, on April 21, 1887. The house is believed to be the third-oldest residence in the city. Henri Bourassa, founder of the newspaper *Le Devoir*, was supposedly once a tenant here. The white section (now divided into two dwellings) still has most of its original characteristics, such as the large porch topped with a gallery, the dormer window wedged between the two chimneys and the small windows. At number 268 is Maison Gravel, designed by a Toronto architect named Ralston for an architecture competition, a good example of the international Bauhaus style. This influential school of thought from the 1920s emphasized functionalism and greatly affected the art and science of architecture.

··· ⋏ *Turn right on Chemin de la Côte-Sainte-Catherine.*

This area of Chemin de la Côte-Sainte-Catherine once again becomes lined with homes, some of undeniable architectural interest. This is certainly the case for number 325, which has a very large balcony and numerous ornamental details, and number 356, home of architect Roger D'Astous, who added an aviary. D'Astous, a student of celebrated architect Frank Lloyd Wright, came up with the designs for Montréal's Olympic Village and Château Champlain.

Parc Beaubien is located on the site of a farming estate once owned by the important Beaubien family of Outremont, the members of which included several prominent figures on the Québec scene. The members of the Beaubien clan lived near one another on the hillside, overlooking their land (part of which is now occupied by the Terrasses Les Hautvilliers). Among the family members were Justine Lacoste-Beaubien, founder of the renowned Hôpital Sainte-Justine for children, and Louis Beaubien, federal and provincial Member of Parliament and his wife, Lauretta Stuart. Louis Riel, the Métis chief from Manitoba whose trial and execution became famous throughout North America, apparently worked on the Beaubiens' land between 1859 and 1864.

··· ⋏ *Walk to Avenue Davaar and turn right.*

The building that houses Outremont's former **city hall** (1817) *(543 Chemin de la Côte-Ste-Catherine)* alternately served as a warehouse for the Hudson's Bay Company, a school and a prison. A tollbooth used to stand here on Chemin de la Côte-Sainte-Catherine to collect a fee to finance the upkeep of the road, which, like many others in those years, was administered by a private company. The building is now home to the Outremont borough's administrative offices.

··· ⅄ *Go down Avenue Davaar to Avenue Bernard.*

Avenue Bernard ★ *(Outremont metro)* is lined with shops, offices, apartment buildings and houses. This wide avenue with large, grassy medians, curbside landscaping and stately buildings, appears quite imposing and reflects the will of an era to clearly affirm the growing municipality's prestige. The **Théâtre Outremont** *(1234-1248 Avenue Bernard,* ☎ *514-495-9944, www.theatreoutremont. ca)*, once a very popular repertory theatre currently serving as a concert hall, is located on the street. Its interior was designed by Emmanuel Briffa.

Heads Up!

Do you scream for ice scream? For the authentic old-fashioned variety, **Le Bilboquet** (see p 240) is your best choice in the area. This little café/ice-cream maker is renowned for its creative flavours.

The former post office at number 1145 and the **Clos Saint-Bernard**, a large garage now converted into condominiums at numbers 1167 to 1175, are also interesting. Another highlight on this street is the first large-scale grocery store opened by the Steinberg family, who later came to own more than 190 such stores across Québec but nevertheless went bankrupt in 1992. Several residential buildings along Avenue Bernard are architecturally beautiful as well, including the **Montcalm** *(numbers 1040 to 1050)*, the **Garden Court** *(numbers 1058 to 1066)*, the **Royal York** *(numbers 1100 to 1144)* and the **Parklane** *(number 1360)*.

··· ⅄ *Head west on Avenue Bernard to Avenue Rockland to reach the park located along this avenue.*

Parc Joyce was laid out on a vast property formerly owned by James Joyce, a Canadian of British descent who was a confectioner by profession. The buildings, which were of great architectural interest, were demolished because no one could find a use for them after the land was transferred to the City in 1926. The resulting park has gentle hills and mature vegetation dating back to the time of the estate.

It is worth taking the time to see three homes on Avenue Ainslie, which ends at the park. Numbers 18 and 22 are especially impressive, as much for the size of the lots of land upon which they were built as for the dimensions of the buildings and the majesty of their Victorian-inspired design. Number 7 was built in 1936 and represents one of the first attempts at modernism in this country.

··· ⅄ *Back on Chemin de la Côte-Sainte-Catherine, take a moment to walk along Avenue Claude-Champagne.*

On the north side of the street are three residences whose architectural and patrimonial value is obvious: number 637, the country-style **Maison J.B. Aimbault**, built around 1820, is an extremely rare legacy of a bygone era in Outremont; number 645, the neighbouring house, has a sharply pitched roof, the trademark of architect Beaugrand-Champagne and, finally, number 661, built at the very end of the 19th century, whose design, relatively unique for the neighbourhood, is inspired by the New-England Georgian style.

··· ⅄ *Turn onto Avenue Claude-Champagne.*

The **Sœurs des Saints-Noms-de-Jésus-et-de-Marie** housing complex *(Édouard-Montpetit metro)* is a string of big institutional buildings that extends along Avenue Claude-Champagne and beyond, into the mountain and along Boulevard Mont-Royal. It once belonged to a single community of nuns, the Sœurs des Saints-Noms-de-Jésus-et-de-Marie. These women came to Outremont in the 19th century with an essentially educational mission, which they managed to fulfill while this large area was developing.

Walking along Avenue Claude-Champagne, visitors will first see the **Pensionnat du Saint-Nom-de-Marie** (boarding school), built in 1905. It stands out on Chemin de la Côte-Sainte-Catherine thanks to its architecture, which includes a Renaissance-style portico; its silvery roof and dome crowned with a cupola; its massive size and its location on higher ground. Farther up, immediately behind the boarding school, lies the much more modern **Pavillon Marie-Victorin**, which was originally used as a college by the nuns before being purchased by the Université de Montréal for its Faculty of Education.

Even higher, this time right on the mountain, stands the **Pavillon de la Faculté de Musique** (Faculty of Music), which is part of the Université de Montréal. The building's concert hall, **Salle Claude-Champagne**, has exceptionally good acoustics and is used for recordings on a regular basis. The grounds offer a remarkable view of Outremont, as well as the entire northern part of the island of Montréal. Finally, east of and a little below this building, on Boulevard Mont-Royal *(numbers 1360 to 1430)*, the nuns' mother house, built in the 1920s, completes the tableau.

Avenue Claude-Champagne, part of "Outremont-en-haut," is also graced with residential buildings befitting the reputation of this section of the city. The imposing **Villa Préfontaine**, located at number 22, epitomizes the style many local residents wanted to give their property. Higher up, from number 36 to 76, visitors will notice a very well-executed series of twin houses, successfully differentiated from one another by certain ornamental and architectural details.

··· ⊀ *At the end of Avenue Claude-Champagne, turn left on Boulevard Mont-Royal and continue straight ahead at the traffic lights to Avenue Maplewood.*

Also known as the "avenue of power," **Avenue Maplewood** ★ *(Édouard-Montpetit metro)* forms the central axis of the area referred to as "Outremont-en-haut," where various opulent-looking houses with distinctive architecture lie perched in a very hilly landscape, occupied in both the past and the present by influential Quebecers.

On Place Duchastel, numbers 161, 159 and 6 are remarkable for their architecture, inspired by the Tudor and Elizabethan period. The massive structure at number 153, built by architect Randolph C. Betts, is also impressive. The different coloured materials used for the facing and the roof, as well as the organized diversity of the architectural components used in the design, help tone down the building's impact on the landscape. The lovely residences at numbers 118 and 114, from a different period, hem in a lovely little stream, which adds to the beauty of the avenue. This stream once supplied a watering place for horses on Côte-Sainte-Catherine before forming the swamp where Parc Outremont is now located. Today, it disappears into the pipes located below the avenue, and under the property of the Religieuses de l'Imaculée-Conception (Sisters of the Immaculate Conception).

Beyond Avenue McCulloch (where the late former Prime Minister of Canada Pierre Elliott Trudeau lived for a time at number 84), Avenue Maplewood becomes even more picturesque. Its slight slope and gentle twists and turns, combined with the beauty of the residences and careful landscaping of the yards, are examples of how appealing "Outremont-en-haut" has always been for the Québec intelligentsia. Many houses here are worth a quick look: number 77 is a fine example of the Colonial American style; numbers 71 and 69 resemble 1920s-style suburban houses; numbers 49 and 47, twin houses dating back to 1906, have a country look about them (they are the oldest houses on the street), and finally, number 41, where the architectural style

Exploring - Outremont and Mile-End

and large front yard bring to mind the great French manors of the Renaissance.

⋯ 🚶 *Take the footpath between numbers 54 and 52, which leads to Boulevard Mont-Royal via the lane of the same name.*

Boulevard du Mont-Royal is the second major artery of "Outremont-en-haut." It was thus named because the first section of the road led to the Cimetière Protestant Mont-Royal. Although strictly residential, the road now tends to be quite busy with motorists en route to the Université de Montréal. It is also used as a jogging path by neighbourhood residents.

The section of the boulevard included in this tour is an example of the quality of the local architecture and landscaping. Lovely period residences have been built here, some of which were designed while bearing in mind their access to both the boulevard and Avenue Maplewood. This is especially the case with number 1151, which has two well-balanced facades, one facing each street. Number 1139 is typically Art Deco in style. The vast wooded area that has been preserved south of the boulevard adds to the beauty of the neighbourhood. Once threatened with over-development along the lines of the large residential high-rises found on Chemin de la Côte-Sainte-Catherine, the area is now part of Parc du Mont-Royal.

From the end of the street (at the bend in the road) is a beautiful view of the eastern part of Montréal (Plateau Mont-Royal), which also reveals the radical difference between this part of Outremont and the city at its feet. After the turn at the end of this tour, visitors will see the **Couvent des Sœurs de Marie-Réparatrice** on the left. This convent, with its buff-coloured brick, was considered very modern for its time in 1911.

The **Mount Royal Protestant Cemetery** ★ ★ (see p 120) can be reached via Boulevard Mont-Royal and is described in the Mont Royal tour.

⋯ 🚶 🚌 *Return to Boulevard Mont-Royal and head to the corner of Chemin de la Côte-Sainte-Catherine to get back on bus no. 11, which can either take you to the Mont-Royal metro station, in the Plateau Mont-Royal area, or to Parc du Mont-Royal, above the city.*

Tour M: Little Italy
★

🕐 *three hours*

Montréal has a large Italian community. By the beginning of the 19th century, many of the best hotels in town were owned by Italians. At the end of the same century, the first group of immigrants from the poorer regions of southern Italy and Sicily settled in the area around Rue Saint-Christophe, north of Rue Ontario. The largest wave, however, arrived at the end of World War II, when thousands of Italian peasants and workers set foot at the port of Montréal. Many of these settled around Marché Jean-Talon and Église Madonna Della Difesa, thereby creating Little Italy, where visitors will now find cafés, trattorias and specialty food shops. Since the 1960s, many of Montréal's Italians have moved to Saint-Léonard, a separate municipality located in the northeast, though they still return to Little Italy to do their shopping.

⋯ 🚶 Ⓜ *From the Jean-Talon metro station, head east on Rue Jean-Talon.*

Jean-Talon street is named after the man who served as intendant (administrator) of New France from 1665 to 1668 and from 1670 to 1672. During his two short

★ **ATTRACTIONS**

1.	CW	Casa d'Italia
2.	CW	Plaza Saint-Hubert
3.	BX	Rivoli and Château Cinemas (former)
4.	BX	École Sainte-Julienne-Falconieri
5.	BX	Église Madonna della Difesa

6.	BX	École Madonna della Difesa
7.	AX	Caserne de Pompiers no 31
8.	BW	Marché Jean-Talon
9.	BX	Marché des Saveurs

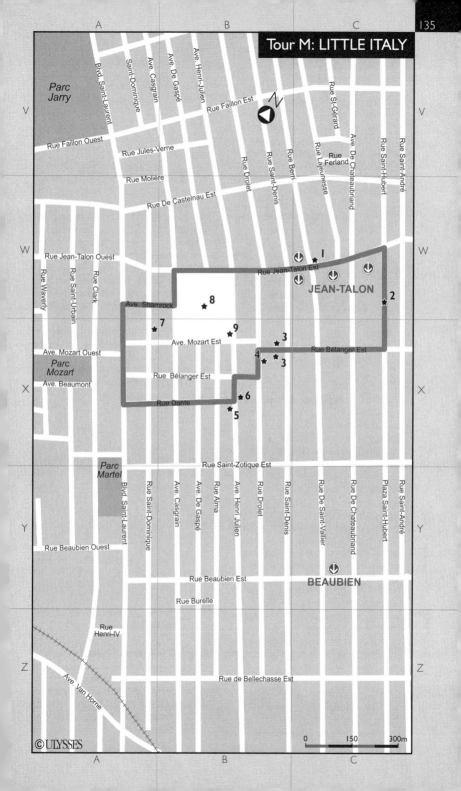

Tour M: LITTLE ITALY

Parc Jarry

Blvd Saint-Laurent
Saint-Dominique
Ave. Casgrain
Ave. De Gaspé
Ave. Henri-Julien
Rue Faillon Est

Rue St-Gérard
Ave. De Chateaubriand
Rue Saint-Hubert
Rue Saint-André

Rue Faillon Ouest

Rue Jules-Verne

Rue Molière

Rue Ferland

Rue Drolet
Rue Saint-Denis
Rue Berri
Rue Lajeunesse

Rue De Castelnau Est

W

Rue Jean-Talon Ouest

Rue Waverly
Rue Saint-Urbain
Rue Clark

1

Rue Jean-Talon Est

JEAN-TALON

2

Ave. Shamrock

8

7

9

Ave. Mozart Est

3

Rue Bélanger Est

Ave. Mozart Ouest

4

3

Parc Mozart

Ave. Beaumont

Rue Bélanger Est

6

Rue Dante

5

Rue Saint-Zotique Est

Parc Martel

Blvd. Saint-Laurent
Rue Saint-Dominique
Ave. Casgrain
Ave. De Gaspé
Rue Alma
Ave. Henri-Julien
Rue Drolet
Rue Saint-Denis
Rue De Saint-Vallier
Rue De Chateaubriand
Plaza Saint-Hubert
Rue Saint-André

Y

Rue Beaubien Ouest

Rue Beaubien Est

Rue Burelle

BEAUBIEN

Rue Henri-IV

Z

Ave. Van Horne

Rue de Bellechasse Est

© ULYSSES

0   150   300m

A   B   C

mandates, Jean Talon was responsible for reorganizing the colony's finances and diversifying its economy.

The **Casa d'Italia** (*505 Rue Jean-Talon Est; Jean-Talon metro*) is the Italian community centre. It was built in 1936 in the Art Moderne style, a variation on Art Deco characterized by rounded, horizontal lines inspired by the streamlined designs of steamships and locomotives. A fascist group briefly took up residence here before the Second World War.

··· 人 *Walk east to Rue Saint-Hubert, and turn right.*

Plaza Saint-Hubert (*Rue Saint-Hubert between Rue de Bellechasse and Rue Jean-Talon; Jean-Talon or Beaubien metro*) is known for its shops, most of which sell inexpensive, low-quality merchandise. The glass awnings were put up over the sidewalks in 1986.

··· 人 *Turn right on Rue Bélanger and walk to Rue Saint-Denis.*

The former **Rivoli and Château Cinemas** (*6906 and 6956 Rue St-Denis; Jean-Talon metro*), located on both sides of Rue Bélanger, are two examples of neighbourhood movie theatres that have been converted for other uses. The Cinéma Château was built in 1931 and designed by architect René Charbonneau. The original decor, executed in an exotic Art Deco style by Emmanuel Briffa, has been preserved. The Cinéma Rivoli, however, was not so lucky—only the Adamesque facade, dating back to 1926, remains; the interior was transformed into a pharmacy. This part of Rue Saint-Denis is lined with typical Montréal apartment buildings with traditional exterior metal and wood staircases. Notice the many finely worked cornices and balconies, as well as the Art Nouveau–style stained glass in the upper part of the windows and doors.

··· 人 *Keep heading west on Rue Bélanger, then turn left on Rue Drolet.*

École Sainte-Julienne-Falconieri (*6839 Rue Drolet; Jean-Talon metro*) was designed

in 1924 by Ernest Cormier, architect of the **Université de Montréal**'s main building (see p 124). The school was clearly influenced by the buildings of American architect Frank Lloyd Wright, erected about 10 years earlier.

··· 人 *Go back to Rue Bélanger and turn left. Take another left on Avenue Henri-Julien.*

The design of **Église Madonna Della Difesa** ★ (*6810 Avenue Henri-Julien; Jean-Talon metro*), or Our Lady of the Defense church, is of Roman-Byzantine inspiration, characterized by small arched openings and varied treatment of the surfaces, arranged in horizontal bands. A basilica-style plan such as this is unusual in Montréal. The church was designed in 1910 by painter, master glass-worker and decorator Guido Nincheri, who spent over 30 years working on it, finishing every last detail of the decor himself. Nincheri was in the habit of depicting contemporary figures in his stained-glass windows and in his vibrantly coloured frescoes, made with egg-wash, a technique he had mastered. One of these, showing Mussolini on his horse, was a source of controversy for many years. It can still be seen above the high altar.

At number 6841, visitors will find the Art Moderne–style **École Madonna Della Difesa** (*Jean-Talon metro*). The bas-relief depicting school children is particularly noteworthy. Parc Dante stretches west of the church, with the place of honour in its centre occupied by a modest bust of the Italian poet, sculpted by Carlo Balboni in 1924. Neighbourhood bocci ball (Italian lawn bowling played on a long narrow dirt court) buffs meet here during the summer months.

··· 人 *Take Rue Dante west to Boulevard Saint-Laurent and turn right.*

Boulevard Saint-Laurent (*Jean-Talon metro*) could be described as Montréal's "immigration corridor." Since 1880, immigrants to the city have been settling along different segments of the boulevard, depending on their ethnic background. After several decades, they usually leave the area and scatter throughout the city or reunite in another neighbourhood. Some communities leave few traces of their passage on Boulevard Saint-Laurent, while others have opened shopping areas where descendants of these first arrivals still come with their families. Between Rue De Bellechasse to the south and Rue Jean-Talon to the north, the boulevard is lined with numerous Italian restaurants and cafés, as well as food stores like **Milano** (see p 289), swarmed by Montrealers of all origins on weekends.

Heads Up!

One of the city's best cappuccinos is served at **Café Italia** (see p 245).

⋯ 🕴 *Turn right on Avenue Shamrock, whose name serves as a reminder that this neighbourhood was predominantly Irish before it became Italian.*

The **Caserne de Pompiers no 31** *(7041 Rue St-Dominique; Jean-Talon metro)*, or Fire Station no. 31, was built as part of a job-creation project initiated after the economic crisis of 1929. The building, which dates back to 1931, was designed by architect E. A. Doucet in the Art Deco style. At the intersection of Avenue Shamrock and Avenue Casgrain, a small, Art Moderne brick building with a rounded corner once served as the Clinique Jean-Talon, where many new arrivals came for care and comfort.

Marché Jean-Talon ★ *(bordered by Avenue Casgrain, Avenue Henri-Julien, Rue Jean-Talon and Avenue Mozart; Jean-Talon metro)* was built in 1933 on the site of the Irish lacrosse field known as Shamrock Stadium. The space was originally intended for a bus station, which explains the platforms with concrete shelters over them. Despite its less-than-attractive appearance, the market is a pleasant place to shop thanks to the constant buzz of activity. It is surrounded with specialty food shops, often set up right in the backyards of buildings facing the neighbouring streets. Among these stores, the **Marché des Saveurs** *(corner Avenue Henri-Julien)*, which stocks a good range of local products, is definitely worth a visit. The market's central area is occupied by farmers who sell their products every day from 8am. Fresh seasonal fruits and vegetables, as well as various other homemade products, are sold here at unbeatable prices. Though the market is open year-round, the best time to visit it is between mid-April and mid-September, when the weather is warmer.

Heads Up!

Time for a bite to eat? You've probably already stocked up on cheese, cold cuts and fruit at Jean-Talon market. Why not settle at one of the market's outdoor tables for a quick picnic? You'll also find many cafés and *trattorias* in the streets that surround the market.

Passing through the neighbourhood, visitors will see vegetable gardens laid out in whatever meagre space is available, Madonnas in their niches and grape-laden vines climbing up trellises on balconies, all of which lend this part of Montréal a Mediterranean feel.

Tour N: Sault-au-Récollet ★

🕐 *three hours*

Around 1950, the Sault-au-Récollet neighbourhood was still a farming village isolated from the city on the banks of Rivière des Prairies. Today, it is easy to reach by metro, at Henri-Bourassa, the northeast terminal station. The history of the "Sault" dates back a long way. In 1610, Monsieur des Prairies headed up the river that now bears his name, thinking it was the St. Lawrence. Then, in 1625, Récollet Nicolas Viel and his Aboriginal guide Ahuntsic drowned in the river's rapids, hence the name of the area, *Sault*, meaning rapids.

In 1696, the Sulpicians established the Fort Lorette Huron mission here. In the

19th century, Sault-au-Récollet became a popular resort area among Montrealers looking for a spot close to the city during the summer months, which explains the existence of the handful of summer cottages that have survived the recent development of the area.

⋯ 🚶 Ⓜ *From the Henri-Bourassa metro station, head east on the boulevard of the same name. Turn left on Rue Saint-Hubert, then right on Boulevard Gouin Est to get to the start of this tour.*

Monseigneur Ignace Bourget, Montréal's second bishop, courted a number of French religious communities during the 1840s in an attempt to get them to establish schools in the Montréal region.

The Dames du Sacré-Cœur were among those who accepted to make the long voyage. In 1856, they settled on the banks of Rivière des Prairies, where they built a convent school for girls. The former day school (1858) at 1105 Boulevard Gouin Est is all that remains of the original complex. After a fire, the convent was rebuilt in stages. The building resembling an austere English manor is the most interesting of the new facilities (1929). The school, **Collège Sophie-Barat** *(1105 and 1239 Boulevard Gouin Est; Henri-Bourassa metro)*, now bears the name of the founder of the Dames du Sacré-Cœur community.

Before reaching the Église de la Visitation, visitors will see a few ancestral homes, such as the **Maison David-Dumouchel**, at number 1737, built between 1838 and 1840 for a carpenter from Sault-au-Récollet. It has high firebreak walls even though there are no buildings adjoining it, showing that this architectural element, once strictly utilitarian, had become a decorative feature and a symbol of prestige and urbanity.

Église de la Visitation ★★ *(every day 8am to 11:30am and 1:30pm to 4:30pm; 1847 Boulevard Gouin Est; Henri-Bourassa metro and bus no. 69)* is the oldest church still in use on the island of Montréal. It was built between 1749 and 1752, but was considerably modified afterwards. Its beautiful Palladian facade, added in 1850, is the work of Englishman John Ostell, who designed the **Maison de la Douane** (customs house; see p 61) on Place Royale and the Vieux Palais de Justice (former courthouse) on Rue Notre-Dame. The degree of refinement here is a tribute to the fierce competition between the parishioners of Sault-au-Récollet and those of Sainte-Geneviève, further west, who had just built a church in the same style.

Viewed as a whole, the interior of the Église de la Visitation is one of the most remarkable works of woodcarving in Québec. Begun in 1764, the interior was not completed until 1837. Philippe Liébert, born in Nemours, France, executed the first decorative elements, including the sculpted doors of the reredos, which are precious Louis-XV-style pieces. It was David-Fleury David, however, who completed the bulk of the work, namely the cornice, Louis-XVI pilasters and finely chiselled vault. The church is adorned with beautiful paintings, such as *La Visitation de la Vierge* (The Visitation of the Virgin), purchased by Curé Chambon in 1756 and painted by Mignard.

At the end of Rue Lambert, visitors will find the former Noviciat Saint-Joseph, now **Collège du Mont-Saint-Louis** *(1700 Boulevard Henri-Bourassa Est)*. The neoclassical building, erected in 1852, was expanded thanks to the addition of a Second Empire–style pavilion in 1872. The heart of the village of Sault-au-Récollet lies along Boulevard Gouin Est, east of Avenue Papineau. There are

★ ATTRACTIONS

1. BY Collège Sophie-Barat
2. CY Maison David-Dumouchel
3. CY Église de la Visitation
4. CY Collège du Mont-Saint-Louis
5. DX Maison du Pressoir
6. DX Parc-Nature de l'Île-de-la-Visitation
7. DX Maison du Meunier
8. DZ TOHU, la Cité des Arts du Cirque

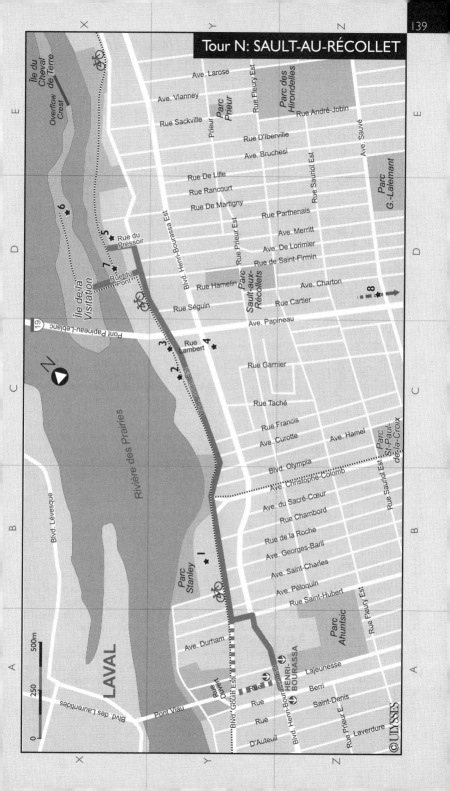

some noteworthy buildings here, including number 1947, the Maison Boudreau, built around 1750; numbers 2012 to 2016, the former general store, which is a small Second Empire building of urban design transposed in a rural setting; and finally, number 2084, the proud Maison Persillier-Lachapelle, former residence of a prosperous miller and bridge-builder, erected around 1840.

››› *Turn left on Rue du Pressoir.*

Around 1806, Didier Joubert built the **Maison du Pressoir** ★ *(free admission; May to Oct every day noon to 6pm; 10865 Rue du Pressoir, ☎514-280-6783)*, a cider press on his property in Sault-au-Récollet. Researchers believe that this is Montréal's only surviving example of half-timbered architecture. The building was restored in 1982 and now houses a history-interpretation centre.

››› *Backtrack along Boulevard Gouin, heading west. Turn right on Rue du Pont to reach Île de la Visitation.*

Parc-Nature de l'Île-de-la-Visitation ★ ★ *(reception centre at 2425 Boulevard Gouin Est; early May to late Aug every day 9:30am to 6pm; early Sep to late Oct every day 9:30am to 4:30pm; ☎514-280-6733; Henri-Bourassa metro and bus no. 69)* encompasses a vast area alongside Rivière des Prairies, as well as the island itself, a long strip of land hemmed in at each end by dykes used to control the level and flow of the river, thus eliminating the famous *sault*, or rapids, for which the area was named. On the way to the island, visitors will cross over the Rue du Pont dyke. Under the French Regime, the Sulpicians built powerful mills along here; unfortunately, however, very little remains of these structures. The **Maison du Meunier** *(free admission; May to Oct every day 10am to 6pm; 10897 Rue du Pont, ☎514-850-0322)* also features a history-interpretation centre that examines the site's former industrial vocation.

Heads Up!

⤳ Feel like strapping on your skis? Cross-country skiers can explore the Parc-Nature de l'Île-de-la-Visitation in winter by following the trails that were set up around the island.

The dyke located at the east end of the island supports Rivière-des-Prairies' hydroelectric power station, built in 1928 by Montreal Island Power. The dam includes a fish trap, which makes it a favourite spot for shad fishing, one of the river's most abundant species.

Outside this tour, in the northern part of the island's Saint-Michel district, is **TOHU, la Cité des Arts du Cirque** ★ *(2345 Rue Jarry Est, ☎514-376-8648, www.tohu.ca; Jarry metro and bus no. 193)*. This "circus district" makes the city one of the world's top sites for circus arts, in addition to contributing to the rehabilitation of a major dumpsite. It includes the new building of the **École Nationale de Cirque** *(8181 2ᵉ Avenue)*, as well as the **Chapiteau des Arts**, a unique performance hall in Canada that is specifically designed for circus arts and also serves as the reception pavilion for the **Complexe Environnemental de Saint-Michel (CESM)** (see p 176). And let's not forget the **Cirque du Soleil headquarters** *(8400 2ᵉ Avenue)* and its lodging establishment for artists. Guided tours *(reservations at ☎514-374-3522, ext. 2233)* provide an overview of the various facets of the TOHU circus complex, which focuses both on creative and environmental endeavours. Visitors get to learn about the history of TOHU, and can enjoy a large public space. The performance hall and Terra Cirqua permanent exhibit, which includes one of the largest private collections of items related to circus arts, can be reached by foot, by bike or by minibus.

››› Ⓜ *To get back to the Henri-Bourassa metro station where this tour started, head west on Boulevard Gouin from the shores of Rivière des Prairies to the corner of Rue Lajeunesse. Turn left to get to the metro station.*

Tour O: Île Sainte-Hélène and Île Notre-Dame ★★

 one day

When Samuel de Champlain reached the island of Montréal in 1611, he found a small rocky archipelago located in front of it. He named the largest of these islands in the channel after his wife, Hélène Boulé. Île Sainte-Hélène later became part of the seigneury of Longueuil. Around 1720, the Baroness of Longueuil chose the island as the site for a country house surrounded by a garden. It is also worth noting that in 1760, the island was the last foothold of French troops in New France, commanded by Chevalier François de Lévis.

Recognizing Île Saint-Hélène's strategic importance, the British army built a fort on the eastern part of the island at the beginning of the 19th century. The threat of armed conflict with the United States having diminished, the Canadian government rented Île Sainte-Hélène to the City of Montréal in 1874, at which time the island was turned into a park and linked to Old Montréal by ferry and, in 1930, by the Jacques-Cartier bridge.

In the early 1960s, Montréal was chosen as the site of the 1967 World's Fair (Expo 67). The city wanted to set up the event on a large, attractive site near the downtown area; a site such as this, however, did not exist. So it became necessary to build one: using soil excavated during the construction of the metro tunnel, Île Notre-Dame was created, doubling the area of Île Sainte-Hélène. From April to November 1967, 45 million visitors passed through Cité-du-Havre, the gateway to the fairground, and criss-crossed both islands. Expo, as Montrealers still refer to it, was more than a jumble of assorted objects; it was Montréal's awakening, during which the city opened itself to the world, and visitors from all over discovered a new art of living, including mini-skirts, colour television, hippies, flower power and protest rock.

⁂ 🚗 🚌 Ⓜ *It is not easy to reach Cité du Havre from downtown. The best way is to take Rue Mill, then Chemin des Moulins, which runs below Autoroute Bonaventure to Avenue Pierre-Dupuy. This last road leads to Pont de la Concorde and then over the St. Lawrence to the islands. It is also possible to take bus no. 168 from the McGill metro station.*

Heads Up!

Feel like exploring the islands' 15km of bike trails? You can rent bicycles in the old port (see p 179) and then head for the Lachine Canal bike trail. Follow the signs for Cité du Havre first, and then for Île Notre-Dame.

Tropique Nord, **Habitat 67** and **Parc de la Cité-du-Havre** ★★ were all built on a spit of land created to protect the port of Montréal from ice and currents. This site also offers lovely views of the city and the water. The administrative offices of the port are located at the entrance to the area, along with a group of buildings that once housed the Expo-Théâtre and Musée d'Art Contemporain. A little farther on, visitors will spot the large glass wall of Tropique Nord, a residential complex composed of apartments with a view of the outdoors on one side and an interior tropical garden on the other.

Next, visitors will see Habitat 67, an experimental housing development built for Expo 67 in order to illustrate construction techniques using prefabricated concrete slabs, and to herald a new art of living. Its architect, Moshe Safdie, was only 23 years old when he drew up the plans. Habitat 67 looks like a gigantic cluster of cubes, each containing one or two rooms. The apartments are as highly prized as ever and are inhabited by a number of notable Quebecers.

At Parc de la Cité du Havre, visitors will find 12 panels containing a brief description of the history of the St. Lawrence River. A section of the bicycle path leading to Île Notre-Dame and Île Sainte-Hélène passes through the park.

Exploring – Île Sainte-Hélène and Île Notre-Dame

⁕⁕⁕ 🚶 *Cross Pont de la Concorde. From spring to autumn, Île Sainte-Hélène can also be reached by river shuttle from Montréal's Old Port ($5; ☎514-281-8000).*

Parc Jean-Drapeau ★★ *(☎514-872-6120, www.parcjeandrapeau.com; Jean-Drapeau metro)* lies on Île Notre-Dame and Île Sainte-Hélène. The latter originally covered an area of 50ha but was enlarged to over 120ha for Expo 67. The original portion corresponds to the raised area studded with breccia boulders. Peculiar to this island, breccia is a very hard, ferrous stone that takes on an orange colour when exposed to air for a long time. In 1992, the western part was transformed into a vast open-air amphitheatre where large-scale shows are presented. In this lovely riverside park, visitors will find *L'Homme*, a large metal sculpture by Alexander Calder, created for Expo 67.

A little farther, close to the entrance to the Jean-Drapeau metro station, is a work by Mexican artist Sebastián entitled *La Porte de l'Amitié* (The Door to Friendship). This sculpture was given to the City of Montréal by Mexico City in 1992 and erected on this site three years later to commemorate the signing of the free-trade agreement between Canada, the United States and Mexico (NAFTA).

⁕⁕⁕ 🚶 *Follow the trails that lead to the heart of the island.*

The pool house, with a facade of breccia stone, and outdoor swimming pools, built during the Great Depression, lie at the edge of the original park. The island's three original pools were taken apart and then rebuilt for the 2005 FINA World Aquatic Championships. The island, with its varied contours, is dominated by the **Tour Lévis**, a simple water tower built in 1936 that looks like a dungeon.

⁕⁕⁕ 🚶 *Follow the signs for the Fort de l'Île Sainte-Hélène.*

After the War of 1812 between the United States and Great Britain, the **Fort de l'Île Sainte-Hélène** ★★ *(Jean-Drapeau metro)* was built so that Montréal could be properly defended if ever a new conflict were

to erupt. Its construction, supervised by military engineer Elias Walker Durnford, was completed in 1825. Built of breccia stone, the fort is in the shape of a jagged *U*, surrounding a drill ground, used today by the Compagnie Franche de la Marine and the 78th Regiment of the Fraser Highlanders as a parade ground. These two costumed mock regiments delight visitors by reviving Canada's French and Scottish military traditions. The drill ground also offers a lovely view of both the port and Pont Jacques-Cartier, inaugurated in 1930 and straddling the island, separating the park from La Ronde.

The fort's arsenal is now occupied by the **Musée Stewart** ★★ *($10; mid-Oct to late May Wed-Mon 10am to 5pm, late May to mid-Oct every day 10am to 5pm; ☎514-861-6701, www.stewart-museum.org; Jean-Drapeau metro)*, which is dedicated to colonial history and the exploration of the New World. The museum exhibits objects from past centuries, including interesting collections of maps, firearms, and scientific and navigational instruments collected by Montréal industrialist David Stewart and his wife Liliane.

The vaults of the former barracks are home to the **Festin du Gouverneur** (see p 249), a dinner-show geared mainly toward large groups. It recreates the atmosphere of a New France feast.

La Ronde ★ *($34; mid-May to late Oct, for schedules call ☎514-397-7777; ☎514-872-2000, www.laronde.com; Jean-Drapeau metro and bus no. 167)*, an amusement park set up for Expo 67 on the former Île Ronde, opens its doors to both the young and the not-so-young every summer. For Montrealers, an annual trip to La Ronde has almost become a pilgrimage. The **L'International des Feux Loto-Québec** (see p 276) international fireworks competition is held here during the months of June and July.

⁕⁕⁕ 🚶 *Head toward the Biosphère on the road that runs along the south shore of the island.*

Built in 1938 as a sports pavilion, **Restaurant Hélène de Champlain** ★ was inspired by the architecture of New France and

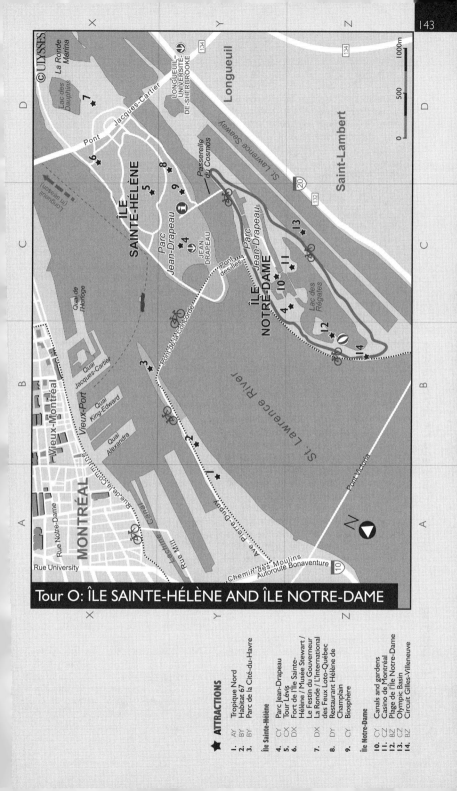

143

Tour O: ÎLE SAINTE-HÉLÈNE AND ÎLE NOTRE-DAME

★ **ATTRACTIONS**

1. AY   Tropique Nord
2. BY   Habitat 67
3. BY   Parc de la Cité-du-Havre

Île Sainte-Hélène

4. CY   Parc Jean-Drapeau
5. CX   Tour Lévis
6. DX   Fort de l'île Sainte-
          Hélène / Musée Stewart /
          Le Festin du Gouverneur
7. DX   La Ronde / L'International
          des Feux Loto-Québec
8. DY   Restaurant Hélène de
          Champlain
9. CY   Biosphère

Île Notre-Dame

10. CY   Canals and gardens
11. CZ   Casino de Montréal
12. BZ   Plage de l'île Notre-Dame
13. CZ   Olympic Basin
14. BZ   Circuit Gilles-Villeneuve

is reminiscent of the summer house of the Baroness of Longueuil, once located in the area. Behind the restaurant is a lovely rose garden planted for Expo 67, which embellishes the view from the dining room. The **former military cemetery** of the British garrison stationed on Île Sainte-Hélène from 1828 to 1870 lies in front of the building. Most of the original tombstones have disappeared; a commemorative monument, erected in 1937, stands in their place.

Very few of the pavilions built for Expo 67 have survived the destructive effects of the weather and the changes in the islands' roles. One that has, however, is the former American pavilion, a veritable monument to modern architecture. The first complete geodesic dome to be taken beyond the stage of a model, it was created by celebrated engineer Richard Buckminster Fuller (1895-1983).

The **Biosphère** ★ ★ *($9.78; late Jun to mid-Sep every day 10am to 6pm; mid-Sep to late Jun Mon, Wed, Thu, Fri 12am to 5pm, Sat-Sun and holidays 10am to 5pm;* ☎ *514-283-5000, www.biosphere.ec.gc.ca; Jean-Drapeau metro)*, built of tubular aluminum and measuring 80m in diameter, unfortunately lost its translucent acrylic skin in a fire back in 1976. An environmental interpretive centre on the St. Lawrence River, the Great Lakes and the different Canadian ecosystems is now located in the dome. The permanent exhibit aims to sensitize the public on issues of sustainable development and the conservation of water as a precious resource. There are several interactive galleries with giant screens and hands-on displays to explore and delight in.

⋯ ⋅ 𝝠 *Cross over to Île Notre-Dame on the Passerelle du Cosmos.*

Île Notre-Dame emerged from the waters of the St. Lawrence in just 10 months, with the help of 15 million tons of rock and soil transported here from the metro construction site. Because it is an artificial island, its creators were able to give it a fanciful form by shaping both the soil and water. The island is traversed by charming **canals** and **gardens** ★ ★ *(Jean-*

Drapeau metro and bus no. 167), laid out for the 1980 Floralies Internationales, an international flower show. Boats can be rented here, enabling visitors to explore the canals.

The **Casino de Montréal** ★ *(see also p 272; free admission, parking and coat check; every day 24hrs;* ☎ *514-392-2746 or 800-665-2274; Jean-Drapeau metro and bus no. 167)* occupies the former French and Québec pavilions of Expo 67. The main building corresponds to the old **French Pavilion** ★, an aluminum structure designed by architect Jean Faugeron. The upper galleries offer some lovely views of downtown Montréal and the St. Lawrence Seaway. Immediately to the west of the former French pavilion, the building shaped like a truncated pyramid is the former **Québec Pavilion** ★ *(every day 9am to 3am)*.

Visitors will find all sorts of things to do at the casino, all in a festive atmosphere; some 15,000 people visit the casino each day. With 3,000 slot machines and 120 gaming tables, it is one of the 10 largest casinos in the world. It is also a popular spot thanks to its bars and cabaret, along with its restaurants, including **Nuances** (see p 249), which is rated as one of the best in Canada. Entrance is reserved for people over 18.

Nearby, visitors will find the entrance to the **Plage de l'Île Notre-Dame** *($7.50, $4.50 after 4pm; mid-Jun to mid-Aug every day 10am to 7pm;* ☎ *514-872-6120; Jean-Drapeau metro and bus no. 167)*, a beach enabling Montrealers to lounge on real sand right in the middle of the St. Lawrence. A natural filtering system keeps the water in the small lake clean, with no need for chemical additives. The number of swimmers allowed on the beach is strictly regulated, however, so as not to disrupt the balance of the system.

There are other recreational facilities here as well, namely the **Olympic Basin** created for the rowing competitions of the 1976 Olympics and the **Circuit Gilles-Villeneuve** *(Jean-Drapeau metro and bus no. 167)*, where Formula One drivers compete every year in the Grand Prix du Canada, part of the international racing circuit, as well as, since 2002, the Champ Car car-racing series.

 To return to downtown Montréal, take the metro from the Jean-Drapeau station.

Tour P: Hochelaga-Maisonneuve
★★

🕐 *one day*

In 1883, the city of Maisonneuve was founded in eastern Montréal by farmers and French-Canadian merchants; port facilities expanded into the area in 1889 and the city's development picked up. Then, in 1918, the formerly autonomous city was annexed to Montréal, becoming one of its major working-class neighbourhoods, with a 90% francophone population. In the course of its history, Maisonneuve has been profoundly influenced by men with grand ideas who wanted to make this part of the province a place where people could thrive together. Upon taking office at the Maisonneuve town hall in 1910, brothers Marius and Oscar Dufresne instituted a rather ambitious policy of building prestigious Beaux-Arts–style public buildings intended to make "their" city a model of development for French Québec. Then, in 1931, Brother Marie-Victorin founded Montréal's Jardin Botanique (botanical garden) in Maisonneuve; it is still one of the largest in the world today. The last major episode in the area's history took place in 1971, when Mayor Jean Drapeau initiated construction of the immense sports complex that was used for the 1976 Olympic Games.

 From the Pie-IX metro station, climb the hill that leads to the corner of Rue Sherbrooke.

The **Jardin Botanique de Montréal** and **Insectarium de Montréal** ★★★ *($11.75, $8.75 in low season, combined ticket for the Biôdome and the Tour de Montréal (Olympic Tower) $28.50, valid for 30 days; Nov to mid-May*

Tue-Sun 9am to 5pm, until 9pm early Sep to late Oct; mid-May to early Sep every day 9am to 6pm; 4101 Rue Sherbrooke Est, ☎514-872-1400, www.ville.montreal.qc.ca; Pie-IX metro). The Jardin Botanique de Montréal, covering an area of 73ha, was first created during the economic crisis of the 1930s on the site of Mont-de-La-Salle, home base of the brothers of the Écoles Chrétiennes, by Brother Marie-Victorin, a well-known Québécois botanist. Behind the Art Deco building occupied by the Université de Montréal's institute of biology, visitors will find a stretch of 10 connected greenhouses open year-round, which shelter, most notably, a precious collection of orchids and the largest grouping of bonsais and *penjings* outside of Asia. The latter includes the famous Wu collection, given to the garden by master Wu Yee-Sun of Hong Kong in 1984. The cucurbitaceae family of vegetables takes the spotlight in the main greenhouse in October: over 600 pumpkins are dressed up to celebrate

Hochelaga: The New *Plateau*?

The historic working-class neighbourhood of Hochelaga has long been "ghettoized" for its stereotypical reputation as a poor area where crime is rampant. Fortunately, the area seems to be shedding this false image. An influx of real-estate developers and urban-planning projects has led to the neighbourhood's new nickname: "Hochelaga-Maisonneuve: the New *Plateau*." This rejuvenation movement does have a flipside though: concerned "anti-gentrification" committees have been formed to defend the neighbourhood's sensitive working-class background. Here's hoping the district's architectural heritage will at least receive the attention it deserves.

Exploring – Hochelaga-Maisonneuve

Halloween, much to the joy of the many young and not-so-young visitors who drop by for this event *(Le Grand Bal des Citrouilles / The Great Pumpkin Ball; Oct every day 9am to 9pm)*.

Thirty outdoor gardens, open from spring to autumn and designed to educate and amaze visitors, stretch to the north and west of the greenhouses. Particularly noteworthy are a beautiful rosary, the Japanese garden and its *sukiya*-style tea pavilion, as well as the very beautiful Chinese Lac de Rêve, or Jardin de Chine garden, whose pavilions were designed by artisans who came here from China specifically for the task. Since Montréal is the twin city of Shanghai, it was deemed appropriate that it should have the largest such garden outside of Asia. During late-summer nights, the Chinese Garden is decorated with hundreds of Chinese lanterns that create a wonderful fairy-tale-like setting of light and flowers *(La Magie des Lanternes; mid-Sep to late Oct every day 9am to 9pm)*.

Another must-see is the First Nations Garden. It is the result of efforts by several contributors, both Aboriginal and non-Aboriginal, including Brother Marie-Victorin, who was hoping to integrate a garden of medicinal plants used by Aboriginal communities. His achievement allows the uninitiated to familiarize themselves with the Aboriginal world, especially their use of plants. Among other things, you will learn how the Huron-Wendat and Mohawk peoples used corn. Québec's 11 First Nations are represented in their natural habitat zones: deciduous forest, coniferous forest and the Arctic zone. An exhibition pavilion completes the tour.

The northern part of the botanical garden is occupied by an arboretum. The **Maison de l'Arbre**, or "tree house," was es-

tablished in this area to educate people about the life of trees. The interactive, permanent exhibit is actually set up in an old tree trunk. There are displays on the yellow birch, Québec's emblematic tree and the building's structure, consisting of different types of wooden beams, reminds us how leafy forests really are. Note the play of light and shade from the frame onto the large white wall, meant to resemble trunks and branches. The terrace in the back is an ideal spot from which to contemplate the arboretum's pond; it also leads to a charming little bonsai garden. To reach the Maison de l'Arbre, climb on board the *Balade*, the shuttle that regularly tours the garden, or use the garden's northern entrance on Boulevard Rosemont.

The **Insectarium de Montréal** *(☎514-872-1400)* is located to the east of the greenhouses. This innovative, living museum invites visitors to discover the fascinating world of insects through short films, interactive games and an impressive collection of insects. Watch for the various activities organized throughout the year. You could, for instance, sample edible insects, if you're so inclined.

⋯ ⋏ *Return to Boulevard Pie-IX. On the western side of the boulevard, just south of Rue Sherbrooke, is Château Dufresne.*

Château Dufresne ★★ *($6; Thu-Sun 10am to 5pm; 2929 Rue Jeanne-d'Arc, ☎514-259-9201, www.chateaudufresne.qc.ca; Pie-IX metro)* is in fact two 22-room private mansions behind the same facade, built in 1916 for brothers Marius and Oscar Dufresne, shoe manufacturers and authors of a grandiose plan to develop Maisonneuve. The plan was abandoned after the onset of World War I, causing the municipality to go bankrupt. Their home, designed by Marius Dufresne and Parisian architect Jules Renard, was sup-

Exploring – Hochelaga-Maisonneuve

★ **ATTRACTIONS**

1.	AW	Jardin Botanique de Montréal
2.	AW	Maison de l'Arbre
3.	BV	Insectarium de Montréal
4.	AW	Château Dufresne
5.	CV	Parc Olympique
6.	BW	Stade Olympique / Tour de Montréal
7.	CW	Biodôme de Montréal
8.	CW	Aréna Maurice-Richard / Univers Maurice «Rocket» Richard
9.	AX	Église Saint-Jean-Baptiste-de-LaSalle
10.	BY	Hôtel de Ville
11.	BY	Marché Maisonneuve / Place du Marché
12.	BY	Bain Morgan
13.	BZ	Théâtre Denise-Pelletier / Salle Fred-Barry
14.	BZ	Parc Morgan
15.	BZ	Caserne de Pompiers no 1
16.	BZ	Église du Saint-Nom-de-Jésus

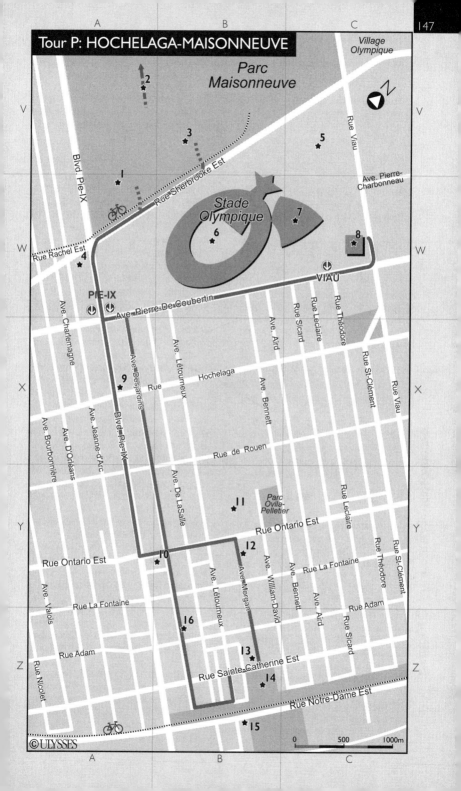

posed to be the nucleus of a residential upper-class neighbourhood, which never materialized. It is one of the best examples of Beaux-Arts architecture in Montréal. Château Dufresne now houses temporary exhibitions as well as a collection of furniture.

⋯ ⚼ *Head back downhill on Boulevard Pie-IX, then turn left on Avenue Pierre-De Coubertin.*

Jean Drapeau was mayor of Montréal from 1954 to 1957, as well as from 1960 to 1986. He dreamed of great things for "his" city. Endowed with an exceptional power of persuasion and unfailing determination, he saw a number of important projects through to a successful conclusion, including the construction of Place des Arts, the metro, Expo 67 and, of course, the 1976 Summer Olympics.For this last international event, however, it was necessary to equip the city with the appropriate facilities.

In spite of the controversy it caused, the city hired Parisian visionary Roger Taillibert, who also designed the Parc des Princes stadium in Paris, to design something completely original. A billion dollars later, the **Parc Olympique** stunned everyone with its curving, organic concrete shapes, and remains one of this renowned architect's major works.

The **Stade Olympique** ★ ★ ★ *($7.50; guided tours, regular departures from 10am; 4141 Avenue Pierre-De Coubertin,* ☎*514-252-4737 or 877-997-0919, www.rio.gouv.qc.ca; Viau metro)* is also known as the Olympic Stadium, a 56,000-seat oval stadium that features a 175m leaning tower. In the distance, visitors will see the two pyramid-shaped towers of the Olympic Village, where athletes were housed in 1976. Each year, the stadium hosts different events. The Montréal Expos professional baseball team played its home games here from 1977 to 2004, when the team was transferred to Washington, DC.

The stadium's tower, which is the tallest leaning tower in the world, was renamed the **Tour de Montréal**. A funicular *($13; every day 9am to 5pm in high season,* *closed early Jan to mid-Feb)* climbs the structure to an interior observation deck that commands a view of the eastern part of Montreal. On the second floor of the observatory are various exhibits, and there is also a rest area known as Salon Montréal. The foot of the tower houses the swimming pools of the Olympic Complex and a cinema.

The former cycling track, known as the Vélodrome, located nearby, has been converted into an artificial habitat for plants and animals called the **Biodôme de Montréal** ★ ★ ★ *($10.50; late Jun to early Sep every day 9am to 6pm, early Sep to late Jun Tue-Sun 9am to 5pm; 4777 Avenue Pierre-De Coubertin,* ☎*514-868-3000, www.biodome.qc.ca; Viau metro).* This new type of museum, associated with the Jardin Botanique, contains four very different ecosystems—the Tropical Rainforest, the Laurentian Forest, the St. Lawrence Marine Ecosystem and the Polar World—within a space of 10,000m². These are complete micro-climates, including plants, mammals and free-flying birds, and close to real climatic conditions.

As for the **Aréna Maurice-Richard** *(2800 Rue Viau,* ☎*514-872-6666; Viau metro),* it precedes the Olympic Village, with which it is now affiliated, by 20 years. Its rink is the only one in Eastern Canada whose area respects international norms. Canada's Olympic speed-skating team practices here, as do several figure-skating champions. A statue of Maurice Richard has stood in front of the entrance to the arena since 1998. Measuring 2.5m in height and cast at the Inverness Atelier du Bronze, it is the work of sculptors Annick Bourgeau and Jules Lasalle. Ice hockey holds a special place in the hearts of Quebecers and many consider Maurice "The Rocket" Richard (1921-2000) the greatest hockey player of all time. **Univers Maurice "Rocket" Richard** *(free admission; Tue-Sun noon to 6pm; 2800 Rue Viau,* ☎*514-251-9930; Viau metro)* is a small museum in his honour. Located in the arena that bears his name, next to the Olympic facilities, the museum contains equipment, trophies and other significant memorabilia that once belonged to this hero of hockey who played for

Exploring ▪ **Hochelaga-Maisonneuve**

the Canadiens from 1942 to 1960. The museum also has a small boutique with hockey paraphernalia.

··· ⚲ *Return to Boulevard Pie-IX and head south.*

The **Église Saint-Jean-Baptiste-de-LaSalle** *(corner of Rue Hochelaga and Boulevard Pie-IX; Pie-IX metro)* was built in 1964 within the context of the Vatican II liturgical revival. In an effort to maintain its following, members of the Catholic clergy cast aside traditions and introduced an audacious style of architecture, which still, however, did not advance their goal. The evocative mitre-like exterior conceals a depressing interior made of bare concrete, which looks like it is falling onto the congregation.

··· ⚲ *Continue south on Boulevard Pie-IX, then turn left on Rue Ontario.*

In 1912, the Dufresne administration kicked off its policy of grandeur by building the **Hôtel de Ville ★** *(4120 Rue Ontario Est)*, a city hall designed by architect Cajetan Dufort. From 1925 to 1967, the building was occupied by the Institut du Radium, which specialized in cancer research. Since 1981, the edifice has served as the Bibliothèque Maisonneuve, which houses one of the City of Montréal's neighbourhood cultural centres. On the second floor, a 1915 bird's-eye-view drawing of Maisonneuve shows the prestigious buildings as they stood back then, as well as those that remained only on paper.

Built directly in line with Avenue Morgan in 1914, the **Marché Maisonneuve ★** *(4445 Rue Ontario Est, ☎514-937-7754, www.marchespublics-mtl.com)* is one of Montréal's many lovely public markets. Since 1995, it has occupied a much newer building than the one next door, where it was once established. The Marché Maisonneuve is in keeping with a concept of urban design inherited from the teachings of the École des Beaux-Arts in Paris, known as the City Beautiful movement in North America. It is a mixture of parks, classical perspectives and civic and sanitary facilities. De-

signed by Cajetan Dufort, the market was Dufresne's most ambitious project. The centre of **Place du Marché** is adorned with an important work by sculptor Alfred Laliberté entitled *La Fermière* (The Woman Farmer).

··· ⚲ *Follow Avenue Morgan.*

Although small, the **Bain Morgan ★** *(1875 Avenue Morgan)* bath house has an imposing appearance due to its Beaux-Arts elements—a monumental staircase, twin columns, a balustrade on the top and sculptures by Maurice Dubert from France. A bronze entitled *Les Petits Baigneurs* (The Little Bathers) is another piece by Alfred Laliberté. Originally, people came to the public baths not only to relax and enjoy the water, but also to wash, since not all houses in working-class neighbourhoods such as this were equipped with bathrooms.

In 1977, the former Cinéma Granada was converted into a theatre and renamed **Théâtre Denise-Pelletier** *(4353 Rue Ste-Catherine Est)* after one of the great actresses of the Quiet Revolution, who died prematurely. The terra cotta facade is decorated in the Italian Renaissance style. The original interior (1928), designed by Emmanuel Briffa, is of the atmospheric type and has been partially preserved. Above the colonnade of the mythical palace encircling the room is a black vault that used to be studded with thousands of stars, making the audience feel as if they were attending an outdoor presentation. A projector was used to create images of moving clouds and even airplanes flying through the night. The theatre also features the **Salle Fred-Barry** hall.

Heads Up!

⟶ Time for lunch? Give **La Bécane Rouge**'s (see p 250) light, market-fresh meals a try. This neighbourhood bistro is located across the street from Théâtre Denise-Pelletier.

Parc Morgan *(at the southernmost end of Avenue Morgan)* was laid out in 1933 on the site of the country house belonging to

Henry Morgan, owner of the stores of the same name. From the cottage in the centre there is an interesting perspective on the Marché Maisonneuve silhouetted by the enormous Olympic Stadium.

›››🚶 *Follow Rue Sainte-Catherine west to Avenue Létourneux and turn left.*

Maisonneuve boasted two firehouses, one of which had an altogether original design by Marius Dufresne (1915). He was trained as an engineer and businessman, but he also took a great interest in architecture. Impressed by the work of Frank Lloyd Wright, he designed the **Caserne de Pompiers no 1** ★ *(on the south side of Rue Notre-Dame)*, or fire station, as an adaptation of the Unity Temple (1906) in Oak Park, on the outskirts of Chicago. The building was one of the first works of modern architecture erected in Canada.

›››🚶 *Turn right on Avenue Desjardins. Due to the unstable ground in this part of the city, some of the houses tilt to an alarming degree.*

Behind the somewhat drab Romanesque Revival facade of the **Église du Saint-Nom-de-Jésus** ★ *(at the corner of Rue Adam and Avenue Desjardins)*, built in 1906, visitors will discover a rich, polychromatic decor, created in part by artist Guido Nincheri, whose studio was located in Maisonneuve. Particularly noteworthy are the large organs built by the Casavant brothers, divided up between the rear jube and the chancel—very unusual in a Catholic church. Because this building stands on the same shifting ground as neighbouring houses, its vault is supported by metal shafts.

›››🚶 *Follow Avenue Desjardins to the Pie-IX metro station.*

Tour Q: Around the Lachine Canal
★

- -

Little Burgundy and Saint-Henri
★

 three hours

Little Burgundy and Saint-Henri are working-class neighbourhoods that were once both autonomous municipalities. In 1905, however, the cities of Saint-Henri-des-Tanneries and Petite-Bourgogne, or Little Burgundy, then officially known as the City of Sainte-Cunégonde, were annexed by Montréal. Saint-Henri was founded at the end of the 18th century around the Rolland family's tannery, which no longer exists (it was located at the corner of Chemin Glen and Rue Saint-Antoine).

After the opening of the Lachine Canal in 1825, the little town grew significantly, with industries clustering in its southern portion, around the canal. Little Burgundy's prosperity was also ensured by the industries along the canal, as well as by rail transport, since the town was crossed by a series of railroad tracks leading up to the Gare Bonaventure on Rue Peel (destroyed in 1952). The tracks were dismantled during the 1970s to make way for housing, the suburban ap-

★ ATTRACTIONS

Little Burgundy

1.	DY	St. Jude's Church
2.	DY	Église Sainte-Cunégonde
3.	DY	Sainte-Cunégonde City Hall (former)
4.	DZ	Théâtre Corona
5.	CY	Église Saint-Irénée

Saint-Henri

6.	CY	Union United Church
7.	CX	Parisian Laundry

8.	BX	Square Saint-Henri
9.	AY	Place Saint-Henri
10.	BY	Art Deco Fire Station no 23
11.	AX	Musée des Ondes Émile Berliner
12.	AY	Église Saint-Zotique
13.	AY	Square Sir-George-Étienne Cartier
14.	BZ	Merchants Manufacturing Company
15.	CZ	Marché Atwater

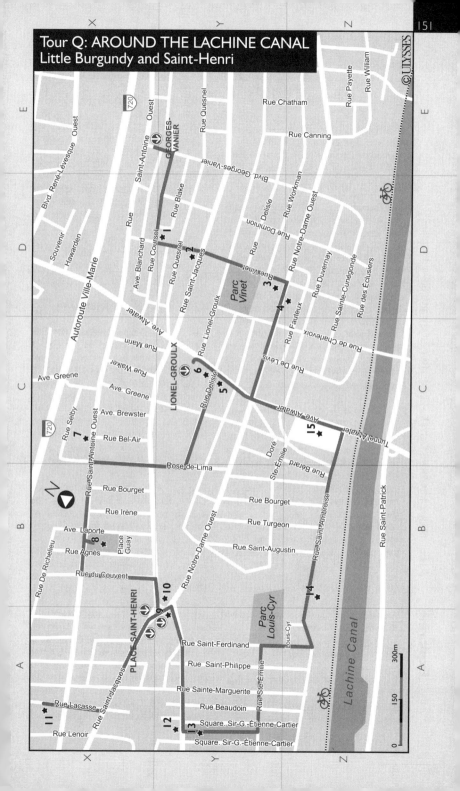

Tour Q: AROUND THE LACHINE CANAL
Little Burgundy and Saint-Henri

© ULYSSES

pearance of which does not at all fit in with the rest of the neighbourhood.

⋯ ⅄ Ⓜ *From the Georges-Vanier metro station, head to the boulevard of the same name. Turn right onto little Rue Coursol.*

The Georges-Vanier metro station and boulevard both honour the memory of General Georges-Philias Vanier (1888-1967), governor general of Canada from 1959 to 1967.

Rue Coursol is lined with charming single-family row houses, built around 1875 for the foremen and semi-skilled workers at the factories in Sainte-Cunégonde. The Second-Empire stone residences on Rue Saint-Antoine Ouest, farther north, were occupied by local notable residents and certain shop owners. Since Sainte-Cunégonde was located near the downtown train stations (**Bonaventure** and **Windsor**, see p 73), a number of houses on these two streets later became boarding houses for railway employees, mainly those who worked on the trains (waiters, packers, cooks, etc.).

Before 1960, most of these employees were black. **Little Burgundy** was thus identified with the black community from the late 19th century on, although there was never a black majority in the neighbourhood. Most of these immigrants, who came here from the United States between 1880 and 1900 in hopes of a better future, contributed greatly to the history of music in Montréal. In fact, Little Burgundy was the birthplace of celebrated jazz pianist Oscar Peterson, as well as the location of a famous cabaret, Rockhead's Paradise, which opened in 1928 at the corner of Rue Saint-Antoine and Rue de la Montagne, and where Louis Armstrong and Cab Calloway played and sang regularly (it closed in 1984).

⋯ ⅄ *Turn left on Rue Vinet.*

On the corner of Rue Vinet is the former **St. Jude's Church** *(2390 Rue Coursol)*, now the Bible-Way Pentecostal Church (1876; Goodwin and Mann, architects).

Église Sainte-Cunégonde ★ *(2641 Rue St-Jacques)*, at the corner of Rue Saint-Jacques, is a large Catholic Beaux-Arts–style church designed by architect Joseph-Omer Marchand in 1906. The building has a remarkable rounded chevet, as well as an ingenious roof with a single-span steel framework that makes it possible to open up the spacious interior, which is completely free of columns and pillars. Decorated with lovely woodwork and vibrantly coloured remounted paintings, which benefit from the natural light coming through the large windows, the interior was damaged when the church was closed in 1971. The building was slated for demolition, but was fortunately saved at the last minute, and is now used, notably, for traditional Catholic services in Latin.

⋯ ⅄ *Take Rue Vinet to Rue Notre-Dame.*

The former **Sainte-Cunégonde City Hall** *(facing Parc Vinet)*, erected at the end of the 19th century, also served as a post office, a firehouse and a police station. Famous strongman Louis Cyr (a statue in his honour can be found at the corner of Rue Saint-Jacques and Rue De Courcelle) was a member of the local police force here for several years.

⋯ ⅄ *Turn right on Rue Notre-Dame.*

The part of **Rue Notre Dame** between Rue Guy to the east and Rue Atwater to the west is nicknamed *"rue des antiquaires"* (antique-dealers row) thanks to the presence of many shops dealing in second-hand goods and, in some cases, local antiques (especially Victorian and Art Deco furniture). These shops, where all sorts of treasures lay hidden, occupy handsome 19th-century commercial buildings, all located on the south side of the street. Behind these sprawl dilapidated factories along the Lachine Canal, some of which were converted into housing complexes during the 1980s. At 2490 Rue Notre-Dame Ouest, visitors can see the facade of the former **Théâtre Corona** (1912; see p 274), whose interior is still intact. It was recently transformed into a concert hall.

Heads Up!

Hunting for antiques? You'll fall head over heels in love with the Victorian and Art Deco items found on Rue Notre-Dame's "antique row," in the Petite-Bourgogne area. While you're there, why not drop by the exotic **Ru de Nam** (see p 253), a boutique which doubles as a restaurant, for lunch?

···🚶 *Turn right on Avenue Atwater.*

Église Saint-Irénée *(3044 Rue Delisle)* is one of those churches whose copper, verdigris-coated bell towers pierce through the low skyline of Montréal's working-class neighbourhoods. It was built in 1912, incorporating a portion of the walls of an earlier church that was built in 1904 and burned down in 1911. Its cramped interior is the work of architects MacDuff and Lemieux. Particularly noteworthy are the exaggerated curves of the arches and the typical Belle Époque motifs used in the decor.

Saint-Henri (a neighbourhood that is colourfully described by Gabrielle Roy in her novel *Bonheur d'occasion*, 1945) starts on the west side of Avenue Atwater.

···🚶 *Head west on Rue Delisle.*

You'll come upon the **Union United Church** *(3007 Rue Delisle)* near the corner of Rue Delisle and Avenue Atwater. The church was built in 1899 and was Québec's first religious institution to be founded by a black community. The church's eventful history makes up for its rather plain architecture: it has welcomed such important figures as Nelson Mandela and Desmond Tutu, and the adjoining house is where famous jazz pianist Oscar Peterson was born. Gospel concerts are sometimes presented here.

···🚶 *Turn right on Rue Rose-de-Lima and then right again on Rue Saint-Antoine.*

Parisian Laundry *(Tue-Fri noon to 6pm, Sat noon to 5pm; 3350 Rue St-Antoine Ouest, ☎514-989-1056, www.parisianlaundry.com;*

Lionel-Groulx metro) follows in the footsteps of the **Fonderie Darling** (see p 63) and the **Craig Pumping Station** (see p 115). All of these are former industrial buildings that have been restored and now feature cultural endeavours. The Laundry Company was a large-scale commercial laundry facility that was purchased by a Montréal collector in 2001. Its concrete-and-steel structure and large windows recall the building's former industrial vocation and provide the perfect setting for artistic exhibits. The prestigious international World Press Photo contest was presented in the art gallery in 2005.

···🚶 *Return to Rue Saint-Antoine and head west. Turn left on Avenue Laporte.*

As in Sainte-Cunégonde, Saint-Henri's upper-class neighbourhood lies along Rue Saint-Antoine. The beautiful **Square Saint-Henri** ★ *(between Avenue Laporte, Place Guay, Rue Agnès and Rue St-Antoine)*, adorned with a cast-iron fountain topped with a statue of Jacques Cartier (1895-1896), was a gathering point for the municipality's affluent residents. Mayor Eugène Guay, who was responsible for laying out these areas, also had a residence built for himself in front of the square, at number 846 Rue Agnès, in 1902. The house was later converted into a quaint bed and breakfast.

···🚶 *Turn left on Rue Saint-Antoine, then left again on Rue du Couvent. Continue southward, then turn right on Rue Saint-Jacques to reach Place Saint-Henri, which is centered around the metro station of the same name.*

The once remarkable **Place Saint-Henri** has been altered beyond recognition. In an unbridled attempt at modernization, the college, school, convent and church, whose Renaissance Revival facade fronted the north side of the square, were torn down in 1969-70 and replaced by a high school and a public pool, concealed behind a blind brick wall. This grouping faces away from the square, which sprung up naturally at the railway crossing of Rue Saint-Jacques and Rue Notre-Dame (the train station was located nearby); at the end of the 18th century, this was the main route to the western part of the island of Montréal.

Only a few buildings have survived the wave of changes that took place in the 1960s. These include the **Art Deco Fire Station no 23**, built in 1931 on the site of the former town hall of Saint-Henri; the **Caisse Populaire** *(4038 Rue St-Jacques Ouest)*, or credit union, which occupies the former post office and the **Banque Laurentienne** *(4080 Rue St-Jacques Ouest)*. The latter used to belong to the City and District Savings Bank of Montréal, whose branches across Montréal display a quality of architecture worthy of special mention.

A detour to the small **Musée des Ondes Émile Berliner** *($3; Fri-Sun 2pm to 5pm; 1050 Rue Lacasse, ☎514-932-9663, www. berliner.montreal.museum; Place St-Henri metro)* will allow you to learn about audiovisual inventions throughout the world. The Musée des Ondes Émile Berliner's mission is to preserve and promote the sound industry's heritage. The exhibits showcase, among other things, television sets and a wide array of radio sets from the 1920s to the 1970s.

››› ⚲ *Return to Place Saint-Henri and cross the square to return to Rue Notre-Dame. Turn right on this street and continue walking to Église Saint-Zotique.*

Église Saint-Zotique *(4565 Rue Notre-Dame Ouest)* was erected in stages between 1910 and 1927 for the least affluent parish in Saint-Henri. This explains the brick facing on the church, a less expensive material than stone. The Baroque Revival steeples rise up from a structure not unlike the industrial buildings along the nearby Lachine Canal. The neighbouring credit-union building oddly resembles some sort of futuristic spaceship.

Square Sir-George-Étienne-Cartier ★ *(Rue Notre-Dame Ouest, in front of Église St-Zotique)* honours the memory of one of the Fathers of Canadian Confederation. It was among the measures approved by the City of Montréal to clean up the neighbourhood and improve the area's reputation, as we shall see a little further.

In 1912, this green space, surrounded by typical Montréal triplexes, replaced the Saint-Henri slaughterhouses, whose putrid stench had permeated the entire area. The pretty cast-iron fountain in the middle of the square is particularly interesting.

››› ⚲ *Cross the square and head east on Rue Sainte-Émilie.*

Rue Sainte-Émilie is lined with typical 19th-century working-class houses. Saint-Henri, like Sainte-Cunégonde and Pointe-Saint-Charles, corresponds to the lower town of Montréal, which, before 1910, was among the poorest areas in North America. Infant mortality was four times higher here than anywhere else on the continent. The workers lived in poverty, steeped in pollution and at the mercy of destructive fires and infectious diseases.

In 1897, local reformist Herbert Browne Ames published *The City Below the Hill*, a work that stands out in the history of urban-renewal movements. It revealed to the world the decrepit state of Montréal's working-class neighbourhoods at the end of the 19th century. Today, renovation and social-assistance programs have put some order back into local streets, but Saint-Henri's future nevertheless remains uncertain since its aging industrial facilities have led to the closing of a number of the factories that provided local families with a living. As if to exaggerate the contrast between the upper and lower city, the hill of Westmount, surrounded by large, luxurious residences shrouded in greenery, is visible to the north if you look straight up most of the streets intersecting with Rue Sainte-Émilie.

››› ⚲ *Turn right on Rue Saint-Ferdinand, and then left on Rue Saint-Ambroise, which runs alongside the Lachine Canal.*

For many years, the **Merchants Manufacturing Company** *(4000 Rue St-Ambroise)* was the main employer in Saint-Henri. Purchased by Dominion Textile in the early 20th century, the factory was used to manufacture fabric, blankets, sheets and clothing. Many women worked in the factory, which, in 1891, was the scene of the first textile strike in Montréal. The long, low building erected in 1880 is a good example of late 19th-century industrial architecture, characterized by large glass windows and staircase towers crowned with brick cornices.

On **Rue Saint-Augustin** *(immediately east of the railroad tracks serving the factories along the Lachine Canal)*, visitors will find some of Saint-Henri's oldest houses, which were inhabited for many years by the poorest local families. Of modest size, they are made of wood (some were recently covered with aluminum siding). The **Maison Clermont** *(110 Rue St-Augustin)*, dating back to 1870, was admirably restored in 1982 and provides a good idea of what this type of working-class dwelling looked like when it was new. It was from these houses, which backed into the railroad tracks, that novelist Gabrielle Roy drew her inspiration.

⋯ 🚶 *Take Rue Saint-Ambroise to Marché Atwater.*

Marché Atwater ★ *(138 Avenue Atwater,* ☎*514-937-7754, www.marchespublic-mtl. com)* is one of Montréal's public markets. Farm-fresh fruits and vegetables are sold outside during summer and fall, while inside, specialty shops sell meat, cheese, fish and bread. The market was built in 1932 as part of job-creation programs initiated during the Great Depression. Designed by architect Ludger Lemieux, it is an elegant Art Deco building.

⋯ 🚶 Ⓜ *Head north on Avenue Atwater to reach the Lionel-Groulx metro station, erected on the Sainte-Cunégonde railroad tracks.*

Pointe-Saint-Charles
★

🕙 *three hours*

The actual point of Pointe-Saint-Charles was named by fur traders Charles Le-Moyne and Jacques LeBer, to whom the piece of land was first granted. They

then sold it to Marguerite Bourgewho built the Ferme Saint-Gabrie the Sœurs de la Congrégation de No Dame here in 1668. The location's toral nature was greatly disrupted by the construction of the Lachine Canal between 1821 and 1825, which attracted various types of mills to the area, turning it into the cradle of the Canadian Industrial Revolution.

The village of Saint-Gabriel sprung up on Saint Charles point, south of the factories. With the construction of the Victoria bridge between 1854 and 1860 and the laying-out of various railroad installations near the St. Lawrence, Saint-Gabriel developed into a veritable little city.

The Irish, omnipresent on the construction sites of these two major projects, settled in large numbers in Saint-Gabriel and other villages farther east (Griffintown, Sainte-Anne and Victoriatown), of which, unfortunately, only a few traces remain. The village of Saint-Gabriel was annexed to Montréal in 1887 and renamed Pointe-Saint-Charles. Though it is located near the downtown area, it is separated from it by the canal and a number of highways, and bisected by railroad tracks. It nevertheless boasts a rich heritage from the Industrial Revolution.

Today, Pointe-Saint-Charles resembles a working-class area whose aging production facilities can barely generate jobs. A few factories have been converted into housing complexes, while the area along the Lachine Canal, which reopened for pleasure boating in 2002, has been transformed into a linear park with a lovely bicycle path.

⋯ 🚶 🚲 Ⓜ *Head east on Rue Centre from the Charlevoix metro station. This tour can also be easily completed by bicycle, starting from the bike path alongside the Lachine canal.*

Victims of a dreadful famine caused by potato blight in the mid-19th century, the Irish fled their country in large numbers to seek refuge in Canada. A lot of them did not make it past Grosse Île, downriver from Québec City, but those who overcame illness went to work on the colonial building sites, forming an inexpensive, unskilled workforce. These people lived in poverty for many years. Their first medieval-looking wooden houses, built in Victoriatown (also known as Village aux Oies), have been torn down and replaced, all in the name of progress.

Église Saint-Gabriel *(2157 Rue Centre; Charlevoix metro)* was built in 1893 by the Irish Catholic community of Pointe-Saint-Charles. At the same time, a French-Canadian Catholic church was being constructed on the neighbouring piece of land. In fact, the two imposing buildings were built side by side by the same architects (Perrault and Mesnard), creating an unusual sight that makes Montréal truly worthy of the nickname "city of a hundred steeples." The original interior decoration of the Saint-Gabriel church was destroyed by fire in 1959, and was replaced by a minimalist decor that highlights the building's thick rubble-stone walls. Next to the church is a lovely Romanesque Revival presbytery with Queen Anne details.

Église Saint-Charles ★ *(2125 Rue Centre; Charlevoix metro)* was consumed by flames in 1913. The following year, it was rebuilt by architects MacDuff and Lemieux, who recreated its Romanesque Revival appearance. The interior, with its columns painted with imitation marble patterns, is worth a short visit. The presbytery of the parish of Saint-Charles is, unlike that of Saint-Gabriel, a symmetrical building with a Beaux-Arts-inspired design.

⋯ ⅄ *Turn left on Rue Island. Cross Rue Saint-Patrick to reach the Parc du Canal de Lachine. Be very careful crossing the bike path, where cycling enthusiasts sometimes ride at high speeds.*

In the 17th century, a farm owned by the Messieurs de Saint-Sulpice, then seigneurs of the island of Montréal, occupied the entire northern part of Pointe-Saint-Charles. In 1689, the Sulpicians, anxious to develop their island, began digging a canal next to Rivière Saint-Pierre, which bordered their property. Their goal was to bypass the famous Lachine rapids, a hindrance to navigation on the St. Lawrence upriver from Montréal. These visionary priests, perhaps too ambitious for their time, launched the project before even asking permission from their order or obtaining funds from the king, both of which they were later denied. Their venture was thus suspended until 1821, when work was begun on the present canal. Later, it was widened twice. However, the opening of the St. Lawrence Seaway in 1959 made the canal obsolete, and it closed in 1970.

In 1978, Parks Canada purchased the canal and its shores and created the **Lachine Canal National Historic Site ★** *(between the Old Port and Lac Saint-Louis, ☎514-283-6054, www.pc.gc.ca/canallachine; Charlevoix or Atwater metro)* in order to preserve the memory of the canal and its role in the country's history. It was later decided that the canal should reopen, its shores redeveloped and its neighbouring districts revitalized. The Lachine Canal was finally opened to pleasure boating in 2002. A lovely multi-purpose path was entirely redone and lines the entire canal over some 15km, from Old Montréal to the **Lachine Visitors Services Centre** (see p 162). As a result, cyclists, pedestrians and in-line skaters can enjoy the canal at their leisure, surrounded by lush greenery.

You can explore the Lachine Canal by taking part in the **Lachine Canal Historical Cruise** *($16.75; late Jun to early Sep every day 1pm and 3:30pm, late May to late Jun and*

★ **ATTRACTIONS**

Pointe-Saint-Charles

1.	CX	Église Saint-Gabriel
2.	CX	Église Saint-Charles
3.	CX	Lachine Canal National Historic Site
4.	DX	Belding Corticelli silk mill
5.	DX	Northern Electric factory (former)
6.	DX	Caserne de Pompiers no. 15
7.	DY	Canadian National Railyards

8.	DY	Grand Trunk houses
9.	CZ	Maison Saint-Gabriel

Verdun

10.	AZ	Vieux Verdun
11.	AZ	Église Notre-Dame-des-Sept-Douleurs
12.	AZ	Île des Sœurs

Tour Q: AROUND THE LACHINE CANAL
Pointe-Saint-Charles and Verdun

Rue Young

Rue Murray

© ULYSSES

Rue Ottawa

Rue du Séminaire

Rue Bridge

Rue de Condé

Rue Basin

Rue de Montmorency

Rue Richmond

Pont des Seigneurs

Rue du Canal

Lachine Canal

Rue Saint-Patrick

Rue Auguste-Cantin

Rue de l'Île

Rue Richardson

Rue Clarendon

Rue Shearer

Rue Grand Trunk

Rue Mullins

Rue Saint-Charles

Rue Ropery

Rue Laprairie

Rue Centre

CHARLEVOIX

Rue Châteauguay

Rue Charlevoix

Rue Knox

Rue Ryde

Rue Coleraine

Rue Rozel

Rue Rushbrooke

Rue Reading

Rue Butler

Ave. Atwater

Saint-Patrick

Rue de Sébastopol

Rue de la Congrégation

Rue Sainte-Madeleine

Rue Bourgeoys

Rue Charon

Ave. Ash

Rue Frank-Selke

Rue Dick-Irving

Rue Wellington

Rue de Paris

Rue Fortune

Rue Liverpool

Rue Hibernia

Hall

Dublin

Pl. Dublin

Rue du Parc-Marguerite-Bourgeoys

Parc Marguerite-Bourgeoys

LASALLE

Rue Henri-Duhamel

Rue Rushbrooke

Rue Wellington

Blvd. LaSalle

Rue Caisse LaSalle

Rue Strathmore

Rue Régina

Rue Dupuis

Rue Claude

Rue Joseph

Rue de Verdun

Rue Evelyn

Rue Gertrude

Rue Ethel

Rue Rhéaume

Rue Lafleur

LaSalle

Troy

Rue Hickson

Rue Ross

Wellington Blvd.

DE L'ÉGLISE

de l'Église

Rue Galt

Rue Gordon

Ave. Rielle

Parc Aqueduc de Montréal

Parc Therrien

St. Lawrence River

Parc Richard

600m

300

0

N

15

15

20

mid-Sep to mid-Oct Sat, Sun and holidays 1pm and 3:30pm; departures near the pedestrian footbridge south of Atwater market; ☎*514-846-0428, www.croisierecanaldelachine.ca).* The cruise takes you through the canal that played such an important role in Canada's industrial development, crossing the Saint-Gabriel lock and Peel basin aboard L'Éclusier, and providing a unique view of the surrounding neighbourhoods.

Heads Up!

→ Why not set sail on the Lachine Canal? Boats, kayaks and pedal-boats can be rented from the kiosk located east of the Atwater market, on the other side of the canal.

››› ⚲ *Walk eastward along the canal and enjoy the view of the industrial buildings and the skyscrapers in the business centre.*

The canal was used not only for navigation but also as a source of power. The former **Belding Corticelli silk mill** ★ *(1790 Rue du Canal; Charlevoix metro)* was one of the establishments that ran its machines on hydraulic energy. The red-brick building has a cast-iron structure. It was erected in 1884 and has since been renovated to make room for apartment lofts. The abandoned former buildings of the Redpath sugar refinery, founded by John Redpath in 1854, stand a little farther along. Redpath, a native of Berwickshire, Scotland, had 17 children and was one of McGill University's principal donors.

››› ⚲ *Head back to Rue Saint-Patrick by walking through the residential complex at the former Belding Corticelli mill, and cross over one of the few arms of the canal that have not been filled in. Turn left on Rue Saint-Patrick, then right on Rue Richmond, which runs alongside the former Northern Electric factory.*

The former **Northern Electric factory** *(1751 Rue Richardson; Charlevoix metro)* houses the Nordelec business "incubator." Dozens of small clothing and contemporary furniture manufacturers share the same secretarial services, as well as the advice of marketing specialists, thereby reducing start-up expenses and making it possible to avoid costly errors while manufacturing their goods or placing them on the market. The huge, monolithic edifice was built between 1913 and 1926 for the Northern Electric Company, which manufactured everyday electrical appliances. The company is now known as Northern Telecom (Nortel). Across the street is the old **Caserne de Pompiers no. 15** *(1255 Rue Richmond)*, a fire station erected in 1903 in a vaguely Romanesque Revival style.

››› ⚲ *Continue south on Rue Richmond.*

In the area around Rue Mullins are some good examples of the residential working-class architecture of Pointe-Saint-Charles. Some houses have even retained their original windows.

››› ⚲ *Turn right on Rue Wellington, then left on Rue de Sébastopol.*

The **Canadian National Railyards** *(east of Rue de Sébastopol; Charlevoix metro)* used to belong to the Grand Trunk Railway, a company founded in London in 1852 with the aim of developing railroads in Canada. It merged with Canadian Northern Railway in 1923 to form Canadian National. The Grand Trunk Railway was behind the construction of the Victoria bridge, and built its repair shops near the bridge exit in 1856.

Rue de Sébastopol borders the railway yard, which was opened in 1855 while the Crimean War, which was marked by the Siege of Sebastopol in Ukraine, was under way in Europe.

The **Grand Trunk houses** *(422 to 444 Rue de Sébastopol; Charlevoix metro)* are among the earliest examples of North-American housing specially designed by a company for its workers. These "company houses," inspired by British models, were built in 1857 by Robert Stephenson (1803-1859), engineer and designer of the Victoria bridge and son of the inventor of the steam engine. Of the seven houses designed by Stephenson, each containing four apartments, only about half remain, while the others are in a sad state of disrepair.

> ⋯ 𝍖 *From Rue de Sébastopol, take Rue Favard.*

Like the neighbouring streets, **Rue Favard** is lined with various examples of residential working-class architecture. Particularly interesting are the patterns of the brick, woodwork and terra cotta inlays. The names of the streets indicate that this area was once owned by the Sœurs de la Congrégation de Notre Dame. The nuns' land was gradually sold off in lots, which explains why the neighbourhood seems newer as you approach the Saint-Gabriel farmhouse.

> ⋯ 𝍖 *Turn left at Place Dublin.*

Maison Saint-Gabriel ★★ *($8, free admission Sat late Jun to early Sep; guided tours mid-Apr to late Jun and early Sep to mid-Dec Tue-Sun 1pm to 5pm; late Jun to early Sep Tue-Sun 11am to 6pm; 2146 Place Dublin, ☎514-935-8136, www.maisonsaint-gabriel. qc.ca; Charlevoix metro and bus no. 57)* offers precious evidence of what daily life was like in New France. The farmhouse and nearby barn, now surrounded by the city, were built between 1662 and 1698. Marguerite Bourgeoys purchased the entire property from the Le Ber family in 1668 as a place of residence for the Dames de la Congrégation de Notre-Dame, a religious community she founded in 1653. The house later served as a school for young Aboriginal girls and as accommodations for the "filles du Roy," who were young women with no families that Louis XIV sent from Paris to Montréal to find husbands here.

In 1966, the house was restored and opened to the public. Since then, it has housed displays of 17th- and 18th-century objects belonging to the community. The building itself is of great interest, as it has, most notably, one of the only authentic 17th-century roof frames in North America, as well as rare sinks made of black stone.

> ⋯ 𝍖 *Head north on Place Dublin, and then along the street of the same name. Turn left onto Rue Wellington.*

Here, visitors will find two Gothic Revival brick churches dating back to the end of the 19th century *(625 Rue Fortune and 2183 Rue Wellington)*, Art-Deco public baths built during the economic crisis of the 1930s *(2188 Rue Wellington)*, and a row of Victorian houses designed around 1875 by the architect of Montréal's City Hall, Henri-Maurice Perrault.

- -
Verdun
★

 one to two hours, not counting an excursion to Île des Sœurs

> ⋯ 𝍖 *The trek from Pointe-Saint-Charles to Verdun will take you about 10min. Follow Rue Wellington to Boulevard LaSalle. Turn left on Avenue Lafleur, which leads to Avenue Troy.*

Until the municipal merger of 2002, Verdun was an autonomous municipality of about 60,000 inhabitants. Many descendants of Irish-Catholic immigrants, along with French Canadians, took up residence here between the two World Wars. Its history began in 1665, when eight militiamen settled alongside the river, west of the Ferme Saint-Gabriel. These armed colonists, nicknamed "les Argoulets," were ultimately massacred by the Iroquois. In 1671, the territory was granted to Zacharie Dupuis, a native of Saverdun, near Carcassonne, France, who named it Verdun in memory of his former village. Between 1852 and 1865, the channel of the aqueduct of Montréal was dug in the northern portion of Verdun. A village emerged south of the aqueduct, but its development was slowed by frequent spring floods. Once a dyke was built along the river (1895), its growth accelerated. Today, 97% of **Vieux Verdun** *(east of Avenue Willibrord; De l'Église metro)* is urbanized. The city contains a large number of buildings

Exploring – Around the Lachine Canal – Verdun

that are typical of Montréal, as well as an astonishing variety of charming loggias.

In the 1930s and 1940s, many families from the Îles de la Madeleine were attracted to this area by the jobs offered at the nearby hospital, the Hôpital du Christ-Roi. In those years, nurses were required to be fully bilingual since the hospital served a population that was half anglophone, half francophone. At the time, the Madelinots, as natives of the Îles de la Madeleine are known, were among the few Quebecers capable of expressing themselves in both of Canada's official languages.

One of the entrances to Parc Therrien, which runs alongside the St. Lawrence, is located at the end of Rue Troy. From the park, visitors can enjoy a lovely view of the skyscrapers of downtown Montréal to the east and the residential high-rises of Île des Sœurs to the south.

⋯ 🚶 *Walk west along Parc Therrien to the Auditorium de Verdun, then take Avenue de l'Église to Rue Wellington.*

The **Église Notre-Dame-des-Sept-Douleurs** ★ *(4155 Rue Wellington; De l'Église metro)* is one of the largest parish churches on the island of Montréal. It was built between 1911 and 1914 and designed by Joseph Venne. The Baroque Revival interior is particularly interesting. A handsome Art-Deco bank (1931) stands across the street.

⋯ Ⓜ *The nearby De L'Église metro station is on the same line as the Charlevoix station, the starting point of this tour.*

⋯ 🚶 🚗 🚌 Ⓜ *Those who wish to visit Île des Sœurs should plan on making a separate trip, as the island is difficult to reach from Verdun. To get there, follow Rue Wellington east to Autoroute 20, heading towards the Champlain bridge. Bus no. 12, which goes to the island from the LaSalle metro station, is a good option for those who aren't driving.*

Île des Sœurs ★, literally translated as "Nun's Island," is sure to interest contemporary-architecture buffs. The island was

originally named "Île Saint-Paul," in honour of Paul de Chomedey. Between 1706 and 1769, the island's various seigniorial facilities were purchased by the nuns of the Congrégation de Notre-Dame religious community. Around 1720, a large stone manor and various farm buildings were erected on the northern part of the island. After the nuns left in 1956, the buildings were destroyed by fire. The island passed into the hands of an important developer who laid out the first streets and built three residential high-rises *(on Boulevard de l'Île des Sœurs, southwest of Rue Corot)*. These were designed in 1967 by celebrated German architect Ludwig Mies van der Rohe, who also drew up the plans for the elegant gas station near Rue Berlioz (1968).

The more recent projects carried out on Île des Sœurs have been more or less successful. The best include the yellow-brick houses on Rue Corot, designed in 1982 by architect Dan Hanganu, and the housing in the "L'Isle" development project *(Chemin du Golf and Chemin Marie-LeBer)*, the work of architect and professor Aurèle Cardinal.

Tour R: West Island and Surroundings ★★

 one day

The only real riverside tour on the island of Montréal, this visit to the "West Island," as the western part of this island is known, will allow visitors to discover old villages and the loveliest panoramic views of the St. Lawrence, Lac Saint-Louis and Lac des Deux Montagnes. Although a number of the towns that make up the West Island were founded by French colonists, many now have an anglophone majority. Therefore, don't be surprised to hear the language of Shakespeare more often than that of Molière in the shops and along residential streets.

This is not considered an urban walking tour since it covers nearly 50km. It can, however, be a bike tour, because a good part of the excursion runs along either a well laid-out bike path or streets with low speed limits. It is possible to reach the starting point of the tour by following the Lachine Canal bike path from Old Montréal. Drivers coming from downtown should take Autoroute 20 Ouest, then Route 138 briefly towards the Mercier Bridge.

Take the exit for Rue Clément in LaSalle. Turn right on Rue Clément, left on Rue Saint-Patrick, then immediately left on Avenue Stirling to reach the river.

Lachine
★ ★

In 1667, the Messieurs de Saint-Sulpice granted some land on the western part of the island of Montréal to explorer Robert Cavelier de La Salle, who, obsessed with the idea of finding a passage to China, later discovered Louisiana at the mouth of the Mississippi. Montrealers mockingly referred to his land as *La Chine* (China), a name that later became official. In 1689, the inhabitants of Lachine were victims of the worst Iroquois massacre of the French Regime. However, instead of leaving the area, the population grew. Two forts were built to protect Lachine, strategically located upriver from the rapids of the same name, which at the time still hindered shipping on the St. Lawrence. Consequently, the precious furs from the hinterland destined for the European market had to be unloaded at Lachine and transported by land to Montréal, located downriver from the rapids. In the years following the opening of the Lachine Canal in 1825, many industries set up shop in Lachine, leading to an important period of urbanization. Today, its aging industry is fortunately counterbalanced by an enchanting location that still charms and attracts enthusiastic residents.

The **Moulin Fleming** *(free admission; late Apr to late Aug Sat-Sun 11am to 5pm; 9675 Boulevard LaSalle, in Parc Stinson,* ☎*514-367-*1000; Angrignon metro and bus no. 110 or 106), although located within the limits of the former city of LaSalle, is closely linked to the development of Lachine, to which it used to belong. Built in 1816 for a Scottish merchant, the mill is cone-shaped, like mills in the United States. An exhibition relates its history.

Fort Rémy, one of the two fortified enclosures in Lachine, stood nearby. It was built to protect the village's first stone church, which was erected in 1703 but no longer exists. The former Burrows-Welcome pharmaceutical factory, which can be seen to the west, is now the town hall for the borough of LaSalle.

Follow Boulevard LaSalle to Chemin du Musée. Turn left to reach the parking lot of the Musée de Lachine, which faces Chemin LaSalle.

The **Musée de Lachine** ★ *(free admission; Apr to Dec Wed-Sun 11:30am to 4:30pm: 1 Chemin du Musée,* ☎*514-634-3471 ext. 346; Angrignon metro and bus no. 110)* is located in a former trading post (**Maison LeBer-LeMoyne**, *110 Chemin LaSalle*) and its fur warehouse (**La Dépendance**), perforated with loopholes for its defence, the oldest extant structures in the entire Montréal region. At the time of their construction in 1670, Lachine was the last inhabited area in the St. Lawrence Valley before the wilderness to the west. It was also the final destination of cargoes of fur, for many years Canada's main natural resource and the true *raison d'être* of the French colonies in North America. The building was erected for Jacques LeBer and Charles LeMoyne, two wealthy Montréal merchants. This history museum has existed since 1948 and also features a visual-arts centre, the **Pavillon Benoît-Verdickt**.

Take Chemin LaSalle, in front of the museum. Turn right on Chemin du Canal, then left on Chemin du Musée, which becomes Boulevard Saint-Joseph.

What is known as the **Musée Plein Air de Lachine** ★ *(*☎*514-634-3471, ext. 346)* is actually some 50 outdoor sculptures scattered throughout Parc René-Lévesque (see below) and other riverside parks along Lac Saint-Louis in Lachine.

Three narrow, man-made spits of land make up the **mouth of the Lachine Canal**, which resembles a sprawling estuary widening at the end. The majestic Lac Saint-Louis extends beyond **Parc René-Lévesque ★ ★**, accessible from Chemin du Canal. The park is dotted with a number of contemporary sculptures. The Lachine Yachting Club occupies the second strip of land, while the **Promenade du Père Marquette ★** and **Parc Monk ★** lie between the original entrance of the canal, opened in 1825, and the widening that was added in 1848.

Located at the entrance to the canal, next to the recently restored lock, the **Lachine Visitors Services Centre** *(free admission; mid-May to early Sep every day 9:30am to 5pm;* ☎*514-283-6054, www.pc.gc.ca)* will allow you to be well prepared for a tour of the canal. Here, you will learn about all the services offered along the canal (on the **Lachine Canal National Historic Site ★**, see p 156), its history and its heritage. There is a snack bar, a sales kiosk and

terraces with great views; there is also an outdoor interpretation trail. In addition, the exhibit *A 300-Year-Old Project* is currently being presented, with old photographs and objects, maps and plans, as well as interactive games. A documentation centre on the canal *(by appointment:* ☎*514-283-6054)* can also be found here, boasting some 3,000 archives.

Heads Up!

Not afraid to get wet? Head to **Descentes sur le Saint-Laurent** (see p 182) in LaSalle for a thrill-a-minute ride on the Lachine rapids.

⋯🚗 *Follow Promenade du Père-Marquette to reach the next attraction.*

The **Fur Trade at Lachine National Historic Site ★** *($4; early Apr to early Oct every day 9:30am to 12:30pm and 1pm to 5pm, mid-Oct to late Nov Wed-Sun 9:30am 12:30pm and 1pm to 5pm, closed Dec to Apr; 1255 Boulevard St-Joseph,* ☎*514-637-7433 or 283-6054 off-season; Angrignon metro and bus*

Exploring – West Island and Surroundings – Lachine

The Lachine Canal: Then and Now

The mainspring of Montréal's industrialization, the 13.5km-long Lachine Canal has been part of the city's heritage since the 19th and 20th centuries, when its excavation and the building of its sluice gates made it possible to bypass the tumultuous Lachine Rapids, after a few fruitless attempts.

François Dollier de Casson, the Superior of the Sulpician order, was the first, in 1689, to believe in the project of a canal bypassing the rapids and leading to the Great Lakes. The project was ultimately abandoned in midstream due to high costs. After the conquest of New France, a similar project was undertaken by the British and, after seven years of studies, negotiations and petitions, was completed between 1812 and 1819.

It was then that Montréal merchants formed the Company of the Lachine Canal in order to finally complete the present canal. The company went bankrupt in 1821, but the project was taken over and the work completed by the government of Lower Canada. The widening of the canal, as well as the restoration and addition of locks, would proceed without interruption between its opening in 1825 and that of the St. Lawrence Seaway in 1959. The Lachine Canal was closed to maritime traffic between 1970 and 2002, when it re-opened to pleasure boats for summer.

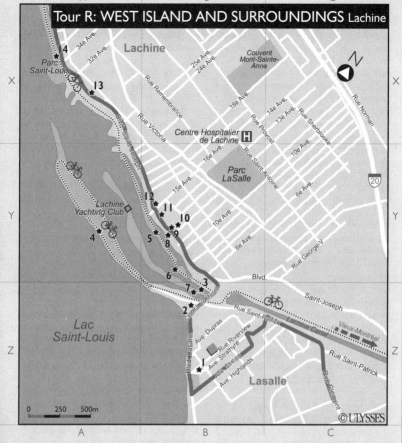

Tour R: WEST ISLAND AND SURROUNDINGS Lachine

★ ATTRACTIONS

1. BZ Moulin Fleming
2. BZ Musée de Lachine / Maison LeBer-LeMoyne / La Dépendance / Pavillon Benoît-Verdickt
3. BZ Mouth of the Lachine Canal
4. AY Parc René-Lévesque
5. BY Promenade du Père-Marquette
6. BY Parc Monk
7. BZ Lachine Visitors Services Centre
8. BY Fur Trade at Lachine National Historic Site
9. BY Couvent Sainte-Anne
10. BY St. Stephen's Anglican Church
11. BY Église des Saints-Anges Gardiens
12. BY St. Andrew's United Church
13. AX Complexe Culturel Guy-Descary / Brasserie Dawes / Pavillon de l'Entrepôt / Maison du Brasseur / Vieille Brasserie
14. AX Fort Rolland

no. 195). For nearly two centuries, the fur trade was the main economic activity in the Montréal region. Lachine played a crucial role in the transportation of pelts to the European market—so much so that the Hudson's Bay Company made it the centre of its operations. The National Historic Site occupies the company's former warehouse, erected in 1803. Various objects and examples of furs and clothing made with these pelts are on display. An interactive exhibition transports visitors back to the 19th century. Temporary ex-

hibits also explore the lives of the trappers, or *voyageurs* (the Aboriginal people who, in the 17th century, caught most of the animals), as well as the heads of the powerful French and English companies who were engaged in a bitter struggle for monopoly on this lucrative trade.

›››🚗 *Continue west on Boulevard Saint-Joseph.*

In 1861, the sisters of Sainte-Anne purchased a house built in 1833 for Sir George Simpson, then head of the

Hudson's Bay Company. They built their mother house, and then a convent school for young girls, the **Couvent Sainte-Anne** ★ *(1300 Boulevard St-Joseph)*, around the original building. This house was later demolished and replaced in 1889 with an imposing, Russian-style chapel topped with a silvery dome designed by architects Maurice Perrault and Albert Mesnard. The interior of the chapel, reminiscent of a Victorian concert hall, can be visited upon request. The convent is also home to the **Musée Sainte-Anne** *(voluntary contribution; mid-May to mid-Jun and Sep to late Nov Thu-Sun 1pm to 4:30pm, mid-Jun to late Aug Wed-Sun 10am to noon and 1pm to 4:30pm; ☎514-637-4616; Angrignon metro and bus no. 195)*, where works of art and religious costumes provide a glimpse of the history of the sisters of Sainte-Anne religious community.

Behind the convent, visitors will find **St. Stephen's Anglican Church** *(25 12ᵉ Avenue)*, built in 1831 to serve the executive personnel of the Hudson's Bay Company. The humble, vaguely Gothic Revival–style building, made of rubble stone, contrasts with the immense Catholic church located nearby.

Until 1865, the Catholic church of Lachine was located farther east, in the enclosure at Fort Rémy. That year, a French Gothic Revival church was inaugurated on the present site, in the centre of the town. Unfortunately, a huge fire destroyed it in 1915. The present **Église des Saints-Anges Gardiens** *(1400 Boulevard St-Joseph)* was erected on the ruins of the former church in 1919, according to plans by architects Dalbé Viau and Alphonse Venne. This huge parish church was built in the Romanesque Revival style.

St. Andrew's United Church *(75 15ᵉ Avenue)*, once Presbyterian, is located near the Catholic church. It was built in the Gothic Revival style in 1832 and designed by John Wells. Its bell tower was damaged by fire a few years ago. At 1560 Boulevard Saint-Joseph, visitors will see the lovely residence of the church's pastor, the Reverend Doctor, whose openings are framed by small, neoclassical columns (1845).

The **Complexe Culturel Guy-Descary** ★★ *(2901 Boulevard St-Joseph, ☎514-634-3471, ext. 302; Angrignon metro and bus no. 195)* is actually comprised of three buildings that once belonged to the Dawes brewery, which established itself in Lachine in the early 19th century: the **Pavillon de l'Entrepôt**, the **Maison du Brasseur** and the **Vieille Brasserie**. It houses a lovely 318-seat concert hall, a temporary-exhibit space and another space for its permanent exhibit on beer making, as well as reception halls.

The **Brasserie Dawes** opened in Lachine in 1811 to provide beer for trappers and traders passing through. The company closed in 1922 after the merger of several small regional breweries. The facilities, among the oldest of their kind in North America, can nevertheless still be found on either side of Boulevard Saint-Joseph. On the lake side, visitors will see the brewery (two rubble-stone buildings erected around 1850), as well as the home of Thomas Amos Dawes, son of the company founder, built in 1862. The great ice house, converted into apartments (1878), and the old warehouse (circa 1820), located at the end of 21ᵉ Avenue, lie on the city side. The remains of the working-class neighbourhood centered around the brewery completes this grouping, which is of exceptional anthropological value.

›››➾ *Continue westward on Boulevard Saint-Joseph.*

A monument reminds visitors that **Fort Rolland** *(west of 34ᵉ Avenue)*, the main trading post in Lachine in the 17th century, was once located on this site. Military troops were stationed here to ensure the protection of local inhabitants and to supervise the transshipment of precious cargoes of fur. On their way, visitors will see some lovely houses dating back to the French Regime, including the **Maison Quesnel** *(5010 Boulevard St-Joseph)*, built around 1750, and the **Maison Picard** *(5430 Boulevard St-Joseph)*, erected in 1719.

››› *Once in the city of Dorval, Boulevard Saint-Joseph is known as Lakeshore Drive. Although sometimes called Chemin du Bord-du-Lac, it is the same road.*

Dorval

★

In 1691, Sieur d'Orval purchased La Présentation, a fort established by the Sulpicians in 1667, from the estate of Pierre Le Gardeur of Repentigny, and named it after himself. Later, from 1790 to 1821, the small **Dorval Island**, located opposite the city, became the point of departure of the Northwest Company's *coureurs des bois* and *voyageurs*, who travelled to the Outaouais and Great Lakes regions in search of beaver pelts each year. Nowadays, Dorval is a comfortable Montréal suburb, known mainly for its international airport (recently renamed after Pierre Elliott Trudeau). It is still possible to find old farmhouses here that have been carefully restored by their residents, who clearly appreciate the decorative elements of Québec's French heritage.

The stone walls at the base of the **Maison Frederick Barlow** *(900 Chemin du Bord-du-Lac)* are supposedly those of the Sulpicians' Fort de La Présentation, erected in the 17th century. At number 940, visitors will see the **Maison André Legault dit Deslauriers**, with its decorative firebreak walls (1817). Before being carefully restored by architect Galt Durnford in 1934, it was the summer home of Lord Strathcona, one of the Canadian Pacific's principal shareholders.

Maison Minnie Louise Davis *(1240 Chemin du Bord-du-Lac)*, built in 1922, reveals the interest certain architects of British descent and their clients had in traditional Québec architecture between the two World Wars. These individuals even went so far as to build new homes in the style of the 18th century. Percy Nobbs, a professor of architecture at McGill University, drew up the plans for the Davis house, which its owner called "Le Canayen" (*Le Canadien*, or The Canadian, as pronounced with a heavy Québecois accent).

A number of sporting clubs once favoured by Montréal's anglophone bourgeoisie are located in Dorval, including the Royal Montreal Golf Club, the oldest golf club in North America (it was founded in 1873), and the Royal St. Lawrence Yacht Club, founded in 1888, whose facilities can still be seen on the edge of Lac Saint-Louis. The most unusual of these clubs, however, is without question the Forest and Stream Club, which occupies the former villa of Alfred Brown, **Maison Brown** *(1800 Chemin du Bord-du-Lac)*, erected in 1872. Though still in existence, the organization has seen better days. Back in the 1920s, tea was served to dozens of guests in its gardens on Saturday and Sunday summer afternoons.

⋯🚐 *Continue to Pointe-Claire.*

Pointe-Claire

★

One of the first missions established by the Sulpicians along the periphery of the island of Montréal, Pointe-Claire has become a comfortable suburb that has nevertheless preserved the core of its original village. Up until 1940, Chemin du Bord-du-Lac, which leads through West-Island municipalities from Lachine to Sainte-Anne-de-Bellevue, passing through Pointe-Claire on the way, was the only route for motorists travelling from Montréal to Toronto.

Stewart Hall *(free admission; park open year-round; art gallery Mon-Fri and Sun 1pm to 5pm, also Mon and Wed 7pm to 9pm; 176 Chemin du Bord-du-lac, ☎514-630-1220)* is a rather long house, built in 1915 for industrialist Charles Wesley MacLean by Robert Findlay. Since 1963, it has served as Pointe-Claire's cultural centre and is therefore open to the public, offering visitors a chance to see its interior and enjoy unobstructed views of Lac Saint-Louis from its back porch, a pleasure previously reserved for its owner alone.

Built in 1710, the tiny **Maison Antoine-Pilon** *(258 Chemin du Bord-du-Lac)* is the oldest house in Pointe-Claire. Recent work has restored its former appearance.

▸▸▸🚗 *Turn left on Rue Sainte-Anne to reach Pointe Claire (the actual point), extending into Lac Saint-Louis. The institutional buildings of the traditional village are clustered here.*

Église Saint-Joachim ★ *(2 Rue Ste-Anne)* is a Gothic Revival church (1882) with an extremely original steeple that dominates the entire institutional grouping. It is one of the last buildings designed by Victor Bourgeau, the architect of dozens of churches in the Montréal area. Its flamboyant, polychrome wooden interior, decorated with numerous statues, is worth a short visit. The **convent** *(1 Rue Ste-Anne)* of the Sœurs de la Congrégation de Notre-Dame was built in 1867 on the southern portion of the windswept point. The **mill** *(1 Rue St-Joachim)*, which could not have been built in a better spot, was erected in 1709 by the Messieurs de Saint-Sulpice.

▸▸▸🚗 *Return to Chemin du Bord-du-Lac and head toward Beaconsfield and Baie d'Urfé. These two municipalities form the heart of the English-speaking West Island. They also, however, include a number of old properties once owned by prosperous French-Canadian families.*

Beaconsfield

Jean-Baptiste de Valois, a direct descendant of the French Royal family, settled in Canada in 1723. His son, Paul Urgèle Gabriel, commissioned **Le Bocage** ★ *(26 Chemin Du Bord-du-Lac)* in 1810. Houses with cut-stone facades were extremely rare in rural areas in the early 19th century, so this one indicates the special status of its owner. In 1874, Le Bocage was sold to Henri Menzies, who converted the property into a vineyard. The experiment was a pitiful failure due to the unproductive soil and, above all, the location's exposure to both warm and cold winds. Menzies was more successful in naming the estate Beaconsfield, in honour of British Prime Minister Disraeli, annointed Lord Beaconsfield by Queen Victoria. From 1888 to 1966, the house was used by a private club before becoming the Beaconsfield Yacht Club's lounge.

Sainte-Anne-de-Bellevue
★

Just like Lachine, Sainte-Anne-de-Bellevue has a more or less compact centre, compressed along the lakeside panoramic road that here takes on the name Rue Sainte-Anne. Visitors will find numerous boutiques and a number of restaurants, most of which have quaint terraces looking out on the water behind the buildings. The houses on Île Perrot

Exploring – West Island and Surroundings – Pointe-Claire

★ **ATTRACTIONS**

Dorval

1. CY Dorval Island
2. CY Maison Frederick Barlow
3. CY Maison André Legault dit Deslauriers
4. CY Maison Minnie Louise Davis
5. CY Maison Brown

Pointe-Claire

6. CY Stewart Hall
7. CY Maison Antoine-Pilon
8. CZ Église Saint-Joachim
9. CZ Sœurs de la Congrégation de Notre-Dame convent
10. CZ Mill

Beaconsfield

11. BZ Le Bocage

Sainte-Anne-de-Bellevue

12. BZ Macdonald College
13. AY Écomuseum

14. AZ Daoust General Store
15. AZ Maison Simon Fraser
16. AZ Lock

Sainte-Geneviève

17. BY Église Sainte-Geneviève
18. BY Maison d'Ailleboust-de Manthet
19. BY Monastère Sainte-Croix (former)

Saint-Laurent

20. DX Pensionnat Notre-Dame-des-Anges
21. DX Église Saint-Laurent
22. DX Chapelle Mariale Notre-Dame-de-l'Assomption, presbytery and former grain warehouse
23. DX Collège de Saint-Laurent
24. DX Salle Émile-Legault
25. DX Musée des Maîtres et Artisans du Québec

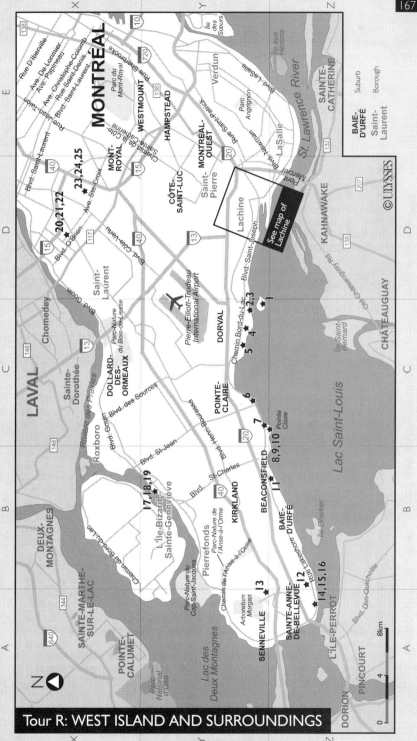

Tour R: WEST ISLAND AND SURROUNDINGS

©ULYSSES

are visible across the water. The village owes its existence to the lock, today used by pleasure crafts to pass from Lac Saint-Louis to the very beautiful Lac des Deux Montagnes, into which the Rivière des Outaouais (Ottawa River) flows. Just east of the old village, visitors will find a comfortable suburb and institutions such as the Veterans' hospital, Macdonald College and John Abbott College, an anglophone CÉGEP (post-secondary college).

Arriving in Sainte-Anne-de-Bellevue, visitors will be surprised to see a whole series of English Baroque Revival buildings faced with orange brick, surrounding a vast, closely trimmed lawn, including **Macdonald College** ★ *(21111 Chemin du Bord-du-Lac)*. Erected between 1905 and 1908, they are part of the Macdonald Campus of McGill University's Department of Agriculture. Some of the buildings belong to John Abbott College, the only English CEGEP west of Vanier College, in Ville St-Laurent.

The goal of the **Écomuseum** ★ *($7; every day 9am to 4pm; from Montréal, take Autoroute 40 Ouest to Exit 41 and follow Chemin Ste-Marie; 21125 Chemin Ste-Marie,* ☎*514-457-9449, www.ecomuseum.ca)* is to educate the public about the flora and fauna of the St. Lawrence plain. In a large, well-laid-out park, visitors can see several different animal species, including foxes and black bears. There is also an aviary for aquatic birds.

In the centre of the village is the **Daoust General Store** *(73 Rue Ste-Anne,* ☎*514-457-5333)*. This once-common type of family business has now practically disappeared in Québec. Founded in 1902, the Daoust store sold everything from flour to boots, wool blankets and snuff. These days they mostly sell knick-knacks and clothing. The best reason to stop in, however, is to see the Lamson money conveyor in action. This system of cables, pulleys and suspended rails, one of the few still in use in Canada, links the various departments of the store to a central cash register. It was installed in 1924.

Around 1960, the **Maison Simon Fraser** *(153 Rue Ste-Anne)* was slated for demolition in order to make way for the ramp of the bridge on Autoroute 20. It was saved by a historical society, but the bridge, built a few years later, passes less than 5m from the house, occupied sporadically by Simon Fraser in the early 19th century. This Montréal merchant was one of the heads of the Northwest Company, which specialized in fur trading. It was here that Irish poet Thomas Moore (1779-1852) stayed during his trip to North America in 1804 and composed his famous *Canadian Boat Song*, in memory of the "voyageurs" who passed through Sainte-Anne-de-Bellevue on their way to the forests of the Canadian shield. The house now serves as a non-profit café run by the Victorian Order of Nurses, a charitable organization founded in the 19th century to provide assistance and home care to sick people.

This is the western tip of the island of Montréal, 50km from the eastern extremity at Pointe-aux-Trembles. Running alongside the **lock** *(mid-May to mid-Oct; 170 Rue Ste-Anne,* ☎*514-457-5546)* is a lovely boardwalk where visitors can watch the doors of the lock opening and closing, and the chambers filling with water and crowded with pleasure craft and Sunday-afternoon captains. A tiny beach and picnic area lie nearby. The Église Sainte-Anne (1853-1875) and the convent face the lock north of the bridges.

▸▸▸ 🚗 *Follow the curve of Rue Sainte-Anne, then turn left on* **Chemin Senneville** ★★.

This road passes through Senneville, the most rural of all of the agglomerations on the island of Montréal. As a matter of fact, it is here that visitors will find the last farms on the island, as well as a number of large properties on the shores of Lac des Deux Montagnes. The country setting lends itself marvellously well to cycling excursions. The road then leads through Pierrefonds, where two important regional parks are located: **Parc-Nature de L'Anse-à-l'Orme** (see p 177), and **Parc-Nature du Cap-Saint-Jacques** ★★ (see p 176).

The Quartier Latin and its main thoroughfare: lively and colourful Rue Saint-Denis.
© *Philippe Renault*

A romantic winter afternoon spent exploring the Parc du Mont-Royal aboard a horse-drawn carriage.
© *Tourisme Montréal, Daniel Choinière*

A few of the famous colourful Victorian houses that border Square Saint-Louis.
© *Patrick Escudero*

Remnants of the Expo 67 World Fair, the Habitat 67 apartments stand over the Cité du Havre area.
© *Philippe Renault*

Pont Jacques-Cartier, one of the Island of Montréal's most emblematic structures.
© *Philippe Renault*

Heads Up!

Feel like skiing? Some 32km of cross-country ski trails are maintained at **Parc-Nature du Cap-Saint-Jacques** (see p 176), while the park's sugar shack provides a sweet resting spot (pun definitely intended) along the way.

''' *In Pierrefonds, Chemin Senneville becomes Boulevard Gouin and keeps this name across the entire island, all the way to the far eastern point.*

Sainte-Geneviève
★

The old village of Sainte-Geneviève is a francophone enclave in the borough of Pierrefonds. Its origins date back to 1730, when a small fort was built here to defend the portage of the Rapides du Cheval-Blanc on Rivière des Prairies, which ran alongside the village. In the 19th century, the *cageux*, robust fellows who floated logs down the river toward Québec, where the largest shipyards were then located, used to stop in Sainte-Geneviève. There they made rafts (called *cages*, hence their name) with the logs in order to pass through the many rapids along Rivière des Prairies. Starting in 1880, this method of floating logs was gradually replaced by rail transport.

Église Sainte-Geneviève ★ ★ *(16037 Boulevard Gouin Ouest)* is the only building designed by the Baillargé family in the Montréal region. Thomas Baillargé designed the church in 1836, giving it an imposing neoclassical facade with two bell towers, thereby influencing the architecture of Catholic churches across the entire region during the 1840s and 1850s. The interior was inspired by a since-vanished church in Rotterdam, built by the architect Guidici. Of particular interest are the tabernacle and the tomb of Ambroise Fournier, as well as the painting in the choir, entitled *Sainte-Geneviève*, by Ozias Leduc. The church is flanked by the convent of Sainte-Anne

and the presbytery, and has outdoor Stations of the Cross made of bronzed cast iron, executed by the Union Artistique de Vaucouleurs in France.

Like the church, the **Maison d'Ailleboust-de-Manthet** *(closed to the public; 15886 Boulevard Gouin Ouest)* is neoclassical in style. It was built in 1845 and occupied by the d'Ailleboust de Manthet family, one of the great French-Canadian families of the 18th and 19th centuries, whose members won fame in both military and civilian circles on a number of occasions.

At the bend in the road, visitors will see the Lombard-style former **Monastère Sainte-Croix ★** *(15693 Boulevard Gouin Ouest)*, which looks like it came straight out of the Middle Ages. It was in fact built for the fathers of Sainte-Croix in 1932 by talented architect Lucien Parent. The cloister in the centre is a haven of peace and serenity. The building was sold in 1968 and is now home to Collège Gérald-Godin.

''' ⊕ *Continue on Boulevard Gouin.*

After crossing the eastern portion of Pierrefonds, the road leads through Roxboro. A little further are two regional parks, **Parc-Nature du Bois-de-Liesse** (see p 176) and Bois-de-Saguenay.

Heads Up!

Feel like a forest stroll? The maintained trails at **Parc-Nature du Bois-de-Liesse** (see p 176) are perfect for nature-hiking buffs.

''' *Turn right on Boulevard O'Brien, then take the fork in the road leading to Avenue Sainte-Croix, the last leg of this tour.*

Saint-Laurent
★

The residential part of Saint-Laurent is concentrated on a fifth of what was once this municipality's territory. The rest is monopolized by a huge industrial park, making it the second-largest industrial city in Québec. Saint-Laurent developed inland after the signing of the peace treaty with the Iroquois tribes in 1701. The arrival of the Fathers, Brothers and Sisters of Sainte-Croix in 1847, encouraged by Monseigneur Ignace Bourget, the second bishop of Montréal, made it possible for the village to grow, dominated by the institutions of this religious community from Le Mans, France.

The former convent school of the Sisters of Sainte-Croix, the **Pensionnat Notre-Dame-des-Anges** *(821 Avenue Ste-Croix)*, was founded in 1862, while the modern chapel by architect Gaston Brault was added in 1953. A wing of the building was once occupied by the Collège Basile-Moreau, one of the only institutions in Québec to offer higher education in French to young women before the Quiet Revolution. In 1970, the convent became Vanier College, an anglophone CÉGEP.

The design of **Église Saint-Laurent ★** *(805 Avenue Ste-Croix)*, built in 1835, was inspired by Montréal's Église Notre-Dame, inaugurated six years earlier. Unfortunately, both the pinnacles and the decorative battlements of the facade and aisles were removed in 1868. What was the oldest extant Gothic Revival interior decor in a Catholic church, executed by François Dugal and Janvier Archambault between 1836 and 1845, was spoiled during the frenzied wave of religious revival of Vatican II in the early 1960s.

South of the church, visitors will find the **Chapelle Mariale Notre-Dame-de-l'Assomption**, the **presbytery** and the **former grain warehouse** (1810), where parishioners could pay their tithe in the form of grain and other foodstuffs. It now serves as the church hall.

When the Fathers and Brothers of Sainte-Croix arrived in Canada in 1847, they were lodged in the house located at number 696 Boulevard Sainte-Croix. In 1852, they moved across the street to their college. The building has been modified and enlarged on several occasions. Over the course of its history, the **Collège de Saint-Laurent ★** *(625 Avenue Ste-Croix; Du Collège metro)* has stood out for its avant-garde policies. Accordingly, it trained businessmen at a time when greater importance was given to the priesthood, law, medicine and the notarial profession. During the 1880s, a biology museum was created here, which was later set up inside an octagonal tower in 1896. That same year, the college built a 300-seat auditorium for the students' theatrical productions. In 1968, as part of the wave of changes stemming from the Quiet Revolution, the college became a CÉGEP, and the priests who had founded the institution and directed it for over a century were only given a few days to pack their bags.

Salle Émile-Legault ★ ★ *(613 Avenue Ste-Croix,* ☎*514-855-6110; Du Collège metro).* In 1928, the administration of the Collège de Saint-Laurent decided to build a new chapel since the old one was overflowing with students. In the meantime, a graduate of the institution, then president of the executive committee of the City of Montréal, suggested purchasing the Presbyterian Church of St. Andrew and St. Paul (then located on Boulevard René-Lévesque, where the Queen Elizabeth Hotel now stands) and reconstructing it in Saint-Laurent. The building, expropriated by the Canadian National railway company in 1926, had to be destroyed to make way for the railroad tracks of the Gare Centrale, so the project was approved, despite its unusual character.

In 1930-31, the Protestant church, erected in 1866 by architect Frederick Lawford, was dismantled stone by stone and reconstructed in Saint-Laurent. Lucien Parent made a few modifications to the structure. For example, the basement was raised to make space for a modern auditorium. During the 1930s and 1940s, this room played an important role in the evolution of the arts in Québec, thanks, notably, to the Compagnons de Saint-Laurent, a theatre company founded by Père Paul-Émile Legault in 1937, which trained a number of the province's actors. Salle Émile-Legault can seat 700 people and its regular schedule features plays, concerts, variety shows, movies and conferences.

In 1968, however, when the college was transformed into a CÉGEP, the church lost its purpose. The Musée d'Art de Saint-Laurent, founded a few years earlier by Gérard Lavallée, was set up there in 1979. It displayed collections of tools, traditional fabrics and Québec furniture, as well as a number of 18th and 19th-century religious artifacts.

After the old chapel was restructured, the **Musée des Maîtres et Artisans du Québec** ★ ★ *($3, Wed free admission; Wed-Sun noon to 5pm; 615 Avenue Ste-Croix,* ☎*514-747-7367,* *www.mmaq.qc.ca; Du Collège metro)* took over the Musée d'Art de Saint-Laurent on April 1, 2003, with a new permanent exhibit on wood, metal and textile trades. It showcases a collection of 8,000 antique and traditional art objects from the 18th and 19th centuries. The museum was given a new name to better indicate its mission and offers an educational program that is more consistent and better adapted to its collection. An on-site gift shop sells arts and crafts.

› › › ⇔ *To get back on the highway, take Avenue Sainte-Croix south to the Autoroute 40 junction. Or, to return to the centre of Montréal, head south on Chemin Lucerne, turn left on*

Outdoors

Parks   174
Outdoor Activities   177

Outdoors

There are parks all over the island of Montréal, providing great opportunities to enjoy a thousand and one activities. In all seasons, Montrealers flock to these green spaces to get away from the urban hustle and bustle while staying close to their city. Nature parks, large and small urban parks, neighbourhood parks and recreational parks are open to all, in both summer and winter.

Parks

Parc La Fontaine ★ *(bordered by Avenue du Parc-La Fontaine, Rue Sherbrooke Est, Rue Rachel and Avenue Papineau; Plateau Mont-Royal; see p 116)* and **Parc René-Lévesque** ★★ *(at the western tip of the Lachine Canal, see p 162)* are lovely spots for a bit of relaxation. In addition, both parks, as well as other parks in Montréal, are linked to the **Route Verte**, a 3,000km bike path that crosses the province of Québec.

Established in 1910, **Parc Jeanne-Mance** *(bordered by Avenue de l'Esplanade, Place du Parc, Avenue du Mont-Royal Ouest and Avenue des Pins; Plateau Mont-Royal)* is named after the co-founder of Montréal and founder of the Hôtel-Dieu, the city's first hospital. A natural extension of Mount Royal's eastern side, Parc Jeanne-Mance has been officially part of Parc du Mont-Royal since 1990. This green space covers nearly 15ha and offers inhabitants numerous equipments and facilities: playgrounds for children and toddlers, including a paddling pool, sports grounds for soccer and tennis, skating rinks and a snowshoeing area.

Parc Sir-Wilfrid-Laurier ★ *(bordered by Avenue Laurier Est, Rue de Mentana, Rue de Brébeuf and Rue St-Grégoire; Plateau Mont-Royal)*, a beautiful 10ha recreational park, is simply known to most people as "Parc Laurier" and was created in 1925. Locals come here in summer to enjoy a very refreshing swimming pool and in winter to take advantage of a maintained skating rink (a second rink is reserved to sports enthusiasts). Kids and toddlers are not left out, as they have their own playground. Parc Laurier also features sports grounds for baseball and soccer, and contains lots of beautiful trees.

Parc Angrignon ★★ *(bordered by Boulevard LaSalle, Boulevard des Trinitaires and Boulevard La Vérendrye; ☎514-872-3066; Angrignon metro)*, covering 110ha, was originally created to feature a large zoo. Its network of pedestrian and cross-country ski trails stretches along some 10km, and a narrow, sinewy road also crosses the park. A trail that links the park to the Lachine Canal bike trail was added in June 2005. In addition to a magnificent green space and a lovely pond, it also features the Ferme Angrignon (see below) and **Fort Angrignon** *(admission fees vary from $6.50 to $12; family activities reserved for groups on weekends; ☎514-872-3816, www. fortangrignon.ca; Angrignon metro)*, which is open year-round and offers fun indoor challenges for children, families and adults. The Centre d'Animation du Parc Angrignon (CAPA) now runs the activities at Fort Angrignon.

An educational farm that is run by the Montréal Botanical Garden, the **Ferme Angrignon** *(mid-June to early Sep every day 9:30am to 5pm; 3400 Boulevard des Trinitaires, corner Rue Lacroix, ☎514-280-3744; Angrignon metro)* has been caring, since 1990, for some 100 farm animals that children can get close to in five aviaries, a rabbit hutch, a henhouse, a sheepfold, a goat shed, a stable and two ponds. Egg gathering, animal feeding, cow milking, guided tours and several activities can be enjoyed at the Ferme Angrignon. In summer, in addition to day camps, the place features farm-themed days with educational food samplings.

Covering 268ha, **Parc Jean-Drapeau** *(☎514-872-6120; Jean-Drapeau metro; see p 142)* encompasses both **Île Sainte-Hélène** and **Île Notre-Dame**. In summer, Montrealers flock here on sunny days to enjoy the beach. Footpaths, in-line skating and bicycle trails criss-cross the park. The

Fête des Neiges (see p 275) is held here in winter, and the park also welcomes the **Grand Prix of Canada** (see p 273) and the **L'International des Feux Loto-Québec** (see p 276) fireworks competition in summer.

All year, Montrealers come to **Parc du Mont-Royal** ★★★ *(to get there, take Avenue du Parc and then Voie Camillien-Houde, or the no. 11 bus from the Mont-Royal metro station;* ☎*514-843-8240),* a huge green expanse in the middle of the city, to enjoy a wide range of athletic activities. During summer, footpaths are open to hikers, and mountain biking is only permitted on Chemin Olmsted. In winter, the paths serve as cross-country ski trails, leading across the snowy slopes of the mountain, and Lac aux Castors becomes a big, beautiful skating rink. In summer, the park's eastern section, along Avenue du Parc near the Sir George Étienne Cartier monument, livens up on Sundays thanks to the sounds of percussionists. An eccentric crowd gathers here to have fun in a warm, friendly atmosphere.

Two Montréal organizations are dedicated to the preservation of Mount Royal: the **Centre de la Montagne** and **Les Amis de la Montagne** *(Maison Smith, 1260 Chemin Remembrance, Parc du Mont-Royal,* ☎*514-843-8240, www.lemontroyal.qc.ca).* Throughout the year, they organize various activities that highlight the park's beauty. Parc du Mont-Royal offers nature-lovers the opportunity to admire and enjoy rich, diverse fauna and flora. Bird-watchers will be thrilled to learn that this small piece of heaven is home to a variety of birds that is unique for such an urban setting as Montréal. Some of the most impressive species include the American kestrel, the downy woodpecker, the scarlet tanager, the white-breasted nuthatch, the Baltimore oriole and the American goldfinch… enough to provoke mild hysteria among bird-watchers everywhere! A wide variety of trees is also found here, such as weeping birch, red oak, sugar maple, chestnut tree, linden and catalpa. Finally, let's not forget to mention the presence of mammals such as squirrels, Eastern chipmunks, woodchucks, racoons, skunks and red foxes.

Covering 80ha, including the **Montréal Botanical Garden** ★★★ *(4101 Rue Sherbrooke Est,* ☎*514-872-1400, see p 145)* and the **Golf Municipal de Montréal**, **Parc Maisonneuve** ★ *(bordered by Boulevard Pie-IX, Rue Sherbrooke E., Boulevard Rosemont and Rue Viau; 4601 Rue Sherbrooke Est,* ☎*514-872-6555; Pie-IX or Viau metro),* a large green space, is ideal for a stroll or a picnic in summer. In winter, a lovely skating rink and cross-country ski trails delight Montrealers.

Parc Jarry *(bordered by Boulevard Saint-Laurent, Rue Faillon Ouest, Rue Jarry and the railway tracks; De Castelneau or Jarry metro)* was laid out where the farm of the clerics of Saint-Viateur once lay; their former Institut des Sourds-Muets (Deaf-Mute Institute) is still visible south of Rue Faillon. The park is known for its stadium, which was home to the Expos baseball team from 1968 to 1976, and now hosts the **Rogers Cup** (see p 274). In addition to playing both indoor and outdoor tennis, it is possible to enjoy in-line skating and skateboarding on a circuit that is specifically designed for these sports.

Though scarcely dotted with trees, it encloses various playing fields, big and small (football, soccer, baseball). There is also a sculpture celebrating world peace.

The **Morgan Arboretum** ★★ *($5; every day 9am to 4pm; Autoroute 40 Ouest, Exit 41, corner Chemin Ste-Marie and Chemin des Pins, Sainte-Anne-de-Bellevue,* ☎*514-398-7811, www.morganarboretum.org)* extends over 245ha, making it the largest arboretum in Canada. An arboretum is an area planted with different tree species for use in experiments on cultivation methods. Visitors can observe 500 plant species, including some 170 different kinds of indigenous trees, along the arboretum's 20km of forest paths and ecological interpretation.

After visiting the Arboretum, stop by the **Écomuseum** ★ (see p 168), where you can see and gain an appreciation of the flora and fauna of the St. Lawrence valley (birds of prey, wolves, lynx, bears, caribou, etc.).

Outdoors – Parks

Parc Linéaire du Complexe Environnemental Saint-Michel *(bordered by Avenue Papineau, Rue Jarry, 2ᵉ Avenue and Rue Champdoré; access at the corner of D'Iberville and Louvain streets)* includes, in addition to several playgrounds, bike paths in summer and cross-country ski trails in winter over a 55ha territory. The Complexe itself covers approximately 192ha. This former limestone quarry was a dumpsite before its current transformation by the City of Montréal through a huge environmental rehabilitation project. The site will eventually be converted into an immense urban park with several purposes: cultural, educational, sports, commercial and industrial. The project has already begun; in addition to the linear park, the site is home to **TOHU, la Cité des Arts du Cirque** ★ (see p 140) and various environmental organizations.

Parc de la Promenade Bellerive ★ *(bordered by the St. Lawrence River, Rue Bellerive, Avenue Georges-V and Rue Liébert;* ☎514-493-1967) is now, thanks to the Société d'Animation de la Promenade Bellerive, responsible for activities in the park and on the river; it is one of the liveliest urban parks in Montréal, both in summer and winter. In addition, from spring to fall, a shuttle (paying) for pedestrians and cyclists links it to Île Charron, the access to the Parc National des Îles-de-Boucherville, in the middle of the St. Lawrence. This riverside park is 2.2km long and offers a breathtaking view of the river. In summer, water equipment can be rented, and in winter skaters can enjoy a skating rink; a lovely chalet is also available to users.

Located in LaSalle, **Parc des Rapides** ★★ *(bordered by Boulevard LaSalle, the St. Lawrence River, 3ᵉ Avenue and 31ᵉ Avenue; LaSalle; access via 6ᵉ Avenue;* ☎514-367-6540) is the best place to see and hear the famous Lachine rapids, which are always a thrill for observers. Overlooking the river, the park also allows users to observe migrating birds that visit the surroundings, including the largest colony of herons in Québec. Audacious visitors can rent kayaks, while others can enjoy bike paths (for bicycles and in-line skates) and pedestrian trails.

■ Nature Parks

Since the early 1980s, **Parcs-Nature** *(*☎514-280-7272, www.ville.montreal.qc.ca/parcs-nature)* has been operating a network of well-maintained nature parks throughout the island. These parks are open year-round from early morning until nightfall and feature picnic tables. An amateur photography contest is also held throughout the nature-park network.

Note that all reception chalets and interpretation centres are closed from late October to mid-December, as well as Christmas and New Year's Day. Here is a short description of the six existing nature parks; the City of Montréal plans to eventually open others, such as Bois-de-Saraguay, Bois-d'Anjou and Bois-de-la-Roche:

Parc-Nature du Cap Saint-Jacques *(reception chalet at 20099 Boulevard Gouin Ouest, Pierrefonds,* ☎514-280-6871) is located on the north shore of the island of Montréal, on a point measuring 288ha that extends into Lac des Deux-Montagnes. Its shore has a public beach, while trails and an interpretation centre have been established here to highlight the diversity of the flora and wildlife. An **outdoor centre** *(205 Chemin du Cap-St-Jacques, Pierrefonds,* ☎514-280-6778) provides lodging for groups, and the **Ferme Écologique du Cap-Saint-Jacques** *(183 Chemin du Cap-St-Jacques, Pierrefonds,* ☎514-280-6743) offers free tours of its facilities. There is also a sugar shack in the park.

Established on a 159ha site with exceptional flora, **Parc-Nature du Bois-de-Liesse** ★ *(Accueil Pitfield, 9432 Boulevard Gouin Ouest, Pierrefonds,* ☎514-280-6729; Accueil des Champs, 3555 Rue Douglas-B. Floreani, St-Laurent,* ☎514-280-6678) features a lovely hardwood and wild-flower forest. Diverse fauna, both aquatic and winged (attracted by bird feeders) also thrives here. Hiking trails, bike paths and cross-country ski trails criss-cross this green space, which is also equipped for snowshoeing and tobogganing in winter. On the park's peninsula, on the edge of Rivière des Prairies, near the intersection of Boulevard Gouin and Highway 13, stands the **Maison du Ruisseau** *(5 Rue Oakridge, Cartierville,* ☎*514-280-6829)*, a fully equipped lodging establishment that welcomes groups.

Parc-Nature de l'Anse-à-l'Orme *(Chemin de l'Anse-à-l'Orme, corner Boulevard Gouin Ouest, Pierrefonds,* ☎*514-280-6871)* is intended exclusively for windsurfers, as it is swept by exceptional westerly winds. There is also a picnic area.

Covering 201ha, **Parc-Nature du Bois-de-l'Île-Bizard** ★ *(reception pavilion, 2115 Chemin du Bord-du-Lac, L'Île-Bizard,* ☎*514-280-8517)* is located at the western tip of the island of Montréal, on the shore of Lac des Deux Montagnes, the stopping place of log drivers who, in the 19th century, transported logs along Rivière des Prairies to the St. Lawrence River. In addition to hiking and cross-country ski trails, which are dotted with bird feeders, there is a picnic area, a beach, a boat ramp and a dock (boat rental). Finally, a footbridge crosses the park's marsh, allowing visitors to admire its paludal nature.

Covering 34ha, **Parc-Nature de l'Île-de-la-Visitation** ★★ *(reception chalet at 2425 Boulevard Gouin Est, Ahuntsic,* ☎*514-280-6733)* attracts crowds of city-dwellers yearning for nature. They come here to enjoy picnics and walks along short trails dotted with bird feeders (binoculars and bird-watching guides can be rented on site), which can be explored on foot in summer or on cross-country skis in winter, when sleds and "crazy carpets" can also be rented to go sliding. Set along the Rivière des Prairies, the park's landscape is magnificent. On site, two historical buildings, the **Maison du Pressoir** ★ (see p 140) and the **Maison du Meunier** (see p 140) houses history-interpretation centres.

Covering 261ha, **Parc-Nature de la Pointe-aux-Prairies** ★ *(Chalet d'Accueil Héritage, 14905 Rue Sherbrooke Est,* ☎*514-280-6691; Pavillon des Marais, 12300 Boulevard Gouin Est,* ☎*514-280-6688; Chalet d'Accueil Rivière-des-Prairies, 12980 Boulevard Gouin Est,* ☎*514-280-6772)*, which stretches along the eastern tip of the island of Montréal, is home to a lovely network of hiking trails, bike paths and cross-country ski trails (also in winter: snowshoeing area and tobogganing hills, as well as rental of snowshoes, toboggans and sleds). They all cross forested areas and fields, along marshes that are ideal for bird observation; indeed, a large number of feeders attract several species to the park. If you're lucky, you might also spot a deer. The **Pavillon des Marais**, for its part, houses a nature-interpretation centre (guide and binocular rental), while the **Maison Bleau** is a space for artists-residents (visit of the workshop by appointment).

Outdoor Activities

■ Adventure Packages

If you are staying in Montréal and feel the need to escape to wide, green spaces, you can participate in one of the activities organized by **Globe-Trotter Aventure** *(2467 Rue Ste-Catherine Est, Suite 200,* ☎*514-849-8768)*. This young company offers, among other things, various winter and summer packages for horseback riding, canoeing, camping and snowmobiling in various regions around the city. These packages include transportation and equipment rental, which is quite useful for travellers. An experienced guide accompanies groups for both long and short stays. In summer, a fixed schedule allows you to plan your excursions.

■ Bird-Watching

For information on specialized publications, observation sites and group outings, contact the following organization:

Fédération québécoise des groupes d'ornithologues (AQGO)
(bird-watching association)
☎(514) 860-3074
www.aqgo.qc.ca
The island of Montréal features several natural sites and other unique spots where you can observe birds. Here are some of them:

Countless species of birds can be observed along the shores of Lac des Deux-Montagnes in the **Parc-Nature du Bois-de-l'Île-Bizard** ★ (see p 177), particularly American coots and several kinds of ducks.

More than a 100 species of winged creatures can be observed at the **Parc-Nature du Cap Saint-Jacques** ★★ (see p 176), mostly wading birds, raptors and other types of aquatic birds. Wood ducks, eagle owls and red-tailed hawks, among others, also take advantage of these natural surroundings.

More than 125 species of birds nest in **Parc-Nature de la Pointe-aux-Prairies** ★ (see p 177).

The Botanical Garden ★★★ (see p 145) is visited throughout the winter by numerous winged creatures. If you're lucky, you might spot a hawfinch, a woodpecker, a coal tit or a red-breasted nuthatch.

■ Climbing

Centre d'Escalade Horizon Roc *(2350 Rue Dickson,* ☎ *514-899-5000, www.horizonroc. com; Assomption metro)* is one of the world's largest indoor climbing centres. Beginners can practice free climbing with instructors and various competitions are held for advanced climbers.

■ Cross-Country Skiing

Montréal is full of places that are easily accessible by bus or metro where you can enjoy lovely skiing excursions in settings that often make you forget all about the city. In addition, standing on your skis at the top of Mount Royal and admiring the downtown office buildings is an unforgettable experience that few cities can rival!

Over 25km of cross-country ski trails, which run alongside a plantation featuring several species of trees, are maintained throughout the winter season at the **Morgan Arboretum** ★★ (see p 175). In the spring, you can visit the Arboretum's charming *cabane à sucre*; it is considered

to be the oldest sugar shack still in operation on the island of Montréal.

The 32km of hiking trails in **Parc-Nature du Cap-Saint-Jacques** ★★ (see p 176) become beautiful cross-country skiing trails in the winter. Ski rental.

Parc-Nature de la Pointe-aux-Prairies ★ (see p 177) has 23.5km of cross-country ski trails set amidst beautiful and abundant forest and plantlife. Ski rental.

The **Parc-Nature de l'Île-de-la-Visitation** ★★ (see p 177) has 8km of cross-country ski trails, enabling skiers to go all the way around both the park and the island after which it is named. Ski rental.

The **Parc-Nature du Bois-de-Liesse** ★ (see p 176) has 16km of cross-country trails. Ski rental.

The **Parc-Nature du Bois-de-l'Île-Bizard** ★ (see p 177) has 20km of cross-country trails divided into three loops. Ski rental.

There are nearly 6km of trails in the **Montréal Botanical Garden**, offering skiers a chance to familiarize themselves with its many different kinds of trees.

Parc Maisonneuve ★ (see p 175) has about 10km of trails, enabling skiers to go all the way around the park, while admiring the Olympic Stadium tower.

Skiers can explore **Parc du Mont-Royal** ★★★ (see p 175), the city's green lung or, perhaps more appropriately, "white lung" in the winter, on over 25km of trails, all the while enjoying exceptional views of the city.

Parc Angrignon ★★ (see p 174) has two cross-country ski trails, each approximately 12km long.

■ Cycling

The **Société de Transport de Montréal (STM)** *(*☎*514-786-9636, www.stm.info)* allows passengers to board the metro with their bicycle under certain restrictions, which are detailed on their Web site.

At all times, cyclists can park their bicycle near a metro station; the STM provides several bike racks.

In spring, the City of Montréal also provides a large number of bike racks across the island, which are then stored for winter.

You can also travel with your bicycle on commuter trains, which are run by the **Agence Métropolitaine de Transport (AMT)** *(☎514-287-8726, www.amt.qc.ca).*

Note that it is possible to participate in the **Tour de l'Île** (see p 273), which is held on the first Sunday of June and is the largest event held during the **Montréal Bike Fest**. This cycling festival allows amateur and experienced cyclists to pedal to their heart's content.

La Maison des Cyclistes *(1251 Rue Rachel Est,* ☎*514-521-8356)* provides various services. In addition to a café (**Café Bicicletta**, see p 231), it features a specialized shop.

There is another association called **Le Monde à Bicyclette**, whose horizons stretch a little farther *(7235 Rue St-Urbain,* ☎*514-270-9190).*

Vélo Montréal *(3880 Rue Rachel Est,* ☎*514-259-7272, www.velomontreal.com)* specializes in bicycle touring and organizes guided tours of the island.

Cyclists will be thrilled to discover nearly 600km of interesting bicycle paths that traverse the island of Montréal. A map of the paths is available at tourist-information offices. Here are a few places to enjoy:

The area around the **Lachine Canal** has been redesigned in an effort to highlight this communication route, so important during the 19th and early 20th centuries. A lovely bike path was laid out alongside the canal (one section even has a trail on each shore). Very popular with Mont-

realers, especially on Sundays, the path leads from the Old Port to **Parc René-Lévesque** ★ ★ (see p 162), a narrow strip of land jutting out into Lac Saint-Louis that offers splendid views of the lake and surroundings. There are benches and picnic tables in the park. Many birds frequent this side of the park, and if you're lucky, you might get to see great herons and ducks. You can head back to the Old Port by following the river via the **Pôle des Rapides** trail.

To the north of the island (accessible via the bicycle path that crosses the island north-south, or by metro), a bicycle path follows **Boulevard Gouin** and Rivière des Prairies. It leads to **Parc-Nature de l'Île-de-la-Visitation** ★ ★ (see p 177). Continuing alongside the river, the trail then leads to a very peaceful part of Montréal. It is possible to ride all the way to **Parc-Nature de la Pointe-aux-Prairies** ★ (see p 177), and from there follow the path to **Vieux-Montréal** through the southeast part of the city (a good half-day).

Île Notre-Dame and **Île Sainte-Hélène** (see p 141) are accessible from Old Montréal. The path runs through an industrial area, then through the Cité du Havre before reaching the islands (cyclists can cross the river on the Pont de la Concorde). It is easy to ride from one island to the other. The islands are well maintained and are a great place to relax, stroll and admire Montréal's skyline.

Parc-Nature du Bois-de-Liesse ★ (see p 176) is criss-crossed by 8km of bicycle paths through a hardwood forest.

Bicycle Rentals

Many bicycle shops also rent bicycles; here are a few. For others (and there are many), check with **Vélo Québec Association** *(1251 Rue Rachel Est,* ☎*514-521-8356)* or with **regional tourist offices (ATR)**. Purchasing insurance is a good idea. Some places include theft insurance in the rental price; be sure to check when renting.

Outdoors - Outdoor Activities

Bicycletterie J.R.
151 Rue Rachel Est, Plateau Mont-Royal
☎ (514) 843-6989

Ça Roule Montréal
27 Rue de la Commune Est, Vieux-Montréal
☎ (514) 866-0633
www.caroulemontreal.com

La Cordée Plein Air
2159 Rue Ste-Catherine Est
☎ (514) 524-1106
www.lacordee.com

Pignon sur Roues
1308 Avenue du Mt-Royal Est, Plateau Mont-Royal
☎ (514) 523-6480

■ Golf

Much of the 18-hole golf course that once extended north of the present site of the Olympic Stadium in **Parc Maisonneuve** ★ (see p 175) was lost due to the construction of the Olympic Village. The Golf Municipal de Montréal *($20, early May to mid-Oct; main entrance on Rue Viau between Boulevard Rosemont and Rue Sherbrooke, ☎514-872-4653)*, a par-three, nine-hole course does remain, however, and is open to everyone.

■ Hiking

Montréal is easy to explore on foot. However, those who would like to roam about magnificent green spaces that have yet to be taken over by asphalt and concrete will find that Montréal also has hundreds of kilometres of trails, which offer a delightful means of soaking up the beauty of these vast, rolling expanses of land.

To learn more about the city's hiking trails, pick up a copy of *Hiking in Québec*, which includes a chapter on hiking in and around Montréal, by Ulysses Travel Guides. Here are a few spots you can enjoy:

The **Morgan Arboretum** ★★ (see p 175) offers a network of maintained hiking trails that head 3km deep into the forest

and are lined with interpretative panels that provide information on various forestry techniques and the ecosystems that characterize the forest.

The 1km ecological trail features seven interpretative stations that explain the relation between the forest's living organisms and their environment. Another trail, which spreads over 2km, is reserved for member hikers who wish to walk with their dog without having to keep it on a leash. In total, over 20km of trails are available for hikers here. Note that only members of the Arboretum are admitted during the weekends of January and February.

Close to the downtown area, **Parc du Mont-Royal** ★★★ (see p 175) is an oasis of greenery that is ideal for walking and hiking. The park features about 20km of trails, including many secondary trails, as well as the wonderful Chemin Olmsted and the loop at the top of the mountain.

Parc-Nature du Bois-de-Liesse ★ (see p 176) has 11km of walking trails, some of which are nature-interpretation trails. This park is home to the superb **Pitfield House** (1954), as well as a magnificent Japanese footbridge with an unusual design.

Parc-Nature du Cap Saint-Jacques ★★ (see p 176) offers 17km of hiking trails through mature forests (a hickory-sugar maple forest and a beech-maple forest), transition zones (birch and poplar trees) and vast expanses of varied aquatic and riverside plant life.

Parc-Nature de l'Île-de-la-Visitation ★★★ (see p 177) has 8km of ecological hiking trails. Hikers can explore hilly areas, small patches of undergrowth, the banks of the Rivière des Prairies and the very pretty island, Île de la-Visitation.

Parc-Nature de la Pointe-aux-Prairies ★ (see p 177) covers a variety of different ecosystems criss-crossed by 15km of hiking trails. This park shelters the only mature forest east of Mount Royal. Stretching along Rivière des Prairies to the St. Lawrence, it also contains fields and marshes.

Parc-Nature du Bois-de-l'Île-Bizard ★ (see p 177) has 10km of hiking trails. It is divided into two sections, Pointe aux Carrières and the woods, and boasts a lovely sandy beach and a superb 406m footbridge over a marsh.

Parc Maisonneuve ★ (see p 175) has 10km of hiking trails including the Botanical Garden which crisscross the 30 or so outdoor gardens.

There are a few trails running through **Parc La Fontaine** ★★★ (see p 174), where Montrealers come to relax beneath the tall trees or near the lake.

Parc Jean-Drapeau ★★ (see p 174) features some 12km of trails, including footpaths, maintained trails and small paved roads.

Parc Angrignon ★★ (see p 174) has a number of little paths, as well as the small main road, for a total of nearly 10km.

The 14km-long path that runs alongside the **Lachine Canal** (☎514-283-6054), a favourite with cyclists, can also be enjoyed by pedestrians. It links the Old Port to Parc René-Lévesque in Lachine.

The Canal de Sainte-Anne-de-Bellevue is located at the western tip of the island of Montreal. There are 2km of trails here, including the Sainte-Anne-de-Bellevue boardwalk.

■ Ice Skating

Ice skating has not lost any of its popularity in Montréal. This sport is inexpensive and requires a minimum amount of equipment and technique.

During the winter, a number of public skating rinks are set up. Some of the best ones include **Lac aux Castors**, **Parc du Mont-Royal** (see p 175), **Parc La Fontaine** ★ (see p 174), **Bassin Bonsecours** *($4; rental; Vieux-Port, Champ-de-Mars metro,* ☎514-

496-7678, *www.vieuxportdemontreal.com)* and **Parc Maisonneuve** ★ (see p 175).

Atrium
$5.50; $5 for rental
1000 Rue De la Gauchetière Ouest
☎(514) 395-0555
The Atrium, located at 1000 De la Gauchetière (the tallest office building in Montréal), houses a large skating rink with a surface area of 900m² open year-round. The rink is surrounded by food stands and rest areas, and is overlooked by a mezzanine. Above the skating rink is a superb glass dome that lets the sun shine in.

■ In-Line Skating

The growing popularity of in-line skating is particularly evident in Montréal. Unfortunately, the Highway code prohibits in-line skating on the streets of Canadian cities, but it is tolerated on the city's bicycle paths. In-line skating enthusiasts can also flock to the Circuit Gilles-Villeneuve on **Île Notre-Dame** (see p 141), where they have the car-free race track all to themselves.

The craze over this activity and means of transportation has led to the opening of several specialized boutiques that buy and sell skates and all the necessary equipment that goes with them; some even offer lessons. You can rent in-line skates from the following shops. Both are located near the Old Port and the starting point of the very popular Lachine Canal bike trail, which is also open to skaters.

Ça Roule Montréal
$8.50/hour
27 Rue de la Commune Est, Vieux-Montréal
☎(514) 866-0633
www.caroulemontreal.com

Vélo Aventure Montréal
$8.50/hour
Quai des Convoyeurs, Vieux-Montréal, entrance via Boulevard St-Laurent
☎(514) 847-0666

Outdoors - Outdoor Activities

■ Pleasure Boating and Windsurfing

École de Voile de Lachine
3045 Boulevard St-Joseph, Lachine
☎ (514) 634-4326
www.voilelachine.com
The École de Voile de Lachine rents windsurfers and small sailboats and offers private and group lessons.

The **Lachine Canal**, cradle of Canada's industrial history, has recently reopened to pleasure boats.

■ Rafting

Descentes sur le Saint-Laurent
$40
8912 Boulevard LaSalle, LaSalle
☎ (514) 767-2230
www.raftingmontreal.com
Looking for a refreshing activity for the dog days of summer? The young and dynamic staff at Les Descentes sur le Saint-Laurent offers three different excursions on the Lachine rapids. Rafting calls upon a strong sense of teamwork and provides an unforgettable adrenaline rush. Guides supply information on the region while navigating between the river's small islands on the way to the rapids. For those who wish to start off slowly, the outfit also offers a "family" excursion that follows a more tranquil route. A shuttle service is offered free of charge from the **Centre Infotouriste** *(1255 Rue Peel)*. Remember to bring along a change of clothes.

Expéditions sur les Rapides de Lachine
$55
mid-Jun to Sep
47 Rue de la Commune Ouest
☎ (514) 284-9607
www.jetboatingmontreal.com
This company organizes various excursions on the Lachine Rapids.

■ Speleology

The **Site Cavernicole de Saint-Léonard** *($9; May to Oct; Parc Pie-XII, 5200 Boulevard Lavoisier, St-Léonard,* ☎ *514-252-3323; reservations must be made with the Société Québé-coise de Spéléologie)* is located outside this guide's various tours and provides an opportunity to visit a 10,000- to 20,000-year-old rock formation right on the island of Montréal. The guided tour includes a slide show and the exploration of the cave.

■ Swimming

The majority of the city's cegeps and universities have their own sports centre with a swimming pool that is open to the public. In addition, the City of Montréal has established outdoor swimming pools in many neighbourhoods, which are very popular on hot summer days. There are also a few public beaches on the island.

Prices and schedules are subject to change, so it is best to check with the administrative offices before hand.

CÉGEP du Vieux-Montréal
Indoor pool
255 Rue Ontario Est, Quartier Latin
☎ (514) 982-3437

Centre Claude-Robillard
Indoor pool
1000 Rue Émile-Journault, Ahuntsic
☎ (514) 872-6905

Université de Montréal
Indoor pool
2100 Boulevard Édouard-Montpetit, Outremont
☎ (514) 343-6150

John-Abbott College
Indoor pool
21275 Chemin Bord du Lac, Ste-Anne-de-Bellevue
☎ (514) 457-6610

Parc Olympique
Indoor pool
3200 Rue Viau, Maisonneuve
☎ (514) 252-4622

The three Olympic-size pools (recreational, competitive and diving) at **Complexe Aquatique de l'Île Sainte-Hélène** *(Île Sainte-Hélène Aquatic Complex;* ☎ *514-872-6120; www.parcjeandrapeau.com)* were inaugurated in 2005 when Montréal hosted the FINA World Aquatic Championships.

Beaches

Located on the shore of Lac des Deux Montagnes, the fine-sand beach at **Parc-Nature du Cap-Saint-Jacques ★★** (see p 176) is ideal for swimming.

Parc-Nature du Bois-de-l'Île-Bizard ★ (see p 177) features a lovely beach where you can enjoy various watersports and activities.

On Île Notre-Dame, the water at the **Parc Jean-Drapeau ★★** (see p 174) beach is naturally filtered, allowing beach-goers to swim in clean, chemical-free water. If you're heading to the beach on a particularly sunny day, we recommend you arrive early, as the number of bathers admitted on site is limited.

■ Tennis

Several urban and recreational parks provide tennis courts for enthusiasts in summer. Some have a cover charge; others are free.

Stade Uniprix
285 Rue Faillon Ouest, De Castelneau metro
☎ (514) 273-1234
www.stadeuniprix.com

With indoor and outdoor courts, the Stade Uniprix is more than well equipped to satisfy tennis buffs at any time of the year. Built for Tennis Canada, which presents the Rogers Cup competition, it is open to the public. Some of its services and facilities include showers, changing rooms, lockers and a restaurant.

Accommodations

Vieux-Montréal	188	Plateau Mont-Royal	206
Downtown and Golden Square Mile	193	Notre-Dame-de-Grâce	206
Shaughnessy Village	199	Côte-des-Neiges	206
The McGill Ghetto and "The Main"	201	Hochelaga-Maisonneuve	207
Quartier Latin	201	West Island and Surroundings	207
The Village	205		

Travellers will discover a wide variety of comfortable lodging in all categories in Montréal. Rates vary greatly from one season to the next. For example, the weeks of the Grand Prix of Canada, in mid-June, and the International Jazz Festival, in early July, are the busiest of the year; we recommend making reservations well in advance if you plan on being in Montréal during these events.

The choice of accommodations in Montréal is extensive. Prices vary according to the type of accommodation, but remember to add 7% GST (Federal Goods and Services Tax) and 7.5% QST (Québec Services Tax). These taxes are refundable for non-residents (see p 51). A new tax has also been added to all accommodations in Montréal; the revenue from the *Taxe spécifique sur l'hébergement* is used to maintain the area's tourist infrastructure. The tax represents a flat rate of $2 per night (regardless of the price of your room). It is non-refundable and does not apply to campgrounds and youth hostels.

When making reservations, a credit card is indispensable, and a deposit for the first night is often required in advance.

Hospitality Canada *(☎866-363-6647, www.hospitality-canada.com)* offers a free reservation service for accommodation and tourism packages in Québec and elsewhere in Canada.

■ Prices and Symbols

Unless otherwise noted, all prices indicated in this guide apply to a **standard room for two people in peak season**.

$	less than $60
$$	from $60 to $100
$$$	from $101 to $150
$$$$	from $151 to $225
$$$$$	more than $225

The prices that are given in this guide are those that were in effect at press time. Of course, rates may fluctuate and are subject to change at all times. Be sure to ask about corporate and other discounts as they are often very easy to obtain.

The various services offered by each establishment are indicated by a small symbol, explained in the legend in the last pages of this guidebook. By no means is this an exhaustive list of what the establishment offers, but rather the services we consider to be the most important.

Please note that the presence of a symbol does not mean that all rooms feature this service; you will sometimes have to pay extra to get, for example, a whirlpool tub.

The Ulysses Label

The Ulysses Label is awarded to our favourite establishments (hotels and restaurants). While every establishment recommended in this guide was included because of its high quality and/or uniqueness, as well as its high value, every once in a while we come across an establishment that simply wows us. These, our favourite establishments, are awarded a Ulysses Label. You'll find those labels in all price categories from exclusive, high-price to budget establishments. Regardless of the price, each of these establishments offers the most for your money. Look for them first.

■ Hotels

Montréal boasts a great number of accommodation options varying from modest hotels to luxurious palaces, and hotel rooms usually come with their own private bathroom. Prices in this guide are based on high-season rates.

Many establishments offer special weekend rates with discounts of up to 50%, as most of their clientele is made up of business travellers who only rent rooms during the week. Members of professional associations, automobile clubs and seniors can also take advantage of significant discounts. When making your reservations, we recommend that you inquire about any special package deals or discounts that may be available.

■ Bed & Breakfasts

Unlike hotels, bed and breakfast rooms don't always have their own bathroom. You'll find many of these establishments in Montréal. Besides their usually low rates, they offer the advantage of a family-style setting and a complimentary homemade breakfast. Be aware, however, that credit cards are not always accepted. The Fédération des Agricotours produces an annual guide entitled *Inns and Bed & Breakfasts Québec*, which lists the names and telephone numbers of all members who provide rooms for travellers. The rooms have been selected according to the federation's standards of quality and are also fairly economical. The book is available in bookstores throughout Canada, the United States and Great Britain.

Réseau de Gîtes Centre-ville de Montréal
$$ bkfst incl.
3458 Avenue Laval
☎ (514) 289-9749 or 800-267-5180
🖶 (514) 287-7386
www.bbmontreal.qc.ca
Since its first days of existence, almost 25 years ago, the Réseau de Gîtes Centre-ville de Montréal collaborates with bed and breakfasts in the downtown, Old Montréal, Quartier Latin and Plateau Mont-Royal districts. It brings together about 80 establishments, a large number of which are located in Victorian homes. In order to make sure that all rooms are comfortable and satisfactory, the organization takes the time to visit each B&B. Reservations are required.

■ Youth Hostels

Youth hostels are rare in Montréal, though a few bed and breakfasts also double as hostels. Hostelling International, a major network of inexpensive accommodations for travellers on a tight budget, has a branch downtown.

■ University Residences

Due to certain restrictions, this can be a complicated alternative. Residences are only available during the summer (mid-May to mid-August), and making reservations in advance is strongly recommended. This type of accommodation, however, is less

Accommodations

costly than the "traditional" alternatives, and can be a pleasant experience. Visitors with valid student cards can expect to pay approximately $25 plus tax (slightly more for non-students). Bedding is included in the price, and there is usually a cafeteria in the building (meals are not included in the price).

■ Camping

Camping and RVing cannot be enjoyed in Montréal per se, but enthusiasts will find several campgrounds around the island, either in Laval, the Montérégie region, the Laurentians or the Lanaudière region. The ***www.campingquebec.com*** Web site and the **Centre Infotouriste** *(☎514-873-2015)* can help travellers find outdoor accommodations.

Ulysses' Favourites

■ Montréal Classics

Fairmont Queen Elizabeth p 197
Le Ritz-Carlton Montréal p 199

■ For History Buffs

Auberge-Restaurant Pierre du Calvet p 190
L'Auberge du Vieux-Port p 190

■ For the Friendly Service

Anne Ma Sœur Anne p 206
L'Auberge de la Fontaine p 206

■ For Business Travellers

Le Centre Sheraton p 197
Hilton Montréal Bonaventure p 197
Hôtel Godin p 196
Hôtel Inter-Continental Montréal p 189
Hôtel Omni Mont-Royal p 198
Loews Hôtel Vogue p 198
Montréal Marriott Château Champlain p 199
Novotel Montréal Centre p 196

■ For the Pool

Hilton Montréal Bonaventure p 197
Hôtel de la Montagne p 198

Vieux-Montréal

Since the beginning of the 21st century, Old Montréal has become fertile ground for a wide array of high-end hotels. This unusual trend is mostly comprised of hotels known as **boutique hotels**, whose design is highly innovative and creative. Several of the old buildings in this area have thus undergone major renovations to recapture their former glory; as a

result, each hotel is more beautiful and original than the next, and their rooms are all equipped to cater to the needs of both business travellers and vacationers. Almost all of these establishments also offer condos for longer stays.

L'Auberge Alternative
$ bkfst incl.
sb ☞ ☜
358 Rue St-Pierre
☎ (514) 282-8069

www.auberge-alternative.qc.ca
Located in Old Montréal and opened in 1996, L'Auberge Alternative is run by a young couple and housed in a renovated building dating from 1875. The 34 beds in the rooms and dormitories are rudimentary but comfortable, and the bathrooms are very clean. A friendly atmosphere is provided by brightly coloured walls, lots of space and a large common room and

Accommodations

kitchen with stone walls and old wooden floors. Guests have laundry machines at their disposal. Twenty-four-hour access.

Passants du Sans-Soucy
$$$-$$$$ bkfst incl.
≡ ◎ @

171 Rue St-Paul Ouest
☎ (514) 842-2634
▤ (514) 842-2912
www.lesanssoucy.com

Passants du Sans-Soucy is a lovely inn set in the heart of the old city whose nine charming rooms are furnished with antiques. Built in 1723, the building was renovated about 15 years ago. Reservations required. No smoking in the establishment.

L'Auberge Bonaparte
$$$$ bkfst incl.
◎ ≡ ♨ @

447 Rue St-François-Xavier
☎ (514) 844-1448
▤ (514) 844-0272
www.bonaparte.ca

Well known for its delicious French cuisine, the **Le Bonaparte** restaurant (see p 214) now features a 30-room inn on its upper floors. In addition to providing Internet access, they are all quite comfortable and feature a lovely decor, although the beds don't look quite as inviting as they should. The rooms at the rear of the building, which dates from 1886, overlook the Jardin des Sulpiciens, behind the Notre-Dame basilica. Breakfast is served at the restaurant.

Marriott SpringHill Suites Vieux-Montréal
$$$$ bkfst incl.
☀ ♨ ≋ ≡ ☂ @

445 Rue St-Jean-Baptiste
☎ (514) 875-4333 or
866-875-4333
▤ (514) 875-4331
www.springhillsuites.com

Nestled on a small street in Old Montréal, the Marriott SpringHill Suites Vieux-Montréal is quite imposing. It features 124 suites, all equipped with kitchenette, sofa, desk and modems. Because this is Old Montréal, the suites are not very large, and their decor, similar from one room to another, will probably remind you of hotel chains, but they are comfortable. The hotel has established a partnership with its neighbour, the **Vieux Saint-Gabriel** restaurant (see p 214), so an indoor passageway links the two establishments.

Hôtel Inter-Continental Montréal
$$$$-$$$$$
≋ ☂ ♨ ⫸ ≡ ⚅ ☛ @

360 Rue St-Antoine Ouest
☎ (514) 987-9900 or
800-361-3600
▤ (514) 847-8730
www.montreal.intercontinental.com

This hotel, located on the edge of Old Montréal, is linked to the Centre de Commerce Mondial (World Trade Centre) and several shops. The Palais des Congrès (convention centre) is right nearby. The hotel has an original look thanks to its turret with multiple windows, where the living rooms of the suites are located. The 357 rooms are taste-fully decorated with simple furniture. Each one is equipped with a spacious bathroom, among other nice touches. Business people will enjoy all the necessary services, such as computer hook-ups, fax machines and photocopiers. Service is attentive and professional.

Le Saint-Sulpice
$$$$-$$$$$
≡ ♨ ⚅ △ ☀ ☛ Y @ ☂

414 Rue St-Sulpice
☎ (514) 288-1000 or
877-785-9423
▤ (514) 288-0077
www.lesaintsulpice.com

Enter the huge lobby of the Saint-Sulpice hotel and discover a world of luxury and comfort with a touch of Old Montréal. Throughout the establishment, decorative elements remind guests that the site is steeped in history: amber and mahogany woodwork, stone walls, rugs with *fleur de lys* motif, fireplace, etc. After all, the Sulpicians played a major role in the city's history. In fact, their basilica and seminary are located next door to the hotel, whose courtyard features a fountain and offers direct access to the beautiful Jardin des Sulpiciens. Because it is an all-suite hotel (there are 108), you will have enough room to move around and a kitchenette to boot. Best of all, some of the suites have a balcony or a roof patio.

Accommodations - Vieux-Montréal

L'Auberge du Vieux-Port
$$$$$ bkfst incl.
≡ ⚠ ◎ ☞ ⚏ @

97 Rue de la Commune Est
☎ (514) 876-0081 or
888-660-7678
▤ (514) 876-8923
www.aubergeduvieuxport.com

The Auberge du Vieux-Port stands right in front of the Old Port. Opened in 1996, this place is a real gem. It occupies a historic building dating from 1882 whose stone walls have been left exposed in the chic, attractively decorated lobby. The building's construction and the way the rooms were divided highlight its many wood beams and stone walls. The 27 rooms have been decorated so as to pay tribute to the past, with outstanding results. There is also a French restaurant in the basement, where you can see a segment of the fortifications of the old city. In addition to hypoallergenic bedding, each room features a telephone with voice mail. No smoking.

Auberge-Restaurant Pierre du Calvet
$$$$$ bkfst incl.
⚠ ≡ ⚏

405 Rue Bonsecours
☎ (514) 282-1725 or
866-544-1725
▤ (514) 282-0456
www.pierreducalvet.ca

Located near the Champ-de-Mars metro station, this establishment is set in one of Montréal's oldest homes (1725), discreetly tucked away at the intersection of Bonsecours and Saint-Paul streets. It

has recently been entirely renovated, as have many other older houses in the neighbourhood. The nine rooms, all different and featuring a fireplace, exude a refined charm with lovely antique wood panelling accentuated by stained glass and beautiful antiques. Furnishings include canopy beds and mahogany armoires with gold leaf. Moreover, the bathrooms are tiled in Italian marble. A pretty indoor courtyard and day room allow guests to escape from the crowds. Breakfast is served in a lovely Victorian greenhouse, and service is attentive and meticulous. This inn, located in the heart of the city's historic district, is a real gem that will make your stay absolutely unforgettable. And let's not forget that the restaurant's chef is a master of French cuisine. Note that the establishment features a smoking room.

Delta Centre-Ville
$$$$$
≋ ⚏ ⑅ ⚓ ᕓ ≡ @ ⅄

777 Rue University
☎ (514) 879-1370 or
877-814-7706
▤ (514) 879-1831
www.deltahotels.com

The Delta is visible when arriving in Montréal via the Autoroute Bonaventure. Its 711 rooms are attractive but small, and feature Internet access. On the top floor is a revolving panoramic restaurant offering regional cuisine and a spectacular view of the city.

Hôtel Gault
$$$$$ bkfst incl.
≡ ⚓ ☞ @ ᕓ

449 Rue Ste-Hélène
☎ (514) 904-1616 or
866-904-1616
▤ (514) 904-1717
www.hotelgault.com

Established in June 2002, Hôtel Gault is a small, 30-room hotel reminiscent of a private mansion... one could get used to living here. It features designer furnishings and accessories that were created especially for its innovative decor. The lobby features large windows that give an impression of space, and there is a cozy reading nook at the rear. Breakfast is served communal style at a large table. All the rooms, occupying four floors, are decorated by theme; each is unique, though all share a similar contemporary style. With the exception of the lofts, the rooms are not very big, but the space is well designed and very comfortable. The lovely, modern bathrooms are equipped with tubs, a heated floor and all the amenities to pamper yourself. Some rooms have a patio and all windows open onto the street and the pretty flower boxes that enhance the facade.

Hôtel Nelligan
$$$$$ bkfst incl.
≡ ⚏ ⚠ ⚓ @ ◎

106 Rue St-Paul Ouest
☎ (514) 788-2040 or
877-788-2040
▤ (514) 788-2041
www.hotelnelligan.com

It's anyone's guess what the famous poet would have thought of the luxury hotel bearing his

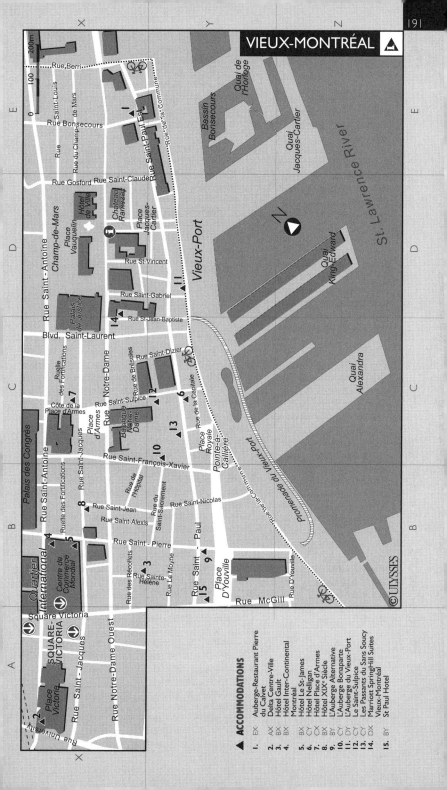

| 191 |

VIEUX-MONTRÉAL ▲

▲ **ACCOMMODATIONS**

1. EX Auberge-Restaurant Pierre du Calvet
2. AX Delta Centre-Ville
3. BX Hôtel Gault
4. BX Hôtel Inter-Continental Montréal
5. BX Hôtel Le St-James
6. CX Hôtel Nelligan
7. CX Hôtel Place d'Armes
8. BY Hôtel XIXᵉ Siècle
9. CY L'Auberge Alternative
10. CY L'Auberge Bonaparte
11. DY L'Auberge du Vieux-Port
12. CY Le Saint-Sulpice
13. CY Les Passants du Sans Soucy
14. DX Marriott Spring Hill Suites Vieux-Montréal
15. BY St Paul Hotel

© ULYSSES

name, but one thing's for sure: this place is something else. Recently opened in Old Montréal, this boutique hotel boasts 60 all-equipped, very comfortable rooms and suites. The establishment belongs to a family that owns many others in the neighbourhood and, as such, has the know-how to make a place special. Between the lobby and the restaurant is a lovely inner courtyard where breakfast is served. Some of the rooms overlook the courtyard, which, despite the lack of view, makes for a quieter environment. The rooms are attractive, with stone and/or brick walls, wood blinds, modern bathrooms (some of which feature a double whirlpool) and down-filled duvets. Wine and cheese are served in the courtyard from 5pm to 7pm, next to an inviting reading nook. In fact, the poetry theme is found throughout the hotel; for instance, the rooms are decorated with canvases on which Nelligan's poems have been hand-written. A complimentary continental breakfast is served in the morning.

Hôtel Place d'Armes
$$$$$ bkfst incl.
≋ ⯑ ≡ ⯑ ⊚ @ ⯑
701 Côte de la Place d'Armes
☎ (514) 842-1887 or
888-450-1887
▤ (514) 842-6469
www.hotelplacedarmes.com

Among the new boutique hotels that have taken over Old Montréal, one of the first to open (2002) was the Hôtel Place d'Armes, standing at the corner of

the square of the same name and facing the magnificent Notre-Dame basilica. The establishment's 136 rooms are spread out over three towers where the decor varies from elegant dark woodwork to rich cream tones and brick walls. Equipped with CD and DVD players, a home-movie theatre and modern bathrooms, all rooms are comfortable and practical. In addition to breakfast, wine and cheese are served in the lobby before dinner. Non-smoking establishment.

Hôtel Le Saint-James
$$$$$
≡ ⊚ ⯑ ⫻ ✳ ⯑ ⯑ @
355 Rue St-Jacques
☎ (514) 841-3111 or
866-841-3111
▤ (514) 841-1232
www.hotellestjames.com

A magnificent hotel that exudes luxury, Le Saint-James opened its doors in the spring of 2002 and is the delight of a well-off clientele who wishes to explore Montréal while enjoying a comfortable stay in a sumptuous, refined environment. Fittingly, it stands in the very heart of Montréal's former business district, in a gorgeous building that has seen many a financial transaction and, in the past few years, has undergone major renovations. While its designers were busy restoring the building's former lustre and adding modern amenities, a team of specialists was scouring Europe, the Far East and the rest of the planet to handpick furnishings and

art. Antiques, paintings, sculptures and furnishings now richly decorate the hotel's lobby, hallways, 61 rooms and suites. The result will please even the most demanding guest. The building's architecture, with its friezes and mouldings, is accentuated by the decor's warmth and richness, as well as top-quality services and amenities, such as a spa.

Hôtel XIXᵉ Siècle
$$$$$ bkfst incl.
≡ ⊚ @
262 Rue St-Jacques Ouest
☎ (514) 985-0019
▤ (514) 985-0059
www.hotelxixsiecle.com

Housed in a former bank of Second Empire architecture, the Hôtel XIXᵉ Siècle has both old-fashioned charm and modern attributes. Its 59 rooms are spacious, and high ceiling and large windows add to this feeling of grandeur. Warm hues, stylish furnishings, lovely fabrics and gorgeous bathrooms provide each room with a cozy, comfortable decor. There is also Internet access. The breakfast room dazzles in black and white, while the lobby features armchairs and books to welcome visitors.

St-Paul Hotel
$$$$$
≡ ⯑ ⯑ ⯑ ⯑ @
355 Rue McGill
☎ (514) 380-2222 or
866-380-2202
▤ (514) 380-2200
www.hotelstpaul.com

The St-Paul Hotel's 96 rooms and 24 suites are housed in a superb historic building that has been entirely renovated. Consequently, the interior decor is very modern, and various materials blend harmoniously to create a stunning effect. With alabaster and fire, fur and vinyl, black tiling and cream-coloured fabrics, each room has been created with utmost care. The result is an audacious, avant-garde design, making it a unique place where wealthy, fashionable guests can get together. Despite the bold decor, some of the spaces are quite warm and inviting. For example, in some rooms, the bed area is delimited by a curtain that lends a cozy effect. The hotel's restaurant, **Cube** (see p 215), is already internationally renowned.

Downtown and Golden Square Mile

L'Abri du Voyageur
$-$$
sb ≡
9 Rue Ste-Catherine Ouest
☎ (514) 849-2922 or
866-302-2922
▤ (514) 499-0151
www.abri-voyageur.ca
This is the perfect hotel for young travellers. It is located on the bustling Rue Sainte-Catherine, near the corner of Boulevard Saint-Laurent, right in the heart of Montréal's nightlife. There are only four bathrooms in the two-storey hotel, but all 28 rooms have sinks. The rooms are simple and clean, and the welcome is friendly.

Auberge de Jeunesse
$-$$
☞ ≡
1030 Rue Mackay
☎ (514) 3843-3317
▤ (514) 934-3251
www.hostellingmontreal.com
This youth hostel, located a stone's throw from the downtown area, offers 250 beds in rooms for four to 10 people, as well as 15 private rooms equipped with bathrooms. This is one of the cheapest establishments in Montréal. Guests have the use of a washer and dryer, as well as a kitchen, a luggage check-room, a TV room and a pool table. This is a non-smoking hostel.

McGill University
$-$$
sb ✳ ☞ ৬
mid-May to mid-Aug
3935 Rue University
☎ (514) 398-6367
▤ (514) 398-4854
www.residences.mcgill.ca/summer.html
If you wish to stay within the downtown core, you can opt for McGill University's student residences, on the flank of Mount Royal. There are 1,100 rooms, each containing one or two beds, in six residence halls. The rooms are small, but each has a large chest of drawers and a desk, and some offer a magnificent view of Mount Royal. Most are equipped with a miniature refrigerator, and all the windows open. There are two kitchenettes and two large bathrooms on each floor. For an additional fee, guests can use the university pool, gym and tennis courts.

Hôtel du Nouveau Forum
$$ bkfst incl.
pb/sb ≡ ৬
1320 Rue St-Antoine Ouest
☎ (514) 989-0300 or
888-989-0300
▤ (514) 931-3090
www.nouveau-forum.com
Located right next to the Bell Centre and not far from Old Montréal, the Hôtel du Nouveau Forum, opened in 1996, has some 38 small, modest but decent rooms, including six with shared bathrooms. It occupies a historic storehouse that has been renovated inside and out. Fortunately, the friendly staff adds a little warmth to the rather sterile atmosphere of the hallways and dining room, where a hearty breakfast is served. There is a public telephone on each floor, and guests can communicate with the reception desk by intercom. Note that the rooms do not have bathtubs.

Hôtel Casa Bella
$$-$$$ bkfst incl.
pb/sb ≡ @
264 Rue Sherbrooke Ouest
☎ (514) 849-2777 or
888-453-2777
▤ (514) 849-3650
www.hotelcasabella.com
Located near Place des Arts on Rue Sherbrooke, Hôtel Casa Bella is a charming hotel housed in a century-old home. It offers good value for the money in the downtown area. The 20 rooms are quaint and reflect the care that has gone into decorating them. Breakfast is served in guests' rooms. There is free laundry service and free parking, and the friendly welcome makes guests quickly feel at ease.

Le Manoir Ambrose
$$-$$$ bkfst incl.
pb/sb ≡ @
3422 Rue Stanley
☎ (514) 288-6922
🖹 (514) 288-5757
www.manoirambrose.com
Le Manoir Ambrose is set in two Victorian houses, side by side on a peaceful street. It has 22 small rooms scattered all over the house, 20 of which feature private bathrooms. The outdated decor will amuse some guests, but the renovated rooms are well kept and the service is friendly. Laundry service for a fee. This is a non-smoking establishment.

Gîte Saint-Dominique
$$-$$$ bkfst incl.
sb
1074 Rue St-Dominique
☎ (514) 876-3960 or
866-808-3960
🖹 (514) 876-3926
www.gitesaintdominique.com
Located near Chinatown, Gîte Saint-Dominique is a five-room bed and breakfast run by a new owner and her cat and set in a beautifully decorated Victorian townhouse. The establishment was entirely redecorated and offers air conditioning and free Internet access. Vegetarian breakfasts are available. Laundry service. Non-smoking.

Courtyard Marriott Montréal
$$$
≈ 🛏 ♨ ≡ ♦ Y ♿ @
410 Rue Sherbrooke Ouest
☎ (514) 844-8855 or
800-449-6654
🖹 (514) 844-0912
www.courtyard.com
Located at the edge of the downtown area, the

Courtyard Marriott has 180 rooms, but no more than nine per floor, which gives this hotel the feeling of a small inn. The attractively decorated rooms offer views of either the mountain or the river. Conference rooms.

Travelodge Montréal Centre
$$$
≡ 🛏 ♨ @ ♿
50 Boulevard René-Lévesque Ouest
☎ (514) 874-9090 or
800-365-6535
🖹 (514) 874-0907
www.travelodge.com
The Travelodge Montréal Centre has 242 comfortable rooms with modern, though conventional, decor. Its location and rates make this place a good deal. The restaurant serves breakfast.

Holiday Inn Select Montréal Centre-Ville
$$$-$$$$
♨ ≈ ♒))) Y ≡ ♿ @
99 Avenue Viger Ouest
☎ (514) 878-9888 or
888-878-9888
🖹 (514) 878-6341
www.hiselect.com/yul-downtown
Built in 1992, the Holiday Inn provides all the comforts of a high-class hotel. Located in the heart of Chinatown, it is easily identifiable by its pagoda-style roof. The interior is also decorated in an oriental style. In addition to providing hypoallergenic bedding, the 235 rooms are spacious and impeccable, and service is courteous and attentive. The hotel's restaurant, **Chez Chine** (see p 218), is recommended.

Quality Inn Centre-Ville
$$$-$$$$ bkfst incl.
≡ 🛏 @
1214 Rue Crescent
☎ (514) 878-2711 or
800-950-1363
🖹 (514) 878-0030
www.choicehotels.ca
Located on a quiet section of Crescent Street, the Quality Inn Centre-Ville is only steps away from a restaurant- and shop-filled area. Its 96 rooms are simply furnished, offering adequate comfort and a small but lovely balcony.

Castel Durocher
$$$ bkfst incl. rooms
$$$$$ bkfst incl. apartments
pb/sb @ ≡ ♨
3488 Rue Durocher
☎ (514) 282-1697
🖹 (514) 282-0025
www.casteldurocher.com
This elegant Queen Anne-style dwelling was built in 1898 and is located a stone's throw from Rue Sainte-Catherine and Place des Arts. The former home of Emma Tassé (the wife of Guillaume-Alphonse Nantel, a lawyer and politician who was also Anathase David's father-in-law) was converted into a five-room bed and breakfast. The establishment's two floors can also be rented as private apartments that include a bedroom, a living room, a kitchen, a dining room and a private bathroom. This bed and breakfast also offers an extra gourmet touch: its Chic Choc Belgian chocolates are handmade on site.

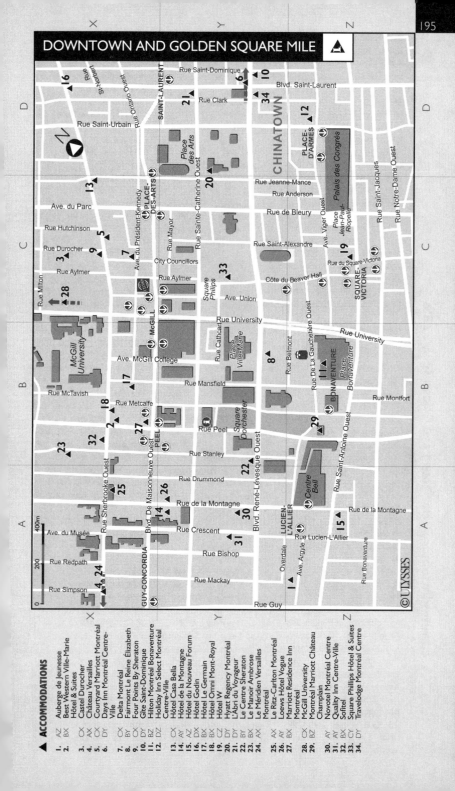

DOWNTOWN AND GOLDEN SQUARE MILE

CHINATOWN

McGill University

Place des Arts

Palais des Congrès

Place Bonaventure

Centre Bell

▲ ACCOMMODATIONS

1.	Auberge de Jeunesse	AZ
2.	Best Western Ville-Marie	BX
3.	Castel Durocher	CX
4.	Château Versailles	AX
5.	Courtyard Marriott Montréal	CX
6.	Days Inn Montréal Centre-Ville	DY
7.	Delta Montréal	CX
8.	Fairmont Le Reine Élizabeth	BY
9.	Gîte Saint-Dominique	CX
10.	Hilton Montréal Bonaventure	BZ
11.	Holiday Inn Select Montréal Centre-Ville	DZ
12.		DZ
13.	Hôtel Casa Bella	CX
14.	Hôtel de la Montagne	AY
15.	Hôtel du Nouveau Forum	AZ
16.	Hôtel Godin	DX
17.	Hôtel Le Germain	BX
18.	Hôtel Omni Mont-Royal	BX
19.	Hôtel W	CZ
20.	Hyatt Regency Montréal	DY
21.	L'Abri du Voyageur	DY
22.	Le Centre Sheraton	BY
23.	Le Manoir Ambrose	BX
24.	Le Méridien Versailles	AX
25.	Le Ritz-Carlton Montréal	AX
26.	Loews Hôtel Vogue	AY
27.	Marriott Residence Inn Montréal	BX
28.	McGill University	CX
29.	Montréal Marriott Château Champlain	BZ
30.	Novotel Montréal Centre	AY
31.	Quality Inn Centre-Ville	AY
32.	Sofitel	BX
33.	Square Phillips Hôtel & Suites	CY
34.	Travelodge Montréal Centre	DY

© ULYSSE

Best Western Ville-Marie Hôtel & Suites
$$$$
♿ ⛵ 📶 ✳ @ ≡

3407 Rue Peel
☎ (514) 288-4141 or
800-361-7791
🖨 (514) 288-3021
www.hotelvillemarie.com

Right in the heart of downtown, this hotel offers 160 plainly decorated but comfortable rooms on 19 floors. The lobby, with its assortment of little shops, has a rather cold atmosphere and is not very inviting. Eleven suites are suited specifically to the needs of business people. Massage therapy is also offered.

Four Points By Sheraton
$$$$
⛵ 📶))) ≡ 🕿 ☎ @ @

475 Rue Sherbrooke Ouest
☎ (514) 842-3961 or
800-842-3961
🖨 (514) 842-0945
www.fourpoints.com

The Four Points By Sheraton offers 196 simple but very comfortable rooms.

Novotel Montréal Centre
$$$$
⛵))) 📶 ≡ ♿ ✟ @

1180 Rue de la Montagne
☎ (514) 861-6000 or
800-221-4542
🖨 (514) 861-0992
www.novotelmontreal.com

Novotel is a French hotel chain. The pleasant rooms in its downtown Montréal establishment are equipped with numerous extras, including a large desk and outlets for computers. Special packages are available for guests travelling with children. The emphasis here seems to be on security.

Some rooms are reserved for smokers.

Square Phillips Hôtel & Suites
$$$$ bkfst incl.
⛵ ≋ ≡ @ ☛

1193 Rue du Square-Phillips
☎ (514) 393-1193
🖨 (514) 393-1192
www.squarephillips.com

Still relatively unknown, the Square Phillips hotel opened in 2003, and everything here still seems brand new. Located south of Sainte-Catherine Street, this hotel is a great place for business and leisure travellers who are looking for studios, set up like furnished apartments, that can be rented for the day, week or month. In all, 80 studios and 80 suites with one or two bedrooms are available on 10 floors. You will also find an indoor swimming pool adjoining a lovely terrace that provides an interesting view of the downtown area.

Château Versailles
$$$$-$$$$$ bkfst incl.
📶 @))) ⛵ ≡ ♿ ♿ @

1659 Rue Sherbrooke Ouest
☎ (514) 933-3611 or
888-933-8111
🖨 (514) 933-6867
www.versailleshotels.com

Located in a building that encompasses the Château and the Tour de Versailles, the Château Versailles reopened in 2000 after major renovations. It was converted into a charming boutique hotel whose 65 rooms have preserved some of the old building's elements, such as mouldings, fireplaces and light fixtures, combined with Victorian and modern accessories. The result is

a lovely, relaxing atmosphere.

Hôtel Godin
$$$$$ bkfst incl.
≡ 🕿 ⛵ @ ✟

10 Rue Sherbrooke Ouest
☎ (514) 843-6000 or
866-744-6346
🖨 (514) 843 6810
www.hotelgodin.com

Hôtel Godin's 126 rooms and 10 suites were designed for 21st-century globetrotters, with a focus on functionality that is rarely found in other hotel establishments. Business travellers will appreciate the long wooden mural panels and flat-screen televisions with integrated computers that can transform each room into an office. The hotel has managed to retain the former Godin building's original cachet (see **Édifice Godin**, p 103) while favouring a 1960s design with a minimalist touch that gives the establishment a very modern look. Hôtel Godin is ideally located between the "Main" and the downtown area, and offers a few interesting accommodation/tourism packages such as its *City Smart*, *Relaxation* and *The Main!* packages.

Hôtel W
$$$$$
≡ 📶 🕿 ⛵ ✟ @

901 Rue du Square-Victoria
☎ (514) 395-3100 or
877-946-8357
🖨 (514) 395-3150
www.starwoodhotels.com

Canada's first outlet of the prestigious W chain of hotels was inaugurated in 2004 and occupies the imposing former Bank of Canada building, in the heart of the city's Quartier International. An extra floor, featuring some 30 suites, was added to the building. Comfort and design are the keywords when describing the hotel's 152 rooms. Besides such now-standard amenities as flat-screen television sets, DVD players and high-speed Internet access, the rooms also provide a view of Square Victoria and feature elegant desks, spacious showers and the hotel's emblematic black-and-blue colour scheme. Guests will enjoy the personalized attention provided by the *Top Désirs* service, a 24-hour beck-and-call option that includes extras like dry-cleaning and massage therapy at the hotel's Away spa. They'll even take your dog for a walk! The Détox sports centre, the Wunderbar and the Otto restaurant round out this unique hotel's facilities.

Le Centre Sheraton
$$$$$
≋ ⛵))) ⍦ ≡ ≻ ᵬ ◎ @
1201 Boulevard René-Lévesque Ouest
☎ (514) 878-2000 or 800-325-3535
🖷 (514) 878-3958
www.sheraton.com/lecentre
Standing over 30 stories high, this giant establishment has 825 rooms. Take the time to admire the beautiful lobby, with its picture windows and tropical plants. The rooms are attractively decorated and feature a number of little extras (coffee makers, hair dryers, non-smoking floors) that add to their comfort. Some

rooms are equipped for business travellers.

Days Inn Montréal Centre-Ville
$$$$$
≡ ⍦ ≋ ⛵ ᵬ @
215 Boulevard René-Lévesque Est
☎ (514) 393-3388 or 800-668-3872
🖷 (514) 395-9999
www.daysinnmontreal.com
This Days Inn was renovated in 2005. Its 123 rooms are small, and the location, on the edge of the Quartier Latin, is a little dreary. On the other hand, the hotel is relatively close to Old Montréal, where it is often very difficult to find a place to stay. Furthermore, some of the rooms offer lovely views of the city. A number of floors are reserved for non-smokers. The hotel has a French and a Chinese restaurant. Dry-cleaning available.

Delta Montréal
$$$$$
≋ ⛵ ⍦ ≻ ᵬ ≡))) ᵬ
475 Avenue Président-Kennedy
☎ (514) 286-1986 or 877-286-1986
🖷 (514) 284-4342
www.deltamontreal.com
The Delta Montréal has two entrances, one on Rue Sherbrooke and the other on Avenue du Président-Kennedy. It has 456 pleasant rooms that are attractively decorated with dark wooden furniture. Some rooms are reserved to smokers.

Fairmont Queen Elizabeth
$$$$$
≋ ⍦ ⛵ ᵬ ≡ ᵬ
900 Boulevard René-Lévesque Ouest
☎ (514) 861-3511 or 800-257-7544
🖷 (514) 954-2256
www.fairmont.com
The Fairmont Queen Elizabeth is one Montréal hotel that has set itself apart over the years. The establishment, which includes 1,050 rooms, recently became part of the Fairmont chain of hotels. Its lobby, decorated with fine wood panelling, is magnificent. Visitors will find a number of shops on the main floor where underground corridors provide easy access to the train station and the underground city.

Hilton Montréal Bonaventure
$$$$$
≋ ⛵ ⍦ ≡ ᵬ ᵬ @
1 Place Bonaventure
☎ (514) 878-2332 or 800-267-2575
🖷 (514) 878-3881
www.hiltonmontreal.com
The Hilton Montréal Bonaventure is located between downtown and Old Montréal. Its 395 rooms offer a number of little extras (coffee maker, hair dryer) that make this hotel the perfect place to relax. The hotel has a heated outdoor swimming pool, where guests can swim all year, as well as a lovely garden and access to the underground city. Some rooms are reserved for smokers.

Hôtel de la Montagne
$$$$$
@ ⚕ ⛲ ≡ ⬥ 🐾 @

1430 Rue de la Montagne
☎ (514) 288-5656 or
800-361-6262
🖶 (514) 288-9658
www.hoteldelamontagne.com

Besides its 135 rooms spread over 19 floors, the Hôtel de la Montagne has an excellent restaurant and a bar with friendly and courteous staff, the Thursday's.

Hôtel Le Germain
$$$$$
⚕ ≡ 🚲 🐾 @

2050 Rue Mansfield
☎ (514) 849-2050 or
877-333-2050
🖶 (514) 849-1437
www.hotelboutique.com

Right in the heart of downtown Montréal stands a former office tower that was converted into a hotel in 1999: Hôtel Le Germain. This establishment is part of the new trend of boutique hotels where service is personalized and special care is given to the decor. Each of the 101 rooms has been carefully designed in a minimalist style of earth and cream tones, mahogany or rattan furnishings and fabulous accessories. The overall effect is one of total relaxation. The building's first vocation as an office building is not forgotten, however; it is found in various architectural details (concrete ceilings, for example) and in the hotel's more functional aspects (Internet-equipped desks and ergonomic chairs). Although the corner rooms have great windows, the best view can be enjoyed at the hotel's restaurant, with one windowed wall overlooking Rue Président-Kennedy.

Hôtel Omni Mont-Royal
$$$$$
⛲ 🚲))) ⚕ ≡ 🐾 @

1050 Rue Sherbrooke Ouest
☎ (514) 284-1110 or
800-843-6664
🖶 (514) 845-3025
www.omnihotels.com

One of the most renowned hotels in Montréal, the Omni Mont-Royal offers 299 comfortable, spacious accommodations. Nevertheless, the decor of the standard rooms is mundane and the bathrooms are small for such a prestigious establishment. The hotel is famous for its restaurants. The outdoor pool is heated and open year-round.

Hyatt Regency Montréal
$$$$$ bkfst incl.
⚕ ≡ 🚲 @ ⬤🍴

1255 Rue Jeanne-Mance
☎ (514) 982-1234
🖶 (514) 285-1243
www.montrealregency.hyatt.com

The Hyatt Regency Montréal is part of Complexe Desjardins, where you can find a wide array of shops, restaurants and various services. Facing the Place des Arts and offering a great view of the downtown core from its higher floors (it has 12 in all), the hotel benefits from a great location, especially during the Jazz and Francofolies festivals, which are held on Sainte-Catherine St. Its 605 rooms and suites were recently renovated, are large and very comfortable, and are exactly what you might expect from this kind of hotel. They also feature several amenities (such as desk with ergonomic chair and high-speed Internet access in the suites, two-line telephone and modem in the rooms) that will enhance your stay. The establishment has preserved the French-style charm of the first hotel to occupy this space, Le Méridien. At the hotel, **Le Café Fleuri** (*☎514-285-1450; no dinner*) restaurant is available to clients, while the bar allows them to meet in an intimate atmosphere and features a terrace in summer.

Loews Hôtel Vogue
$$$$
@ 🚲 ⚕ ≡ 🚲 @ 🐾

1425 Rue de la Montagne
☎ (514) 285-5555 or
800-465-6654
🖶 (514) 849-8903
www.loewshotels.com/vogue.html

At first glance, the Loews Hôtel Vogue, a glass-and-concrete building with no ornamentation, looks bare. The lobby, however, embellished with warm-coloured woodwork, gives a more accurate idea of the luxury and elegance of this establishment. The 142 large rooms, with their elegant furniture, reveal the comfort of this hotel. Modems and hypoallergenic bedding in the rooms.

Marriott Residence Inn Montréal
$$$$$ bkfst incl.
🚲 ⛲ ≡ 🚲 ⬥ @ ❄

2045 Rue Peel
☎ (514) 982-6064 or
800-999-9494
🖶 (514) 844-8361

This hotel was completely renovated before it re-

Accommodations – Downtown and Golden Square Mile

opened in early 1997. It has 190 suites and studios, each with a kitchenette complete with stove, microwave oven, refrigerator and dishwasher. These may be rented for a single night or for months at a time. Twenty-four-hour laundry service, a large outdoor terrace and a roof-top swimming pool are all available to guests.

Le Meridien Versailles Montréal
$$$$$
⌕ ♨ ≡ ◎ ❋ ⟁ @
1808 Rue Sherbrooke Ouest
☎ (514) 933-8111 or
888-933-8111
▤ (514) 933-6867
www.versailleshotels.com
Facing the **Château Versailles** (see p 196) and managed by the same team, Le Meridien Versailles Montréal is its sister establishment. It was also renovated, but, contrary to the Château, it is not a boutique hotel. Here, some 100 rooms feature a decor that is pleasant but not unlike that of hotel chains. It offers the full gamut of services to a mostly business clientele, as well as conference rooms. On some evenings, a pianist provides entertainment in the restaurant.

Montréal Marriott Château Champlain
$$$$$
Ψ ⌕ ⫝̸ ♨ ⟁ ≡ ⫶
1050 Rue de la Gauchetière Ouest
☎ (514) 878-9000 or
800-200-5909
▤ (514) 878-6761
www.marriott.com
The Marriott Château Champlain is a white

building with semicircular windows, much resembling a cheese grater. Unfortunately, this renowned establishment's 611 small rooms are somewhat less attractive than what you'd usually expect from this class of hotel. It does however, offer direct access to the underground city.

Le Ritz-Carlton Montréal
$$$$$
⌕ ♨ ≡ ◎ ⟁ ⟁ ⟁
1228 Rue Sherbrooke Ouest
☎ (514) 842-4212 or
800-363-0366
▤ (514) 842-3383
www.ritzcarlton.com
The Ritz Carlton opened in 1912 and has been renovated over the years in order to continue offering its clientele exceptional comfort; it has managed, however, to preserve its original elegance. Worthy of a high-end establishment, the 229 rooms are decorated with superb antique furniture and are very comfortable. In addition, an excellent restaurant (**Café de Paris**, see p 219) features, in summer, a lovely garden where you can have a bite (**Jardin du Ritz**, see p 220).

Sofitel
$$$$$
⌕ ♨ ⫶ ≡ @
1155 Rue Sherbrooke Ouest
☎ (514) 285-9000
▤ (514) 289-1155
www.sofitel.com
Although new to Montréal's hotel scene, Sofitel is already a well-established name. This luxury establishment offers two types of rooms. We recommend choosing the

deluxe rooms if you plan on staying several nights since they are larger, have more storage space and feature a bathtub (contrary to the other rooms, which only have a shower). All of the hotel's 258 rooms are elegant and refined, decorated with teak furnishings and bathed in shades of amber, while the modern bathrooms are enhanced with Italian marble. The multilingual staff is courteous.

Shaughnessy Village

Residence Inn by Marriott Montreal Westmount
$$$
⌕ ⌕ ⟁ ⫶ ≡ @
2170 Avenue Lincoln
☎ (514) 935-9224 or
800-678-6233
▤ (514) 935-5049
www.residencemontreal.com
The Residence Inn by Marriott Montreal Westmount has 218 rooms, each one equipped with a kitchenette. This hotel is somewhat modest-looking, but its location, on a quiet street on the western edge of the downtown area, makes it an excellent place to stay.

Hôtel du Fort
$$$-$$$$
⌕ ≡ ❋ ⟁ ⟁ @
1390 Rue du Fort
☎ (514) 938-8333 or
800-565-6333
www.hoteldufort.com
The Hôtel du Fort offers comfort, security and personalized service. All 124 rooms have kitchenettes equipped with a microwave oven, a refrigerator

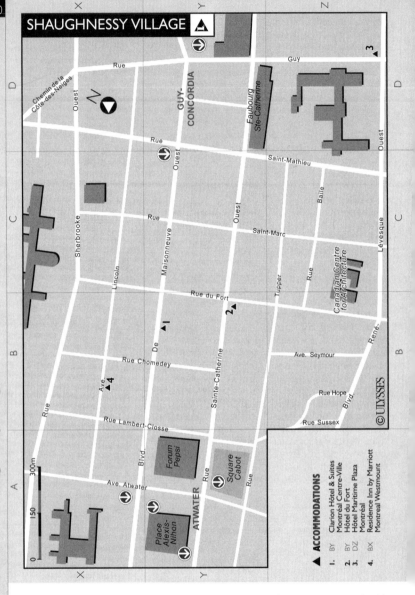

SHAUGHNESSY VILLAGE

ACCOMMODATIONS

1.	BY	Clarion Hôtel & Suites Montréal Centre-Ville
2.	BY	Hôtel du Fort
3.	DZ	Hôtel Maritime Plaza Montréal
4.	BX	Residence Inn by Marriott Montreal Westmount

© ULYSSES

and a coffee maker, as well as a hair dryer, a mini-bar and an Internet hook-up. All the windows in the rooms open.

Clarion Hôtel & Suites Montréal Centre-Ville
$$$$
🛥))) ₩ ≡ ➤ ⚕ @

2100 Boulevard de Maisonneuve Ouest
☎ (514) 931-8861 or 800-361-7191
🖷 (514) 931-7726
www.clarionmontreal.com
Located between the Atwater and Guy-Concordia metro stations, the Clarion Hôtel & Suites Montréal Centre-Ville is a set in a

former apartment building. The establishment offers 266 spacious, brightly lit suites with a somewhat basic decor. All feature a fully equipped kitchen. In addition, the establishment is spotless. The Clarion favours longer stays and offers a sliding scale of weekly and monthly rates.

Hôtel Maritime Plaza Montréal

$$$$

≡ ☕ ⛲ ⚓ @

1155 Rue Guy
☎ (514) 932-1411
🖨 (514) 932-0446
www.hotelmaritime.com

This hotel is only a few steps away from Rue Sainte-Catherine. It features 214 slightly cramped rooms that are nonetheless elegant and well equipped, with all the modern comforts required by both business travellers and vacationers. There are also four luxury suites with kitchenette. In addition, guests can take advantage of the heated indoor swimming pool, exercise room and parking.

The McGill Ghetto and "The Main"

Bienvenue Bed & Breakfast

$$-$$$ bkfst incl.

pb/sb
3950 Avenue Laval
☎ (514) 844-5897 or
800-227-5897
🖨 (514) 844-5894
www.bienvenuebb.com

The Bienvenue Bed & Breakfast is just two steps south of Rue Duluth. Located on a lovely quiet street, this establishment offers 12 small but charmingly decorated rooms with large beds. The well-established bed and breakfast occupies a very pretty, well-maintained house with a peaceful, friendly atmosphere. A very generous breakfast is served in the quaint dining room.

Quartier Latin

Auberge de Jeunesse de l'Hôtel de Paris

$

sb ☕

901 Rue Sherbrooke Est
☎ (514) 522-6861 or
800-567-7217
🖨 (514) 522-1387
www.hotel-montreal.com

The Auberge de Jeunesse de l'Hôtel de Paris, which shares the same owners as the Hôtel de Paris (see below), is divided into dormitories for 4, 8 or 14 people, with a total of 40 beds. A blanket, sheets and a pillow are provided. The communal kitchen is small but has everything you'll need to prepare meals, and there is an outdoor seating area with an attractive view. The place has four showers and toilets, and there's a laundromat right nearby. No curfew.

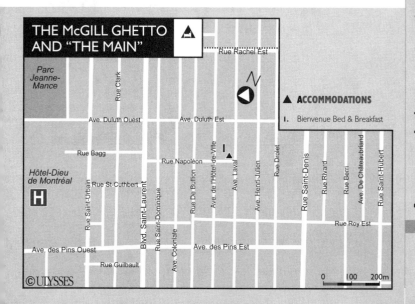

THE McGILL GHETTO AND "THE MAIN"

Rue Rachel Est

Parc Jeanne-Mance

Rue Clark

Ave. Duluth Ouest — Ave. Duluth Est

▲ **ACCOMMODATIONS**

1. Bienvenue Bed & Breakfast

Rue Bagg

Rue Napoléon

Hôtel-Dieu de Montréal

H

Rue St-Cuthbert
Rue Saint-Urbain
Blvd. Saint-Laurent
Rue Saint-Dominique
Ave. Colomale
Rue De Bullion
Ave. de l'Hôtel-de-Ville
Ave. Laval
Ave. Henri-Julien
Rue Drolet
Rue Saint-Denis
Rue Rivard
Rue Berri
Ave. De Châteaubriand
Rue Saint-Hubert

Rue Roy Est

Ave. des Pins Ouest — Ave. des Pins Est

Rue Guilbault

©ULYSSES

0   100   200m

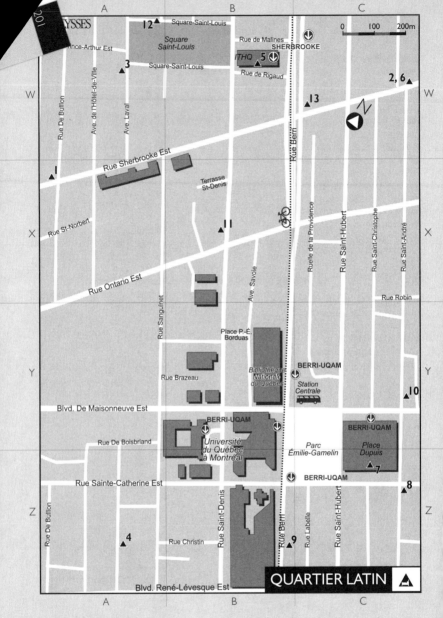

QUARTIER LATIN

▲ ACCOMMODATIONS

1.	AX	Armor Manoir Sherbrooke
2.	CW	Auberge de Jeunesse de l'Hôtel de Paris
3.	AW	Aux Portes de la Nuit
4.	AZ	Gîte Angelica Blue
5.	BW	Hôtel de l'Institut
6.	CW	Hôtel de Paris
7.	CZ	Hôtel Gouverneur Place Dupuis
8.	CZ	Hôtel Le Saint André
9.	BZ	Hôtel Lord Berri
10.	CY	Le Chasseur
11.	BX	Le Jardin d'Antoine
12.	AW	Pierre et Dominique
13.	CW	Plaza Hotel Centre-Ville

Le Chasseur
$$ bkfst incl.

pb/sb ≡

1567 Rue St-André

☎ (514) 521-2238 or
800-451-2238

🖷 (514) 527-0512

www.lechasseur.com

Not too far from the gay village, this B&B offers tastefully decorated rooms and service with a smile. In the summer, the terrace provides a welcome escape from the bustle of the city and a chance to relax. Non-smoking establishment.

Pierre et Dominique
$$ bkfst incl.

sb @

271 Rue du Square St-Louis

☎ (514) 286-0307

www.gitescanada.com/928.html

Square Saint-Louis (see p 105) is a quaint park surrounded by beautiful Victorian houses. This private home stands out for its five extremely comfortable and tastefully decorated rooms. Non-smoking.

Armor Manoir Sherbrooke
$$-$$$ bkfst incl.

pb/sb ◎ ≡ @

157 Rue Sherbrooke Est

☎ (514) 845-0915 or
800-203-5485

🖷 (514) 284-1126

www.armormanoir.com

The Armor Manoir Sherbrooke is an old stone house. The 35 rooms are modest, while the staff is polite and efficient.

Gîte Angelica Blue
$$-$$$ bkfst incl.

1213 Rue Ste-Élisabeth

☎ (514) 844-5048 or
800-878-5048

www.angelicablue.com

The Gîte Angelica Blue is an inviting bed and breakfast that offers six rooms of varying sizes, each with its own theme. They are all, however, equally charming and warm. After a day of touring the city, guests can relax in the living room, which features brick walls and hardwood floors. Non-smoking establishment.

Hôtel de Paris
$$-$$$

≡ ♨ ● ⌨

901 Rue Sherbrooke Est

☎ (514) 522-6861 or
800-567-7217

🖷 (514) 522-1387

www.hotel-montreal.com

A lovely house built in 1870, the Hôtel de Paris has 39 rooms. The renovated house has retained its distinctive character, thanks to the magnificent woodwork in the entryway. The rooms are comfortable.

Aux Portes de la Nuit
$$$ bkfst incl.

3496 Avenue Laval

☎ (514) 848-0833

🖷 (514) 848-9023

www.auxportesdelanuit.com

This bed and breakfast is located in a charming Victorian house that faces Square Saint-Louis and features five attractive rooms. The wood furnishings, visible beams and ochre tones give this place a warm atmosphere. The Bleue, Terrasse and Jaune rooms offer air conditioning in summer. Families should opt for the upper-floor Terrasse room, which includes a large double bed as well as two single beds, and

offers a beautiful view of Mount Royal.

Hôtel de l'Institut
$$$-$$$$ bkfst incl.

≡ ♨ & @

3535 Rue St-Denis

☎ (514) 282-5120 or
800-361-5111

🖷 (514) 873-9893

www.ithq.qc.ca

The Hôtel de l'Institut occupies the upper floors of the Institut de Tourisme et d'Hôtellerie du Québec (ITHQ). It is ideally located across from Square Saint-Louis and at the limits of the Plateau Mont-Royal, "Main" and Quartier Latin neighbourhoods. It reopened in 2005, following major renovations that lasted two years. Its 42 rooms and two suites have undergone a much-needed rejuvenation, with splendid results. The architects have even managed to add balconies to almost every room, a noteworthy asset for a Montréal hotel. The now resolutely modern Hôtel de l'Institut offers very comfortable accommodations and all the major services you would expect from a quality hotel. The hotel is run by students in training who are followed closely by their professors to ensure the top-notch service that is expected from a four-star establishment such as this. Still need some convincing? The delicious buffet breakfast served in the magnificent **Restaurant de l'Institut** (see p 229) should do the trick.

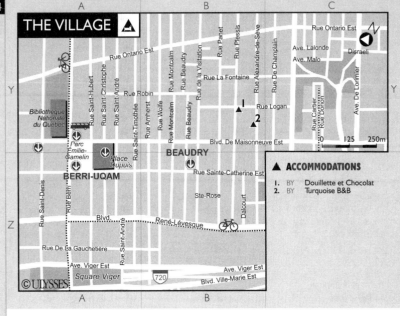

THE VILLAGE

Rue Ontario Est
Rue Panet
Rue Plessis
Ave. Lalonde
Disraeli
Ave. Malo
Rue Alexandre-de-Sève
Rue De Champlain
Ave. De Lorimier
Rue Ontario Est
Rue Saint-Hubert
Rue Saint-Christophe
Rue Saint-André
Rue Robin
Rue Montcalm
Rue Beaudry
Rue de la Visitation
Rue La Fontaine
Rue Logan
Rue Cartier
Rue Dorion
Bibliothèque Nationale du Québec
Rue Saint-Timothée
Rue Amherst
Rue Wolfe
Rue Montcalm
Rue Beaudry
Blvd. De Maisonneuve Est
0   125   250m
Parc Émilie-Gamelin
Place Dupuis
BEAUDRY
BERRI-UQAM
Rue Sainte-Catherine Est
Rue Saint-Denis
Rue Berri
Rue Saint-André
Blvd. René-Lévesque
Ste-Rose
Dalcourt
Blvd.
Rue De La Gauchetière
Ave. Viger Est
Square Viger
720
Ave. Viger Est
Blvd. Ville-Marie Est

▲ ACCOMMODATIONS

1. BY   Douillette et Chocolat
2. BY   Turquoise B&B

Accommodations – Quartier Latin

Hôtel Le Saint André
$$$-$$$$ bkfst incl.
≡ ⛵

1285 Rue St-André
☎ (514) 849-7070 or
800-265-7071
▤ (514) 849-8167
www.hotelsaintandre.ca

A charming little hotel, the Saint André is conveniently located in the Quartier Latin, near the bars and restaurants of Rue Saint-Denis, Old Montréal and downtown. In addition to the warm reception, there are 62 comfortable, well-decorated rooms, all of which have air conditioning, private bathroom and television set. A continental breakfast is served in the room. Stay here once and you'll want to stay here again.

Le Jardin d'Antoine
$$$-$$$$ bkfst incl.
≡ ◎

2024 Rue St-Denis
☎ (514) 843-4506 or
800-361-4506
▤ (514) 281-1491
www.hotel-jardin-antoine.qc.ca

The three-storey Jardin d'Antoine has some 25 lovingly decorated rooms, some with exposed brick walls and hardwood floors. Many comfortable, well-equipped suites are also available. The back garden is rather small, but the balconies are adorned with flower baskets and the effect is very attractive. Hypoallergenic bedding is included in all the rooms.

Hôtel Gouverneur Place Dupuis
$$$$-$$$$$
≋ ⏛ ⱳ ≡ ⛵ ♿

1415 Rue St-Hubert
☎ (514) 842-4881 or
888-910-1111
▤ (514) 842-1584
www.gouverneur.com

The Hôtel des Gouverneurs Place Dupuis, located right in the heart of the Quartier Latin, a stone's throw away from the outdoor cafés on Rue Saint-Denis, is linked to both Place Dupuis, with its many shops, and the Université du Québec à Montréal. Parking lot *($12)* and direct underground access (by way of the metro) to the city. Internet access in all rooms.

Plaza Hotel Centre-Ville
$$$$$
ⱳ ⏛ ≋ ◎ ≡ ⛵))) ⛵ ♿ @

505 Rue Sherbrooke Est
☎ (514) 842-8581 or
800-561-4644
▤ (514) 842-8910
www.cpmontreal.com

The 319 spacious rooms of the Plaza Hotel Centre-Ville have a modern decor and are all equipped with a coffee maker, television and two telephones. The hotel is located near the Quartier Latin, steps away from numerous restaurants, bars and shops. It offers a number of services for business people, including voice mail and secretarial service.

Hôtel Lord Berri
$$$$$
≡ ♨ ✳ & 🚗 @
1199 Rue Berri
☎ (514) 845-9236 or
888-363-0363
🗐 (514) 849-9855
www.lordberri.com
The facade of the Hôtel Lord Berri conceals a slightly plain decor, a simple lobby and 154 large rooms.

The Village

Douillette et Chocolat
$$ bkfst incl.
sb
1631 Rue Plessis
☎ (514) 523-0162
🗐 (514) 523-6795
Douillette et Chocolat is run by a young Frenchman and his two cats who has tastefully renovated an old Victorian house and converted it into a small inn. The two bright, spacious guest rooms have a particularly charming style. One of the rooms has two twin beds that can be transformed into

one large bed, while the other has a double. They share a large bathroom. A generous breakfast is served in the establishment's attractive dining room. No smoking.

Turquoise B & B
$$ bkfst incl.
sb
1576 Rue Alexandre-de-Sève
☎ (514) 523-9943 or
877-707-1576
www.tutquoisebb.com
Located in the heart of the gay village, this Victorian building was completely renovated—only the interior, with its five rooms, is indicative of the period.

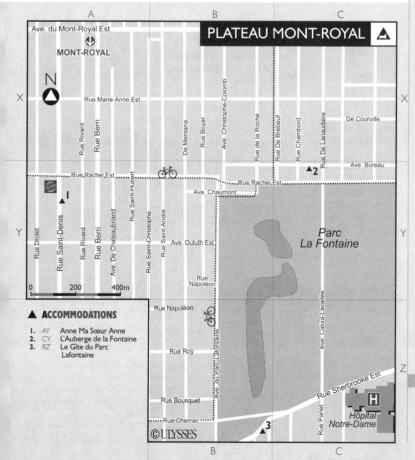

PLATEAU MONT-ROYAL

▲ ACCOMMODATIONS

1. AY Anne Ma Sœur Anne
2. CY L'Auberge de la Fontaine
3. BZ Le Gîte du Parc Lafontaine

©ULYSSES

Accommodations - The Village

The large garden terrace is perfect for enjoying an outdoor buffet-style breakfast on sunny mornings.

Plateau Mont-Royal

Gîte du Parc Lafontaine
$-$$ bkfst incl.
early Jun to late Aug
pb/sb ☞
1250 Rue Sherbrooke Est
☎ (514) 522-3910 or
877-350-4483
▤ (514) 844-7356
www.hostelmontreal.com

This century-old rooming house provides guests with 25 furnished rooms, a kitchen, a living room, a small laundry room, a terrace and a warm welcome. The hostel is ideally located next to Parc Lafontaine, close to Rue Saint-Denis.

Anne Ma Sœur Anne
$$$-$$$$ bkfst incl
☞ ≡ @
4119 Rue St-Denis
☎ (514) 281-3187
▤ (514) 281-1601
www.annemasoeuranne.com

Anne Ma Sœur Anne's 17 studio-apartments are located in a handsome 19th-century stone build-

ing and offer unique accommodations in the heart of the Plateau area. The studio-apartments feature a sober decor and include fully equipped kitchenettes. Each can easily be transformed into an office during the day, thanks to integrated mural furnishings. If possible, try to get one of the four rooms with private rooftop terraces: they're the hotel's best choices. The free coffee and croissants that are delivered to guests' rooms every morning provide a pleasant personal touch, and owner Isabelle Imbert's warm welcome ensures a memorable stay.

L'Auberge de la Fontaine
$$$$-$$$$$ bkfst incl.
◎ ≡ ✵ ⚬
1301 Rue Rachel Est
☎ (514) 597-0166 or
800-597-0597
▤ ▤ (514) 597-0496
www.aubergedelafontaine.com

The Auberge de la Fontaine stands opposite the lovely Parc Lafontaine. Designed with a great deal of care, it has a lot of style. A feeling of peace and relaxation emanates from the 21 rooms, all

of which are attractively decorated. These features have made this a popular place, so it is best to make reservations. Dry-cleaning service.

Notre-Dame-de-Grâce

Concordia University
$-$$
mid-May to mid-Aug
sb
7141 Rue Sherbrooke Ouest
☎ (514) 848-4758
▤ (514) 848-4780
http://residence.concordia.ca/summer.html

Visitors can rent rooms at Concordia University's student residences, located west of the downtown area, 15min by bus from the Vendôme metro station. Weekly and monthly rentals are available.

Côte-des-Neiges

Université de Montréal
$-$$
mid-May to end of Aug
sb ⚬⚓ ✵ ☞
2350 Boulevard Édouard-Montpetit
☎ (514) 343-6531
▤ (514) 343-2353

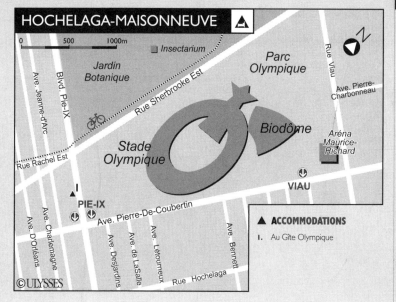

HOCHELAGA-MAISONNEUVE

Insectarium

Jardin
Botanique

Rue Sherbrooke Est

Parc
Olympique

Rue Viau

Ave. Pierre-
Charbonneau

Ave. Jeanne-d'Arc

Blvd. Pie-IX

Stade
Olympique

Biodôme

Aréna
Maurice-
Richard

Rue Rachel Est

VIAU

PIE-IX

Ave. Pierre-De-Coubertin

Ave. D'Orléans

Ave. Chatelmagne

Ave. Desjardins

Ave. de LaSalle

Ave. Létourneux

Ave. Bennett

Rue Hochelaga

© ULYSSES

▲ **ACCOMMODATIONS**

1. Au Gîte Olympique

---

www.resid.umontreal.ca
Available during summer, the rooms in these university residences offer basic comfort: a single bed, a small dresser, a small refrigerator and a sink, but bathrooms are shared. Nevertheless, the price is right. The residences are located at the foot of Mount Royal in a quiet neighbourhood, a few kilometres from downtown and accessible by bus or metro. Weekly and monthly accommodations are available. Reservations recommended.

Hôtel Terrasse Royale
$$$
♨ ≡ ● @
5225 Chemin de la Côte-des-Neiges
☎ (514) 739-6391 or
800-567-0804
▤ (514) 342-2512
www.terrasse-royale.com
The Hôtel Terrasse Royale is located steps away from the Université de

Montréal, in an area full of shops and restaurants. Its 56 rooms are basic and nondescript, but spacious, clean and modern.

Hochelaga-Maisonneuve

Au Gîte Olympique
$$-$$$ bkfst incl.
2752 Boulevard Pie-IX
☎ (514) 254-5423 or
888-254-5423
▤ (514) 254-4753
www.gomontrealgo.com
Although it is located on the very busy Boulevard Pie-IX, Gîte Olympique offers five quiet rooms and a great view of the Olympic Stadium. Two apartments are also available for short or longer stays. There are two sitting rooms where guests can relax or meet other travellers. In summer, breakfast is served on a large rear

terrace. Located two steps from the Pie-IX metro station and the main attractions of the eastern part of the city. No smoking.

West Island and Surroundings

Dorval

Hilton Montréal Aéroport
$$$
⛵ ≋))) ♨ ≡ ☞ ♿ ✳ @
12505 Chemin de la Côte-de-Liesse
☎ (514) 631-2411 or
800-567-2411
▤ (514) 631-0192
www.hilton.com
This Hilton hotel has 486 attractive rooms near the Montréal-Trudeau airport. Dry-cleaning service. Internet access is provided in all the hotel's rooms.

Accommodations - West Island and Surroundings - Dorval

Hôtel Best Western Montréal Aéroport
$$$-$$$$ bkfst incl.
🛏))) ≈ ♨ ≡ ✻

13000 Chemin de la Côte-de-Liesse

☎ (514) 631-4811 or
800-361-2254

🖷 (514) 631-7305

www.bestwestern.com

Thc 110 rooms at the Hôtel Best Western Montréal Aéroport are pleasant and affordable. The hotel also offers an interesting service: after spending the night, guests can park their car here for up to three weeks, free of charge. Free airport shuttle to Montréal-Trudeau service also available.

Restaurants

Vieux-Montréal	211	Outremont and Mile-End	239
Downtown and Golden Square Mile	215	Little Italy	245
Shaughnessy Village	220	Sault-au-Récollet	249
The McGill Ghetto and "The Main"	222	Île Sainte-Hélène and Île Notre-Dame	249
Quartier Latin	227		
The Village	229	Hochelaga-Maisonneuve	250
Plateau Mont-Royal	231	Around the Lachine Canal	252
Westmount, Notre-Dame-de-Grâce and Côte-des-Neiges	238	West Island and Surroundings	254

Restaurants

A s far as food is concerned, Montréal's reputation is enviable, to say the least—it is also well deserved. The culinary traditions of countries from around the world are represented in the city and no matter what your budget, a memorable meal can always be enjoyed. The following descriptions are grouped according to location, in the same order as the tours in the "Exploring" chapter, to make it easier for visitors to find those hidden treasures while they are exploring a particular area.

A lthough you may have learned differently in your French classes, Quebecers refer to breakfast as *déjeuner*, lunch as *dîner* and dinner as *souper*. Many restaurants offer a "daily special" (called *spécial du jour*), a complete meal for one flat price, which is usually less expensive than ordering individual items from the menu. Served only at lunch, it usually includes a choice of appetizers and main dishes, plus coffee and dessert. In the evenings, a table d'hôte (same formula, but slightly more expensive) is also an attractive option.

■ Prices and Symbols

Prices in this guide are for a meal for one person, excluding taxes and tip.

$	less than $15
$$	$15 to $25
$$$	$26 to $50
$$$$	more than $50

The Ulysses Label

The Ulysses Label pictogram is awarded to our favourite establishments (hotels or restaurants). While every establishment recommended in this guide was included because of its high quality and/or uniqueness, as well as its good value, every once in a while we come across an establishment that absolutely wows us. These, our favourite establishments, are awarded a Ulysses Label. You'll find labels in all price categories: from exclusive, high-price to budget establishments. Regardless of the price, each of them offers the most for your money. Look for them first.

■ "Bring Your Own Wine"

Several Montréal restaurants allow you to bring your own wine. This interesting phenomenon is a result of the fact that in order to sell alcohol, a restaurant must have an alcohol permit, which is very expensive. Restaurants that want to offer their clientele a less expensive menu opt for a special type of permit that allows their patrons to bring their own wine. In most cases, a sign in the restaurant window indicates whether alcohol can be purchased on the premises or if you have to bring your own (*apportez votre vin*).

■ Index by type of cuisine

To choose a restaurant according to its specialty, please refer to the index on page 256.

Ulysses' Favourites

■ Montréal's Finest Restaurants

Anise p 244
Les Caprices de Nicolas p 220
Chez la Mère Michel p 222
La Chronique p 244
Nuances p 249
Toqué! p 220

■ For History Buffs

Auberge-Restaurant Pierre
 du Calvet p 215
Le Festin du Gouverneur p 249
Gibby's p 214
Maison George Stephen p 219
Le Vieux Saint-Gabriel p 214

■ For the View

Nuances p 249

■ For the Terrace

Café Méliès p 226
La Moulerie p 242

■ For the Location

Hélène de Champlain p 249

■ For People-Watching

Café Cherrier p 235
Le Continental p 237
Cube p 215
L'Express p 237

■ For Late-Night Dining

La Banquise p 232
Café du Nouveau Monde p 216
Le Continental p 237
Leméac Café Bistrot p 243
Le Saloon p 229
L'Express p 237
Shed Café p 225

■ For Breakfast or Brunch

Beauty's p 224
Café Cherrier p 235
Côté Soleil p 234
Eggspectation p 216, 240
Fruit Folie p 231
Le Petit Alep p 245
Toi Moi et Café p 242

Vieux-Montréal

In summer, you'll have no trouble finding an ice-cream bar in Old Montréal: they're everywhere, especially around Rue de la Commune. Some even have a lovely terrace.

Bio Train
$
410 Rue St-Jacques Ouest
☎(514) 842-9184
For health food, Bio Train is a favourite self-serve restaurant. Things move very quickly at lunchtime, as the restaurant is very popular with business people who work in the neighbourhood.

Crémerie Saint-Vincent
$
153 Rue St-Paul Est
☎(514) 392-2540
Only open in the summertime, the Crémerie Saint-Vincent is one of the rare spots in Montréal where you can enjoy excellent soft maple-sugar-filled ice cream. The

Restaurants - Vieux-Montréal

menu features a wide variety of flavours.

Olive + Gourmando
$
351 Rue St-Paul Ouest
☎ (514) 350-1083
This Saint-Paul street bistro-bakery's two owners used to ply their trade at Toqué!, Montréal's most celebrated restaurant over the last few years. Start your meal off with a mushroom soup, then move onto the beet salad served with a smoked-trout sandwich, and top it all off with a double chocolate and cherry biscuit. You won't be disappointed. This charming bistro is a good choice for an unpretentious gourmet meal in Vieux-Montréal.

Steak-Frites St-Paul
$
12 Rue St-Paul Ouest
☎ (514) 842-0972
Business people crowd into Steak Frites St-Paul at noon, where they feel perfectly comfortable despite the relatively small and noisy dining room. They come here for well-prepared steaks and French fries drenched in a variety of sauces.

Titanic
$
lunch only
445 Rue St-Pierre
☎ (514) 849-0894
Titanic is a very busy lunch spot located in a semi-basement. It offers a multitude of baguette sandwiches and Mediterranean-style salads, feta and other cheeses, smoked fish, *pâtés*, mar-

inated vegetables... delicious.

La Cage aux Sports
$-$$
395 Rue Lemoyne
☎ (514) 288-1115
The Cage aux Sports features an interesting decor strewn with an eclectic mix of bric-a-brac, including a rather imposing airplane. Menu staples are spare ribs and chicken—very North American. Generous portions, inexpensive beer and friendly, efficient service. Major sporting events are shown on a giant screen.

Boris Bistro
$$
465 Rue McGill
☎ (514) 848-9575
Boris Bistro regulars will probably tell you that they come to this Old Montréal restaurant for the setting: the two-storey terrace provides this eatery with lots of charm. Simple, unassuming bistro-style fare and a laid-back atmosphere are the other reasons why they flock here for lunch.

Gandhi
$$
230 Rue St-Paul Ouest
☎ (514) 845-5866
This Indian restaurant in Old Montréal is a real gem. The decor and tables are so elegant that you feel you're seated at a maharaja's table, while the staff, worthy of an Indian palace, fits right into this refined environment. Indeed, conversing with the servers might lead you to think they've probably officiated in Pondicherry. Despite all of this, how-

ever, the cuisine is slightly disappointing due to its lack of audacity and imagination, but the dishes do credit to the best Indian traditions. In the end, eating at Gandhi is an experience that rivals top Indian restaurants, and at the same prices.

Casa de Mateo
$$
440 Rue St-Francois-Xavier
☎ (514) 844-7448
Decorated with hammocks, cacti and Latin-American knick-knacks, Casa de Mateo is a delightful Mexican restaurant. The restaurant's staff will be glad to help you bone up on your rusty Spanish. The food is authentic and delicious.

La Gargote
$$
351 Place D'Youville

☎ (514) 844-1428
La Gargote is not what you would expect from its name, which means "a cheap place to eat" in French. Rather, it is a small French restaurant that attracts a regular clientele and curious newcomers. The decor is inviting, the cuisine tasty and the prices affordable.

Le Petit Moulinsart
$$
139 Rue St-Paul Ouest
☎ (514) 843-7432
Le Petit Moulinsart is a Belgian bistro that could easily pass for a small museum devoted to the characters of the *Tintin* comic books by Georges Rémi, a.k.a. Hergé. All

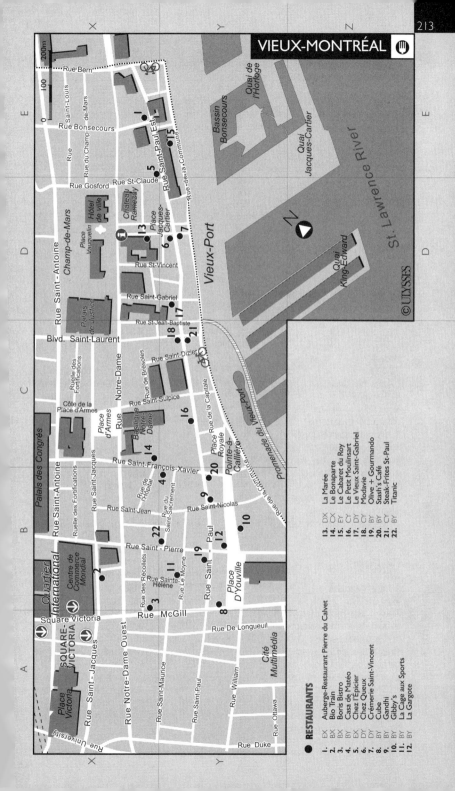

VIEUX-MONTRÉAL

RESTAURANTS

1. EX   Auberge-Restaurant Pierre du Calvet
2. BX   Bio Train
3. BX   Boris Bistro
4. BY   Casa de Matéo
5. EX   Chez l'Épicier
6. DY   Chez Queux
7. DY   Crémerie Saint-Vincent
8. BY   Cube
9. BY   Gandhi
10. BY Gibby's
11. BY La Cage aux Sports
12. BY La Gargote

13. DX   La Marée
14. CX   Le Bonaparte
15. EY   Le Cabaret du Roy
16. CY   Le Petit Moulinsart
17. DY   Le Vieux Saint-Gabriel
18. CY   Modavie
19. BY   Olive + Gourmando
20. BY   Stash's Café
21. CY   Steak-Frites St-Paul
22. BY   Titanic

©ULYSSES

sorts of objects and posters related to the *Tintin* books decorate the walls, menus and tables of the establishment. Service is friendly but slow. Besides the traditional dish of mussels and French fries, don't miss Colonel Sponz's sorbet and Capitaine Haddock's salad.

Stash's Café
$$

200 Rue St-Paul Ouest
☎ (514) 845-6611

This charming little Polish restaurant with a simple, cozy decor is the ideal choice for delicious cheese-stuffed pirogies, sausage and sauerkraut. The vodka is also excellent.

Modavie
$$-$$$

1 Rue St-Paul Ouest
☎ (514) 287-9582

You will recognize Modavie, at the corner of Boulevard Saint-Laurent and Rue St-Paul, by the awning above its windows. Its beautiful decor, both modern and antique, creates a soothing atmosphere. Mediterranean-style meat, pasta and fish dishes are served here.

Chez L'Épicier
$$$

311 Rue St-Paul Est
☎ (514) 878-2232

This is a wonderful spot to savour fresh products and market-inspired cuisine. L'Épicier ("the grocer"), which doubles as a gourmet store, is first and foremost a restaurant that serves good, creative food in a spectacular way. Stone walls, large windows overlooking the

magnificent architecture of the Bonsecours Market and a bistro-style decor give the place an atmosphere that is both lively and intimate. L'Épicier's wine bar also features some interesting selections.

Le Bonaparte
$$$

443 Rue St-François-Xavier
☎ (514) 844-4368

The varied menu of French restaurant Le Bonaparte always includes some delicious surprises. Guests can savour them in one of the establishment's three rooms, all richly decorated in the Empire style. The largest offers the warmth of a fireplace in winter, while another, named "La Serre" (the greenhouse), reveals a subdued ambiance thanks to its many potted plants.

Le Cabaret du Roy
$$$

363 Rue de la Commune Est
☎ (514) 907-9000

If you plan on dining at this Old Montréal restaurant, don't expect an ordinary night out. After all, you're at Cabaret du Roy, and you're not alone. A crowd of characters right out of Montréal's golden age awaits diners in an old-fashioned decor and involves them in an entertaining historical re-enactment. Rest assured, you don't have to participate if you don't feel like it. You might not learn the city's entire history in one night, but the entertainment is worthwhile—not to mention the food.

Traditional dishes with a twist make up a fantastic menu.

Le Vieux Saint-Gabriel
$$$

426 Rue St-Gabriel
☎ (514) 878-3561

The attraction of the Vieux Saint-Gabriel lies above all in its enchanting decor reminiscent of early New France; the restaurant is set in an old house that served as an inn in 1754 (see p 64). The French and Italian selections from the somewhat predictable menu are adequate.

Chez Queux
$$$

158 Rue St-Paul Est
☎ (514) 866-5194

Ideally located in Old Montréal and overlooking Place Jacques-Cartier, Chez Queux serves classic French cuisine in the finest tradition. Refined service in an elegant setting guarantee a positive culinary experience.

Gibby's
$$$-$$$$

298 Place d'Youville
☎ (514) 282-1837

Gibby's is located in a renovated old stable. Its menu offers generous servings of beef or veal steaks served at wooden tables set around a glowing fire and surrounded by low brick-and-stone walls. In the summer months, patrons can eat comfortably outdoors in a large inner courtyard. All in all, an extraordinary decor, which is reflected in the rather high prices. Vegetarians beware.

Cube
$$$$
355 Rue McGill
☎ (514) 276-2823
Cube came close to becoming a featureless shape following a conflict between the restaurant's owners. Fortunately, the famous polygon managed to retain its purity with the arrival of Éric Gonzalez, one of the most talented chefs this city has had the privilege of welcoming. Since then, the establishment has maintained its chic, well-kept allure, with impeccable service, a tasteful decor and furnishings that provide the perfect setting for the real reason food aficionados come here: to revel in an unforgettable culinary experience that compares favourably with any of the world's top gourmet dining establishments. If money is no object, don't hesitate to choose the seven-course meal. The combination of marvellous flavours will leave you breathless. Among the many splendid offerings are roasted veal sweetbread and asparagus with hazelnut-butter juice; simply prepared sea salt-seasoned duck foie gras; melt-in-your-mouth, slow-cooked salmon, as light as mousse and served with a stunning veal stock and lobster sauce; and Angus beef filet served with truffle-flavoured egg-yolk ravioli. The wine list and the wine steward's judicious suggestions round out an exquisite meal.

La Marée
$$$$
404 Place Jacques-Cartier
☎ (514) 861-9794
Located on bustling Place Jacques-Cartier, La Marée has managed to maintain an excellent reputation over the years. The chef prepares fish and seafood to perfection. The dining room is spacious, so everyone is comfortable.

Auberge-Restaurant Pierre du Calvet
$$$$
401 Rue Bonsecours
☎ (514) 282-1725
The old jewel among Montréal restaurants, the inn **Auberge-Restaurant Pierre du Calvet** (see p 190) boast one of the best dining rooms in the city. The establishment is particularly recommended for its delicious and imaginative French cuisine. Its menu, based on game, poultry, fish and beef, changes every two weeks. The elegant surroundings, antiques, ornamental plants and discrete service further add to the pleasure of an evening meal at the **Maison Pierre du Calvet** (see p 69) built in 1725.

Downtown and Golden Square Mile

Ben's Delicatessen
$
900 Boulevard De Maisonneuve Ouest
☎ (514) 844-1000
In the beginning of the 20th century, a Lithuanian immigrant modified a recipe from his native country to suit the needs of workers and thus introduced the smoked-meat sandwich to Montréal, creating in the process Ben's Delicatessen. Over the years, the restaurant has become a Montréal institution, attracting a motley crowd. This is where people come when the bars close. The worn Formica tables and yellowed photographs give the restaurant an outdated appearance. Don't expect much from the service either.

Café Starbuck's
$
1171 Rue Ste-Catherine Ouest, in the Chapters bookstore
☎ (514) 843-4418
Café Starbuck's, set in a corner of the downtown branch of Chapters, has a lot going for it: there is of course the excellent coffee, and then there are the books. What better way to pass the time before the shops open or after they close than to find a good book or magazine (the magazine section is right next to the café) and savour a good cup of coffee?

Café Daylight Factory
$
1030 Rue St-Alexandre
☎ (514) 871-4774
This hip bar and restaurant caters to the young professionals who work in the Quartier International. They come here for a quick sandwich and salad at lunch time or to celebrate Happy Hour with colleagues after work. The minimalist decor

has retained the historic cachet of the Unity building, an architectural marvel that was designed by David Jerome Spence and built in 1912-1913.

Nocochi
$
2156 Rue Mackay
☎(514) 989-7514
Desserts are the main draw at this refined-looking little café. Delicate tea-, almond- and chocolate-flavoured tidbits, pistachio or rose-water macaroons... all of these can be bought to go or enjoyed on site, with a cup of flavourful coffee, of course. Nocochi also offers light meals (salads, omelettes and sandwiches) that cater to its student clientele from nearby Concordia University.

Eggspectation
$
1313 Boulevard de Maisonneuve Ouest
☎(514) 842-3447
Eggspectation is an excellent spot for weekend brunch. In addition to eggs, they have good waffles, crêpes and French toast, all topped with fruit and whipped cream and served in an eclectic decor and lively ambiance.

Man-Na
$
1421 Rue Bishop
☎(514) 288-1703
This neighbourhood eatery is popular with local Concordia University students. They come here for classic Korean fare: grilled meats, noodles, consommé of mushroom and sautéed vegetables,

among other spicy dishes.

La Brûlerie Saint-Denis
$
2100 Rue Stanley, in the Maison Alcan
☎(514) 985-9159
This Brûlerie Saint-Denis branch serves the same delicious coffee blends, light meals and desserts as the other Brûleries. Even though the coffee is not roasted on the premises, it does come fresh from the roasters on Rue Saint-Denis (see also p 232).

Le Lutétia
$
1430 Rue de la Montagne
☎(514) 288-5656
Le Lutétia offers breakfast every day until 11am in the chic Victorian decor of **Hôtel de la Montagne** (see p 198).

Le Grand Comptoir
$-$$
1225 Rue Square-Phillips
☎(514) 393-3295
At lunchtime, the place to be is Le Grand Comptoir, not for its decor, which is rather nondescript, but for the bistro menu at unbeatable prices.

Mangia
$-$$
1101 Boulevard De Maisonneuve Ouest
☎(514) 848-7001
Mangia is one of the few places in downtown Montréal where you'll find good, reasonably priced meals to enjoy in an attractive atmosphere. Salads and pasta dishes, each more enticing than the other, are sold by weight, and sandwich-

es and more elaborate meals, like steak with bell peppers, are also on the menu.

Café du Nouveau Monde
$$
84 Rue Ste-Catherine Ouest
☎(514) 866-8669
The Café du Nouveau Monde is a lovely addition to this part of town. Sip a glass of wine or a cup of coffee, sample a dessert in the deconstructionist decor of the ground-floor dining room, or enjoy a good meal upstairs in the atmosphere of a Parisian brasserie. The menu matches the decor: classic French bistro cuisine. Impeccable service, beautiful presentation and excellent food.

Jardin Sakura
$$
2114 Rue de la Montagne
☎(514) 288-9122
With a name like Jardin Sakura, diners might expect a more refined decor (sakura is the beautiful flower on Japanese cherry trees). The menu offers decent Japanese cuisine, though the sushi is not always a success. The service is very attentive.

Le Commensal
$$
1204 Avenue McGill College
☎(514) 871-1480
Le Commensal is a buffet-style vegetarian restaurant where the food is sold by weight. Le Commensal is open every day until late in the evening. The inviting, modern decor and big windows looking out on the downtown streets

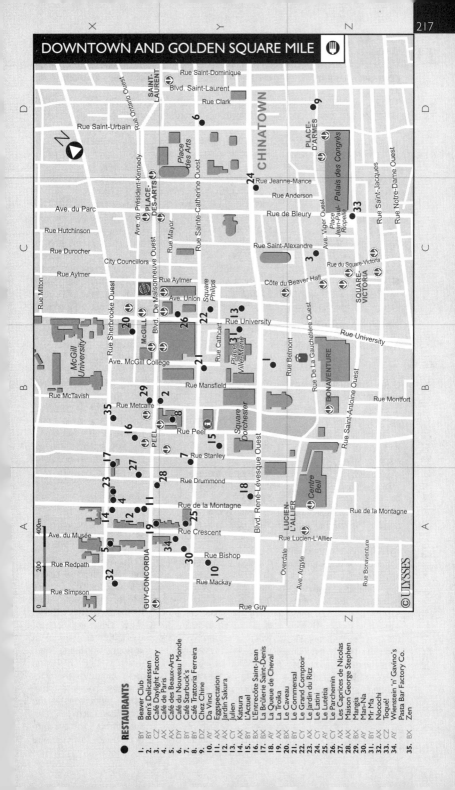

DOWNTOWN AND GOLDEN SQUARE MILE

Rue Saint-Dominique

SAINT-LAURENT

Blvd. Saint-Laurent

Rue Ontario Ouest

Rue Clark

Rue Saint-Urbain

6

CHINATOWN

9

PLACE-D'ARMES

Place des Arts

Rue Saint-Jacques

Place Jean-Paul-Riopelle Palais des Congrès

Rue Notre-Dame Ouest

Ave. du Parc

Ave. du Président-Kennedy

PLACE-DES-ARTS

Rue Sainte-Catherine Ouest

24 Rue Jeanne-Mance

Rue Anderson

Rue de Bleury

Ave. Viger Ouest

33

Rue Hutchinson

Rue Durocher

Rue Mayor

Rue Saint-Alexandre

3

Rue Aylmer

Rue Milton

City Councillors

3

Rue du Square-Victoria

SQUARE-VICTORIA

Rue Aylmer

Côte du Beaver Hall

Rue Sherbrooke Ouest

Blvd. De Maisonneuve Ouest

Ave. Union

Square Philips

20

McGILL

McGill University

26

22

3 Rue University

Rue University

Rue Cathcart

Rue McTavish

Ave. McGill College

21

Place Ville-Marie

Rue Belmont

Rue De La Gauchetière Ouest

BONAVENTURE

Rue Mansfield

29

2

35

Rue Metcalfe

8

Square Dorchester

Rue Saint-Antoine Ouest

Rue Montfort

16

PEEL

Rue Peel

15

Rue De La Gauchetière Ouest

17

7 Rue Stanley

27

28 Rue Drummond

18

Centre Bell

Rue de la Montagne

23

4

11

Rue de la Montagne

14

12

25

19

LUCIEN-L'ALLIER

Blvd. René-Lévesque Ouest

Ave. du Musée

34

Rue Crescent

Rue Lucien-L'Allier

5

GUY-CONCORDIA

30 Rue Bishop

Overdale

Ave. Argyle

Rue Bonaventure

Rue Redpath

10

Rue Mackay

32

Rue Simpson

Rue Guy

© ULYSSES

400m

200

0

● RESTAURANTS

1. BY Beaver Club
2. BY Ben's Delicatessen
3. CZ Café Daylight Factory
4. AX Café de Paris
5. AX Café des Beaux-Arts
6. DY Café du Nouveau Monde
7. BY Café Starbuck's
8. BY Café Trattoria Ferreira
9. DZ Chez Chine
10. AY Da Vinci
11. AX Eggspectation
12. AX Jardin Sakura
13. CY Julien
14. AX Katsura
15. BY L'Actuel
16. BX L'Entrecôte Saint-Jean
17. BX La Brûlerie Saint-Denis
18. AY La Queue de Cheval
19. AX La Troïka
20. BX Le Caveau
21. CY Le Commensal
22. CY Le Grand Comptoir
23. CY Le Jardin du Ritz
24. CY Le Latini
25. AY Le Lutéria
26. CY Le Parchemin
27. AX Les Caprices de Nicolas
28. AX Maison George Stephen
29. BX Mangia
30. BX Man-Na
31. BY Mr Ma
32. AX Nocochi
33. AY Toqué!
34. AY Wienstein 'n' Gavino's
35. BX Zen

make it a pleasant place to be.

L'Entrecôte Saint-Jean
$$
2022 Rue Peel
☎ (514) 281-6492
The menu of L'Entrecôte Saint-Jean is very simple, and therefore inexpensive: rib-steak (*entrecôte*) prepared in a variety of ways.

Café des Beaux-Arts
$$-$$$
in the Montreal Museum of Fine Arts; enter via 1380 or 1384 Rue Sherbrooke Ouest
☎ (514) 843-3233
The Café des Beaux-Arts, located in the Montreal Museum of Fine Arts, offers creative, mouth-watering cuisine and attentive service. The bistro's "private salon," Le Collectionneur, is great for groups who can rent it for events, launches, cocktail parties and conferences.

Da Vinci
$$-$$$
closed Sundays
1180 Rue Bishop
☎ (514) 874-2001
Da Vinci is an established family restaurant that caters to an upscale crowd (which, incidentally, often includes hockey stars past and present). The menu is classic Italian, and though you won't find too many surprises on it, everything served is prepared with the finest ingredients. The extensive wine list contains the perfect bottle for every meal. Rich, subdued lighting and beautifully set tables create a refined and inviting atmosphere.

L'Actuel
$$-$$$
closed Sundays
1194 Rue Peel
☎ (514) 866-1537
L'Actuel, the most authentic Belgian restaurant in Montréal, is always full for lunch and dinner. It has two large dining rooms, one of which is lively and fairly noisy, where affable waiters rush to serve a clientele of business people. The restaurant serves mussels, of course, as well as a number of other specialties.

Le Caveau
$$-$$$
2063 Rue Victoria
☎ (514) 844-1624
Le Caveau occupies a charming white house nestled between downtown skyscrapers. The restaurant serves fine, skilfully prepared, French cuisine. Unfortunately, the service is somewhat aloof and the desserts are disappointing.

Wienstein 'n' Gavino's Pasta Bar Factory Co.
$$-$$$
1434 Rue Crescent
☎ (514) 288-2231
Wienstein 'n' Gavino's Pasta Bar Factory Co. occupies a modern building that visitors and locals alike might believe has been part of the streetscape for years. The look is just as effective inside, where exposed brick walls, bright yet weathered Mediterranean floor tiles and ventilation ducts in the rafters give the place the feel of an old warehouse. Each table receives a loaf of fresh French bread along with olive oil for dipping and roasted garlic for spreading. Among the menu offerings, the pizza is decent, if a little bland, but the pasta dishes are delicious.

Café Trattoria Ferreira
$$$
closed Sundays
1446 Rue Peel
☎ (514) 848-0988
This is a friendly, excellent downtown-area restaurant that offers Portuguese specialties prepared with the kind of refinement that is rare, even in Portugal. The top-quality *caldo verde*, cabbage soup that warms the heart and soul, and the generous rice with seafood are definitely worth a mention. Now accustomed to Montréal, our Lusitanian friends are losing some of the aloofness that somewhat characterizes the Portuguese, and that's a good thing. Lonely hearts can eat at the bar, where they will enjoy the most delightful company.

Chez Chine
$$$
99 Avenue Viger Ouest
☎ (514) 878-9888
Located at the edge of Chinatown, the **Holiday Inn Select Montréal Centre-Ville** (see p 194) features one of the district's best restaurants, Chez Chine. Here, delicious Chinese specialties are served in an immense dining room next to the reception area. Although the windowless space is somewhat impersonal, the decor is attractive. Tables are placed around an indoor pond, in the centre

of which is a pagoda with a large table in it. You can also reserve small private dining rooms, which are ideal for receptions.

Julien
$$$
closed Sundays
1191 Rue Union
☎ (514) 871-1581

Julien is a Montréal institution, thanks largely to its *bavette à l'échalote*, or steak with shallots, which is one of the best in the city. But it isn't just the *bavette* that attracts patrons, since each dish is more succulent than the next. For that matter, everything here is impeccable, from the service to the decor to the wine list.

Katsura
$$$
2170 Rue de la Montagne
☎ (514) 849-1172

At Katsura, located in the heart of downtown, visitors can savour refined Japanese cuisine. The main dining room is furnished with long tables, making this a perfect place for groups. Smaller, more intimate rooms are also available.

La Troïka
$$$
closed Sundays and Mondays
2171 Rue Crescent
☎ (514) 849-9333

La Troïka epitomizes the typical Russian restaurant. Hanging tapestries, mementos, dark and intimate corners and live accordion music conjure up images of the old country. The food is authentic and excellent.

Le Parchemin
$$$
closed Sundays
1333 Rue University
☎ (514) 844-1619

Occupying the former rectory of the Christ Church Cathedral, Le Parchemin is distinguished by its stylish decor and smooth atmosphere. Guests enjoy carefully prepared French cuisine, suitable for the finest of palates. The four-course table d'hôte, with its wide range of choices, is an excellent option.

Maison George Stephen
$$$
1440 Rue Drummond
☎ (514) 849-7338

Founded in 1884, the **Maison George Stephen** (see p 93) houses the Mount Stephen Club, which only opens its restaurant to the public on Sundays, when it serves a musical brunch. The decor dates back to another era, with superb panelled walls adorned with 19th-century stained glass. You will have the privilege of treating both your taste buds and your ears to a feast, as classical music interpreted by conservatory students wafts through the air.

Mr Ma
$$$
closed Sundays
1 Place Ville-Marie
☎ (514) 866-8000

With two dining rooms, including one that is wonderfully bathed in natural light during the day, Mr Ma makes Szechuan cuisine that is nothing extraordinary but offers good value, especially for the downtown area. The sea-

food dishes are a good choice.

Zen
$$$-$$$$
1050 Rue Sherbrooke Ouest
☎ (514) 499-0801

The decor at Zen is modern minimalism taken to the extreme; one might even find it conducive to a Zen experience. Each of the excellent Chinese dishes is beautifully presented. If you can't decide, opt for the "Zen Experience," an unlimited choice of smaller portions of the 40-odd dishes on the menu.

Beaver Club
$$$$
Fairmont Queen Elizabeth
900 Boulevard René-Lévesque Ouest
☎ (514) 861-3511

Magnificent woodwork confers a refined atmosphere to the Beaver Club, a restaurant with an international reputation located in one of Montréal's best-known hotels. The changing table d'hôte may include fresh lobster or fine cuts of beef or game. Everything is prepared with finesse and every detail, including the presentation, is seen to with the utmost care. There is a wine cellar, as well as dancing on Saturday nights.

Café de Paris
$$$$
1228 Rue Sherbrooke Ouest
☎ (514) 842-4212

The Café de Paris is the renowned restaurant at the magnificent **Le Ritz-Carlton Montréal** (see p 199). Its sumptuous blue-and-ochre decor is absolutely beautiful. The carefully thought-out menu is delicious.

La Queue de Cheval
$$$$
1221 Boulevard René-Lévesque Ouest
☎ (514) 390-0090

A haven for meat-lovers, La Queue de Cheval is impressive thanks to its opulent decor of woodwork, wainscoting and chandeliers hanging from high, vaulted ceilings. Needless to say, a rather "masculine" atmosphere prevails here during the meals of businessmen and influential people. The menu features a lovely selection of dry-aged beef from the best cattle breeders in the American Midwest. While you wait for your table, head to the intimate, cozy bar, a great spot to sip a whisky while discussing foreign politics to the sounds of fitting music. Fish, seafood and veal are also offered on the menu. In short, the ideal place for hearty appetites and sturdy stomachs. The stylish, thoughtful staff is most courteous.

Le Jardin du Ritz
$$$$
1228 Rue Sherbrooke Ouest
☎ (514) 842-4212

Le Jardin du Ritz is the perfect escape from the summer heat and the fast pace of downtown. Classic French cuisine is featured on the menu, with tea served on a patio surrounded by flowers and greenery, next to the pond with its splashing ducks. Only open during the summer months, the Jardin is an extension of the hotel's other restaurant, le **Café de Paris** (see p 219).

Le Latini
$$$$
1130 Rue Jeanne-Mance
☎ (514) 861-3166

Italian restaurant Le Latini is known as much for its excellent, deliciously refined cuisine as for its sometimes snobby service. The wine list is sure to please even the most discerning patrons.

Les Caprices de Nicolas
$$$$
2072 Rue Drummond
☎ (514) 282-9790

Les Caprices de Nicolas is one of the very best restaurants in Montréal, with highly innovative and sophisticated French cuisine. There is an interesting arrangement whereby, for the price of a bottle of wine, you can sample different wines by the glass to accompany every course of the meal. The service is friendly and impeccable, and the decor is like an indoor garden. Non-smoking establishment.

Toqué!
$$$$
closed Sundays and Mondays
Centre CDP Capital
900 Place Jean-Paul Riopelle
(on the western side of Rue De Bleury, between Avenue Viger and Rue St-Antoine)
☎ (514) 499-2084

Formerly located on Rue Saint-Denis, Toqué! moved in early 2004 to the new **Centre CDP Capital** (see p 80). If you're looking for a new culinary experience, Toqué is without a doubt the place to go. Chef Normand Laprise insists on the freshest ingredients, and prepares and serves dishes with great care. And then there are the desserts, which are veritable modern sculptures. The service is exceptional, the wine list good, the new decor elegant, and the high prices do not seem to deter anyone. One of the most original dining establishments in Montréal.

Shaughnessy Village

Calories
$
4114 Rue Ste-Catherine Ouest
☎ (514) 933-8186

Calories, which welcomes a noisy, mostly English-speaking clientele late into the night, features delicious cakes served in generous portions.

Bar-B-Barn
$-$$
1201 Rue Guy
☎ (514) 931-3811

The Bar-B-Barn serves delicious pork ribs cooked just to perfection. The food is hardly refined, especially since you have to eat it with your hands, but it appeals to many Montrealers. Those planning to come here on the weekend should prepare to be patient; there is often a long wait.

Le Pique-Assiette
$-$$
2201 Rue Ste-Catherine Ouest
☎ (514) 932-7141

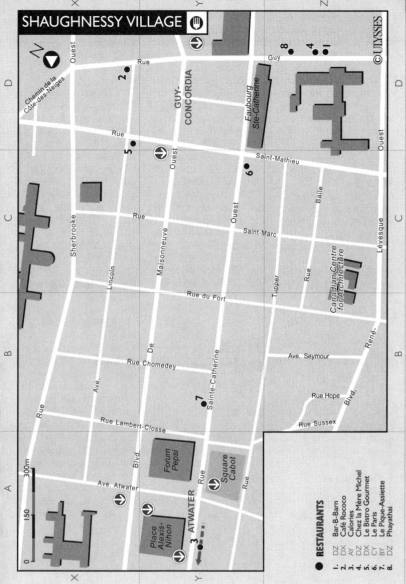

SHAUGHNESSY VILLAGE

© ULYSSES

● **RESTAURANTS**

1. DZ Bar-B-Barn
2. DX Café Rococo
3. AY Calories
4. DZ Chez la Mère Michel
5. DX Le Bistro Gourmet
6. CY Le Paris
7. BY Le Pique-Assiette
8. DZ Phayathai

Le Pique-Assiette has an Indian-style decor and a quiet atmosphere. The lunchtime Indian buffet is well worth the trip, as the menu focuses on excellent curries and Tandoori specialties. In addition, diners can have as much nan bread as they please. Those with a weak stomach should stay away, however, because the food is very spicy. English beer washes it down nicely.

Café Rococo
$$
1650 Avenue Lincoln
☎ (514) 938-2121
Café Rococo is a charming little Hungarian restaurant mostly frequented by a Magyar-speaking clientele. The food is de-

cent and served with lots of paprika. The pink and scarlet drapes and table-cloths give this place a cute Eastern-European decor that would be even more romantic with candles on each table. Excellent selection of cakes.

Le Paris
$$
1812 Rue Ste-Catherine Ouest
☎ (514) 937-4898
If you like *boudin*, *foie de veau* or mackerel in white wine, Le Paris is the place to enjoy such French delicacies in a friendly and relaxed ambiance. As for the decor, well, that hasn't changed in years. The wine list is, however, quite respectable and up to date.

Phayathai
$$
1235 Rue Guy
☎ (514) 933-9949
A small Thai restaurant, Phayathai has a simple, tasteful layout and serves good, exotic-tasting cuisine.

Le Bistro Gourmet
$$-$$$
2100 Rue St-Mathieu
☎ (514) 846-1553
Le Bistro Gourmet is a quaint little French restaurant where visitors can savour delicious dishes, always prepared with fresh ingredients and carefully served.

Chez La Mère Michel
$$$-$$$$
1209 Rue Guy
☎ (514) 934-0473
Considered by many as one of Montréal's best

restaurants, Chez La Mère Michel is the definition of fine French dining. Inside a lovely old house on Rue Guy are three exquisitely decorated, intimate dining rooms. Banquettes and chairs covered in richly printed fabrics welcome patrons to their elegantly set tables, and a cozy fireplace and profusion of plants set the mood. Chef Micheline creates delightful French regional specialties and an alternating five-course seasonal table d'hôte menu with market-fresh ingredients. The service is friendly and attentive. The wine cellar has some of the finest bottles in the city.

The McGill Ghetto and "The Main"

Coco Rico
$
3907 Boulevard St-Laurent
☎ (514) 849-5554
Coco Rico specializes in barbecue chicken and is perfect for anyone on a tight budget. For a few dollars, treat yourself to a quarter chicken with salad. Perfect for picnics, whole chickens are sold at a reduced price on Mondays and Tuesdays.

Euro Deli
$
3619 Boulevard St-Laurent
☎ (514) 843-7853
Euro Deli is where the hip St-Laurent crowd hangs out and is the best choice for a ready-made meal of pasta or pizza at any time of the day or night.

La Chilenita
$
152 Rue Napoléon
☎ (514) 286-6075
64 Rue Marie-Anne Ouest
☎ (514) 982-9212
La Chilenita is a small bakery-restaurant that prepares, among others, *empanadas*. Fresh pastries stuffed with various ingredients, such as beef, sausage, tomatoes, eggplant, olives and cheese, are served with a delicious homemade salsa. Latin American-style sandwiches and a few tasty Mexican dishes are also served.

Schwartz's Montréal Hebrew Delicatessen
$
3895 Boulevard St-Laurent
☎ (514) 842-4813
Montréal is famous for its smoked meat and, according to many people, the best can be found at Schwartz's Montréal Hebrew Delicatessen. Patrons come here for a sandwich on the go and to rub elbows with carnivorous connoisseurs who often travel a long ways for this delicacy. The small establishment is not exactly welcoming, but authenticity is guaranteed.

Tay Do
$
bring your own wine
300 Avenue Duluth Est
☎ (514) 281-6788
This restaurant on Duluth Avenue offers adequate Vietnamese cuisine served in very generous portions and at low prices. Service is very friendly and exotic background music will

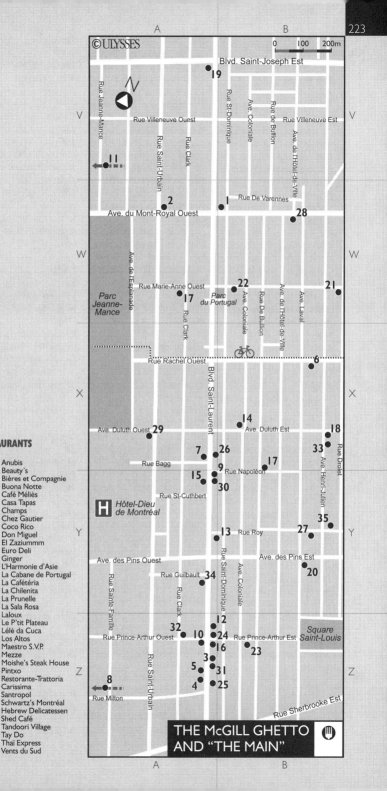

© ULYSSES

223

0   100   200m

Blvd. Saint-Joseph Est

19

Rue Jeanne-Mance

Rue St-Dominique

Ave. Coloniale

Rue de Bullion

Ave. de l'Hôtel-de-Ville

Rue Villeneuve Ouest

V

Rue Villeneuve Est

V

Rue Saint-Urbain

Rue Clark

11

2

Ave. du Mont-Royal Ouest

1

Rue De Varennes

28

Ave. de l'Esplanade

W

Parc Jeanne-Mance

Rue Marie-Anne Ouest

17

Rue Clark

22

Parc du Portugal

Ave. Coloniale

Rue De Bullion

Ave. de l'Hôtel-de-Ville

Ave. Laval

21

W

Rue Rachel Ouest

6

X

Blvd. Saint-Laurent

Ave. Duluth Ouest **29**

14

Ave. Duluth Est

18

33

Rue Drolet

X

● RESTAURANTS

7   **26**

Rue Bagg

9   Rue Napoléon

17

15

30

Ave. Henri-Julien

Rue St-Cuthbert

H Hôtel-Dieu de Montréal

35

1.	BW	Anubis
2.	AW	Beauty's
3.	AZ	Bières et Compagnie
4.	AZ	Buona Notte
5.	AZ	Café Méliès
6.	BX	Casa Tapas
7.	AX	Champs
8.	AZ	Chez Gautier
9.	AY	Coco Rico
10.	AZ	Don Miguel
11.	AV	El Zaziumm
12.	AZ	Euro Deli
13.	AY	Ginger
14.	BX	L'Harmonie d'Asie
15.	AY	La Cabane de Portugal
16.	AZ	La Cafétéria
17.	AW, BX	La Chilenita
18.	BX	La Prunelle
19.	AV	La Sala Rosa
20.	BY	Laloux
21.	AZ	Le P'tit Plateau
22.	BW	Lélé da Cuca
23.	BZ	Los Altos
24.	AZ	Maestro S.V.P.
25.	AZ	Mezze
26.	AX	Moishe's Steak House
27.	BY	Pintxo
28.	BW	Restorante-Trattoria Carissima
29.	AX	Santropol
30.	AY	Schwartz's Montréal Hebrew Delicatessen
31.	AZ	Shed Café
32.	AZ	Tandoori Village
33.	BX	Tay Do
34.	AY	Thaï Express
35.	BY	Vents du Sud

13   Rue Roy

27

Y

Ave. des Pins Ouest

Ave. des Pins Est

20

Rue Guilbault **34**

Rue Sainte-Famille

Rue Clark

Rue Saint-Dominique

Ave. Coloniale

32

12

10   **24**

16

Rue Prince-Arthur Ouest

Rue Prince-Arthur Est

23

Square Saint-Louis

Z

3

5   **31**

8

Rue Saint-Urbain

4   **25**

Rue Milton

Rue Sherbrooke Est

THE McGILL GHETTO AND "THE MAIN"

enhance your culinary experience.

Thaï Express
$
3710 Boulevard St-Laurent
☎ (514) 287-9957
In a simple setting with a strong Thai atmosphere, choose from a menu that offers a host of combinations. The place is a sure bet, with all dishes prepared to order from fresh ingredients. Moreover, the open kitchen allows you to watch the cooks at work. Adventurous souls can order their dishes "spicy," although they are actually very mild compared to what you would get in Bangkok. A good place for an inexpensive meal.

Champs
$-$$
3956 Boulevard St-Laurent
☎ (514) 987-6444
Sports fans gather at Champs to enjoy simple meals and cold beer while watching their favourite sport on the giant screen or on one of the many television sets. Sports vary with the seasons: hockey, baseball, football, etc.

La Cabane du Portugal
$-$$
3872 Boulevard St-Laurent
☎ (514) 843-7283
The restaurant-bar La Cabane is the ideal place to savour a cold pint of microbrewed beer and simple but mouth-watering dishes.

La Sala Rosa
$-$$
4848 Boulevard St-Laurent
☎ (514) 844-4227
Run by Mauro and Kiva of the **Casa del Popolo** (see p 265) and located on the ground floor of a former Spanish community centre, La Sala Rosa has managed to retain its distinctive family atmosphere while attracting young, hip diners who drop by for a bite on their way to one of the shows that are presented in the upper floor's concert hall or at the Casa, across the street. In addition to the traditional tapas and paellas, you can also savour unpretentious, honest Spanish fare among the market-fresh daily specials. A tasty brunch is served on weekends.

L'Harmonie d'Asie
$-$$
bring your own wine
65 Avenue Duluth Est
☎ (514) 289-9972
L'Harmonie d'Asie is a tiny Vietnamese restaurant with a charming staff and a solid menu. Though the service is a bit slow, the meals are not necessarily prepared upon request. The vegetarian dishes are composed of perfectly cooked, crunchy vegetables, and the meat and fish dishes are low in fat. The soups are especially tasty.

Lélé da Cuca
$-$$
bring your own wine
70 Rue Marie-Anne Est
☎ (514) 849-6649
This tiny restaurant serves Mexican and Brazilian dishes. It can only accommodate about 30 people, but exudes a relaxed and laid-back ambiance.

Santropol
$-$$
3990 Rue St-Urbain
☎ (514) 842-3110
Popular with groovy diners of all ages, Santropol serves enormous sandwiches, quiches and salads, always with plenty of fruits and vegetables. It is also known for its wide variety of herbal teas and coffees. Fair-trade coffee can also be purchased here to go. Laid-back atmosphere and pleasant service.

Anubis
$$
35 Avenue du Mont-Royal Est
☎ (514) 843-3391
Head to Anubis if you're looking for something out of the ordinary. Asian-French-Italian fusion cuisine is served in a warm atmosphere, with a singer providing entertainment on some evenings.

Beauty's
$$
93 Avenue du Mont-Royal Ouest
☎ (514) 849-8883
Beauty's is known for its hearty, delicious brunches. The place is often crowded on weekend mornings. It is only open for breakfast, lunch and brunch, and serves classic North-American fare.

Bières et Compagnie
$$
3547 Boulevard St-Laurent
☎ (514) 888-0210
See description p 234

Don Miguel
$$
20 Rue Prince-Arthur Ouest
☎ (514) 845-7915

In a setting that will transport you to some remote Spanish province, Don Miguel himself serves you delicious cuisine from his native land, such as irresistible paella, served in very generous portions. Patrons are offered some cultural immersion at the same time, so feel free to brush up on your Spanish.

El Zaziummm
$$
4581 Avenue du Parc
☎ (514) 499-3675
See description p 234

La Cafétéria
$$
3581 Boulevard St-Laurent
☎ (514) 849-3855
Cafétéria attracts young professionals who come here for burgers and people-watching through the big picture windows that look onto Boulevard Saint-Laurent. The tasty, healthy vegetarian burger is definitely worth a try, while the 1950s decor is the epitome of kitsch.

Los Altos
$$
124 Rue Prince-Arthur Est
☎ (514) 843-6066
Los Altos is one of the most interesting restaurants on Rue Prince-Arthur, a pedestrian street that is not particularly renowned for the quality of its establishments. In summer, candle-lit tables are placed at the front of the restaurant, while the servers, most of whom are Mexican, twirl around carrying high-quality, well-presented dishes. The menu only offers specialties from the land

of Moctezuma, including chicken *mole poblano*, prepared with cocoa and spices, all at reasonable prices.

Shed Café
$$
3515 Boulevard St-Laurent
☎ (514) 842-0220
The Shed Café serves salads, burgers and desserts with creative presentations. The interior, which definitely plays a role in attracting the restaurant's clientele, a terminally trendy crowd that comes here to be seen, is wacky and avant-garde. A down side, however, is the loud, indigestible music.

Tandoori Village
$$
27 Rue Prince-Arthur Ouest
☎ (514) 842-8044
Located in a modest setting in a neighbourhood livened up by McGill University students, among others, Tandoori Village satisfies a growing number of clients with its delicious, affordable Indian cuisine.

Vents du Sud
$$
bring your own wine
323 Rue Roy Est
☎ (514) 281-9913
These "southern winds" are warm, gentle and carry a thousand and one mouth-watering aromas. In the depths of winter, when you've had enough of the cold and need a good, hearty meal, head to this little Basque restaurant. Basque cuisine, dominated by tomatoes, red peppers and onions, is hearty and tasty. And if you're still in need of

warming up at the end of the meal, the ebullient owner will be happy to explain how to play *pelota*.

Chez Gautier
$$-$$$
closed Sundays
3487 Avenue du Parc
☎ (514) 845-2992
Chez Gautier occupies a long woodwork-adorned space. The menu offers excellent traditional bistro fare and a variety of desserts from the next-door Belgian pastry shop. Charming terrace.

Mezze
$$-$$$
3449 Boulevard St-Laurent
☎ (514) 281-0275
Located in a strip of pretentious restaurants that attract an even more pretentious clientele, Mezze offers excellent Greek cuisine in a simple atmosphere. People come here to eat well, rather than show off their luxury cars in the parking lot. We can only hope that some of its neighbours will follow Mezze's example.

Restorante-Trattoria Carissima
$$-$$$
222 Avenue du Mont-Royal Est
☎ (514) 844-7283
Opened in 1998, Carissima is a fine Italian restaurant decorated with dark wood that is enhanced by a cozy fireplace in the dining room and large sliding windows facing Avenue du Mont-Royal. Prices are reasonable and there is a table-d'hôte menu during the week. Good selection of desserts. Italian foodstuffs

Restaurants - The McGill Ghetto and "The Main"

for sale are displayed next to the kitchen.

Buona Notte
$$$
3518 Boulevard St-Laurent
☎ (514) 848-0644

It is impossible to walk down Boulevard Saint-Laurent without noticing Buona Notte. And once up close, it is nearly impossible to resist the temptation to go inside. Buona Notte is Italy rediscovered, a combination of Little Italy and Soho, a piece of New York in Montréal. The prices are high, but, the punters don't seem to mind.

Café Méliès
$$$
3536 Boulevard St-Laurent
☎ (514) 847-9218

Café Méliès followed Cinéma Parallèle into **Ex-Centris** (see p 103), a beautiful, modern building on Boulevard Saint-Laurent. Located on two floors, the café overlooks the street from its magnificent windows and has become one of Montréal's most creative eateries. Its cinematographic decor is impressive (especially the majestic staircase).

Casa Tapas
$$$
266 Rue Rachel Est
☎ (514) 848-1063

Casa Tapas serves exquisite traditional Spanish cuisine. Tapas are little appetizers which the Spanish eat mainly with drinks in late afternoon. Combined, they are a meal in themselves. Meals of tapas are served here, so you can taste a selection of the specialties of this sun-drenched country.

Ginger
$$$
16 Avenue des Pins Est
☎ (514) 844-2121

A little ways off "The Main," Ginger serves sushi, rolls, maki and sashimi, as well as salads, dumplings and noodles. Its wide selection of refined Japanese cuisine is served in an atmosphere that is exotic rather than uptight, and the very attractive decor has a distinctively Asian flavour. Ginger also has a summer terrace on Rue des Pins, where the bustling traffic may provide an unpleasant distraction.

Laloux
$$$
250 Avenue des Pins Est
☎ (514) 287-9127

Occupying a superb residence, Laloux resembles a chic and elegant Parisian-style bistro. People come here to enjoy nouvelle cuisine of consistently high quality, which is one of the best in Montréal.

La Prunelle
$$$
bring your own wine
327 Avenue Duluth Est
☎ (514) 849-8403

La Prunelle is one of the best restaurants in the area and occupies a space that looks right onto the street, which is especially pleasant in the summer. La Prunelle serves attractively presented, classic French cuisine with a few innovative touches.

Patrons can even bring their own wine, a real perk in a land where restaurant owners pay more for wine than do consumers. So dust off that good bottle you've been saving for a special occasion and enjoy a lovely evening at La Prunelle.

Le P'tit Plateau
$$$
bring your own wine
330 Rue Marie-Anne Est
☎ (514) 282-6342

A neighbourhood restaurant, Le P'tit Plateau offers a family atmosphere and attentive service. Simple and unpretentious cuisine.

Maestro S.V.P.
$$$
3615 Boulevard St-Laurent
☎ (514) 842-6447

Maestro S.V.P. is remarkable for the quality of its oyster bar, seafood and ultra-dynamic staff, which really seems to get into the uplifting jazz music.

Pintxo
$$$
256 Rue Roy Est
☎ (514) 844-0222

Run, don't walk to this charming little restaurant: a friendly, and frankly surprising, dining experience awaits. Here, you'll be greeted by the gas fireplace that stands in the boudoir entrance and separates the establishment's two sober but cozy dining rooms. Pintxo seems to be able to magically lend itself to almost any occasion: whether it's a festive meal for a large group, a friendly night out among friends or a romantic dinner with your better half, this is the place to be. At the helm in the kitchen is chef Alonso Ortiz, a proud Mexican who's studied with some of the no-less proud masters of Basque cuisine. He'll delight you with his exquisite bite-sized offerings (the famous *pintxos*, the Basque Country's variation on the traditional Spanish tapas) and many refined dishes. You'll be probably be invited to abandon yourself to the chef's whims; don't hesitate to go along!

Moishe's Steak House
$$$-$$$$
3961 Boulevard St-Laurent
☎ (514) 845-3509
You may find Moishe's exterior rather garish and, well, downright unattractive. But you shouldn't judge this book by its cover though because Moishe's serves the best steaks in town, bar none. The secret of its deliciously tender meat lies in the aging process. Another specialty is chopped liver with fried onions.

Quartier Latin

La Brioche Lyonnaise
$
1593 Rue St-Denis
☎ (514) 842-7017
Brioche Lyonnaise is a pastry shop and café offering an extremely wide selection of pastries, cakes and sweetmeats, all the more appealing because everything really is as delicious as it looks!

La Brûlerie Saint-Denis
$
1587 Rue St-Denis
☎ (514) 286-9159
See description p 232

Camellia Sinensis
$
351 Rue Émery
☎ (514) 286-4002
This small tea shop provides a haven of calm and tranquillity in the Quartier Latin area. Don't expect to munch on pastries or scones here: they only serve fine teas imported from China, Japan and India... seventh heaven for tea purists. Visitors can also stop by the small adjacent boutique to get a whiff of the shop's various teas before buying their favourite to go.

La Paryse
$
302 Rue Ontario Est
☎ (514) 842-2040
In a 1950s-style decor, La Paryse is regularly frequented by a young, eclectic crowd, and by looking at its menu, you will understand why: delicious burgers and home fries are served in generous portions.

Le Pèlerin-Magellan
$
330 Rue Ontario Est
☎ (514) 845-0909
Located near Rue Saint-Denis, Le Pèlerin-Magellan's young and friendly ambiance attracts a disparate crowd that comes here to meet friends and have a bite. Wooden furniture, made to look like mahogany, and works

of modern art create a friendly atmosphere.

Les Gâteries
$
3443 Rue St-Denis
☎ (514) 843-6235
A stone's throw from Square Saint-Louis, this small café serves tasty, light dishes like sandwiches and salads, as well as a healthy, flavourful daily menu. The dessert counter literally overflows with delicious treats. Open for several years, this place has the atmosphere of a neighbourhood café with an intimate, pleasant ambiance created partially by low-key lighting. A terrace is open in the summertime.

Le Commensal
$-$$
1720 Rue St-Denis
☎ (514) 845-2627
This well-known vegetarian restaurant offers a self-serve, buffet-style array of tasty, healthy dishes sold by weight. Its large bay windows in the front, brick walls and different levels lack warmth, but the fare is good and the atmosphere is relaxed.

Zyng
$-$$
1748 Rue St-Denis
☎ (514) 284-2016
This branch of the Toronto chain of friendly noodle and dim sum restaurants brings flair to this overly commercial part of Rue St-Denis. Regulars appreciate the funky decor, amusing and original menu and fresh, creative dishes where vegetables are given the spotlight. The flavours of

Restaurants - Quartier Latin

QUARTIER LATIN

Square Saint-Louis

Rue Prince-Arthur Est

Square Saint-Louis

Square-Saint-Louis

Rue de Malines

SHERBROOKE

Rue de Rigaud

ITHQ

Rue De Bullion

Ave. de l'Hôtel-de-Ville

Ave. Laval

Rue Cherbrooke Est

Rue Berri

Terrasse St-Denis

Rue St-Norbert

Ruelle de la Providence

Rue Saint-Hubert

Rue Saint-Christophe

Rue Saint-André

Rue Ontario Est

Rue Sanguinet

Ave. Savoie

Rue Robin

Rue Émery

Place P.-É. Borduas

Rue Brazeau

Bibliothèque Nationale du Québec

BERRI-UQAM

Station Centrale

Blvd. De Maisonneuve Est

BERRI-UQAM

Rue De Boisbriand

Université du Québec à Montréal

Parc Émilie-Gamelin

BERRI-UQAM

Place Dupuis

Rue Sainte-Catherine Est

BERRI-UQAM

Rue De Bullion

Rue Saint-Denis

Rue Berri

Rue Labelle

Rue Saint-Hubert

Blvd. René-Lévesque Est

Ave. de l'Hôtel-de-Ville

Rue Sainte-Élisabeth

Rue De La Gauchetière Est

©ULYSSES

Ave. Viger Est

CHAMP-DE-MARS

0   100   200m

● RESTAURANTS

1.	BX	Camellia Sinensis
2.	BX	La Brioche Lyonnaise
3.	BX	La Brûlerie Saint-Denis
4.	BW	La Paryse
5.	BW	La Sila
6.	BW	Le Commensal
7.	BW	Le Pèlerin-Magellan
8.	AZ	Le Piémontais
9.	BV	Les Gâteries
10.	BW	Mikado
11.	BV	Restaurant de l'Institut
12.	BW	Zyng

China, Japan, Thailand, Korea and Vietnam meet and mix here, resulting in very original dishes.

Mikado
$$
1731 Rue St-Denis
☎ (514) 844-5705
This area has not weathered the years very well, but the worst seems to be over, and with its theatres, concert venues and cinemas nearby, it is drawing locals who had once forsaken it. Mikado has stayed the course and continues to serve the same excellent Japanese cuisine as it always has, with sushi and sashimi at the forefront. There are no fashionable trappings here and so much the better; even the prices don't follow the astronomical curve of other Japanese restaurants, some of which are obviously only taking advantage of the current trend for this type of cuisine. Indeed, true-blue Asians patronize this place in droves, a sure sign of its authenticity.

Le Piémontais
$$$
1145-A Rue de Bullion
☎ (514) 861-8122
All true lovers of Italian cuisine know and adore this restaurant. The dining room is narrow and the tables are close together, making this place very noisy, but the soft, primarily pink decor, the kind, good-humoured and efficient staff, and the works of culinary art on the menu make dining here an unforgettable experience.

La Sila
$$$
2040 Rue St-Denis
☎ (514) 844-5083
La Sila serves traditional Italian cuisine in an elegant setting, which includes an inviting bar and an outdoor terrace for warm summer evenings.

Restaurant de l'Institut
$$$
3535 Rue St-Denis
☎ (514) 282-5120 or
800-361-5111
www.ithq.qc.ca
Recent major renovations have given the Institut de Tourisme et d'Hôtellerie du Québec's restaurant a much needed facelift, and provided the institute's students with splendid new digs where they can practice what they have been taught. Located on the ground floor of the institute, behind large bay windows that face Square Saint-Louis, the restaurant is a daytime haven of light and a nighttime hot spot in the heart of one of Montréal's liveliest districts. The atmosphere is warm and unhurried here, with a suspended ceiling that recalls a pergola, and oak and maple walls and ceilings. Chef William Chacon and his students prepare six menus per year, and always favour local products. Be it for breakfast, lunch or dinner, the institute's restaurant offers one of the best values for your money in Montréal.

The Village

Le Bangkok
$
1201 Boulevard De Maisonneuve Est
☎ (514) 527-9777
There aren't many Siamese in Montréal, yet they rule the kitchen at Le Bangkok, a small, unpretentious restaurant serving dishes that will transport diners to the shores of the Chao Phraya River. With Thai Express on Saint-Laurent Boulevard, this is the best quality/price ratio for Thai cuisine in Montréal. In a simple yet pleasant decor, enjoy friendly, unpretentious service.

Kilo
$
1495 Rue Ste-Catherine Est
☎ (514) 596-3933
See description p 240

Le Saloon
$
1333 Rue Ste-Catherine Est
☎ (514) 522-1333
Le Saloon serves burgers, Mexican dishes and sophisticated salads in a saloon-type decor, in the heart of the gay village.

La Piazzetta
$-$$
1101 Rue Ste-Catherine Est
☎ (514) 526-2244
See description p 232

Bato Thaï
$$
1310 Rue Ste-Catherine Est
☎ (514) 524-6705
Bato Thaï boasts a pretty decor, as warmly painted walls and ceiling enclose it in design and style. The food is always good, even if the menu is a

Restaurants - The Village

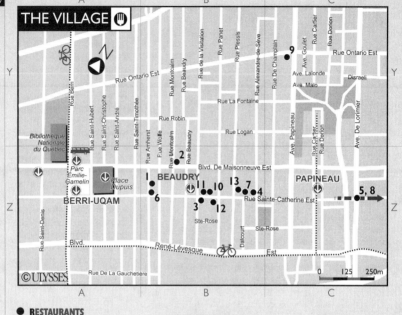

THE VILLAGE

● **RESTAURANTS**

1.	BZ	Area	6.	BZ	La Piazzetta	11.	BZ	Mi Burri to Café
2.	BZ	Bangkok	7.	BZ	La Strega du Village	12.	BZ	Piccolo Diavolo
3.	BZ	Bato Thaï	8.	CZ	Le Grain de Sel	13.	BZ	Planète
4.	BZ	Kilo	9.	CY	Le Petit Extra			
5.	CZ	L'Entre-Miche	10.	BZ	Le Saloon			

little too easy to decode: it amounts to little more than chicken, fish, shrimp, beef and vegetables, each prepared with a selection of the same sauces: coconut milk, peanut sauce or curry. Unless you are there every week, this lack of variety is not a problem, especially considering the charming staff and relaxed mood of this temple of Thai cuisine.

La Strega du Village
$$
1477 Rue Ste-Catherine Est
☎(514) 523-6000

Always packed thanks to its "complete meal at a low price" formula, La Strega is a busy, lively place. This can sometimes affect the quality of ser-

vice, but you will always be served with a smile. The dishes range from ordinary to good, but at these prices, no one can complain.

Le Petit Extra
$$
1690 Rue Ontario Est
☎(514) 527-5552

Le Petit Extra is a large European-style bistro and a distinguished spot for a good meal in a lively setting. A different and always good table d'hôte is offered every day. The clientele includes many regulars. We should also mention the particularly friendly service.

Piccolo Diavolo
$$
1336 Rue Ste-Catherine Est
☎(514) 526-1336

Piccolo Diavolo is an Italian restaurant that offers a warm decor, providing the required privacy for a lovely dinner for two. Service is efficient and discreet, while dishes testify to the chef's creativity and are a treat for the taste buds.

Planète
$$
1451 Rue Ste-Catherine Est
☎(514) 528-6953

Planète serves innovative fusion cuisine. The menu offers more than 30 choices of entrées from all five continents, though the service can be slow and the quality of the fare is rather uneven.

Mi Burri to Café
$$
1327 Rue Ste-Catherine Est
☎(514) 525-8138
With *ensaladas*, nachos, burritos and fajitas, this small Gay Village café promises "laid-back Mexican cuisine." The basic yet colourful decor, with cacti and generous lighting, provides a Latin-American ambiance. Discreet, friendly service.

L'Entre-Miche
$$-$$$
2275 Rue Ste-Catherine Est
☎(514) 521-0036
A lovely modern decor and very high ceiling give this local French restaurant a touch of class. The service is friendly, attentive and professional.

Area
$$$
1429 Rue Amherst
☎(514) 890-6691
Some say this is one of the city's best restaurants, a rather bold statement for an eatery located in the Village, which is more renowned for it bars and night life. Much thought seems to have gone into this attractive establishment's refined decor, and the menu boasts a definite personal touch, with its pureed cauliflower blintzes and Îles de la Madeleine lobster.

Le Grain de Sel
$$$
2375 Rue Ste-Catherine Est
☎(514) 522-5105
Le Grain de Sel is a little French bistro serving an unpretentious table d'hôte. The delicious food is always fresh and beautifully prepared.

Plateau Mont-Royal

Aux Entretiens
$
1577 Avenue Laurier Est
☎(514) 521-2934
A large room with only a few posters, an old tin ceiling and an atmosphere conducive to conversation awaits diners at Aux Entretiens. This neighbourhood café serves all sorts of sandwiches and salads.

Byblos
$
closed Mondays
1499 Rue Laurier Est
☎(514) 523-9396
A small, modest-looking restaurant whose walls are decorated with Persian handicrafts, Byblos appears both simple and exotic. The light, refined dishes are marvels of Iranian cuisine. The service is attentive and friendly.

Café Bicicletta
$
Maison des Cyclistes
1251 Rue Rachel Est
☎(514) 521-8356
For a coffee break or a quick lunch on the go in the heart of the Plateau Mont-Royal neighbourhood, stop by Café Bicicletta. Tasty Italian-style coffee, pastries, sandwiches and empanadas can be enjoyed on the café's small terrace facing Parc La Fontaine.

Café Rico
$
969 Rue Rachel Est
☎(514) 529-1321
Café Rico is a small coffee-roasting joint whose policy is to use fair-trade coffee exclusively. So why not drop by this charming café, with its casual decor consisting of a few tables, a hammock and plants, to savour its delicious blends? As an accompaniment, you'll have to make do with a simple sandwich or cookie, but to compensate, you can linger for hours in this convivial setting that serves as a gathering place for a fair share of socially conscious associations.

Frite Alors
$
1562 Avenue Laurier Est
☎(514) 524-6336
433 Rue Rachel
☎(514) 843-2490
See description p 240

Fruit Folie
$
3817 Rue St-Denis
☎(514) 840-9011
Patrons flock to Fruit Folie for its spectacular breakfasts, which are not only delicious but also very affordable. You'll simply go crazy (*"folie"*) for their fruit-filled plates! If you sleep in on Sundays and only arrive after 11am, expect to wait in line; this is especially true if you have your heart set on a table on the terrace. Fruit Folie also serves simple dishes such as pasta and salads for lunch and dinner.

Restaurants - Plateau Mont-Royal

La Binerie Mont-Royal

$

367 Avenue du Mont-Royal Est

☎ (514) 285-9078

With its decor made up of four tables and a counter, Binerie Mont-Royal looks like a modest little neighbourhood restaurant. It is known for its specialty, baked beans (*fèves au lard* or "*binnes*") and also as the backdrop of Yves Beauchemin's novel, *Le Matou (The Alley Cat)*.

La Brûlerie Saint-Denis

$

3967 Rue St-Denis

☎ (514) 286-9158

The Brûlerie imports its coffees from all over the world and offers one of the widest selections in Montréal. The coffee is roasted on the premises, filling the place with a very distinctive aroma. The menu offers light meals and desserts (see also p 216 and p 227).

L'Anecdote

$

801 Rue Rachel Est

☎ (514) 526-7967

L'Anecdote serves burgers and vegetarian club sandwiches made with quality ingredients. The place has a 1950s-style decor, with movie posters and old Coca-Cola ads on the walls.

La Banquise

$

994 Rue Rachel Est

☎ (514) 525-2415

This charming and colourful little restaurant is open day an night, and is renowned among Plateau residents who come here for a quick bite after a night out on the town. The specialty here is *poutine*, offered in fifteen different varieties that include everything from the Elvis *poutine* (ground beef with sautéed peppers and mushrooms) to the Obélix *poutine* (with smoked meat). Daily specials such as salads and hamburgers are also offered for under $10.

Orienthé

$

4511 Rue St-Denis

☎ (514) 995-6533

Leave your shoes—and your worries—at the entrance, and slip into some oriental slippers. You're entering a tea room where time stands still and relaxation is king, a veritable haven of peace and quiet in the Quartier Latin area. The refined decor, warm colours and scattered cushions may make you want to stay all day. So take your time, let the knowledgeable staff recommend a special blend

and savour your tea while you watch passersby on Rue Saint-Denis. A selection of oriental pastries is also served.

Ambala

$-$$

3887 Rue St-Denis

☎ (514) 499-0446

Ambala is a typical Montréal Indian restaurant, with affordable menu selections, quality, although predictable, Indian cuisine, English beers, rare French wines and cordial, reserved service. Beyond all of this though, it is the deliciously aromatic and exotic curries and tandooris that keep the faithful coming back.

La Piazzetta

$-$$

4097 Rue St-Denis

☎ (514) 847-0184

Piazzetta serves pizza made in the true Italian style, with a thin, crispy crust. The prosciutto-and-melon salad is worth a try, and the restaurant's decor is funky and attractive.

La Selva

$-$$

bring your own wine

862 Rue Marie-Anne Est

☎ (514) 525-1798

Restaurants - Plateau Mont-Royal

● RESTAURANTS

1.	AY	Ambala
2.	BX	Au 917
3.	AY	Au Pied de Cochon
4.	CV	Aux Entretiens
5.	AX	Bières et Compagnie
6.	AY	Bistrot Cocagne
7.	CV	Byblos
8.	AW	Cactus
9.	CX	Café Bicicletta
10.	AZ	Café Cherrier
11.	BW	Café El Dorado
12.	BX	Café Rico
13.	AY	Chu Chai
14.	AY	Côté Soleil
15.	BX	Crêperie Bretonne
		Ty-Breiz
16.	CV	El Zaziummm
17.	AX	Fondue Mentale
18.	AX	Frite Alors
19.	AZ	Fruit Folie
20.	AY	Khyber Pass
21.	AX	L'Anecdote
22.	BW	L'Avenue
23.	AY	L'Express
24.	BX	La Banquise
25.	AW	La Binerie Mont-Royal
26.	AY	La Brûlerie Saint-Denis
27.	AV	La Colombe
28.	AV	La Gaudriole
29.	AV	La Petite Marche
30.	AY	La Piazzetta
31.	BV	La Raclette
32.	BX	La Selva
33.	AX	Le Continental
34.	AX	Le Flambard
35.	AY	Le Jardin de Panos
36.	AZ	Le Nil Bleu
37.	AX	Le Piton de la Fournaise
38.	BW	Misto
39.	BW	Modigliani
40.	AV	Orienthé
41.	AW	Ouzeri
42.	CW	Pistou
43.	CW	Pizzédélic
44.	BW	Tampopo
45.	CV	Un Monde Sauté
46.	AW	Vintage Tapas et Porto
47.	CW	Zyng

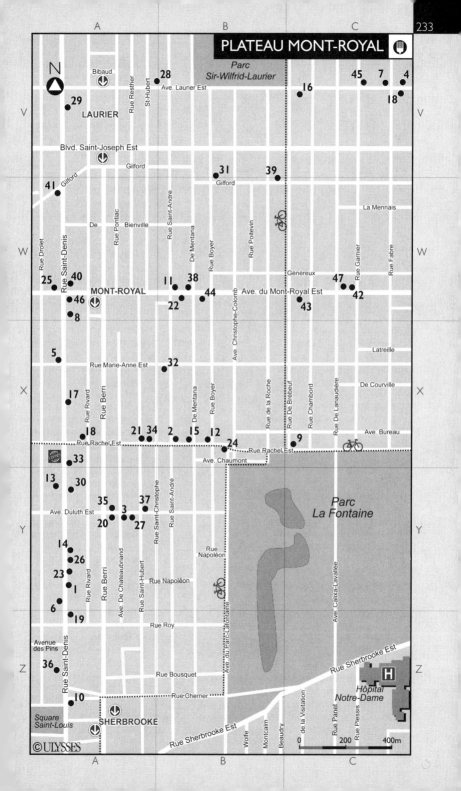

Good, inexpensive food is served at La Selva, a simple Peruvian restaurant. The place is often filled with regulars, and reservations are recommended.

Tampopo
$-$$
4449 Rue Mentana
☎ (514) 526-0001

Tampopo's tiny space is a constant beehive of activity. A multitude of people from the Plateau and beyond come here at practically all hours of the day to chow down on good Asian food. Bountiful Tonkinese soups share menu space with a series of noodle dishes. Behind the counter, cooks sauté vegetables, meat and seafood done to a turn in huge woks. Have a seat on a small stool at the counter or on a floor mat at one of three low tables and be sure to savour the Oriental-style decor as well.

Zyng
$-$$
1371 Avenue du Mt-Royal Est
☎ (514) 523-8883
See description p 227

Au 917
$$
bring your own wine
917 Rue Rachel Est
☎ (514) 524-0094

For quality French cuisine at reasonable prices, try Au 917. The large mirrors on the walls, close-set tables and waiters in aprons create a bistro atmosphere that perfectly matches the cuisine. Giblets, kidneys and calf sweetbread are particular-

ly well prepared here and will melt in your mouth.

Bières et Compagnie
$$
4350 Rue St-Denis
☎ (514) 844-0394

Let yourself be seduced by an excellent meal: sausages, grilled dishes, mussels, ostrich, bison and caribou burgers. Add to this one of the establishment's 115 local and imported beers, and you have everything you need to fully enjoy the musical ambiance this place has to offer.

Cactus
$$
4461 Rue St-Denis
☎ (514) 849-0349

Cactus prepares refined Mexican food. Though servings are small, the ambiance is cozy and very pleasant. The restaurant's little terrace is very popular during the summer.

Café El Dorado
$$
921 Avenue du Mont-Royal Est
☎ (514) 598-8282

Locals in the know head over to Café El Dorado for a coffee or a quick, tasty bite in its spectacular, curvilinear decor. The desserts here are particularly tasty.

Chu Chai
$$
4088 Rue St-Denis
☎ (514) 843-4194

Chu Chai deserves praise for breaking the monotony and daring to be innovative. The Thai vegetarian menu is quite a surprise: vegetarian shrimp, vegetarian fish, and even vegetarian beef and pork.

The resemblance to the real thing is so extraordinary that you'll spend the evening wondering how they do it! The chef affirms that they really are made of vegetable-based products like seitan and wheat. The delicious results delight the clientele that squeezes into the modest dining room or onto the terrace. The establishment also has inexpensive lunch specials. Next door is Chu Chai's little sister, **Chuch**, which offers ready-made delicacies of the same quality to enjoy in tasteful, relaxing surroundings.

Côté Soleil
$$
3979 Rue St-Denis
☎ (514) 282-8037

Coté Soleil offers consistently fresh items from a menu that changes every day and never misses the mark. Excellent, occasionally inventive French cuisine is served at prices so affordable that this is probably the best value in the neighbourhood. The service is attentive and friendly, and the setting, although simple, is quite warm. In summer, there are two sunny terraces: one on the busy street and the other in the lovely garden.

El Zaziummm
$$
1276 Avenue Laurier Est
☎ (514) 598-0344

El Zaziummm is unlike any other restaurant in Montréal. The decor is highly eccentric and includes, for example, a table made from a glass-topped old bathtub that showcases postcards and plane tickets half-buried in sand. The toilet-paper rolls on each table and the countless knick-knacks placed haphazardly here and there confer an undeniable, though unusual, charm to the restaurant. The menu offers a long list of typical Mexican dishes, with a clear Californian influence, prepared in new and original ways. The service is about as slow as it gets, though.

Fondue Mentale
$$
4325 Rue St-Denis
☎ (514) 499-1446

Fondue Mentale occupies an old house with superb woodwork, which is typical of the Plateau Mont-Royal. As the restaurant's name suggests, fondue is the specialty here—and what a choice, each one more appetizing than the last! The Swiss fondue with pink pepper is particularly delicious.

Khyber Pass
$$
bring your own wine
506 Avenue Duluth Est
☎ (514) 849-1775

Exotic and inviting, Khyber Pass restaurant offers traditional Afghani cuisine featuring a cornucopia of surprising, delicious flavours. For starters, the morsels of pumpkin covered with a yogurt, mint and garlic sauce, and the boiled ravioli smothered in a tomato-lentil sauce are especially delectable. This savoury adventure continues with a selection of grilled lamb, beef and chicken dishes, prepared with a marinade that blends perfectly with the fragrant rice. Attentive service and outdoor dining in summer.

La Petite Marche
$$
5035 Rue St-Denis
☎ (514) 842-1994

One of the few small café-style neighbourhood restaurants on St-Denis, a street that is becoming increasingly commercialized, La Petite Marche is a good place to have a reasonably priced meal in a casual atmosphere. The table d'hôte menu is varied and offers generous portions of French- and Italian-inspired dishes. The service is courteous and efficient. Breakfast also available.

Le Jardin de Panos
$$
bring your own wine
521 Avenue Duluth Est
☎ (514) 521-4206

A Greek *brochetterie*, Le Jardin de Panos serves simple cuisine made with quality ingredients. Inside a house with a large rear terrace surrounded by greenery, this restaurant is extremely pleasant in the summer.

Le Nil Bleu
$$
3706 Rue St-Denis
☎ (514) 285-4628

The amazingly delicious food at this Ethiopian restaurant is certainly worth the trip, if only to dine in the traditional manner, with your right hand on a choice of meat or vegetables rolled in an enormous crêpe, called *injera*

amharic. The decor is extremely inviting.

Ouzeri
$$
4690 Rue St-Denis
☎ (514) 845-1336

Ouzeri set out on a mission to offer its clientele refined Greek cuisine, and succeeded. The food is excellent, and the menu includes several surprises, such as vegetarian moussaka and scallops with melted cheese. With its high ceilings and long windows, this is an attractive place where you'll be tempted to linger on and on, especially as the Greek music sets your mind wandering.

Pizzédélic
$$
1250 Avenue du Mont-Royal Est
☎ (514) 522-2286

Pizzédélic serves delicious thin-crust pizza with a fabulous selection of toppings. The large windows are open in summer and let in a nice breeze.

Café Cherrier
$$-$$$
3635 Rue St-Denis
☎ (514) 843-4308

The meeting place *par excellence* for many fifty-something professionals, the terrace and dining room at Café Cherrier are always packed. The atmosphere is reminiscent of a French *brasserie*, highly animated and busy, which can lead to fortuitous meetings. The menu features bistro-type meals that are generally quite tasty, but the service can be uneven.

Crêperie Bretonne Ty-Breiz
$$-$$$
933 Rue Rachel Est
☎ (514) 521-1444
Crêperie Bretonne Ty-Breiz serves wonderful crêpes, both regular and whole wheat, with a wide selection of stuffings. The decor is typical of northwestern France, but you might mistake it for Austrian or Swiss. Good wine list, and for dessert... more crepes! Table-d'hôte menu for lunch and dinner during the week. Probably the best *crêperie* in Montréal and the best known.

La Raclette
$$-$$$
bring your own wine
1059 Rue Gilford
☎ (514) 524-8118
La Raclette is a popular neighbourhood restaurant on warm summer evenings, thanks to its attractive terrace. The menu includes raclette (of course), but also Zurich-style sliced filet of pork, salmon with *Meaux* mustard and cherry clafoutis. Those with a hearty appetite can opt for the *menu dégustation*, which includes appetizer, soup, main dish, dessert and coffee.

L'Avenue
$$-$$$
922 Avenue du Mont-Royal Est
☎ (514) 523-8780
L'Avenue has become a sanctuary for beautiful people in search of hearty meals. Arrive early to avoid the line-up. The service is attentive and polite.

Le Flambard
$$-$$$
bring your own wine
851 Rue Rachel Est
☎ (514) 596-1280
A quaint bistro decorated with woodwork and mirrors, Le Flambard excels in the preparation of quality French cuisine. Though the place is charming, the narrow dining room and closely set tables offer little room for intimacy.

Misto
$$-$$$
929 Avenue du Mont-Royal Est
☎ (514) 526-5043
Misto is an Italian restaurant patronized by a hip clientele that comes here to savour delicious and imaginative Italian cooking. The decor features exposed brick walls and shades of green, and the noisy atmosphere and crowded tables only add to the ambiance and the attentive and friendly service.

Pistou
$$-$$$
1453 Avenue du Mont-Royal Est
☎ (514) 528-7242
With its large, high-ceilinged dining room and modern decor, Pistou is certainly not cozy, and it is usually too packed to have a quiet conversation. But the noise isn't bothersome when dining with friends and conversations get animated. The menu lists some classics like delicious salad with warm goat cheese and honey *(salade de chèvre chaud au miel)* and steak tartar. Another good choice is the daily table d'hôte.

Un Monde Sauté
$$-$$$
1481 Avenue Laurier Est
☎ (514) 590-0897
This restaurant has an original but simple concept: an internationally inspired menu (mostly sautés, hence the name), an intimate and colourful decor and unparalleled, friendly service. An exotic place that will brighten up even the coldest winter day.

Au Pied de Cochon
$$$
536 Avenue Duluth Est
☎ (514) 281-1114
This bistro is located in the heart of the Plateau and serves delicious and resolutely hearty meals. Try the "happy pig" (*cochon heureux*) pork chops or the candied lamb shanks, or, if you're feeling adventurous, order the *poutine* with duck *foie gras*. Some may call this dish a culinary sacrilege, but wait till you've tried it!

Bistrot Cocagne
$$$
3842 Rue St-Denis
☎ (514) 286-0700
After several years spent working at another renowned eatery, master chef Alexandre Loiseau invites food lovers to his own restaurant, located in Toqué!'s former digs on Rue Saint-Denis. He's passionate about his local ingredients and strives to offer the freshest and highest-quality products. His ingenious talent for unexpected combinations includes such masterful creations as citrus-fla-

voured scallops, and his creative presentations make each dish a veritable work of art. The restaurant's attractive woodwork, tastefully subtle furnishings and soft lighting make this the perfect spot for an intimate dinner. This is an excellent choice for a gourmet dinner without the usual stuffy atmosphere. A separate dining room that can seat as many as 18 diners is also available.

La Gaudriole
$$$
825 Avenue Laurier Est
☎(514) 276-1580
La Gaudriole is located in cramped and somewhat uncomfortable quarters, but serves excellent "hybrid" French cuisine, which incorporates flavours from around the world. The menu is constantly changing, so the ingredients are always fresh, allowing chef Marc Vézina's creativity to shine through.

Le Continental
$$$
4169 Rue St-Denis
☎(514) 845-6842
The staging is very subtle at the Continental. Some evenings, the restaurant is positively charming, with its attentive, courteous staff, stylish clientele and modern 1950s-style decor. The varied menu always includes nice surprises. The cuisine can be sublime, and the presentation is always excellent.

Le Piton de la Fournaise
$$$
bring your own wine
835 Avenue Duluth Est
☎(514) 526-3936
Tiny and charming, Le Piton de la Fournaise sparkles with life and is a treat for the senses. Here, you can sample ingeniously prepared cuisine from Reunion Island that is full of surprises, thanks to its aromas, spices and textures. In order to fully enjoy a meal here, it's best to come unhurried and to make a night of it.

L'Express
$$$
3927 Rue St-Denis
☎(514) 845-5333
A yuppie gathering place during the mid-1980s, L'Express is still highly rated for its locomotive dining-car decor and lively Parisian-bistro atmosphere, which few restaurants have managed to recreate. In addition to the consistently appealing menu, the above-mentioned factors have earned this restaurant a solid reputation over the years.

Le Symposium Psarotaverna
$$$
3829 Rue St-Denis
☎(514) 842-0867
Symposium Psarotaverna transports its guests to the islands of the Aegean Sea, with its blue-and-white decor, and warm, friendly service. Of course, fish (striped bass, porgy, red and white snapper) and seafood are the specialties here. Try the delicious moussaka and the *saganaki*. And don't miss

the sinful *galatoboureco* for dessert.

Modigliani
$$$
1251 Rue Gilford
☎(514) 522-0422
Located off the beaten track, this Italian restaurant has an inviting atmosphere and a warm, plant-filled decor. The food is original and consistently good.

Vintage Tapas et Porto
$$$
4475 Rue St-Denis
☎(514) 849-4264
Behind a discreet facade is a restaurant that is very much appreciated by Montrealers. Vintage serves classic Portuguese cuisine, including grilled veal, beef, fish and seafood dishes, as well as tapas, which are delicious appetizers. As is to be expected, the restaurant features a good wine and port list.

La Colombe
$$$$
bring your own wine
554 Avenue Duluth Est
☎(514) 849-8844
A hallmark veteran of the restaurant wars, La Colombe has long been welcoming patrons in a tiny and intimate setting, and serving market-fresh cuisine with North-African influences. As is the case in many of the neighbouring restaurants on the same street, you can bring your own wine.

Westmount, Notre-Dame-de-Grâce and Côte-des-Neiges

Pizzafiore
$
3518 Rue Lacombe
☎(514) 735-1555
Upon entering Pizzafiore, visitors will see the cook standing beside the wood-burning pizza oven. He makes pizza for every taste, with every different kind of sauce, topped with the widest range of ingredients imaginable. This good restaurant is often filled with locals and students from Université de Montréal.

Al Dente Tratorria
$$
bring your own wine
5768 Avenue Monkland
☎(514) 486-4343
Well established on Monkland Avenue for many years, Al Dente is a popular and friendly Italian eatery. The menu features a good selection of pizza, soups and fresh salads, as well as a list of pasta and accompanying sauces that you can mix and match. The decor is simple and the ambiance laid back. Diners come here for the solid food and the no-fuss service.

La Pasta Casareccia
$$
5849 Rue Sherbrooke Ouest
☎(514) 483-1588
The bright red-and-yellow decor of La Pasta Casareccia attracts a diverse crowd in the heart of the mainly English-speaking Notre-Dame-de-Grâce neighbourhood. Fresh pasta is the specialty here and the service is courteous and professional.

Le Claremont
$$
5032 Rue Sherbrooke Ouest
☎(514) 483-1557
Claremont is a lively place, to say the least. A fine menu offers a wide range of choices from one of the best and freshest pestos around to a delicious and savoury mulligatawny soup. You might also prefer, as many here do, just to enjoy a drink and a platter of nachos with fresh salsa. The loud music rules this place out as a spot for a quiet dinner, but if you don't mind a little excitement, you won't be disappointed. The decor is enhanced by changing exhibits of works by local artists and photographers.

Mess Hall
$$
4858 Rue Sherbrooke Ouest
☎(514) 482-2167
With the same owners as the **Cafétéria** (see p 225), Mess Hall boasts a similarly striking decor, the *pièce de résistance* being an exquisite starburst chandelier in the centre of the room. The menu is both original and standard with great salads, burgers and pasta, as well as a few more refined dishes. Westmount's young professionals come here to see and be seen.

Pizzédélic
$$
5556 Avenue Monkland
☎(514) 487-3103
5153 Chemin de la Côte-des-Neiges
☎(514) 739-2446
An affirmation of Monkland Avenue coming of age was the opening of a branch of the trendy pizzeria Pizzédélic. The same funky decor, great thin-crust pizza and eclectic choice of toppings have made the Monkland branch, one of the biggest, just as popular as the others.

La Louisiane
$$-$$$
closed Mondays
5850 Rue Sherbrooke Ouest
☎(514) 369-3073
A meal at La Louisiane is like a trip to the Bayou. You can start with a plate of authentic hush puppies, continue with something spicy like crayfish *étouffée* or shrimp magnolia, and finish up with an order of heavenly bananas Foster. Huge paintings of New Orleans street scenes adorn the walls and the sounds of jazz complete the mood. Unfortunately, the food here doesn't always meet expectations.

Le Maistre
$$-$$$
5700 Avenue Monkland
☎(514) 481-2109
Firmly established on Monkland for many years, Le Maistre serves French cuisine that is always impeccable. The choice of wines to accompany your meal is always good and well priced. In summer, there is a lovely terrace overlooking the comings and goings on the street.

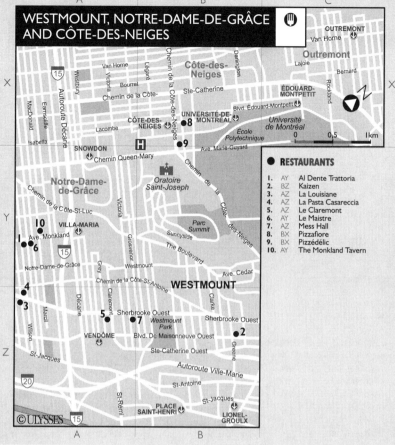

WESTMOUNT, NOTRE-DAME-DE-GRÂCE AND CÔTE-DES-NEIGES

● **RESTAURANTS**

1.	AY	Al Dente Trattoria
2.	BZ	Kaizen
3.	AZ	La Louisiane
4.	AZ	La Pasta Casareccia
5.	AZ	Le Claremont
6.	AY	Le Maistre
7.	AZ	Mess Hall
8.	BX	Pizzafiore
9.	BX	Pizzédélic
10.	AY	The Monkland Tavern

The Monkland Tavern
$$$

5555 Avenue Monkland
☎ (514) 486-5768

Established in a former neighbourhood tavern, this local favourite attracts a crowd of young professionals who come here for the terrace that faces onto western Montréal's latest popular artery, Avenue Monkland. The menu is limited, but is complemented by ever-changing daily specials that offer good value. Unfortunately, the quality has suffered a bit since chef Steve Leslie opened a second restaurant in Westmount. One of the best offerings here is the *crostini*, small slices of French bread spread with *tapenade* and topped with sun-dried tomatoes and bocconcini cheese. Simply divine!

Kaizen
$$$$

4120 Rue Ste-Catherine Ouest
☎ (514) 932-5654

The best Japanese restaurant in Westmount, Kaizen serves all the classics from the land of the rising sun. The prices are high but the portions are gargantuan. The staff won't mind if you share your plate.

Outremont and Mile-End

Café Romolo
$

272 Avenue Bernard Ouest
☎ (514) 272-5035

People go to Café Romolo to talk endlessly while sipping delicious cafés au lait served Portuguese- and Spanish-style in tall glasses.

Restaurants - Outremont and Mile-End

Café Souvenir
$

1261 Avenue Bernard Ouest
☎ (514) 948-5259

Maps of large European cities like Paris decorate the walls of the Café Souvenir. The ambiance of a French café pervades this comfortable little restaurant, which is open 24 hours a day on weekends. Rainy Sundays bring out droves of locals for a quick coffee and a chat. The menu is not extraordinary, but the meals are well prepared.

Chez Claudette
$

351 Avenue Laurier Est
☎ (514) 279-5173

A cozy family bistro, Chez Claudette is decorated with posters, a long counter and an open kitchen. Classic North-American fare is served here.

Eggspectation
$

198 Avenue Laurier Ouest
☎ (514) 278-6411
See description p 216

Fairmount Bagel Bakery
$

74 Avenue Fairmount Ouest
☎ (514) 272-0667

The St. Viateur Bagel Shop's most famous competitor is the Fairmount Bagel Bakery, which offers an impressive 20 or so different takes on the classic Montréal bagel. Salty or sweet, these include chocolate, muesli and sun-dried-tomato bagels. Another plus: this bakery stays open 24 hours a day, 365 days

a year. The perfect late-night stop when you've got the munchies.

Frite Alors
$

5235-A Avenue du Parc
☎ (514) 948-2219

Frite Alors is a re-creation of a typical *friterie belge*, or Belgian fry-stand, where patrons can stop by at any time of the day for fries and a sausage. Though service can be a bit slow, this is where you'll find some of the best fries in town.

Kilo
$

5206 Boulevard St-Laurent
☎ (514) 277-5039

Kilo looks like a contemporary fairy-tale house with its beautifully displayed array of sweets, grey walls, metal furnishings and high ceiling. A young, dynamic clientele can be found here at all hours enjoying a sandwich or a piece of the establishment's famous gargantuan cakes. People don't come here to relax, but rather to mingle with the beautiful people.

La Croissanterie
$

5200 Rue Hutchison
☎ (514) 278-6567

A charming café, La Croissanterie is one of those neighbourhood treasures that are so delightful to discover. Small marble tables, old-fashioned chandeliers and beautiful wood panelling make up a decor that is perfectly suited for leisurely breakfasts and intimate

conversations when you wish time could stand still. The bright morning sun streams through large windows. This café almost seems right out of a bygone era, and regulars include struggling artists and distracted intellectuals.

Le Bilboquet
$

1311 Avenue Bernard Ouest
☎ (514) 276-0414

Ice-cream lovers of all ages flock to Bilboquet for its countless different flavours. This small café, located in the heart of Outremont, has a fun little terrace that is always full on summer nights.

Le Paltoquet
$

1464 Avenue Van Horne
☎ (514) 271-4229

Le Paltoquet is both a pastry shop and a café. Run by a friendly French couple, it serves delicious treats that will satisfy your sweet tooth.

Lester's
$

1057 Avenue Bernard Ouest
☎ (514) 276-6095

Lester's is famous for its smoked-meat sandwiches. There is not much decor to speak of, creating a sterile and cold atmosphere, but who cares—it doesn't take long to eat a good smoked-meat sandwich!

St. Viateur Bagel Shop
$

263 Avenue St-Viateur Ouest
☎ (514) 276-8044

Montréal's reputation for bagels can be traced directly to this little bakery in

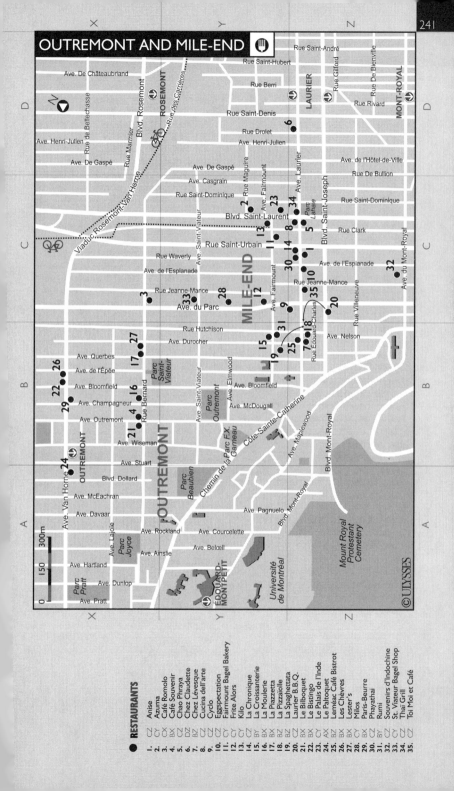

OUTREMONT AND MILE-END

ROSEMONT

LAURIER

MONT-ROYAL

MILE-END

OUTREMONT

Mount Royal Protestant Cemetery

Université de Montréal

ÉDOUARD-MONTPETIT

© ULYSSES

● RESTAURANTS

1.	Anise	CZ
2.	Azuma	CY
3.	Café Romolo	CX
4.	Café Souvenir	BX
5.	Chao Phraya	CZ
6.	Chez Claudette	DZ
7.	Chez Lévesque	BZ
8.	Cucina dell'arte	CZ
9.	Cyclo	CZ
10.	Eggspectation	CZ
11.	Fairmount Bagel Bakery	CY
12.	Frite Alors	CY
13.	Kilo	CY
14.	La Chronique	CZ
15.	La Croissanterie	BY
16.	La Moulerie	BX
17.	La Piazzetta	BX
18.	La Pizzaiolle	BZ
19.	La Spaghettata	BZ
20.	Laurier B.B.Q.	BX
21.	Le Bilboquet	BX
22.	Le Bistingo	BX
23.	Le Palais de l'Inde	CY
24.	Le Paltoquet	AX
25.	Leméac Café Bistrot	BZ
26.	Les Chèvres	BX
27.	Lester's	BX
28.	Milos	CY
29.	Pains-Beurre	BX
30.	Phayathai	CZ
31.	Rumi	BZ
32.	Souvenirs d'Indochine	CZ
33.	St. Viateur Bagel Shop	CY
34.	Thaï Grill	CY
35.	Toi Moi et Café	CZ

the heart of the Outremont borough. Connoisseurs know that New York-style bagels are no match for these wood-oven baked treats. You can choose between regular, sesame, poppy-seed, raisin or cinnamon bagels, and rest assured that you won't be disappointed. If you'd prefer to sit down and enjoy a classic bagel with cream cheese or smoked salmon, head to **St. Viateur Bagel & Café** *(1127 Avenue du Mont-Royal Est, ☎514-528-6361)*, in the Plateau Mont-Royal area. There is also another outlet at 5629 Avenue Monkland *(☎514-487-8051)*.

Toi Moi et Café
$

244 Avenue Laurier Ouest
☎(514) 279-9599

Toi Moi et Café is a charming place decorated in warm tones where hours can be spent sipping excellent coffee roasted on the premises. The café's Sunday brunches are extremely popular, so arrive early to avoid waiting in line.

Cucina dell'arte
$-$$

5134 Boulevard St-Laurent
☎(514) 495-1131

This Italian restaurant has an austere decor and prepares delicious pizza baked in a wood oven with a local or international flavour. A variety of pasta offerings round out the menu.

La Piazzetta
$-$$

1105 Avenue Bernard Ouest
☎(514) 278-6465
See description p 232

La Pizzaïolle
$-$$

5100 Rue Hutchison
☎(514) 274-9349

Pizzaïolle was one of the first restaurants in Montréal to serve pizza cooked in a wood-burning oven. They also do the best job at it. The tables are a little close together, but the atmosphere is still very pleasant.

Laurier B.B.Q.
$-$$

381 Avenue Laurier Ouest
☎(514) 273-3671

Laurier B.B.Q. has been a favourite with Montréal families for years. The menu includes delicious, golden barbecue chicken. Meals are a bit expensive, however.

Azuma
$$

5263 Boulevard St-Laurent
☎(514) 271-5263

At this charming restaurant, visitors can sample such delicious Japanese classics as sushi and sashimi. The service is polite and attentive.

Chao Phraya
$$

50 Avenue Laurier Ouest
☎(514) 272-5339

Chao Phraya has a very modern decor enhanced by big bay windows. Delicious Thai food.

Cyclo
$$

5136 Avenue du Parc
☎(514) 272-1477

Many consider Cyclo one of the best Vietnamese restaurants in its category. Indeed, this establish-

ment always delights its clientele thanks to delicious, classic Vietnamese cuisine. The dining-room decor is sober and elegant, bathed in shades of white. Excellent quality-price ratio.

La Moulerie
$$

1249 Avenue Bernard Ouest
☎(514) 273-8132

La Moulerie is an Outremont institution where exquisitely prepared mussels are given the spotlight. Among the many choices are the classic *moules marinières* (mussels cooked in their own juice with white wine and shallots), the Madagascar-style mussels and the horseradish-flavoured mussels. The restaurant's elegant dining room features large bay windows, which provide a nice view of Rue Bernard, and the superb terrace is very popular in summertime. The menu also includes a section entitled *j'haïs les moules* ("I hate mussels") for those who, well, hate mussels.

Le Bistingo
$$

1199 Avenue Van Horne
☎(514) 270-6162

Some say Avenue Van Horne is among Outremont's least attractive streets. It is nonetheless lined with some of the city's most charming bistros, of which Le Bistingo is probably the best. The food is always delicious at this intimate establishment, which only has a few tables, large bay windows and attentive service. The menu varies

according to what fresh ingredients are available, which is why people come back again and again.

Le Palais de l'Inde
$$
5125 Boulevard St-Laurent
☎ (514) 270-7402
The Palais de l'Inde is one of the many great Indian restaurants along St-Laurent near Avenue Laurier. The menu includes a wide range of main dishes, which, though prepared with quality ingredients, lack originality. The service is a bit aloof.

Paris-Beurre
$$
1226 Avenue Van Horne
☎ (514) 271-7502
Though the menu at Paris-Beurre has remained unchanged for some time, regulars keep coming back to savour the classic dishes that have stood the test of time, like *côte de boeuf* (beef) with mustard sauce, salmon with sorrel or the delectable vanilla *crème brulée*, which is always a hit. Diners also delight in the attractive dining room, despite the drab view of Avenue Van Horne from the large bay windows.

Phayathai
$$
107 Avenue Laurier Ouest
☎ (514) 272-3456
See description p 222

Rumi
$$
5198 Rue Hutchison
☎ (514) 490-1999
What if the renowned Silk Road actually passed through Hutchison street?

You may come to that conclusion after setting foot in this restaurant named after a famous 13th-century Sufi master. The decor, featuring Persian wall coverings and fabrics, and the splendid scents of the many marvellously fragrant dishes make this the perfect spot for a quiet, succulent dinner.

Chez Lévesque
$$-$$$
1030 Avenue Laurier Ouest
☎ (514) 279-7355
Avenue Laurier Ouest has several restaurants that have stood the test of time and maintained their enviable reputations, and Chez Lévesque is one of them. Its menu includes traditional French dishes; there are no surprises here but the food is high quality and always very tasty.

La Spaghettata
$$$
399 Avenue Laurier Ouest
☎ (514) 273-9509
La Spaghettata's new staff offers a refreshing and creative variety of dishes in a completely redesigned decor. The restaurant's many faithful regulars come here for the quality daily lunch and dinner specials and the top-notch service.

Nonya
$$-$$$
Tue-Sun from 5pm
151 Rue Bernard Ouest
☎ (514) 875-9998
www.nonya.ca
Surprisingly enough, Nonya is Montréal's, and indeed the whole province's, only Indonesian

restaurant. A selection of some of the archipelago's most refined dishes are served here in an elegant setting. Family recipes are the inspiration behind the daily specials and "discovery menu" *(35-45)*. Some of the restaurant's gourmet treats include *udang mangga* (sautéed shrimp served on a bed of banana leaves with a coconut-milk and red-curry sauce), satays (chicken or lamb brochettes with peanut sauce) and black-rice pudding served with hot coconut cream. Adventurous Asian-food buffs will find much to love here, and the warm welcome and charming service should keep them coming back.

Leméac Café Bistrot
$$$
1045 Avenue Laurier Ouest
☎ (514) 270-0999
This classic Outremont café-bistro was designed by architect Luc Laporte, and is named after the famous Montréal publishing house that used to occupy this pleasant spot on Avenue Laurier. The woodwork, garden terrace and large bay windows give this typical European café a particularly luminous ambiance. A vast selection of excellent wines accompanies a classic menu of French fare (including calf's liver, flank steak and duck confit).

Souvenirs d'Indochine
$$$
243 Avenue du Mont-Royal Ouest
☎ (514) 848-0336

In a most refined setting, Monsieur Ha serves a cuisine that is simply wonderful. Far from the insipid clichés of Vietnamese dishes that are served elsewhere, the offerings here follow the finest of Indo-Chinese traditions, with a touch of French influence. Don't skip the appetizers, such as fried calamari and crab-mousse soup. As for main dishes, the shrimp with green curry and the salmon will please your taste buds. Even the rice is fabulously unique! As for the service, it is rather uneven and cold.

Thaï Grill
$$$
5101 Boulevard St-Laurent
☎(514) 270-5566

It is no surprise that Thaï Grill won an award for its design; here, patrons never grow weary of admiring the decor. Traditional Thai elements have been skilfully integrated into a modern environment that manages to maintain a quiet elegance despite the animation all around. The service is friendly and attentive. The innovative food is based on traditional Thai cuisine and includes such dishes as green-papaya salad with lime and exquisitely seasoned rice noodles with chicken.

Anise
$$$$
closed Sundays and Mondays
104 Avenue Laurier Ouest, corner Rue St-Urbain
☎(514) 276-6999

Heading the kitchen at Anise, chef Rasha Bassoul is surprisingly masterful and has a great sense of originality, which translates into a refined menu featuring Mediterranean-inspired culinary creations. Diners will surely be tempted by the roasted rack of lamb or the pan-seared breast of Peking duck. The polished, contemporary decor, created by famous Québec designer Jean-Pierre Viau, features an array of orange and yellow hues. A must for any self-respecting gourmet.

Les Chèvres
$$$$
1201 Avenue Van Horne
☎(514) 270-1119

Walking into Les Chèvres, what will first hit your eye is the armoire/closet that seems to be covered in seal skin... just an illusion! The *maître d'hôtel*, a stern, old-fashioned character, will then take you to your table in one of two dining rooms, where you can sit comfortably, far enough from the other diners thanks to ample space. You might be surprised by the decor, which is refined and modern but seems incomplete. You will then receive the large menu, proportionate to the tables and the restaurant, as well as the actual dishes. And the surprises continue. The description of dishes will definitely puzzle diners who, without a dictionary of vegetables and mushrooms, might have a hard time figuring out the contents of their meal. But not to worry: although the establishment's prices make it one of the most expensive in the city, you won't be disappointed by your culinary experience, as the chef's skillful creations will allow you to discover the most sublime of flavours. The refined presentation is both surprising and charming, and service is efficient and friendly, even though you might feel like you've stepped into a culinary contemporary art show.

La Chronique
$$$$
closed Sundays and Mondays
99 Avenue Laurier Ouest, corner Rue St-Urbain
☎(514) 271-3095

Hip Montrealers will tell you that La Chronique always lives up to its reputation as one of the best restaurants in the city by going beyond the standards of fine dining. The establishment's famous Belgian-born chef, Marc De Canck, favours Québec products and offers market-style cuisine that is constantly evolving and features undeniably fresh ingredients that soothe the soul. In an unpretentious decor enhanced by those popular black-and-white photographs, diners can enjoy such fine dishes as roasted Atlantic halibut and duck hotchpotch. The wine list will please all connoisseurs, while service is professional, thoughtful and unassuming.

Milos
$$$$
5357 Avenue du Parc
☎(514) 272-3522

Milos puts your standard Montréal Greek *brochetterie* to shame; this is real

Greek cuisine. This establishment's reputation rests firmly on the quality of its exceptional selection of fresh fish and seafood from around the globe. The decor retains the air of the simple *psarotaverna* that this place started out as, but with a certain rustic elegance that appeals to a wealthy clientele. The portions are large, but if you have any room left, the traditional baklava is well worth it.

Little Italy

Café Italia
$
6840 Boulevard St-Laurent
☎ (514) 495-0059
People don't go to Café Italia for the decor, which consists of mismatched chairs and a large television, but for the comfortable atmosphere, the excellent sandwiches and most of all the cappuccino, considered by many to be the best in the city.

Boulangerie & Pâtisserie Motta
$
303 Avenue Mozart Est
☎ (514) 270-5952
This bakery doubles as a *trattoria* and is popular with Marché Jean-Talon regulars. The Gallo family offers homemade meals to go, delicious tiramisu, fresh pasta and deli meats. A daily special is served at lunchtime in the bakery's adjoining dining room or on the fun little terrace.

Aux Derniers Humains
$-$$
6950 Rue St-Denis
☎ (514) 272-8521
Nestled in the former **Cinéma Château** (see p 136), with its Art-Deco architecture, the decor at Derniers Humains features a touch of originality that suits this establishment: Milky Way ceiling, stained glass, lovely, elongated ceiling lamps, paintings by various artists that change every week... This neighbourhood café has a friendly atmosphere, and the food is inspired and creative.

Le Petit Alep
$-$$
191 Rue Jean-Talon Est
☎ (514) 270-9361
Mouhamara, *tabouli*, hummus, vine leaves, shish kebab, *shish taouk*... is your mouth watering yet? You'll find all of these Middle-Eastern and North-African dishes at Petit Alep. It's called "little" (*petit*) because big brother Alep is right next door. This café-bistro mainly specializes in delicious Syrian food. Awaken your taste buds with honey, oil or cayenne pepper. With its large garage door opening onto Rue Jean-Talon, the place looks like a loft. Temporary exhibits adorn the walls and are sometimes interesting, and the newspapers and magazines just might make you want to stay a while. Weekend brunches are also available.

Punjab Palace
$-$$
bring your own wine
920 Rue Jean-Talon Ouest
☎ (514) 495-4075
Though generally ignored by the city's gourmet critics, Punjab Palace remains many Montrealers' favourite Indian eatery. They come here for the friendly service, honest fare, generous servings and, especially, ridiculously low prices. The menu includes such traditional fare as nan bread, chicken or shrimp curry, beef *korma* served with almond and raisin sauce, as well as a wide variety of vegetarian dishes.

La Tarantella
$$
184 Rue Jean-Talon Est
☎ (514) 278-3067
What distinguishes La Tarantella from other good Italian restaurants is its location. This is a good place to eat a copious breakfast, savour a delicious dinner or sip a café au lait on the flowered terrace of this restaurant, which looks out onto the activity of the Jean-Talon market.

L'Auberge du Dragon Rouge
$$
8870 Rue Lajeunesse
☎ (514) 858-5711
Located near the Crémazie metro station, in the heart of a residential district, L'Auberge du Dragon Rouge welcomes an eccentric mix of clients who come to taste typical medieval fare while enjoying period music played by troubadours. Not to be missed are the "*pétaques*" (sliced potatoes cooked

Restaurants - Little Italy

LITTLE ITALY

Parc Jarry

Rue Faillon Ouest

Rue Jules-Verne

Rue Molière

Rue De Castelnau Est

Blvd Saint-Laurent

Saint-Dominique

Ave. Casgrain

Ave. De Gaspé

Ave. Henri-Julien

Rue Faillon Est

Rue Drolet

Rue Saint-Denis

Rue Berri

Rue Lajeunesse

Rue St-Gérard

Rue Ferland

Rue De Chateaubriand

Rue Saint-Hubert

Rue Saint-André

15

7

9

13
Rue Jean-Talon Ouest

Rue Waverly

Rue Saint-Urbain

Rue Clark

10

5 **8**

Ave. Shamrock

Marché Jean-Talon

12

Ave. Mozart Est

Rue Jean-Talon Est

JEAN-TALON

2

1

Rue Bélanger Est

Ave. Mozart Ouest

Parc Mozart

Ave. Beaumont

4

14

Rue Bélanger Est

Rue Dante

11

3

Parc Martel

Rue Saint-Zotique Est

6

Blvd. Saint-Laurent

Rue Saint-Dominique

Ave. Casgrain

Ave. De Gaspé

Rue Alma

Ave. Henri-Julien

Rue Drolet

Rue Saint-Denis

Rue De Saint-Valier

Rue De Chateaubriand

Plaza Saint-Hubert

Rue Saint-André

Rue Beaubien Ouest

Rue Beaubien Est

BEAUBIEN

Rue Burelle

© ULYSSES

0   150   300m

● **RESTAURANTS**

1.	BY	Aux Derniers Humains
2.	BY	Boulangerie & Pâtisserie Motta
3.	AY	Café International
4.	AY	Café Italia
5.	BX	Casa Cacciatore
6.	BZ	Il Mulino
7.	CW	L'Auberge du Dragon Rouge
8.	BX	La Tarantella

9.	CX	Le Gavroche
10.	BX	Le Petit Alep
11.	BY	Pizzeria Napoletana
12.	AY	Primo e Secundo
13.	AX	Punjab Palace
14.	AY	Quelli Della Notte
15.	BW	Tapeo

in oil, then sprinkled with cinnamon). On the second floor, the Échoppe du Dragon Rouge boutique sells medieval crafts.

Pizzeria Napoletana
$$
bring your own wine
189 Rue Dante
☎ (514) 276-8226

Pizzeria Napoletana is small and nondescript but usually overrun with a large, lively crowd. These regulars return for the consistently good pasta and pizza, not to mention that they can bring their own wine and choose from an inexpensive menu.

Le Gavroche
$$-$$$
closed Sundays and Mondays
2098 Rue Jean-Talon Est
☎ (514) 725-9077

Le Gavroche is an intimate French restaurant with a devoted neighbourhood clientele that appreciates its beautifully presented, refined classic French dishes. The personalized service is overseen by the restaurant's attentive and friendly owner.

Tapeo
$$-$$$
511 Rue Villeray
☎ (514) 495-1999

Tapeo's tapas bar is located in the Villeray neighbourhood, a few streets north of Little Italy, and has been garnering rave reviews lately. Groups of diners invade this warm and sometimes noisy restaurant to share delicious Spanish tapas. Chef Marie-Fleur St-Pierre's

market-fresh menu offers a variety of small dishes, including several vegetarian selections. Among the many outstanding offerings are delicate vine tomatoes served with goat cheese, wild mushrooms, grilled sardines, toasted tilapia, veal flank steak and fried squid. Seafood lovers can also share a delicious *paella* for two. Top off your meal with a traditional Spanish *chourros* served with a divine chocolate sauce. The service is attentive, and the wine list includes an interesting selection of Spanish wines. This recent addition to the city's gourmet landscape is well worth the detour: make sure you reserve well in advance because the small dining room fills up quickly.

Café International
$$$
6714 Boulevard St-Laurent
☎ (514) 495-0067

Stop by Café International if you're exploring the Little Italy district. Marco Arcaro welcomes his regulars with his market-fresh fare, and his menu includes traditional pasta, served with a variety of classic sauces, and fried squid. End your meal with a cup of tasty Italian coffee and some delicious cannolis.

Casa Cacciatore
$$$
170 Rue Jean-Talon Est
☎ (514) 274-1240

For years, Casa Cacciatore has kept up Montréal's Italian culinary traditions near the Jean-Talon market. The decor is warm

and intimate with tablecloths, candles and professional service. The enticing menu lists various quality dishes such as pasta and meats carefully prepared by the chef.

Il Mulino
$$$
236 Rue St-Zotique Est
☎ (514) 273-5776

Many local Italians choose to eat at Il Mulino for its fine, typical Italian cuisine.

Quelli Della Notte
$$$
6834 Boulevard St-Laurent
☎ (514) 271-3929

Quelli Della Notte brings a touch of class to Little Italy. Velour wall coverings, mirrors and a Venetian chandelier provide a resolutely Italian backdrop for a cuisine that honours such classic Southern-Italian dishes as veal medallions with prosciutto.

Primo e Secundo
$$$$
7023 Rue St-Dominique
☎ (514) 908-0838

Aficionados of fine Italian cuisine flock to Primo e Secundo. A stone's throw from the Jean-Talon market, the establishment is housed in a restored private residence. The menu is written on the walls and changes according to new arrivals, but always features fish, seafood and veal dishes, as well as sublime pasta. The wine list, for its part, offers a wide selection of great vintages.

Restaurants - Little Italy

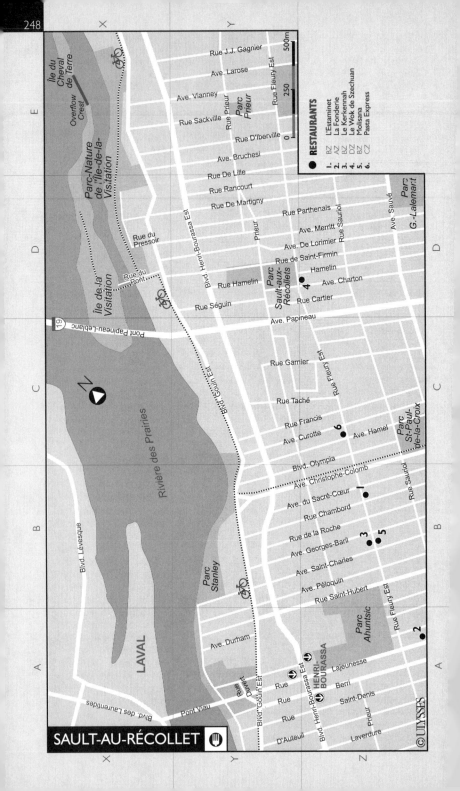

Sault-au-Récollet

La Fonderie
$

10145 Rue Lajeunesse
☎ (514) 382-8234

La Fonderie enjoys a solid reputation for its many delicious fondues.

Le Wok de Szechuan
$

1950 Rue Fleury Est
☎ (514) 382-2060

Le Wok de Szechuan, as you may have guessed, serves good Szechuan food to a local clientele, including Asians.

Pasta Express
$

1501 Rue Fleury Est
☎ (514) 384-3174

Pasta Express, a small restaurant that serves unpretentious Italian cuisine, is frequented by neighbourhood residents. Pasta dishes are inexpensive and always delicious.

Le Kerkennah
$$

1021 Rue Fleury Est
☎ (514) 387-1089

Generous portions of Tunisian food are served at this neighbourhood restaurant. Couscous, fish and shrimp figure on the menu.

L'Estaminet
$$

1340 Rue Fleury Est
☎ (514) 389-0596

L'Estaminet is a friendly little café that serves salads, soups and desserts.

Molisana
$$

1014 Rue Fleury Est
☎ (514) 382-7100

This Italian restaurant features a quiet atmosphere. The menu is not particularly original, consisting mainly of pasta dishes and pizza cooked in a wood-burning oven, but the food is good and the portions generous. Musicians liven up weekend evenings with a few songs.

Île Sainte-Hélène and Île Notre-Dame

Hélène de Champlain
$$$

☎ (514) 395-2424

Located on Île Sainte-Hélène, Hélène de Champlain lies in an enchanting setting, without question one of the loveliest in Montréal. The large dining room, with its fireplace and view of the city and river, is extremely pleasant. Each corner has its own unique charm, overlooking the season-changing surrounding landscape. Though the restaurant does not serve the fanciest of gastronomic cuisine, the food is very good. Service is courteous and attentive.

Le Festin du Gouverneur
$$$$

Fort de l'Île Ste-Hélène
☎ (514) 879-1141

Festin du Gouverneur creates feasts like those prepared in New France at the beginning of colonization. Characters in period costumes and traditional Québec dishes transport diners to a bygone era. The restaurant only serves groups and reservations are required.

Nuances
$$$$

Casino de Montréal, Île Notre-Dame
☎ (514) 392-2708

On the fifth floor of Montréal's casino, Nuances is one of the best dining establishments in the city, perhaps even the country. Refined and imaginative cuisine is served in a decor bathed in mahogany, brass, leather and views of the city lights. Of particular note on the menu are the lobster *chartreuse* with green-asparagus appetizer, as well as roast-duck magret, Québec lamb tenderloin and pan-seared duck foie gras in its own juice. The delectable desserts are always exquisitely presented. The plush and classic ambiance of this award-winning restaurant is perfect for business meals or special occasions. The casino also has three less expensive restaurants: **Via Fortuna (*$$*)**, **La Bonne Carte (*$$*)**, a buffet with *à la carte* service and **L'Entre-Mise (*$*)**, a snack bar.

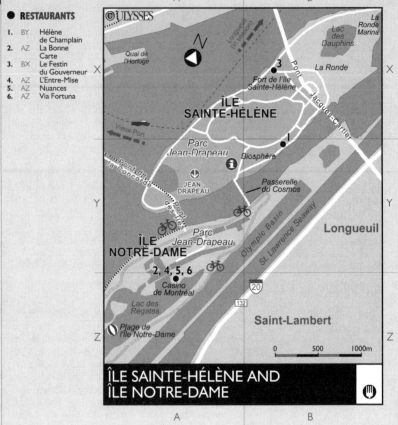

● **RESTAURANTS**

1.	BY	Hélène de Champlain
2.	AZ	La Bonne Carte
3.	BX	Le Festin du Gouverneur
4.	AZ	L'Entre-Mise
5.	AZ	Nuances
6.	AZ	Via Fortuna

ÎLE SAINTE-HÉLÈNE AND
ÎLE NOTRE-DAME

Hochelaga-Maisonneuve

La Piazzetta
$-$$
6770 Rue Sherbrooke Est
☎ (514) 254-2535
See description p 232

Moe's Deli & Bar
$$
3950 Rue Sherbrooke Est
☎ (514) 253-6637

Moe's Deli & Bar is particularly prized for its "happy hour," which fills up the bar; the restaurant is often just as crowded, however. The menu is extremely varied, which does not always ensure quality fare, though we would recommend the salads, sandwiches and grilled specialties. Diners with a healthy appetite can choose from a variety of original desserts. The music is loud, the atmosphere lively and the decor reminiscent of an English pub. The Olympic Stadium is just a few steps away.

La Bécane Rouge
$$
4316 Rue Ste-Catherine Est
☎ (514) 252-5420

La Bécane Rouge is a friendly neighbourhood eatery where waiters rush through the restaurant's two floors and summer terrace in typical French bistro style. Local residents and theatre buffs on their way to Théâtre Denise-Pelletier like to meet here for a drink, a cup of coffee or a tasty selection from the daily menu. In summer, try to get a table on the terrace that overlooks Parc Morgan.

Les Cabotins
$$$
4821 Rue Ste-Catherine Est
☎ (514) 251-8817

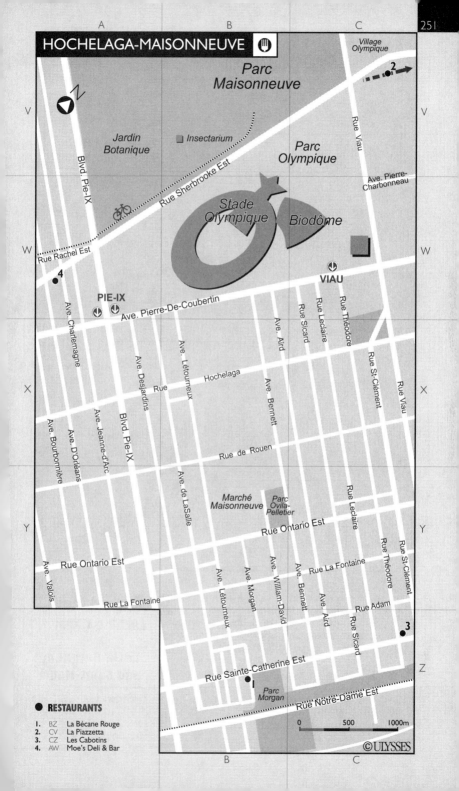

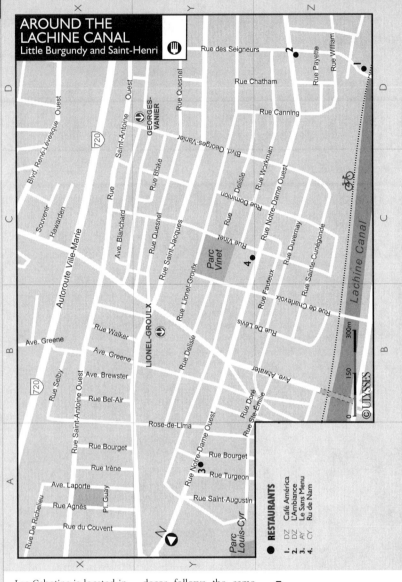

AROUND THE LACHINE CANAL

Little Burgundy and Saint-Henri

Rue des Seigneurs

Rue Chatham

Rue Canning

Blvd. Georges-Vanier

Rue Quesnel

Rue des Seigneurs

Rue Payette

Rue William

GEORGES-VANIER

Saint-Antoine Ouest

Rue Workman

Rue Delisle

Rue Notre-Dame Ouest

Rue Dominion

Rue Duvernay

Rue Blake

Rue Quesnel

Rue Saint-Jacques

Rue Vinet

Rue

Parc Vinet

Rue Fauteux

Rue de Charlevoix

Rue Sainte-Cunégonde

Lachine Canal

Rue Lionel-Groulx

LIONEL-GROULX

Rue Walker

Ave. Greene

Ave. Greene

Ave. Blanchard

Rue De Lévis

Autoroute Ville-Marie

Souvenir

Hawarden

Blvd René-Lévesque Ouest

Rue

Ave. Brewster

Rue Delisle

Ave. Atwater

Rue Selby

Rue Saint-Antoine Ouest

Rue Bel-Air

Rose-de-Lima

Rue Doré

Rue Sainte-Émilie

Rue Bourget

Rue Bourget

Ave. Laporte

Rue Irène

Rue Notre-Dame Ouest

Rue Turgeon

Rue De Richelieu

Rue Agnès

Pl. Guay

Rue Saint-Augustin

Rue du Couvent

Parc Louis-Cyr

300m

150

0

© ULYSSES

RESTAURANTS

- 1. Café America DZ
- 2. L'Ambiance DZ
- 3. Le Sans Menu AY
- 4. Ru de Nam CY

Les Cabotins is located in a former haberdasher's shop and has retained a few elements from the previous decor. Traditional French cuisine is served here, with a slightly eccentric twist. The mix of flavours (like salmon and citrus fruit, strawberry-and-Ricard-flavoured escargots) is always refined and well balanced. The decor follows the same logic, marrying both kitsch and chic elements, such as Formica tables and mismatched lamps, while retaining a tasteful and intimate atmosphere.

Around the Lachine Canal

Little Burgundy and Saint-Henri

Café America

$

every day until 3pm

20 Rue des Seigneurs

☎ (514) 937-9983

Café America boasts a large terrace overlooking the Lachine Canal bicycle path. This is a good stop for cyclists and those out on a stroll in the park. Quality dishes, with an accent on health food, are served in the old-fashioned decor of a renovated warehouse.

Le Sans Menu
$-$$
3714 Rue Notre-Dame Ouest
☎ (514) 933-4782

Le Sans Menu is a tiny bistro that is just that—sans menu. The choice of dishes changes every day, and can include rabbit, lamb,

juicy steaks and pasta with a variety of original and innovative sauces. The decor is reminiscent of a plain old Chinese restaurant, but there is nothing boring about the food and the friendly staff.

Ru de Nam
$-$$
2499 Rue Notre-Dame Ouest
☎ (514) 989-2002

A nice addition to the neighbourhood's rather restricted choice of restaurants is Ru de Nam, which also doubles as a boutique. Take a look at the shop's various Asian-imported decorative ob-

jects before entering the restaurant, which serves contemporary Vietnamese cuisine. The simple fare includes papaya and dried-beef salad, tamarind shrimp and pineapple-flavoured fish soup. Try the daily lunch special, which includes a starter, main course, dessert and tea or coffee for only $12.

L'Ambiance
$$
1874 Rue Notre-Dame Ouest
☎ (514) 939-2609

L'Ambiance is both a tea room and an antique shop. Diners here can enjoy their meal among

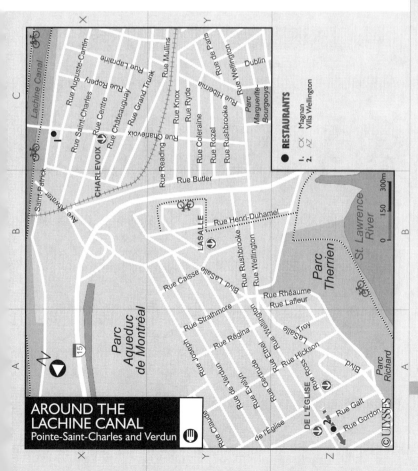

AROUND THE LACHINE CANAL
Pointe-Saint-Charles and Verdun

RESTAURANTS
1. CX Magnan
2. AZ Villa Wellington

Restaurants – Around the Lachine Canal – Little Burgundy and Saint-Henri

the rather outdated dining room's many antiques.

Pointe-Saint-Charles and Verdun

Villa Wellington
$
4701 Rue Wellington
☎(514) 768-0102

A Peruvian restaurant in Verdun? Why not! Villa Wellington offers very tasty traditional Peruvian cuisine mainly composed of fish and seafood. The

portions are generous and the prices reasonable.

Magnan
$$-$$$
2602 Rue St-Patrick
☎(514) 935-9647

Right in the heart of industrial Pointe-Saint-Charles is Magnan, one of the best-known taverns in Montréal. The house specialty is steak, ranging from six to 22 ounces (170 grams to 625 grams); why not get your yearly ration of red meat in one sitting? The high-quality beef and lobster festival, as well as the shrimp fes-

tival, attract large crowds. Arrive by 11:30am to get a table for lunch.

West Island and Surroundings

Lachine

Il Fornetto
$$
1900 Boulevard St-Joseph
☎(514) 637-5253

Il Fornetto's location near Lachine's marina is perfect for taking a stroll

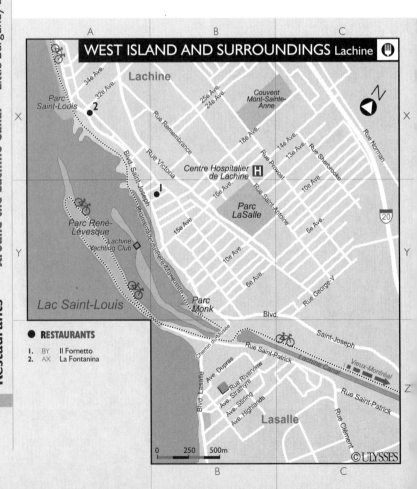

WEST ISLAND AND SURROUNDINGS Lachine

RESTAURANTS
1. BY Il Fornetto
2. AX La Fontanina

©ULYSSES

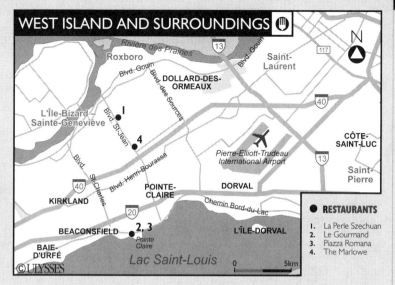

WEST ISLAND AND SURROUNDINGS

● RESTAURANTS
1. La Perle Szechuan
2. Le Gourmand
3. Piazza Romana
4. The Marlowe

©ULYSSES

along Lac Saint-Louis after a generous meal. With its noisy crowd and friendly service, the place is reminiscent of a *trattoria*. The pizza cooked in a wood-burning oven is worth a try.

La Fontanina
$$
3194 Boulevard St-Joseph
☎ (514) 637-2475
For good Italian food, head to La Fontanina, located in a charming, renovated old house.

Pointe-Claire

Piazza Romana
$$
339 Lakeshore Rd.
☎ (514) 697-3593
Piazza Romana is another favourite Italian restaurant in the Pointe-Claire Village. Inside, the decor is quaint and modern, while

a terrace is open outside during the warm summer months. The menu consists of a reliable choice of standard dishes.

The Marlowe
$$
981 Boulevard St-Jean
☎ (514) 426-8713
The Marlowe is possibly one of the hippest resto-bars on the West Island. Its menu offers a wide choice of interesting dishes: the dumplings with peanut sauce make a nice starter, while the smoked-salmon sandwich and the spinach salad are just two of the tasty possibilities for the main course. The desserts are equally inviting. The volume can be high, so be prepared for a noisy evening.

Le Gourmand
$$$-$$$$
42 Rue Ste-Anne
☎ (514) 695-9077

Located inside a beautiful, old stone house, Le Gourmand is the perfect place for a hot soup for lunch on a crisp fall day, or a fresh salad and cool iced tea on a bright summer afternoon. The evening menu features French, Cajun and Californian dishes. You can also pick up some delicious fixings for a picnic by Lac Saint-Louis at the deli counter.

Dollard-des-Ormeaux

La Perle Szechuan
$-$$
4230 Boulevard St-Jean Nord
☎ (514) 624-6010
La Perle Szechuan is the most inviting of the scores of Szechuan places on the West Island. The menu features unusual dishes.

Restaurants – West Island and Surroundings – Dollard-des-Ormeaux

Index of Restaurants by Type of Cuisine

■ Afghan

Khyber Pass 235

■ Asian

Ru de Nam 253
Tampopo 234
Zyng 227, 234

■ Bakeries

Boulangerie & Pâtisserie Motta 245
Fairmount Bagel Bakery 240
Olive + Gourmando 212
St. Viateur Bagel Shop 240

■ Basque

Pinxto 226
Vents du Sud 225

■ Belgian

L'Actuel 218
Bières et Compagnie 224, 234
Frite Alors 231, 240
Le Petit Moulinsart 212

■ Brazilian

Lélé da Cuca 224

■ Breakfast and Brunch

L'Ambiance 253
Aux Entretiens 231
Beauty's 224
Café Cherrier 235
Café Souvenir 240
Chez Claudette 240
La Croissanterie 240
Eggspectation 216, 240
Fruit Folie 231
Le Jardin du Ritz 220
Le Pèlerin-Magellan 227
Le Petit Alep 245

■ Breton

Crêperie Bretonne Ty-Breiz 236

■ Cafés and Tea Rooms

L'Ambiance 253
Aux Entretiens 231
Le Bilboquet 240
La Brioche Lyonnaise 227
La Brûlerie Saint-Denis 216, 227, 232
Café Bicicletta 231
Café Daylight Factory 215
Café El Dorado 234
Café Méliès 226
Café Rico 231
Café Romolo 239
Café Souvenir 240
Café Starbuck's 215
Calories 220
Camellia Sinensis 227
Fruit Folie 231
Les Gâteries 227
Kilo 240, 229
Le Paltoquet 240
Nonochi 216
St. Viateur Bagel & Café 242
Toi Moi et Café 242

■ Cajun

La Louisiane 238
Wienstein 'n' Gavino's Pasta
  Bar Factory Co. 218

■ Chicken and Ribs

Bar-B-Barn 220
La Cage aux Sports 212
Champs 224
Coco Rico 222
Laurier B.B.Q. 242

■ Chilean

La Chilenita 222

■ Chinese

Chez Chine 218
Mr Ma 219
La Perle Szechuan 255
Le Wok de Szechuan 249
Zen 219

■ Creative

Anise 244
Anubis 224
Area 231
Café des Beaux-Arts 218
Les Caprices de Nicolas 220
Les Chèvres 244
Chez L'Épicier 214
La Chronique 244
Chu Chai 234
Le Claremont 238
Le Continental 237
Cube 215
Aux Derniers Humains 245
Le Gourmand 255
The Marlowe 255
Mess Hall 238
Un Monde Sauté 236
The Monkland Tavern 239
Planète 230
Wienstein 'n' Gavino's Pasta
    Bar Factory Co. 218

■ Ethiopian

Le Nil Bleu 235

■ Fondue

La Fonderie 249
Fondue Mentale 235

■ French

Au 917 234
Auberge-Restaurant Pierre
    du Calvet 215
La Bécane Rouge 250
Le Bistingo 242
Le Bistro Gourmet 222
Le Bonaparte 214
Boris Bistro 212
Café Cherrier 235

Café de Paris 219
Le Caveau 218
Chez Gautier 225
Chez La Mère Michel 222
Chez Lévesque 243
Chez Queux 214
La Colombe 237
Le Continental 237
Côté Soleil 234
L'Entre-Miche 231
L'Estaminet 249
L'Express 237
Le Festin du Gouverneur 249
Le Flambard 236
La Gargote 212
Le Gavroche 247
Le Grain de Sel 231
Le Grand Comptoir 216
Hélène de Champlain 249
Le Jardin du Ritz 220
Julien 219
Laloux 226
Leméac Café Bistrot 243
Le Lutétia 216
Le Maistre 238
Nuances 249
Le Parchemin 219
Paris-Beurre 243
La Petite Marche 235
Le Petit Extra 230
Au Pied de Cochon 236
Pistou 236
Planète 230
Le Sans Menu 253
Le Vieux Saint-Gabriel 214

■ Greek

Le Jardin de Panos 235
Mezze 225
Milos 244
Ouzeri 235
Le Symposium Psarotaverna 237

■ Hamburgers

L'Anecdote 232
L'Avenue 236
La Banquise 232
La Cafétéria 225
La Cage aux Sports 212
Champs 224
Frite Alors 231, 240

Restaurants – Index of Restaurants by Type of Cuisine

Moe's Deli & Bar 250
La Paryse 227
Le Saloon 229
Shed Café 225

■ Health Food/Vegetarian

Aux Entretiens 231
Bio Train 211
Café America 252
Chu Chai 234
Le Commensal 216, 227
Le Gourmand 255
Le Pèlerin-Magellan 227
Santropol 224

■ Hungarian

Café Rococo 221

■ Ice Cream

Le Bilboquet 240
Crémerie Saint-Vincent 211

■ Indian

Ambala 232
Gandhi 212
Le Palais de l'Inde 243
Le Pique-Assiette 220
Punjab Palace 245
Tandoori Village 225

■ Indonesian

Nonya 243

■ Iranian

Byblos 231

■ Italian

Al Dente Tratorria 238
Buona Notte 226
Café International 247
Café Italia 245
Casa Cacciatore 247

Cucina dell'arte 242
Da Vinci 218
Euro Deli 222
La Fontanina 255
Il Fornetto 254
Le Latini 220
Mangia 216
Misto 236
Modigliani 237
Molisana 249
Il Mulino 247
La Pasta Casareccia 238
Pasta Express 249
La Petite Marche 235
Piazza Romana 255
Piccolo Diavolo 230
Le Piémontais 229
Primo e Secundo 247
Quelli Della Notte 247
Restorante-Trattoria Carissima 225
La Sila 229
La Spaghettata 243
La Strega du Village 230
La Tarantella 245
Le Vieux Saint-Gabriel 214
Wienstein 'n' Gavino's Pasta
  Bar Factory Co. 218

■ Japanese

Azuma 242
Ginger 226
Jardin Sakura 216
Kaizen 239
Katsura 219
Mikado 229

■ Korean

Man-Na 216

■ Market-Fresh Cuisine

Le Bistingo 242
Chez L'Épicier 214
Chez la Mère Michel 222
La Chronique 244
La Colombe 237
Primo e Secundo 247
Toqué! 220

■ Medieval

L'Auberge du Dragon Rouge 245

■ Mediterranean

Anise 244
Côté Soleil 234
Modavie 214
Titanic 212

■ Mexican

Cactus 234
Casa de Mateo 212
El Zaziummm 225, 234
Los Altos 225
Mi Burri to Café 231

■ Middle Eastern

Rumi 243

■ Peruvian

La Selva 232
Villa Wellington 254

■ Pizza

La Piazzetta 232, 242, 229, 250
Pizzafiore 238
La Pizzaïolle 242
Pizzédélic 235, 238
Pizzeria Napoletana 247

■ Polish

Stash's Café 214

■ Portuguese

Café Trattoria Ferreira 218
Vintage Tapas et Porto 237

■ Reunionese

Le Piton de la Fournaise 237

■ Russian

La Troïka 219

■ Seafood & Fish

La Marée 215
La Moulerie 242
Maestro S.V.P. 226
Milos 244

■ Smoked Meat

Ben's Delicatessen 215
Schwartz's Montréal Hebrew
  Delicatessen 222
Lester's 240
Moe's Deli & Bar 250

■ Spanish

Casa Tapas 226
Don Miguel 224
La Sala Rosa 224
Tapeo 247

■ Steak

Gibby's 214
La Cabane du Portugal 224
L'Entrecôte Saint-Jean 218
Magnan 227
Moishe's Steak House 227
La Queue de Cheval 220
Steak-Frites St-Paul 212

■ Swiss

La Raclette 236

■ Syrian

Le Petit Alep 245

■ Thai

Le Bangkok 229
Bato Thaï 229
Chao Phraya 242

Restaurants - Index of Restaurants by Type of Cuisine

Chu Chai 234
Phayathai 222, 243
Thaï Express 224
Thaï Grill 244

■ Traditional Québécois

La Binerie Mont-Royal 232
Le Cabaret du Roy 214
Chez Claudette 240
Le P'tit Plateau 226

■ Tunisian

Le Kerkennah 249

■ Vietnamese

Cyclo 242
L'Harmonie d'Asie 224
Ru de Nam 253
Souvenirs d'Indochine 243
Tay Do 222

Entertainment

Bars and Nightclubs   262
Gaming and Activities   271
Cultural Activities   272

Montréal's reputation as a vibrant and unique North-American city is well established. Whether it's for cultural activities, huge festivals or simply countless bars and nightclubs of all kinds, Montréal is a fascinating city with something for everyone. Sports enthusiasts will also get their fill thanks to professional hockey, football and soccer, as well as international sporting events that take place here each year.

Bars and Nightclubs

From sundown until early morning, Montréal is alive with the sometimes boisterous, sometimes romantic rhythm of its bars. There are bars designed to suit everyone's tastes, from the sidewalk bars along Rue Saint-Denis and the underground bars of Boulevard Saint-Laurent to the chic clubs on Rue Crescent and the gay bars in the "Village."

Some bars have a cover charge and coat-check fees. Québec nightlife is particularly lively—of course, it doesn't hurt that the sale of alcohol continues until 3am! Some bars remain open past this hour, but serve only soft drinks (soda or pop). Drinking establishments that only have a tavern or brasserie permit must close at midnight.

Vieux-Montréal

Les Deux Pierrots
104 Rue St-Paul Ouest
☎ (514) 861-1270
Les Deux Pierrots is a veritable Montréal institution. If your idea of a fun night out entails drinking massive quantities of beer and standing on your chair to sing popular songs in French, this is the place for you. Those who do not speak French may not get everything that's going on, but they will get a taste of a certain type of traditional Québécois nightlife; the lively atmosphere here is contagious.

Downtown and Golden Square Mile

Altitude 737
1 Place Ville-Marie
☎ (514) 397-0737
If you are one of those people who love reaching high places, you must ascend to the top of Place Ville-Marie. Altitude 737 is jam-packed on weeknights, especially on Thursdays and Fridays, when a clientele of thirtysomething professionals comes here for drinks before dinner. The comfortable room and two terraces offer breathtaking views of the city and the river that unquestionably justify the place's popularity. Later at night, clubbers have to climb another storey to the hip club.

Brutopia
1219 Rue Crescent
☎ (514) 393-9277
Between Sainte-Catherine and René-Lévesque streets is a cozy Irish pub that breaks away from the posh ambiance that characterizes Crescent Street. This unpretentious establishment brews its own beer (bottled beer is not sold here) and is the ideal place to begin the evening before heading off to another trendy spot. On weekends, musicians liven up the atmosphere with traditional Irish tunes. And if hunger should strike, the kitchen offers homemade pasta.

Carlos & Pepes
1420 Rue Peel
☎ (514) 288-3090
Carlos & Pepes, patronized by a predominantly twenty-something, English-speaking crowd of Montrealers, has two floors, the first of which features a Mexican-Californian restaurant. The second floor is equipped with televisions that keep fans up-to-date on their preferred spectator sport. The dance floor is rather small.

Le Dôme
32 Rue Ste-Catherine Ouest
☎ (514) 875-5757
This futuristic-looking nightclub reflects its rather young clientele. Lots of beautiful people come here, and the music is a

blend of hip, commercial dance tunes and techno.

Les Foufounes Électriques
87 Rue Ste-Catherine Est
☎ (514) 844-5539
Montréal's underground music scene's once-mighty Foufounes Électriques sure isn't what it used to be: the graffiti-laden decor may have stayed the same, but the crowd has become much more mainstream and the DJs are not exactly at the cutting edge of current musical tastes. Though Foufounes' traditionally eclectic clientele has left for other, less commercial venues, the bar remains popular with a younger crowd.

Funkytown
1454-A Rue Peel
☎ (514) 282-8387
Funkytown is frequented by a twenty-something clientele nostalgic for the sounds of the 1980s. The disco ball hanging from the ceiling, the illuminated floor and the disco and rock music mixed with current hits make this a great place to dance and perhaps make new acquaintances.

The Hard Rock Cafe
1458 Rue Crescent
☎ (514) 987-1420
The famous Hard Rock Cafe is decorated with objects that were once owned by highly acclaimed musicians. It has a relatively small dance floor. Get there early on the weekend, or you'll find yourself waiting in line to get in.

Hurley's Irish Pub/ Hurley's Medieval
1225 Rue Crescent
☎ (514) 861-4111
Discreetly tucked away south of Rue Sainte-Catherine among innumerable Crescent Street restaurants and bars, Hurley's Irish Pub and Hurley's Medieval succeed in recreating an atmosphere worthy of traditional Irish pubs. This is largely due to excellent amateur Irish folk musicians (The Paddingtons, Jim & Gary) and the quality of the world-famous Guinness beer.

Loft
1405 Boulevard St-Laurent
☎ (514) 281-8058
A large nightclub with a sombre "techno" decor and touches of purple where alternative music reigns, the Loft attracts clients between the ages of 18 and 30. It also features temporary exhibits that are somewhat interesting. Some patrons come here to play pool, and the rooftop terrace is also quite pleasant.

Luba Lounge
2109 Rue de Bleury
☎ (514) 288-5822
For a relaxing evening comfortably seated with a glass of port, try Luba Lounge, which features a DJ and bands a couple of nights a week. This place is packed with 20- to 30-year-olds on Fridays, partly because there is no cover charge.

McKibbin's Irish Pub
1426 Rue Bishop
☎ (514) 288-1580
McKibbin's Irish Pub features wooden stools and

booths, brick walls and plenty of knick-knacks, trophies and period photos that lend the place plenty of Old World charm. Live Irish folk music is featured on some evenings, and the mix of traditional Irish beer and music attracts a regular crowd of revellers. If you enjoy throwing a dart or two, there's a dartboard at the back of the place. The rear terrace is tailor-made for private discussions.

Newtown
1476 Rue Crescent
☎ (514) 284-6555
Owned by Québec's favourite Formula 1 pilot, Jacques Villeneuve, Newtown draws crowds of patrons who feel the urge to see and be seen. Guests can eat in the beautiful restaurant, dance at the nightclub or have a drink in the lush ambiance of the lounge in this huge, splendidly designed complex.

Peel Pub
1107 Rue Ste-Catherine Ouest
☎ (514) 844-6769
The most popular place in town for fans of sports and draught beer. If you have a victory to celebrate, a defeat to mourn, or simply feel like letting loose, head on over to Peel Pub.

Pub The Old Dublin
1219-A Rue University
☎ (514) 861-4448
Irish pub with live Celtic music and an impressive selection of draught beer. Live singers provide the entertainment and merry atmosphere.

Entertainment – Bars and Nightclubs - Downtown and Golden Square Mile

Happy Hour!

Cocktail or Happy Hour is a Montréal institution. The downtown area features several trendy bars that attract crowds of young professionals who meet there for a drink after work. The secret to their popularity lies in their "Happy Hours," when drinks are sold at reduced prices or "two for one" specials are offered. The most popular Happy Hours can be found at **Altitude 737**, whose terrace offers a breathtaking view of the city; **Newtown**, which is owned by famous race-car driver Jacques Villeneuve and where you may run into a few celebrities; **Pub Winston Churchill**, an English-style pub where Happy Hour extends to the dance floor; and **Thursday's**, which is mostly frequented by an English-speaking crowd of business people.

Pub Sir Winston Churchill
1459 Rue Crescent
☎ (514) 288-3814
An English-style bar, the Sir Winston Churchill attracts crowds of singles who come here to cruise and meet people. It has pool tables and a dance floor.

Thursday's
1449 Rue Crescent
☎ (514) 288-5656
Thursday's bar is very popular, especially among the city's English-speaking population. It is a favourite meeting place for business people and professionals.

Upstairs Jazz Club
1254 Rue Mackay
☎ (514) 931-6808
Located in the heart of downtown Montréal, Upstairs hosts jazz and blues shows seven days a week. During summer, the walled terrace behind the bar is a wonderful place to take in the sunset.

Vocalz Karaoke
1421 Rue Crescent
☎ (514) 288-9119
In the heart of Crescent Street, Vocalz Karaoke is the ideal spot for those who want to have fun and let go of their inhibitions. Here, clients can choose from a vast repertory of over 3,000 songs and try to sing as best they can. Giant screens broadcast the performances of these wannabe stars.

McGill Ghetto and "The Main"

Balattou
4372 Boulevard St-Laurent
☎ (514) 845-5447
Smoky, jam-packed, hot, hectic and noisy, Le Balattou is without a doubt the most popular African nightclub in Montréal. Shows are presented only during the week, when the cost of admission varies.

Belmont sur le Boulevard
4483 Boulevard St-Laurent
☎ (514) 845-8443
A clientele composed mainly of junior executives crowds into the Belmont sur le Boulevard. On weekends, the place is literally overrun with customers.

Les Bobards
4328 Boulevard St-Laurent
☎ (514) 987-1174
Les Bobards, an unassuming neighbourhood bar, is the perfect location for people-watching along Saint-Laurent while enjoying one of many beers on tap. All-you-can-eat peanuts are another reason to stop in, and the inevitable shells covering the floor add colour and charm to the place.

Café Sarajevo
2080 Rue Clark
☎ (514) 284-5629
Café Sarajevo hosts gypsy bands on Thursdays, Fridays and Saturdays, and jazz musicians the rest of the week. The crowd is a mix of bohemian students and, of course, Yugoslavians, and the atmosphere is decidedly laid-back. While sipping a beer or a glass of red Hungarian wine, why not try some Balkan specialities, such as *bourek* (meat and filo pastry roll), *pleckavica* (hamburger) and *cevapcici* (meatballs) served with *ajvar* (red-pepper spread). There is a patio out back that is pleasant during the

summer. Meet Osman, the charismatic owner, who bears an uncanny resemblance to Sean Connery! Cover charge later in the evening for performances.

Casa del Popolo
4873 Boulevard St-Laurent
☎ (514) 284-3804
Casa del Popolo is a vegetarian restaurant, café and performance venue. Its owners, Mauro Pezzente (a member of renowned Montréal band Godspeed You! Black Emperor) and Kiva Stimac, have played a major role in the city's booming music scene over the last few years. The concerts they have presented at Casa del Popolo, **La Sala Rosa** (see p 224) and El Salon, all of which are located on Boulevard Saint-Laurent, cover a wide array of genres from pop, rock and folk to jazz, avantgarde and electronic music, as well as poetry readings and a monthly "comix jam." The first two weeks of June are dedicated to the **Suoni Per Il Popolo** festival (see p 275). Take a look at the famous Distroboto at the bar's entrance: this converted cigarette machine offers a variety of works by local artists, from mini-comics and CDs to prose and poetry, all for a mere $2.

Dieu du Ciel
29 Avenue Laurier Ouest
☎ (514) 490-9555
Although slightly far from the downtown core, Dieu du Ciel is a friendly microbrewery that is definitely worth the detour, as the establishment of-

fers an excellent selection of house beers. Here, the clientele is often composed of young idealists who exchange world views between two pints of hemp ale. If you're hungry, you can order cheese nachos.

Else's
156 Rue Roy Est
☎ (514) 286-6689
You'll immediately feel at home upon entering Else's: its perfect location at the corner of two quiet streets, warm, cozy ambiance and friendly, unpretentious crowd make it a great place for a relaxed night out away from Boulevard Saint-Laurent's bustling bar scene.

Laïka
4040 Boulevard St-Laurent
☎ (514) 842-8088
Named after the first Russian dog to have travelled to space, Laïka is a trendy café-restaurant during the day and a cool, hip lounge at night. In a refined decor, the DJ spins the sharpest drum & bass, house, funk and electronica tunes. This place is also quite popular for its hearty Sunday brunch.

Saphir
3699 Boulevard St-Laurent
☎ (514) 284-5093
Saphir certainly deserves the award for most difficult Montréal club to describe. Its musical offerings range from punk, industrial, glam, hip-hop, new wave and dark wave, making it, in short, ideal for fringe clubbers.

Le Sergent Recruteur
4801 Boulevard St-Laurent
☎ (514) 287-1412
This microbrewery is worth the trip. Here, you can savour a delicious house beer while treating yourself to a pizza with Portobello mushrooms or whelk (sea snails), among many other unique toppings. Jazz concerts are occasionally presented. A small terrace located at the back adds to the establishment's charm. *Dimanches du Conte* storytelling sessions on Sundays at 7:30pm.

Tokyo Bar
3709 Boulevard St-Laurent
☎ (514) 842-6838
This popular Main nightclub features two rooms: the first is a discotheque, while the second is a lounge. The music varies from retro hits to house and hip hop. Get a seat on the large rooftop terrace in summertime, and watch the crowd go by on Boulevard Saint-Laurent.

Upper Club
3519 Boulevard St-Laurent
☎ (514) 285-4464
The Upper Club caters to a clientele composed of lovely ladies and young executives who like to speak loudly into their cell phones. Service is provided by curvy waitresses with a propensity to attract attention, while the flawless musical selection invites merry patrons to unwind on the dance floor. Dress accordingly.

Entertainment - Bars and Nightclubs - McGill Ghetto and "The Main"

Quartier Latin

Aria
1280 Rue St-Denis
☎ (514) 987-6712
Located in the space that was once occupied by the old Berri movie theatre, Aria is the top after-hour destination for clubbers who don't want to go home at 3am. Here, night owls can dance on three floors that pound to the sounds of the hottest tunes of the day. One room is reserved for techno fans, while another is filled with the rhythms of hip-hop. An absolute must on the Montréal scene for any self-respecting clubber.

Baloo's
403 Rue Ontario Est
☎ (514) 843-5469
At the corner of Ontario and Saint-Denis you'll find Baloo's, a very appealing watering hole with a friendly staff, frequented by a crowd of 18-30. Low prices on beer and shooters are their specialty, as the bartender will be sure to point out. French and English rock, alternative music, and rhythm and blues are played here. A second bar and a dance floor are open for partyers from Thursday to Saturday, when rock bands also play. The establishment also has a pool table, a table football game (foosball) and a few televisions frequently showing sporting events and the popular American animated series *The Simpsons.*

Café Chaos
2031 Rue St-Denis
☎ (514) 844-1301
The cooperatively run Café Chaos attracts a packed crowd of young, energetic students who like to chat about music and life. The music here includes every imaginable style: garage, rock, surf, alternative, techno-industrial, etc. Local musicians present their newest creations beginning at about 9pm. Local groups such as Caféine and WD-40 made their debuts here.

Le Cheval Blanc
809 Rue Ontario Est
☎ (514) 522-0211
Le Cheval Blanc is a Montréal tavern and microbrewery that does not appear to have been renovated since the 1940s, hence its unique style! Excellent seasonal beers are brewed on the premises. The establishment has its faithful cast of regulars, and the space can also be rented out for cultural events.

Jello Bar
151 Rue Ontario Est
☎ (514) 285-2621
Jello Bar is strewn with an unusual mix of furniture and knick-knacks straight out of the 60s and 70s. The bar serves a selection of 32 different martini cocktails that can be sipped to the mellow sounds of jazz or blues. Great musical acts are regularly featured.

L'Amère à Boire
2049 Rue St-Denis
☎ (514) 282-7448
Between Ontario and Sherbrooke streets, L'Amère à Boire is a small, friendly brewpub that produces almost a dozen lagers and ales. The establishment features a tiny back terrace for those who prefer taking a break from the hustle and bustle of Saint-Denis Street. Note to foodies: the place also serves stout-flavoured crème brûlée and "beer cheese."

Les 3 Brasseurs
1660 Rue St-Denis
☎ (514) 845-1660
A stone's throw from Théâtre Saint-Denis, Les 3 Brasseurs is a Montréal franchise of a French chain of establishments that has gained quite a reputation. Thanks to its rustic decor and friendly service, the place welcomes a crowd of students and young executives who come here to quench their thirst. You can sample delicious Alsatian specialties, such as *flams* (flambéed pie topped with pieces of chicken, lardoons or vegetables). In summer, the two terraces (one on the roof, and the other at street level) are the ideal spot to sip a cold beer and watch passersby on Rue Saint-Denis.

Île Noire Pub
342 Rue Ontario Est
☎ (514) 982-0866
The Île Noire Pub is a beautiful bar in the purest Scottish tradition. The abundance of precious wood used for the decor gives the place a cozy charm and sophisticated atmosphere. The knowledgeable staff guides guests through the im-

pressive list of scotches. The bar also has a good selection of imported draught beer. Unfortunately, prices are high.

L'Ours Qui Fume
2019 Rue St-Denis
☎ (514) 845-6998
Hear ye! Hear ye! Fans of Québécois songs and poetry commune at L'Ours Qui Fume. Local writers and musicians drop in here to discuss, sometimes quite loudly, their most recent artistic discoveries or simply to relax. Decorated with photographs of these same artists, this extremely appealing little place, which occasionally presents live music, is well worth checking out.

Le Pèlerin-Magellan
330 Rue Ontario Est
☎ (514) 845-0909
Located right next to the Île Noire Pub, Le Pèlerin-Magellan is a small bar and restaurant that will awaken the explorer in you thanks to its Old World woodwork, curtains with African motif, portholes and old atlases and travel memoirs tucked away on a bookcase with a globe and other assorted objects. World music, jazz and live performances add to the atmosphere. Forego the usual beer and try the tasty rum coffee or such evocatively-named house cocktails as *Le Planteur* or the *Marie-Galante*. Weeknights are generally quiet and well-suited for an intimate tête-à-tête.

Le Medley
1170 Rue St-Denis
☎ (514) 842-6557 (bar)
☎ (514) 842-7469 (concert info)
Several big names in the music business have performed at Le Medley. Indeed, such musicians as Bob Walsh, Jimmy James and other notable blues singers have attracted large, enthusiastic crowds. Artists from south of the border, such as Marilyn Manson, and icons of a not-too-distant past, like Chuck Berry and James Brown, have also come here to perform their classics. Covering two floors, Le Medley offers lots of room, both seated and standing, and the beer flows freely.

Le P'tit Bar
3451 Rue St-Denis
☎ (514) 281-9124
Facing Square Saint-Louis, the P'tit Bar is the perfect place to discuss literature, philosophy, photography, etc. The former hangout of the late Gérald Godin, celebrated Québec poet, this place will appeal to fans of French music. Photo exhibits make up the sober decor and Québécois and French singers sometimes perform here..

Quartier Latin Pub
318 Rue Ontario Est
☎ (514) 845-3301
Is the Quartier Latin Pub overshadowed by its neighbours, L'Île Noire and Le Pèlerin-Magellan? Maybe not, since the bar has, on more than one occasion, been chosen as a filming location for several Québec television shows. Perhaps it's the meticulously designed

but rather cold decor that brings it so much attention, or maybe it's the clientele, as prim as the surroundings: clean-cut "preppies" in their early 30s that seem right out of a beer commercial. Terrace in summer.

Le Sainte-Élisabeth
1412 Rue Ste-Élisabeth
☎ (514) 286-4302
It's a shame that this charming pub is so out of the way; when you first walk in, you almost feel like you're in Ireland! The decor is warm and the first floor looks like an actual living room, with sofas and coffee tables; a large, round window overlooks a friendly, intimate terrace, while multiple tables, chairs and stools are scattered around the small bar. The second floor is also filled with tables and chairs, as well as another bar. Needless to say, the place is often packed on weekends with students from the nearby university and cegep. And in summer, this is one of the best terraces in the Quartier Latin district.

Saint-Sulpice
1680 Rue St-Denis
☎ (514) 844-9458
The Saint-Sulpice occupies all three floors of an old house and is tastefully decorated. Its front and rear terraces are the perfect place to get the most out of summer evenings.

Yer' Mad!
901 Boulevard De Maisonneuve
☎ (514) 522-9392
Located in a basement, Yer' Mad! will transport

Entertainment - Bars and Nightclubs - Quartier Latin

you to the heart of Ireland thanks to folk music and painted gnomes and elves on the walls. People come to Yer' Mad! for its casual ambiance, but mostly for its great selection of delicious beer and cider.

The Village

Jet Club
1003 Rue Ste-Catherine Est
☎ (514) 842-2582
The Jet Club is one of the hippest nightlife addresses in Montréal. Its huge dance floor is taken over by hysterical clubbers who come here to dance to the feverish beats of R&B, hip-hop and house music. There is also a VIP lounge, where the beautiful people strut their stuff, roaring with laughter and exchanging whispered secrets. Admission and dress code are quite strict.

■ Gay Bars and Nightclubs

Le Cabaret Mado
1115 Rue Ste-Catherine Est
☎ (514) 525-7566
Frequented by a mixed, lively clientele, Le Cabaret Mado presents, among other things, drag shows. Guaranteed fun with the famous Mado!

Gotham Bar
1641 Rue Amherst
☎ (514) 526-1270
This is a quiet, friendly bar—the kind that will make you wish there were more of in the gay village! Background music inspires conversation and the warm reception makes everyone

feel comfortable. Modern, cozy furnishings invite you to stay a little longer and sip a house cocktail or beer on tap.

Le Parking
1296 Rue Amherst
☎ (514) 282-1199
Le Parking is all about choices: funky house at the *Nightclub*, rock in the *Lounge* or hip hop in the basement *Garage*. Young and hip Village district revellers come out in hordes for the bar's famous *Traffic* and *Perfect Sunday* nights. Don't miss the Tuesday-night *Bunkers* event, with $3 drinks from 4pm to 3am.

Pub Magnolia
1329 Rue Ste-Catherine Est
☎ (514) 526-6011
A trendy, women-only lounge, Pub Magnolia regularly presents quality shows, while its dance floor livens up as the night progresses.

Stéréo Club
856-858 Rue Ste-Catherine Est
☎ (514) 286-0300
Young members of the gay community who go to sleep in the wee hours of the morning don't miss the chance to drop by Stéréo on the weekend. This after-hours club opens at 2am and is well known for the quality of its sound equipment... you guessed it: it's loud! The clientele here is hip and quite young.

Sky Pub and Sky Club
1474 Rue Ste-Catherine Est
☎ (514) 529-6969
This busy gay bar boasts an elaborate decor that lacks a certain unity,

and the loud, uninspired music leaves a bit to be desired. The ground-floor Sky Pub attracts a crowd of young dancers, while the Sky Club is spread over the two upper floors and is one of the city's main gay nightspots where revellers dance to a variety of musical styles. The atmosphere can seem rather cold in such a vast space, but the young crowd makes the most of it and doesn't let this get in the way of their partying. In summer, however, its huge, wonderful rooftop terrace allows guests to observe the hustle and bustle of Sainte-Catherine Street. Another sore spot is the unusually high cover charge that seems to vary for no apparent reason.

La Track
1574 Rue Ste-Catherine Est
☎ (514) 521-1419
This lively gay disco welcomes men of all ages.

Unity II
1171 Rue Ste-Catherine Est
☎ (514) 523-4429
Unity is a large gay club that is mainly frequented by a young masculine crowd. Its architecture is very interesting, with different levels, including a mezzanine from which you can watch the dance floor and the entrancing light show. In addition to the main dance floor, there are also two other dance floors, including the Bamboo, where the music tends to be quieter, and another featuring the trendiest of tunes. On the main floor, there is a lovely bar decorated

Cafés

In the past few years, "fast-food" cafés have been springing up everywhere in the United States and Canada, and Montréal has its fair share of them. Although these establishments are not nearly as charming as other local cafés, they offer a unique concept: some have take-out counters, some are Internet cafés, and all serve many different kinds of coffee, juices, ice teas—even muffins and gigantic desserts. The clientele is young and lively, and the decor is modern. You'll surely come across several of them while in Montréal. note that some are open 24 hours.

with plenty of woodwork and carefully thought-out lighting. For warm summer nights there is a huge rooftop terrace.

Plateau Mont-Royal

Bacci
4205 Rue St-Denis
☎ (514) 844-3929
Bacci has about 30 pool tables, as well as a varied but rather bland menu. That's not what people come here for, however: a pleasure-hungry crowd packs in here to chat, seduce, fall in love and drink beer, though not necessarily in that order.

L'Barouf
4171 Rue St-Denis
☎ (514) 844-0119
If you can, take a seat at one of the wicker chairs near the large open window that overlooks Rue Saint-Denis in summertime: you'll have a front-row seat to watch this commercial artery's many passersby and a good view of this guidebook's very own travel bookstore across the street! L'Barouf serves a large array of imported and micro-brewed

beers, as well as wine sold by the glass, and the service is always friendly. Live radio shows and CD launches are sometimes held here.

Bily Kun
354 Avenue du Mont-Royal Est
☎ (514) 845-5392
The second bar opened by the Cheval Blanc microbrewery, Bily Kun offers a wide selection of beers, including the excellent and good-value house brand. With an original decor of mounted ostrich necks, this hip place has a friendly and very lively atmosphere and is always packed.

Le Boudoir
850 Avenue du Mont-Royal Est
☎ (514) 526-2819
The inviting atmosphere at Le Boudoir is sure to appeal to a broad audience. A large selection of micro-brewed beers is offered, and Monday and Tuesday nights feature scotch specials between 8pm and 3am. The bar also has a pool table and a foosball table.

Café Campus
57 Rue Prince-Arthur Est
☎ (514) 844-1010

Mostly frequented by students, Café Campus spreads over three floors in a large place on Rue Prince Arthur. The rather forgettable decor doesn't prevent a horde of regulars from dancing the night away or waiting their turn to play at the bar's first-floor billiards table. An array of rock and blues shows, including several local acts, are presented at the bar's concert room, Le Petit Café Campus. Theme nights include francophone, 1980s alternative, and modern rock offerings.

Le Big Cheeze
4479 Rue St-Denis
☎ (514) 845-9010
A former unpretentious jazz bar, Le Big Cheeze is another meeting place for students in need of a little rock'n'roll, since alcoholic beverages are inexpensive here, although there is a cover charge. The first floor is home to **Quai des Brumes** *(☎514-499-0467)*, which is quieter and features a warm decor and a jazz Happy Hour on Sundays.

Entertainment – Bars and Nightclubs – Plateau Mont-Royal

Au Diable Vert

4557 Rue St-Denis
☎ (514) 849-5888

Au Diable Vert is the place to go to let loose on a large dance floor. Because it is very popular with students, there is often a lineup. Cover charge is $2 (including coat-check) on Wednesday and Thursday nights, and $3 on Friday and Saturday nights.

Chez Baptiste

1045 Avenue du Mt-Royal Est
☎ (514) 522-1384

You'll feel right at home in this unassuming neighbourhood bar. Chez Baptiste is perfect for a quiet late-afternoon drink or a slightly livelier evening out when a younger crowd invades the premises.

Le Dogue

4177 Rue St-Denis
☎ (514) 845-8717

Le Dogue is the ideal place to dance, dance, dance! The music is the delight of a rather young, high-spirited crowd thirsting for cheap beer. There are two pool tables, which are a bit in the way, but keep pool sharks entertained. The place is jam-packed seven days a week, so you are strongly advised to get here early.

El Zaz Bar

4297 Rue St-Denis
☎ (514) 288-9798

El Zaz Bar is owned by the same people who run the El Zaziumm restaurants. There is a small, popular dance floor where the crowd can let loose to almost every style of music, from French crooners to disco, salsa and techno.

The unusual decor is composed of a multitude of mismatched objects. The service is nothing to write home about, but if you are interested in a change of scenery, this is the place to be!

L'Escogriffe

4467-A Rue St-Denis
☎ (514) 842-7244

Located near the Mont-Royal metro station, L'Escogriffe is that place where everybody knows your name and where regulars drop by for a drink after a hard day's work. The ambiance is sometimes enhanced by a harmonica player or musicians who enchant their audience with a bit of jazz or blues.

Le Passeport

4156 Rue St-Denis
☎ (514) 842-6063

Le Passeport is very dark and intimate. A twenty-something crowd comes here to dance to 1980s and 1990s tunes or simply have a beer with friends. This unpretentious place is packed on the weekend, especially during summer.

Le Réservoir

9 Avenue Duluth Est
☎ (514) 849-7779

A microbrewery at night and a bistro at lunch time, Le Réservoir also offers a tasty brunch menu on Saturday and Sunday mornings. We like the bar's location on charming little Avenue Duluth, its second-floor terrace and its quality microbrewed beer.

Sofa

451 Rue Rachel Est
☎ (514) 285-1011

Sofa invites you into a lounge atmosphere where a crowd between the ages of 20 and 35 comes to sip port and scotch. As the name indicates, this establishment is scattered with comfortable plush couches that are perfect for enjoying a drink with old friends and new acquaintances. A small stage allows some local bands to transport the audience to the worlds of jazz, soul and R&B.

Taverne Inspecteur Épingle

4051 Rue St-Hubert
☎ (514) 598-7764

Another good place for a beer and some great blues is Inspecteur Épingle. This tavern, which became famous as the occasional hangout of controversial Québec singer Plume Latraverse, presents good local musicians

Le Verre Bouteille

2112 Avenue du Mt-Royal Est
☎ (514) 521-9409

Established in the heart of the Plateau Mont-Royal district since 1942, Le Verre Bouteille is one of the last bastions of Québécois music in the neighbourhood. On weekends, singer-songwriters take to the stage to entertain the audience. Casual ambiance and quality service.

Zinc Café Bar Montréal

1148 Avenue du Mt-Royal Est
☎ (514) 523-5432

Looking for a good place to talk about everything and nothing while enjoying a *picon bière*? The Zinc Café Bar is an inviting place that serves a variety of unusual drinks.

Westmount, Notre-Dame-de-Grâce and Côte-des-Neiges

La Grande Gueule

5615-A Chemin de la Côte-des-Neiges
☎ (514) 733-3512

La Grande Gueule, located near the Université de Montréal, has a light menu, cheap draught beer and four pool tables. A number of board games are also available. On Mondays and Tuesdays you can play pool for free when you buy a drink.

La Maisonnée

5385 Rue Gatineau
☎ (514) 733-0412

La Maisonnée is always packed with Université de Montréal students who flock here after class to talk and drink. French fries and pizza are also served, while television sets broadcast popular sports games.

Typhoon Lounge

5752 Avenue Monkland
☎ (514) 482-4448

Come sip a beer on the comfy couches at Typhoon Lounge. Lounge music takes over on Tuesdays and Saturdays, while Wednesdays are devoted to favourites from the 70s and 80s, Thursdays feature reggae and ska, and Saturdays play world beat.

Outremont and Mile-End

L'Assommoir

112 Rue Bernard Ouest
☎ (514) 272-0777

This combination bar and restaurant is a recent addition to the Mile-End nightlife scene. A regular crowd of thirty-some-things comes here for the popular happy hour, the long list of cocktails and the mini-fashion shows that feature some of the many local designers that have recently set up shop in the neighbourhood.

BU

5245 Boulevard St-Laurent
☎ (514) 276-0249

This Mile-End wine bar has a distinctly laid back atmosphere. The wine menu offers a daily selection of some 30 wines sold by the glass. An array of antipasti is served until 2am, for those who would also like a quick bite to eat.

Fûtenbulle

273 Avenue Bernard Ouest
☎ (514) 276-0473

The Fûtenbulle is frequented by a mixed crowd. Besides the simple menu, patrons can choose from one of the largest selection of beers in Montréal.

Whisky Café

5800 Boulevard St-Laurent / 3 Rue Bernard Ouest
☎ (514) 278-2646

The Whisky Café is so conscientiously decorated that even the bathrooms are a strange tourist attraction. The warm colours used in a modern setting, the tall columns covered with woodwork and 1950s-style chairs all create a sense of comfort and elegance. The well-off, well-bred clientele is mainly gilded youth between the ages of 20 and 35.

Rosemont

Chez Roger

2300 Rue Beaubien Est
☎ (514) 723-5939

Contrary to what its rather plain name suggests, this place is actually one of Montréal's hottest bar-lounges. Located near Cinéma Beaubien, Chez Roger is a former neighbourhood tavern that attracts its fair share of colourful characters and trendsetters who discuss their trials and tribulations while sipping a cocktail. The place is a little out of the way, but that doesn't keep regulars from coming back again and again. This establishment also features a restaurant: Roger BBQ.

Gaming and Activities

Laser Quest *($8; closed Mon except for groups; 1226 Rue Ste-Catherine Ouest,* ☎*514-393-3000)* will thrill people of all ages who relish interactive science-fiction games. Two teams battle it out with laser light guns in a labyrinth spread out over three floors. Laser Quest can welcome up to 32 people and offers some 40 different games.

Each year, the **Shed 16 Labyrinth** *($12; Old Port,* ☎*514-499-0099)* is restructured so that its users can experience a new theme adventure; its itinerary and clues are regularly changed. Amateur explorers can enjoy loads of obstacles, traps and play areas.

The **Forum Pepsi** *(2313 Rue Ste-Catherine Ouest,* ☎*514-933-6786)* is housed in the former Forum of the Montréal Canadiens hockey team. You can visit the theme gallery and celebrity walk of fame that honours hockey and entertainment stars. In addition, the Forum Pepsi presents the latest movies thanks to 22 theatres and features a few restaurants and terraces serving international cuisine.

The **La Ronde** (see p 142) amusement park is chockfull of world-class roller coasters, Ferris wheels and rides that will delight thrill-seekers young and old.

With 2,700 slot machines and 100 gaming tables (blackjack, roulette, baccarat, poker, etc.), the **Casino de Montréal** *(free admission; every day 9am to 5am;* ☎*514-392-2746)* is without a doubt a major player in the city's nightlife. The casino is now one of the 10 largest in the world in terms of gaming equipment. Its concert hall, the **Cabaret du Casino**, presents colourful variety acts.

Cultural Activities

Montréal has an intense cultural scene. Various shows and exhibitions provide Montrealers with a large variety of cultural events to choose from. Shows and films from all over the world, exhibitions of all styles of art and festivals for all tastes and ages are presented throughout the year. Free weekly newspapers *Voir*, *Ici*, *The Mirror* and *Hour* provide listings and reviews of the main events.

■ Cultural Centres

Cultural centres have been established to help young Montréal artists practice and promote their craft on a professional level. In order to make these exhibits and shows accessible to all, admission is free. Most of the time, though, you will need to purchase your tickets ahead of time to get a seat. Schedules of specific exhibits at the Maisons de la Culture are published in free weekly entertainment publications such as *Ici*, *Voir*, *The Mirror* and *Hour*, which are distributed every Thursday.

Ahuntsic–Cartierville
10300 Rue Lajeunesse
☎(514) 872-8749

Côte-des-Neiges
5290 Chemin de la Côte-des-Neiges
☎(514) 872-6889

Maisonneuve
4200 Rue Ontario Est
☎(514) 872-2200

Mercier
8105 Rue Hochelaga
☎(514) 872-8755

Notre-Dame-de-Grâce
3755 Rue Botrel
☎(514) 872-2157

Plateau Mont-Royal
465 Avenue du Mont-Royal Est
☎(514) 872-2266

Pointe-aux-Trembles
14001 Rue Notre-Dame Est
☎(514) 872-2240

Rivière-des-Prairies
9140 Boulevard Perras
☎(514) 872-9814

Rosemont–La Petite patrie
6707 Avenue De Lorimier
☎(514) 872-1730

Sud-Ouest
Marie-Uguay
6052 Boulevard Monk
☎(514) 872-2044

Ville-Marie
Frontenac
2550 Rue Ontario Est
☎(514) 872-7882

Villeray–Saint-Michel–Parc-Extension
911 Rue Jean-Talon Est
☎(514) 872-6131

■ Movie Theatres

Montréal has many movie theatres. Special rates are offered on Tuesdays, Wednesday and matinees. Here is a list of the major downtown theatres.

In French

Cinéma Beaubien
2396 Rue Beaubien Est
☎(514) 721-6060

The strikingly innovative architecture of the Stade Olympique, which hosted the 1976 Summer Olympic Games.
© *Tourisme Montréal*

The Jardin de Chine (Chinese Garden), one of the Jardin Botanique's several splendid theme gardens.
© *Philippe Renault*

Young Montrealers at play on one of the city's many outdoor ice rinks.
© *Philippe Renault*

The Chalet du Mont-Royal's belvedere offers a breathtaking view of downtown Montréal.
© *Tourisme Montréal*

Le Parisien
480 Rue Ste-Catherine Ouest
☎(514) 866-0111

Le Quartier Latin
305 Rue Émery
☎(514) 849-4422

In English

AMC
2313 Rue Ste-Catherine Ouest
☎(514) 904-1250

Paramount
977 Rue Ste-Catherine Ouest
☎(514) 842-5828

Repertory

Cinémathèque Québécoise
335 Boulevard De Maisonneuve Est
☎(514) 842-9763
See p 108

Ex-Centris
3536 Boulevard St. Laurent
☎(514) 847-9272
See p 103

Impérial
1430 Rue de Bleury
☎(514) 848-0300
This is the oldest movie theatre in Montréal.

Specialty

Cinéma IMAX
Centre des Sciences de Montréal, Old-Port
☎(514) 496-4629
Films are presented on a giant screen here (see p 64).

Canadian and Québécois

**ONF Montréal
(National Film Board)**
1564 Rue St-Denis
☎(514) 496-6895

■ Sporting Events

Car Racing

Circuit Gilles-Villeneuve
☎(514) 350-0000 (tickets)
www.grandprix.ca
The month of June is marked by an international-scale event that captivates a massive crowd of Formula 1 amateurs who come from all over the world: the **Grand Prix of Canada**, held in the middle of June at the Circuit Gilles-Villeneuve of Parc Jean-Drapeau, on Île Notre-Dame. Without a doubt, this is one of the most popular events of the summer. For three days, you can attend various car races, notably the high-energy and spectacular Formula 1 race.

Cycling

**Montréal Bike Fest
(Féria du vélo de Montréal)**
☎(514) 521-8687 or
800-567-8356 (tickets)
www.velo.qc.ca/tour
The Montréal Bike Fest is held in late May-early June, and ends with the **Tour de l'Île** on the first Sunday in June. This cycling tour attracts some 30,000 cyclists who travel over approximately 50km. During the Bike Fest, three other events are also presented: the Défi Métropolitain, the Tour de l'Île des Enfants and Un Tour La Nuit.

Football

Percival-Molson Stadium
475 Avenue des Pins Ouest
☎(514) 871-2255 (tickets)
www.montrealalouettes.com

The **Montréal Alouettes** (Canadian Football League) have been playing at the Percival-Molson Stadium since 1998. Regular season begins in late May and ends in late October. You should attend at least one Alouettes games to enjoy the breathtaking view of downtown Montréal and, of course, to support the team, along with 20,000 other spectators!

Hockey

Bell Centre
1260 Rue De La Gauchetière Ouest
☎(514) 790-1245 or
800-361-4595 (tickets)
www.canadiens.com
The world-famous **Montreal Canadiens** National Hockey League team plays at the Bell Centre. There are 82 games during the regular season, 41 of which are played at home, then come the playoffs, at the end of which the winning team takes home the legendary Stanley Cup.

Soccer

Complexe Sportif Claude-Robillard
1000 Rue Émile-Journault
☎(514) 328-3668 or
790-1245 (tickets)
www.impactmontreal.com
The **Montréal Impact**, the city's soccer team, plays at the Complexe Sportif Claude-Robillard from mid-May to late August. A professional team, member of the international A-League, the Impact presents great soccer just like in Europe.

Entertainment – Cultural Activities

Tennis

Stade Uniprix
285 Rue Faillon Ouest
☎ (514) 790-1245 or
800-361-4595 (tickets)
www.tenniscanada.com
At Parc Jarry, located at the corner of Saint-Laurent Boulevard and Jarry Street, the best tennis players in the world participate, each year in early August, in the **Rogers Cup** competition. Even years are reserved to women's competitions.

■ Theatres and Concert Halls

Prices vary greatly from one theatre to the next. Most of the time, however, there are discounts for students.

L'Agora de la Danse
840 Rue Cherrier
☎ (514) 525-1500

Le Cabaret Music-Hall
2111 Boulevard St-Laurent
☎ (514) 845-2014

La Tulipe
4530 Avenue Papineau
☎ (514) 529-5000

Centaur Theatre
453 Rue St-François-Xavier
☎ (514) 288-3161

Le Gesù–Centre de créativité
1200 Rue de Bleury
☎ (514) 861-4378

Monument-National
1182 Boulevard St-Laurent
☎ (514) 871-2224

Place des Arts
175 Rue Ste-Catherine Ouest
☎ (514) 842-2112
The complex contains five performance spaces: Salle Wilfrid-Pelletier, Théâtre Maisonneuve, Théâtre Jean-Duceppe, Studio-théâtre and the Cinquième Salle. The Orchestre Symphonique de Montréal (☎ 514-842-9951), Opéra de Montréal (☎ 514-985-2258), Compagnie Jean-Duceppe (☎ 514-842-8681), Grands Ballets Canadiens (☎ 514-849-0269) and the Festival International de Jazz de Montréal hold performances here.

Spectrum
318 Rue Ste-Catherine Ouest
☎ (514) 861-5851
Shows usually begin around 9pm.

Théâtre Corona
2490 Rue Notre-Dame Ouest
☎ (514) 931-2088

Théâtre d'Aujourd'hui
3900 Rue St-Denis
☎ (514) 282-3900

Théâtre Denise-Pelletier
4353 Rue Ste-Catherine Est
☎ (514) 253-8974

Théâtre des Deux Mondes
7285 Rue Chabot
☎ (514) 593-4417

Théâtre Espace GO
4890 Boulevard St-Laurent
☎ (514) 845-4890

Théâtre Espace Libre
1945 Rue Fullum
☎ (514) 521-4191

Théâtre La Chapelle
3700 Rue St-Dominique
☎ (514) 843-7738

Théâtre La Licorne
4559 Rue Papineau
☎ (514) 523-2246

Théâtre du Nouveau Monde
84 Rue Ste-Catherine Ouest
☎ (514) 866-8668

Théâtre Olympia
1004 Rue Ste-Catherine Est
☎ (514) 287-7884

Théâtre Outremont
1248 Avenue Bernard Ouest
☎ (514) 495-9944

Théâtre Prospero
1371 Rue Ontario Est
☎ (514) 526-6582

Théâtre de Quat'Sous
100 Avenue des Pins Est
☎ (514) 845-7277

Théâtre du Rideau Vert
4664 Rue St-Denis
☎ (514) 844-1793

Théâtre Saint-Denis
1594 Rue St-Denis
☎ (514) 849-4211

Théâtre de Verdure
Parc La Fontaine
☎ (514) 872-2644
Set up in the heart of Parc La Fontaine, the Théâtre de Verdure features free open-air shows all summer long.

Saidye Bronfman Centre
5170 Chemin de la Côte-Ste-Catherine
☎ (514) 739-2301

Usine C
1345 Avenue Lalonde
☎ (514) 521-4493

■ Ticket Sales

Two major ticket agencies sell tickets for shows, concerts and other events in Montréal over the telephone or Internet. You'll need to pay by credit card to buy tickets online, though various ticket

outlets where you can pay cash can be found throughout the city. Service charges, which vary according to the show, are added to the price of tickets.

Admission
☎ (514) 790-1245 or 800-361-4595
www.admission.com

Ticketpro
☎ (514) 908-9090 or 866-908-9090
www.ticketpro.ca

Festivals and Cultural Events

During summer, festival fever takes hold of Montréal and its visitors. From May to September, the city hosts a whole series of festivals, each with a different theme. One thing is certain: there is something for everyone. As the summer season draws to a close, the events become less frequent but remain just as interesting.

■ January

Winter's cold does not preclude the festival spirit; it merely provides an opportunity to organize another festival in Montréal, this time to celebrate the pleasures and activities of the frosty season. The **Fête des Neiges** *(☎514-872-6120, www.fetedesneiges.com)* takes place in Parc Jean-Drapeau from late January to early February. Skating rinks and giant toboggans are available for the enjoyment of Montréal families. The snow-sculpture competition also attracts a number of curious onlookers.

■ February

The **Montréal High Lights Festival** (Festival Montréal En Lumière) *(☎514-288-9955, www.montrealenlumiere.com)* brings a bit of magic to the deepest frost of Québec's winter. In mid-February, light shows draw attention to the city's architecture and fireworks are presented outdoors. In the *Art de la Table* part of the festival, top chefs from all over the world prepare samples, meals and workshops. The festival also showcases concerts, dance and theatre.

■ April

Vues d'Afrique *(☎514-990-3201, www.vuesdafrique.org)* promotes African and Creole cinema. Films are presented in late April in Montréal's movie theatres, such as the ONF Montréal (National Film Board). All summer long, at dusk, Vues d'Afrique features outdoor concerts followed by movies at Théâtre de Verdure, in Parc Lafontaine.

■ June

The most important festival of its kind in North America, **Mondial de la Bière (Montréal Beer Festival)** *(☎514-722-9640, www.festivalmondialbiere.qc.ca)* is now well-known in Montréal. This event encourages a responsible approach to alcohol consumption and is held at Windsor Station in early June, giving you the chance to taste some 250 beers from around the world.

Another great initiative undertaken by Mauro Pezzente and Kiva Stimac is the **Suoni Per Il Popolo** (Sounds For The People) festival *(4873 Boulevard St-Laurent, ☎514-284-0122, www.casadelpopolo.com)*, which offers a nice alternative to what some consider a rather conservative and commercial Montréal Jazz Festival. The festival is held during the month of June at **Casa**

del Popolo (see p 265) and at the concert hall located on the second floor of **La Sala Rosa** (see p 224), across the street on Boulevard Saint-Laurent. Marked by the decidedly eclectic tastes of its programmers, Suoni Per Il Popolo presents the latest up-and-comers on the city's music scene as well as some of the biggest names in jazz, underground rock and electronic and left-field music. The last few editions of the festival have featured everything from Peter Brötzmann's free jazz workouts and Taqaq's traditional Inuit throat singing to trumpeter Wadada Leo Smith's subtle minimalist improvisations. For open ears and minds.

The **Nuit Blanche sur Tableau Noir** event (☎514-522-3797, www.tableaunoir. com) is held in the heart of the Plateau Mont-Royal district in mid-June. To the delight of passers-by, painters and musicians take over the street and transform the urban landscape into a colourful collective work of art. Activities are offered throughout the day and, come nightfall, people can observe the live creation of a fresco right on the asphalt.

The **First Peoples' Festival** (☎514-278-4040, www.nativelynx.qc.ca) is presented by the Land InSight Aboriginal association and held every year in Parc Émilie-Gamelin. A stage and a small village of Aboriginal craftspeople and artisans are set up in the park, where various plays, concerts, traditional dances and exhibits provide an overview of Native-American and Inuit know-how. The celebrations end every year on National Aboriginal Day, June 21st. The festival also presents several Aboriginal films. The screenings take place at ONF (NFB) Montréal and at the Cinémathèque Québécoise, and include many world premieres. Attendees can also meet some of the filmmakers whose works are shown.

Every summer in June, the **Saint-Ambroise Montréal Fringe Festival** (☎514-849-3378) showcases an impressive number of avant-garde shows and plays. They are often presented in cramped venues, but tickets are cheap, allowing everyone to enjoy this creative event.

■ July

L'International des Feux Loto-Québec (international fireworks competition) (☎514-397-2000, www.internationaldesfeuxloto-quebec.com) starts around mid-June and ends in late July. The world's top pyrotechnists present at La Ronde (île Sainte-Hélène) high-quality pyromusical shows every Saturday in June and every Wednesday and Saturday in July. Montrealers head to the La Ronde amusement park (where admission fees must be paid), Pont Jacques-Cartier or along the river in the Old Port (both at no cost) to admire the spectacular fireworks display that colours the sky above the city for over 30min.

During the **Festival International de Jazz de Montréal** (☎514-871-1881, www. montrealjazzfest.com), hundreds of shows set to the rhythm of jazz and its variations are presented on stages around Place des Arts. From late June to mid-July, this part of the city and a fair number of theatres are buzzing with activity. The event offers people an opportunity to take to the streets and be carried away by the festive atmosphere of fantastic, free outdoor shows that attract Montrealers and visitors in large numbers. The FIJM also presents various concerts outside the festival season.

Humour and creativity are highlighted during the **Festival Juste pour Rire/Just for Laughs Festival** (☎514-845-3155), which is held in mid-July. Theatres host comedians from a variety of countries for the occasion. Outdoor activities take place in the Quartier Latin, on Rue Saint-Denis south of Rue Sherbrooke, which is closed to traffic, while indoor shows are presented at the Théâtre Saint-Denis.

Montréal takes on a festive air during the **Festival International Nuits d'Afrique** (☎514-499-9239, *www.festivalnuits dafrique.com)*, which is held in mid-July and presents several outdoor concerts and activities. The biggest names in African, West-Indian and Caribbean music also offer indoor concerts.

The **FrancoFolies de Montréal** (☎514-523-3378, *www.francofolies.com)* are organized to promote French-language music and song. In late July, artists from francophone countries (Europe, Africa, the French Antilles, Québec and French Canada) perform, providing spectators with a unique glimpse of the French-speaking world's musical talent.

■ August

From the end of August until early September, the **Festival des Films du Monde de Montréal (World Film Festival)** (☎514-845-3883, *www.ffm-montreal. org)* takes over various Montréal movie theatres. During this competition, films from different countries are presented to Montréal audiences. At the end of the competition, prizes are awarded to the best films. The most prestigious category is the Grand Prix des Amériques. During the festival, films are shown from 9am to midnight, much to the delight of moviegoers across the city. An outdoor screening also takes place at Place des Arts during the festival.

■ October

Held in mid-October mainly at the Ex-Centris complex, but also at Cinéma Impérial, Cinéma du Parc and Concordia University's Théâtre Hall, the **Festival du Nouveau Cinéma** (☎514-282-0004, *www.nouveaucinema.ca)* aims to promote and develop digital creation and independent and avant-garde cinema.

■ December

Every year in December, at Place Bonaventure *(901 Rue De La Gauchetière Ouest)*, is the **Salon des Métiers d'Art du Québec** (☎514-861-2787). This exhibit lasts about 15 days and features Québécois artisans who exhibit and sell their work.

Entertainment - Festivals and Cultural Events

Shopping

Accessories	280	Food	286
Antiques	280	Gifts	289
Art	281	Home Decor	290
Children	282	Music	292
Cigars	283	Outdoor Equipment	292
Computers	283	Pet Stores	293
Curiosities	283	Reading	293
Electronics	283	Sex Shops	294
Fashion	283	Travel Accessories	294

D ie-hard shoppers will find much to love about Montréal. Among the many hunting grounds they can choose from are Rue Sainte-Catherine, the city's shopping mecca and main commercial artery, the maze-like halls of the underground city and its myriad boutiques, the Mile-End area where local designers have set up shop to sell their wares, Vieux-Montréal and its antique shops, and Avenue du Mont-Royal, where they'll find several funky second-hand clothing, book and music stores. To help you organize your shopping expeditions, we have chosen shops and boutiques that stand out for the quality, originality or value of their products. You're likely to encounter the phrases "*en vente*" or "*en solde*" in Montréal shops; both mean "on sale."

Accessories

■ Hats

For all kinds of hats in any size, shape or colour, here are two great places in Montréal:

Chapofolie
3944 Rue St-Denis
☎ (514) 982-0036

Henri Henri
189 Rue Ste-Catherine Est
☎ (514) 288-0109

■ Jewellery

Birks
1240 Rue du Square Phillips
☎ (514) 397-2511
A veritable Montréal institution, Birks has everything for the romantic spouse in search of the perfect gem to celebrate a special occasion.

Argent Tonic
138 Avenue Laurier Ouest
☎ (514) 274-5668
This charming jewellery store's cramped space is probably the inspiration for the nickname its owners have given it: *bar à bijoux*, or "jewel

bar." Thankfully, quality, originality and creativity are not measured by the square metre here, but unfortunately, neither are the prices.

Agatha
1054 Avenue Laurier Ouest
☎ (514) 272-9313
For fancy costume jewellery of silver or molten glass, check out Agatha.

Clio Blue
1468 Rue Peel
☎ (514) 281-3112
This boutique is part of a French chain of jewellery shops that specializes in silver.

Oz Bijoux
3915 Rue St-Denis
☎ (514) 845-9568
Oz Bijoux is a good choice if you're looking for something more creative.

■ Shoes

Brown's
1191 Rue Ste-Catherine Ouest
☎ (514) 987-1206
Not many Montréal shoe stores stand out for their selection of footwear. Brown's is an exception:

you'll find a vast array of choices here, both for men and women.

La Godasse
3686-B Boulevard St-Laurent
☎ (514) 286-8900
The large green centipede on the window of this small boutique should catch your eye. Step inside and you'll find the latest in hip urban footwear, from Adidas and Puma to Le Coq Sportif and Nike.

Antiques

Montréal's antique and second-hand shops offer a wide variety of odds-and-ends for every taste. Those who are on the lookout for antiques and have money to spare can stroll down the section of Rue Sherbrooke that crosses Westmount and where several quality antique dealers are located. If budget is an issue, try the second-hand stores on Rue Notre-Dame near Guy. The following shops sell beautiful antique furniture:

David S. Brown
995 Rue Wellington, Suite 203
☎(514) 844-9866

Henrietta Anthony
4192 Rue Ste-Catherine Ouest
☎(514) 935-9116

Le Petit Musée
1494 Rue Sherbrooke Ouest
☎(514) 937-6161

Art

■ Art Galleries

Art galleries are found everywhere in Montréal. It is hard to describe them since they obviously vary depending to the exhibition. It is better to go there in person and let the art speak for itself.

Galerie Clarence Gagnon
301 Rue St-Paul Est
☎(514) 875-2787

Galerie Claude Lafitte
1270 Rue Sherbrooke Ouest
☎(514) 842-1270

Galerie Dominion
1438 Rue Sherbrooke Ouest
☎(514) 845-7471

Galerie Jean-Pierre Valentin
1490 Rue Sherbrooke Ouest
☎(514) 939-0500

Waddington & Gore
372 Rue Ste-Catherine Ouest
☎(514) 847-1112

Contemporary and Modern Art

Centre d'Art et de Diffusion Clark
The Fashion Plaza
5455 Avenue de Gaspé, Suite 114
☎(514) 288-4972

Édifice Belgo
372 Rue Ste-Catherine Ouest
This former commercial building now houses a dynamic arts centre that features such art galleries as **Centre des Arts Actuels Skol** *(room 314, ☎514-398-9322)* as well as theatre and dance studios.

Espace Pepin
350 Rue St-Paul Ouest
☎(514) 844-0114
www.pepinart.com
This gallery stands out for the way its works are presented: visitors enter artist Lysanne Pepin's real home apartment, where paintings, furnishings and decorative objects are creatively displayed.

Galerie Michel-Ange
430 Rue Bonsecours
☎(514) 875-8281

Galerie Oboro
4001 Rue Berri
☎(514) 844-3250

Galerie Samuel Lallouz
4295 Boulevard St-Laurent
☎(514) 849-5844

Galerie Simon Blais
5420 Boulevard St-Laurent
☎(514) 849-1165

Community cultural centres and the Université du Québec à Montréal (UQAM) also host exhibitions of various Québec artists.

Glasswork

Elena Lee
1460 Rue Sherbrooke Ouest, Suite A
☎(514) 844-6009

■ Art Supplies

To find charcoal, pastels, tempera, sketchbooks, India ink, easels and other materials for your masterpiece, head to:

Omer DeSerres
334 Rue Ste-Catherine Est
☎(514) 842-6637
2134 Rue Ste-Catherine Ouest
☎(514) 938-4777

■ Crafts

Le Chariot
448 Place Jacques-Cartier
☎(514) 875-6134
Le Chariot exhibits fantastic artworks by Inuit and other native peoples, which are also sold here. It is really worth visiting just to take a look.

Dix Mille Villages
4128 Rue St-Denis
☎(514) 848-0538
Fair trade is this little arts-and-crafts boutique's *raison d'être*. The shop sells decorative objects from Asia, Africa and South America, including ceramics from Vietnam, sculptures from Kenya and vases from Peru. The selection is somewhat slim, and not all of the objects stand out. Rue Saint-Denis strollers can also stop by for a fresh cup of fair-trade coffee.

L'Empreinte Coopérative
272 Rue St-Paul Est
☎(514) 861-4427
Set up in a historic building in Vieux-Montréal, L'Empreinte is a Québec artisan co-op that sells fashion accessories, clothing, artwork and decorative household objects. This is a good spot to dis-

Shopping - Art

cover the latest trends in Québec arts and crafts.

Galerie Ima
3839A Rue St-Denis
☎ (514) 499-2904
Iranian artisans chisel, decorate and weave small, delicate treasures with geometric designs in bronze, silk, wood and mother-of-pearl. Some art objects from this far-away country are sold at Galerie Ima.

Giraffe
3997 Rue St-Denis
☎ (514) 499-8436
From Africa, the cradle of humanity, striking masks, dazzling fabrics and fascinating hand-crafted objects are all available at Giraffe, a shop whose merchandise is irresistibly appealing.

Canadian Guild of Crafts
1460 Rue Sherbrooke Ouest
☎ (514) 849-6091
The Canadian Guild of Crafts has a shop that sells hand-crafted Québécois and Canadian objects. As well, there are two small galleries that deal in Inuit and other native art.

Bonsecours Market
390 Rue St-Paul Est
☎ (514) 878-2787
The Bonsecours Market is the place to shop for crafts and exclusive designer items. Among the boutiques-galeries to visit, keep in mind the Galerie des métiers d'art *(☎514-878-2787)* and the Galerie de l'Institut de Design Montréal *(☎514-866-2436)*.

Each year in December at Place Bonaventure *(901 Rue De La Gauchetière Ouest)* artists from Québec display and sell their work in a giant exposition hall during the **Salon des Métiers d'Art du Québec**. If you miss the show, the **Le Rouet** *(1500 Avenue McGill College, ☎514-843-5235)* boutique sells sculptures, pottery and ceramics by several Québec artists.

Children

■ Children's Wear

Boutique La Petite Ferme du Mouton Noir
2160 Rue Beaubien Est
☎ (514) 271-9760
From her own experience as a mother of two little ones, the young designer of the Mouton Noir clothing line has developed a collection that is a perfect blend of beauty, comfort and practicality. Her secret: clothes that move with the child and fabrics that are easy to care for and that kids will like to wear, but especially, design (one must not forget the active mother!).

Enfants Deslongchamps
1007 Avenue Laurier Ouest
☎ (514) 274-2442
Parents who want to spoil their children will love Enfants Deslongchamps. Beware: this store doesn't cater to the budget-minded.

Fiou
3922 Rue St-Denis
☎ (514) 844-0444
Fiou offers clothing for infants and children up to eight years old. The owner is familiar with the children's wear business and sells attractive clothing from well-known manufacturers.

Peek a Boo
807 Rue Rachel Est
☎ (514) 890-1222
Peek a Boo is an attractive second-hand children's clothing and accessory store. Everything you need for pampering baby, from pajamas to baby carriers, is available in good condition at affordable prices.

Pom'Canelle
4860 Rue Sherbrooke Ouest
☎ (514) 483-1787
Pom'Canelle is another good spot for dressing your little ones.

■ Games and Toys

La Cerf-Volanterie
4039 Rue Ste-Catherine Est
☎ (514) 845-7613
For kites, why not go to the experts? La Cerf-Volanterie custom-makes them in every size and colours for everyone. On summer weekends, customers can try out their kite-flying skills at the Old Port.

Coin du Cheminot
5354 Rue Bélanger Est
☎ (514) 728-8443
Model-train collectors should check out Coin du Cheminot.

Au Diabolo
1390 Avenue du Mont-Royal Est
☎ (514) 528-8889
A veritable treasure-trove of games and toys for infants, children and kids at heart.

Franc Jeu
4152 Rue St-Denis
☎ (514) 849-9253
Pinocchio and Capucine, Babar and Milou will delight children at Franc Jeu, which has a vast assortment of toys for all ages, from babies to those who are enjoying their second chilhood.

Valet de Coeur
4408 Rue St-Denis
☎ (514) 499-9970
Playing is not only for children, and Valet de Coeur has games for everyone, from three-dimensional puzzles, Chinese checkers and chess sets to a variety of parlour games.

Cigars

Casa del Habano
1434 Rue Sherbrooke Ouest
☎ (514) 849-0037
This cigar shop and smoking room is located in the heart of the museum district.

Computers

The latest computers, software, printers and other computer products can be purchased at the following stores:

Camelot Info
1191 Rue du Square-Phillips
☎ (514) 861-5019

Dumoulin Informatique
8990 Boulevard de l'Acadie
☎ (514) 384-1022
2050 Boulevard St-Laurent
☎ (514) 288-7755

Micro Boutique
6615 Avenue du Parc
☎ (514) 270-4477

Softmagic Computer Software
9760 Boulevard Henri-Bourassa Ouest
☎ (514) 335-0195

Curiosities

Excalibor
122 Rue St-Paul Est
☎ (514) 393-7260
4400 Rue St-Denis
☎ (514) 843-9993
Excalibor has an impressive selection of armour, swords, hats, costumes, books and many other articles inspired by the period from the Middle Ages to the Renaissance.

L'Échoppe du Dragon Rouge
8874 Rue Lajeunesse
☎ (514) 858-5711
3804 Rue St-Denis
☎ (514) 840-9030
L'Échoppe du Dragon Rouge sells replicas of medieval objects and clothes.

Electronics

Espace Bell
705 Rue Ste-Catherine Ouest
☎ (514) 288-8436
Place Dupuis
1475 Rue St-Hubert
☎ (514) 844-1313
When it comes to telephones, it's best to consult the experts at Espace Bell.

Future Shop
470 Rue Ste-Catherine Ouest
☎ (514) 393-2600
For televisions, computers and other electronic appliances, one establishment claims to have the lowest prices: Future Shop. They frequently do have bargains, but shop around a bit before buying.

On **Boulevard Saint-Laurent**, between Rue Ontario and Rue Sherbrooke, several stores sell all kinds of electronic equipment. Bargaining is recommended; count on getting 10% to 20% off the listed price.

Fashion

The fashion industry is flourishing in Montréal. The city is a multi-ethnic crossroads where Québécois and Canadian designers show their latest creations alongside those from the United States, Italy, France and the world. Streets like Rue Saint-Denis, Avenue Laurier, Boulevard Saint-Laurent and Rue Sherbrooke stand out for the numerous fashion boutiques that line their sidewalks. A visit to the shops is sure to turn up something that is just your style.

■ Clothing

Downtown Montreal has exceptionally fine clothing stores for the well-dressed man, such as **Eccetera... & Co** *(2021 Rue Peel,* ☎*514-845-9181)*, **Uomo** *(1452 Rue Peel,* ☎*514-844-1008)* and **Il n'y a que deux** *(1405 Rue Crescent,* ☎*514-843-5665)*. For something more casual, head to **Old**

River *(1115 Rue Ste-Catherine Ouest,* ☎*514-843-7828).*

Aime Com Moi
150 Avenue du Mont-Royal Est
☎ (514) 982-0088
Ready-to-wear clothes for women.

American Apparel
3523 Boulevard St-Laurent
☎ (514) 286-0091
American Apparel is owned by native Montrealer Dov Charney. The shop sells simple, distinctive clothing such as their signature Made-in-L.A. cotton T-shirts.

Billie
141 Avenue Laurier Ouest
☎ (514) 270-5415
Conviviality and timelessness are the keywords in this new women's wear boutique located on chic Avenue Laurier. The shop's clothing and accessories are created by local designers or imported from around the world. The Carla collection is exclusive to Billie and features impeccably cut, sophisticated dresses that are well suited to this elegant boutique. Men have not been left out here: game consoles are available for them to play while their sweethearts go about shopping!

Boutique Nadya Toto
2057 Rue de la Montagne
☎ (514) 350-9090
Ready-to-wear clothes for women. Artwork exhibits are also held here.

La Cache
3941 Rue St-Denis
☎ (514) 842-7693
1353 Avenue Green
☎ (514) 935-4361

La Cache is a Canadian chain of quality clothing stores. Their clothes are handmade in India from colourful and original fabrics with patterns inspired by traditional Indian themes.

Dubuc Mode de Vie
4451 Rue St-Denis
☎ (514) 282-1424
Ready-to-wear clothing and accessories for men and women.

Henriette L.
1031 Avenue Laurier Ouest
☎ (514) 277-3426
You don't have to go to extremes to find something original: just head to Henriette L. in Outremont.

Lola & Emily
3475 Boulevard St-Laurent
☎ (514) 288-8239
We have a soft spot for this boutique-apartment that provides a refreshing twist on the art of shopping. With classic styles for Emily and a rock touch for Lola, the clothing that is chosen by the shop's two owners is sold alongside various accessories, furnishings and beauty products.

Lyla Collection
400 Avenue Laurier Ouest, Suite 200
☎ (514) 271-0763
For women: lingerie, swimsuits and accessories. Artists' exhibits.

Mains Folles
4427 Rue St-Denis
☎ (514) 284-6854
The attractive bas-relief in the storefront at Mains Folles is just the beginning. The real reason

for shopping here is the beautiful apparel: colourful dresses, skirts and shirts imported from Bali. There is also a small selection of jewellery that complements the clothing.

Morales
5392 Boulevard St-Laurent
☎ (514) 271-5061

Falbala
122 Rue Bernard Ouest
☎ (514) 948-4523
You'll find these two ready-to-wear designers' creations in the heart of the hip Mile-End area: Falbala *(www.falbaladesign. com)* is owned by sisters Mélanie and Sophie Veilleux, who previously worked for designer Marie Saint-Pierre, an institution in Québec fashion, while Renata Morales' *(www.renatamorales.com)* Mexican origins are the inspiration behind her baroque and sensual line of clothing.

Muse
4467 Rue St-Denis
☎ (514) 848-9493
Ready-to-wear clothes for the free-spirited, romantic woman.

Musky Design
3917-B Rue St-Denis
Ready-to-wear clothes for women.

Pierre, Jean, Jacques
158 Avenue Laurier Ouest
☎ (514) 270-8392
The men's clothing store Pierre, Jean, Jacques has moved to the more exclusive Avenue Laurier, where the friendly, highly professional owner gives good advice to male customers of any age. Don't be shy to ask for help

when trying to find the perfect fit.

Revenge
3852 Rue St-Denis
☎ (514) 843-4379
Not every inspired creation comes from Paris. Revenge sells lovingly crafted originals and accessories created by talented Québec designers for both men and women.

Rudsak
1400 Rue Ste-Catherine Ouest
☎ (514) 399-9925
Ready-to-wear clothing for men and women. Leather accessories and clothing.

U & I
3650-2 Boulevard St-Laurent
☎ (514) 844-8788
This sparsely decorated store was recently named one of the city's most fashionable boutiques and features several currently popular designers, such as Comme des garçons, Martin Margiela, Mackage and Denis Gagnon. For both men and women.

Urban Outfitters
1250 Rue Ste-Catherine Ouest
☎ (514) 874-0063
Urban Outfitters brings the 1970s back to life with its popular line of clothing, accessories and books sold in what can only be called a luxury thrift-store decor. Each object here is a find, from funky lamp shades and shoes to colourful shower curtains.

■ Fur

Well known for years as *the* spot to buy furs, Montréal is home to designers who create up-to-date fashions from the most luxurious pelts.

Desjardins Fourrure
325 Boulevard René-Lévesque Est
☎ (514) 288-4151

Fourrure Oslo
2863A Boulevard Rosemont
☎ (514) 721-1271

Harricana Atelier-Boutique
3000 Rue St-Antoine Ouest
☎ (514) 287-6517
Clothing and accessories made from recycled fur.

McComber
402 Boulevard De Maisonneuve Ouest
☎ (514) 845-1167

■ Jeans

All kinds of jeans are available in Montréal, often at lower prices than in Europe.

Levi's
705 Rue Ste-Catherine Ouest, Centre Eaton
☎ (514) 286-1574
1241 Rue Ste-Catherine Ouest
☎ (514) 288-8199
Those who won't wear anything but Levi's will love these two shops that sell this brand exclusively.

■ Leather

MO 851
3526 Boulevard St-Laurent
☎ (514) 849-9759
Leather clothing and accessories, including some colourful, close-fitting soft-leather styles.

■ Lingerie

Looking for something lacy? **Deuxième Peau** *(4457 Rue St-Denis,* ☎*514-842-0811),* **Lyla Collection** *(400 Avenue Laurier Ouest,* ☎*514-271-0763)* and **Madame Courval** *(4861 Rue Sherbrooke Ouest,* ☎*514-484-5656)* have lovely selections of lingerie. They also sell swimsuits.

■ Shopping Centres and Department Stores

Several downtown shopping centres and department stores offer a good selection of clothing by well-known fashion designers, including Jean-Claude Chacok, Cacharel, Guy Laroche, Lily Simon, Adrienne Vittadini, Mondi, Ralph Lauren and many others. The young and the young at heart will find relatively inexpensive clothing such as comfortable casual wear, wool sweaters, jeans and shirts at major chains such as Gap, Jacob, Bedo, America and Tristan et Iseut.

Les Ailes de la Mode
677 Rue Ste-Catherine Ouest
☎ (514) 282-4537

The Bay
585 Rue Ste-Catherine Ouest
☎ (514) 281-4422

Eaton Centre
705 Rue Ste-Catherine Ouest
☎ (514) 288-3759
The largest urban mall in Montréal, the Eaton Centre features 175 shops,

Shopping - Fashion

services and restaurants, a foreign-exchange office and indoor parking.

Les Cours Mont-Royal
1445 Rue Peel
☎ (514) 842-7777

Holt Renfrew
1300 Rue Sherbrooke Ouest
☎ (514) 842-5111

Ogilvy
1307 Rue Ste-Catherine Ouest
☎ (514) 842-7711

Place Montréal Trust
1500 Avenue McGill College
☎ (514) 843-8000

Place Ville-Marie
1 Place Ville-Marie
☎ (514) 861-9393

Les Promenades de la Cathédrale
625 Rue Ste-Catherine Ouest
☎ (514) 849-9925

Simons
977 Rue Ste-Catherine Ouest
☎ (514) 282-1840
Established in Québec City in 1840, the Simons retail chain has long been a staple among many Quebecers. In 1999, Simons finally opened in Montréal, an event that had long been awaited by the city's most avid shoppers. In this large department store with lovely designer decor, you'll find head-to-toe clothing for men, women and children in a wide range of styles, as well as fashion accessories and bedding.

Some department stores offer couture creations in a wide range of prices. There are Canadian creations by designers such as Simon Chang, Jean-

Claude Poitras and Alfred Sung, and international designers such as Mondi, Liz Claiborne, Jones New York and Adrienne Vittadini. These stores also feature beautiful leather clothing at reasonable prices.

Food

■ Bakeries

Boulangerie Monsieur Pinchot
4354 Rue de Brébeuf
☎ (514) 522-7192
Boulangerie Monsieur Pinchot is just the place to stock up for an impromptu picnic off the bicycle path. This charming old-fashioned bakery has delicious quality products.

But how can we talk about Montréal bakeries without mentioning bagels? Montréal is world famous for these little delicacies, as they are probably the best bagels on the planet! Whether or not this is true, they are certainly delicious and much loved. Many bakeries, especially in Outremont and Mile-End, make several varieties of them in a wood-burning oven. Among these are the famous **Fairmount Bagel Bakery** *(74 Avenue Fairmount Ouest, ☎ 514-272-0667)*, which is open 24hrs, and **St. Viateur Bagel Shop** *(263 Avenue St-Viateur Ouest, ☎ 514-276-8044)*.

Faubourg Saint-Catherine
1616 Rue Ste-Catherine Ouest
☎ (514) 939-3663

Faubourg Saint-Catherine is a modern shopping complex that has various specialty shops selling excellent quality foods.

Le Fromentier *(1375 Avenue Laurier Est, ☎ 514-527-3327)* is a home-style bakery that offers a wide selection of absolutely delicious breads. It is still possible to observe bakers hard at work at the ovens.

Première Moisson can't really be called an artisan bakery because it is in fact a chain of bakeries. However, each one prepares fresh, delicious baked goods daily, straight from a wood-burning oven. Deli meats, cakes, chocolates, desserts and delicious ready-made dishes are also sold here. Première Moisson has outlets in Montréal's three public markets, as well as the Gare Centrale *(895 Rue de la Gauchetière)*, at 1271 Avenue Bernard Ouest and at 860 Avenue du Mont-Royal Est.

For its part, **Boulangerie Au Pain Doré** *(3075 Rue de Rouen, ☎ 514-528-8877)* provides baguettes and bread, as well as pastries and cakes, to several good restaurants in Montréal that swear by this bakery. Its number of shops testifies to its success! Here are some addresses: 556 Rue Sainte-Catherine Est, 3611 Boulevard Saint-Laurent, 6850 Rue Marquette, 1415 Rue Peel, 1145 Avenue Laurier Ouest and 1357 Avenue du Mont-Royal Est

■ Butcher Shops

La Queue de Cochon
1375 Avenue Laurier Est
☎(514) 527-2525
6400 Rue St-Hubert
☎(514) 527-2252
Foodies will definitely like the excellent products at La Queue de Cochon, a small craft-style *charcuterie* (butcher shop). A variety of terrines and sausages such as *boudin blanc* and *boudin noir* (white-pudding and blood-pudding sausages), as well as several prepared dishes, are available here. Pork products are obviously the speciality here, and after the owner (from Vendée, France) and his family tell you all about them, you won't want to leave without buying something!

■ Cheese

La Foumagerie
4906 Rue Sherbrooke Ouest
☎(514) 482-4100
La Foumagerie boasts a large assortment of cheeses, including different kinds of brie, goat's-milk and raw-milk cheese.

Fromagerie Hamel
220 Rue Jean-Talon Est
☎(514) 272-1161
There is a panoply of little shops worth mentioning around the Jean-Talon Market. One of these is Fromagerie Hamel, one the best cheese shops in the city, which is known for the fine quality and wide selection of its products, as well as its excellent service. You should definitely sample their cheeses if offered. Despite the lineup, the staff

always sees to its customers' every need.

Another excellent neighbourhood cheese shop is **Maître Affineur Maître Corbeau** *(1375 Avenue Laurier Est, ☎514-528-3293).*

■ Chocolate

Les Chocolats de Chloé
375 Rue Roy Est
☎(514) 849-5550
Chloé Germain-Fredette, an artisan chocolate maker and the owner of this ravishing Plateau Mont-Royal boutique, comes up with some daring combinations when making her chocolates: some of her original flavours include green tea, Espelette pepper and *fleur de sel*. Ask for an assortment and enjoy the wide variety of tastes.

Chocolats Geneviève Grandbois
162 Avenue St-Viateur Ouest
☎(514) 394-1000
Marché Atwater,
138 Rue Atwater, 2nd floor
☎(514) 933-1331
Geneviève Grandbois is renowned for her devilishly divine chocolates. Each little cube is a marvel, with stunningly creative varieties running the gamut from Chai tea and *fleur de sel*-flavoured caramel (homemade, of course) to black truffle and olive oil. Connoisseurs will appreciate the refined choice of ingredients and the high-quality cocoa beans. The pure pleasure of discovering your new favourite can be enjoyed again and again, as delicious new

creations are presented each season.

Au Festin de Babette
4085 Rue St-Denis
☎(514) 849-0214
In summer, the terrace at Au Festin de Babette is a charming spot to sip an espresso or savour a sorbet or ice cream. And in all seasons, there is a veritable treasure trove to browse through: marvellous olive oils, exotic preserves, flavourful condiments and many other delightful items. Their mouth-watering Belgian pralines are simply to die for!

Succulent Belgian pralines are also available at **Daskalidès** *(377 Avenue Laurier, ☎514-272-3447)* and **Léonidas** *(605 Boulevard De Maisonneuve Ouest, ☎514-849-2620).*

Neuhaus
1442 Rue Sherbrooke Ouest
☎(514) 849-7609
For a few dollars more, Belgian-praline lovers will be lured to Neuhaus where scrumptious cocoa morsels are elegantly presented.

Confiserie Louise Décarie
4424 Rue St-Denis
☎(514) 499-3445
Children of all ages will like the colourful displays of candy, soft caramels, barley sugar and other sweet delights at Confiserie Louise Décarie.

■ Health Food

Rachelle-Béry
505 Rue Rachel Est
☎(514) 524-0725

Originally located at the corner of Rachel and Berri streets (hence the name), Rachelle-Béry now has a few other stores in the city *(4660 Boulevard St-Laurent, ☎514-849-4118; 2510 Rue Beaubien Est, ☎514-727-2327 and 1332 Rue Fleury Est, ☎514-388-5793)*. These are large grocery stores that sell natural products such as food, vitamins and cosmetics.

Tau
4238 Rue St-Denis
☎(514) 843-4420
Tau sells a vast array of soaps, health products, bulk foods, organically grown fruit and vegetables, as well as prepared dishes. In short, they have everything necessary to maintain good health.

■ Pastry Shops

La Brioche Lyonnaise
1593 Rue St-Denis
☎(514) 842-7017
At La Brioche Lyonnaise, delicious pastries and coffee can be enjoyed right on the premises. But don't worry—there are also plenty left to bring home.

Pâtisserie Belge
3487 Avenue du Parc
☎(514) 845-1245
1075A Avenue Laurier Ouest
☎(514) 279-5274
Belgian in name only, Pâtisserie Belge offers a wide assortment of wonderful little morsels made of chocolate, cream and mousse, and many other sinful delights that are the perfect finishing touch to a meal.

Pâtisserie de Nancy
5655 Avenue Monkland
☎(514) 482-3030
Pâtisserie de Nancy is prized by neighbourhood residents who love good, warm, buttery croissants on Saturday and Sunday mornings. Many other treats are also available.

Duc de Lorraine
5002 Chemin de la Côte-des-Neiges
☎(514) 731-4128
Duc de Lorraine is another classic Montréal *pâtisserie* that has captivated the taste buds of many local gourmets thanks to its delicious Grand Marnier–glazed treats and almond croissants.

Pâtisserie de Gascogne
6095 Boulevard Gouin Ouest
☎(514) 331-0550
4825 Rue Sherbrooke Ouest
☎(514) 932-3511
237 Avenue Laurier Ouest
☎(514) 490-0235
For years, the Pâtisserie de Gascogne has been considered one of the city's best. The new location on Laurier Street is easy to reach and has tables where you can have a coffee and pastry. *Miroir Cassis* and *Indulgent*, popular French nouvelle-cuisine desserts, are their specialty.

■ Public Markets

Montréal still has public markets where local farmers come to sell their produce. Imported products are also available in some of these markets.

Les Marchés Publics de Montréal
www.marchespublics-mtl.com

Marché Atwater
138 Avenue Atwater
☎(514) 937-7754

Marché Lachine
1865 Rue Notre-Dame, corner 18e Avenue
☎(514) 937-7754

Marché de Maisonneuve
4445 Rue Ontario Est
☎(514) 937-7754

Marché Jean Talon
7075 Rue Casgrain
☎(514) 277-1588

In summer, you can also find little outdoor markets here and there, such as the one at the Mont-Royal metro station. **Kiosque Mont-Royal** *(May to late Oct)* sells fruit, vegetables and plants.

■ Specialty Grocers

L'Aromate
1106 Avenue du Mont-Royal Est
☎(514) 521-6333
L'Aromate sells seasonings, spices, herbs, jams, jellies and ketchup, as well as decorative objects to spice up the kitchen.

Atlantic Meat & Delicatessen
5060 Chemin de la Côte-des-Neiges
☎(514) 731-4764
Atlantic Meat & Delicatessen is a German grocery store that is popular for its traditional foods like sauerkraut and sausages.

L'épicerie Gourmet Laurier
1042 Avenue Laurier Ouest
☎(514) 274-5601
L'épicerie Gourmet Laurier grocery store has a large selection of cheeses.

Shopping - Food

Maison des Pâtes Fraîches
865 Rue Rachel Est
☎ (514) 527-5487
Maison des Pâtes Fraîches sells quality Italian food: cheese, olives and capers, cold cuts, biscotti and gelati, as well as delicious fresh pasta and savoury sauces. Here you can buy all the ingredients for concocting a quick, delicious homemade meal. Also, tasty, reasonably priced hot dishes are prepared and served on the premises or to go, much to the delight of neighbourhood workers.

Milano
6862 Boulevard St-Laurent
☎ (514) 273-8558
Located in the heart of Little Italy, Milano's charming grocery store overflows with fine European products such as fresh pasta, chocholate, prosciutto and provolone.

Supermarché Andes Gloria
4387 Boulevard St-Laurent
☎ (514) 848-1078
Supermarché Andes Gloria sells dishes like salsa, empanadas and tortillas, as well as other Latin-American products.

La Vieille Europe
3855 Boulevard St-Laurent
☎ (514) 842-5773
Salami, smoked lard, chorizo, vegetarian sausages, foie gras, olives... homesick for authentic European food? Head to La Vieille Europe, where you'll also find a huge selection of cheeses at impossibly low prices and a wide variety of fine coffees.

Looking for that elusive ingredient for your traditional Chinese cuisine recipe? You'll find everything you need in the city's **Chinatown** district.

Gifts

The city's **Économusées** feature lovely shops with enticing works of art that make great gifts for a loved one... or why not for yourself?

Galerie Parchemine – Économusée de l'Encadrement
40 Rue St-Paul Ouest
☎ (514) 845-3368
The Galerie Parchemine – Économusée de l'Encadrement's boutique sells several attractive frames, and the gallery also offers framing workshops and features a permanent exhibit on antique and modern framing techniques.

If you're walking down Boulevard Saint-Laurent, you'll come upon La Tranchefile – Économusée de la Reliure *(5251 Boulevard St-Laurent, ☎514-270-9313).* This book-binding workshop and museum provides an opportunity to discover the vitality of an ancient trade that explores contemporary forms of expression. A variety of beautifully bound books are exposed in the shop, and the delicate leather aromas that permeate the establishment are enticing. A few steps further is a vitrified glass-making workshop and museum called **Hectarus – Économusée du**

Verre Vitrifié *(5329 Boulevard St-Laurent, ☎514-495-2629).* Hectarus reveals the secrets of the art of vitrified glass-making by presenting the different processes and techniques of the trade. You'll get to see a few of Hectarus' stunning works, including his popular vitrified-glass washbasins. Finally, across the street from Hectarus is **Les Brodeuses – Économusée de la Broderie** *(5364 Boulevard St-Laurent, ☎514-276-4181),* an embroidery shop and museum. Discover the art of needlework and its harmonious blend of threads and colours. A small gallery displays the tools of the trade, various embroidered objects and documents on the history of this secular art, while the shop sells embroidered products and everything you need to start making your own embroideries.

Montréal's museum gift shops are almost like museums in themselves, and sell various reproductions lovely enough to embellish any home. Here are two to remember:

Boutique du Musée d'art Contemporain
185 Rue Ste-Catherine Ouest
☎ (514) 847-6904

Montreal Museum of Fine Arts Boutique and Bookstore
1390 Rue Sherbrooke Ouest
☎ (514) 285-1600

Céramique
4201B Rue St-Denis
☎ (514) 848-1119
If you're looking for an original gift, at Céramique Art-Café you can paint a

clay object yourself while comfortably seated and enjoying a light meal or a drink. The experienced staff is there to help you.

L'Essence du Papier
4160 Rue St-Denis
☎ (514) 288-9691
Ogilvy, 1307 Rue Ste-Catherine Ouest
☎ (514) 842-7711
Onion skin, tissue, stationery and wrapping: every kind of paper imaginable is available at Essence du Papier. Postcards, ribbons, famous brand-name pens—even inkwells and feathers are sold here.

Farfelu
843 Avenue du Mont-Royal Est
☎ (514) 528-6251
Still searching for the perfect gift wrapping? Try Farfelu. It's packed with coloured ribbons, wrapping paper and everything else to embellish that special something.

Kamikaze
4156 Rue St-Denis
☎ (514) 848-0728
A tiny boutique by day, Kamikaze becomes a lively bar by night (Le Passeport). It stocks fashionable costume jewellery (earrings, necklaces and other imaginative creations) and clothing (scarves, hosiery and hats).

Mortimer Snodgrass
209 Rue St-Paul Ouest
☎ (514) 499-2851
5737 Avenue Monkland
☎ (514) 485-9777
There's something for everyone in Mortimer Snodgrass' boutiques. You'll find every delightfully useless and striking-

ly original gift idea you could imagine here, from colourful electrical switch plates to neoprene wine bags to a unique collection of items for kids. For the humorous gift-giver in search of that perfect catch.

Aux Papiers Japonais
21 Avenue Fairmount Ouest
☎ (514) 276-6863
The art of making paper is still very popular at Aux Papiers Japonais, which sells paper with textures unlike any others; they are perfect for origami or fancy letters. Paper-making courses are sometimes offered.

Aux Plaisirs de Bacchus
1225 Avenue Bernard Ouest
☎ (514) 273-3104
Wine connoisseurs should definitely stop by Aux Plaisirs de Bacchus, where a large selection of accessories for wine cellars is available. Wine-tasting glasses are also sold here.

Senteurs de Provence
4077 Rue St-Denis
☎ (514) 845-6867
Senteurs de Provence sells Provençal soaps, aromatic oils, potpourris, perfumes, fabrics and many other charming items from this Mediterranean region.

There are also specialty paper shops in Westmount and Outremont: **Origami Plus** *(1369 Avenue Greene,* ☎*514-938-4688)* and **Papillote** *(1126 Avenue Bernard Ouest,* ☎*514-271-6356).*

Home Decor

12° En Cave
367 Rue St-Paul Est
☎ (514) 866-5722
If you've decided to set up a wine cellar in your home, drop by 12° En Cave: you'll find everything an expert wine taster may need, from glasses and vineyard maps to hygrometers and storerooms.

Arthur Quentin
3960 Rue St-Denis
☎ (514) 843-7513
To entertain in style, Arthur Quentin has the finest selection of dishware, table linens and kitchen accessories—everything from garlic crushers to sugar tongs.

Artisans du Meuble Québécois
88 Rue St-Paul Est
☎ (514) 866-1836
The craftspeople at Artisans du Meuble Québécois create new, antique-looking furniture that blends in well with the decor of modern houses.

Atelier
4247 Rue St-André
☎ (514) 843-7513
Open only from Thursday to Saturday, the small Atelier on Rue Saint-André is a discount store for **Arthur Quentin** (see above) and **Bleu Nuit** (see p 291) on Rue Saint-Denis. It is a great spot for reasonably priced items to decorate your home.

Caban
777 Rue Ste-Catherine Ouest
☎ (514) 844-9300
Caban sells top-of-the-line home decoration items.

You'll find everything you need to make your home a palace in this three-storey shop located in the heart of commercial Rue Sainte-Catherine: refined furniture, accessories, decorative objects, plants, tableware and even a line of clothing.

La Cache
3941 Rue St-Denis
☎ (514) 842-7693
1353 Avenue Green
☎ (514) 935-4361
La Cache sells lovely objects for the home, including linens.

Caplan Duval 2000
5800 Boulevard Cavendish
☎ (514) 483-4040
Caplan Duval 2000 has a wide choice of reasonably priced crystal vases, glassware and china to complete your trousseau.

Côté Sud
4338 Rue St-Denis
☎ (514) 289-9443
Whether your decorating style is baroque, classical or more exotic, Côté Sud will suit your taste. Furniture, mirrors, draperies and wall hangings, stylish doorknobs, bathroom carpets, dishes and candle holders... the list goes on!

Interversion
4273 Boulevard St-Laurent
☎ (514) 284-2103
Interversion has three stories full of furniture and other crafts made in Québec. These lovely, affordably priced objects are contemporary, yet timeless, and most are made out of wood. They will add originality and creativity to any home.

Jeune d'Ici Meubles
134 Avenue Laurier Ouest
☎ (514) 270-5512
Children, as well as adults, deserve lovely furniture. Jeune d'Ici Meubles has functional and imaginative items for children.

Maison d'Émilie
1073 Avenue Laurier Ouest
☎ (514) 277-5151
It's hard to leave Maison d'Émilie empty-handed. Its exquisite table linens and settings, glassware, china and kitchen accessories are tempting and sometimes costly.

Nordsouth
50 Rue St-Paul Ouest
☎ (514) 288-1292
Nordsouth is chock full of modern furniture and other household items by Québec designers.

Quincaillerie Dante
6851 Rue St-Dominique
☎ (514) 271-2057
Quincaillerie Dante set up shop in the Little Italy district in 1956, and its owner, Elena Venditelli-Faita, appears regularly on trendy Québec cooking shows. You won't find any hammers or power drills in this *quincaillerie* (French for hardware store). Surprisingly enough, the shop sells the latest kitchen and home accessories imported from Europe as well as a selection of quality hunting and fishing items.

Zone
4246 Rue St-Denis
☎ (514) 845-3530
5014 Rue Sherbrooke Ouest
☎ (514) 489-8901
Looking for the perfect gift but fresh out of ideas?

Head straight for Zone, where off-beat key chains, stylish candle holders, Art Deco soap dishes and mood-enhancing lamps will inspire you!

■ Flowers

La Boutique du Fleuriste
1011 Avenue Bernard Ouest
☎ (514) 276-3058

Fauchois Fleurs
3933-A Rue St-Denis
☎ (514) 844-4417

Fleuriste Pourquoi Pas
3629 Boulevard St-Laurent
☎ (514) 844-3233

Madame Lespérance
1135A Rue Laurier Ouest
☎ (514) 277-2173

Marcel Proulx
3835 Rue St-Denis
☎ (514) 849-1344

Marie Vermette
801 Rue Laurier Est
☎ (514) 272-2225

Westmount Florist
360 Avenue Victoria
☎ (514) 488-9121

Here are two shops that not only sell flowers and plants, but also lovely terracotta vases from Mexico, Thailand and Indonesia: **Alpha** *(230 Rue Peel,* ☎*(514) 935-1812)* and **Caméléon Vert** *(1300 Rue St-Antoine Ouest,* ☎*(514) 937-2481).*

■ Linens

Bleu Nuit
3913 Rue St-Denis
☎ (514) 843-5702
Suffering from bedtime blues? The pretty cotton

sheets at Bleu Nuit will hush you right to sleep. A bit pricey, though.

Carré Blanc
3999 Rue St-Denis
☎ (514) 847-0729
White includes all the colours in the spectrum, which are all available at Carré Blanc, in affordably priced sheets and pillowcases that will give you a good night's sleep.

Décor Marie Paule
1090 Avenue Laurier Ouest
☎ (514) 273-8889
In hot and refined colours, Décor Marie Paule has down comforter covers and sheets.

Linen Chest
Promenades de la Cathédrale
625 Rue Ste-Catherine Ouest
☎ (514) 282-9525
The Linen Chest is the "supermarket" of bedding for those who prefer a wide array of choices.

■ Posters

À L'Affiche
4415 Rue St-Denis
☎ (514) 845-5723
To plaster your walls with movie posters, go to À L'Affiche.

For reproductions of Renoirs, Van Goghs, Fortins or Borduas, check out **L'Atelier 68** *(5170 Boulevard St-Laurent, ☎514-276-2872)* or **Galerie Montréal Images** *(3854 Rue St-Denis, ☎514-284-0192; 3620 Boulevard St-Laurent, ☎514-842-1060).*

Music

■ CDs

The following megastores have the largest selection of compact discs of all musical genres at the lowest prices:

Archambault
500 Rue Ste-Catherine Est
☎ (514) 849-6201
Place des Arts
175 Rue Ste-Catherine Ouest
☎ (514) 281-0367

HMV
1020 Rue Ste-Catherine Ouest
☎ (514) 875-0765

Smaller music shops may specialize in used CDs or more wide-ranging musical genres. The reception and service is generally more personalized than in major chain stores, and the knowledgeable staff can help you track down that elusive album or recommend the best up-and-coming acts on the bustling Montréal music scene. The following record shops will appeal to music fans who aren't necessarily looking for the latest Top 40 hit.

Atom Heart Records
364B Rue Sherbrooke Est
☎ (514) 843-8484
Good selection of electronic and alternative CDs and vinyl records.

Cheap Thrills
2044 Rue Metcalfe
☎ (514) 844-8988
Cheap Thrills has a large selection of both new and used blues, jazz, hip hop and avant-garde CDs and vinyl records. You'll

also find a nice selection of second-hand books in English.

L'Oblique
4333 Rue Rivard
☎ (514) 499-1323
A mainstay in the Plateau Mont-Royal area, L'Oblique offers a wide array of alternative rock, punk and avant-garde music CDs and records, including a nice selection of titles by local acts.

Pop Shop
4081 Boulevard St-Laurent
☎ (514) 848-6300
Pop Shop sells both new and used alternative rock CDs and records.

■ Musical Instruments

Steve's Music Store
51 Rue St-Antoine Ouest
☎ (514) 878-2216
For years now, Steve's Music Store has been the place to go for musical instruments and accessories.

Outdoor Equipment

Altitude
4140 Rue St-Denis
☎ (514) 847-1515
Altitude is small but full of tents, backpacks, hiking boots, clothing, etc. The salespeople are friendly and knowledgeable.

Atmosphere
1610 Rue St-Denis
☎ (514) 844-2228
Located in the gleaming Quartier Latin movie theatre, Atmosphere offers all

kinds of outdoor accessories in a large, airy space. Among other goods, you will find the top Québec brand for clothing and accessories, Chlorophylle. Atmosphere specializes in watersports and sells canoes and kayaks.

Azimut
1781 Rue St-Denis
☎ (514) 844-1717
Azimut sells outdoor clothing and apparel by popular brand names such as Kanuk, which has been in business in Québec for about 20 years. They also sell other top-of-the-line clothing and sports equipment: tents, backpacks, rain gear, etc.

La Cordée
2159 Rue Ste-Catherine Est
☎ (514) 524-1106
La Cordée opened in 1953 to outfit the Boy Scouts and Girl Guides of Québec. Now they serve just about anyone who wants the best quality outdoor equipment. Renovated and expanded in 1997, the store is the largest of its kind in Montréal, and its layout and design make it a very pleasant place to shop.

Kanuk
485 Rue Rachel Est
☎ (514) 527-4494
Kanuk makes backpacks, sleeping bags and outdoor clothing and accessories. You can buy their merchandise at their huge outlet, located right above the factory on Rue Rachel. Kanuk winter coats come in various styles and are extremely warm.

La Maison des Cyclistes
1251 Rue Rachel Est
☎ (514) 521-8356
La Maison des Cyclistes, as its name implies, has a lot to offer cyclists. There is a café and a store that sells guides, maps and small accessories—perfect for exploring Montréal by bicycle.

Mountain Equipment Co-op
Marché Central
8989 Boulevard L'Acadie
corner Rue Legendre
☎ (514) 788-5878
Mountain Equipment Co-op, a Canadian chain specializing in outdoor gear, has finally opened its long-awaited branch in Montréal. The shop is well-respected for its high-quality line of outdoor wear, in particular. If you want to buy anything here, you have to join the co-op ($5, valid for life)—some 127,000 Quebecers already have.

Le Yéti
5190 Boulevard St-Laurent
☎ (514) 271-0773
Le Yéti is a large, attractive store that sells bicycles, as well as outdoor clothing and accessories.

Pet Stores

The following stores have everything to help care for animal companions: food in bulk, sweaters, winter booties, down-filled wicker baskets and much more.

Mondou
4310 Rue de la Roche
☎ (514) 521-9491
90 Rue Jean-Talon Est
☎ (514) 271-5503

Little Bear
4205 Rue Ste-Catherine Ouest
☎ (514) 935-3425

Pattes à Poil
4810 Rue St-Denis
☎ (514) 282-9886

Reading

Montréal has both French and English bookstores. Books from Québec, Canada and the United States are available at reasonable prices, while books from Europe are slightly more expensive because of import costs. Anyone interested in Québécois literature will find a large selection in Montréal stores.

■ Bookstores

General

Archambault
(French)
500 Rue Ste-Catherine Est
☎ (514) 849-6201
Place des Arts, 175 Rue Ste-Catherine Ouest
☎ (514) 281-0367

Chapter's
(French and English)
1171 Rue Ste-Catherine Ouest
☎ (514) 849-8825

Indigo
(French and English)
1500 Avenue McGill
☎ (514) 281-5549

Coles
(French and English)
Place Ville-Marie
☎ (514) 861-1736
Promenades de la Cathédrale
625 Rue Ste-Catherine Ouest
☎ (514) 289-8737

Shopping - Reading

Librairie Gallimard
(French)
3700 Boulevard St-Laurent
☎ (514) 499-2012

Paragraphe
(English)
2220 McGill College
☎ (514) 845-5811

Le Parchemin
(French)
505 Rue Ste-Catherine
☎ (514) 845-5243

Librairie Renaud-Bray
(French)
5252 Chemin de la Côte-des-Neiges
☎ (514) 342-1515
4380 Rue St-Denis
☎ (514) 844-2587
4301 Rue St-Denis
☎ (514) 499-3656
Complexe Desjardins
☎ (514) 288-4844
5117 Avenue du Parc
☎ (514) 276-7651
1432 Rue Ste-Catherine Ouest
☎ (514) 876-9119
1155 Rue Ste-Catherine Est
☎ (514) 527-4477
1691 Rue Fleury Est
☎ (514) 384-9920

Specialty

Éditions Paulines
(religion)
4362 Rue St-Denis
☎ (514) 849-3585

Librairie Boule de Neige
(esoteric and New Age books)
4433 Rue St-Denis
☎ (514) 849-0959

Librairie C.EstC. Michel Fortin
(education and languages)
3714 Rue St-Denis
☎ (514) 849-5719

Librairie du Centre Canadien d'Architecture
(architecture)
1920 Rue Baile
☎ (514) 939-7028

Librairie Italiana
(Italian books)
6792 Boulevard St-Laurent
☎ (514) 277-2955

Librairie Las Américas
(Spanish, Latin American books)
10 Rue St-Norbert
☎ (514) 844-5994

Librairie Nouvel Âge
(esoteric and New Age books)
1707 Rue St-Denis
☎ (514) 844-1719

Librairie-Bistrot Olivieri
(foreign literature, humanities)
5219 Chemin de la Côte-des-Neiges
☎ (514) 739-3639

**Librairie Olivieri
(Librairie du Musée d'Art Contemporain)**
(art)
185 Rue Ste-Catherine Ouest
☎ (514) 847-6903

Librairie Ulysse
(travel)
4176 Rue St-Denis
☎ (514) 843-9447
560 Avenue du Président-Kennedy
☎ (514) 843-7222
Ulysses has a large selection of city and road maps, as well as travel guides.

Maison de la Bible
(religion)
Promenades de la Cathédrale
625 Rue Ste-Catherine Ouest
☎ (514) 848-9777

Quatre Points Cardinaux
551 Rue Ontario Est
☎ (514) 843-8116

For topographical maps of Québec, drop by Quatre Points Cardinaux.

■ Newspapers and Magazines

Maison de la Presse Internationale
550 Rue Ste-Catherine Est
☎ (514) 842-3857

Sex Shops

Capoterie
2061 Rue St-Denis
☎ 845-0027
Everything goes at Capoterie, the only shop specialized in condoms in Montréal. There are coloured, fluorescent and even fruit-flavoured condoms that come in all sizes. Kinky types should not miss it!

Priape
1311 Rue Ste-Catherine Est
☎ (514) 521-8451
When love is gay the place to go is Priape for accessories and erotic literature. The hot selection of sexy clothes will have you fighting off potential suiters.

Travel Accessories

Jet-Setter
66 Avenue Laurier Ouest
☎ (514) 271-5058
Whether you are planning a weekend in Québec City, two weeks in the Dominican Republic or a sabbatical year in a remote paradise, Jet-Setter has suitcases, trunks and backpacks to meet your travel needs.

Appendix

Index	296	General Orientation	318
English-French Glossary	304	Table of Distances	319
Our Guides	312	Weights and Measures	319
Contact Information	314	Map Symbols	320
Write to Us	314	Symbols Used In This Guide	320
Notes	315	The Metro	Inside Cover

Appendix

Index

Bold numbers refer to maps.

Numerals

1000 De La Gauchetière (Downtown) 74
1250 Boulevard René-Lévesque (Downtown) 73

A

Académie Querbes (Outremont and Mile-End) 130
Accessories 280
Accommodations 185
  Abri du Voyageur, L' 193
  Anne Ma Sœur Anne 206
  Armor Manoir Sherbrooke 203
  Auberge-Restaurant Pierre du Calvet 190
  Auberge Alternative, L' 188
  Auberge Bonaparte, L' 189
  Auberge de Jeunesse 193
  Auberge de Jeunesse de l'Hôtel de Paris 201
  Auberge de la Fontaine, L' 206
  Auberge du Vieux-Port, L' 190
  Au Gîte Olympique 207
  Aux Portes de la Nuit 203
  Aux portes de la nuit 202
  Best Western Ville-Marie Hôtel & Suites 196
  Bienvenue Bed & Breakfast 201
  Castel Durocher 194
  Centre Sheraton, Le 197
  Chasseur, Le 203
  Château Versailles 196
  Clarion Hôtel & Suites Montréal Centre-Ville 200
  Concordia University 206
  Courtyard Marriott Montréal 194
  Days Inn Montréal Centre-Ville 197
  Delta Centre-Ville 190
  Delta Montréal 197
  Douillette et Chocolat 205
  Fairmont Queen Elizabeth 197
  Four Points By Sheraton 196
  Gîte Angelica Blue 203
  Gîte du Parc Lafontaine 206
  Gîte Saint-Dominique 194
  Hilton Montréal Aéroport 207
  Hilton Montréal Bonaventure 197
  Holiday Inn Select Montréal Centre-Ville 194
  Hôtel Best Western Montréal Aéroport 208
  Hôtel Casa Bella 193
  Hôtel de l'Institut 203
  Hôtel de la Montagne 198
  Hôtel de Paris 203
  Hôtel du Fort 199
  Hôtel du Nouveau Forum 193
  Hôtel Gault 190
  Hôtel Godin 196
  Hôtel Gouverneur Place Dupuis 204
  Hôtel Inter-Continental Montréal 189
  Hôtel Le Germain 198
  Hôtel Le Saint-James 192
  Hôtel Le Saint André 204
  Hôtel Lord Berri 205
  Hôtel Maritime Plaza Montréal 201
  Hôtel Nelligan 190
  Hôtel Omni Mont-Royal 198
  Hôtel Place d'Armes 192
  Hôtel Terrasse Royale 207
  Hôtel W 196
  Hôtel XIXe Siècle 192
  Hyatt Regency Montréal 198
  Jardin d'Antoine, Le 204
  Loews Hôtel Vogue 198
  Manoir Ambrose, Le 194
  Marriott Residence Inn Montréal 198
  Marriott SpringHill Suites Vieux-Montréal 189
  McGill University 193
  Meridien Versailles Montréal, Le 199
  Montréal Marriott Château Champlain 199
  Novotel Montréal Centre 196
  Passants du Sans-Soucy 189

  Pierre et Dominique 203
  Plaza Hotel Centre-Ville 204
  Quality Inn Centre-Ville 194
  Residence Inn by Marriott Montreal Westmount 199
  Ritz-Carlton Montréal, Le 199
  Saint-Sulpice, Le 189
  Sofitel 199
  Square Phillips Hôtel & Suites 196
  St-Paul Hotel 192
  Travelodge Montréal Centre 194
  Turquoise B & B 205
  Université de Montréal 206
Adventure Packages 177
Agora de la Danse (Plateau Mont-Royal) 116
Ailes de la Mode, Les (Downtown) 76
Airports
  Mont-Tremblant International Airport 40
  Montréal-Pierre Elliott Trudeau International
    Airport 39
Alcohol 54
Antiques 280
Architecture Garden (Shaughnessy Village) 97
Aréna Maurice-Richard (Hochelaga-Maisonneuve) 148
Art 281
Art Deco Fire Station no 23
  (Little Burgundy and Saint-Henri) 154
Art Galleries 281
Art Supplies 281
Atrium (Downtown) 74
Auberge Saint-Gabriel (Vieux-Montréal) 64
Avenue Bernard (Outremont and Mile-End) 132
Avenue du Mont-Royal (Plateau Mont-Royal) 115
Avenue Greene (Westmount) 125
Avenue Laurier (Outremont and Mile-End) 130
Avenue Laval (Quartier Latin) 105
Avenue Maplewood (Outremont and Mile-End) 133
Avenue McDougall (Outremont and Mile-End) 131
Avenue McGill College (Downtown) 75
Avenue Seymour (Shaughnessy Village) 97

B

Baie, La (Downtown) 76
Bain Morgan (Hochelaga-Maisonneuve) 149
Bakeries 286
Banks 46
Banque de Montréal (Vieux-Montréal) 58
Banque Laurentienne (Little Burgundy and Saint-Henri) 154
Banque Laurentienne Tower (Downtown) 75
Banque Molson (Vieux-Montréal) 57
Banque Royale (Vieux-Montréal) 57
Bars and Nightclubs 262
  3 Brasseurs, Les 266
  Altitude 737 262
  Amère à Boire, L' 266
  Aria 266
  Assommoir, L' 271
  Au Diable Vert 270
  Bacci 269
  Balattou 264
  Baloo's 266
  Barouf, L' 269
  Belmont sur le Boulevard 264
  Big Cheeze, Le 269
  Bily Kun 269
  Bobards, Les 264
  Boudoir, Le 269
  Brutopia 262
  BU 271
  Cabaret Mado, Le 268
  Café Chaos 266
  Café Sarajevo 264
  Carlos & Pepes 262
  Casa del Popolo 265
  Cheval Blanc, Le 266
  Chez Baptiste 270
  Chez Roger 271

Deux Pierrots, Les 262
Dieu du Ciel 265
Dogue, Le 270
Dôme, Le 262
Else's 265
El Zaz Bar 270
Escogriffe, L' 270
Foufounes Électriques, Les 263
Funkytown 263
Fûtenbulle 271
Gay Bars and Nightclubs 268
Gotham Bar 268
Grande Gueule, La 271
Hard Rock Cafe, The 263
Hurley's Irish Pub 263
Hurley's Medieval 263
Île Noire Pub 266
Jello Bar 266
Jet Club 268
Laïka 265
Loft 263
Luba Lounge 263
Maisonnée, La 271
McKibbin's Irish Pub 263
Medley, Le 267
Newtown 263
Ours Qui Fume, L' 267
P'tit Bar, Le 267
Parking, Le 268
Passeport, Le 270
Peel Pub 263
Pèlerin-Magellan, Le 267
Pub Magnolia 268
Pub Sir Winston Churchill 264
Pub The Old Dublin 263
Quartier Latin Pub 267
Réservoir, Le 270
Saint-Sulpice 267
Sainte-Élisabeth, Le 267
Saphir 265
Sergent Recruteur, Le 265
Sky Club 268
Sky Pub 268
Sofa 270
Stéréo Club 268
Taverne Inspecteur Épingle 270
Thursday's 264
Tokyo Bar 265
Track, La 268
Typhoon Lounge 271
Unity II 268
Upper Club 265
Upstairs Jazz Club 264
Verre Bouteille, Le 270
Vocalz Karaoke 264
Whisky Café 271
Yer' Mad! 267
Zinc Café Bar Montréal 270
Basilique Notre-Dame (Vieux-Montréal) 60
Bateau-Mouche (Vieux-Montréal) 63
Bay, The (Downtown) 76
Beaches 183
Beaconsfield (West Island and Surroundings) 166
Beaver Lake (Mont Royal) 120
Beer 54
Belding Corticelli silk mill (Pointe-Saint-Charles) 158
Belvédère Camillien-Houde (Mont Royal) 119
Belvédère Kondiaronk (Mont Royal) 120
Bibliothèque Centrale de Montréal, former
    (Plateau Mont-Royal) 116
Bibliothèque Nationale, former (Quartier Latin) 106
Bibliothèque Nationale du Québec (Quartier Latin) 108
Bicycle Rentals 179
Biodôme de Montréal (Hochelaga-Maisonneuve) 148
Biosphère (Île Sainte-Hélène and Île Notre-Dame) 144
Bird-Watching 177
BNP Tower (Downtown) 75
Boat 42
Bocage, Le (Beaconsfield) 166
Bookstores 293
Botanical Garden (Maisonneuve) 175
Boulevard du Mont-Royal (Outremont and Mile-End) 134
Boulevard Saint-Laurent (Little Italy) 136

Boulevard Saint-Laurent
    (McGill Ghetto and "The Main") 99
Brasserie Dawes (Lachine) 164
Bus 42
Business Hours 44
Butcher Shops 287

C

Caisse Populaire (Little Burgundy and Saint-Henri) 154
Canadian Centre for Architecture (Shaughnessy Village) 97
Canadian National Railyards (Pointe-Saint-Charles) 158
Canal de Lachine (Vieux-Montréal) 63
Car Rental 41
Casa d'Italia (Little Italy) 136
Caserne de Pompiers no I (Hochelaga-Maisonneuve) 150
Caserne de Pompiers no 15 (Pointe-Saint-Charles) 158
Caserne de Pompiers no 31 (Little Italy) 137
Casino de Montréal
    (Île Sainte-Hélène and Île Notre-Dame) 144
Cathédrale Marie-Reine-du-Monde (Downtown) 72
Cathédrale Schismatique Grecque Saint-Nicolas
    (Vieux-Montréal) 67
Cathedral of St. Peter and St. Paul (The Village) 113
CDs 292
Centre Bell (Downtown) 74
Centre Canadien d'Architecture (Shaughnessy Village) 97
Centre CDP Capital (Downtown) 80
Centre d'Exposition de la Prison-des-Patriotes
    (The Village) 115
Centre d'Histoire de Montréal (Vieux-Montréal) 62
Centre de Céramique Bonsecours (Vieux-Montréal) 64
Centre de Commerce Mondial (Downtown) 81
Centre des Sciences de Montréal (Vieux-Montréal) 64
Centre Eaton (Downtown) 76
Centre Infotouriste (Downtown) 70
Chalet du Mont Royal (Mont Royal) 120
Champ-de-Mars (Vieux-Montréal) 66
Chapelle Mariale Notre-Dame-de-l'Assomption
    (Saint-Laurent) 170
Chapelle Notre-Dame-de-Bonsecours
    (Vieux-Montréal) 67
Chapelle Notre-Dame-de-Lourdes (Quartier Latin) 109
Chapiteau des Arts (Sault-au-Récollet) 140
Château, Le (Golden Square Mile) 92
Château Champlain (Downtown) 74
Château Cinema (Little Italy) 136
Château Dufresne (Hochelaga-Maisonneuve) 146
Château Ramezay (Vieux-Montréal) 66
Cheese 287
Chelsea Place (Golden Square Mile) 91
Chemin de la Côte-Sainte-Catherine
    (Outremont and Mile-End) 128
Chemin Senneville (Sainte-Anne-de-Bellevue) 168
Children 46, 282
Children's Wear 282
Chinatown (Downtown) 79
Chocolate 287
Christ Church Cathedral (Downtown) 76
Church of Saint Michael's and Saint Anthony's
    (Outremont and Mile-End) 130
Church of St. Andrew and St. Paul (Golden Square Mile) 92
Church of St. James The Apostle (Golden Square Mile) 94
Church of The Ascension of Our Lord (Westmount) 125
Cigars 283
Cimetière Notre-Dame-des-Neiges (Mont Royal) 120
Cinémathèque Québécoise (Quartier Latin) 108
Cinérobothèque (Quartier Latin) 106
Circuit Gilles-Villeneuve
    (Île Sainte-Hélène and Île Notre-Dame) 144
Circus Arts 34
Cirque du Soleil 35
Cirque du Soleil headquarters (Sault-au-Récollet) 140
Cirque Éloize 35
Cirque Éos 35
Cité du Commerce Électronique (Downtown) 74
Cité Multimédia de Montréal (Vieux-Montréal) 63
City Hall (Westmount) 125
City Hall, former (Outremont) 132
Climate 46
Climbing 178
Clos Saint-Bernard (Outremont and Mile-End) 132
Clothing 283

Cognicase building (Vieux-Montréal) 63
Collège de Saint-Laurent (Saint-Laurent) 170
Collège du Mont-Saint-Louis (Sault-au-Récollet) 138
Collège Rachel (Plateau Mont-Royal) 118
Collège Sophie-Barat (Sault-au-Récollet) 138
Colonne Nelson (Vieux-Montréal) 65
Commuter Trains 43
Complexe Culturel Guy-Descary (Lachine) 164
Complexe Desjardins (Downtown) 78
Complexe La Cité (McGill Ghetto and "The Main") 100
Concert Halls 274
Concordia University (Golden Square Mile) 94
Conseil des Arts de Montréal
  (McGill Ghetto and "The Main") 103
Consulates 45
Contemporary Art 281
Côte-des-Neiges
  Accommodations 206, **206**
  Bars and Nightclubs 271
  Restaurants 238, **239**
Côte Saint-Antoine (Westmount) 127
Cours Le Royer (Vieux-Montréal) 61
Cours Mont-Royal (Downtown) 70
Couvent des Soeurs de Marie-Réparatrice
  (Outremont and Mile-End) 134
Couvent des Soeurs Grises (Shaughnessy Village) 98
Couvent Sainte-Anne (Lachine) 164
Crafts 281
Craig Pumping Station, former (The Village) 115
Credit Cards 46
Cross-Country Skiing 178
Cultural Centres 272
Cultural Events 275
Currency 47
Customs 38
Cycling 178

D

Daoust General Store (Sainte-Anne-de-Bellevue) 168
Dawson College (Shaughnessy Village) 96
Department Stores 285
Dépendance, La (Lachine) 161
Disabled Travellers 53
Dorval (West Island and Surroundings) 165
  Accommodations 207
Dorval Island (Dorval) 165
Downtown 70, **71**
  Accommodations 193, **195**
  Bars and Nightclubs 262
  Restaurants 215, **217**
Driving 40
Drugs 46

E

Eaton (Downtown) 76
École des Hautes Études Commerciales, former
  (Quartier Latin) 109
École Le Plateau (Plateau Mont-Royal) 116
École Madonna Della Difesa (Little Italy) 136
École Nationale de Cirque (Sault-au-Récollet) 140
École Sainte-Brigide (The Village) 113
École Sainte-Julienne-Falconieri (Little Italy) 136
Écomusée du Fier Monde (The Village) 110
Écomuseum (Sainte-Anne-de-Bellevue) 168
Économusée de la Lutherie
  (McGill Ghetto and "The Main") 104
Economy 26
Édifice Ernest-Cormier (Vieux-Montréal) 64
Édifice Godin (McGill Ghetto and "The Main") 103
Édifice Grothé (McGill Ghetto and "The Main") 104
Édifice Sun Life (Downtown) 72
Église de la Visitation (Sault-au-Récollet) 138
Église des Saints-Anges Gardiens (Lachine) 164
Église du Gesù (Downtown) 77
Église du Saint-Nom-de-Jésus
  (Hochelaga-Maisonneuve) 150
Église Madonna Della Difesa (Little Italy) 136
Église Notre-Dame-des-Sept-Douleurs (Verdun) 160
Église Saint-Charles (Pointe-Saint-Charles) 156

Église Saint-Enfant-Jésus du Mile-End
  (Outremont and Mile-End) 130
Église Saint-Gabriel (Pointe-Saint-Charles) 156
Église Saint-Irénée (Little Burgundy and Saint-Henri) 153
Église Saint-Jean-Baptiste (Plateau Mont-Royal) 118
Église Saint-Jean-Baptiste-de-LaSalle
  (Hochelaga-Maisonneuve) 149
Église Saint-Joachim (Pointe-Claire) 166
Église Saint-Laurent (Saint-Laurent) 170
Église Saint-Léon (Westmount) 127
Église Saint-Louis-de- France (Plateau Mont-Royal) 118
Église Saint-Pierre-Apôtre (The Village) 112
Église Saint-Sauveur (Quartier Latin) 110
Église Saint-Viateur (Outremont and Mile-End) 130
Église Saint-Zotique (Little Burgundy and Saint-Henri) 154
Église Sainte-Cunégonde
  (Little Burgundy and Saint-Henri) 152
Église Sainte-Geneviève (Sainte-Geneviève) 169
Electricity 46
Electronics 283
Embassies 45
Emergencies 46
Engineering, Computer Science and Visual Arts Complex
  (Concordia University) 99
Entertainment 261
Entrance Formalities 38
Erskine & American United Church
  (Golden Square Mile) 92
Ethnic Communities, Montreal's 28
Ex-Centris (McGill Ghetto and "The Main") 103

F

Fashion 283
Faubourg Sainte-Catherine (Shaughnessy Village) 99
Ferme Angrignon (Parc Angrignon) 174
Ferme Écologique du Cap-Saint-Jacques 176
Ferme OutreMont (Outremont and Mile-End) 131
Festival des Films du Monde de Montréal 277
Festival du Nouveau Cinéma 277
Festival International de Jazz de Montréal 276
Festival Juste pour Rire 276
Festivals 275
Fête des Neiges 275
Film 32
Financial Services 46
First Peoples' Festival 276
First Presbyterian Church
  (McGill Ghetto and "The Main") 100
Flowers 291
Fonderie Darling (Vieux-Montréal) 63
Food 286
Foreign Consulates 47
Fort Angrignon (Parc Angrignon) 174
Fort de l'Île Sainte-Hélène
  (Île Ste-Hélène and Île Notre-Dame) 142
Fort Rolland (Lachine) 164
FrancoFolies de Montréal 277
French Pavilion, former
  (Île Sainte-Hélène and Île Notre-Dame) 144
Fringe Festival 276
Fur 285
Fur Trade at Lachine National Historic Site (Lachine) 162

G

Games 282
Garden Court (Outremont and Mile-End) 132
Gare Centrale (Downtown) 75
Gare Dalhousie (Vieux-Montréal) 67
Gare Maritime Iberville du Port de Montréal
  (Vieux-Montréal) 64
Gare Viger (Vieux-Montréal) 67
Gare Windsor (Downtown) 73
Gay and Lesbian Life 47
Gay Village 112
Getting Around 39
Getting There 39
Gifts 289
Glasswork 281

Index - C

Golden Square Mile 86, **87**
  Accommodations 193, **195**
  Bars and Nightclubs 262
  Restaurants 215, **217**
Golf 180
Grain Silos (Vieux-Montréal) 64
Grand Séminaire (Shaughnessy Village) 96
Grand Trunk houses (Pointe-Saint-Charles) 158
Guided Tours 47

H

Habitat 67 (Île Sainte-Hélène and Île Notre-Dame) 141
Hats 280
Health 49
Health Food 287
Hélène de Champlain, Restaurant
  (Île Sainte-Hélène and Île Notre-Dame) 142
Hiking 180
History 14
  Between the Two Wars 21
  From 1960 to Today 24
  *Industrialization and Economic Power
    (1850-1914) 20*
  Origins 15
  Renewed Growth (1945-1960) 22
  The Fur Trade (1665-1760) 17
  Transitional Years (1763-1850) 19
  Ville-Marie (1642-1665) 16
Hochelaga-Maisonneuve 145, **147**
  Accommodations 207, **207**
  Restaurants 250, **251**
Holt Renfrew (Golden Square Mile) 92
Home Decor 290
Hôpital Général des Soeurs Grises (Montréal) 62
Hôpital Notre-Dame (Plateau Mont-Royal) 116
Hospice Auclair (Plateau Mont-Royal) 118
Hôtel-Dieu (McGill Ghetto and "The Main") 102
Hôtel de Ville (Vieux-Montréal) 66
Hôtel de Ville, former (Hochelaga-Maisonneuve) 149

I

Ice Skating 181
Île des Sœurs (Verdun) 160
Île Notre-Dame 143, 144
  Restaurants 249, **250**
Île Sainte-Hélène 141, **143**
  Restaurants 249, **250**
In-Line Skating 181
Insectarium de Montréal (Hochelaga-Maisonneuve) 146
Institut des Sourdes-Muettes (Plateau Mont-Royal) 118
Institut de Tourisme et d'Hôtellerie du Québec
  (Quartier Latin) 104
Insurance 49
International des Feux Loto-Québec, L' 276

J

Jacques-Cartier Bridge (The Village) 114
Jardin Botanique de Montréal
  (Hochelaga-Maisonneuve) 145
Jeans 285
Jewellery 280
Jules Saint-Michel, Luthier
  (McGill Ghetto and "The Main") 104
Just for Laughs Festival 276
Just for Laughs Museum
  (McGill Ghetto and "The Main") 104

K

King George Park (Westmount) 127

L

La Baie (Downtown) 76
Lac aux Castors (Mont Royal) 120
Lachine (West Island and Surroundings) 161, **163**
  Restaurants 254, **254**
Lachine Canal (Vieux-Montréal) 63
Lachine Canal Historical Cruise (Pointe-Saint-Charles) 156

Lachine Canal National Historic Site
  (Pointe-Saint-Charles) 156
Language 25, 49
La Ronde (Île Sainte-Hélène and Île Notre-Dame) 142
Laundromats 50
Leather 285
Linens 291
Lingerie 285
Linton, Le (Golden Square Mile) 92
Literature 30
Little Burgundy (Around the Lachine Canal) 150, **151**
  Restaurants 252, **252**
Little Italy 134, **135**
  Restaurants 245, **246**

M

Macdonald College (Sainte-Anne-de-Bellevue) 168
Magazines 294
Maison Alcan (Golden Square Mile) 93
Maison André Legault dit Deslauriers (Dorval) 165
Maison Antoine-Pilon (Pointe-Claire) 165
Maison Atholstan (Golden Square Mile) 93
Maison Baumgarten (Golden Square Mile) 88
Maison Baxter (Golden Square Mile) 93
Maison Brown (Dorval) 165
Maison Clarence de Sola (Golden Square Mile) 91
Maison Clermont (Little Burgundy and Saint-Henri) 155
Maison Cormier (Golden Square Mile) 91
Maison d'Ailleboust-de-Manthet (Sainte-Geneviève) 169
Maison David-Dumouchel (Sault-au-Récollet) 138
Maison de l'Arbre (Hochelaga-Maisonneuve) 146
Maison de l'OACI (Downtown) 81
Maison de la Douane (Vieux-Montréal) 61
Maison de Radio-Canada (The Village) 112
Maison du Brasseur (Lachine) 164
Maison du Meunier (Sault-au-Récollet) 140
Maison du Pressoir (Sault-au-Récollet) 140
Maison Fréchette (Quartier Latin) 105
Maison Frederick Barlow (Dorval) 165
Maison George Stephen (Golden Square Mile) 93
Maison Hamilton (Golden Square Mile) 89
Maison Hans Selye (McGill Ghetto and "The Main") 100
Maison Hosmer (Golden Square Mile) 89
Maison J.B. Aimbault (Outremont and Mile-End) 132
Maison James Ross (Golden Square Mile) 88
Maison James Thomas Davis (Golden Square Mile) 89
Maison John Kenneth L. Ross (Golden Square Mile) 88
Maison Lady Meredith (Golden Square Mile) 89
Maison LeBer-LeMoyne (Lachine) 161
Maison Linton (Golden Square Mile) 92
Maison Minnie Louise Davis (Dorval) 165
Maison Mortimer B. Davis (Golden Square Mile) 89
Maison Notman (McGill Ghetto and "The Main") 103
Maison Papineau (Vieux-Montréal) 69
Maison Peter Lyall (Golden Square Mile) 94
Maison Picard (Lachine) 164
Maison Pierre du Calvet (Vieux-Montréal) 69
Maison Quesnel (Lachine) 164
Maison Raymond (Golden Square Mile) 91
Maison Rodolphe-Forget (Golden Square Mile) 91
Maison Saint-Gabriel (Pointe-Saint-Charles) 159
Maison Shaughnessy (Shaughnessy Village) 97
Maison Simon Fraser (Sainte-Anne-de-Bellevue) 168
Maison Smith (Mont Royal) 120
Maison William Alexander Molson (Golden Square Mile) 86
Marché Atwater (Little Burgundy and Saint-Henri) 155
Marché Bonsecours (Vieux-Montréal) 69
Marché des Saveurs (Little Italy) 137
Marché Jean-Talon (Little Italy) 137
Marché Maisonneuve (Hochelaga-Maisonneuve) 149
Masonic Temple (Shaughnessy Village) 96
McCord Museum of Canadian History
  (Golden Square Mile) 86
McGill Ghetto 99, **101**
  Accommodations 201, **201**
  Bars and Nightclubs 264
  Restaurants 222, **223**
McGill University (Golden Square Mile) 86
Measures 53
Merchants Manufacturing Company
  (Little Burgundy and Saint-Henri) 154
Metro 42

Mile-End **129**, 130
   Bars and Nightclubs 271
   Restaurants 239, **241**
Modern Art 281
Molson Bank (Vieux-Montréal) 57
Molson Brewery (The Village) 113
Monastère Sainte-Croix (Sainte-Geneviève) 169
Mondial de la Bière 275
Mont-Saint-Louis (Quartier Latin) 105
Mont-Tremblant International Airport 40
Montcalm (Outremont and Mile-End) 132
Montréal-Pierre Elliott Trudeau International Airport 39
Montreal Diocesan Theological College
   (McGill Ghetto and "The Main") 100
Montréal High Lights Festival 275
Montreal Holocaust Memorial Centre (Mont Royal) 124
Montréal Jazz Festival 276
Montreal Museum of Fine Arts 82
   19th- and 20th-century European Art 83
   Canadian Art 84
   Canadian Decorative Arts 84
   Contemporary Art 84
   Contemporary Decorative Arts 85
   Galleries of Ancient Cultures 84
   Inuit Art 84
   Max and Iris Stern Sculpture Garden 85
   Mediterranean Archaeology 85
   Native American Art 85
   Old Masters 83
   Pre-Columbian Art 84
Mont Royal 119, **121**
Monument-National (Downtown) 79
Monument to Maisonneuve (Vieux-Montréal) 57
Monument to the Patriotes (The Village) 114
Morrice Hall (Golden Square Mile) 88
Moulin Fleming (Lachine) 161
Mount Royal 119
Mount Royal Club (Golden Square Mile) 93
Mount Royal Cross (Mont Royal) 119
Mount Royal Protestant Cemetery (Mont Royal) 120
Movie Theatres 272
Musée d'Art Contemporain de Montréal (Downtown) 78
Musée de Lachine (Lachine) 161
Musée des Beaux-Arts de Montréal 82
Musée des Hospitalières
   (McGill Ghetto and "The Main") 102
Musée des Maîtres et Artisans du Québec
   (Saint-Laurent) 171
Musée des Ondes Émile Berliner
   (Little Burgundy and Saint-Henri) 154
Musée du Château Ramezay (Vieux-Montréal) 66
Musée Juste Pour Rire (McGill Ghetto and "The Main") 104
Musée Marc-Aurèle-Fortin (Vieux-Montréal) 63
Musée Marguerite-Bourgeoys (Vieux-Montréal) 68
Musée Plein Air de Lachine (Lachine) 161
Musée Sainte-Anne (Lachine) 164
Musée Stewart
   (Île Sainte-Hélène and Île Notre-Dame) 142
Muse McCord d'Histoire Canadienne
   (Golden Square Mile) 86
Museums 50
Music 33, 292
Musical Instruments 292

N

National Film Board of Canada (Quartier Latin) 106
Nature Parks 176
Newspapers 50, 294
NFB Montréal (Quartier Latin) 106
Northern Electric factory (Pointe-Saint-Charles) 158
Notre-Dame-de-Grâce
   Accommodations 206
   Bars and Nightclubs 271
   Restaurants 238, **239**
Nuit Blanche sur Tableau Noir 276
Numismatic Museum (Vieux-Montréal) 58

O

Ogilvy's (Golden Square Mile) 93
Old Montréal 56

Old Port (Vieux-Montréal) 63
Olympic Basin (Île Sainte-Hélène and Île Notre-Dame) 144
Oratoire Saint-Joseph (Mont Royal) 123
Ouimetoscope (The Village) 112
Outdoor Activities 177
Outdoor Equipment 292
Outdoors 173
   Outdoor Activities 177
   Parks 174
Outremont 128, **129**
   Bars and Nightclubs 271
   Restaurants 239, **241**

P

Palais de Justice (Vieux-Montréal) 64
Palais de Justice, former (Vieux-Montréal) 65
Palais des Congrès de Montréal (Downtown) 80
Parc-Nature de l'Île-de-la-Visitation (Sault-au-Récollet) 140
Parc Beaubien (Outremont and Mile-End) 131
Parc de la Cité-du-Havre
   (Île Sainte-Hélène and Île Notre-Dame) 141
Parc du Mont-Royal (Mont Royal) 119
Parc Émilie-Gamelin (Quartier Latin) 109
Parc Jean-Drapeau
   (Île Sainte-Hélène and Île Notre-Dame) 142
Parc Joyce (Outremont and Mile-End) 132
Parc La Fontaine (Plateau Mont-Royal) 116
Parc Monk (Lachine) 162
Parc Morgan (Hochelaga-Maisonneuve) 149
Parc Olympique (Hochelaga-Maisonneuve) 148
Parc Outremont (Outremont and Mile-End) 131
Parc René-Lévesque (Lachine) 162
Parc Summit (Mont Royal) 123
Parisian Laundry (Little Burgundy and Saint-Henri) 153
Parklane (Outremont and Mile-End) 132
Parks 174
   Angrignon 174
   Anse-à-l'Orme 177
   Bois-de-l'Île-Bizard 177
   Bois-de-Liesse 176
   Cap Saint-Jacques 176
   Complexe Environnemental Saint-Michel 176
   Île-de-la-Visitation 177
   Jarry 175
   Jean-Drapeau 174
   Jeanne-Mance 174
   La Fontaine 174
   Maisonneuve 175
   Mont-Royal 175
   Morgan Arboretum 175
   Nature Parks 176
   Parcs-Nature 176
   Pointe-aux-Prairies 177
   Promenade Bellerive 176
   Rapides 176
   René-Lévesque 174
   Sir-Wilfrid-Laurier 174
Passport 38
Pastry Shops 288
Pavillon Benoît-Verdickt (Lachine) 161
Pavillon de l'Entrepôt (Lachine) 164
Pavillon de la Faculté de Musique
   (Outremont and Mile-End) 133
Pavillon Jacques-Cartier (Vieux-Montréal) 69
Pavillon Marie-Victorin (Outremont and Mile-End) 133
Pensionnat du Saint-Nom-de-Marie
   (Outremont and Mile-End) 133
Pensionnat Notre-Dame-des-Anges (Saint-Laurent) 170
Pets 50
Pet Stores 293
Pharmacie Montréal (The Village) 110
Pilon Clothing Store (The Village) 110
Pitfield House (Parc-Nature du Bois-de-Liesse) 180
Place Alexis-Nihon (Shaughnessy Village) 96
Place Bonaventure (Downtown) 75
Place Charles-de-Gaulle (Plateau Mont-Royal) 116
Place d'Armes (Vieux-Montréal) 57
Place d'Youville (Vieux-Montréal) 62
Place De La Dauversière (Vieux-Montréal) 66
Place des Arts (Downtown) 77
Place du 6-Décembre-1989 (Mont Royal) 124
Place du Canada (Downtown) 72

Place du Marché (Hochelaga-Maisonneuve) 149
Place Dupuis (The Village) 110
Place Jacques-Cartier (Vieux-Montréal) 65
Place Jean-Paul-Riopelle (Downtown) 80
Place Montréal Trust (Downtown) 75
Place Royale (Vieux-Montréal) 61
Place Saint-Henri (Little Burgundy and Saint-Henri) 153
Place Vauquelin (Vieux-Montréal) 66
Place Ville-Marie (Downtown) 75
Plage de l'Île Notre-Dame
   (Île Sainte-Hélène and Île Notre-Dame) 144
Plane 39
Planétarium de Montréal (Downtown) 74
Plateau Mont-Royal 115, **117**
   Accommodations **205**, 206
   Bars and Nightclubs 269
   Restaurants 231, **233**
Plaza Saint-Hubert (Little Italy) 136
Pleasure Boating 182
Pointe-à-Callière, Musée d'Archéologie et d'Histoire
   de Montréal (Vieux-Montréal) 62
Pointe-Claire (West Island and Surroundings) 165
   Restaurants 255
Pointe-Saint-Charles (Around the Lachine Canal) 155, **157**
   Restaurants **253**, 254
Politics 26
Pont Jacques-Cartier (The Village) 114
Posters 292
Prison du Pied-du-Courant (The Village) 114
Promenade du Père Marquette (Lachine) 162
Promenades de la Cathédrale (Downtown) 76
Public Holidays 50
Public Markets 288
Public Transportation 42

Q

Quai Jacques-Cartier (Vieux-Montréal) 65
Quartier des Spectacles (Downtown) 77
Quartier International de Montréal (Downtown) 79
Quartier Latin 104, **107**
   Accommodations 201, **202**
   Bars and Nightclubs 266
   Restaurants 227, **228**
Québec Pavilion, former
   (Île Sainte-Hélène and Île Notre-Dame) 144

R

Rafting 182
Ravenscrag (Golden Square Mile) 89
Reading 293
Redpath Museum (Golden Square Mile) 88
Refus Global 85
Résidence Forget (Golden Square Mile) 93
Restaurants 209
   Actuel, L' 218
   Al Dente Tratorria 238
   Ambala 232
   Ambiance, L' 253
   Anecdote, L' 232
   Anise 244
   Anubis 224
   Area 231
   Au 917 234
   Auberge-Restaurant Pierre du Calvet 215
   Auberge du Dragon Rouge, L' 245
   Au Pied de Cochon 236
   Aux Derniers Humains 245
   Aux Entretiens 231
   Avenue, L' 236
   Azuma 242
   Bangkok, Le 229
   Banquise, La 232
   Bar-B-Barn 220
   Bato Thaï 229
   Beauty's 224
   Beaver Club 219
   Bécane Rouge, La 250
   Ben's Delicatessen 215
   Bières et Compagnie
      McGill Ghetto and "The Main" 224
      Plateau Mont-Royal 234

Bilboquet, Le 240
Binerie Mont-Royal, La 232
Bio Train 211
Bistingo, Le 242
Bistro Gourmet, Le 222
Bistrot Cocagne 236
Bonaparte, Le 214
Bonne Carte, La 249
Boris Bistro 212
Boulangerie & Pâtisserie Motta 245
Brioche Lyonnaise, La 227
Brûlerie Saint-Denis, La
   Downtown and the Golden Square Mile 216
   Plateau Mont-Royal 232
   Quartier Latin 227
Buona Notte 226
Byblos 231
Cabane du Portugal, La 224
Cabaret du Roy, Le 214
Cabotins, Les 250
Cactus 234
Café America 252
Café Bicicletta 231
Café Cherrier 235
Café Daylight Factory 215
Café de Paris 219
Café des Beaux-Arts 218
Café du Nouveau Monde 216
Café El Dorado 234
Café International 247
Café Italia 245
Café Méliès 226
Café Rico 231
Café Rococo 221
Café Romolo 239
Café Souvenir 240
Café Starbuck's 215
Cafétéria, La 225
Café Trattoria Ferreira 218
Cage aux Sports, La 212
Calories 220
Camellia Sinensis 227
Caprices de Nicolas, Les 220
Casa Cacciatore 247
Casa de Mateo 212
Casa Tapas 226
Caveau, Le 218
Champs 224
Chao Phraya 242
Chèvres, Les 244
Chez Chine 218
Chez Claudette 240
Chez Gautier 225
Chez L'Épicier 214
Chez La Mère Michel 222
Chez Lévesque 243
Chez Queux 214
Chilenita, La 222
Chronique, La 244
Chu Chai 234
Claremont, Le 238
Coco Rico 222
Colombe, La 237
Commensal, Le
   Downtown and the Golden Square Mile 216
   Quartier Latin 227
Continental, Le 237
Côté Soleil 234
Crémerie Saint-Vincent 211
Crêperie Bretonne Ty-Breiz 236
Croissanterie, La 240
Cube 215
Cucina dell'arte 242
Cyclo 242
Da Vinci 218
Don Miguel 224
Eggspectation
   Downtown and the Golden Square Mile 216
   McGill Ghetto and "The Main" 240
El Zaziummm
   McGill Ghetto and "The Main" 225
   Plateau Mont-Royal 234
Entre-Miche, L' 231
Entre-Mise, L' 249

Entrecôte Saint-Jean, L' 218
Estaminet, L' 249
Euro Deli 222
Express, L' 237
Fairmount Bagel Bakery 240
Festin du Gouverneur, Le 249
Flambard, Le 236
Fonderie, La 249
Fondue Mentale 235
Fontanina, La 255
Frite Alors
    Outremont and Mile-End 240
    Plateau Mont-Royal 231
Fruit Folie 231
Gandhi 212
Gargote, La 212
Gâteries, Les 227
Gaudriole, La 237
Gavroche, Le 247
Gibby's 214
Ginger 226
Gourmand, Le 255
Grain de Sel, Le 231
Grand Comptoir, Le 216
Harmonie d'Asie, L' 224
Hélène de Champlain 249
Il Fornetto 254
Il Mulino 247
Jardin de Panos, Le 235
Jardin du Ritz, Le 220
Jardin Sakura 216
Julien 219
Kaizen 239
Katsura 219
Kerkennah, Le 249
Khyber Pass 235
Kilo
    Outremont and Mile-End 240
    The Village 229
Laloux 226
Latini, Le 220
Laurier B.B.Q. 242
Lélé da Cuca 224
Leméac Café Bistrot 243
Lester's 240
Los Altos 225
Louisiane, La 238
Lutétia, Le 216
Maestro S.V.P. 226
Magnan 254
Maison George Stephen 219
Maistre, Le 238
Man-Na 216
Mangia 216
Marée, La 215
Marlowe, The 255
Mess Hall 238
Mezze 225
Mi Burri to Café 231
Mikado 229
Milos 244
Misto 236
Modavie 214
Modigliani 237
Moe's Deli & Bar 250
Moishe's Steak House 227
Molisana 249
Monkland Tavern, The 239
Moulerie, La 242
Mr Ma 219
Nil Bleu, Le 235
Nocochi 216
Nonya 243
Nuances 249
Olive + Gourmando 212
Orienthé 232
Ouzeri 235
P'tit Plateau, Le 226
Palais de l'Inde, Le 243
Paltoquet, Le 240
Parchemin, Le 219
Paris, Le 222
Paris-Beurre 243

Paryse, La 227
Pasta Casareccia, La 238
Pasta Express 249
Pèlerin-Magellan, Le 227
Petit Alep, Le 245
Petite Marche, La 235
Petit Extra, Le 230
Petit Moulinsart, Le 212
Phayathai 222, 243
Piazza Romana 255
Piazzetta, La
    Hochelaga-Maisonneuve 250
    Outremont and Mile-End 242
    Plateau Mont-Royal 232
    The Village 229
Piccolo Diavolo 230
Piémontais, Le 229
Pintxo 226
Pique-Assiette, Le 220
Pistou 236
Piton de la Fournaise, Le 237
Pizzafiore 238
Pizzaiolle, La 242
Pizzédélic
    Plateau Mont-Royal 235
    Westmount, Notre-Dame-de-Grâce
        and Côte-des-Neiges 238
Pizzeria Napoletana 247
Planète 230
Primo e Secundo 247
Prunelle, La 226
Punjab Palace 245
Quelli Della Notte 247
Queue de Cheval, La 220
Raclette, La 236
Restaurant de l'Institut 229
Restorante-Trattoria Carissima 225
Ru de Nam 253
Rumi 243
Sala Rosa, La 224
Saloon, Le 229
Sans Menu, Le 253
Santropol 224
Schwartz's Montréal Hebrew Delicatessen 222
Selva, La 232
Shed Café 225
Sila, La 229
Souvenirs d'Indochine 243
Spaghettata, La 243
St. Viateur Bagel & Café 242
St. Viateur Bagel Shop 240
Stash's Café 214
Steak-Frites St-Paul 212
Strega du Village, La 230
Symposium Psarotaverna, Le 237
Tampopo 234
Tandoori Village 225
Tapeo 247
Tarantella, La 245
Tay Do 222
Thaï Express 224
Thaï Grill 244
Titanic 212
Toi Moi et Café 242
Toqué! 220
Troïka, La 219
Un Monde Sauté 236
Vents du Sud 225
Via Fortuna 249
Vieux Saint-Gabriel, Le 214
Villa Wellington 254
Vintage Tapas et Porto 237
Wienstein 'n' Gavino's Pasta Bar Factory Co. 218
Wok de Szechuan, Le 249
Zen 219
Zyng
    Plateau Mont-Royal 234
    Quartier Latin 227
Riopelle, Jean-Paul 80
Ritz-Carlton (Golden Square Mile) 93
Rivoli Cinema (Little Italy) 136
Ronde, La (Île Sainte-Hélène and Île Notre-Dame) 142
Rosemont
    Bars and Nightclubs 271

Royal Bank (Vieux-Montréal) 57
Royal Victoria College (McGill Ghetto and "The Main") 100
Royal York (Outremont and Mile-End) 132
Rue Coursol (Little Burgundy and Saint-Henri) 152
Rue Crescent (Golden Square Mile) 94
Rue Dalcourt (The Village) 113
Rue Favard (Pointe-Saint-Charles) 159
Rue Notre-Dame (Little Burgundy and Saint-Henri) 152
Rue Prince-Arthur (McGill Ghetto and "The Main") 103
Rue Saint-Amable (Vieux-Montréal) 65
Rue Saint-Augustin (Little Burgundy and Saint-Henri) 155
Rue Saint-Denis (Plateau Mont-Royal) 118
Rue Saint-Jacques (Vieux-Montréal) 57
Rue Saint-Paul (Vieux-Montréal) 61
Rue Sainte-Catherine (Downtown) 76
Rue Sainte-Émilie (Little Burgundy and Saint-Henri) 154

S

Saint-Ambroise Montréal Fringe Festival 276
Saint-Henri (Around the Lachine Canal) 150, **151**
    Restaurants 252, **252**
Saint-Jacques (Quartier Latin) 106
Saint-Laurent (West Island and Surroundings) 169
Sainte-Anne-de-Bellevue
    (West Island and Surroundings) 166
Sainte-Cunégonde City Hall, former
    (Little Burgundy and Saint-Henri) 152
Sainte-Geneviève (West Island and Surroundings) 169
Salle Claude-Champagne (Outremont and Mile-End) 133
Salle Émile-Legault (Saint-Laurent) 170
Salle Pierre-Mercure (Quartier Latin) 108
Salon des Métiers d'Art du Québec 277
Sanctuaire du Saint-Sacrement (Plateau Mont-Royal) 115
SAT (Downtown) 79
Sault-au-Récollet 137, **139**
    Restaurants **248**, 249
Seasons 29
Sex Shops 294
Shaughnessy Village 94, **95**
    Accommodations 199, **200**
    Restaurants 220, **221**
Shoes 280
Shopping 279
Shopping Centres 285
Sir George-Étienne-Cartier National Historic Site
    (Vieux-Montréal) 67
Smokers 44
Sœurs des Saints-Noms-de-Jésus-et-de-Marie
    housing complex (Outremont and Mile-End) 132
Specialty Grocers 288
Speleology 182
Sporting Events 273
Square Cabot (Shaughnessy Village) 96
Square Dorchester (Downtown) 70
Square Phillips (Downtown) 76
Square Saint-Henri (Little Burgundy and Saint-Henri) 153
Square Saint-Louis (Quartier Latin) 105
Square Sir-George-Étienne-Cartier
    (Little Burgundy and Saint-Henri) 154
Square Victoria (Downtown) 81
Square Viger (Quartier Latin) 109
St. Andrew's United Church (Lachine) 164
St. George's Anglican Church (Downtown) 73
St. James United Church (Downtown) 76
St. John Church (McGill Ghetto and "The Main") 100
St. Jude's Church (Little Burgundy and Saint-Henri) 152
St. Patrick's Basilica (Downtown) 77
St. Stephen's Anglican Church (Lachine) 164
Stade Olympique (Hochelaga-Maisonneuve) 148
Stewart Hall (Pointe-Claire) 165
Suoni Per Il Popolo 275
Swimming 182

T

Taxes 51
Taxis 43
Tax Refunds for Non-Residents 51
Telecommunications 51
Tennis 183
Terrasse Saint-Denis (Quartier Latin) 106

Théâtre Corona (Little Burgundy and Saint-Henri) 152
Théâtre Denise-Pelletier (Hochelaga-Maisonneuve) 149
Théâtre National (The Village) 112
Théâtre Outremont (Outremont and Mile-End) 132
Theatres 274
Théâtre Saint-Denis (Quartier Latin) 106
The Bay (Downtown) 76
Ticket Sales 274
Time Zone 52
Tipping 52
TOHU, la Cité des Arts du Cirque
    (Sault-au-Récollet) 36, 140
Tour CIBC (Downtown) 72
Tour de l'Horloge (Vieux-Montréal) 69
Tour de la Bourse (Downtown) 80
Tour de Montréal (Hochelaga-Maisonneuve) 148
Tourist Information 52
Tour Lévis (Île Sainte-Hélène and Île Notre-Dame) 142
Toys 282
Train 42
Travel Accessories 294
Traveller's Cheques 46
Travellers with Disabilities 53
Tropique Nord
    (Île Sainte-Hélène and Île Notre-Dame) 141
TVA (The Village) 113

U

Underground City (Downtown) 73
Union Française (Quartier Latin) 109
Union United Church
    (Little Burgundy and Saint-Henri) 153
Université de Montréal (Mont Royal) 124
Université du Québec à Montréal (Quartier Latin) 108
Univers Maurice "Rocket" Richard
    (Hochelaga-Maisonneuve) 148
UQAM (Quartier Latin) 108

V

Verdun (Around the Lachine Canal) **157**, 159
    Restaurants **253**, 254
Vieille Brasserie (Lachine) 164
Vieux-Montréal 56, **59**
    Accommodations 188, **191**
    Bars and Nightclubs 262
    Restaurants 211, **213**
Vieux-Port de Montréal (Vieux-Montréal) 63
Vieux Séminaire Saint-Sulpice (Vieux-Montréal) 61
Vieux Verdun (Verdun) 159
Village, The 110, **111**
    Accommodations **204**, 205
    Bars and Nightclubs 268
    Restaurants 229, **230**
Villa Préfontaine (Outremont and Mile-End) 133
Visa 38
Visual Arts 34
Vues d'Afrique 275

W

Weights 53
West Island 160, **167**
    Accommodations 207
    Restaurants 254, **255**
Westmount 125, **126**
    Bars and Nightclubs 271
    Restaurants 238, **239**
Westmount Library (Westmount) 127
Westmount Park (Westmount) 127
Westmount Square (Westmount) 125
Windsor, Le (Downtown) 72
Windsor Station (Downtown) 73
Windsurfing 182
Wine 54
World Film Festival 277
World Trade Centre (Downtown) 81

English-French Glossary

■ Greetings

Hi (casual)	*Salut*
How are you?	*Comment ça va?*
I'm fine	*Je vais bien*
Hello (during the day)	*Bonjour*
Goodbye, See you later	*Bonjour, Au revoir, À la prochaine*
Yes	*Oui*
No	*Non*
Maybe	*Peut-être*
Please	*S'il vous plaît*
Thank you	*Merci*
You're welcome	*De rien, Bienvenue*
Excuse me	*Excusez-moi*
I am a tourist	*Je suis touriste*
I am American (m/f)	*Je suis Américain(e)*
I am Canadian (m/f)	*Je suis Canadien(ne)*
I am British	*Je suis Britannique*
I am sorry, I don't speak French	*Je suis désolé(e), je ne parle pas le français*
Do you speak English?	*Parlez-vous l'anglais ?*
Slower, please	*Plus lentement, s'il vous plaît*
What is your name?	*Comment vous appelez-vous?*
My name is...	*Je m'appelle...*
spouse (m/f)	*époux(se)*
brother, sister	*frère, sœur*
friend (m/f)	*ami(e)*
son, boy	*garçon*
daughter, girl	*fille*
father	*père*
mother	*mère*
single (m/f)	*célibataire*
married (m/f)	*marié(e)*
divorced (m/f)	*divorcé(e)*
widower/widow	*veuf(ve)*

■ Directions

Is there a tourism office near here?	*Est-ce qu'il y a un bureau de tourisme près d'ici?*
There is no...	*Il n'y a pas de...,*
Where is...?	*Où est le/la ... ?*
straight ahead	*tout droit*
to the right	*à droite*
to the left	*à gauche*
beside	*à côté de*
near	*près de*
here there, over there	*ici, là, là-bas*
into, inside	*à l'intérieur*
outside	*à l'extérieur*
far from	*loin de*

between	entre
in front of	devant
behind	derrière

■ Getting Around

airport	aéroport
on time	à l'heure
late	en retard
cancelled	annulé
plane	avion
car	voiture
train	train
boat	bateau
bicycle	bicyclette, vélo
bus	autobus
train station	gare ferroviaire
bus stop	arrêt d'autobus
The bus stop, please	L'arrêt, s'il vous plaît
street	rue
avenue	avenue
road	route, chemin
highway	autoroute
rural route	rang
path, trail	sentier
corner	coin
neighbourhood	quartier
square	place
tourist office	bureau de tourisme
bridge	pont
building	immeuble
safe	sécuritaire
fast	rapide
baggage	bagages
schedule	horaire
one way ticket	aller simple
return ticket	aller retour
arrival	arrivée
return	retour
departure	départ
north	nord
south	sud
east	est
west	ouest

■ Cars

for rent	à louer
a stop	un arrêt
highway	autoroute
danger, be careful	attention
no passing	défense de doubler
no parking	stationnement interdit
no exit	impasse

English-French Glossary - Cars

Stop!	Arrêtez!
parking	stationnement
pedestrians	piétons
gas	essence
slow down	ralentir
traffic light	feu de circulation
service station	station-service
speed limit	limitation de vitesse

■ Money

bank	banque
credit union	caisse populaire
exchange	change
money	argent
I don't have any money	Je n'ai pas d'argent
credit card	carte de crédit
traveller's cheques	chèques de voyage
The bill please	L'addition, s'il vous plaît
receipt	reçu

■ Accommodation

inn	auberge
youth hostel	auberge de jeunesse
bed and breakfast	gîte touristique
hot water	eau chaude
air conditioning	climatisation
accommodation	logement, hébergement
elevator	ascenseur
bathroom	toilettes, salle de bain
bed	lit
breakfast	déjeuner
manager, owner	gérant, propriétaire
bedroom	chambre
pool	piscine
floor (first, second...)	étage
main floor	rez-de-chaussée
high season	haute saison
off season	basse saison
fan	ventilateur

■ Shopping

open	ouvert(e)
closed	fermé(e)
How much is this?	C'est combien?
I would like...	Je voudrais...
I need...	J'ai besoin de...
a store	un magasin
a department store	un magasin à rayons
the market	le marché
salesperson (m/f)	vendeur(se)

the customer (m/f)	le / la client(e)
to buy	acheter
to sell	vendre
T-shirt	t-shirt
skirt	jupe
shirt	chemise
jeans	jeans
pants	pantalon
jacket	blouson
blouse	blouse
shoes	chaussures
sandals	sandales
hat	chapeau
eyeglasses	unettes
handbag	sac à main
gifts	cadeaux
local crafts	artisanat local
sunscreen	crème solaire
cosmetics and perfumes	cosmétiques et parfums
camera	appareil photo
photographic film	pellicule
records, cassettes	disques, cassettes
newspapers	journaux
magazines	revues, magazines
batteries	piles
watches	montres
jewellery	bijouterie
gold	or
silver	argent
precious stones	pierres précieuses
fabric	tissu
wool	laine
cotton	coton
leather	cuir

■ Miscellaneous

new	nouveau
old	vieux
expensive	cher, dispendieux
inexpensive	pas cher
pretty	joli
beautiful	beau
ugly	laid(e)
big, tall (person)	grand(e)
small, short (person)	petit(e)
short (length)	court(e)
low	bas(se)
wide	large
narrow	étroit(e)
dark	foncé
light (colour)	clair
fat (person)	gros(se)
slim, skinny (person)	mince
a little	peu

a lot	*beaucoup*
something	*quelque chose*
nothing	*rien*
good	*bon*
bad	*mauvais*
more	*plus*
less	*moins*
do not touch	*ne pas toucher*
quickly	*rapidement*
slowly	*lentement*
big	*grand*
small	*petit*
hot	*chaud*
cold	*froid*
I am ill	*Je suis malade*
pharmacy, drugstore	*pharmacie*
I am hungry	*J'ai faim*
I am thirsty	*J'ai soif*
What is this?	*Qu'est-ce que c'est?*
Where?	*Où?*
fixed price menu	*table d'hôte*
order courses separately	*à la carte*

■ Weather

rain	*pluie*
clouds	*nuages*
sun	*soleil*
It is hot out	*Il fait chaud*
It is cold out	*Il fait froid*

■ Time

When?	*Quand?*
What time is it?	*Quelle heure est-il?*
minute	*minute*
hour	*heure*
day	*jour*
week	*semaine*
month	*mois*
year	*année*
yesterday	*hier*
today	*aujourd'hui*
tomorrow	*demain*
morning	*matin*
afternoon	*après-midi*
evening	*soir*
night	*nuit*
now	*maintenant*
never	*jamais*
Sunday	*dimanche*
Monday	*lundi*
Tuesday	*mardi*
Wednesday	*mercredi*

Thursday	jeudi
Friday	vendredi
Saturday	samedi
January	janvier
February	février
March	mars
April	avril
May	mai
June	juin
July	juillet
August	août
September	septembre
October	octobre
November	novembre
December	décembre

■ Communications

post office	bureau de poste
air mail	par avion
stamps	timbres
envelope	enveloppe
telephone book	bottin
long distance call	appel outre-mer
collect call	appel à frais virés (PCV)
fax	télécopieur, fax
rate	tarif
dial the regional code	composer l'indicatif régional
wait for the tone	attendre la tonalité

■ Activities

recreational swimming	baignade
beach	plage
scuba diving	plongée sous-marine
snorkelling	plongée-tuba
fishing	pêche
recreational sailing	navigation de plaisance
windsurfing	planche à voile
bicycling	faire du vélo
mountain bike	vélo tout-terrain (VTT)
horseback riding	équitation
hiking	randonnée pédestre
to walk around	se promener
museum or gallery	musée
cultural centre	centre culturel
cinema	cinéma

■ Touring

river	fleuve, rivière
waterfall	chute
viewpoint	belvédère

English-French Glossary - Touring

hill	*colline*
garden	*jardin*
wildlife reserve	*réserve faunique*
peninsula	*péninsule, presqu'île*
south/north shore	*côte sud/nord*
town or city hall	*hôtel de ville*
court house	*palais de justice*
church	*église*
house	*maison*
manor	*manoir*
bridge	*pont*
basin	*bassin*
workshop	*atelier*
historic site	*lieu historique*
train station	*gare ferroviaire*
stables	*écuries*
convent	*couvent*
door, archway, gate	*porte, porche, portail*
customs house	*bureau de douane*
market	*marché*
seaway	*voie maritime*
museum	*musée*
cemetery	*cimetière*
mill	*moulin*
windmill	*moulin à vent*
hospital	*hôpital*
high school	*école secondaire*
lighthouse	*phare*
barn	*grange*
waterfall	*chute*
sandbank	*batture*
neighbourhood	*quartier*
region	*région*

■ Numbers

1	*un*
2	*deux*
3	*trois*
4	*quatre*
5	*cinq*
6	*six*
7	*sept*
8	*huit*
9	*neuf*
10	*dix*
11	*onze*
12	*douze*
13	*treize*
14	*quatorze*
15	*quinze*
16	*seize*
17	*dix-sept*
18	*dix-huit*
19	*dix-neuf*

English-French Glossary - Touring

20	*vingt*
21	*vingt et un*
22	*vingt-deux*
23	*vingt-trois*
24	*vingt-quatre*
25	*vingt-cinq*
26	*vingt-six*
27	*vingt-sept*
28	*vingt-huit*
29	*vingt-neuf*
30	*trente*
40	*quarante*
50	*cinquante*
60	*soixante*
70	*soixante-dix*
80	*quatre-vingt*
90	*quatre-vingt-dix*
100	*cent*
200	*deux cents*
500	*cinq cents*
1,000	*mille*
10,000	*dix mille*
1,000,000	*un million*

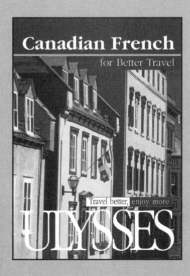
English-French Glossary - Numbers

Our Guides

Fabulous

Fabulous Québec	$29.95 CAD	$22.95 USD

Ulysses Green Escapes

Cross-Country Skiing and Snowshoeing in Ontario	$24.95 CAD	$22.95 USD
Cycling in France	$24.95 CAD	$17.95 USD
Cycling in Ontario	$24.95 CAD	$17.95 USD
Hiking in Ontario	$24.95 CAD	$19.95 USD
Hiking in Québec	$24.95 CAD	$19.95 USD
Ontario's Bike Paths and Rail Trails	$19.95 CAD	$17.95 USD
The Trans Canada Trail in Québec	$24.95 CAD	$19.95 USD

Ulysses Non-Series Titles

Bed and Breakfasts in Ontario	$17.95 CAD	$12.95 USD
Inns and Bed and Breakfasts in Québec 2004	$17.95 CAD	$12.95 USD

Ulysses Phrasebooks

Canadian French for Better Travel	$9.95 CAD	$6.95 USD
French for Better Travel	$9.95 CAD	$6.95 USD
Italian for Better Travel	$9.95 CAD	$7.95 USD
Spanish for Better Travel in Latin America	$9.95 CAD	$7.95 USD
Spanish for Better Travel in Spain	$9.95 CAD	$7.95 USD

Ulysses Travel Guides

Acapulco	$14.95 CAD	$9.95 USD
Alberta's Best Hotels and Restaurants	$14.95 CAD	$12.95 USD
Arizona and Grand Canyon	$24.95 CAD	$17.95 USD
Atlantic Canada	$24.95 CAD	$19.95 USD
The Islands of The Bahamas	$24.95 CAD	$17.95 USD
Beaches of Maine	$12.95 CAD	$9.95 USD
Belize	$16.95 CAD	$12.95 USD
Biking Montréal	$3.95 CAD	$2.95 USD
Boston	$17.95 CAD	$12.95 USD
British Columbia's Best Hotels and Restaurants	$14.95 CAD	$12.95 USD
Calgary	$16.95 CAD	$12.95 USD
California	$29.95 CAD	$21.95 USD
Canada	$29.95 CAD	$22.95 USD
Cancún-Riviera Maya	$19.95 CAD	$17.95 USD
Cape Cod, Nantucket and Martha's Vineyard	$17.95 CAD	$12.95 USD
Cartagena	$12.95 CAD	$9.95 USD
Chicago	$19.95 CAD	$14.95 USD
Chile	$27.95 CAD	$17.95 USD
Costa Rica	$27.95 CAD	$19.95 USD
Cuba	$24.95 CAD	$17.95 USD
Dominican Republic	$24.95 CAD	$17.95 USD
Ecuador - Galapagos Islands	$24.95 CAD	$17.95 USD
Guadalajara	$17.95 CAD	$12.95 USD
Guadeloupe	$24.95 CAD	$17.95 USD
Guatemala	$24.95 CAD	$17.95 USD
Havana	$16.95 CAD	$12.95 USD
Hawaii	$29.95 CAD	$21.95 USD
Honduras	$24.95 CAD	$17.95 USD
Huatulco & Puerto Escondido	$17.95 CAD	$12.95 USD
Las Vegas	$17.95 CAD	$12.95 USD
Lisbon	$18.95 CAD	$13.95 USD
Los Angeles	$19.95 CAD	$14.95 USD
Los Cabos and La Paz	$14.95 CAD	$10.95 USD
Louisiana	$29.95 CAD	$21.95 USD
Martinique	$24.95 CAD	$17.95 USD

New England	$29.95 CAD	$21.95 USD
New Orleans	$17.95 CAD	$12.95 USD
Nicaragua	$24.95 CAD	$17.95 USD
Ontario	$29.95 CAD	$22.95 USD
Ontario's Best Hotels & Restaurants	$16.95 CAD	$12.95 USD
Ottawa-Hull	$14.95 CAD	$12.95 USD
Panamá	$27.95 CAD	$19.95 USD
Peru	$27.95 CAD	$19.95 USD
Phoenix	$16.95 CAD	$12.95 USD
Porto	$17.95 CAD	$12.95 USD
Portugal	$24.95 CAD	$17.95 USD
Provence and the Côte d'Azur	$29.95 CAD	$21.95 USD
Puerto Plata, Sosúa, Cabarete	$14.95 CAD	$9.95 USD
Puerto Rico	$24.95 CAD	$17.95 USD
Puerto Vallarta	$14.95 CAD	$10.95 USD
Québec	$29.95 CAD	$22.95 USD
Quebec And Ontario With Via	$9.95 CAD	$7.95 USD
Québec City	$24.95 CAD	$19.95 USD
San Diego	$17.95 CAD	$12.95 USD
San Francisco	$17.95 CAD	$12.95 USD
Seattle	$17.95 CAD	$12.95 USD
St. Lucia	$17.95 CAD	$12.95 USD
St. Martin - St. Barts	$17.95 CAD	$12.95 USD
Toronto	$22.95 CAD	$17.95 USD
Tunisia	$27.95 CAD	$19.95 USD
Vancouver, Victoria and Whistler	$19.95 CAD	$14.95 USD
Washington D.C.	$19.95 CAD	$14.95 USD
Western Canada	$29.95 CAD	$22.95 USD

Ulysses Travel Journals

Travel Journal: 80 Days	$14.95 CAD	$9.95 USD
Travel Journal: The Lighthouse	$12.95 CAD	$9.95 USD

Titles	Quantity	Price	Total
Name:	Subtotal		
	Shipping		$4.85CAD/$5.75 USD
Address:	GST in Canada 7%		
	Total		
E-mail:			

Payment: ☐ Cheque ☐ Visa ☐ MasterCard

Card number _____ Expiry date _____

Signature _____

To place an order, please send this order form to one of our offices (the adresses appear on the following page), or visit our Web site: **www.ulyssesguides.com**.

Contact Information

Offices

Canada: Ulysses Travel Guides, 4176 St. Denis Street, Montréal, Québec, H2W 2M5, ☎(514) 843-9447, ▤(514) 843-9448, info@ulysses.ca, www.ulyssesguides.com

Europe: Les Guides de Voyage Ulysse SARL, 127 rue Amelot, 75011 Paris, France, ☎01 43 38 89 50, voyage@ulysse.ca, www.ulyssesguides.com

U.S.A.: Ulysses Travel Guides, 305 Madison Avenue, Suite 1166, New York, NY 10165, info@ulysses.ca, www.ulyssesguides.com

Distributors

U.S.A.: Hunter Publishing, 130 Campus Drive, Edison, NJ 08818, ☎800-255-0343, ▤(732) 417-1744 or 0482, comments@hunterpublishing.com, www.hunterpublishing.com

Canada: Ulysses Travel Guides, 4176 St. Denis Street, Montréal, Québec, H2W 2M5, ☎(514) 843-9882, ext. 2232, ▤514-843-9448, info@ulysses.ca, www.ulyssesguides.com

Great Britain and Ireland: Roundhouse Publishing, Millstone, Limers Lane, Northam, North Devon, EX39 2RG, ☎1 202 66 54 32, ▤1 202 66 62 19, roundhouse.group@ukgateway.net

Other countries: Ulysses Travel Guides, 4176 St. Denis Street, Montréal, Québec, H2W 2M5, ☎(514) 843-9882, ext.2232, ▤514-843-9448, info@ulysses.ca, www.ulyssesguides.com

Write to Us

The information contained in this guide was correct at press time. However, mistakes may slip by, omissions are always possible, establishments may move, etc. The authors and publisher hereby disclaim any liability for loss or damage resulting from omissions or errors.

We value your comments, corrections and suggestions, as they allow us to keep each guide up to date. The best contributions will be rewarded with a free book from Ulysses Travel Guides. All you have to do is write us at the following address and indicate which title you would be interested in receiving (please refer to the list provided in the previous pages).

Ulysses Travel Guides

4176, Saint-Denis Street
Montréal (Québec)
Canada H2W 2M5

305 Madison Avenue
Suite 1166, New York
NY 10165

www.ulyssesguides.com
E-mail: text@ulysses.ca

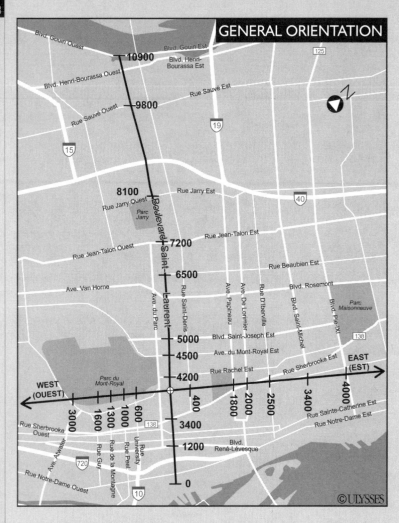

Blvd. Gouin Ouest

10900

Blvd. Gouin Est

Blvd. Henri-Bourassa Est

Blvd. Henri-Bourassa Ouest

Rue Sauvé Est

9800

Rue Sauvé Ouest

125

19

15

Rue Jarry Est

8100

Rue Jarry Ouest

Parc Jarry

Boulevard Saint-Laurent

40

Rue Jean-Talon Est

7200

Rue Jean-Talon Ouest

Rue Beaubien Est

6500

Ave. Van Horne

Ave. Papineau

Ave. De Lorimier

Rue D'Iberville

Blvd. Rosemont

Blvd. Saint-Michel

Blvd. Pie-IX

Parc Maisonneuve

Rue Saint-Denis

Ave. du Parc

138

Blvd. Saint-Joseph Est

5000

Ave. du Mont-Royal Est

4500

Parc du Mont-Royal

Rue Rachel Est

Rue Sherbrooke Est

EAST (EST)

4200

WEST (OUEST)

3000 1600 1300 1000 600

400 1800 2000 2500 3400 4000

Rue Sainte-Catherine Est

Rue Sherbrooke Ouest

Ave. Atwater

720

Rue Guy

Rue de la Montagne

Rue Peel

Rue University

138

3400

Rue Notre-Dame Est

Blvd. René-Lévesque

1200

Rue Notre-Dame Ouest

10

0

©ULYSSES

Traversing the Island of Montréal from north to south, Boulevard Saint-Laurent, which is commonly referred to as "The Main," serves as the city's dividing point between east and west. South of the boulevard, near the St. Lawrence River, civic addresses start at 0 and increase gradually as you head north. Civic adresses also start at 0 at Boulevard Saint-Laurent and increase gradually as you head either east or west.

General Orientation

Table of Distances

Distances in kilometres, via the shortest route

Example: The distance between Montréal and Boston (Mass.) is 512km.

	Toronto (Ont.)	Sherbrooke	Saguenay	Rouyn-Noranda	Québec City	Niagara Falls (Ont.)	New York (N.Y.)	Montréal	Halifax (N.S.)	Gatineau / Ottawa	Gaspé	Chibougamau	Charlottetown (P.E.I.)	Boston (Mass.)	Baie-Comeau
Boston (Mass.)															1040
Charlottetown (P.E.I.)														1081	724
Chibougamau													1347	1152	679
Gaspé												1214	867	1247	293
Gatineau / Ottawa											1124	725	1404	701	869
Halifax (N.S.)										1488	952	1430	265	1165	807
Montréal									1290	205	924	700	1194	512	674
New York (N.Y.)								608	1508	814	1550	1308	1421	352	1239
Niagara Falls (Ont.)							685	670	1919	543	1590	1298	1836	767	1334
Québec City						925	834	259	1056	461	700	521	984	648	414
Rouyn-Noranda					872	858	1246	636	1916	522	1551	517	1833	1136	1171
Saguenay				860	210	1126	1045	463	1076	666	636	363	992	849	316
Sherbrooke			445	786	240	827	657	157	1271	356	906	757	1187	426	656
Toronto (Ont.)		693	1000	606	802	141	823	546	1828	399	1476	1124	1746	906	1224
Trois-Rivières	688	155	334	742	130	814	750	138	1173	322	809	577	1089	566	544

Weights and Measures

Land Measure

1 acre = 0.4 hectare (ha)
1 hectare (ha) = 2.47 acres
10 square feet (ft^2) = 1 square metre (m^2)

Linear Measure

1 inch (in) = 2.5 centimetres (cm)
1 foot (ft) = 30 centimetres (cm)
1 mile (mi) = 1.6 kilometre (km)
1 kilometre (km) = 0.63 miles (mi)
1 metre (m) = 39.37 inches (in)

Volume Measure

1 U.S. gallon (gal) = 3.79 litres

Weights

1 pound (lb) = 454 grams (g)
1 kilogram (kg) = 2.2 pounds (lbs)

Temperature

To convert °F into °C:
subtract 32, divide by 9, multiply by 5.

To convert °C into °F:
multiply by 9, divide by 5, add 32.

100°F	40°C
70°F	30°C
50°F	20°C
32°F	10°C
20°F	0°C
0°F	-10°C
-20°F	-18°C
	-30°C

Map Symbols

★	Attractions				
▲	Accommodations	⊘	Beach	🏛	Museum
●	Restaurants	🚲	Bike path		Optional tour
	Sea, lake, river		Building		Passenger ferry
	Forest or park	🚌	Bus station	≡	Stairs
	Place	🚗	Car ferry		Suggested tour
✪	National capital	H	Hospital	❶	Tourist information
✪	Provincial or state capital	✈	International airport		Train station
	International border		Lookout		ULYSSES bookstore
	Provincial or regional border	◐	Metro station		
	Train track				
	Tunnel				

Symbols Used In This Guide

≡	Air conditioning
bkfst incl.	Breakfast included
♠	Casino
⊰	Fan
▤	Fax number
△	Fireplace
⚓	Fitness centre
☕	Kitchenette
@	Internet access in the room
#	Mosquito net
P	Parking
🐾	Pets allowed
≈	Pool
pb/sb	Private and shared bathrooms
❄	Refrigerator
♜	Restaurant
)))	Sauna
sb	Shared bathroom
⅄	Spa
☎	Telephone number
🚲	Travel by bike
🚌	Travel by bus
🚗	Travel by car
🚶	Travel by foot
Ⓜ	Travel by metro
🔅	Ulysses favourite
♿	Wheelchair access
◎	Whirlpool

Attraction Classification

★ ★ ★	Not to be missed
★ ★	Worth a visit
★	Interesting

Accommodation Classification

Unless otherwise noted, all prices indicated in this guide apply to a standard room for two people in peak season.

$	less than $60
$$	from $60 to $100
$$$	from $101 to $150
$$$$	from $151 to $225
$$$$$	more than $225

Restaurant Classification

Prices in this guide are for a meal for one person, excluding taxes and tip.

$	less than $15
$$	$15 to $25
$$$	$26 to $50
$$$$	more than $50

All prices in this guide are in Canadian dollars.

This guide's practical section features a grey border and lists this destination's useful addresses. You can refer to the following pictograms to find the information you need:

▲	**Accommodations**
♜	**Restaurants**
♪	**Entertainment**
🎁	**Shopping**